LAND REGISTRATION FOR THE TWENTY-FIRST CENTURY
A Conveyancing Revolution

LAND REGISTRATION BILL AND COMMENTARY

Laid before Parliament by the Lord High Chancellor pursuant to section 3(2) of the Law Commissions Act 1965

Ordered by The House of Commons *to be printed*
9 July 2001

LAW COMMISSION
LAW COM NO 271

H M LAND REGISTRY

LONDON: The Stationery Office
£45

HC 114

The Law Commission was set up by section 1 of the Law Commissions Act 1965 for the purpose of promoting the reform of the law.

Her Majesty's Land Registry, a separate department of government and now an Executive Agency, maintains the land registers for England and Wales and is responsible for delivering all land registration services under the Land Registration Act 1925.

The terms of this report were agreed on 31 May 2001.

The text of this report is available on the Internet at:
http://www.lawcom.gov.uk

---

*   Mr Stuart Bridge was appointed Law Commissioner with effect from 2 July 2001. The terms of this report were agreed on 31 May 2001, while Mr Charles Harpum was a Law Commissioner.

LAND REGISTRATION FOR THE TWENTY-FIRST CENTURY
A Conveyancing Revolution

CONTENTS

	Paragraph	Page
PART I: THE LAND REGISTRATION BILL AND ITS OBJECTIVES		**1**
INTRODUCTION	1.1	1
THE OBJECTIVES OF THE BILL	1.4	2
SOME KEY FEATURES OF THE BILL	1.11	4
Electronic conveyancing	1.12	4
Adverse possession	1.13	4
Other changes	1.14	5
THE BACKGROUND TO THE BILL	1.15	6
STRUCTURE OF THE REPORT	1.21	8
PART II: SUMMARY OF THE MAIN CHANGES MADE BY THE BILL		**9**
INTRODUCTION	2.1	9
FIRST REGISTRATION	2.4	10
CAUTIONS AGAINST FIRST REGISTRATION	2.14	13
POWERS OF DISPOSITION	2.15	13
REGISTRABLE DISPOSITIONS	2.16	14
PRIORITIES	2.17	14
NOTICES AND RESTRICTIONS	2.19	15
CHARGES	2.23	16
OVERRIDING INTERESTS	2.24	16
REGISTRATION	2.28	18
SPECIAL CASES	2.32	19
ALTERATION, RECTIFICATION AND INDEMNITY	2.38	20
CONVEYANCING: GENERAL MATTERS	2.40	21
ELECTRONIC CONVEYANCING	2.41	21
Introduction	2.41	21
Present conveyancing practice in relation to registered land	2.43	22
Electronic conveyancing: the anticipated model	2.48	23
Introduction	2.48	23
How a typical conveyancing transaction might operate	2.52	24
Compulsory use of electronic conveyancing	2.59	26
Finance	2.62	28
Stamp duty	2.64	28

	Paragraph	Page
Electronic conveyancing and first registration	2.65	28
Do-it-yourself conveyancing	2.68	29
ADVERSE POSSESSION	2.69	30
Introduction	2.69	30
Why do we have a doctrine of adverse possession?	2.71	30
An outline of the new scheme in the Bill	2.74	32
JUDICIAL PROVISIONS	2.75	33
RULES	2.76	33

PART III: FIRST REGISTRATION

		35
INTRODUCTION	3.1	35
THE LEGAL SCOPE OF TITLE REGISTRATION ANDTHE EXTENT OF LAND THAT MAY BE REGISTERED UNDER IT	3.3	35
The legal scope of title registration	3.3	35
The extent of land that may be registered	3.5	36
VOLUNTARY FIRST REGISTRATION	3.6	37
Registrable estates	3.6	37
Who may apply for first registration?	3.6	37
Which legal estates may be registered with their own titles?	3.9	38
A fee simple absolute in possession	3.9	38
Certain leases	3.10	38
Rentcharges	3.18	40
Franchises	3.19	41
Profits à prendre in gross	3.20	41
Manors no longer to be registrable	3.21	42
COMPULSORY REGISTRATION	3.22	42
Introduction	3.22	42
Events that trigger the compulsory registration of title	3.23	43
Introduction	3.23	43
Transfers	3.24	43
Transfer of a qualifying estate	3.24	43
Transfers to which section 171A of the Housing Act 1985 applies	3.28	45
Grants	3.29	45
Leases granted for a term of more than seven years from the date of grant	3.30	45
Reversionary leases	3.32	46
Grant of a right to buy lease under Part V of the Housing Act 1985	3.33	47
Grant of a lease to which section 171A of the Housing Act 1985 applies	3.34	47
Protected first legal mortgages	3.35	47
Crown grants out demesne land	3.36	47
The power to extend the triggers to compulsory registration	3.37	48
The effect of failure to register	3.38	48
The duty to register	3.38	48
The effect of non-compliance with the duty to register	3.40	49

	Paragraph	Page
THE EFFECT OF FIRST REGISTRATION	3.42	50
Classes of title	3.42	50
Introduction	3.42	50
Freehold titles	3.43	50
Leasehold titles	3.44	51
The effect of first registration	3.45	52
Freehold title	3.45	52
Registration with absolute title	3.45	52
Qualified title	3.49	54
Possessory title	3.50	54
Leasehold title	3.51	54
Miscellaneous rule-making powers	3.52	55
CAUTIONS AGAINST FIRST REGISTRATION AND THE CAUTIONS REGISTER	3.54	56
The nature of cautions against first registration under the present law	3.54	56
Cautions against first registration under the Bill	3.56	57
The right to lodge a caution	3.56	57
The effect of a caution against first registration	3.60	59
Cancellation of cautions	3.63	60
The cautions register	3.65	61
PART IV: DISPOSITIONS OF REGISTERED LAND		**63**
INTRODUCTION	4.1	63
POWERS OF DISPOSITION	4.2	63
Introduction	4.2	63
The principles adopted in the Bill	4.4	64
The provisions of the Bill	4.5	65
Owner's powers	4.5	65
Protection for disponees	4.8	66
REGISTRABLE DISPOSITIONS	4.12	67
Introduction	4.12	67
The general principle	4.13	68
Dispositions required to be registered and the registration requirements that apply to them	4.16	69
Introduction	4.16	69
Transfers of a registered estate	4.17	69
The grant of certain leases	4.20	71
Leases of franchises and manors	4.23	72
Express grant or reservation of an easement, right or privilege	4.24	72
Express grant or reservation of a rentcharge or legal right of re-entry	4.27	74
The grant of a legal charge	4.29	75
Dispositions of a registered charge	4.30	75
Applications for registration	4.31	76
PART V: PRIORITIES		**77**
INTRODUCTION	5.1	77
PRIORITY UNDER THE BILL	5.5	78
The general rule	5.5	78

	Paragraph	Page
The principal exception: registrable dispositions that have been registered	5.6	78
The exception	5.6	78
Applicable only to registrable dispositions	5.7	79
Made for valuable consideration	5.8	79
Priority conferred	5.10	79
When the priority of an interest will be protected	5.11	80
The priority of registered charges	5.14	81
The grant of leases that are not registrable dispositions	5.15	81
The irrelevance of notice	5.16	82
SPECIAL CASES	5.22	84
Inland Revenue Charges	5.23	84
Rights of pre-emption	5.26	85
An equity arising by estoppel	5.29	87
A mere equity	5.32	89
Inchoate rights arising under the Prescription Act 1832	5.37	90

PART VI: NOTICES AND RESTRICTIONS

		92
INTRODUCTION	6.1	92
THE PROPOSALS IN THE CONSULTATIVE DOCUMENT	6.2	92
THE PROVISIONS OF THE BILL	6.3	93
Prospective abolition of cautions against dealings	6.3	93
Notices	6.5	94
Introduction	6.5	94
Nature and effect of a notice	6.6	94
Interests which may not be protected by notice	6.8	95
Interests under trusts of land and settlements	6.9	95
Short leases	6.10	96
A restrictive covenant between landlord and tenant	6.13	97
An interest which is registrable under the Commons Registration Act 1965	6.14	97
An interest in any coal or coal mine or ancillary rights	6.15	98
A PPP lease	6.16	98
The circumstances in which a notice may be entered on the register	6.17	98
Introduction	6.17	98
Burdens entered on the register on first registration	6.18	99
Entry in respect of an overriding interest	6.19	99
Entry in respect of a registrable disposition	6.20	100
Where the entry is necessary to update the register	6.21	100
Applications for the entry of a notice	6.22	101
Unilateral notices	6.26	102
The nature of unilateral notices	6.26	102
Protection against the improper entry of a unilateral notice	6.27	103
Abolition of inhibitions as a separate form of entry	6.32	104
Restrictions	6.33	105
Introduction	6.33	105
The nature and effect of a restriction	6.34	105
When a restriction may or must be entered	6.38	107

	Paragraph	Page
Introduction	6.38	107
When the registrar may or must enter a restriction	6.39	107
Where the registrar may enter a restriction	6.40	108
Where the registrar must enter a restriction	6.46	111
Applications for the entry of a restriction	6.47	111
Where the court may order the entry of a restriction	6.51	113
Notifiable applications for a restriction	6.54	114
Withdrawal of restrictions	6.58	116
Pending land actions, writs, orders and deeds of arrangement	6.59	116

PART VII: CHARGES — 118

INTRODUCTION	7.1	118
THE POWER TO CREATE CHARGES AND THE POWERS OF THE CHARGEE	7.2	118
Legal Charges	7.2	118
The creation of charges and the powers of the chargee	7.2	118
The definition of "charge"	7.5	120
Powers of chargees and the need for a deed	7.6	121
Dispositions made by chargees and the protection of disponees	7.7	121
Equitable charges	7.9	122
SUB-CHARGES AND THE POWERS OF THE SUB-CHARGEE	7.11	123
PRIORITIES	7.13	124
Priority of registered charges	7.13	124
Registered sub-charges	7.16	125
Equitable charges	7.17	125
Tacking and further advances	7.18	126
Present law and practice	7.18	126
Provisions of the Bill	7.28	130
Further advances made with the agreement of subsequent chargees	7.29	130
Further advances where the prior chargee has not received notice of the subsequent charge	7.30	130
Where there is an obligation to make a further advance	7.31	131
Further advances up to a maximum amount	7.32	131
Statutory charges	7.37	132
Types of statutory charge	7.38	133
Overriding statutory charges	7.39	133
Charges which are local land charges	7.42	134
MISCELLANEOUS	7.43	135
Application of proceeds of sale	7.43	135
Consolidation	7.44	136
Power to give receipts	7.46	136

PART VIII: OVERRIDING INTERESTS — 137

INTRODUCTION	8.1	137
THE NATURE OF OVERRIDING INTERESTS	8.3	138
UNREGISTERED INTERESTS WHICH MAY BE OVERRIDING: INTRODUCTION	8.6	139

	Paragraph	Page
UNREGISTERED INTERESTS WHICH OVERRIDE FIRST REGISTRATION	8.8	140
Introduction	8.8	140
Short leases	8.9	141
PPP Leases	8.11	142
Interests of persons in actual occupation	8.14	144
Legal easements and *profits à prendre*	8.23	147
Customary and public rights	8.26	148
Local land charges	8.29	149
Mines and minerals	8.31	150
Rights to coal	8.32	150
Certain mineral rights where the title was registered before 1926	8.33	151
Miscellaneous	8.35	152
Introduction	8.35	152
Franchises and manorial rights	8.40	154
Crown rents	8.43	155
Certain rights in respect of embankments and sea and river walls	8.45	156
A right to payment in lieu of tithe	8.46	157
UNREGISTERED INTERESTS WHICH OVERRIDE REGISTERED DISPOSITIONS	8.47	158
Introduction	8.47	158
Categories of overriding interest that are the same as those that apply on first registration	8.48	158
Categories of overriding interest that differ from those that apply on first registration	8.49	159
Short leases	8.50	159
Interests of persons in actual occupation	8.53	161
Introduction	8.53	161
The general principle	8.54	161
Qualification: Protection is restricted to the land in actual occupation	8.55	162
Exception 1: No protection for settled land	8.59	163
Exception 2: Rights not disclosed on reasonable enquiry	8.60	163
Exception 3: Rights of persons whose occupation is not apparent	8.61	164
Exception 4: Leases granted to take effect in possession more than three months after grant	8.63	165
Transitional provisions	8.64	165
Legal easements and *profits à prendre*	8.65	166
The problem	8.65	166
Only legal easements and profits may be overriding interests	8.67	167
Legal easements and profits that are not easily discoverable should not be overriding interests	8.68	168
Transitional arrangements	8.73	169
REDUCING THE IMPACT OF OVERRIDING INTERESTS	8.74	170
Introduction	8.74	170
Categories of overriding interests that are to be abolished	8.75	170
Introduction	8.75	170
Squatters' rights	8.76	171
Rights excepted from the effect of registration	8.79	172
Categories of overriding interests that are to be phased out	8.81	173
The principle of phasing out overriding statues and the objections to it	8.81	173

	Paragraph	Page
The views expressed on consultation	8.85	175
The scheme adopted in the Bill	8.86	175
Human rights	8.89	177
Ensuring that overriding interests are protected on the register when they come to light	8.90	178

PART IX: THE REGISTER AND REGISTRATION — 180

INTRODUCTION	9.1	180
THE REGISTER	9.3	181
REGISTRATION AS PROPRIETOR	9.4	181
Conclusiveness	9.4	181
Dependent entries	9.7	182
Effective date of registration	9.8	182
BOUNDARIES	9.9	183
The general boundaries rule	9.9	183
Accretion and diluvion	9.14	185
QUALITY OF TITLE	9.16	186
Introduction	9.16	186
When title can be upgraded	9.17	186
Upgrading freehold title which has possessory title	9.17	186
Upgrading freehold title which has qualified title	9.18	187
Upgrading leasehold title which has a good leasehold title	9.19	188
Upgrading leasehold title which has a possessory title	9.20	188
Upgrading leasehold title which has a qualified title	9.21	188
No power to upgrade where there is an outstanding adverse claim	9.22	188
Who may apply for the upgrading of a title	9.23	189
Effect of upgrading title	9.25	189
Indemnity	9.28	190
Use of register to record defects in title	9.29	190
ACCESSING INFORMATION	9.36	193
Introduction	9.36	193
Open registers and their inspection	9.37	193
The significance of the open register	9.37	193
The rights conferred by the Bill	9.38	193
The limitations on the rights to inspect and copy	9.43	195
Official copies	9.44	195
Conclusiveness of filed copies	9.48	196
Introduction	9.48	196
The preconditions	9.50	197
Conclusiveness	9.52	198
Index	9.54	198
Historical information	9.58	199
Official searches	9.61	200
PRIORITY PROTECTION	9.62	201
The present law	9.62	201
Priority protection under the Bill	9.67	203
The circumstances in which priority protection will be available	9.68	203
The meaning of priority protection	9.70	204
Rules	9.73	206

	Paragraph	Page
APPLICATIONS	9.76	206
The form and content of applications	9.76	206
Registered charges and company charges	9.81	208
LAND CERTIFICATES	9.83	209
The nature of a land or charge certificate under the present law	9.83	209
Present practice	9.86	210
The impact of the Bill	9.88	211
Abolition of charge certificates	9.89	211
Land Certificates	9.90	212

PART X: ALTERATION, RECTIFICATION AND INDEMNITY — 213

	Paragraph	Page
INTRODUCTION	10.1	213
THE EFFECT OF THE BILL: ALTERATION	10.5	214
Introduction	10.5	214
The circumstances in which the register may be altered	10.6	215
The meaning of alteration and rectification	10.6	215
Powers of alteration	10.9	216
The powers of the court	10.10	216
The circumstances in which the court may order alteration of the register	10.10	216
Qualified indefeasibility: the protection for the proprietor who is in possession	10.13	216
The powers of the registrar	10.19	222
The circumstances in which the registrar may alter the register	10.19	222
Qualified indefeasibility: the protection for the proprietor who is in possession	10.22	224
Alteration under network access agreements	10.23	224
Costs in non-rectification cases	10.24	225
The circumstances in which the register of cautions may be altered	10.26	225
Alteration of documents	10.27	226
THE EFFECT OF THE BILL: INDEMNITY	10.29	227
Introduction	10.29	227
The grounds on which indemnity is payable	10.30	227
Loss by reason of rectification	10.31	228
Loss by reason of a mistake	10.32	228
Mistake in an official search	10.33	229
Mistake in an official copy	10.34	229
Mistake in a document kept by the registrar which is not an original	10.35	230
Loss or destruction of a document lodged at the registry	10.36	230
Mistake in the register of cautions against first registration	10.37	230
Failure to notify a chargee of an overriding statutory charge	10.38	231
Mines and minerals	10.39	231
The measure of indemnity	10.40	232
Introduction	10.40	232
Elements to be taken into account in assessing indemnity	10.41	232
General	10.41	232
Valuing the loss of an estate, interest or charge	10.42	232

	Paragraph	Page
Interest	10.44	234
Costs	10.45	234
Factors that will bar a claim for indemnity or reduce the amount that can be recovered	10.47	235
When a claim will be barred	10.47	235
When a claim will be reduced	10.48	236
The mechanism for determining indemnity	10.49	236
Rights of recourse	10.51	237

PART XI: SPECIAL CASES — 239

INTRODUCTION	11.1	239
THE CROWN	11.2	239
Acknowledgements	11.2	239
Crown land	11.3	239
The issues addressed by the Bill	11.4	240
Registration of land held in demesne	11.5	241
The present law	11.5	241
Voluntary registration under the Bill	11.11	243
Compulsory registration under the Bill	11.13	243
Cautions against the first registration of demesne land	11.17	244
Escheat	11.20	246
The nature of escheat	11.20	246
The circumstances in which escheat occurs	11.23	248
The treatment of escheat in the Bill	11.26	250
Crown and Duchy land: representation	11.31	252
The disapplication of certain requirements in relation to Duchy land	11.33	253
Introduction	11.33	253
The present law	11.34	253
The Duchy of Cornwall	11.34	253
The Duchy of Lancaster	11.36	254
The provisions of the Bill	11.37	255
Matters for which the Bill makes no provision	11.38	255
BANKRUPTCY	11.39	256
Introduction	11.39	256
Procedure in relation to bankruptcy petitions	11.40	256
Procedure in relation to bankruptcy orders	11.41	257
Protection for disponees in good faith	11.42	257
SETTLEMENTS	11.45	258

PART XII: CONVEYANCING 1: GENERAL PROVISIONS — 259

INTRODUCTION	12.1	259
PROOF OF TITLE	12.2	259
Introduction	12.2	259
What proof of title must a seller deduce?	12.4	260
What title is a buyer entitled to see?	12.9	262
COVENANTS FOR TITLE	12.14	264
Introduction	12.14	264
No liability for matters on the register	12.16	265

	Paragraph	Page
Rules	12.20	266
Covenants implied on the assignment of a lease prior to 1996	12.21	267

PART XIII: CONVEYANCING 2: ELECTRONIC CONVEYANCING

		268
INTRODUCTION	13.1	268
FORMAL REQUIREMENTS FOR ELECTRONIC DISPOSITIONS	13.5	269
Introduction	13.5	269
THE DRAFT LAW OF PROPERTY (ELECTRONIC COMMUNICATIONS) ORDER	13.7	270
THE PROVISIONS OF THE BILL	13.11	272
Introduction	13.11	272
The applicability of Clause 91	13.12	272
The four conditions	13.13	273
Deemed execution	13.18	276
Deeds	13.19	276
Execution by agents	13.20	276
Notice of assignments	13.22	277
Execution by corporations	13.24	278
Execution by corporations which are companies for the purposes of the Companies Act 1985	13.25	278
Execution by other corporations	13.30	280
Rights of a purchaser as to execution	13.31	280
Supplementary rule-making powers	13.32	280
PROVISIONS GOVERNING THE LAND REGISTRY NETWORK	13.34	281
Introduction	13.34	281
Access to the network	13.36	282
Network access agreements	13.36	282
The level of access will be variable	13.38	283
Authority may be given to perform registrar's functions	13.39	283
Criteria for entry into a network access agreement	13.40	283
Terms of access	13.47	286
The purposes for which the power to authorise may be used	13.48	286
To require transactions to be conducted electronically	13.49	286
To regulate ancillary purposes	13.50	286
To enable transactions to be monitored	13.51	287
The obligation to comply with network transaction rules	13.52	287
The power to regulate terms of access by rules	13.54	288
Termination of access	13.55	288
Appeals	13.57	289
Overriding nature of network access obligations	13.58	289
Presumption of authority	13.60	290
Managing network transactions	13.63	291
Rules	13.66	292
Introduction	13.66	292
Why a rules-based approach is necessary	13.67	292
Safeguards	13.70	293
Do-it-yourself conveyancing	13.72	294

THE POWER TO MAKE ELECTRONIC CONVEYANCING
COMPULSORY AND TO REQUIRE THAT ELECTRONIC
DISPOSITIONS SHOULD BE SIMULTANEOUSLY REGISTERED 13.74 294
The objective of the power   13.74 294
The application of the power   13.80 296
Registration requirements   13.84 297
Rules   13.85 298

PART XIV: ADVERSE POSSESSION   299

INTRODUCTION   14.1   299

THE EFFECT OF THE BILL   14.9   305
Adverse possession shall not extinguish the title to a registered estate   14.9   305
  The governing principle   14.9   305
  The principle applies only in relation to registered estates and rentcharges 14.10 305
  *Provisions of the Limitation Act 1980 which depend on the accrual of
a cause of action or the limitation period will not apply*   14.11 306
  Mortgagors in possession   14.12 307
  Mortgagees in possession   14.15 308
The right to apply for registration after ten years' adverse possession   14.19 310
  The prerequisites for an application: the general position   14.19 310
  Where no valid application to be registered can be made   14.24 313
    Where there are possession proceedings against the squatter
that are still current   14.25 313
    Where the proprietor is an enemy or held in enemy territory 14.28 314
    Where the proprietor is suffering from mental disability or
physical impairment   14.29 314
  Notification of the registered proprietor and others   14.32 315
  Registration where no counter-notice is served   14.34 318
  No registration where a counter-notice is served   14.35 318
  Special case: registration even where a counter-notice is served 14.36 318
    General summary   14.36 318
    Estoppel   14.39 319
      The principle   14.39 319
      Examples   14.42 321
    Some other right to the land   14.43 321
    Reasonable mistake as to boundary   14.44 322
      The principle   14.44 322
      When will this exception be invoked?   14.46 323
      What has to be established to fall within the exception —
factual elements   14.48 324
      What has to be established to fall within the exception —
the mental element   14.50 325
The right to make a further application for registration after two
more years' adverse possession   14.53 325
  Introduction   14.53 325
  The right to make a further application to be registered   14.57 327
    Where the squatter remains in adverse possession two years
after the rejection of his application to be registered   14.58 327
    Where the proprietor obtains a judgment against the squatter
but fails to enforce it within two years   14.59 328

Where proceedings are discontinued or struck out more than
two years after the squatter's application was rejected — 14.61 — 329
The status of a right to be registered — 14.63 — 330
The effect of registration — 14.65 — 331
  Introduction — 14.65 — 331
  The legal background — 14.66 — 331
  The recommendations in the Consultative Document and the response
  on consultation — 14.68 — 332
  The provisions in the Bill — 14.70 — 334
    No trust — 14.70 — 334
    The squatter is successor in title to the previous proprietor — 14.71 — 334
    Registration of the squatter and the effect on registered charges — 14.74 — 335
    Where the squatter will be bound by charges — 14.76 — 336
    Apportionment — 14.77 — 336
Possession proceedings — 14.82 — 338
  Introduction — 14.82 — 338
  The general rule: the registered proprietor is entitled to possession as
  against the squatter — 14.83 — 338
  Exceptions: defences to possession proceedings — 14.84 — 338
    Defences which are unconnected with the squatter's adverse
    possession — 14.84 — 338
    Other defences — 14.85 — 339
      Reasonable mistake as to boundary — 14.86 — 339
      Where the squatter has become entitled to be registered
      even though his or her application to be registered was
      rejected — 14.87 — 339
Special cases — 14.88 — 340
  Rentcharges — 14.89 — 340
  Trusts — 14.91 — 341
    Adverse possession by a stranger of land held in trust — 14.91 — 341
    Adverse possession by a trustee or beneficiary of land held
    in trust — 14.95 — 342
  Crown foreshore — 14.97 — 343
Transitional provisions — 14.101 — 345
  Introducing the new system — 14.102 — 345
  Preserving vested rights — 14.104 — 345

PART XV: THE LAND REGISTRY — **347**

INTRODUCTION — 15.1 — 347

THE LAND REGISTRY — 15.2 — 347

CONDUCT OF BUSINESS — 15.5 — 348

ANNUAL REPORT — 15.8 — 348

FEES — 15.9 — 349

MISCELLANEOUS FUNCTIONS — 15.11 — 349
Power to publish information about land — 15.11 — 349
Consultancy and advisory services — 15.12 — 349

PART XVI: JUDICIAL PROVISIONS — **351**

INTRODUCTION — 16.1 — 351

	Paragraph	Page
THE ADJUDICATOR	16.3	352
The office of Adjudicator	16.3	352
Jurisdiction	16.6	353
The general right to object an application to the registrar and the		
registrar's duty to refer to contested applications to the Adjudicator	16.6	353
Other matters	16.8	354
PROCEEDINGS	16.11	355
Proceedings before the registrar	16.11	355
Proceedings before the Adjudicator	16.15	357
Power for the Adjudicator to direct a hearing before the court	16.20	358
Right of appeal	16.23	360
THE ROLE OF THE COURT	16.24	360
OFFENCES	16.26	361
The present law	16.26	361
The offences under the Bill	16.28	362
Suppression of information	16.28	362
Improper alteration of the registers	16.29	362
Dishonestly inducing another to change or authorise		
a change to the register	16.30	362
Intentionally or recklessly making an unauthorised		
change in the register	16.32	363
Privilege against self-incrimination	16.33	363
PART XVII: RULES AND ORDERS		**364**
INTRODUCTION	17.1	364
RULES	17.2	364
The present law	17.2	364
The approach to rule-making powers adopted in the Bill	17.4	365
The rule-making powers under the Bill	17.5	365
Land registration rules	17.5	365
Other rules and regulations	17.10	368
ORDERS	17.12	369
APPENDIX A: DRAFT LAND REGISTRATION BILL		**371**
APPENDIX B: LIST OF RESPONDENTS TO CONSULTATIVE DOCUMENT LAW COM NO 254		**602**

THE LAW COMMISSION AND HM LAND REGISTRY

Item 5(a) of the Law Commission's Seventh Programme of Law Reform

To the Right Honourable the Lord Irvine of Lairg, Lord High Chancellor of Great Britain

PART I
THE LAND REGISTRATION BILL AND ITS OBJECTIVES

INTRODUCTION

1.1 The Land Registration Bill is the final outcome of six years' joint work by the Law Commission and HM Land Registry.[1] The purpose of the Bill is a bold and striking one. It is to create the necessary legal framework in which registered conveyancing can be conducted electronically. The move from a paper-based system of conveyancing to one that is entirely electronic is a very major one and it will transform fundamentally the manner in which the process is conducted. The Bill will bring about an unprecedented conveyancing revolution within a comparatively short time. It will also make other profound changes to the substantive law that governs registered land. These changes, taken together, are likely to be even more far-reaching than the great reforms of property law that were made by the 1925 property legislation. Not only will the Bill introduce a wholly different method of conveyancing, but, as we explain below, it will also alter the way in which title to land is perceived.[2] The Land Registration Bill is the largest single law reform Bill and project that has been undertaken in the Law Commission since its foundation in 1965.

1.2 When the Law Commission and HM Land Registry first began planning the Bill, the possibility that conveyancing might be conducted electronically had scarcely been mooted. The Consultative Document from which the Bill derives, "Land Registration for the Twenty-First Century", which the Law Commission and HM Land Registry published in 1998,[3] set the agenda for the development of dematerialised conveyancing and stimulated a good deal of public debate. There is now wide support, both within the property industry and from many legal practitioners, for the introduction of a system of dealing with land in dematerialised form. Indeed, such a system has come to be regarded as inevitable.

---

[1] The collaboration has already resulted in Land Registration Act 1997, which (amongst other things) extended the triggers to compulsory first registration and recast the provisions on indemnity.

[2] See below, para 1.10.

[3] (1998) Law Com No 254, referred to throughout this Report as "the Consultative Document". See below, para 1.15.

The Bill provides the necessary changes to the law at precisely the time when they are needed. It will enable those who deal with property to take full advantage of the developments in information technology unconstrained by out-of-date legislation.

1.3   In this Part we explain—

    (1)   the objectives of the Bill and the thinking behind them;

    (2)   some key features of the Bill; and

    (3)   the background to the Bill and how it has come about.

THE OBJECTIVES OF THE BILL

1.4   We have explained above that a system of conveyancing conducted in dematerialised form is now regarded as inevitable.[4] Dealings with land cannot remain unaffected by the general development of electronic commerce. Nevertheless, however inevitable it may now seem, there is a legitimate public expectation that the change to an electronically based system for dealings with land will produce clear and demonstrable benefits. The public rightly seeks a more expeditious and much less stressful system of dealing with land. It also wants to see better protection for title to land and for the rights and interests that exist in land. The Bill attempts to meet these expectations.

1.5   **The fundamental objective of the Bill is that, under the system of electronic dealing with land that it seeks to create, the register should be a complete and accurate reflection of the state of the title of the land at any given time, so that it is possible to investigate title to land on line, with the absolute minimum of additional enquiries and inspections.**

1.6   Although that ultimate objective[5] may seem an obvious one, its implications are considerable, and virtually all the changes that the Bill makes to the present law flow directly from it. The Bill is necessarily limited in its scope to registered land or to dealings with unregistered land in England and Wales that will trigger first registration. Although the great majority of titles are in fact now registered, there are still substantial amounts of land (particularly in rural areas) that are unregistered. However, as we explain in Part II, unregistered land has had its day.[6] In the comparatively near future, it will be necessary to take steps to bring what is left of it on to the register.[7]

1.7   The process of registration of title is conducted by the State through the agency of HM Land Registry. Indeed, the State guarantees the title to registered land. If, therefore, any person suffers loss as a result of some mistake or omission in the

---

[4]   See above, para 1.2.

[5]   It will not be achieved at once.

[6]   See below, para 2.9.

[7]   See below, para 2.13.

register of title, he or she is entitled to be indemnified for that loss. At present, there is no requirement that a disposition of registered land has to be entered in the register if it is to be effective. Even without registration, dispositions are valid not only between the parties to them, but as against many but not necessarily all third parties who subsequently acquire an interest in the same registered land. This is a necessity under the present law because there is a hiatus — called the "registration gap" — between the making of any disposition and its subsequent registration. The transfer or grant has to be submitted to the Land Registry for registration, which inevitably takes some time.[8] It would be wholly unacceptable for the transfer or grant to have no legal effect in that interim period. It should be noted that there are some interests in registered land, presently known as overriding interests, which are not protected in the register at all but which nonetheless bind *any* person who subsequently acquires an interest in the land affected. This is so whether or not that person knew of, or could readily have discovered, the existence of these interests.

1.8   If it is to be possible to achieve the fundamental objective of the Bill mentioned in paragraph 1.5 above—

(1)   all express dispositions of registered land will have to be appropriately protected on the register unless there are very good reasons for no doing so;

(2)   the categories of overriding interests will have to be very significantly reduced in scope; and

(3)   dispositions of registered land will have to be registered simultaneously, so that it becomes impossible to make most dispositions of registered land except by registering them.

The aim stated in (3) will be possible only if conveyancing practitioners are authorised to initiate the process of registration when dispositions of registered land are made by their clients. This is a very significant departure from present practice.

1.9   To achieve the goals stated in paragraph 1.8 will also require a change in attitude. There is a widely-held perception that it is unreasonable to expect people to register their rights over land. We find this puzzling given the overwhelming prevalence of registered title. Furthermore, the law has long required compliance with certain formal requirements for the transfer of interests in land and for contracts to sell or dispose of such interests. The wisdom of these requirements is not seriously questioned. We cannot see why the further step of registration should be regarded as so onerous. In any event, under the system of electronic conveyancing that we envisage (and for which the Bill makes provision), not only will the process of registration become very much easier, but the execution of the

---

[8]   Registration is effective from the time when an application is taken to have been received in the Registry.

transaction in electronic form and its simultaneous registration will be inextricably linked.

1.10   These changes will necessarily alter the perception of title to land. It will be the fact of registration and registration alone that confers title. This is entirely in accordance with the fundamental principle of a conclusive register which underpins the Bill.[9]

SOME KEY FEATURES OF THE BILL

1.11   It may be helpful to list some of the most striking changes that the Bill will either introduce as soon as it is brought into force or allow to be introduced subsequently. Two of the main changes—in relation to the introduction of electronic conveyancing and the recasting of the law on adverse possession—call for specific comment.

Electronic conveyancing

1.12   The Bill will create a framework in which it will be possible to transfer and create interests in registered land by electronic means. It is envisaged that, within a comparatively short time, it will it will be the only method of conducting registered conveyancing. As we have indicated above,[10] an essential feature of the electronic system when it is fully operational is that it will be impossible to create or transfer many rights in or over registered land expressly except by registering them. Investigation of title will be almost entirely online. It is intended that the secure electronic communications network on which the system will be based, will be used to provide information about properties for intending buyers. It will also provide a means of managing a chain of transactions by monitoring them electronically. This will enable the cause of delays in any chain to be identified and remedial action encouraged. It is anticipated that far fewer chains will break in consequence and that transactions will be considerably expedited. Faster conveyancing is also likely to provide the most effective way of curbing gazumping. The process of registration under the electronic system will be initiated by solicitors and licensed conveyancers, though the Land Registry will exercise control over the changes that can be made to the register. Electronic conveyancing will not come into being as soon as the Bill is brought into force. It will be introduced over a number of years, and there will be a time when both the paper and electronic systems co-exist.

Adverse possession

1.13   The Bill abandons the notion that a squatter acquires title once he or she has been in adverse possession for 12 years. It creates new rules in relation to registered land that will confer greater protection against the acquisition of title by persons in adverse possession. This is consistent with one of the objectives of the Bill—that it is registration alone that should confer title.[11] The essence of the new scheme is

---

[9]   See above, para 1.5

[10]   See para 1.8.

[11]   See above, para 1.10.

that a squatter will be able to apply to be registered as proprietor after 10 years' adverse possession. However, the registered proprietor will be notified of that application and will, in most cases, be able to object to it.[12] If he or she does, the application will be rejected. However, the proprietor will then have to take steps to evict the squatter or otherwise regularise his or her position within two years. If the squatter is still in adverse possession after two years, he or she will be entitled to be registered as proprietor. We consider that this new scheme strikes a fairer balance between landowner and squatter than does the present law. It also reflects the fact that the basis of title to registered land is the fact of registration, not (as is the case with unregistered land) possession.

Other changes

1.14 Some of the other striking changes that the Bill makes can be summarised as follows—

- the requirement of compulsory registration of title is to be extended to leases granted for more than 7 years, with power to reduce the length of registrable leases still further;

- in favour of those dealing with them, owners of registered land will be presumed to have unrestricted powers of disposition in the absence of any entry on the register;

- the rules as to the competing priority of interests in registered land will be clarified and simplified;

- the protection for rights in or over registered land will be simplified and improved by the extension of notices and restrictions and the prospective abolition of cautions and inhibitions;

- the range of overriding interests will be significantly restricted in their scope: the ambit of particular categories of overriding interests will be narrowed, some categories will be abolished altogether and others will be phased out after 10 years;

- it will become possible to access the history of a registered title (to the extent that the Registry has it) if there is a reason to see it;

- charge certificates will be abolished and land certificates will have a much less important role;

- Crown land, including much of the foreshore around England and Wales, that is not presently registrable will become so; and

- a new system of independent adjudication of disputes arising out of disputed applications to the registrar will be set up.

---

[12] If there is no objection to the application, the squatter will be registered.

1.15   As we have indicated above,[13] the Land Registration Bill has its genesis in the Consultative Document, "Land Registration for the Twenty-First Century", which was published by the Law Commission and HM Land Registry in 1998.[14] This was part of the continuing work of the Law Commission and Land Registry on the reform of the law on land registration.[15] That Document was prompted by three factors—

(1)   the need to create the legal environment in which it was possible to conduct conveyancing in electronic form and which reflected the possibilities that electronic conveyancing could offer;[16]

(2)   the unsatisfactory nature of the legislation that governs land registration;[17]

(3)   the need to create principles that reflected the fact that registered land was different from unregistered land and rested on different principles.[18]

The Document set out in great detail the present law and made proposals for the reform of almost all aspects of it, having regard to the three matters listed above.

1.16   The Consultative Document attracted a good deal of interest and attention. There were nearly 70 written responses, many of them very detailed and well-informed. We list those who kindly responded in Appendix B to this Report. In addition to these written responses, the Law Commission and Land Registry had the benefit of the views that were expressed at three very well-attended seminars that were held to discuss the proposals, namely—

(1)   a seminar for members of the Bar held at Falcon Chambers and kindly organised by Derek Wood, CBE, QC;

(2)   a meeting of the Chancery Bar Association; and

(3)   a meeting of the Property Litigation Association.

Furthermore, both Steve Kelway, the General Counsel to the E-Conveyancing Taskforce at HM Land Registry, and Charles Harpum, the relevant Law Commissioner, have spoken regularly to firms of solicitors around the country, to seek their views on the development of electronic conveyancing. We are very

---

[13]   See para 1.2.

[14]   (1998) Law Com No 254.

[15]   The Consultative Document was the second report produced by the Law Commission and HM Land Registry. The recommendations contained in the first, Land Registration: Land Registration: First Report of a Joint Working Group (1995) Law Com No 235, were implemented by Land Registration Act 1997. For the background to this joint collaboration, see Law Com No 254, paras 1.7—1.9.

[16]   Law Com No 254, para 1.2.

[17]   Principally the Land Registration Act 1925. See Law Com No 254, para 1.3.

[18]   Law Com No 254, para 1.6.

grateful to all of those who went to so much time and trouble to assist us. It will be apparent from the Bill and the commentary on it that their efforts were not wasted. We gratefully acknowledge the assistance that we have received from others on specific aspects of the Bill elsewhere in this Report.

1.17   The great majority of the recommendations contained in the Consultative Document were accepted on consultation. Where different or better views were expressed, they have been accepted in preference, as the Report makes clear. There is only one issue upon which we have diverged from the views of respondents, and that concerns the length of registrable leases.[19] Having regard to other, compelling policy objectives, we did not follow the trend of responses.

1.18   There are two matters on which we sought views in the Consultative Document which were supported on consultation which we have nevertheless not taken forward.

1.19   First, the proposals contained in Part X of the Consultative Document[20] on prescription have been abandoned for three reasons—

(1)   there was not a compelling case for the reform of the law of prescription in the context of registered land alone as there was in relation to the law of adverse possession;

(2)   the Law Commission is now undertaking a comprehensive review of easements and land obligations which will include prescription and it seems better to view prescription as a totality; and

(3)   some of the conveyancing concerns that informed our proposals[21] have been addressed in more direct ways in the Bill.[22]

1.20   Secondly, we have not made any specific recommendations in relation to a problem thrown up by the decision of the Court of Appeal in *Brown & Root Technology Ltd v Sun Alliance & London Assurance Co Ltd*.[23] The particular problem there was as follows. A tenant had assigned a registered lease. The assignee did not register the assignment. The assignor then exercised a break clause and successfully determined the lease. This case caused considerable concern and we explored a number of ways in which it might be resolved in the Consultative Document.[24] However, we have decided that no reform is needed because the law already provides an adequate remedy. Where a seller of land[25] has executed a transfer of a registered title, he or she holds that land on a bare trust

---

[19]   See below, para 3.14.

[20]   See Law Com No 254, paras 10.79 and following.

[21]   See Law Com No 254, para 10.89(2).

[22]   See below, para 8.66.

[23]   [2000] 2 WLR 566.

[24]   See Law Com No 254, paras 11.26—11.29.

[25]   Including an assignor of a lease for valuable consideration.

for the buyer until the buyer is registered as proprietor. If the seller purports to dispose of the land after it has been transferred but before registration, he or she commits a breach of trust for which the usual remedies exist. The problem thrown up by the *Brown & Root* case will disappear when electronic conveyancing is introduced, because the making of dispositions and their registration will occur simultaneously.[26]

STRUCTURE OF THE REPORT

1.21 In Part II of this Report we explain the principal changes to the law which the Bill will make.[27] In Parts III—XVII, we provide a detailed commentary on the Bill and explain how it is intended to operate. That commentary follows the structure of the Bill in most respects, but not slavishly.

---

[26] See above, para 1.12.

[27] We have not included a statement of the present law on land registration because the matter was exhaustively considered in the Consultative Document, Law Com No 254, to which reference should be made.

PART II
SUMMARY OF THE MAIN CHANGES
MADE BY THE BILL

INTRODUCTION

2.1 In Part I of this Report, we stated that the Land Registration Bill would bring about the most fundamental changes to conveyancing and land law since the reforms of 1925.[1] Indeed, the effect of the Bill may be even more profound than the changes made in 1925. Three of its features are particularly striking—

(1) It creates a new system of electronic conveyancing that is quite different from, and will supersede, the present paper-based practice. One of its main aims is to make it possible to investigate title as far as possible on-line, with a minimum of additional enquiries.

(2) When the system of electronic conveyancing is fully operative, the transfer or creation of many interests in land will only be effective when registered. An electronic system means that these two distinct steps will in fact occur simultaneously. This overcomes the difficulties that presently exist because of the so-called "registration gap"[2] and means that the register will become conclusive as to the priority of most expressly created interests in registered land.

(3) It introduces a new system of adverse possession, applicable only to registered estates and registered rentcharges. This system is based upon the recognition that registration is the basis of title to registered land and not possession (as is the case in relation to unregistered land).

2.2 In this Part, as a necessary prelude to the technical commentary on the Bill that follows, we summarise the main changes that the Bill will make to the present law. For the convenience of readers, we examine the topics in the order in which they appear in the Report.[3] That order is determined partly, but by no means exclusively, by the arrangement of clauses in the Bill, rather than by the intrinsic importance or novelty of the provisions. Indeed the explanations of both electronic conveyancing and the new provisions on adverse possession appear towards the end of the Report.

2.3 The matters addressed in this Part are as follows—

(1) first registration;

---

[1] See above, para 1.1.

[2] See below, para 2.45.

[3] Certain matters, such as the Land Registry, which is the subject of a short Part of the Report, require no comment here, as it is not the subject of any significant change.

(2)   cautions against first registration;

(3)   powers of disposition;

(4)   registrable dispositions;

(5)   priorities;

(6)   notices and restrictions;

(7)   charges;

(8)   overriding interests;

(9)   registration;

(10)   special cases;

(11)   alteration, rectification and indemnity;

(12)   conveyancing: general matters;

(13)   electronic conveyancing;

(14)   adverse possession;

(15)   judicial provisions; and

(16)   rules.

In the course of this review, we make one recommendation. This relates to the future extension of compulsory registration of title,[4] and it is for future action.

FIRST REGISTRATION

2.4   The provisions governing first registration were recast comparatively recently by the Land Registration Act 1997. This Act was the first result of the joint work on land registration by HM Land Registry and the Law Commission and it greatly extended the dispositions which trigger the compulsory registration of land.[5] The Bill does make further changes to the law, but they are less extensive than those made by the 1997 Act.[6] Four of these changes are, however, particularly noteworthy.

2.5   First, in response to views expressed on consultation, the Bill permits the voluntary registration in two cases where it is not presently possible. Profits *à prendre* in gross[7] and franchises[8] may be registered with their own titles, provided

---

[4]   See below, para 2.13.

[5]   See Land Registration Act 1925, ss 123, 123A.

[6]   See generally, Part III of this Report.

[7]   Such as fishing or shooting rights.

that they are held for an interest equivalent to a fee simple or under a lease of which there are still 7 years to run.[9] Such rights often have considerable economic value and, particularly in the case of certain profits (such as fishing rights), are not infrequently bought and sold. At present such rights can only be noted in the register.

2.6 Secondly, the length of leases that are subject to compulsory registration is reduced. Leases granted for more than 7 years (rather than for more than 21 years as at present) will be subject to the requirement of registration,[10] with a power to reduce the period still further.[11] At present, most business leases — the most common form of commercial dealing with land — are granted for periods of less than 21 years[12] and are therefore incapable of registration. We can see no justification for excluding such leases from the benefits of land registration and, in particular, electronic conveyancing. Furthermore, it is absurd to continue to maintain two separate systems of conveyancing — the registered and unregistered — particularly as these will become much more divergent as a result of this Bill. Unregistered conveyancing must be given its quietus as soon as possible.

2.7 Thirdly, the Bill makes it possible for the Crown to register for the first time land that is held in demesne — in other words land that it holds in its capacity as ultimate feudal overlord. At present only estates in land can be registered,[13] and land which the Crown holds in demesne is not held for an estate.[14] The Bill enables the Crown to grant itself a freehold estate so that it can register it.[15] This is of some practical importance because the amount of land held in demesne is considerable. In particular, most of the foreshore is so held and cannot at present be registered. If such land is registered, it will be easier for the Crown to protect it against adverse possession[16] under the provisions explained below.[17] This is very much in the public interest, as it preserves the foreshore from incursions.

2.8 Fourthly, the territorial extent of the land that can be registered is significantly increased by the Bill so that some submarine land will become registrable.[18]

---

[8] Such as the right to hold a market.

[9] Cl 3; see below, paras 3.19, 3.20.

[10] Cl 4; see below, paras 3.13—3.16.

[11] Cl 116; see below, para 3.17.

[12] See, eg, BPF/IPD, *Annual Lease Review 2000*, p 6: "Considerably shorter terms are evident in new lease agreements with almost three-quarters of new leases... now lasting just 15 years".

[13] Land Registration Act 1925, s 2.

[14] This has a number of other consequences for land registration that the Bill also addresses: see paras 11.20 and following.

[15] Cl 79; below, para 11.11.

[16] Typically by persons building jetties and piers out into the sea.

[17] See paras 2.69 and following.

[18] Cl 127; below, para 3.5. This was prompted by our discussions with the Crown Estate, which is anxious to have this extension.

2.9   We consider that, in principle, the remaining unregistered land should be phased out as quickly as possible and that all land in England and Wales should be registered. As we have indicated above,[19] the continuation of two parallel systems of conveyancing, registered and unregistered, has absolutely nothing to commend it. Furthermore, as a result of the change to an open register in 1990, the contents of the register are now public.[20] The register is no longer something of concern only to conveyancers but provides an important source of publicly available information about land, a resource in which there is an increasing interest. However, the Bill does not introduce any system to compel the registration of all land that is presently unregistered. This may at first sight appear paradoxical, but there are three particularly compelling reasons for not doing so at this juncture.

2.10   First, we consider that it would be premature to do so. Not only have the changes made by the 1997 Act only recently started to have effect, but the present Bill will offer considerable additional benefits to those whose titles are registered, quite apart from the conveyancing advantages should they wish to sell or deal with their land.[21] We therefore anticipate a very significant rise in voluntary first registrations as a result.[22] Compulsion should not be employed in our view until it is clear that existing provisions have been given an opportunity to work.

2.11   Secondly, compulsory registration is at present triggered by the making of many of the commonest dispositions of unregistered land. It is not at all easy to devise a system of compelling compulsory registration of title other than one that operates on a disposition of the land in question. The mechanisms of compulsion in such situations are not self-evident and there are dangers in devising a system that could be heavy handed. Any such system would obviously have to comply with the European Convention on Human Rights. The means employed would therefore have to be proportionate to the desired ends.

2.12   Thirdly, the implementation of the present Bill, which makes such striking and fundamental changes to the law governing registered land and the methods of conveyancing that apply to it, is likely to stretch the resources of both the conveyancing profession and HM Land Registry for some years after its introduction. We doubt that it would be possible to accommodate a programme for the compulsory registration of all the remaining unregistered land at the same time.

2.13   Nevertheless, we recognise that total registration is a goal that should be sought within the comparatively near future. **We therefore recommend that ways in which all remaining land with unregistered title in England and Wales**

---

[19]   Para 2.6.

[20]   The change was made pursuant to the Land Registration Act 1988.

[21]   In particular, the protection that the Bill offers against acquisition of title by adverse possession: see below, paras 2.69 and following.

[22]   As a result of the changes made by the Land Registration Act 1997, it is cheaper to register land voluntarily than if compulsory registration is triggered by a disposition.

might be brought on to the register should be re-examined five years after the present Bill is brought into force.

CAUTIONS AGAINST FIRST REGISTRATION

2.14 As the name suggests, cautions against first registration provide a means by which a person, having some estate or interest in the land affected, may be notified of an application for first registration.[23] Such cautions exist under the present law.[24] The principal changes to the present law that the Bill makes are as follows. First, it places the register of such cautions on a statutory footing and makes provision for its alteration by analogy with the provisions applicable to the register of title. Secondly, it makes it impossible for a person to lodge a caution against first registration in relation to his or her own estate, where that estate is registrable.[25] The entry of a caution against first registration is not intended to be a substitute for the registration of an estate where such registration is possible.[26]

POWERS OF DISPOSITION

2.15 As we have indicated,[27] one of the goals of the Bill is to make it possible for title to land to be investigated almost entirely on-line. The register must therefore provide all the necessary information about the title. One ground on which a disposition of land might be challenged is that the party who made it was acting outside his or her powers in some way, as for example, where a statutory body such as a local authority made a disposition that it was not permitted to make.[28] The present law is not entirely clear on this point. However, it has been assumed that a registered proprietor is to be taken to have all the powers of disposition that an absolute owner of a registered estate or charge would have under the general law, unless there is some entry in the register, such as a restriction or caution, which limits those powers.[29] The Bill gives statutory effect to that assumption.[30] At the same time, it makes it clear that, although a disponee's title will be protected if some limitation on those powers has not been entered in the register,[31] this does not make the disposition lawful.[32] The protection given to the disponee's title does not

---

[23] For cautions against first registration under the Bill, see paras 3.54 and following. For the relevant provisions of the Bill, see Cls 15—22.

[24] See Land Registration Act 1925, s 53.

[25] This prohibition takes effect two years after the Bill is brought into force.

[26] There are, however, special provisions dealing with Crown land that is held in demesne: see paras 11.17 and following.

[27] See above, para 2.1(1).

[28] For a case involving an *ultra vires* disposition of registered land by a charity, see *Hounslow London Borough Council v Hare* (1990) 24 HLR 9.

[29] Cf *State Bank of India v Sood* [1997] Ch 276, 284.

[30] See Cls 23, 26, 52. See below, paras 4.5—4.11 and 7.7, respectively.

[31] For the future, the appropriate entry will be a restriction, because cautions are prospectively abolished: see below, paras 2.19 and following.

[32] See Cls 26, 52. See below, paras 4.8—4.11 and 7.7, respectively.

therefore prejudice any claims that may arise in relation to the improper exercise of that power.[33]

REGISTRABLE DISPOSITIONS

2.16 The Bill lists the transactions that are registrable dispositions, in other words, those dispositions that transfer or create a legal estate and which should, therefore, be completed by registration.[34] There are two novelties in the Bill. First, the concept of registrable dispositions is extended to leases granted for more than 7 years or (rather than for more than 21 years, as at present),[35] with a power to reduce that period still further.[36] This echoes the position in relation to first registration.[37] Secondly, Schedule 2 sets out precisely what the registration requirements are for registrable dispositions.

PRIORITIES

2.17 At present, the law that governs the priority of interests in registered land is partly a matter of express provision in the Land Registration Act 1925 and partly a matter of common law where that Act is silent. Although the relevant common law principles have been clarified by judicial decision, they are still in some respects uncertain. The Bill therefore sets out in statutory form the principles of priority that apply in relation to interests in registered land. The effect of the general principle stated in the Bill is that the date of the creation of an interest determines its priority, whether or not it is protected in the register.[38] However, by way of exception, where a registrable disposition is registered, it takes priority over any interest that affected the estate immediately prior to the disposition that is not protected at the time of registration.[39] Subject to certain exceptions, of which overriding interests are the most important, an interest will only be protected if it is a registered charge or the subject of a notice in the register. When electronic conveyancing becomes the norm, it is likely to become impossible to create or transfer many interests in registered land except by simultaneously registering them.[40] In this way, creation and registration will coincide so that the register will in fact become conclusive as to the priority of many interests and not just, as now, of interests under registered dispositions.

2.18 The Bill also clarifies the status of certain rights for the purposes of registered land, namely rights of pre-emption, an equity arising by estoppel and a mere

---

[33] If, for example, trustees sell land without obtaining the consent of a beneficiary that is required by the trust instrument, the transfer to the buyer will be unimpeachable. However, the trustees will remain liable for their breach of trust.

[34] Cl 27.

[35] Cl 27(2)(b)(i).

[36] Cl 116.

[37] See above, para 2.6.

[38] See Cl 28; below, para 5.5.

[39] Cls 29, 30; below, paras 5.6 and following.

[40] See below, para 2.59.

equity. All are treated as proprietary interests from the time of their creation for the purposes of the Bill.[41]

NOTICES AND RESTRICTIONS

2.19 Not only does the Bill seek to make title to registered land more secure, but it also attempts to enhance substantially the protection given to the interests of third parties over registered land. The Bill does this by simplifying the methods of protecting such interests in the register and, at the same time, extending the protection that an entry in the register gives. Two of the existing forms of protection — cautions against dealings and inhibitions — are prospectively abolished, subject to transitional provisions.[42] Cautions against dealings do not protect the priority of an interest, but merely give the cautioner a right to be notified of an impending dealing with the registered land. However, where a person who wishes to protect his or her interest in the register cannot obtain the consent of the registered proprietor to the entry of a notice or restriction, a caution is the only available option. Inhibitions are merely one form of restriction on a registered proprietor's powers. They prevent the registration of *any* disposition of a registered estate or charge.[43] There is no good reason for retaining them as a separate form of entry.

2.20 The only two forms of protection under the Bill are notices and restrictions.[44] A notice is appropriate to protect incumbrances on land that are intended to bind third parties, such as the burden of a lease, an easement or a restrictive covenant.[45] A restriction regulates the circumstances in which a disposition of a registered estate or charge may be the subject of an entry in the register.[46] It can be used for many purposes, for example to ensure that—

(1) where there is a disposition of land held on a trust of land or a settlement, the proceeds are paid to at least two trustees or to a trust corporation, thereby overreaching the interests under the trust or settlement;

(2) where any consents are required to a disposition, they are obtained; or

(3) where a corporation or other body has limited powers, to indicate this limitation.[47]

---

[41] See Cls 113, 114; below, paras 5.26 and following.

[42] Schedule 12, para 2(2)—(4). Cautions *against dealings* are not be confused with cautions *against first registration* which are, as we have explained above, retained under the Bill: see para 2.14.

[43] Land Registration Act 1925, s 57.

[44] See Cls 32—47, discussed in Part VI of this Report.

[45] See Cl 32; below, para 6.6.

[46] See Cl 40; below, para 6.34.

[47] Cf above, para 2.15.

2.21 Under the Bill it will be possible either to enter a notice or apply for a restriction without the consent of the registered proprietor.[48] However, in such a case, the proprietor will be notified—

(1) in the case of a notice, of its entry and will be able to apply for its cancellation;[49] and

(2) in the case of a restriction, of the application, to which he may then object.[50]

2.22 The Bill also imposes a duty on a person to act reasonably in exercising the right to apply for the entry of a notice or restriction. The duty is owed to any person who suffers damages in consequence of the breach of that duty.[51]

CHARGES

2.23 Such changes as the Bill makes in relation to charges are mainly of a technical kind.[52] Two are, however, significant. First, the law that governs the priority of further advances made by chargees is recast so that it coincides with present practice. A new method of making further advances is also offered.[53] Secondly, the Bill imposes a duty on the registrar (for breach of which indemnity is payable) to inform existing chargees whose charges are protected in the register, of any overriding statutory charge when it is registered.[54]

OVERRIDING INTERESTS

2.24 Overriding interests are interests that are not protected in the register but are, nonetheless, binding on any person who acquires an interest in registered land, whether on first registration or where there has been a registrable disposition of a registered estate that has been completed by registration. The range of interests that are presently overriding is significant. They include many easements (whether or not these have been expressly granted or reserved),[55] the rights of persons in actual occupation,[56] leases granted for 21 years or less,[57] as well as some obscure interests that may have very serious effects on the registered proprietor (such as manorial rights). Overriding interests therefore present a very significant impediment to one of the main objectives of the Bill, namely that the register

---

[48] It will not be necessary to produce the land certificate or otherwise obtain the proprietor's consent as it is now.

[49] See Cls 35; 36; below, paras 6.26—6.31

[50] See Cl 45; below, para 6.56.

[51] Cl 77; below, paras 6.28, 6.55.

[52] See Part VII of the Report.

[53] See Cl 49; below, paras 7.28 and following.

[54] See Cl 50; below, para 7.40.

[55] Land Registration Act 1925, s 70(1)(a).

[56] *Ibid*, s 70(1)(g).

[57] *Ibid*, s 70(1)(k).

should be as complete a record of the title as it can be, with the result that it should be possible for title to land to be investigated almost entirely on-line.

2.25 The Bill seeks to restrict such interests so far as possible.[58] The guiding principle on which it proceeds is that interests should be overriding only where it is unreasonable to expect them to be protected in the register.[59] The Bill incorporates a number of strategies to achieve this objective. These include, in particular, the following—

(1) defining the categories of overriding interests more narrowly;

(2) excluding some expressly created interests from overriding status;

(3) phasing out the overriding status of the more obscure interests after 10 years and allowing for them to be entered on the appropriate register without charge in the interim;[60] and

(4) strengthening mechanisms for ensuring that overriding interests are protected in the register if they are capable of being so protected.

2.26 The move to electronic conveyancing, described below,[61] will itself facilitate the process of eliminating overriding interests. This is because it is envisaged that many interests in land will only be capable of being created when simultaneously registered.[62] Such interests will never be overriding, therefore.

2.27 It may be helpful to summarise the likely extent of overriding interests that will be binding on registered disponee of registered land ten years after the Bill is brought into force and the provisions mentioned in paragraph 2.25(3) have taken effect. They are likely to comprise—

(1) most leases granted for three years or less;

(2) the interests of persons in actual occupation where—

(a) that actual occupation is apparent; and

(b) the interest—

(i) is a beneficial interest under a trust; or

(ii) arose informally (such as an equity arising by estoppel);

---

[58] See below, Part VIII.

[59] See below, para 8.6.

[60] At the end of that period, the interests in question would not be extinguished. But if they were not appropriately protected, they would be vulnerable.

[61] See paras 2.41 and following.

[62] See above, para 2.1 (2) and below, paras 2.59 and following.

(3)   legal easements and *profits à prendre* that have arisen by implied grant or reservation or by prescription;

(4)   customary and public rights;

(5)   local land charges; and

(6)   certain mineral rights.

Each of these can be justified under the guiding principle mentioned above in paragraph 2.25.

REGISTRATION

2.28   As would be expected, the Bill contains extensive provisions relating to registration, the register and searches of the register.[63] These are provisions of considerable practical importance, though most of them are similar to existing provisions. There are some new provisions, however.

2.29   First, there is a power to record in the register the fact that a right to determine a registered estate has become exercisable. The main case that this is intended to cover is where the owner of a freehold subject to a rentcharge has failed to pay the rentcharge and the owner of that rentcharge has a power to re-enter in consequence.[64] This accords with our policy of trying so far as possible to make the register conclusive as to title, so that inquiries outside of the register are kept to a minimum.[65]

2.30   Secondly, in response to representations that were made to us on consultation, the Bill gives the registrar power to disclose information about the history of a title.[66] The register is a record of the title as it stands at any given moment. It does not explain the history of the title, nor is that history relevant in most cases. However, there are occasions when it is necessary to discover how title devolved and the Bill will enable those who have reason to discover this to be able to do so to the extent that the registrar has the information.

2.31   Thirdly, at present, land and charge certificates have to be produced on various occasions in relation to particular transactions or entries in the register. The Bill abolishes (by making no provision for) charge certificates. The role of land certificates is considerably reduced.[67]

---

[63]   See Part 6 of the Bill and below, Part IX of the Report.

[64]   See Cl 64 and below, paras 9.29—9.35, where we explain how this power will be made effective.

[65]   See above, para 2.1(1).

[66]   Cl 69; below, paras 9.58—9.60.

[67]   See Schedule 10, para 4; below, paras 9.83—9.91.

SPECIAL CASES

2.32 The Bill makes provision for certain special cases.[68] Of these, the only one where the Bill makes significant changes to the present law is in relation to the Crown.[69] The Bill addresses three difficulties that presently exist.

2.33 First, much of the land which the Crown holds is not held by it in freehold tenure but in demesne. In other words it holds the land in its capacity as ultimate feudal overlord of whom all freehold land in England and Wales is directly (or perhaps very occasionally indirectly) held. However, as we have mentioned,[70] it is only possible to register a freehold or leasehold estate, so that much of the land that the Crown holds, cannot be registered.[71] The Crown Estate wishes to be able to register land held in demesne. The Bill makes provision by which the Crown may grant to itself a fee simple for this purpose.[72]

2.34 Secondly, the Bill makes provision for the Crown to lodge cautions against the first registration of land held in demesne.[73] Although "Crown cautions" have been lodged in the past, there is no express right to do so under the present legislation and the Bill places the matter beyond doubt.

2.35 Thirdly, there are occasions when an estate in fee simple determines and the land escheats to the Crown.[74] At present, if the title to such land is registered, it should be removed from the register because it ceases to be held in fee simple and is, instead, held in demesne.[75] The Bill contains provisions to ensure that entries in the register in relation to such escheated land remain until the land is disposed of by the Crown or pursuant to an order of the court.[76]

2.36 Our discussions with those representing Her Majesty, the Crown Estate and the Duchies of Cornwall and Lancaster were necessarily both detailed and protracted. As will become clear from Part XI of this Report, this is because of the complexities of—

(1) the application of principles of feudal tenure in relation to the Crown; and

---

[68] See Part 7 of the Bill and below, Part XI of this Report.

[69] The other provisions, such as those on bankruptcy, differ from the present law only in minor details.

[70] See above, para 2.7.

[71] Cf *Scmlla Properties Ltd v Gesso Properties (BVI) Ltd* [1995] BCC 793, 798.

[72] Cl 79; below, para 11.11. Such provision is needed because at common law the Crown cannot grant itself a fee simple. It cannot hold directly of itself as feudal tenant.

[73] Cl 81; below, para 11.17. Grants by the Crown out of demesne land will, as now, be subject to the provisions on compulsory first registration: see Cl 80.

[74] There are, we understand, in the region of 500 such cases every year and they normally arise out of the insolvency of a company. In such cases, the liabilities that affect the land normally exceed its value.

[75] The Crown incurs no responsibility for escheated land unless the escheat has been completed by some act of entry or management by it in relation to the land.

[76] Cl 82; below, paras 11.28 and following.

(2)	the legislation governing dispositions of property by the Royal Duchies.

It was either difficult or, in some cases, impossible, to achieve the straightforward and sensible outcomes that all parties desired.[77] This was partly because of these complexities and in part because the feudal character of the applicable rules of law was fundamentally at variance with the way in which land is now transferred or granted. Both the Crown and the Royal Duchies have important public functions in relation to land. They also have large commercial property portfolios. The rules of law under which they are presently required to operate impede the efficient conduct of their functions. They also create difficulties for those who deal with the Crown and the Duchies.

2.37	We consider that there is a strong case for creating a clear and comprehensive legislative framework that would govern—

(1)	the holding of land by the Crown and the Royal Duchies;

(2)	the circumstances in which land passes to the Crown and the Duchies because it is ownerless; and

(3)	the rights and responsibilities of the Crown and the Duchies in relation to such property, particularly when (as is usually the case) it is of an onerous character.

We cannot immediately see any good reason for the retention of the remaining aspects of feudalism in England and Wales. We note that the Scottish Parliament recently abolished the admittedly more pervasive feudal system that applied in Scotland.[78]

ALTERATION, RECTIFICATION AND INDEMNITY

2.38	Mistakes do occasionally occur in the register[79] and it is also necessary to update it to take account of interests that have determined. The Bill does not make major changes to the present law and practice on the alteration of the register. What it does do is to codify that present practice in a way that makes its working apparent.[80] The present legislation obscures what actually occurs.

2.39	The law governing the payment of indemnity for mistakes that have occurred in the register and other losses for which the Registry is responsible was revised by the Land Registration Act 1997. The Bill does not, therefore, make anything more than minor changes to the present law.[81]

---

[77]	It was on occasions not possible to be sure what the relevant principles of law were.

[78]	Abolition of Feudal Tenure etc (Scotland) Act 2000.

[79]	They are in practice few, as the small number of successful claims for indemnity makes clear.

[80]	See Schedule 4; discussed in Part X of this Report.

[81]	See Schedule 8, discussed below, paras 10.29 and following.

CONVEYANCING: GENERAL MATTERS

2.40 The fact that the register is a public document that is readily and cheaply accessible means that the provisions of the Land Registration Act 1925 that prescribe what proof of title a seller of a registered estate must deduce[82] are now badly out of date. They were conceived at a time when the register was closed and could be inspected only with the permission of the registered proprietor and when searches in the register had to be conducted in person at HM Land Registry in London.[83] These prescriptive rules are not replicated in the Bill, though there is a power to make rules as to the obligations of a seller in relation to the proof and perfection of his or her title.[84]

ELECTRONIC CONVEYANCING

Introduction

2.41 The move from a paper-based system of conveyancing to one that is entirely electronic is the most important single feature of the Bill.[85] However, it should not be thought that this is something sudden. It is in fact the logical culmination of a process that has been going on for a number of years.[86] The land register has been progressively computerised and almost all registered titles have now been entered on the computer. A system of direct access to the computerised register was first introduced in 1995. It is now known as Land Registry Direct.[87] Even electronic conveyancing has begun. It is already possible to notify the Registry of the discharge of a registered charge by electronic means,[88] and applications to register dealings with registered land can be lodged electronically.[89] The development of electronic conveyancing is occurring simultaneously and in tandem with the development of the National Land Information Service, which is an on-line system of access to a range of sources of information about property that are held in disparate places. NLIS provides a means of searching other registers that relate to property such as local authority registers of local land charges and the details of coal mines that are kept by the Coal Authority. It is worth emphasising that electronic conveyancing will employ well-established computer technology and it will be capable of operation from the personal computers that most practitioners already have. The move to electronic conveyancing will not require any great capital outlay by them.

---

[82] Land Registration Act 1925, s 110(1)—(3), (5). Section 110 applies "on a sale or other disposition of registered land to a purchaser other than a lessee or chargee".

[83] Postal searches of the register were introduced in 1930. For their impact on conveyancing, see Alain Pottage, "The Originality of Registration" (1995) 15 OJLS 371.

[84] Schedule 10, para 2; below, para 12.8.

[85] For an explanation of the provisions governing electronic conveyancing, see Part XIII of this Report. For the relevant provisions of the Bill, see Cls 91—94; Schedule 5.

[86] Cf Ruoff & Roper, *Registered Conveyancing*, 1-11.

[87] For the conditions of use, see Ruoff & Roper, *Registered Conveyancing*, F-11, F-12.

[88] Land Registration Rules 1925, r 151A.

[89] See Land Registration Rules 2001, SI 2001 No 619.

2.42   We begin by giving a brief summary of the present practice in relation to dealings with registered land and then explain how electronic conveyancing may work.

Present conveyancing practice in relation to registered land

2.43   In many transactions, typically the sale of a freehold or leasehold property, there is a contract of sale that precedes the eventual transfer or other disposition. At present, on a sale of registered land, it is not the usual practice to protect this estate contract by the entry of a notice or caution in the register. The buyer protects his or her position more effectively instead by making a priority search under the Land Registration (Official Searches) Rules 1993.

2.44   Transfers and other dispositions of a legal estate are made in paper form by deed. They are then submitted in that format by the disponee to the Land Registry for the appropriate form of registration.

2.45   When it is executed, the transfer (or other disposition) operates only in equity until it is registered or entered in the register. In other words, the disposition creates an interest in registered land even before it is registered.[90] Furthermore, there is an inevitable hiatus between the disposition and its entry in the register and this so-called "registration gap" has been a source of problems.[91] When the relevant registration or entry in the register is made, it takes effect from the date on which, under rules, the application for registration is deemed to be delivered to the Registry.[92] This is so even though, in those more complicated transactions in which HM Land Registry raises requisitions, that date may be considerably earlier than the actual date of registration. In practice it is important that the disposition is taken to be registered from the date of deemed delivery of the application.[93] In complex transactions, it often takes some time to sort out matters such as cross-easements and other ancillary rights, and this tends to be done after the application has been submitted for registration.

2.46   The Land Registry only becomes involved in a transaction *after* a disposition has been made. It is only at that stage that problems come to light and requisitions are raised because applications are in some way found to be defective.[94]

---

[90]   This is reflected in the rule that governs the priority of competing minor interests, namely that such an interest takes its priority from the date of its creation and not from the date of its protection in the register. See Law Com No 254, para 7.17.

[91]   Rights may be created in relation to, or dispositions may be made of, the land during the period. For some examples of these difficulties, see *Abbey National Building Society v Cann* [1991] 1 AC 56; *Brown & Root Technology Ltd v Sun Alliance and London Assurance Co* [2000] 2 WLR 566.

[92]   Land Registration Rules 1925, r 83.

[93]   From our discussions we are aware that this is particularly the case in relation to conveyancing transactions that are fiscally driven (and which have to be registered before the start of the next fiscal year) and in complex commercial property transactions.

[94]   Cf Land Registration Rules 1925, r 317. About 50% of applications are defective in some way or another. Fewer mistakes occur with the new-style land registry forms, which are likely to be the model for electronic instruments.

2.47   The actual process of registration after receipt of an application is conducted entirely by the staff of HM Land Registry. The solicitor or licensed conveyancer who submits the application for registration has no part in that process and acts solely as agent for his or her client.

Electronic conveyancing: the anticipated model

Introduction

2.48   The way in which it is visualised that electronic conveyancing will operate is strikingly different.[95] Before examining how a typical dematerialised conveyancing transaction involving registered land[96] might work, two points should be emphasised.

2.49   The first is that the Land Registry's involvement in the conveyancing process will begin earlier than at present. This will be either —

   (1)   before the parties to a disposition of either—

        (a)   registered land; or

        (b)   unregistered land that will trigger compulsory registration;

        conclude a contract that is to precede that disposition;[97] or if there is no such contract,[98]

   (2)   before the relevant disposition is made.

2.50   In many cases the disposition and, where title is already registered, its simultaneous registration will be the *last* stage of the conveyancing process. That means that all the conveyancing work must be completed by that date.[99] One of the intended objectives of the new system is to identify errors and discrepancies at the earliest possible stage, and to resolve any difficulties so far as possible before registration.[100]

---

[95]   See generally Steve Kelway, "Etherlinks in the conveyancing belt" *Estates Gazette*, 2 December 2000, p 104. Mr Kelway is the General Counsel to the E-Conveyancing Taskforce at HM Land Registry.

[96]   For electronic conveyancing and applications for first registration, see below, para 2.65.

[97]   In other words, an estate contract such as a contract to sell land.

[98]   As where a registered proprietor intends to charge his land, or where (as is commonly the case) there is to be a lease without any prior agreement for a lease.

[99]   Ironically, this will bring the registered system into line with what formerly happened with unregistered conveyancing, where the deed of conveyance was the final stage of the conveyancing process. Many dispositions of unregistered land now trigger compulsory registration, so that the deed of conveyance is no longer the final stage. There has to be an application for first registration and the registrar will need to be satisfied as to the title before he can register the disposition. See Ruoff & Roper, *Registered Conveyancing*, 12-45.

[100] We have been told by many practitioners that it is not always possible for them to finalise the details of ancillary rights (typically cross-easements) in a complex conveyancing transaction and that such matters are presently resolved *after* the application for registration is made.

2.51   The second point is that changes to the register will be made as a result of the actions of the solicitors or licensed conveyancers acting for the parties to the transactions. This is explained more fully below.[101] We also explain that do-it-yourself conveyancers will not be excluded from electronic conveyancing.[102]

How a typical conveyancing transaction might operate

2.52   The manner in which electronic conveyancing might operate may be illustrated by the example of a typical contract to sell a parcel of registered land and its subsequent completion. It should be stressed that this is necessarily tentative and that what eventually appears is likely to differ in some details at least from what is set out here.[103] The system is likely to be based on a secure electronic communications network that will only be accessible by contractually authorised professionals, whether those are solicitors, licensed conveyancers, estate agents or mortgage lenders.[104] The network will not just be used for the specifically legal stages of the transaction, but also for the provision of information about the property. It is also likely to be employed to co-ordinate and manage chains of transactions,[105] provided that those transactions are dispositions of registered land or are of a kind that will trigger the requirement of compulsory registration. It is anticipated that some body — which might or might not be the Land Registry — will be made responsible for managing chain sales in order to facilitate them. When a party instructs a solicitor or licensed conveyancer to act on his or her behalf in a purchase or sale of a property in circumstances in which there is likely to be a chain, that agent will be required[106] to notify the "chain manager" of the fact of that instruction. There will be further requirements for that agent to provide information to the chain manager as to the completion of the various pre-contractual stages of the transaction, such as investigating title, carrying out local searches, obtaining mortgage offers, etc. The chain manager will then be able to build up a picture of the chain and so that he can identify any persons in the chain who are delaying the process. This information will be made available via the secure Intranet to all parties in the chain. Although it is not anticipated that the chain manager will have any compulsive powers,[107] he will be able to encourage the offending parties to complete the steps that are still to be performed. There will

However, in future, such matters could be resolved by contract between the parties. That contract will be protected in the register, so that its priority is preserved. When the details are finalised between the parties, the easements or other rights can then be entered in the register.

[101]   See below, para 2.57.

[102]   See below, para 2.68.

[103]   Formal consultation on the Land Registry's model for electronic conveyancing is planned for the autumn of this year.

[104]   The extent to which professionals may be permitted to access the secure Intranet will obviously depend on their role.

[105]   In particular a chain of house sales. There may be no need for "chain management" in relation to a chain of commercial transactions.

[106]   The basis of this requirement will be contractual.

[107]   Indeed, it is not easy to see what effective forms of compulsion there could be.

inevitably be pressure from others in the chain who are ready to contract. The power to manage chains in this way is an important feature of our proposals on electronic conveyancing. Chains are a major cause of disquiet in the conveyancing process, particularly in relation to domestic conveyancing. By providing a means of controlling and expediting chains, the Bill should do much to alleviate the frustrations that are suffered by so many buyers and sellers of land. It is anticipated that it should prevent chains from collapsing.

2.53   When the parties have agreed the terms of the contract,[108] they will send a copy in electronic form to HM Land Registry, where it will be checked electronically. This will enable any discrepancies in the contract on matters such as property address, title number and seller's name to be identified at that stage and rectified before the contract is concluded.

2.54   The contract will be made in electronic form and signed electronically by the parties or their agents. It is anticipated that, under the Bill, estate contracts will be required to be protected in the register by the entry of a notice as a pre-requisite to their validity. This noting in the register will occur simultaneously with the making of the contract and one effect of it will be to confer priority protection on the buyer.[109] The form of notice will have been agreed with the Registry in advance. The Registry will store the contract in electronic form and this is likely to be for a period that will be set in accordance with rules and is likely to reflect the nature of the contract.[110]

2.55   In relation to the disposition itself, a similar process will be undertaken. The draft transfer and any charge will be prepared in electronic form and agreed between the parties. Once again, the draft will be submitted to the Registry. The details in the transfer will be checked electronically against the contract to ensure that there are no discrepancies. A "notional" register will then be prepared by the Registry in consultation with the parties to indicate the form that the register will take when the transaction is completed. Completion, when it occurs, will entail the simultaneous occurrence of the following events—

   (1)   the execution of the transfer and any charges in electronic form and their transmission to the Registry, where they will be stored;

   (2)   the registration of the dispositions so that the register conforms with the notional register previously agreed with the Registry; and

---

[108]   The draft contract will be an electronic document.

[109]   See Cl 72(6)(a)(ii) of the Bill, below, para 9.68.

[110]   In the case of a normal estate contract, the period of storage is likely to be comparatively short. This is because most contractual obligations are merged on completion. Where the contract is likely to have a longer life, such as an option or a right of pre-emption, the period of storage will be longer. It will be possible to obtain official copies of such contracts.

(3)   the appropriate (and automatic) movement of funds[111] and the payment of stamp duty[112] and Land Registry fees.

2.56   The proposed system will eliminate the "registration gap". There will no longer be any period of time between the disposition and its registration. In time it will also mean that the register becomes conclusive as to the priority of all expressly created interests. This is because, if it is only possible to create interests validly if they are registered simultaneously, the date on which they are created will be the date of their registration. The register will therefore become a record of the priority of such rights.

2.57   As we have indicated above—

(1)   Changes to the register will be made automatically as a consequence of electronic documents and applications created by solicitors or licensed conveyancers, who are acting for the parties to the transactions.[113]

(2)   Only those solicitors or licensed conveyancers who have been authorised to do so will be permitted to conduct electronic conveyancing.[114] The relationship with the Registry will be contractual, under a "network access agreement",[115] and the Registry will be obliged to contract with any solicitor or licensed conveyancer who meets the specified criteria.[116] Those specified criteria will be the subject of wide consultation and discussion with the relevant professional and other interested bodies. One of the important aims of those criteria is, as we explain in Part XIII of this Report, to raise the standards of conveyancing.[117]

2.58   However, it will also be noted from the examples given above,[118] that the Registry will still exercise a substantial measure of control over the registration process. This is because it will not be possible to change the register except in the form agreed in advance with the Registry.

Compulsory use of electronic conveyancing

2.59   There is power in the Bill to make the use of electronic conveyancing compulsory. The way that the power will operate, if exercised, is that a disposition (or a contract to make such a disposition) will only have effect if it is—

---

[111]   See below, para 2.62.

[112]   See below, para 2.64.

[113]   See para 2.51.

[114]   See para 2.52.

[115]   For such agreements, see Schedule 5, para 1; below, para 13.36.

[116]   The criteria are necessary to ensure the integrity of the register. For the criteria, see Schedule 5, para 10; below, paras 13.40 and following.

[117]   See below, para 13.42.

[118]   See paras 2.54, 2.55.

(1) made by means of an electronic document;

(2) communicated in electronic form to the Registry; and

(3) simultaneously registered.[119]

2.60 This is a power that will not be exercised lightly. When solicitors and licensed conveyancers enter into network access agreements with the Registry, they will be required to conduct electronic conveyancing in accordance with network transaction rules.[120] Those transaction rules are likely to provide that the dispositions and contracts to make dispositions are made in the manner explained in the previous paragraph. In other words, those rules will ensure that electronic dispositions are simultaneously registered, which is the single most important technical objective of the Bill. However, as we explain in Part XIII of this Report,[121] it may be necessary to exercise the statutory power to secure that technical objective notwithstanding what can be done under the network transaction rules.[122]

2.61 There are, in any event, other reasons why the Bill has to contain a power to make electronic conveyancing compulsory. It is inevitable that the move from a paper-based to an all-electronic system of conveyancing will take some years and that the two systems will necessarily co-exist during this period of transition. However, that period of transition needs to be kept to a minimum for two principal reasons. The first is that it will be very difficult both for practitioners and for the Land Registry to have to operate two distinct systems side by side. Secondly, if electronic conveyancing is to achieve its true potential and deliver the savings and benefits that it promises, it must be the only system. This can be illustrated by the example of a typical chain of domestic sales. As we have indicated above, it will be possible to manage chains in an all-electronic system.[123] However, if just one link in that chain is conducted in the conventional paper-based manner, the advantages of electronic chain management are likely to be lost. A chain moves at the speed of the slowest link. A paper-based link is in its nature likely to be slower than an electronic one[124] and will not be subject to the scrutiny and controls of those links in the chain that are electronic and therefore managed. There must, therefore, be a residual power to require transactions to be conducted in electronic form. It is hoped that the eventual exercise of the power will be merely a formality because solicitors and licensed conveyancers will have chosen to conduct conveyancing electronically in view of the advantages that it offers to them and to their clients. Not only will it make the conduct of conveyancing easier

---

[119] Cl 93; below, para 13.75.

[120] See Schedule 5, paras 2, 5; below, paras 13.47, 13.52.

[121] See below, paras 13.74 and following.

[122] This could be quite important in relation to priorities: see above, para (2).

[123] See para 2.52.

[124] Because it will not be able to take advantage of the time-saving features that electronic conveyancing will be able to offer.

and faster for them, but they will also have to compete with other practitioners who have elected to adopt the electronic system.

Finance

2.62 An effective system of electronic conveyancing requires not only that dispositions can be made and registered electronically but also that the necessary funds can be transferred simultaneously. The absence of any discussion of the funding arrangements in the Consultative Document caused concern to at least one respondent.[125] However, this aspect had not been overlooked. It was considered that any discussion of banking arrangements at that stage would have been hopelessly premature. The function of the Consultative Document was to raise the *legal* issues that had to be addressed in any reform of the land registration system and in the introduction of a system of electronic conveyancing. The creation of the supporting banking arrangements does not require legislation.[126]

2.63 HM Land Registry has in fact been exploring ways in which a system of banking arrangements to complement electronic conveyancing might be set up.[127] It has (for example) looked at the CREST system that applies to share dealings and has also been considering the possibility of an escrow bank. However, until a definite model of electronic conveyancing is settled in more detail than it has been to date,[128] it is unlikely that it will be possible to devise the necessary technical requirements that any banking system will have to meet.

Stamp duty

2.64 At present the Stamp Duty on land transactions depends upon the existence of documents in paper form.[129] On 8 November, 2000, the Inland Revenue announced that there would be legislation to extend the Stamp Duty regime to cover transfers of land that are made in electronic form. A technical advisory group, comprising members of the relevant representative organisations, has been set up to assist in taking this work forward. A comprehensive set of proposals, containing drafts of clauses, regulations and user guidance, will be published later this year.

Electronic conveyancing and first registration

2.65 The impact of electronic conveyancing on the process of first registration is likely to be comparatively slight.

---

[125] The Conveyancing and Land Law Committee of The Law Society.

[126] The Uncertificated Securities Regulations 1995, SI 1995 No 3272, which created the legal framework for CREST, the system for the electronic transfer of and settlement of trades in securities, say nothing about the supporting banking arrangements.

[127] It has been in discussion with representatives of the lending industry.

[128] For the timetable for the introduction of electronic conveyancing, see above, para 2.52.

[129] See Stamp Act 1891, ss 3, 122(1); Finance Act 1999, s 112(3); Schedule 13.

(1) First, where first registration is triggered by a disposition of unregistered land, it will become possible to use one instrument that may be in electronic form, both to make the disposition and to apply for first registration.

(2) Secondly, where first registration is voluntary, it will be possible to make the application for registration in electronic form.

However, whether first registration is compulsory or voluntary, the necessary muniments of title will still have to be sent to the Registry. The registrar will then have to satisfy himself as to the title before he registers it. Given the nature of the state guarantee of title, the continued involvement of the registrar on first registration is inevitable.

2.66 There may however be cases where, even in relation to first registrations, the disposition can be effected electronically and the registration made by the solicitor or licensed conveyancer acting for the disponee. This is likely to be the case in relation to the grant of short leases out of unregistered land. As we have explained above,[130] the requirement of compulsory registration will, under the Bill, be extended to leases granted for more than seven years. It is also anticipated that this period may be further reduced, perhaps to include all leases that are required to be made by deed. In relation to short leases there are unlikely to be complex issues of title. There is, therefore, no reason why they should not be granted and registered electronically.

2.67 Furthermore, in relation to dispositions of unregistered land that trigger compulsory first registration, it is anticipated that the secure electronic communications network could be used to provide information in relation to the transaction.[131]

Do-it-yourself conveyancing

2.68 There are a number of people who prefer to undertake their own conveyancing, though they account for less than 1 per cent of all registered transactions. They will not be excluded from the benefits of electronic conveyancing. Once there is a land registry network, the registrar will be obliged to provide assistance to "do-it-yourself" conveyancers. It is envisaged that the registrar will carry out the electronic transactions on their directions, and that this service will be available from district land registries.

[130] See para 2.6.

[131] This would be particularly important in relation to chain sales. See above, para 2.52.

ADVERSE POSSESSION

Introduction

2.69   As the law stands, if a squatter is in adverse possession of land, he or she will usually extinguish the owner's title to that land after 12 years.[132] At that point, the squatter's title becomes unassailable, because no one has a better right to possess than he or she does.

2.70   As we have indicated above, the Bill introduces a new system of adverse possession applicable only to registered estates and registered rentcharges.[133] The changes that the Bill makes to the law of adverse possession are in fact scarcely less striking than those that it makes to the conveyancing process. There are two main reasons why we consider that we should introduce a new system. First, at the practical level, there is a growing public disquiet about the present law. It is perceived to be too easy for squatters to acquire title.[134] Perhaps precisely because it is so easy, adverse possession is also very common. Although the popular perception of a squatter is that of a homeless person who takes over an empty house (for whom there is understandable sympathy), the much more typical case in practice is the landowner with an eye to the main chance who encroaches on his or her neighbour's land. Secondly, as a matter of legal principle, it is difficult to justify the continuation of the present principles in relation to registered land. These two reasons are in fact interconnected.

Why do we have a doctrine of adverse possession?

2.71   The reasons why there is a doctrine of adverse possession are well known and often stated, but they need to be tested. For example, it is frequently said that the doctrine is an embodiment of the policy that defendants should be protected from stale claims and that claimants should not sleep on their rights. However, it is possible for a squatter to acquire title by adverse possession without the owner realising it. This may be because the adverse possession is either clandestine or not readily apparent.[135] It may be because the owner has more land than he or she can realistically police. Many public bodies fall into this category. A local authority, for example, cannot in practice keep an eye on every single piece of land that it owns to ensure that no one is encroaching on it.[136] But the owner may not even realise that a person is encroaching on his or her land. He or she may think that someone is there with permission[137] and it may take an expensive journey to the Court of

---

[132] See Limitation Act 1980, ss 15, 17. This will not always be so. If, for example, he or she has been in adverse possession of leasehold land, the tenant's title will have been extinguished, but not the landlord's. The squatter will have to remain in adverse possession for a further 12 years after the duration of the period of the lease.

[133] See above, para (3). See Part XIV of this Report for the discussion of adverse possession.

[134] See below, paras 14.1, 14.2.

[135] As where a squatter takes over a basement or a cellar: *Rains v Buxton* (1880) 14 ChD 537.

[136] The leading modern case — *Buckinghamshire County Council v Moran* [1990] Ch 623 — involved a wealthy businessman who enclosed a piece of land that was owned by a County Council and was being kept by them as a "land bank" for future road widening purposes.

[137] Particularly where the person is a neighbour.

Appeal to discover whether or not this is so.[138] In none of these examples is a person in any true sense sleeping on his or her rights. Furthermore, even if a landowner does realise that someone — typically a neighbour — is encroaching on his or her land, he or she may be reluctant to take issue over the incursion, particularly if it is comparatively slight. He or she may not wish to sour relations with the neighbour and is, perhaps, afraid of the consequences of so doing. It may not only affect relations with the neighbour but may also bring opprobrium upon him or her in the neighbourhood. In any event, even if the policy against allowing stale claims is sound, the consequences of it under the present law — the loss for ever of a person's land — can be extremely harsh and have been judicially described as disproportionate.[139]

2.72   There are other grounds for the doctrine of adverse possession that have greater weight. Land is a precious resource and should be kept in use and in commerce. A person may be in adverse possession where the true owner has disappeared and there is no other claimant for the land. Or he or she may have acquired the land informally so that the legal ownership is not a reflection of the practical reality. A person may have innocently entered land, quite reasonably believing that he or she owned it, perhaps because of uncertainties as to the boundaries.

2.73   In relation to land with unregistered title, there are cogent legal reasons for the doctrine. The principles of adverse possession do in fact presuppose unregistered title and make sense in relation to it. This is because the basis of title to unregistered land is ultimately possession. The person best entitled to the land is the person with the best right to possession of it. As we explain below, the investigation of title to unregistered land is facilitated (and therefore costs less) because earlier rights to possess can be extinguished by adverse possession.[140] However, where title is registered, the basis of title is primarily the fact of registration rather than possession.[141] It is the fact of registration that vests the legal title in the registered proprietor. This is so, even if the transfer to the proprietor was a nullity as, for example, where it was a forgery.[142] The ownership of land is therefore apparent from the register and only a change in the register can take that title away. It is noteworthy that, in many Commonwealth states which have systems of title registration, these considerations have led to changes in the law governing acquisition of title by adverse possession. In some states it has been abolished altogether. In others, it has been modified.[143] As we have indicated

---

[138]   For a striking recent illustration, see *J A Pye (Oxford) Holdings Ltd v Graham* [2001] EWCA Civ 117; [2001] 2 WLR 1293, below, para 14.1, where the issue was whether what had initially been possession under licence (in that case a grazing licence) had ceased to be so.

[139]   *J A Pye (Oxford) Holdings Ltd v Graham* [2000] Ch 676, 710, *per* Neuberger J (at first instance).

[140]   See below, para 14.2, and see generally Law Com No 254, paras 10.5—10.10.

[141]   See Law Com No 254, para 10.11.

[142]   See Land Registration Act 1925, s 69(1) (present law); Cl 58(1) (under the Bill); below, para 9.4.

[143]   See Law Com No 254, para 10.17.

above,[144] the doctrine of adverse possession does have benefits and we do not therefore favour outright abolition in relation to registered land. However, we consider that the balance between landowner and squatter needs to be adjusted to overcome some of the deficiencies outlined above,[145] while maintaining the advantages it can offer. We have therefore devised a modified scheme of adverse possession that attempts to achieve that balance and is at the same time appropriate to the principles of registered title.[146]

An outline of the new scheme in the Bill

2.74 The essence of the new scheme in the Bill is that it gives a registered proprietor one chance, but only one chance, to terminate a squatter's adverse possession.[147] In summary, a squatter will be able to apply to be registered as proprietor after 10 years' adverse possession. The registered proprietor and certain other persons (such as a chargee) who are interested in the property will be notified of the application. If any of them object, the squatter's application will be rejected, unless he or she can establish one of the very limited exceptional grounds which will entitle him or her to be registered anyway. Of these exceptional grounds, the only significant one is where a neighbour can prove that he or she was in adverse possession of the land in question for ten years and believed on reasonable grounds for that period that he or she owned it. This exception is intended to meet the case where the physical and legal boundaries do not coincide. Even if the squatter's application is rejected, that is not necessarily the end of the matter. If the squatter remains in adverse possession for a further two years, he or she will be entitled to apply once more to be registered, and this time the registered proprietor will not be able to object. If the proprietor has been notified of the squatter's adverse possession and has been given the opportunity to terminate it within two years,[148] we consider that the squatter should obtain the land. It should be noted that our scheme places the onus on the squatter to take the initiative.[149] If he or she wants to acquire the land, he or she must apply to be registered. This is because the registered proprietor's title will never be barred by mere lapse of time. One point should be stressed about the provisions of the Bill on adverse possession. They are very carefully constructed to ensure that there is consistency between the way in which applications for registration are treated and what happens when the registered proprietor takes proceedings for possession against the squatter. The scheme stands or falls as an entity.

---

[144] See para 2.72.

[145] See para 2.71.

[146] Our starting point was the law applicable in Queensland, but our eventual model is very different.

[147] See below, Part XIV.

[148] Either by taking possession proceedings to recover the land or by reaching an agreement with the squatter that he or she will become the owner's tenant or licensee.

[149] This is a significant point in a case involving neighbours. A neighbour cannot be criticised for objecting to such an application and acting upon it, where he or she might have been regarded as a trouble maker if he or she had taken steps on his or her own initiative against the encroaching neighbour. See above, para 2.71.

JUDICIAL PROVISIONS

2.75 The Bill makes one striking change to the judicial provisions that are presently applicable to land registration. It creates a new office, that of Adjudicator to HM Land Registry.[150] The Adjudicator will be appointed by the Lord Chancellor and he will be independent of HM Land Registry. His task will be to determine objections that are made to any application to the registrar that cannot be resolved by agreement.[151] The Adjudicator will be subject to the supervision of the Council of Tribunals.

RULES

2.76 Much of the process of land registration is, necessarily, conducted in accordance with rules made under the Land Registration Act 1925, of which there are several sets.[152] There are well over 300 such rules and they are amended regularly. They are concerned with the detail of how land registration is conducted and the flexibility that they have provided has enabled land registration to evolve from a system where transactions and searches were conducted in person at HM Land Registry in London to the present computerised system under which it is possible to search the register from a computer in an office anywhere. Rules are made by statutory instrument by the Lord Chancellor on the advice of the Rules Committee.[153] This is a body of experts, chaired by a High Court Judge, that scrutinises all rules before they are laid before Parliament. One problem with the present legislation is that there is not always a very clear demarcation between what is in the Land Registration Act 1925 and what is in the rules made under it. Some remarkably important matters are found in the rules.

2.77 The Bill follows the model of the present legislation in conferring extensive rule-making powers on the Lord Chancellor to make land registration rules. These will, as now, relate to the technical aspects of how registered conveyancing is to be conducted — forms of application, contents of notices, etc. As now, these rules will be subject to scrutiny by the Rules Committee, on whose advice the Lord Chancellor will continue to act.[154] However, the Bill strikes a much more principled balance between what is in rules and what is in primary legislation. The rule-making powers are also much more sharply defined.

2.78 The Bill confers other rule-making powers which relate to matters of substance, such as the possible reduction in length of leases that are registrable.[155] These rules

---

[150] See Part 11 and Schedule 9 of the Bill; and see Part XVI of the Report.

[151] See Cls 73, 106. These functions are presently performed by the Solicitor to HM Land Registry.

[152] Land Registration Rules 1925; Land Registration (Open Register) Rules 1991; Land Registration (Official Searches) Rules 1993; Land Registration (Overriding Leases) Rules 1995; Land Registration (Matrimonial Home Rights) Rules 1997; Land Registration (Hearings Procedure) Rules 2000.

[153] Land Registration Act 1925, s 144(1).

[154] See Cl 124; below, para 17.5.

[155] See Cl 116.

will be made by the Lord Chancellor only after consultation and will be subject to annulment in pursuance of a resolution of either House of Parliament.[156]

[156] Cl 125(4).

PART III
FIRST REGISTRATION

INTRODUCTION

3.1 In this Part we examine five issues—

    (1)   the legal scope of title registration and the extent of land that may be registered under it;

    (2)   the circumstances in which an owner of an interest in unregistered land may apply to register it with its own title;

    (3)   the circumstances in which a disposition of unregistered land must be registered and the consequences of a failure to do so;

    (4)   the effect of first registration; and

    (5)   cautions against first registration and the cautions register.

3.2 The principal concern of this Part is with first registration. The first registration of a title may be either voluntary or compulsory. Registration is presently compulsory on the making of certain dispositions of unregistered land, and the range of such dispositions was extended substantially by the Land Registration Act 1997.[1] In other cases it may be made voluntarily, provided that the interest is one which may be registered. As a result of changes made by the Land Registration Act 1997,[2] there are now fee incentives to encourage voluntary first registration and it is intended that these will continue under the Bill.[3]

THE LEGAL SCOPE OF TITLE REGISTRATION AND THE EXTENT OF LAND THAT MAY BE REGISTERED UNDER IT

The legal scope of title registration

3.3 The Bill describes the scope of title registration in Clause 2.[4] First, Clause 2(a), reflects the fact that the Bill makes provision about the registration of title to the following unregistered legal estates—

    (1)   an estate in land;[5]

---

[1]   Section 1 substituted a new Land Registration Act 1925, s 123 and inserted a new s 123A.

[2]   See Land Registration Act 1925, s 145(3) (substituted by Land Registration Act 1997, s 3). See Land Registration Fees Order 2001 (2001 SI No 1179), art 2(5). Fees for voluntary first registration are 25% lower than those applicable to compulsory first registration.

[3]   The fee-making powers under the Bill are couched in more general terms that will permit this, but do not have an explicit provision equivalent to Land Registration Act 1925, s 145(3): see Cl 101; below, para 15.9

[4]   The provision is merely descriptive. It simply highlights the fact that the Bill makes provision for the matters it describes.

(2)   a rentcharge;[6]

(3)   a franchise;[7]

(4)   a *profit à prendre* in gross;[8]

(5)   any other interest or charge which subsists for the benefit of, or is a charge on, an interest the title to which is registered.[9]

It is these matters that are addressed in the first section of this Part.

3.4   Secondly, Clause 2(b) describes the provision that the Bill makes about the registration of title to legal estates that are created by a disposition of a legal estate the title to which is itself registered. This provision relates to registrable dispositions. These are considered in Part IV of this Report.[10]

The extent of land that may be registered

3.5   At present, the land which can be registered under the Land Registration Act 1925 is, in practice, determined by reference to local government administrative areas. This means the counties of England or Wales,[11] Greater London and the Isles of Scilly.[12] Although the seaward limit of a county (or administrative area) is generally the low water mark, there are tidal waters which are within the body of a county, as (for example) where there is an estuary. The county boundary is at the seaward limit of that estuary as determined by the Ordnance Survey.[13] The Bill applies (as now) to land covered by internal waters which are within the administrative area of England or Wales.[14] However, it extends the scope of the land that may be registered beyond those administrative areas and applies additionally to land covered by internal waters which are adjacent to England or Wales and which are specified for the purposes by order made by the Lord Chancellor.[15] This power to extend registration of title to land under adjacent

---

[5]   That is, a fee simple absolute in possession or a term of years absolute: see Law of Property Act 1925, s 1(1).

[6]   See *ibid*, s 1(2)(b).

[7]   See *ibid*, s 1(2)(a).

[8]   *Ibid*.

[9]   This will include the benefit of a legal easement or a profit appendant or appurtenant, a legal right of re-entry and charge by way of legal mortgage.

[10]   See below, para 4.12.

[11]   As defined by the Local Government Act 1972.

[12]   Cf the definitions of "England" and "Wales" respectively in Interpretation Act 1978, Schedule 1.

[13]   We received some fascinating evidence as to how the seaward limit of an estuary was determined. It was not quite as scientific as we had imagined that it would be.

[14]   Cl 127(a).

[15]   Cl 127(b). Such an order is to be made by statutory instrument, subject to annulment in pursuance of a resolution of either House of Parliament: Cl 125(4).

internal waters was included following discussions with the Crown Estate. The Crown Estate would, in due course, wish to be able to register submarine land not only within the body of a county, but under waters on the landward side of the baselines, fixed in accordance with Article 4 of the Convention on the Territorial Sea of 1958. These baselines are employed for the purposes of defining the territorial limits of the United Kingdom. The reason why the Crown Estate wishes to be able to register such lands is to protect them against encroachments by adverse possessors who might (for example) construct pipelines or other works within internal waters but outside the body of a county.[16] At present, although HM Land Registry could presently resource the registration of submarine land within the body of a county it would be in difficulties if submarine land became registrable as far out as the baselines. However, as and when resources permit, it would, in principle, be willing to register submarine land within the baselines. In those circumstances, the power explained above, could be exercised.

VOLUNTARY FIRST REGISTRATION

Registrable estates

Who may apply for first registration?

3.6 Under the Land Registration Act 1925,[17] only legal estates may be registered with their own titles. Clause 3 of the Bill, which explains the circumstances in which a person may apply for the voluntary first registration of an unregistered legal estate, adheres to that principle but extends the range of such estates that may be registered. It should be noted that, at present, the Crown is unable to register the title to a substantial amount of land which it holds. This is the land that it holds in demesne as feudal lord paramount and not for any estate.[18] As we explain in Part XI of this Report, the Bill addresses this shortcoming and provides a mechanism by which the Crown may grant itself a fee simple in order to register that estate.[19]

3.7 A person may apply to the registrar to be registered as first registered proprietor of a legal estate in two situations. The first is where he or she is the legal owner of it. The second is where he or she is entitled to have the legal estate vested in him or her, as (for example) where the title is vested in a nominee for him or her.[20] However, a person who has contracted to buy land cannot apply for voluntary first registration under this provision.[21] This is because the contract will be completed by a conveyance, and that conveyance will be subject to the requirements of compulsory registration that are explained below.[22] As we have explained above,

---

[16] For the provisions of the Bill on adverse possession, see Part XIV of this Report.

[17] Section 2(1).

[18] See below, para 11.5.

[19] Cl 79; below, para 11.11.

[20] Cl 3(2). The Bill makes no change in the law as to who may apply to be registered: see Land Registration Act 1925, ss 4, 8(1).

[21] Cl 3(6). This replicates the effect of the present law: see Land Registration Act 1925, ss 4(b), 8(1)(b).

[22] See para 3.24.

the fees payable on voluntary first registration are lower than they are on compulsory first registration.[23]

3.8 It should be noted that first registration arises from an application. As we explain in Part XVI of this Report,[24] the Bill confers a right for anyone to object to an application,[25] though it is a right that must not be exercised without reasonable cause.[26] Where an objection cannot be disposed of by agreement and is not groundless, the registrar must refer the matter to the Adjudicator for resolution.[27]

Which legal estates may be registered with their own titles?

A FEE SIMPLE ABSOLUTE IN POSSESSION

3.9 The first legal estate that may be registered with its own title is, as now,[28] a fee simple absolute in possession.[29]

CERTAIN LEASES

3.10 The second estate that may be registered is a term of years absolute. However, not every leasehold estate is capable of being registered with its own title. The relevant principles are as follows.

3.11 First, a lease granted for a term of years under which the tenant's right to possession is discontinuous, is registrable, however many (or few) years are unexpired at the time of the application for registration. This provision is new. Although discontinuous leases are not very common, they are sometimes used for time-share arrangements under which (for example) the tenant is entitled to occupy premises for a specified number of weeks every year for a certain number of years.[30]

---

[23] See para 3.2.

[24] See below, para 16.6.

[25] Cl 73(1).

[26] Cl 77(1)(c)

[27] Cl 73(6), (7); below, paras 16.6, 16.7. For the office of Adjudicator, see below, para 16.3.

[28] See Land Registration Act 1925, ss 2, 4.

[29] Cl 3(1)(a).

[30] See, eg, *Cottage Holiday Associates Ltd v Customs and Excise Commissioners* [1983] QB 735. As Woolf J pointed out in that case, other methods were commonly used to give effect to time-share arrangements, such as the grant of "licences or holiday certificates coupled with memberships of a proprietary club", or the use of trusts: *ibid*, at p 739. Although it is not material in the context of voluntary first registration, it should be noted that the length of a discontinuous lease is apparently determined by aggregating the periods that the tenant is entitled to occupy the premises and not by reference to the commencement and termination dates during which the property was to be made available: *ibid*, at p 740. This point is material in the context of *compulsory* first registration because, as we explain below, under the Bill, leases granted for a term of more than seven years are required to be registered: see Cl 4(1)(c); below, para 3.30.

3.12   Secondly, where a mortgage has been created by demise or sub-demise, the mortgage term is never registrable, provided that there is a subsisting right of redemption.[31] This replicates the present law.[32] It would make no sense to register a mortgage term where the estate charged was an unregistered freehold or leasehold and the mortgage might still be redeemed.

3.13   Thirdly, subject to what is said in paragraphs 3.11 and 3.12 above, a legal lease which has more than seven years unexpired at the time of the application may be registered.[33] It sometimes happens that a person holds under one lease but has been granted another lease to take effect on or shortly after the first. Under the present law, it is possible to add together the terms of the lease in possession and the reversionary lease in determining whether the lease is of a sufficient length to be registrable.[34] The Bill makes similar provision. Provided that the reversionary lease is to take effect in possession on, or within one month of, the end of the lease in possession, the terms may be added together. If, taken together, the terms exceed seven years, the lease is registrable.[35]

3.14   The power to register a lease with more than seven years unexpired involves a significant change to the present law. At present, only a lease with more than 21 years to run may be registered voluntarily.[36] In the Consultative Document, we sought views on whether there should be a reduction in the length of leases that were registrable, but without making any recommendations as such.[37] There was in fact no clear consensus from the answers of those who responded to the point, though there was support for having a power to reduce the length of registrable leases at a later date if, after consultation, there was support for such a change.[38] This is the *only* point of significance where we have decided to go against the views expressed on consultation. Our reasons for doing so, which follow from certain policy decisions as to the future of title registration that we have set out in Part II of this Report,[39] can be summarised as follows.

3.15   It is absurd to continue to maintain two distinct and already very different systems of conveyancing, the registered and the unregistered. These two systems will diverge still further not only as a result of the introduction of electronic conveyancing,[40] but also because of the other reforms that this Bill will bring

---

[31]   Cl 3(5). Mortgages by demise or sub-demise are in practice obsolete. Cf below, para 7.3

[32]   See Land Registration Act 1925, s 8(1).

[33]   Cl 3(1)(a), (3). No application for registration under Cl 3 may be made in respect of a PPP lease (which relates to transport in London) under Greater London Authority Act 1999: see Cl 90(1). For PPP leases, see below, para 8.11.

[34]   See Land Registration Rules 1925, r 47.

[35]   Cl 3(7).

[36]   Land Registration Act 1925, s 8(1).

[37]   See Law Com No 254, para 3.10.

[38]   See below, para 3.17.

[39]   See above, paras 2.6, 2.9.

[40]   Which will apply only to registered land.

about. In principle, as we have recommended in Part II, we should move to a system of total registration as soon as is reasonably practicable.[41]

3.16 The business lease is, in commercial terms, one of the most significant dealings with land. However, it is currently excluded from the benefits of registration, because such leases are almost invariably granted for periods of 21 years or less. This is an indefensible omission. First, it is a considerable barrier to our eventual goal of total registration. Secondly, it means that it will not be possible to grant and make dispositions of such leases electronically. Thirdly, the register of title is a public document and an increasingly important source of public information about land. There is no obvious justification for excluding a significant body of leasehold property from this source of information.

3.17 As we mentioned above,[42] there was support on consultation for the recommendation in the Consultative Document, that the Bill should confer a power, exercisable by statutory instrument, to reduce the length of lease that was capable of being registered voluntarily.[43] The Bill implements that proposal,[44] and confers power on the Lord Chancellor to reduce the term by order after prior consultation.[45] It is likely that, when electronic conveyancing is fully operative, the period will be reduced to include all leases that have to be made by deed — in other words, those granted for more than three years.[46] The move to electronic conveyancing should make it possible to register such short leases and ensure that they are removed when they have terminated. This will virtually eliminate the need to have recourse to unregistered conveyancing for the future.[47]

RENTCHARGES

3.18 The third legal estate that may be registered is a rentcharge. A rentcharge will be a legal estate if it is perpetual or granted for a term of years.[48] Subject to certain exceptions, the Rentcharges Act 1977 prevents the creation of any new rentcharges after 21 August 1977.[49] Most existing rentcharges will be extinguished in 2037. The only ones remaining are those permitted by the 1977 Act,[50] of which "estate rentcharges" are the most important.[51] These are created to enable the

---

[41] See above, para 2.13.

[42] See para 3.14.

[43] See Law Com No 254, paras 3.14, 3.15.

[44] Cl 116(1)(a).

[45] Cl 116(3). Any such order is to be made by statutory instrument that is subject to annulment in pursuance of a resolution of either House of Parliament: Cl 125(4).

[46] See Law of Property Act 1925, ss 52, 54(2).

[47] There are likely to be few dealings with leases granted for three years or less, and such as there are, will almost certainly be straightforward.

[48] Law of Property Act 1925, s 1(2)(b).

[49] Rentcharges Act 1977, s 2.

[50] See *ibid*, s 2(3).

[51] See *ibid*, s 2(3)(c), (4), (5).

enforcement of positive covenants and to secure the payment of service charges. Under the Bill, it will continue to be possible to register rentcharges voluntarily provided that it is perpetual or granted for a term of years with more than seven years unexpired.[52]

FRANCHISES

3.19   The fourth legal estate that may be registered is a franchise. A franchise, which is an incorporeal hereditament, is "a royal privilege or branch of the royal prerogative subsisting in the hands of a subject, by grant from the King".[53] It may be acquired by royal grant or by prescription. The franchises that tend to be encountered nowadays include those to hold a market or fair, or to take tolls.[54] At present, the only way in which a franchise may be protected on the register is if the land subject to it is itself registered, when a notice or caution may be entered against that registered title. A franchise cannot be independently registered with its own title, even though it could be a very valuable right.[55] In the Consultative Document, we sought views as to whether franchises should be capable of being registered voluntarily with their own titles, without making any recommendation on the issue.[56] Nearly three-fifths of those who responded to the point considered that there should be a power to register franchises. The Bill accordingly provides that a franchise may be registered with its own title if it is held for an interest equivalent to a fee simple absolute in possession or a term of years absolute with more than seven years unexpired.[57]

PROFITS À PRENDRE IN GROSS

3.20   The fifth legal estate that may be registered with its own title is a *profit à prendre* in gross. Like franchises, *profits à prendre* are incorporeal hereditaments. Many exist for the benefit of other land in the same way as easements. However, unlike easements, some profits can exist in gross. In other words, they can exist independently, in their own right, and do not have to benefit a dominant tenement. The profits that can exist in gross include the profits of pasture, piscary,[58] and of hunting and shooting game. Such rights are fairly common and can be very valuable. They are often sold and leased. At present, such profits in

---

[52]   Cl 3(1)(b), (3).

[53]   *Spook Erection Ltd v Secretary of State for the Environment* [1989] QB 300, 305, *per* Nourse LJ, referring to Joseph Chitty, *A Treatise on the Law of the Prerogatives of the Crown* (1820), p 119. In fact Chitty's definition can be traced back to 2 *Blackstone's Commentaries*, p 37, which, in turn is derived from still earlier sources.

[54]   See, *eg, Sevenoaks District Council v Pattullo & Vinson Ltd* [1984] Ch 211 (franchise of market). Where the Crown granted a franchise of treasure trove, that franchise is now for treasure under Treasure Act 1996, ss 4, 5. The concept of "treasure" under the 1996 Act is wider than "treasure trove" at common law: see *ibid*, ss 1, 2.

[55]   Franchises are undoubtedly bought and sold. Cf *Sevenoaks District Council v Pattullo & Vinson Ltd*, above.

[56]   See Law Com No 254, paras 3.17—3.19.

[57]   Cl 3(1)(c), (3). Cf Law of Property Act 1925, s 1(2)(a).

[58]   Fishing rights.

41

gross, like franchises, cannot be registered with their own titles,[59] but can only be protected by an appropriate entry against the title of the estate affected by them if that estate is registered. In the Consultative Document, we asked whether it should be possible for *profits à prendre* to be registered voluntarily with their own titles.[60] As with our inquiry on franchises, we made no recommendation one way or the other. Again, there was support for such a power of registration from nearly 60 per cent of those who responded to the question.[61] The Bill therefore makes similar provision for *profits à prendre* as it does for franchises. It permits a *profit à prendre* to be registered with its own title if it is held for an interest equivalent to a fee simple absolute in possession or a term of years absolute with more than seven years unexpired.[62]

Manors no longer to be registrable

3.21 At present a manor — that is the lordship of the manor — is registrable with its own title.[63] In the Consultative Document, we drew attention to the fact that manors are wholly incorporeal and impose no burden on the land within the manor.[64] Because the registration of manors gives rise to many practical difficulties at HM Land Registry but offers few, if any, advantages in return, we recommended that manors should cease to be registrable.[65] This proposal was accepted by 90 per cent of those who responded to the point. Accordingly, the Bill contains no power to register a manor. It also contains a power for the registrar to remove the title of a manor from the register on the application of the registered proprietor of that manor.[66]

COMPULSORY REGISTRATION

Introduction

3.22 As we have explained above,[67] the Land Registration Act 1997 substantially extended the range of dispositions of unregistered land that will trigger compulsory registration of title.[68] Given these recent changes, the Bill largely replicates the present law as set out in sections 123 and 123A of the Land

---

[59] Cf Land Registration Rules 1925, r 257.

[60] See Law Com No 254, paras 3.17—3.19.

[61] Those who supported registration were, on the whole, those bodies and practitioners who encountered such rights most often, and for whom the inability to register the title was a practical problem, such as CLA, Farrer & Co and Holborn Law Society.

[62] Cl 3(1)(d), (3). Cf Law of Property Act 1925, s 1(2)(a).

[63] Land Registration Rules 1925, rr 50, 51.

[64] Law Com No 254, para 3.20.

[65] *Ibid*, drawing an analogy with advowsons, which ceased to be registrable as a result of Patronage (Benefices) Measure 1986, s 6(2).

[66] Cl 117.

[67] See para 3.2.

[68] The Land Registration Act 1997 implemented the joint recommendations of the Law Commission and HM Land Registry in Transfer of Land: Land Registration (1995) Law Com No 235.

Registration Act 1925. What follows is, therefore, no more than a summary of the provisions of the Bill, with comment only where the Bill changes the law.

Events that trigger the compulsory registration of title

Introduction

3.23 The events that trigger the requirement of compulsory registration under the Bill are set out in the following paragraphs.[69] As now, these provisions do not apply to mines and minerals that are held apart from the surface.[70] In the Consultative Document we explained the peculiar difficulties that, largely for historical reasons, apply in relation to the registration of mineral rights and why we felt unable to address these at this stage.[71] Under the present law, the requirements of compulsory registration do not apply to either an incorporeal hereditament (such as a franchise or a *profit à prendre*)[72] or to "corporeal hereditaments which are part of a manor and included in the sale of the manor as such".[73] Neither of these exceptions is replicated in the Bill. Although the grant or transfer of incorporeal hereditaments would not fall within any of the triggers to compulsory registration under the Bill,[74] many transfers of manorial land would do so. In the Consultative Document we explained the reason for this exception of manorial lands to the extent that we understood it,[75] and we recommended that it be abrogated.[76] There were not many responses to the point, but over four-fifths of them agreed with the recommendation.

Transfers

TRANSFER OF A QUALIFYING ESTATE

3.24 Where there is a transfer of a "qualifying estate" — that is, of either a legal freehold estate in land or a legal lease which has more than seven years to run[77] — the requirement of compulsory registration applies if the transfer was made—

(1) for valuable or other consideration;

(2) by way of gift;

(3) in pursuance of an order of any court; or

---

[69] The Bill refers to "events" which trigger compulsory registration, whereas Land Registration Act 1925, s 123, is couched in terms of "dispositions". "Events" is obviously wider in its ambit than "dispositions", and this may be significant for the future: cf below, para 3.37.

[70] Cl 4(9). Cf Land Registration Act 1925, s 123(3)(b).

[71] See Law Com No 254, paras 3.13—3.15.

[72] Land Registration Act 1925, s 123(3)(a).

[73] *Ibid*, s 123(3)(c).

[74] But see the power to extend the triggers that is explained below, para 3.37.

[75] See Law Com No 254, para 3.22.

[76] *Ibid*, para 3.23.

[77] Cl 4(1), (2).

(4)   by means of an assent (including a vesting assent).[78]

The significant change here from the present legislation is that compulsory registration will apply to leases granted for more than seven years, instead of for more than 21 years, as now. The reasons for this have been explained above, in the context of voluntary first registration.[79] There is a power for the Lord Chancellor, after consultation, to reduce the period of seven years by order.[80]

3.25   The following transfers are not within the provisions in paragraph 3.24—

(1)   a transfer by operation of law (as where a deceased's property vests in his or her executors);[81]

(2)   the assignment of a mortgage term (in other words, where there is a mortgage by demise or sub-demise, and the mortgagee assigns the mortgage by transferring the mortgage term);[82] and

(3)   the assignment or surrender of a lease to the immediate reversion where the term is to merge in that reversion (because the estate transferred disappears).[83]

3.26   If an estate transferred has a negative value it is still to be regarded as having been transferred for valuable consideration.[84] The typical case in which this might happen is where there is an assignment of a lease under which the rent exceeds what would be the market rental for the property, perhaps because of the operation of a rent review clause or due to onerous repairing obligations.

3.27   The Bill clarifies what constitutes a "gift" for the purposes of paragraph 3.24, above.

(1)   A transfer by way of gift will include a transfer by a settlor which constitutes a trust under which the settlor does not retain the whole of the beneficial interest.[85] Thus, if S transfers unregistered land to T1 and T2, to hold on a trust of land for S for life, thereafter to U absolutely, that transfer will trigger compulsory registration. However, a transfer by S to

---

[78]   Cl 4(1)(a)(i). For the meaning of a vesting assent, see Cl 4(9); Settled Land Act 1925, s 117(1)(xxxi).

[79]   See paras 3.14—3.16.

[80]   Cl 116(1)(b), (3). Any such order is to be made by statutory instrument that is subject to annulment in pursuance of a resolution of either House of Parliament: Cl 125(4). Cf above, para 3.17.

[81]   Cl 4(3).

[82]   Cl 4(4)(a).

[83]   Cl 4(4)(b).

[84]   Cl 4(6).

[85]   Cl 4(7)(a).

T1 and T2 to hold on trust for her as her nominee will not trigger compulsory registration.

(2) A transfer by way of gift will also include the situation where a beneficiary becomes absolutely entitled to unregistered land that is held on trust for him or her, and he or she requires the trustees to convey the legal estate to him or her.[86] Thus, if T1 and T2 hold unregistered land on trust for A for life, thereafter for B absolutely, and A dies, so that the trustees hold the land on trust for B absolutely, a transfer of that land by T1 and T2 to B will trigger compulsory registration. However, this will not be the case where, on the constitution of the trust, the trustees held the land on trust for the settlor absolutely, and subsequently the land is transferred either to the settlor or to the person entitled to the interest (as, for example, under the settlor's will or intestacy).[87]

The exception in each case reflects the fact that the creation of a nomineeship by a landowner does not involve any element of gift.

TRANSFERS TO WHICH SECTION 171A OF THE HOUSING ACT 1985 APPLIES

3.28 As under the present law, if there is a transfer of an unregistered legal estate in land in circumstances in which section 171A of the Housing Act 1985 applies, that transfer is subject to the requirement of compulsory registration even if it would not otherwise be.[88]

Grants

3.29 In the circumstances set out in the following paragraphs, the grant of a legal lease will trigger the requirement of compulsory registration.

LEASES GRANTED FOR A TERM OF MORE THAN SEVEN YEARS FROM THE DATE OF GRANT

3.30 The first situation is where a lease[89] is granted for a term of more than seven years from the date of the grant, and the grant is made—

(1) for valuable or other consideration;

(2) by way of gift; or

(3) in pursuance of an order of any court.[90]

---

[86] Cl 4(7)(b).

[87] *Ibid.*

[88] Cl 4(1)(b). Cf Housing Act 1985, Schedule 9A, para 2(1) (which the Bill repeals: see Schedule 13). A transfer falls within s 171A, where a person ceases to be a secure tenant of a dwelling-house because his or her landlord disposes of an interest in that house to a private sector landlord. The tenant's right to buy under Part 5 of the 1985 Act is preserved in such circumstances: cf Housing Act 1985, s 171B.

[89] Other than (i) the grant of a mortgage term (that is, where there is a mortgage by demise or sub-demise): Cl 4(5); or (ii) a PPP lease: see Cl 90(2). For PPP leases, see below, para 8.11.

Once again, there is a very significant change to the present law here, namely the reduction of the length of leases that are subject to the requirement of compulsory first registration from those granted for more than 21 years to those granted for more than seven years.[91] We have explained the reasons for this in the context of voluntary first registration.[92] One of the main and intended effects is to bring most business leases on to the register in future.[93] There is a power for the Lord Chancellor, after consultation, to reduce still further the period of seven years by order.[94]

3.31 If a lease granted has a negative value, it is still to be regarded as having been granted for valuable consideration.[95] The comments above as to when a transfer will be regarded as a gift (and so subject to compulsory registration) apply equally to a grant of a lease by way of a gift.[96]

REVERSIONARY LEASES

3.32 The Bill introduces a new category of leases that are registrable, namely any lease granted for a term of whatever length, which takes effect in possession after a period of more than three months beginning with the date of the grant.[97] The reason for this new category is to avoid a conveyancing trap that such reversionary leases may create under the present law.[98] At present, where a lease has been granted for a period of 21 years or less, but has not yet taken effect in possession, it cannot be registered with its own title nor protected by the entry of a notice on the title of the reversion.[99] Any buyer of the land affected may not be able to discover the existence of the lease because the tenant will not be in possession. By making reversionary leases registrable, these problems are overcome.[100] In this

---

[90] Cl 4(1)(c).

[91] Cf above, para 3.24.

[92] See above, paras 3.14—3.16.

[93] See above, para 3.16.

[94] Cl 116(1)(b), (3). Any such order is to be made by statutory instrument that is subject to annulment in pursuance of a resolution of either House of Parliament: Cl 125(4). Cf above, paras 3.17, 3.24.

[95] Cl 4(6). Cf above, para 3.26 (transfer of an estate for negative value).

[96] See Cl 4(7); above, para 3.27.

[97] Cl 4(1)(d). Cf below, para 8.10.

[98] Cf *Brickdale and Stewart-Wallace's The Land Registration Act, 1925* (4th ed 1939), pp 193, 194, commenting on Land Registration Act 1925, s 70(1)(k).

[99] See Land Registration Act 1925, ss 19(2), 22(2), 48(1). Such leases take effect as overriding interests under *ibid*, s 70(1)(k).

[100] It is, in practice, normal for leases to be granted to take effect in possession a short time after they are created, and these cause no significant conveyancing difficulties so far as we are aware. That is why the requirement of compulsory registration does not apply to leases granted to take effect within three months, if they are not otherwise registrable. There *is* a problem in relation to leases that take effect in possession at some more distant date.

regard, the Bill gives effect to a recommendation in the Consultative Document that was unanimously supported by those who responded to it.[101]

GRANT OF A RIGHT TO BUY LEASE UNDER PART V OF THE HOUSING ACT 1985

3.33 The Bill replicates the present provision[102] by which the grant of a "right to buy" lease under Part V is subject to the requirement of compulsory registration, regardless of whether the lease would otherwise be registrable because of its length.[103]

GRANT OF A LEASE TO WHICH SECTION 171A OF THE HOUSING ACT 1985 APPLIES

3.34 If there is the grant of a lease out of an unregistered legal estate in land in circumstances in which section 171A of the Housing Act 1985 applies, that grant is subject to the requirement of compulsory registration even if it would not otherwise be.[104] Once again, this replicates the effect of the present law.[105]

Protected first legal mortgages

3.35 Compulsory registration is also triggered by the creation of a protected first legal mortgage of either a legal freehold estate in land or a legal lease which has more than seven years to run.[106] A legal mortgage is protected for these purposes if it takes effect on creation as a mortgage to be protected by the deposit of documents relating to the mortgage estate.[107] A first legal mortgage is one which, on its creation, ranks in priority ahead of other mortgages affecting the mortgaged estate.[108] This provision differs from the present law in that it applies to mortgages of a leasehold estate with more than seven years to run, rather than more than 21 years as at present.

Crown grants out of demesne land

3.36 We explain in Part XI of this Report that—

(1) at present, when the Crown makes a grant of a freehold estate out of demesne land,[109] that grant is subject to the requirement of compulsory registration under section 123 of the Land Registration Act 1925;

---

[101] See Law Com No 254, paras 5.91, 5.94.

[102] Presently found in Housing Act 1985, s 154, the relevant parts of which the Bill repeals in Schedule 13.

[103] Cl 4(1)(e).

[104] Cl 4(1)(f). See above, para 3.28.

[105] See Housing Act 1985, Schedule 9A, para 2(1) (which the Bill therefore repeals: see Schedule 13).

[106] Cl 4(1)(g), (2).

[107] Cl 4(8)(a).

[108] Cl 4(8)(b).

[109] That is, the land which it holds as feudal lord paramount and in which it has no estate.

47

(2)   such a grant does not fall within the wording of the provisions of the Bill on compulsory registration that we have explained above;[110] but

(3)   special provision is made for such grants to be subject to compulsory registration.[111]

The power to extend the triggers to compulsory registration

3.37   Clause 5 of the Bill empowers the Lord Chancellor, by order, to add new events to those that presently trigger compulsory registration.[112] This is similar to a power that exists under the present law.[113] However, under the Bill, it is provided that the Lord Chancellor may only exercise this power after consultation.[114] Under the Bill, an event that might be added to the list of those that trigger compulsory registration would have to be an event relating to an unregistered interest that is an interest of any of the following kinds—

(1)   an estate in land;

(2)   a rentcharge;

(3)   a franchise; and

(4)   a *profit à prendre* in gross.[115]

The only event that would otherwise fall within this list but is expressly excluded, is to require a mortgagee to register his or her interest.[116] It would be pointless to require the registration of a charge over land if the title to the estate affected remained unregistered.

The effect of failure to register

The duty to register

3.38   There is a duty to apply for registration of the registrable estate within the period of registration if the requirement of compulsory registration applies.[117] That duty applies as follows—

---

[110]   See paras 3.24 and following.

[111]   See Cl 80; below, para 11.14.

[112]   Cl 5(1)(a). He may also make such consequential amendments of any legislation as he thinks fit: Cl 5(1)(b). The power is exercisable by statutory instrument that is subject to annulment in pursuance of the resolution of either House of Parliament: Cl 125(2), (4).

[113]   See Land Registration Act 1925, s 123(4), (5).

[114]   Cl 5(4). Although this is not stated explicitly in Land Registration Act 1925, s 123(4), (5), the power to extend the triggers would not in practice be exercised without extensive prior consultation.

[115]   Cl 5(2).

[116]   Cl 5(3).

[117]   Cl 6(1). Cf Land Registration Act 1925, s 123A(2).

(1)   where compulsory registration is triggered by a protected legal mortgage,[118] the mortgagor must apply for the registration of the estate charged by the mortgage;[119] and

(2)   in every other case, the transferee or grantee must apply for the registration of the estate transferred or granted.[120]

As regards (1), there is (as now) a power by rules to make provision enabling the mortgagee to require the registration of the estate charged by the mortgage to be registered, whether or not the mortgagor consents.[121]

3.39   The period of registration is two months, beginning with the date on which the relevant event occurs.[122] It may, however, be a longer period if, on application to the registrar by any interested person, the registrar is satisfied that there is a good reason for such a longer period as he may specify by order.[123]

The effect of non-compliance with the duty to register

3.40   The effect of non-compliance with the requirement of registration is as follows—

(1)   where the event is a transfer, the transfer becomes void and the transferor holds the legal estate on a bare trust for the transferee;[124] and

(2)   where the event is the grant of a lease or the creation of a protected mortgage, the grant or creation is void and takes effect instead as a contract made for valuable consideration to grant or create the lease or mortgage concerned.[125]

If a transfer, a grant of a lease or the creation of a mortgage has become void under these provisions, and the registrar then makes an order extending the

---

[118]   See above, para 3.35.

[119]   Cl 6(2).

[120]   Cl 6(3).

[121]   Cl 6(6). Cf Land Registration Act 1925, s 123A(10)(b); Land Registration Rules 1925, r 19(2).

[122]   Cl 6(4).

[123]   Cl 6(4), (5). As regards any dealings made by a person entitled to be registered as proprietor, see below, para 17.9(1).

[124]   Cl 7(1), (2)(a). Where the transfer is of a fee simple, the possibility of reverter to which Cl 7(1) gives rise is disregarded for the purposes of determining whether a fee simple is a fee simple absolute: Cl 7(4). This avoids any possibility that Cl 7(1) might have the unintended effect of converting any unregistered fee simple into a determinable fee simple so that it was merely equitable.

[125]   Cl 7(2).

period in which an application for registration can be made,[126] the disposition is treated as never having become void.[127]

3.41 If it is necessary to repeat a disposition because it became void under the provisions mentioned in paragraph 3.40, the transferee, grantee or martgagor is liable to the transferor, grantor or mortgagee for all the proper costs of and incidental to the repeated disposition.[128] He or she is also liable to indemnify the transferor, grantor or mortgagee in respect of any other liability reasonably incurred by him or her because of the failure to comply with the requirement of registration.[129]

THE EFFECT OF FIRST REGISTRATION

Classes of title

Introduction

3.42 The Bill replicates the principle of the Land Registration Act 1925, that there are different classes of title with which an applicant may be registered. The effect of first registration continues to depend upon that class of title. We explain in Part IX the circumstances in which the class of title may or must be upgraded.[130]

Freehold titles

3.43 Under the Bill, where a person applies to be registered as proprietor of a freehold estate, he or she may (as now) be registered with an absolute, qualified or possessory title.[131] The Bill does not change the substance of what amounts to an absolute, qualified or possessory title.

(1) A person may be registered with absolute title if the registrar considers that his or her title is such as a willing buyer could properly be advised by a competent professional adviser to accept.[132] Even if the title is defective in some way, the registrar may still register the applicant with an absolute title if he considers that the defect will not cause the holding under the title to be disturbed.[133] Almost all freehold titles are, in practice, absolute.

---

[126] Under Cl 6(5).

[127] Cl 7(3).

[128] Cl 8(a).

[129] Cl 8(b).

[130] See below, paras 9.17 and following.

[131] Cl 9(1).

[132] Cl 9(2).

[133] Cl 9(3). In practice therefore, the registrar will register a title with an absolute title if the title is a good title (one that can be forced on an unwilling buyer under open contract) or a good holding title (technically a bad title, but the holding under which is unlikely to be challenged). He may register the applicant with an absolute title even if his or her title is doubtful (one that he or she cannot prove to be good).

(2)   A person may, however, be registered merely with qualified title, if the registrar considers that the applicant's title can only be established for a limited period, or subject to certain reservations that are such that the title is not a good holding title.[134] Qualified title is extremely rare, but it might be appropriate where, for example, the transfer to the applicant had been in breach of trust.

(3)   Possessory title is only appropriate where the applicant is either in actual possession, or in receipt of the rents and profits and there is no other class of title with which he or she may be registered.[135] In practice, the registrar tends to register land with a possessory title where the basis of the applicant's title is his or her adverse possession, or where the applicant cannot prove his or her title, usually because the title deeds have been lost or destroyed.

Leasehold titles

3.44   A person who applies to be registered as proprietor of a leasehold estate may be registered as proprietor with an absolute, good leasehold, qualified or possessory title.[136] Again, the Bill does not change the substance of the present law.

(1)   A person may be registered with absolute title if the registrar—

(a)   considers that his or her title is such as a willing buyer could properly be advised by a competent professional adviser to accept; and

(b)   approves the lessor's title to grant the lease.[137]

Absolute title is appropriate, therefore, only where the superior title is either registered with absolute title or, if unregistered, has been deduced to the registrar's satisfaction. The registrar may register an applicant with absolute title even where his or her title is defective, if he considers that the defect will not cause the holding under it to be challenged.[138]

(2)   The applicant may be registered with good leasehold title if the registrar considers that his or her title is such as a willing buyer could properly be advised by a competent professional adviser to accept.[139] Good leasehold will be appropriate where the superior title is neither registered nor deduced. The registrar may register an applicant with good leasehold title

[134] Cl 9(4).

[135] Cl 9(5).

[136] Cl 10(1).

[137] Cl 10(2).

[138] Cl 10(4).

[139] Cl 10(3).

even if the title is open to objection, if he considers that the defect will not cause the holding under it to be challenged.[140]

(3) A person may be registered with qualified title, if the registrar considers that either the applicant's title or the lessor's title to the reversion can only be established for a limited period, or subject to certain reservations that are such that the title is not a good holding title.[141]

(4) The circumstances in which an applicant for the registration of a leasehold title may be registered with a possessory title are the same as those that apply in relation to a freehold title.[142]

The effect of first registration

Freehold title

REGISTRATION WITH ABSOLUTE TITLE

3.45 The effects of first registration under the Bill are not identical with the present law. Registration of title is concerned with both the benefits conferred on the registered proprietor and the burdens subject to which he or she takes the title. On the "credit side", where a person is registered as the first registered proprietor of a freehold estate, it vests the legal estate in him or her together with all the interests subsisting for the benefit of the estate (such as easements).[143] On the "debit side", first registration vests the estate in the proprietor subject only to the interests affecting the estate *at the time of registration* that are set out below.[144] Those interests are as follows.

(1) *Interests which are the subject of an entry in the register in relation to the estate.* As this provision applies only to first registrations under the Bill, the entries in question will be registered charges,[145] notices and restrictions.[146] Cautions and inhibitions are prospectively abolished under the Bill.[147]

(2) *Unregistered interests which fall within any of the paragraphs of Schedule 1.* The interests which override first registration are explained in detail in Part VIII of this Report.[148]

---

[140] Cl 10(4).

[141] Cl 10(5).

[142] Cl 10(6); see above, para 3.43(3).

[143] Cl 11(3).

[144] Cl 11(4). The relevant time must, of course, be the time of registration. As we have explained in this Part, first registration may be voluntary and so not triggered by any disposition of the land.

[145] For registered charges, see Part VII of this Report.

[146] For notices and restrictions, see below, Part VI of this Report.

[147] See below, paras 6.3, 6.32.

[148] See below, paras 8.8 and following.

(3) *Interests acquired under the Limitation Act 1980 of which the proprietor has notice.* This is new and is explained in paragraphs 3.46 and 3.47.

3.46   The matter listed in paragraph 3.45(3) above, has been included primarily to meet the following factual situation.[149] A squatter, A, takes adverse possession of certain unregistered land belonging to B. After 12 years' adverse possession, A extinguishes B's title and becomes herself the owner of the land.[150] A then abandons the land and B resumes possession of it. At some stage before B has been back in possession of the land for 12 years,[151] he sells the land to C. B sells as paper owner in accordance with the title deeds whereas the reality is quite different: the true owner is A. That sale triggers compulsory first registration and C applies to be registered. As we explain in Part VIII of this Report,[152] subject to transitional provisions to protect vested rights, the rights of a squatter will not constitute an overriding interest under the Bill as at present they do.[153] As a result of the matter listed in paragraph 3.45(3), C will take the land free of A's rights unless, at the time of registration, he had notice of them.

3.47   It may be helpful to explain the implications of whether or not C has notice of A's rights. It is relevant to the issue of whether A can seek to have the register altered under the provisions that we explain in Part X of this Report.[154]

   (1)   If C does *not* have notice of A's rights, A will not be able to seek alteration of the register because C is not bound by her rights and there is, therefore, no mistake in the register that requires rectification.

   (2)   By contrast, if C *does* have notice of A's interest, C *is* bound by her rights and she *will* be able to seek alteration of the register. The register is inaccurate and should therefore be altered to give effect to her rights by registering her as proprietor in place of C.[155]

---

[149]   Cf Law Com No 254, para 5.47, where we discussed the analogous position in relation to dispositions of registered land, and see below, para 8.77.

[150]   See Limitation Act 1980, ss 15, 17.

[151]   So that A is still the legal owner of the land.

[152]   See below, paras 8.76 and following.

[153]   See Land Registration Act 1925, s 70(1)(j).

[154]   See below, paras 10.6 and following.

[155]   As C was bound by A's rights, the alteration to the register will not be *rectification* of the register for the purposes of the Bill. As we explain at para 10.6 below, rectification is the correction of a mistake that prejudicially affects the title of the registered proprietor: see Schedule 4, para 1. The change does not prejudicially affect C's title and he will not, therefore, have any claim to indemnity.

For these purposes, notice will have its usual meaning and will include matters that the first registered proprietor ought to have discovered from reasonable inspections and inquiries, as well as matters that he or she actually knows.[156]

3.48 If the registered proprietor is not entitled to the estate for his or her own benefit (or not solely for his or her benefit) then as between him or herself and the persons beneficially entitled to the estate, the estate is vested in him or her subject to such of the interests of which he or she has notice.[157] The sort of case that this is intended to cover is where the first registered proprietor holds the land on trust, whether or not he or she is also one of the beneficiaries under that trust.

QUALIFIED TITLE

3.49 Registration of a freeholder with qualified title has the same effect as registration with absolute title, except that it does not affect the enforcement of any estate, right or interest which appears from the register to be excepted from the effect of registration.[158]

POSSESSORY TITLE

3.50 Registration of a freeholder with possessory title has the same effect as registration with absolute title, except that it does not affect the enforcement of any estate, right or interest that—

(1) is adverse to or in derogation of the proprietor's title; and

(2) is either subsisting at the time of first registration or is capable of arising.[159]

Leasehold title

3.51 The registration of a proprietor of a leasehold estate has the effects set out in the following sub-paragraphs.

(1) Where registration is with an absolute title, it has the same effect as the registration of a freeholder with an absolute title,[160] except that the estate is vested in the leaseholder subject to implied and express covenants, obligations and liabilities incident to the estate.[161] The burden of covenants and other obligations contained in leases that create proprietary rights, such as the landlord's right of re-entry for breach of covenant or restrictive covenants relating to the premises leased are not set out as such on the

---

[156] Cf Law of Property Act 1925, s 199(1)(ii)(a). Under the Bill, where a person is required to have actual knowledge of some matter before he or she can be bound by a right, this is made explicit: see, *eg*, Schedule 3, paras 2(1)(c)(ii); 3(1)(a).

[157] Cl 11(5). Cf Land Registration Act 1925, s 5(c).

[158] Cl 11(6).

[159] Cl 11(7).

[160] See above, paras 3.45—3.48.

[161] Cl 12(3), (4). Cf Land Registration Act 1925, s 9(a).

register.[162] As a lease is referred to in the register, it forms part of the register. Furthermore, any person dealing with leasehold property will inspect the lease.

(2) Registration of a lease with a good leasehold title has the same effect as its registration with an absolute title, except that it does not affect the enforcement of any estate, right or interest affecting, or in derogation of, the title of the lessor to grant the lease.[163]

(3) Registration of a lease with qualified or possessory title has the same effect as registration with absolute title but subject to the exceptions and qualifications that have been explained in relation to qualified and possessory freehold titles.[164]

Miscellaneous rule-making powers

3.52 The Bill confers on the Lord Chancellor certain miscellaneous rule-making powers relating to first registration.[165] First, rules may make provision in relation to the registration of dependent estates.[166] These rules are intended to cover the following cases.

(1) The first is where, on or subsequent to first registration, a registered proprietor has, or is granted, the benefit of a legal estate, such as an easement or a *profit à prendre*, over unregistered land. The rules may make provision as to the entry on the register of the benefit of such an estate.[167]

(2) The second is where—

    (a) on first registration, the land is already subject to a legal mortgage; or

    (b) subsequent to first registration, a charge is created that does not have to be registered to have effect at law, as is the case in relation to certain local land charges.[168]

Rules may make provision for the registration of the mortgagee as the proprietor of a registered charge.[169]

---

[162] The Bill specifically prohibits the entry of a notice in respect of a restrictive covenant in a lease: see Cl 33(c); below, para 6.13.

[163] Cl 12(6).

[164] Cl 12(7), (8). See above, paras 3.49—3.50.

[165] In each case, the rules will be land registration rules, made by the Lord Chancellor, and will be required to be laid before Parliament only. See Cls 125, 129(1).

[166] Cl 13.

[167] Cl 13(a).

[168] See below, para 7.42.

[169] Cl 13(b).

3.53   Secondly, there is a power to make rules relating to what might be described as the mechanics of first registration.[170] These may make provision about the following matters—

(1)   the making of applications for first registration (whether registration is voluntary or compulsory);

(2)   the functions of the registrar following the making of an application in relation to matters such as the examination of title and the entries to be made where he approves the title; and

(3)   the effect of any entries made by the registrar in pursuance of such an application.

CAUTIONS AGAINST FIRST REGISTRATION AND THE CAUTIONS REGISTER

The nature of cautions against first registration under the present law

3.54   Cautions against first registration provide a means by which a person with an interest in *unregistered* land can be informed of an application for first registration of the title to an estate in that land.[171] Under the present law, any person having or claiming to have an interest in unregistered land of a kind that entitles him or her to object to a disposition being made without his or her consent, may apply to lodge a caution with the registrar.[172] In practice, in relation to the circumstances when the applicant's consent is required, this provision has been very liberally interpreted by the registrar and almost any person interested in the unregistered land can in fact apply to lodge such a caution.[173] Once a caution against first registration has been entered,[174] no registration of the estate affected will be made until notice has been served on the cautioner and he or she has had an opportunity to appear before the registrar and oppose the application for first registration.[175] There is no mechanism for "warning off" cautions against first registration.[176] The cautioner will only be required to defend his or her caution when an application for first registration is made.[177] Cautions against first

---

[170]   Cl 14.

[171]   See Law Com No 254, paras 6.24—6.27.

[172]   Land Registration Act 1925, s 53(1).

[173]   See Ruoff & Roper, *Registered Conveyancing*, 13-04.

[174]   See Land Registration Rules 1925, r 64, as to the form of cautions against first registration. The registrar prepares a record, under a distinguishing number, of the details of the caution and of the statutory declaration that must be lodged in support of it, and a plan showing the extent of the land affected by the caution: *ibid*, r 64(4).

[175]   Land Registration Act 1925, s 53(3). In practice, there may not be a hearing. Cf Land Registration Rules 1925, r 299(2) (which gives the registrar authority to determine a question in dispute without an oral hearing).

[176]   As there is at present in relation to cautions against dealings. Cautions against dealings are prospectively abolished under the Bill: see below, para 6.3.

[177]   See Ruoff & Roper, *Registered Conveyancing*, 13-07.

registration are recorded on the index map[178] and may be discovered by an official search of that map.[179]

3.55 In the Consultative Document, we proposed that cautions against first registration should be retained, but should be rationalised.[180] We recommended that—

(1) any person having an interest in unregistered land should be able to lodge a caution against first registration (thereby codifying present practice);

(2) the landowner or other person having a legal estate in the land affected should be able to challenge a caution at any time after it had been lodged and not merely when an application for first registration is made; and

(3) cautions against first registration should continue to be recorded on the index map.

Our recommendations were unanimously supported by those who responded to them. We have in fact modified one of these recommendations in the course of the preparation of the Bill for the reasons that we explain below.[181]

Cautions against first registration under the Bill

The right to lodge a caution

3.56 Subject to the important qualification mentioned below, in paragraph 3.58, the Bill confers a right to lodge a caution against first registration on the following persons—

(1) a person who claims to be the owner of a legal estate that is—

(a) an estate in land;[182]

(b) a rentcharge;

(c) a franchise; or

(d) a *profit à prendre* in gross;

which relates to the land to which the caution relates; or

(2) a person who claims to be entitled to an interest[183] affecting any of the legal estates mentioned in (1).[184]

---

[178] Land Registration Rules 1925, r 8.

[179] See Land Registration (Open Register) Rules 1991, r 9.

[180] See Law Com No 254, paras 6.62—6.64.

[181] See para 3.58.

[182] That is, a fee simple absolute in possession or a term of years absolute: Law of Property Act 1925, s 1(1).

This provision gives effect to the recommendation mentioned above in paragraph 3.55(1). There are special provisions applicable to cautions against the first registration of the Crown's demesne land, and these are explained in Part XI of this Report.[185]

3.57   Some examples may be given of the operation of this provision—

(1)   a tenant under a lease could lodge a caution against the first registration of the title of the reversionary freehold estate;

(2)   a person having the benefit of an option or a charging order in relation to a freehold estate might lodge a caution against the first registration of that estate;[186] and

(3)   a person who claimed to be a beneficiary under (say) a resulting or constructive trust could lodge a caution against the first registration of the estate in which he or she claimed to be beneficially interested.

3.58   There is a significant exception to the principle set out in paragraph 3.56 that is new to the Bill.[187] Subject to the transitional arrangements mentioned below, a caution against first registration may not be lodged by—

(1)   the owner of a freehold estate in land in respect of that estate; or

(2)   the owner of a lease granted for a term of which more than seven years are unexpired in respect of that estate.[188]

The reason for this exclusion is that cautions against first registration are not intended to provide a substitute for first registration. If, therefore, a person has an unregistered legal estate that is registrable, he or she should register it. This is in accordance with our ultimate goal of total registration.[189] This prohibition on

---

[183]   An interest is, for the purposes of the Bill, an adverse right affecting the title to the estate or charge: Cl 129(3)(b).

[184]   See Cl 15(1), (2).

[185]   See below, paras 11.17 and following.

[186]   Both options and charging orders in relation to unregistered land are registrable as land charges under the Land Charges Act 1972. However, a person having the benefit of such a right might wish to lodge a caution either in addition to or instead of the registration of a land charge. The extension of the triggers to compulsory registration by the Land Registration Act 1997 has made cautions against first registration an effective method of protecting interests in unregistered land, even though, as we explain below (see para 3.62), a caution against first registration does not confer any priority on the cautioner's interest.

[187]   It was not the subject of consultation in Law Com No 254.

[188]   This states the effect of Cl 15(3). There is a power to reduce the period of 7 years under Cl 116(1)(c). This power and the reasons for it have been explained above: see para 3.17.

[189]   See above, paras 2.9, 2.13.

lodging cautions against first registration will not, however, apply for two years after the provisions on first registration are brought into force.[190]

3.59 The right to lodge a caution is exercisable by application to the registrar.[191] The form, content, and manner of application will be determined by rules made under the general rule-making power concerning applications that is explained in Part IX of this Report.[192] Furthermore, anyone may object to the application and, if the objection is not groundless and cannot be disposed of by agreement, the registrar must refer the matter for determination to the Adjudicator.[193] In fact, as we explain below, the person who is most likely to object to the lodgement of a caution against first registration — the owner of the legal estate to which it relates — is given a specific right to apply for cancellation of the caution in any event.[194] A person may not exercise his or her right to lodge a caution without reasonable cause.[195] A breach of this statutory duty will be actionable by any person who suffers damage in consequence of it.[196] The cautioner has a right to withdraw a caution against first registration by application to the registrar.[197]

The effect of a caution against first registration

3.60 Where a caution against first registration has been lodged, the registrar must notify the cautioner[198] of any application for first registration and of his right to object to it.[199] The period within which the cautioner may object to the application will be such as is specified by rules.[200] The registrar cannot determine the application for first registration until the end of that period, unless before that time, the cautioner has either exercised his or her right to object to the application[201] or given the registrar notice that he or she does not intend to do so.[202] Where the cautioner objects, the matter must be referred to the Adjudicator for determination unless the registrar is satisfied that the objection is groundless,

---

[190] Schedule 12, para 14(1). For the special provisions applicable to cautions against first registration lodged by the Crown in respect of demesne land and the reasons for them, see below, para 11.18.

[191] Cl 15(4).

[192] See Schedule 10, para 6; below, para 9.77.

[193] Cl 73(1), (6), (7); below, para 16.6. For the office of Adjudicator, see below, para 16.3.

[194] See para 3.63.

[195] Cl 77(1)(a).

[196] Cl 77(2). Cf below, paras 6.28, 6.55, 16.6.

[197] Cl 17.

[198] Which means not only the person who lodged the caution, but also his or her personal representative: Cl 22.

[199] Cl 16(1).

[200] Cl 16(2). The rules will be land registration rules and will be required to be laid before Parliament only. See Cls 125, 129(1).

[201] Under Cl 73(1); see below, para 16.6.

[202] Cl 16(2).

or the matter can be determined by agreement.[203] If the cautioner does not object to the application for first registration, the registrar will proceed to determine it in the usual way.

3.61   The Bill makes provision by which an agent for the applicant for first registration may give notice of the application to the cautioner and for this notice to be treated as having been given by the registrar.[204] The purpose of this provision is to enable a solicitor or licensed conveyancer who is acting for an applicant for first registration to give notice at the time that the application is made. This will help to expedite the conveyancing process because it will not be necessary to wait for the registrar to serve notice on the cautioner. Such a notice will only be regarded as having been given by the registrar if it was given by a person who is of a description provided by rules (which is likely to include solicitors and licensed conveyancers) and the notice is given in such circumstances as rules may provide.[205] This means that rules can define (for example) the time at which the notice must be served, having regard to the purpose of the power.

3.62   The effect of a caution against first registration is limited. It merely gives the cautioner a right to be notified of an application for first registration so that he or she can object to that application. It has no effect on the validity or priority of any interest that the cautioner may have in the legal estate to which the caution relates.[206]

Cancellation of cautions

3.63   The Bill creates a procedure whereby the owner of a legal estate to which a caution relates, and persons of such other description as rules may provide,[207] may apply to the registrar for the cancellation of a caution against first registration.[208] Where such an application is made, the registrar will be required to serve notice on the cautioner of—

(1)   the application; and

---

[203]   Cl 73(6), (7); below, para 16.6.

[204]   Cl 16(4).

[205]   Cl 16(4)(a), (b). The rules will be land registration rules and will be required to be laid before Parliament only. See Cls 125, 129(1). There is a power for rules to make provision about the form, content and service of notice under the Bill: Schedule 10, para 5.

[206]   Cl 16(3). But the mere fact that the cautioner has to be notified and can object to the first registration is, nonetheless, a very useful form of protection. In respect of some rights that cannot be protected by the registration of a land charge, as where a person claims to have an interest under a trust, it may be the only effective way of ensuring that his or her rights are properly protected on first registration by the entry of a restriction.

[207]   This is likely to include persons with an interest in the land affected, such as a mortgagee or a receiver.

[208]   Cl 18(1).

(2)   the fact that, if he or she does not exercise his or her right to object to the application before the end of such period as rules may provide, the registrar must cancel the caution.[209]

This is one of just two cases under the Bill where the general right for *any* person to object to an application[210] does not apply. Only the cautioner may do so.[211] If the cautioner does object, the matter must be referred to the Adjudicator for determination in the usual way, unless it can be resolved by agreement or the registrar is satisfied that the objection is groundless.[212]

3.64   Where the owner of a legal estate[213] has consented to the lodging of the caution,[214] he or she would not normally be able to apply for the cancellation of the caution under the procedure explained in paragraph 3.63.[215] However, even in such a case where the owner had consented, there might be circumstances in which it was appropriate for him or her to seek the cancellation of a caution, and these would be specified in rules.[216] An obvious case would be where the interest protected by the caution had terminated.[217]

The cautions register

3.65   Under the Bill, cautions against first registration will continue be recorded on the index map.[218] However, the Bill also requires the registrar to create a register of cautions against first registration.[219] How the register is kept will be a matter for rules.[220] These are likely to make provision about—

(1)   the information to be kept in the register;

---

[209] Cl 18(3), (4).

[210] Under Cl 73(1); below, para 16.6.

[211] See Cl 73(2); below, para 16.6.

[212] Cl 73(6), (7); below, para 16.6.

[213] Or any person who derives title from him or her by operation of law, such as a trustee in bankruptcy or an executor.

[214] In such manner as rules may provide. The rules will be land registration rules and will be required to be laid before Parliament only. See Cls 125, 129(1).

[215] Cl 18(2). This is in accordance with a recommendation in Law Com No 254, para 6.64, which was supported by all those who responded to it.

[216] Cl 18(2). The rules will be land registration rules and will be required to be laid before Parliament only. See Cls 125, 129(1).

[217] As where A, a freeholder, granted B an option to purchase her land that was exercisable for a period of five years and A agreed that B should lodge a caution against first registration in respect of that option. A would be entitled to apply for the cancellation of the caution after five years notwithstanding her consent.

[218] See Cl 68(1)(c); below, para 9.55. The index map contains the title number of any caution in the cautions register.

[219] Cl 19(1).

[220] Cl 19(2). The rules will be land registration rules and will be required to be laid before Parliament only. See Cls 125, 129(1).

(2)   the form in which information included in the register is to be kept; and

(3)   the arrangement of that information.[221]

At present, details of cautions against first registration are kept on a "caution title", which records the following matters—

(a)   the name and up to three separate addresses for service of the cautioner;

(b)   the name and address of the solicitors or licensed conveyancers, if any, who lodged the application;

(c)   the estate against which the caution has been registered, including in the case of a leasehold estate particulars of the lease in question;

(d)   an extract from the statutory declaration in support of the caution showing the nature of the cautioner's interest in the estate subject to the caution.

It is anticipated that the cautions register will contain similar information. It is intended that it will be kept in dematerialised form.

3.66   The Bill makes provision for the alteration of the register in similar ways to those that apply to the register of title.[222] These provisions are explained in Part X of this Report.[223] There is also a right to indemnity where a person suffers loss by reason of a mistake in the cautions register which is also explained in Part X.[224]

---

[221]   Cf Cl 1 (register of title); considered below, para 9.3.

[222]   Cls 20, 21.

[223]   See below, para 10.26.

[224]   Schedule 8, para 1(1)(g); below, para 10.37.

PART IV
DISPOSITIONS OF REGISTERED LAND

INTRODUCTION

4.1 In this Part we examine two matters—

   (1)   the powers of disposition of a registered proprietor or a person who is entitled to be registered as proprietor; and

   (2)   the dispositions of a registered estate or charge that are required to be registered.

POWERS OF DISPOSITION

Introduction

4.2 In Part IX of this Report, we explain that there are at least four ways in which a title to land may, in some way, be defective and we summarise how the Bill deals with each of them.[1] The matters are as follows—

   (1)   the person who appears to be owner may not be;

   (2)   the owner may have limited powers and may make a disposition that he or she has no power to make;

   (3)   the property may be subject to incumbrances; and

   (4)   events may occur which mean that a registered proprietor's estate has become determinable.

4.3 Our concern here is with the situation in paragraph 4.2(2). A registered proprietor's powers of disposition may be limited, for example, by statute (perhaps because it is a statutory body), if it is a corporation, by its public documents, or where the proprietors are trustees, by the terms of the trust upon which they hold the land. At present it is not entirely clear what powers of disposition a proprietor of a registered estate is to be taken to have.[2] In *State Bank of India v Sood*,[3] Peter Gibson LJ cited with approval a statement in the standard textbook on registered land that—

---

[1]   See below, paras 9.29—9.35.

[2]   The Land Registration Act 1925 contains numerous, very specific provisions as to what a registered proprietor can do with the estate or charge vested in him or her. When taken together, he or she appears to have the same powers as the owner of a legal estate where title to the land is unregistered.

[3]   [1997] Ch 276, 284.

in registered conveyancing it is fundamental that any registered proprietor can exercise all or any powers of disposition unless some entry on the register exists to curtail or remove those powers... .[4]

This may be illustrated by the provisions of the Land Registration Act 1925 and the Land Registration Rules 1925 that relate to trusts. Any limitations on the powers of the tenant for life (where the land is settled) or the trustees (where the land is held on a trust of land) should be protected by the entry of a restriction.[5] The necessary implication from these provisions is that the powers of the tenant for life or trustees would otherwise be unfettered. Similarly, the registrar may enter a restriction where the dispositionary powers of a registered proprietor are limited by statute or where there are limitations on the powers of a corporation or of personal representatives.[6] We consider that the principle stated by Peter Gibson LJ should be the correct one. It means that a person can rely upon the register to tell him or her whether there are any limitations on the powers of a registered proprietor and can safely act in reliance upon it. However, the present legislation does not explicitly state that principle. Indeed, in at least one case, there has been an attempt to rectify the register against a buyer, where—

(1)   the disposition to her was one that, by statute, the seller had no power to make; but

(2)   the register was silent as to this fact.[7]

The principles adopted in the Bill

4.4   The Bill lays down the following principles—

(1)   A registered proprietor (or a person who is entitled to be registered as proprietor) should be taken to have unlimited dispositive powers.

(2)   If those powers are in fact limited for whatever reason, that limitation should be reflected by an entry on the register.

(3)   If there is no entry, any disponee is entitled to assume that there are no limitations on the powers of the disponor.

(4)   If there were in fact limitations on the disponor's powers that were not reflected by an entry on the register, the disponee's title cannot be called into question. However, the disposition will not be rendered lawful. The consequences of acting beyond his or her powers can therefore be visited

---

[4]   The quotation came from the looseleaf edition Ruoff & Roper, *Registered Conveyancing*, para 32-05, as it then was.

[5]   See in relation to settlements, Land Registration Act 1925, s 86(3); Land Registration Rules 1925, rr 56—58, 104, Schedule 2, Forms 9—11; and for trusts of land, Land Registration Act 1925, s 94(4); Land Registration Rules 1925, rr 106A, 236, Schedule 2, Form 11A.

[6]   Land Registration Rules 1925, r 236A.

[7]   *Hounslow London Borough Council v Hare* (1990) 24 HLR 9. Fortunately, the attempt was unsuccessful.

upon the disponor. The disponee may not escape liability if he or she was privy to the disponor's conduct.

In the following paragraphs, we explain these points in more detail.

The provisions of the Bill

Owner's powers

4.5 The Bill employs the concept of "owner's powers". A person is entitled to exercise owner's powers if he or she is either—

(1) the registered proprietor of an estate or charge; or

(2) entitled to be registered as the proprietor.[8]

The right conferred by (2) is subject to rules.[9]

4.6 By Clause 23, owner's powers consist of power—

(1) to make a disposition of any kind permitted by the general law in relation to the interest which the person has, other than a mortgage by demise or sub-demise (in the case of a registered estate) or a legal sub-mortgage[10] (in relation to a registered charge); and

(2) to charge the estate at law with the payment of money (in the case of a registered estate) or to charge at law with the payment of money, indebtedness that is secured by the registered charge.[11]

4.7 As regards the exception of a mortgage by demise or sub-demise in (1), in the Consultative Document,[12] we recommended that because such mortgages were in practice obsolete, they should be prospectively abolished in relation to charges over registered land. This proposal was supported by all but one of those who responded to the point. Clause 23 implements this recommendation.[13] Both the exception for a legal sub-mortgage in (1) and the reason for the express powers

---

[8] Cl 24(1).

[9] Cl 24(2). Such rules are likely to explain how owner's powers are to be exercised in such a case. They will be land registration rules, made by the Lord Chancellor, and will be laid before Parliament only: Cls 125(3), 129(1). It should be noted that, under Land Registration Act 1925, s 37, a person who is entitled to be registered as proprietor, may, in the prescribed manner, dispose of the registered estate or charge before he or she is registered as proprietor of it.

[10] A legal sub-mortgage is, for these purposes, a transfer by way of mortgage, a sub-mortgage by sub-demise, and a charge by way of legal mortgage: Cl 23(3).

[11] Cl 23(1) (registered estates), (2) (registered charges).

[12] Law Com No 254, para 9.5.

[13] See further below, para 7.3.

mentioned in (2) are explained in the context of charges in Part VII of this Report.[14]

Protection for disponees

4.8   Clause 26 provides protection for disponees.[15] As a general principle, a person's right to exercise owner's powers in relation to a registered estate or charge is to be taken to be free from any limitation affecting the validity of a disposition.[16] However, that does not apply to a limitation reflected by an entry in the register, or imposed by or under the Bill.[17] For the future, a limitation on owner's powers will be made by the entry of a restriction.[18] At present it is also possible to limit owner's powers by the entry of a caution or an inhibition. As we explain in Part VI—

(1)   both cautions and inhibitions are prospectively abolished under the Bill;

(2)   existing cautions will remain on the register;[19] and

(3)   although existing inhibitions will remain on the register, they will be treated thereafter as restrictions.[20]

4.9   This general principle that a person's right to exercise owner's powers is unlimited unless there is some entry in the register or limitation imposed by, or under, the Bill, has effect for one specific purpose only. This is to prevent the title of the disponee being questioned.[21] It follows that, if the person exercising owner's powers did not have unlimited powers, but there was no entry in the register to reflect this fact—

(1)   the disponee's title could not be challenged; but

(2)   the disposition would not be rendered lawful.

Those two points merit further explanation.

4.10   First, the protection given to the disponee's title is complete and cannot be called into question. For example, if—

---

[14]   In relation to sub-mortgages, see below, para. 7.11. As regards the power to charge with the payment of money, see below, paras 7.2—7.4.

[15]   Cf Cl 52; below, paras 7.7, 7.8.

[16]   Cl 26(1).

[17]   Cl 26(2). For the restrictions imposed by the Bill, see Cls 24(2) (right to exercise owner's powers subject to rules; above, para 4.5) and 25 (obligation to comply with registration requirements; below, para 4.15).

[18]   See below, para 6.40.

[19]   See below, para 6.3.

[20]   See below, para 6.32.

[21]   Cl 26(3).

(1)   W and X held land on a bare trust as nominee for Y, on terms that they could not make any disposition of the land without Y's written consent;

(2)   Y, who was in actual occupation of the land held in trust, did not protect her interest by the entry of a restriction; and

(3)   W and X fraudulently charged the land to Z without Y's consent in breach of trust;

Z's charge would be valid and could not be called into question by Y. The fact that Y was in actual occupation at the time of the charge would not change this, because W and X's right to exercise owner's powers is taken to be free of limitation. It follows that Y cannot claim that her beneficial interest under the trust was an overriding interest[22] because her prior consent to the charge was not obtained.

4.11   Secondly, where the disposition is in fact unlawful, the consequences of that unlawfulness can be pursued so long as these do not call into question the validity of the disponee's title. The example may be given of trustees of land, A and B, who had limited powers of disposition,[23] but who failed to enter a restriction on the register to reflect this fact. If they transferred the land to a buyer, C, in circumstances that were prohibited by the trust, they would commit a breach of trust. Furthermore, although C's title could not be impeached, the protection given by Clause 26 does not extend to any independent forms of liability to which she might be subject. Thus if C knew of the trustees' breach of trust when the transfer was made, she might be personally accountable in equity for the knowing receipt of trust property transferred in breach of trust.[24]

REGISTRABLE DISPOSITIONS

Introduction

4.12   Clause 27 is one of the most important in the Bill. It defines those dispositions of registered land that must be completed by registration. It corresponds to, but is not identical with, similar provisions in the Land Registration Act 1925.[25] Registrable dispositions have a particular significance under the Bill (as indeed do their equivalents — called "registered dispositions" — under the Land Registration Act 1925[26]). Not only do they take effect at law as legal estates, but they are also given special priority, as we explain in Part V of this Report.[27]

---

[22]   Under Schedule 3, para 2 (interests of persons in actual occupation); see below, para 8.54.

[23]   Cf Trusts of Land and Appointment of Trustees' Act 1996, s 8.

[24]   For the most recent utterance as to degree of knowledge required for knowing receipt, see *Bank of Credit and Commerce International (Overseas) Ltd v Akindele* [2000] 3 WLR 1423. It seems unlikely to be the final word on the subject.

[25]   See in particular ss 18 and 21.

[26]   Cf Land Registration Act 1925, s 3(xxii).

[27]   See below, paras 5.6 and following.

The general principle

4.13 The general principle, stated in Clause 27(1), is that if a disposition of a registered estate or charge is required to be completed by registration, it does not operate at law until the relevant registration requirements are met. We explain below which dispositions are registrable and the registration requirements that apply in relation to each of them.[28] When electronic conveyancing has been introduced, this general principle is likely, in time, to be superseded. This is because it will not apply to dispositions which are required to be communicated electronically to the registrar and simultaneously registered under Clause 93,[29] a provision that we explain in Part XIII of this Report.[30] The reason why the general principle in Clause 27(1) has to be disapplied is because under 93, a disposition has *no* effect whatever, either at law or in equity, until the registration requirements are met.[31]

4.14 It will be apparent from the general principle that the concept of a registrable disposition is concerned with those dealings with registered land that transfer or create legal estates. In principle, there must be a presumption that *all* dispositions of registered land that themselves create or transfer a legal estate should be subject to some form of registration, whether with their own titles or by the entry of some form of notice on the title which is subject to them.[32] Under the Bill there are necessary exceptions to this general rule (as there are under the Land Registration Act 1925), but they are kept to a minimum. It is because registrable dispositions, when registered, confer a legal estate that they are given special priority,[33] much as dispositions of legal estates enjoy special priority in unregistered conveyancing.[34]

4.15 Under the Bill, a registrable disposition of a registered estate or charge only has effect if it complies with such requirements as to form and content as rules may provide.[35] This is, in other words, a power to prescribe the form and content of *any* registrable disposition. Under the present law, it is not possible to prescribe the form of a registered charge,[36] nor has any form ever been prescribed for a lease, though it could be.[37]

---

[28] See below, paras 4.16 and following.

[29] See Cl 93(4).

[30] See below, paras 13.74 and following.

[31] Cl 93(2). See below, para 13.84.

[32] Cf above, para 1.5

[33] Cls 29, 30; below, paras 5.6 and following.

[34] Cf *Megarry & Wade's Law of Real Property* (6th ed 2000), 4-061.

[35] Cl 25(1). The rules will be land registration rules, and will be laid before Parliament only: Cls 125(3), 129(1). Rules may apply Cl 25(1) to any other kind of disposition which depends for its effect on registration: Cl 25(2).

[36] See Land Registration Act 1925, s 25(2).

[37] See Land Registration Act 1925, ss 18(1), 21(1).

Dispositions required to be registered and the registration requirements that apply to them

Introduction

4.16   The Bill lists the dispositions that are required to be completed by registration[38] and, in Schedule 2, it sets out what the registration requirements are for the specified dispositions.[39] Although the range of dispositions that are registrable appears at first sight to be complex, the effect of the provisions is in fact straightforward and can be summarised as follows. Subject to certain limited exceptions,[40] any transfer of, or the grant or reservation of any legal estate out of, registered land,[41] is a registrable disposition. This is in accordance with the policy, explained above in paragraph 4.14, that all dispositions of registered land that transfer or create a legal estate should, in principle, be registrable unless there are good reasons why this should not be the case. The dispositions that are subject to compulsory registration include dispositions by operation of law, but with certain limited exceptions.[42]

Transfers of a registered estate

4.17   Subject to the exceptions mentioned below in paragraph 4.19, any transfer of a registered estate must be completed by registration.[43] A registered estate is a legal estate the title to which is entered in the register other than a registered charge.[44] The following are the registered estates which may or (in some cases) must have their own titles on the register—

(1)   a fee simple absolute in possession;[45]

(2)   a leasehold estate that may be registered with its own title;[46]

(3)   a rentcharge;[47]

(4)   a franchise;[48]

(5)   a *profit à prendre* in gross;[49] and

---

[38]   Cl 27(2), (3).

[39]   Cf Cl 27(4).

[40]   See below, paras 4.19, 4.22, 4.29.

[41]   Registered land means a registered estate or a registered charge: Cl 129(1).

[42]   See Cl 27(5); below, paras 4.19, 4.29.

[43]   Cl 27(2)(a).

[44]   Cl 129(1).

[45]   See above, para 3.9.

[46]   See above, paras 3.10—3.13, 3.30—3.34; and below, paras 4.20 and following.

[47]   See above, para 3.18; and below, para 4.27.

[48]   See above, para 3.19; and below, para 4.24.

[49]   See above, para 3.20; and below, para 4.26.

(6)   a manor.[50]

4.18   The transferee (or his or her successor in title) must be entered in the register as proprietor.[51] Where there is a transfer of part only of a registered estate, such details as may be provided for by rules, must be entered in the register in relation to the registered estate out of which the transfer is made.[52] The Registry makes certain entries on the register of a registered estate in a case where the proprietor disposes of part of it, for example, as to rights reserved or granted. It is anticipated that the practice is unlikely to be different under the Bill.

4.19   There are three exceptions to the principle stated in paragraph 4.17, that a transfer of a registered estate is a registrable disposition, and each of them involves a disposition by operation of law.

(1)   The first is a transfer on the death of a sole individual proprietor.[53] Title to the deceased's estate vests by operation of law in his or her executors (if any) or in the Public Trustee until such time as there is a grant of administration. Once the legal title is vested in the personal representatives, they may apply to the registrar[54] to alter the register to bring it up to date by registering the applicant as proprietor.[55]

(2)   The second is a transfer on the bankruptcy of a sole individual proprietor.[56] When an individual becomes insolvent, his or her estate will vest without any conveyance or transfer in his or her trustee in bankruptcy, immediately on his or her appointment (or in the Official Receiver in default of any such appointment).[57] Once again, the trustee in bankruptcy may then apply to the registrar to alter the register to bring it up to date by registering the applicant as proprietor, as in (1).

(3)   The third is a transfer on the dissolution of a sole corporate proprietor.[58] When a company is dissolved, its property is deemed to be bona vacantia and therefore vests in the Crown (or one of the Royal Duchies).[59] The Crown (or Duchy) may apply to the registrar to alter the register to bring it up to date by registering the applicant as proprietor, again as in (1).

---

[50]   See above, para 3.21.

[51]   Schedule 2, para 2(1).

[52]   *Ibid*, para 2(2). The rules will be land registration rules, and will be laid before Parliament only: Cls 125(3), 129(1).

[53]   Cl 27(5)(a).

[54]   See Schedule 4, para 7; below, para 10.20.

[55]   Under Schedule 4, para 5(b); below, para 10.19.

[56]   Cl 27(5)(a).

[57]   Insolvency Act 1986, s 306.

[58]   Cl 27(5)(b).

[59]   Companies Act 1985, s 654. The property falls to be administered by the Treasury Solicitor: *ibid*, s 656.

These exceptions also apply to the transfer of registered charges, which are explained below, at paragraph 4.30(1).

The grant of certain leases

4.20   The grant of most leases is a registrable disposition and must, therefore be completed by registration. This will be the case in relation to the following—

(1)   leases granted for more than seven years from the date of the grant;[60]

(2)   reversionary leases that are to take effect in possession more than three months after they have been granted;[61]

(3)   discontinuous leases;[62]

(4)   leases granted in pursuance of the right to buy provisions of Part V of the Housing Act 1985;[63] and

(5)   leases granted in circumstances where section 171A of the Housing Act 1985 applies.[64]

It is unnecessary to comment on these categories of leases because an explanation has already been given in relation to them in Part III of this Report.[65] It may be noted that, as regards (1), there is a power for the Lord Chancellor, after consultation, to reduce further the period of seven years by order.[66]

4.21   Where a lease is a registrable disposition, the grantee of the lease or his or her successor in title must be entered in the register as the proprietor of the lease, and a notice in respect of the lease must also be entered.[67]

4.22   It will be clear from paragraph 4.20 that the grant of most leases is a registrable disposition. There are, however, two categories of lease granted out of a registered estate that are not registrable. The first, which follows from what has been said above,[68] is a lease granted for seven years or less unless it falls within one of the classes of lease listed in paragraph 4.20(2)—(5). The second is a PPP lease[69] — in

---

[60]   Cl 27(2)(b)(i). Cf above, para 3.30.

[61]   Cl 27(2)(b)(ii). Cf above, para 3.32.

[62]   Cl 27(2)(b)(iii). Cf above, para 3.11.

[63]   Cl 27(2)(b)(iv). Cf above, para 3.33.

[64]   Cl 27(2)(b)(v). Cf above, para 3.34.

[65]   Any lease which, if granted out of *unregistered* land, either may or must be registered, will, if granted out of *registered* land, be a registrable disposition.

[66]   Cl 116(1)(d), (3). Any such order is to be made by statutory instrument that is subject to annulment in pursuance of a resolution of either House of Parliament: Cl 125(4). Cf above, paras 3.17, 3.30.

[67]   Schedule 2, para 3.

[68]   See para 4.20(1).

[69]   See Cl 90(6).

essence a lease of an underground railway and ancillary property — granted under the Greater London Authority Act 1999.[70] As we have indicated above,[71] in principle *all* dispositions of registered land that create a legal estate should be required to be registered. As regards these two types of lease, there are policy reasons why they are not registrable, but take effect instead as overriding interests. We say more about both types of lease[72] and the policy reasons for excluding them from the requirement of registration[73] in Part VIII of this Report.

Leases of franchises and manors

4.23   So far as we are aware, it would not now be possible to create new manors. Even if it were, as we have explained, such a manor could not be registered with its own title under the Bill.[74] Although the Crown might, in the exercise of its prerogative, grant a new franchise in fee simple, that would be a grant of an unregistered legal estate. As such, it would be subject to the provisions on voluntary first registration that we have already explained.[75] It follows that the Bill does not need to make provision for the creation of manors or franchises as registrable dispositions. However, it does need to make provision in relation to the grant of a lease of a manor or franchise which is itself a registered estate. Under the Bill, where the registered estate is a franchise or a manor, *any* lease of that estate is a registrable disposition.[76] The nature of such incorporeal rights is such that the existence of a lease of them may not be apparent to any person dealing with the land affected unless it is registered. The registration requirements vary according to whether the lease is for a term of—

(1)   more than seven years; or

(2)   seven years or less;

from the date of grant. As regards (1), the grantee of the lease or his or her successor in title must be entered in the register as the proprietor of the lease, and a notice in respect of the lease must also be entered.[77] As regards (2), a notice in respect of the lease must be entered in the register.[78]

Express grant or reservation of an easement, right or privilege

4.24   The express grant or reservation of an interest of a kind falling within section 1(2)(a) of the Law of Property Act 1925, other than one which is capable of being

---

[70]   Cl 90(3)(a).

[71]   See para 4.14.

[72]   See Schedule 3, para 2; Cl 90(5); below, paras 8.11—8.13, 8.48, 8.50.

[73]   See below, paras 8.9, 8.13, 8.50.

[74]   See above, para 3.21.

[75]   See above, para 3.19.

[76]   Cl 27(2)(c).

[77]   Schedule 2, para 4.

[78]   Schedule 2, para 5.

registered under the Commons Registration Act 1965, is a registrable disposition.[79] Section 1(2)(a) of the Law of Property Act 1925 refers to—

> an easement, right or privilege in or over land for an interest equivalent to an estate in fee simple absolute in possession or a term of years absolute...

4.25 The interests that will be registrable will be easements and *profits à prendre*, whether those are in gross or are appurtenant to an estate.[80] There are two qualifications to this. First, rights of common which are capable of being registered under the Commons Registration Act 1965 are excluded. This is because the Commons Registration Act 1965 prohibits the registration under the Land Registration Act 1925 of rights of common that are registrable under the 1965 Act.[81] This prohibition will continue under the Bill.[82] Secondly, where an easement, right or privilege is granted through the operation of section 62 of the Law of Property Act 1925,[83] that grant is not regarded as an express grant for these purposes, so as to require registration. Section 62 is a so-called "word-saving provision" that is taken to import certain words into a conveyance of land unless its effect is excluded.[84] It is therefore treated for some purposes at least as a form of express grant,[85] though in practice it tends to operate without an appreciation of its effect by the parties to the conveyance.[86]

4.26 The registration requirements will depend upon the nature of the grant or reservation.

> (1) Where the disposition involves the creation of a legal *profit à prendre* in gross with its own title,[87] whether that grant is for an interest equivalent to an estate in fee simple or for a term of years for more than seven years—

---

[79] Cl 27(2)(d).

[80] Cl 27(2)(d) *may* include other incorporeal hereditaments, but this is, in practice, very unlikely. This is because the Bill makes express provision in relation to the grant of a lease of manor or a franchise (see above, para 4.23). The grant or reservation of rentcharges is not within Law of Property Act 1925, s 1(2)(a), but s 1(2)(b). Rentcharges are dealt with by Cl 27(2)(e): see below, para 4.27.

[81] Commons Registration Act 1965, s 1(1).

[82] Cf Schedule 11, para 7.

[83] Cl 27(7).

[84] For Law of Property Act 1925, s 62, and its operation, see *Megarry & Wade's Law of Real Property* (6th ed 2000), 18-108 and following.

[85] See *Quicke v Chapman* [1903] 1 Ch 659; *Megarry & Wade's Law of Real Property* (6th ed 2000), 18-113.

[86] For a striking recent example of this, see *Hair v Gillman* [2000] 3 EGLR 74 (acquisition of car-parking rights).

[87] "Creation" will include both grant and reservation. It will also include the case where the registered proprietor of a legal *profit à prendre* in gross that has been registered with is own title grants a lease of that profit for more than seven years.

(a) the grantee or his or her successor in title must be entered in the register as the proprietor of the interest created; and

(b) a notice in respect of the profit must also be entered in the register.[88]

(2) Where the disposition involves the grant or reservation of any other interest falling within those listed in paragraph 4.25,[89] a notice in respect of the interest must be entered in the register. Furthermore, where the interest is for the benefit of a registered estate, the registered proprietor must be entered in the register[90] as the proprietor of the interest.[91]

Express grant or reservation of rentcharge or legal right of re-entry

4.27 The express grant or reservation of the following types of interest are registrable dispositions—

(1) a rentcharge in possession issuing out of or charged on land being either perpetual or for a term of years absolute; and

(2) a right of entry exercisable over or in respect of a legal term of years absolute, or annexed, for any purpose to a legal rentcharge.[92]

As we have explained in Part III of this Report, the circumstances in which a rentcharge can now be created are in fact very limited.[93]

4.28 The registration requirements are as follows—

(1) Where the disposition involves the creation[94] of a legal rentcharge with its own title, whether that grant is for an interest equivalent to an estate in fee simple or for a term of years for more than seven years—

(a) the grantee or his or her successor in title must be entered in the register as the proprietor of the interest created; and

(b) a notice in respect of the rentcharge must also be entered in the register.[95]

---

[88] Schedule 2, para 6.

[89] Such as the grant or reservation of an easement or a profit that is not registered with its own title (whether that profit is appurtenant or in gross), or the lease for seven years or less of a *profit à prendre* in gross (whether or not that profit is registered with its own title).

[90] That is, in the register of the land benefited.

[91] Schedule 2, para 7.

[92] Cl 27(2)(e). Cf Law of Property Act 1925, s 1(2)(b), (e).

[93] See Rentcharges Act 1977, s 2; above, para 3.18.

[94] Whether by grant or reservation.

[95] Schedule 2, para 6.

(2) In every other case — in other words where a rentcharge is granted or reserved for a term not exceeding seven years, or in any case where a right of entry is reserved — a notice in respect of the interest must be entered in the register.[96] Where the interest is for the benefit of a registered estate, the registered proprietor must also be entered in the register[97] as the proprietor of the interest.[98] However, there is a power to modify these registration requirements by rules in relation to a right of entry over or in respect of a term of years absolute.[99] It is not the current practice of HM Land Registry to record the benefit of a right of entry on the title of the reversion to a lease. That practice may change in the future, but the power to modify the requirements means that the present position can be maintained.

The grant of a legal charge

4.29 The grant of a legal charge is a registrable disposition.[100] To register the charge, the chargee or his or her successor in title must be entered in the register as its proprietor.[101] By way of an exception, the creation of a legal charge that is also a local land charge does not require registration.[102] The reasons for this exception are more fully explained in Part VII of this Report,[103] but may be summarised as follows—

(1) local land charges take effect as overriding interests, and are, therefore, binding on any disponee of registered land without registration;[104] but

(2) those local land charges that are charges on land to secure the payment of money, cannot be enforced as charges unless and until they are registered.[105]

It follows, therefore, that such local land charges are not required to be registered when created, but must be registered as charges prior to realisation.

Dispositions of a registered charge

4.30 There are two types of disposition of a registered charge that are registrable dispositions.

---

[96] Schedule 2, para 7(2)(a).

[97] That is, in the register of the land benefited.

[98] Schedule 2, para 7(2)(b).

[99] Schedule 2, para 7(3). Such rules will be land registration rules, made by the Lord Chancellor, and will be laid before Parliament only: Cls 125(3), 129(1).

[100] Cl 27(2)(f).

[101] Schedule 2, para 8.

[102] Cl 27(5)(c).

[103] See below, para 7.42.

[104] Schedule 3, para 6; below, paras 8.29, 8.48.

[105] Cl 55.

(1)   The first is a transfer of the charge.[106] The registration requirement is that the transferee or his or her successor in title must be entered in the register as proprietor.[107]

(2)   The second is the creation of a sub-charge.[108] In this case, the sub-chargee, or his or her successor in title must be registered as the proprietor of the sub-charge. We explain the nature of sub-charges in Part VII of this Report.[109]

Applications for registration

4.31   As might be expected, the Bill confers power for rules to make provision about applications to the registrar for the purposes of meeting registration requirements under Clause 27.[110] It should be noted that, under the present law, where the proprietor's land certificate is outstanding,[111] it has to be produced to the registrar on the application for the registration of a disposition of registered estate or charge.[112] As we explain in Part IX of this Report, this requirement is unlikely to apply under any rules made pursuant to the power mentioned above.[113] There is no provision in the Bill for the issue of charge certificates (which will therefore cease to have any function),[114] and although land certificates will continue to be issued, their role is likely to be much more limited than at present.[115]

---

[106] Cl 27(3)(a). For certain exceptions in relation to transfers by operation of law that have already been explained, see above, para 4.19.

[107] Schedule 2, para 10.

[108] Cl 27(3)(b).

[109] See below, para 7.11.

[110] Cl 27(6). The rules will be land registration rules, and will be laid before Parliament only: Cls 125(3), 129(1).

[111] In other words, where the certificate is not deposited with the Registry under Land Registration Act 1925, s 63. As we explain below, para 9.85, when a certificate is "deposited" with the Registry, the practice is not to hold a document as such, but not to issue a land certificate at all.

[112] Land Registration Act 1925, s 64(1).

[113] See below, para 9.88.

[114] See below, para 9.89.

[115] See below, para 9.90—9.91.

PART V
PRIORITIES

INTRODUCTION

5.1 In this Part we consider the principles that determine the priority of interests in registered land under the Bill.[1] In the Consultative Document we examined the rules that presently governed such priority.[2] We did not consider that major changes were required to the law, though we did consider that there should be a clear statutory statement of what the relevant principles were.[3]

5.2 The essence of the present law is that the priority of interests in registered land is normally determined by the date of their creation, and this is so regardless of whether or not they are protected on the register.[4] This has been laid down in relation to minor interests on the basis that such interests are equitable.[5] The rules that determine the priority of competing minor interests[6] are therefore the traditional rules that govern competing equitable interests. These are compendiously expressed by the maxim, "where the equities are equal, the first in time prevails".[7] That maxim is not always easy to apply because of the uncertainty as to when the equities are *not* equal, namely in cases of negligence or gross carelessness. By way of an exception to this general principle, what the Land Registration Act 1925 calls "registered dispositions",[8] are given "special effect or priority" when made for valuable consideration.[9] The "special effect or priority" is that any interests not protected on the register are subordinated to a registered disposition unless such unregistered interests are overriding interests.[10]

5.3 The main reason why we did not consider that any elaborate new scheme was needed to determine the priority of interests in registered land was because of the impact of the scheme of electronic conveyancing that we proposed in the Consultative Document. The essential feature of that scheme, which we explain in detail below,[11] is that it will not be possible to create or transfer many interests in registered land expressly except by simultaneously registering them or protecting

---

[1] For issues relating to the priority of charges and of further advances, see below, Part VII.

[2] See Law Com No 254, Part VII.

[3] *Ibid*, paras 7.32—7.34.

[4] *Ibid*, paras 7.12, 7.18.

[5] As we pointed out in the Consultative Document, the principles that govern the priority of overriding interests (other than leases granted for 21 years or less for which specific provision is made) are obscure: see Law Com No 254, paras 7.12—7.14.

[6] The Bill has no explicit concept of minor interest.

[7] See Law Com No 254, para 7.17, where the authorities are summarised.

[8] These are dispositions that create or transfer legal estates.

[9] Land Registration Act 1925, s 3(xxii).

[10] See *ibid*, ss 20, 23.

[11] See Cl 93; paras 13.74 and following.

them by a notice in the register. The necessary corollary of that is that the register will in time become conclusive as to the priority of such interests because the date of the creation of an interest and its registration will be one and the same. The proposals in the Consultative Document were supported by nearly 70 per cent of those who responded to them.

5.4 In the Consultative Document, we also made recommendations in relation to certain specific "rights of uncertain status".[12] These proposals were directed at protecting the priority of the interests in question. We explain the provisions of the Bill in relation to these rights below.[13]

PRIORITY UNDER THE BILL

The general rule

5.5 Clause 28(1) states the general principle of priority under the Bill. Subject to the rules on registrable dispositions and Inland Revenue charges explained below,[14] the priority of an interest affecting a registered estate or charge is not affected by a disposition of the estate or charge. This is so whether or not the interest or disposition is registered.[15] It follows therefore, that in cases that fall within this general rule, the priority of *any* interest in registered land is determined by the date of its creation. Unlike the first in time rule that presently applies to competing minor interests, this rule is an absolute one, subject only to the exceptions provided for by the Bill. No question arises as to whether "the equities are equal". References in the Bill to an interest affecting an estate or charge are to an adverse right affecting the title to the estate or charge.[16]

The principal exception: registrable dispositions that have been registered

The exception

5.6 As now, there is, under the Bill, a significant exception to this general principle. If a registrable disposition of either a registered estate or a registered charge is made for valuable consideration, completion of the disposition by registration has the effect of postponing to the interest under the disposition any interest affecting the estate or charge immediately before the disposition whose priority is not protected

---

[12] *Ibid*, paras 3.28—3.38. The rights in question were rights of pre-emption, an equity arising by estoppel before effect had been given to it by a court order, and an inchoate right under the Prescription Act 1832. For reasons that we explain below, at paras 5.37—5.38, the Bill does nothing in relation to the last of the three rights in question.

[13] See paras 5.26 and following.

[14] See paras 5.6, 5.23, respectively.

[15] Cl 28(2).

[16] Cl 129(3)(b). Petitions in bankruptcy and bankruptcy orders are not interests for the purposes of the Bill: see Cl 86(1); below, paras 5.20, 11.42.

at the time of registration.[17] The various elements of this important principle require explanation.

Applicable only to registrable dispositions

5.7 First, the exception applies only to *a registrable disposition* of a registered estate or charge. We have explained in Part IV of this Report that registrable dispositions are dispositions of a registered estate or charge that transfer or create a legal estate.[18] Such dispositions are required to be completed by registration and do not operate at law until they are registered.[19]

Made for valuable consideration

5.8 Secondly, the principle applies only to registrable dispositions made *for valuable consideration*. Valuable consideration does not include either—

(1) marriage consideration; or

(2) a nominal consideration in money.[20]

As regards the first but not the second of these exceptions, the Bill changes the law.[21] It implements a recommendation in the Consultative Document[22] which was supported by all of those who responded to the point. As we explained, marriage consideration is an anachronism. A transfer of land in consideration of marriage is normally a wedding gift and we cannot see why one particular category of gifts should be treated as if it were not a gift.

5.9 Where a registrable disposition is made *other* than for valuable consideration, the general rule of priority, explained in paragraph 5.5 above, applies.

Priority conferred

5.10 When the exception applies it gives the disposition priority over any interest—

(1) that affects the estate or charge *immediately prior to the disposition*; and

(2) whose priority is not protected *at the time of registration.*

---

[17] Cls 29(1) (dispositions of registered estates), 30(1) (dispositions of registered charges). The Bill necessarily refers to the prior interest being postponed to the later registered disposition. The disponee will thereby take free of the unprotected interest. That does not mean that the interest is necessarily destroyed. It may still remain valid as against interests other than that of the disponee under the registered disposition.

[18] See Cl 27; above, para 4.16.

[19] Cl 27(1).

[20] Cl 129(1).

[21] See Land Registration Act 1925, s 3(xxxi).

[22] See Law Com No 254, para 3.43.

A consequence of this is that if, in the period between the disposition and its registration, the *disponee* created an interest in favour of a third party,[23] the disponee would *not* be able to claim priority over it and the general principle in paragraph 5.5, above, would apply.[24] That is, of course, as it should be. The disponee should not be able to create an interest and then claim to take free of it because it had not been protected in the register before he or she happened to be registered as proprietor of the estate or charge.[25] In this context, there is one special case that has caused difficulties in the past,[26] namely the unpaid vendor's lien. An unpaid vendor's lien arises when the seller contracts to sell the land to the buyer and not on completion when the transfer is executed.[27] For that reason, it will not take effect as a right created by the transferee between transfer and registration. Because it pre-dates the transfer, it will not therefore be binding on the transferee when he or she is registered as proprietor unless the seller protects the lien by the entry of a notice against his or her own title prior to the registration of the transfer.[28] We gave this issue considerable thought. In the end, however, we have concluded that it is unnecessary to create any special regime to ensure that a buyer does not take free of an unpaid vendor's lien when the transfer to him or her is registered. Unpaid vendors' liens that are intended to survive completion are uncommon. It should be enough if practitioners are alerted to the need to enter a notice in respect of them prior to or simultaneously with the registration of the transfer.

When the priority of an interest will be protected

5.11 The Bill explains when the priority of an interest will be protected so that it will not be postponed to a registered disposition for valuable consideration.[29] This will be so in any case where that interest—

(1) is a registered charge;

(2) is the subject of a notice in the register;[30]

---

[23] Which, of course, he or she may do: see Cl 24(1)(b); above, para 4.5.

[24] This does, of course, mean that where a person acquires land in circumstances in which he or she holds it on a resulting or constructive trust for some third party as a result of a contribution to the cost of the acquisition by that third party, the disponee cannot claim to take free of the trust. Cf David Wilde, "Resulting trusts of registered land: when is recognising them consistent with the terms of the Land Registration Act 1925" [1999] Conv 382.

[25] The problem will disappear in due course because, electronic dispositions will take effect and be registered simultaneously: see Cl 93; above, para 5.3; below, paras 13.74 and following.

[26] See *Orakpo v Manson Investments Ltd* [1977] 1 WLR 347; at pp 360, 369 respectively, discussed in Law Com No 254, para 7.36.

[27] "As soon as a binding contract for sale of land is entered into the vendor has a lien on the property for the purchase money and a right to remain in possession of the property until payment is made. The lien does not arise on completion but on exchange of contracts. It is discharged on completion to the extent that the purchase money is paid": *Barclays Bank Plc v Estates & Commercial Ltd* [1997] 1 WLR 415, 419, 420, *per* Millett LJ.

[28] A registered proprietor can of course apply for entries to be made on his or her own title.

[29] See Cls 29(2), 30(2).

(3)   is an unregistered interest that overrides a registered disposition under Schedule 3;[31] or

(4)   appears from the register to be excepted from the effect of registration.[32]

5.12   The Bill provides that if an interest has been the subject of a notice in the register at any time since the coming into force of the Bill, it will not fall within paragraph 5.11(3).[33] In other words, if a notice were entered in the register in respect of an interest that fell within Schedule 3, it could never again become an overriding interest, even if the notice were, by mistake, removed from the register.[34] This is one facet of the policy of the Bill to reduce the numbers of overriding interests.[35]

5.13   Furthermore, in the case of a disposition of a leasehold estate, or of a charge relating to such an estate, the burden of any interest incident to that estate will also be protected.[36] This will include, for example, the burden of restrictive covenants affecting that estate. Such matters are not entered on the register, as there is no need for them to be. Any person dealing with the property will, in practice, always examine the lease.

The priority of registered charges

5.14   The Bill makes specific provision as to how registered charges on the same registered estate or charge are to rank between themselves.[37] This is explained in Part VII of this Report.[38]

The grant of leases that are not registrable dispositions

5.15   The Bill makes special provision for the effect of the grant of a lease out of a registered estate that is not a registrable disposition, such as the grant of a lease for seven years or less that is not otherwise required to be registered.[39] The exception to the general principle of priority that is set out above at paragraph 5.5, applies to the grant of such leases as if that grant did involve the making of a registrable disposition that was registered at the time of the grant.[40] This replicates

---

[30]   For the circumstances in which a notice may be entered in the register, see below, para 6.17.

[31]   See below, paras 8.53 and following, where such overriding interests are explained.

[32]   This will be the case where there is a disposition of a registered estate or of a registered charge affecting such an estate, where that estate is registered with some title other than an absolute one. See Cls 11, 12; above, paras 3.49 and following.

[33]   Cls 29(3), 30(3).

[34]   See below, para 8.95

[35]   For that policy, see above, paras 2.24, 2.25; and below, para 8.1.

[36]   Cls 29(2)(b), 30(2)(b). Cf Land Registration Act 1925, s 23(1)(a).

[37]   Cl 48.

[38]   See below, paras 7.13—7.15.

[39]   For the leases that *are* registrable dispositions, see Cl 27(2)(b), (c); above, para 4.20. For leases that are not required to be registered, see below, paras 8.9, 8.50.

[40]   Cl 29(4).

the effect of the present law.[41] As regards other unregistered interests,[42] their priority when they are created or arise is, of course, determined by the general principle explained in paragraph 5.5 above.[43]

The irrelevance of notice

5.16 As a general principle, the doctrine of notice, which still has a residual role in relation to the priority of certain interests in unregistered land, has no application whatever in determining the priority of interests in registered land.[44] Whether or not a disponee of an interest in registered land is bound by a prior interest is determined by the principles set out above. Under those rules, subject to what is said below,[45] issues as to whether that disponee had knowledge or notice of a prior interest, or whether he or she acted in good faith, are irrelevant. Although the point is not completely free from doubt, we do not consider that this approach involves a change in the law.[46] It accords with a recommendation in the Consultative Document[47] that was overwhelmingly supported by those who responded to it.[48] It also accords with one of the principal objectives of the Bill, that all conveyancing inquiries should, so far as is possible, be capable of being conducted on line.[49]

5.17 In a number of very limited situations, issues of knowledge, notice and good faith do have a role under the Bill. These are set out in the following paragraphs.

5.18 First, whether a first registered proprietor is bound by interests acquired under the Limitation Act 1980 depends upon whether that first registered proprietor has notice of those interests.[50] We have explained in Part III of this Report why this is so.[51] It will be noted that in this situation, the issue is whether the first registered proprietor is bound by interests that arose when the title was unregistered.

---

[41] Land Registration Act 1925, ss 19(2), 22(2). Cf Law Com No 254, para 7.10.

[42] That is overriding interests within Schedules 1 and 3; see below, Part VIII.

[43] We explained in Law Com No 254 that the priority of such interests is uncertain under the present law, but that issues of priority in relation to such interests when they come into being will seldom if ever arise: see Law Com No 254, paras 7.12—7.14.

[44] See *Megarry & Wade's Law of Real Property* (6th ed 2000), 6-105 (where the authorities are collected).

[45] See paras 5.17 and following.

[46] See Law Com No 254, para 3.44.

[47] Law Com No 254, para 3.50.

[48] 83% of those who responded to the point supported the recommendation.

[49] Above, para 2.1. The Bill preserves the principle, presently found in Land Registration Act 1925, s 74, whereby the registrar is not affected with notice of any trust: see Cl 78.

[50] Cls 11(4)(c), 12(4)(d).

[51] See paras 3.46 and 3.47.

5.19   Secondly, the effect of a disposition of registered land on an Inland Revenue charge is determined in accordance with the provisions of the Inheritance Tax Act 1984, under which principles of good faith are relevant. This is explained below.[52]

5.20   Thirdly, the effect of a disposition of a registered estate or charge after the proprietor has become bankrupt depends upon principles of good faith and notice. As we explain in Part XI of this Report, the Bill follows the provisions of the Insolvency Act 1986 in this regard.[53] It should be noted that neither a petition in bankruptcy nor a bankruptcy order is an interest affecting an estate or charge for the purposes of the Bill.[54] Such matters are, therefore, necessarily outside the priority provisions explained above.

5.21   Fourthly, in relation to two categories of unregistered interests that override a registered disposition, the disponee's knowledge of the interest is relevant as to whether or not he or she is bound by it. The disponee will not be bound by—

(1)   an interest belonging to a person in actual occupation where—

(a)   that person's occupation would not have been obvious on a reasonably careful inspection of the land at the time of the disposition; and

(b)   the disponee does not have actual knowledge of the interest at that time;[55]

(2)   a legal easement, or a *profit à prendre* not registered under the Commons Registration Act 1965, which at the time of the disposition—

(a)   is not within the actual knowledge of the disponee; and

(b)   would not have been obvious on a reasonably careful inspection of the servient tenement at the time of the disposition.[56]

What is in issue in each of these cases is, of course, whether a disponee is bound by an *unregistered* interest. However, the principles that determine this in relation to these two classes of interests are not drawn from the notice-based principles of priority applicable to unregistered land. They are, instead, derived by analogy from the rule of conveyancing law that a seller of land must disclose to the buyer prior to contract any irremovable latent incumbrances of which the buyer does not actually know.[57] An incumbrance is latent if it is not obvious on a reasonably

---

[52]   See para 5.23.

[53]   See below, para 11.42.

[54]   Cl 86(1).

[55]   Schedule 3, para 2(1)(c); see below, para 8.61.

[56]   Schedule 3, para 3(1); see below, para 8.68

[57]   For these principles, see *Megarry & Wade's Law of Real Property* (6th ed 2000), 12-068. The leading case is *Yandle & Sons v Sutton* [1922] 2 Ch 199. It should be noted in relation to

careful inspection of the land. An incumbrance may be latent therefore — so that the seller is obliged to disclose it — even though a buyer has constructive notice of it.[58] It follows that a disponee may take free of an overriding interest falling within (1) or (2) above, even though he or she has constructive notice of it. This is in accordance with the policy of the Bill to reduce the burden of enquiries that have to be made when dealing with a registered estate or charge and to limit, so far as possible, those inquiries that cannot be conducted on line.[59]

SPECIAL CASES

5.22　There are a number of interests for which the Bill makes particular provision that directly or indirectly affects their priority.

Inland Revenue charges

5.23　Under the Inheritance Tax Act 1984 inheritance tax is chargeable on the value transferred by a chargeable transfer.[60] A chargeable transfer is a transfer of value which is made by an individual that is not an exempt transfer.[61] A transfer of value is, in essence, a disposition that brings about the diminution of the transferor's estate,[62] and the value transferred is the difference between the value of a person's estate immediately before the transfer and its value afterwards.[63] The persons liable to pay the charge include (for example) the transferor and any person whose estate is increased by the transfer.[64]

5.24　Under section 237 of the Inheritance Tax Act 1984, a charge is imposed on specified property in respect of unpaid tax[65] on the value transferred by a chargeable transfer. Where there is a disposition of property subject to an Inland Revenue charge, it takes effect subject to that charge.[66] This general principle is, however, subject to certain exceptions. In particular, where there is a disposition to a purchaser of registered land that is subject to such a charge and the charge is not protected by a notice in the register, the land ceases to be subject to the charge which attaches instead to the proceeds.[67] For these purposes, a purchaser is defined as "a purchaser in good faith for consideration in money or money's

---

(1)(a) above, that it is not the *interest* that has to be apparent but the *occupation* of the person having the benefit of that interest. See below, para 8.62.

[58] See, *eg, Caballero v Henty* (1869) LR 9 Ch App 447.

[59] See above, paras 2.24, 2.25, 5.16; and below, para 8.1.

[60] Inheritance Tax Act 1984, s 1.

[61] *Ibid*, s 2. For exempt transfers, see *ibid*, Part 2.

[62] *Ibid*, s 3. A person's estate is the aggregate of all the property to which that person is beneficially entitled: *ibid*, s 5.

[63] *Ibid*, s 3.

[64] *Ibid*, s 199.

[65] Plus interest.

[66] Inheritance Tax Act 1984, s 237(6).

[67] *Ibid*, s 238(1)(a).

worth other than a nominal consideration and includes a lessee, mortgagee or other person who for such consideration acquires an interest in the property in question".[68]

5.25   The principles explained in paragraph 5.24 are presently applied to dispositions of registered land by section 73 of the Land Registration Act 1925.[69] Clause 31 of the Bill similarly provides that the effect of a disposition of a registered estate or charge on an Inland Revenue charge under section 237 of the Inheritance Tax Act 1984 is to be determined in accordance with the relevant provisions of that Act,[70] and not under Clauses 28 to 30 of the Bill, explained in paragraphs 5.5— 5.15, above.

Rights of pre-emption

5.26   In the Consultative Document[71] we gave the following critical explanation of the present legal position of rights of pre-emption—

> A right of pre-emption is a right of first refusal. The grantor undertakes that he or she will not sell the land without first offering it to the grantee. It is similar to but not the same as an option, because the grantee can purchase the property only if the grantor decides that he or she wants to sell it.
>
> The precise status of a right of pre-emption was uncertain until the decision of the Court of Appeal in *Pritchard v Briggs*,[72] an uncertainty that that decision has not wholly dispelled. In some cases it had been held that it was merely a contractual right and could never be an equitable proprietary interest.[73] In others, the right was held to create an equitable interest in land from its inception.[74] There are also a number of statutory provisions which were enacted on the assumption that rights of pre-emption created interests in land.[75]
>
> In *Pritchard v Briggs*,[76] a majority of the Court of Appeal expressed the view that a right of pre-emption did not confer on the grantee any interest in land. However, when the grantor chose to sell the property, the right of pre-emption became an option and, as such, an equitable

---

[68]   *Ibid*, s 272.

[69]   As amended.

[70]   Summarised above, para 5.24.

[71]   Law Com No 254, paras 3.29—3.31. Some footnotes have been abbreviated and references have been updated.

[72]   [1980] Ch 338.

[73]   See, *eg, Murray v Two Strokes Ltd* [1973] 1 WLR 823. This was also the view of Goff LJ, dissenting, in *Pritchard v Briggs*.

[74]   See, *eg, Birmingham Canal Co v Cartwright* (1879) 11 ChD 421. This was also the view of Walton J at first instance in *Pritchard v Briggs* [1980] Ch 338.

[75]   See, *eg*, Law of Property Act 1925, s 186; Land Charges Act 1972, s 2(4)(iv).

[76]   [1980] Ch 338.

interest in land.[77] It should be noted that the remarks of the Court of Appeal were only obiter[78] and have been recognised as such.[79] They have been much criticised,[80] and this criticism has not escaped judicial attention.[81] Not only was there no previous authority for "this strange doctrine of delayed effectiveness,"[82] but if it is correct its effects can be unfortunate—

(1) It can lead to something "which a sound system of property law ought to strive at all costs to avoid: the defeat of a prior interest by a later purchaser taking with notice of the conflicting interest,"[83] as indeed happened in *Pritchard v Briggs* itself. For example, if A grants B a right of pre-emption which B immediately registers, and A then mortgages the land to C, it seems likely that C will not be bound by the right of pre-emption because the execution of the mortgage probably does not cause the pre-emption to crystallise into an equitable interest. C could therefore, in exercise of his paramount powers as mortgagee, sell the land free from B's right of pre-emption.

(2) Although the person having the benefit of a right of pre-emption may register it at the time it is created either as a land charge (where the title is unregistered)[84] or as a minor interest (where the title is registered),[85] the right is effective for the purposes of priority only from the moment when the grantor demonstrates an animus to sell the land, not from the date of registration.[86]

(3) Similarly, if the grantee of the right of pre-emption is in actual occupation of the land to which it relates and the title is registered, the right of pre-emption takes effect as an overriding interest under section 70(1)(g) of the Land Registration Act 1925 only when the grantor does something to indicate an intention to sell.[87] The precise

---

[77] Goff LJ dissented, holding that a right of pre-emption was a mere contractual right and could never be an equitable interest in land.

[78] The conflict in that case was between a right of pre-emption and an option that was granted subsequently. The terms of the right of pre-emption and the option were such that they did not in fact conflict: the former was exercisable only prior to the death of the grantor, the latter only after his death. The view of the majority of the Court of Appeal, that the option would have taken priority over the right of pre-emption in any event (because it created an equitable interest in land when it was granted, whereas the right of pre-emption created no equitable interest until the grantor decided to sell the land), was therefore necessarily obiter.

[79] See *London & Blenheim Estates Ltd v Ladbroke Retail Parks Ltd* [1994] 1 WLR 31, 38.

[80] See especially HWR Wade, "Rights of Pre-Emption: Interests in Land" (1980) 96 LQR 488; *Megarry & Wade's Law of Real Property* (6th ed 2000), 12-061—12-063.

[81] See the remarks of Peter Gibson LJ in *London & Blenheim Estates Ltd v Ladbroke Retail Parks Ltd* [1994] 1 WLR 31, 38, in which both Beldam and Ralph Gibson LJJ concurred.

[82] HWR Wade, "Rights of Pre-Emption: Interests in Land" (1980) 96 LQR 488, 489.

[83] *Ibid.*

[84] Land Charges Act 1972, s 2(4)(iv).

[85] Land Registration Act 1925, ss 49(1)(c), 59.

[86] Ruoff & Roper, *Registered Conveyancing*, 35-18.

[87] *Kling v Keston Properties Ltd* (1983) 49 P & CR 212.

time when that occurs is uncertain, but it will be no later than the time when the contract to sell to a third party is executed.[88]

5.27 In the Consultative Document, we recommended that a right of pre-emption in registered land should take effect from the time when it was created and not, as *Pritchard v Briggs* suggested, only from the time when the grantor decided to sell.[89] This recommendation was supported by 96 per cent of those who responded to the point. It was clear from the tenor of the responses that the result in *Pritchard v Briggs*[90] was not well regarded because of the practical difficulties to which it gave rise.

5.28 The Bill provides that a right of pre-emption in relation to registered land has effect from the time of creation as an interest capable of binding successors in title (subject to the rules, explained above, about the effect of dispositions on priority[91]).[92] In other words, it takes its priority from the date of its creation. If the dicta in *Pritchard v Briggs* do represent the present law, then the Bill changes the law in its application to registered land.[93] The change is therefore prospective only. It applies to rights of pre-emption created on or after the Bill comes into force.[94]

An equity arising by estoppel

5.29 In the Consultative Document[95] we explained how the doctrine of proprietary estoppel operated,[96] as follows—

> The owner of land, A, in some way leads or allows the claimant, B, to believe that he or she has or can expect some kind of right or interest over A's land. To A's knowledge, B acts to his or her detriment in that belief. A then refuses B the anticipated right or interest in circumstances that make that refusal unconscionable. In those circumstances, an "equity" arises in B's favour. This gives B the right to go to court and seek relief. The court has a very wide discretion as to how it will give effect to this equity, but in so doing it will "analyse the minimum equity to do justice" to B.[97] It will not give him or her any greater rights than he or she had expected to receive. The range of

---

[88] *Ibid,* at p 217.

[89] Law Com No 254, para 3.32.

[90] [1980] Ch 338.

[91] See paras 5.5—5.15.

[92] Cl 113(1).

[93] In an ideal world we would make provision for both registered and unregistered land. However that is not possible within the scope of the present Bill. We consider that the opportunity should be taken to change the law in relation to registered land, particularly as unregistered land is unlikely to have an extended future.

[94] Cl 113(2).

[95] Law Com No 254, para 3.34.

[96] For an account of the law, see *Megarry & Wade's Law of Real Property* (6th ed 2000), Chapter 13.

[97] *Crabb v Arun District Council* [1976] Ch 179, 198, *per* Scarman LJ.

remedies that the courts have shown themselves willing to give is very wide. At one extreme, they have ordered A to convey the freehold of the land in issue to B.[98] At the other, they have ordered A to make a monetary payment to B (in some cases secured on A's land).[99]

5.30 Our concern was with the status of B's "inchoate equity" that arises after he or she has acted to his or her detriment but before the court can make an order giving effect to it. Although the point is not finally settled, the weight of authority firmly favours the view that such an equity is a proprietary and not merely a personal right.[100] HM Land Registry treats it as such, permitting the entry of a caution or notice in relation to such equities.[101] It has also been assumed that a person in actual occupation can protect such an equity in relation to land as an overriding interest.[102] We pointed out in the Consultative Document that proprietary estoppel is increasingly important as a mechanism for the informal creation of property rights. To put the matter beyond doubt, we recommended that the proprietary status of an equity arising by estoppel should be confirmed in relation to registered land.[103] It could therefore be protected by the entry of a notice in the register or, where the claimant was in actual occupation of the land in relation to which he or she claimed an equity, as an overriding interest. This recommendation was more contentious than our proposal in relation to rights of pre-emption. It was supported by 55 per cent of those who responded to the point (of whom there were not many). Those who opposed it were mainly academics, several of whom were defending their published views. On the other hand members of the legal profession generally supported the proposal.[104] We have therefore decided to take the proposal forward, particularly as we consider that we are merely confirming what is probably the present law.

5.31 The Bill declares for the avoidance of doubt that, in relation to registered land, an equity by estoppel has effect from the time when the equity arises as an interest capable of binding successors in title (subject to the rules about the effect of

---

[98] See, *eg, Pascoe v Turner* [1979] 1 WLR 431.

[99] See, *eg, Baker v Baker* [1993] 2 FLR 247.

[100] See *Megarry & Wade's Law of Real Property* (6th ed 2000), 13-028—13-032, where the authorities are collected. Those who support the view that an equity is merely a personal right point to the fact that the court may not grant a proprietary but merely a personal remedy, such as an award of monetary compensation: see Law Com No 254, para 3.35. However, the same may be said of an estate contract. This creates an equitable interest in land because the contract is specifically enforceable. However, specific performance is a discretionary equitable remedy and it may be refused, leaving the claimant to his or her remedy in damages. Cf *Voyce v Voyce* (1991) 62 P & CR 290, 293.

[101] See Ruoff & Roper, *Registered Conveyancing*, 8-02, 35-33, 36-13.

[102] Under Land Registration Act 1925, s 70(1)(g), see *eg Lee-Parker v Izzett (No 2)* [1972] 1 WLR 775, 780. For the rights of occupiers under the Bill, see Schedule 1, para 2; Schedule 3, para 2; below, paras 8.14 and following and paras 8.53 and following.

[103] Law Com No 254, para 3.36.

[104] Both the Conveyancing and Land Law Committee of The Law Society and the Bar Council were in favour of it.

dispositions on priority[105]).[106] As the provision is merely declaratory, there are no transitional provisions.

A mere equity

5.32 Although we did not make any specific recommendations in relation to mere equities in the Consultative Document,[107] it became clear to us that some provision would be needed in relation to them in the Bill. It has been said that—

> The Court of Equity has been careful to distinguish between two kinds of equities, first an equity which creates an estate or interest in land and, secondly, an equity which falls short of that.[108]

5.33 Although it is difficult to define a "mere equity" with clarity, it appears to have the following characteristics—

(1) it is an equitable proprietary right that is capable of binding successive owners of land;[109]

(2) as such it is capable of existing as an overriding interest in relation to registered land;[110]

(3) it is "ancillary to or dependant upon an equitable estate or interest in the land";[111]

(4) it appears to be used to denote a claim to discretionary equitable relief in relation to property, such as a right to sct aside a transfer for fraud[112] or undue influence,[113] a right to rectify an instrument for mistake,[114] or a right to seek relief against the forfeiture of a lease after a landlord has peaceably re-entered;[115] and

(5) where title is unregistered, it is capable of being defeated by a bona fide purchaser of either a legal estate or an equitable interest for value without notice.[116]

---

[105] See above, paras 5.5—5.15.

[106] Cl 114.

[107] They are briefly mentioned: see Law Com No 254, para 7.17.

[108] *Westminster Bank Ltd v Lee* [1956] Ch 7, 19, *per* Upjohn J.

[109] *National Provincial Bank Ltd v Ainsworth* [1965] AC 1175, 1238.

[110] *Nurdin & Peacock Plc v D B Ramsden & Co Ltd* [1999] 1 EGLR 119.

[111] *National Provincial Bank Ltd v Ainsworth, supra,* at p 1238, *per* Lord Upjohn.

[112] *Phillips v Phillips* (1861) 4 De GF & J 208, 218; 45 ER 1164, 1167.

[113] *Bainbridge v Browne* (1881) 18 ChD 18.

[114] *Nurdin & Peacock Plc v D B Ramsden & Co Ltd, supra.*

[115] *Fuller v Judy Properties Ltd* (1991) 64 P & CR 176, 184.

[116] See, *eg, Phillips v Phillips, supra,* at p 218; 45 ER 1164, 1167; *Mid-Glamorgan County Council v Ogwr BC* (1993) 68 P & CR 1, 9.

5.34 There is no clear authority as to the priority of a mere equity in relation to registered land as against a later equitable interest. However, there seems to be nothing to displace the rule applicable to unregistered land that is explained above at paragraph 5.33(5). If this is so, then a mere equity will be defeated by the buyer of a later equitable interest without notice of that equity.[117] If this is so, it is intrinsically unsatisfactory, given that questions of notice are irrelevant as to the priority of interests in registered land.[118]

5.35 The present law governing mere equities has not escaped criticism. In particular, the rule that a mere equity can be defeated by a bona fide purchaser of an equitable interest for value without notice is considered to be anomalous. This is because the distinguishing characteristic of a mere equity — that it is a claim to discretionary equitable relief — does not justify treating it differently from other equitable interests. Thus an estate contract creates an equitable interest in land even though it is in fact dependent upon the availability of specific performance.[119]

5.36 The effect of the Bill is as follows.

(1) It declares for the avoidance of doubt that, in relation to registered land, a mere equity has effect from the time when the equity arises as an interest capable of binding successors in title (subject to the rules about the effect of dispositions on priority[120]).[121] In one sense this is, of course, no more than declaratory of the present law, because it is not disputed that a mere equity is a proprietary right of some kind.[122]

(2) Because a mere equity is an interest for the purposes of the Bill, it is brought within the general principles of priority applicable to registered land that are explained above in paragraphs 5.5— 5.15. If our analysis in paragraph 5.34 above, is correct, this *will* involve a change in the law. It means that a mere equity will not be defeated by a later equitable interest in registered land that is created for valuable consideration, where the grantee was a buyer in good faith and without notice of the mere equity.

Inchoate rights arising under the Prescription Act 1832

5.37 There is one matter that we raised in the Consultative Document that we do not now propose to take forward because, on further examination of the relevant legal principles, we have concluded that no change to the law is needed. The matter was concerned with a facet of the law relating to prescription and was as follows.[123] There are three methods by which easements and *profits à prendre* may be acquired

---

[117] Cf Law Com No 254, para 7.17.

[118] See above, para 5.16.

[119] See R J Smith, *Property Law* (3rd ed 2000), p 26.

[120] See above, paras 5.5—5.15.

[121] Cl 114. Cf above, para 5.31.

[122] There are, therefore, no transitional provisions.

[123] See Law Com No 254, paras 3.37, 3.38.

by prescription — at common law, by the doctrine of lost modern grant, and under the Prescription Act 1832. There is some uncertainty as to the status of rights in the course of acquisition by prescription over registered land under the 1832 Act due to the provisions of that Act. It provides that certain rights are deemed to be either free from challenge on the ground that they had not been enjoyed since 1189, or "absolute and indefeasible", depending on the nature of the right asserted and the length of time that it has been exercised without interruption.[124] However, each of the specified periods is "deemed and taken to be the period next before suit or action" in which "the claim or matter to which such period may relate shall have been brought into question."[125] This provision has been taken to mean that it is only on the commencement of legal proceedings that "the enjoyment... shall ripen into a right."[126] As a result of this, however long the period of enjoyment may have been, no indefeasible right can be acquired until it is put in issue in legal proceedings. Until then, if it is a right at all, it is an inchoate one.[127]

5.38   The concern that we raised in the Consultative Document was that a person, who had been exercising a right over registered land for more than the relevant period prescribed by the Prescription Act 1832,[128] might find that his or her right was defeated. We thought that this might be so because that right might be regarded as being too shadowy to exist as an overriding interest[129] and so not bind a buyer of the servient land. We are now satisfied that there is no such problem. The issue is not about whether a person is bound by an existing property right at all, but whether there has been user of a kind that satisfies the requirements for prescription[130] for the period and in the manner prescribed by the Prescription Act 1832.[131] Once prescription has begun against a freehold estate, it will not normally be interrupted by a disposition of the land affected.

---

[124]   Sections 1 (rights of common and *profits à prendre*); 2 (rights of way and other easements); and 3 (rights of light).

[125]   Prescription Act 1832, s 4.

[126]   *Cooper v Hubbuck* (1862) 12 CB(NS) 456, 467; 142 ER 1220, 1225, *per* Willes J.

[127]   *Hyman v Van den Bergh* [1907] 2 Ch 516, 524—525; approved on appeal: [1908] 1 Ch 167. See too *Colls v Home and Colonial Stores Ltd* [1904] AC 179, 189—190; *Newnham v Willison* (1987) 56 P & CR 8, 12.

[128]   The different periods laid down in that Act are measured backwards from the time when proceedings are brought in which the right is in issue: s 4.

[129]   For the overriding status of certain unregistered easements and *profits à prendre*, see below, paras 8.23, 8.68 and following.

[130]   See *Megarry & Wade's Law of Real Property* (6th ed 2000), 18-122—18-131.

[131]   Cf *Megarry & Wade's Law of Real Property* (6th ed 2000), 18-128, and see *Pugh v Savage* [1970] 2 QB 373.

PART VI
NOTICES AND RESTRICTIONS

INTRODUCTION

6.1 Part 4 of the Bill contains provisions on notices and restrictions. It is concerned primarily, but not exclusively, with the protection of third party rights over or in relation to a registered estate or charge.[1] This Part of the Bill has its origins in Part VI of the Consultative Document.[2] The aims of the changes that were proposed in that Part, which were amongst the most sweeping in the whole of the Consultative Document, can be summarised as follows—

    (1)   to simplify the law;

    (2)   to clarify the concepts that were employed; and

    (3)   to improve significantly the protection given to third party rights where an appropriate entry had been made on the register.

THE PROPOSALS IN THE CONSULTATIVE DOCUMENT

6.2 The main recommendations in the Consultative Document, which were overwhelmingly supported on consultation,[3] can be summarised as follows.

    (1)   Cautions against dealings should be prospectively abolished,[4] though existing cautions would be retained on the register.[5] Cautions were an inadequate form of protection for interests in registered land because they conferred no priority and merely gave the cautioner an opportunity to object to a transaction.[6]

    (2)   The existing system of notices[7] should be extended so that there would be two types of notice, those that were entered consensually,[8] and those that were entered unilaterally by the party claiming the interest. In relation to

---

[1] In other words, what in the Land Registration Act 1925 are called "minor interests": see s 3(xv). The Bill does not use the term.

[2] "The Protection of Minor Interests and Restrictions on Dealings with Registered Land".

[3] As regards (1) and (2), below, 93% of those who responded to our proposals supported the scheme which the Bill now adopts. As regards (3), all of those who responded agreed with our recommendations.

[4] Cautions against first registration are preserved by the Bill: see above, para 3.56.

[5] Law Com No 254, paras 6.50—6.54, 6.69.

[6] See Law Com No 254, paras 6.10—6.23, 6.45.

[7] For the present law, see Law Com No 254, paras 6.3—6.9.

[8] Under the present law, notices can only be entered with the agreement of the registered proprietor (Land Registration Act 1925, s 48(1)) or pursuant to an order of the court (*ibid*, s 48(2)).

the latter, the registered proprietor would be informed of the registration and would be able to apply for its cancellation.[9]

(3) Inhibitions are in reality just one form of restriction and there is therefore no need to retain them as a separate category of entry. The only method of reflecting any limitation on the power of the registered proprietor to make a disposition should be by the entry of a restriction.[10]

The Bill implements these recommendations. In this Part we therefore examine the following matters—

(a) the prospective abolition of cautions;

(b) notices under the Bill;

(c) the prospective abolition of inhibitions;

(d) restrictions under the Bill; and

(e) the special treatment of pending land actions, writs, orders and deeds of arrangement.

THE PROVISIONS OF THE BILL

Prospective abolition of cautions against dealings

6.3 The proposal in the Consultative Document to abolish cautions against dealings was almost unanimously supported on consultation. There is therefore no power to lodge further cautions under the Bill. However, in relation to existing cautions against dealings, those parts of the Land Registration Act 1925 that deal with their operation[11] continue to have effect under the transitional provisions of the Bill.[12] Furthermore, the 1925 Act will continue to apply in relation to any applications for a caution that are pending at the time when the Bill is brought into force.[13] The Land Registration Rules 1925 also contain provisions relating to the operation of cautions.[14] The Bill therefore contains a power to make rules in relation to existing cautions,[15] so that the effect of the existing rules can be replicated.

6.4 For the future, notices and restrictions will do the work of cautions. The choice of entry will obviously depend upon the nature of the interest to be protected and

---

[9] See Law Com No 254, para 6.52.

[10] See Law Com No 254, paras 6.55—6.57.

[11] That is, ss 55 (the effect of cautions) and 56 (general provisions as to cautions).

[12] Schedule 12, para 2(3).

[13] Schedule 12, para 5.

[14] See, in particular, rr 217—219, 221, 222.

[15] Schedule 12, para 2(4). The rules will be land registration rules and will be required to be laid before Parliament only. See Cls 125, 129(1).

the form of protection that is required. As we explain below,[16] the two forms of entry perform very different functions and in most cases only one of the two will be possible.

Notices

Introduction

6.5 The Bill makes provision as to the following matters—

  (1) the nature and effect of a notice;

  (2) the interests which may and may not be protected by the entry of a notice;

  (3) the circumstances in which a notice may be entered on the register; and

  (4) unilateral notices and their cancellation.

These are explained below.

Nature and effect of a notice

6.6 Clause 32 of the Bill explains the nature and effect of a notice. It is an entry in the register in respect of the burden of an interest affecting a registered estate or charge.[17] The interest in question may of course be another registered estate, as where a registrable lease is granted out of a registered freehold and a notice is entered in respect of it on the title to that freehold estate.[18] The notice is entered in relation to the registered estate or charge affected by the interest concerned.[19] As now, the fact that a notice has been entered does not necessarily mean that the interest protected is in fact valid.[20] If, for example, parties had entered into an agreement that was not in fact a valid contract,[21] the entry of a notice in respect of that agreement would not validate it.[22] However, where an interest *is* valid, the entry of a notice *will* protect its priority as against a registered disposition of an

---

[16] See paras 6.9, 6.44.

[17] Cl 32(1).

[18] See Schedule 2, para 3(2); above, para 4.21.

[19] Cl 32(2).

[20] Cl 32(3). For the equivalent provision in the present legislation, see Land Registration Act 1925, s 52(1).

[21] As where it did not comply with the formal requirements of s 2 of the Law of Property (Miscellaneous Provisions) Act 1989.

[22] Another example might be where A, a registered proprietor of land that was subject to a registered charge in favour of B, contracted to sell that estate to C, but without the prior consent of B. C applied for the entry of a notice on A's title. B then exercised its power of sale and conveyed the land to D, who was registered as proprietor. D would not be bound by C's estate contract because it would have been overreached by B's sale to D. All that A could sell to C without B's consent was her equity of redemption. The entry of the notice could not enhance its status. Cf *Duke v Robson* [1973] 1 WLR 267.

estate or charge.[23] As we explain below, notices will either be agreed or unilateral.[24] The entry of the latter can be challenged by the registered proprietor or a person entitled to be registered as proprietor.[25]

6.7 The form and content of notices in the register is to be a matter for rules.[26] Because the Bill does not change the nature of existing notices, there is no need for any transitional provisions. The Bill applies to notices entered under the Land Registration Act 1925 as much as it does to those entered under the provisions of the Bill.[27]

Interests which may not be protected by notice

6.8 The Bill defines negatively the nature of those interests that can be protected by the entry of a notice by setting out those interests that *cannot* be so protected. There are in fact six categories of excluded interest. Five of these are listed in Clause 33 and the sixth in Clause 90(4). With one significant exception, the Bill replicates the effect of the present law.

INTERESTS UNDER TRUSTS OF LAND AND SETTLEMENTS

6.9 The first exception is in respect of interests under either a trust of land or a settlement under the Settled Land Act 1925.[28] It will not, therefore, be possible to enter a notice in respect of *any* interest under *any* form of trust.[29] This exception is, in some senses, the most important of the six because it makes it clear what the nature of a notice is intended to be. A notice protects an interest in registered land when it is intended to bind any person who acquires the land. It is therefore apposite in relation (for example) to the burden of a restrictive covenant or an easement. It is not the appropriate means of protecting beneficial interests under trusts.[30] A buyer wishes to take free of such interests which should be overreached and bind the proceeds of sale. Beneficial interests are capable of being overreached[31] on payment of any purchase money by the buyer to the trustees, of

---

[23] Cl 32(3). Cf Land Registration Act 1925, s 52(1). See too Cls 29(2)(a)(i); 30(2)(a)(i); above, paras 4.5, 4.11.

[24] See para 6.22.

[25] See below, para 6.30.

[26] Cl 39. The rules will be land registration rules and will be required to be laid before Parliament only. See Cls 125, 129(1).

[27] Schedule 12, para 2(1). Such notices take effect as agreed notices under Cl 34(2)(a). For agreed notices, see below, para 6.23.

[28] Cl 33(a).

[29] This will include a charging order over an interest under a trust. This may be protected by the entry of a restriction under the Bill: see below, para 6.43.

[30] One of the fundamental principles of the 1925 property legislation was that trusts should be kept off the title. The Bill adheres to that principle.

[31] For the nature of overreaching, see *State Bank of India v Sood* [1997] Ch 276.

whom there should either be at least two or a trust corporation.[32] A restriction is the proper form of entry to ensure that this occurs.[33]

SHORT LEASES

6.10 The second exception is in respect of leases which are granted for a term of three years or less[34] and are not required to be registered.[35]

6.11 As the law stands, a notice cannot be entered in respect of a lease granted for 21 years or less,[36] unless it falls within certain statutory exceptions. The reduction in the length of leases, the burden of which may be noted on the register, is the one significant change that the Bill makes to the present law. We have explained elsewhere that the Bill reduces the length of leases that are required to be registered from those granted for more than 21 years to those granted for more than 7 years.[37] However, as we have explained, it is likely that there will be a further reduction[38] once electronic conveyancing is fully operative, so that leases granted for more than 3 years will be required to be registered.[39] Furthermore, under the Bill, *all* easements that are expressly granted or reserved out of a registered estate are registrable dispositions, whatever their duration.[40] If, for example, a lease is granted for seven years (and so takes effect without registration),[41] but various easements are granted in relation to the property let, it will in practice be necessary to note all those easements on the register. We strongly suspect that, if the tenant is required to enter a notice in respect of the easements that are ancillary to his or her lease, he or she will also wish to do likewise in respect of the lease itself. The Bill enables him or her to do so, and, at the same time, anticipates the likely reduction in the length of registrable leases.

6.12 We have already explained that certain leases, however short their duration, are either subject to the requirement of compulsory registration[42] or are registrable dispositions.[43] It necessarily follows that, in relation to such leases, it must be possible to enter a notice—

---

[32] See Settled Land Act 1925, s 94(1); Law of Property Act 1925, s 27(2).

[33] See Cl 42(1)(b); below, para 6.41. See too Cl 44; below, para 6.42.

[34] In other words, those leases that can be created orally: see Law of Property Act 1925, s 54(2).

[35] Cl 33(b).

[36] In other words, where the lease is an overriding interest under Land Registration Act 1925, s 70(1)(k): see *ibid*, s 48(1).

[37] See Cl 27(2)(b)(i); above, para 4.20.

[38] Under Cl 116(1); above, paras 3.17, 4.20.

[39] See above, para 3.30.

[40] Cl 27(2)(d); above, para 4.24.

[41] See Schedule 3, para 1; below, para 8.50.

[42] See Cl 4(1)(c)—(f); above, paras 3.30 and following.

[43] See Cl 27(2)(b); above, para 4.20.

(1)   where the lease is granted out of an unregistered estate when that estate is itself eventually registered;[44] and

(2)   where the lease is granted out of a registered estate, when first granted.[45]

A RESTRICTIVE COVENANT BETWEEN LANDLORD AND TENANT

6.13   The third exception is in relation to a restrictive covenant made between a lessor and lessee, so far as relating to the property leased.[46] It is unnecessary to note such covenants, because they are normally apparent from the lease. The Bill accordingly provides that a person to whom a disposition of a registered leasehold estate or of a registered charge over such an estate is made, takes it subject to the burden of an interest[47] that is incident to the estate.[48] A rather wider version of this third exception exists under the present law. A restrictive covenant "made between a lessor and lessee" cannot be protected by the entry of a notice.[49] However, that exception has given rise to some difficulty. It means that no notice can be entered in respect of a restrictive covenant made between lessor and lessee that relates to land that is *not* comprised in the lease, such as other adjacent property owned by the landlord.[50] Such covenants appear, therefore, to be unprotectable. The Bill avoids this difficulty by confining the exception to restrictive covenants "so far as relating to the demised premises".[51]

AN INTEREST WHICH IS REGISTRABLE UNDER THE COMMONS REGISTRATION ACT 1965

6.14   As we have explained,[52] rights of common, which are registrable under the Commons Registration Act 1965, cannot be registered under the Land Registration Act 1925,[53] and this limitation is replicated in the Bill.[54] The fourth exception, by which a notice cannot be entered in respect of an interest capable of being registered under the Commons Registration Act 1965,[55] is the necessary concomitant of this.

---

[44]   Cf Cls 11(4)(a); 12(4)(b); above, para 3.45.

[45]   See Schedule 2, para 3.

[46]   Cl 33(c).

[47]   Such as a restrictive covenant.

[48]   Cls 29(2)(b) (disposition of registered estate); 30(2)(b) (disposition of registered charge). See above, para 5.13.

[49]   Land Registration Act 1925, s 50(1).

[50]   See *Oceanic Village Ltd v United Attractions Ltd* [2000] Ch 234, 252—254.

[51]   Cl 33(c). The point had in fact been foreseen by the Law Commission and HM Land Registry and Parliamentary Counsel had been instructed on it some months before the *Oceanic Village* case was heard.

[52]   See above, para 4.25.

[53]   Commons Registration Act 1965, s 1.

[54]   See Cl 27(2)(d).

[55]   Cl 33(d).

AN INTEREST IN ANY COAL OR COAL MINE OR ANCILLARY RIGHTS

6.15 The fifth exception also replicates one that exists under the present law.[56] It is, in practice, impossible to locate and map all rights to coal. It would, therefore, be impossible to register such rights. For this reason, it has been the policy since the Coal Act 1938 to make rights to coal and the necessary ancillary rights overriding interests,[57] and to provide that such rights cannot be noted on the register. Under the Bill, it is not possible to enter a notice in respect of an interest in any coal or coal mine, the rights attached to any such interest, and the rights of any person under sections 38,[58] 49[59] or 51[60] of the Coal Industry Act 1994.[61]

A PPP LEASE

6.16 The sixth exception concerns PPP leases, granted under the provisions of the Greater London Authority Act 1999.[62] As we explain elsewhere, it is intended that future arrangements for the operation and development of the London underground railway network will be made by means of public-private partnership agreements.[63] PPP leases will be employed as part of that strategy. They will be leases of the underground railways and other ancillary properties. The Bill, once again replicating the present law,[64] provides that no notice may be entered in respect of an interest under a PPP lease.[65]

The circumstances in which a notice may be entered on the register

INTRODUCTION

6.17 Under the Bill, a notice may be entered on the register in at least five circumstances,[66] namely—

(1) on the first registration of an estate, in respect of an interest that burdens it;

(2) where it appears to the registrar that a registered estate is subject to an overriding interest;

---

[56] See Land Registration Act 1925, s 70(4).

[57] See Law Com No 254, paras 5.97, 5.98. For the overriding status of rights to coal, see below, para 8.32; and Schedule 1, para 7; and Schedule 3, para 7.

[58] Right to withdraw support.

[59] Rights to work coal in former copyhold land.

[60] Additional rights in relation to underground land.

[61] Cl 33(e).

[62] For the definition of PPP leases, see Greater London Authority Act 1999, s 218.

[63] See Greater London Authority Act 1999, s 210; below, para 8.11.

[64] See Land Registration Act 1925, s 70(3A), inserted by Greater London Authority Act 1999, s 219(7)(b).

[65] Cl 90(4).

[66] This may not be a comprehensive list.

(3) where it is necessary to complete the registration of a registrable disposition;

(4) where such an entry is necessary to update the register; and

(5) on application to the registrar.

We comment on each of these in turn.

BURDENS ENTERED ON THE REGISTER ON FIRST REGISTRATION

6.18 As we have already explained,[67] on the first registration of an estate, whether freehold or leasehold, the registrar will note against the title the burden of any interest which affects the land of which he is aware, unless the interest is one that cannot be protected by notice.[68] The circumstances in which the registrar will enter a notice on first registration are likely to be clarified by rules made under Clause 14(b)(ii) (entries to be made in the register where an application for first registration is approved).[69]

ENTRY IN RESPECT OF AN OVERRIDING INTEREST

6.19 Where it appears to the registrar that a registered estate is subject to an overriding interest[70] that—

(1) falls within any of the paragraphs of Schedule 1;[71] and

(2) is not excluded by Clause 33;[72]

he may enter a notice in the register in respect of that interest.[73] As we explain in Part VIII of this Report, this power to note overriding interests is part of the strategy to eliminate such interests so far as possible.[74]

---

[67] See above, para 3.45.

[68] Cf Cls 11(4)(a); 12(4)(b). For interests that cannot be protected by notice, see above, paras 6.8 and following.

[69] See above, para 3.53.

[70] Or, as the Bill describes it, "an unregistered interest": see Cl 37. For overriding interests, see below, Part VIII.

[71] See below, paras 8.8 and following, where the categories of interest that override first registration are explained. It is the overriding interests within Schedule 1, rather than those which override a registered disposition under Schedule 3, that are relevant for these purposes. This is because in exercising this power, the registrar is not concerned with the effect of a disposition, but merely with whether there is an overriding interest at the relevant time. The interest might have arisen after the last disposition of the land in question. Cf below, para 8.3.

[72] See above, paras 6.8 and following.

[73] Cl 37.

[74] See below, para 8.95.

ENTRY IN RESPECT OF A REGISTRABLE DISPOSITION

6.20 We have explained in Part IV of this Report that, in order to register certain registrable dispositions, it is necessary to enter a notice in respect of that interest on the title of a registered estate that is burdened by it.[75] The Bill therefore provides that, where a person is registered as proprietor of an interest under a disposition of any of the following kinds, the registrar *must* enter a notice in the register in respect of that interest.[76] The relevant dispositions to which it applies are as follows—

(1) the grant of any lease that is required to be registered;[77]

(2) where the registered estate is a franchise or manor, the grant of any lease of that franchise or manor;[78]

(3) the express grant or reservation of an easement, right or privilege for an interest equivalent to an estate in fee simple absolute in possession or a term of years absolute,[79] other than a right of common which is capable of being registered under the Commons Registration Act 1965;[80]

(4) the express grant or reservation of a rentcharge in possession which is either perpetual or for a term of years absolute;[81] and

(5) the express grant or reservation of a right of entry exercisable over or in respect of a legal lease, or annexed, for any purpose, to a legal rentcharge.[82]

As we have explained above,[83] the notice will be entered against the title of the estate out of which the interest was granted or reserved.[84]

WHERE THE ENTRY IS NECESSARY TO UPDATE THE REGISTER

6.21 There will be occasions where the entry of a notice is necessary in order to update the register. The following examples may be given—

(1) If a court or the Adjudicator[85] determines that a person is entitled to a right over the registered estate of another, the burden of which should be

---

[75] See above, para 4.14.

[76] Cl 38.

[77] Schedule 2, para 3(2); see Cl 27(2)(b); above, para 4.20.

[78] Schedule 2, paras 4(2), 5(2); see Cl 27(2)(c); above, para 4.23.

[79] See Law of Property Act 1925, s 1(2)(a).

[80] Schedule 2, para 6(2); see Cl 27(2)(d); above, para 4.24. Cf above, para 6.14.

[81] Schedule 2, para 7(2); see Cl 27(2)(e); above, para 4.27. The circumstances in which a rentcharge can now be created are very limited: see Rentcharges Act 1977, s 2.

[82] Schedule 2, para 7(2); see Cl 27(2)(e); above, para 4.27. See Law of Property Act 1925, s 1(2)(e).

[83] See para 6.6.

[84] Cl 32(2).

protected by the entry of a notice, an agreed notice will be entered by the registrar.[86]

(2) The registrar might discover that, due to some mistake, the burden of a registered disposition was not protected on the register as it should have been by the entry of a notice.[87] He may then enter a notice.[88]

APPLICATIONS FOR THE ENTRY OF A NOTICE

6.22 A notice may be entered on application to the registrar by a person who claims to be entitled to the benefit of an interest in relation to a registered estate or charge that can be registered as a notice.[89] Subject to rules, that application may be for either an agreed notice or for a unilateral notice.[90] For reasons that we explain below, rules may provide that, in certain circumstances, a notice should *always* be an agreed notice.[91]

6.23 The registrar may only approve an application for an agreed notice in three situations. The first is where the applicant is either the registered proprietor or the person entitled to be registered as proprietor of the estate or charge that is burdened by the interest to be noted.[92] The second is where either the registered proprietor or the person entitled to be registered as proprietor of the estate or charge consents to the entry of the notice.[93] These first two cases are therefore consensual. There is, however, to be no requirement that the land certificate has to be produced in order that a notice should be entered, as is the case now where the land certificate is not deposited with the registry.[94] As we explain in Part IX of this Report, the role of land certificates is to be considerably reduced under the Bill, and they are likely to be little more than an indication that a person is the registered proprietor.[95] They will never be required to be produced in order to secure the registration of an entry on the register. There is no power to issue charge certificates under the Bill and they will therefore become obsolete.

[85] For the role of the Adjudicator, see below, paras 16.6 and following.

[86] Cf Schedule 4, paras 2 and 5; below, paras 10.10; 10.19.

[87] Cf Schedule 2, where the registration requirements are set out; see above, para 4.28.

[88] See Schedule 4, para 5(a).

[89] Cl 34(1). For interests that cannot be protected by notice, see above, paras 6.8 and following.

[90] Cl 34(2). The rules will be land registration rules and will be required to be laid before Parliament only. See Cls 125, 129(1).

[91] See para 6.25. The power could in theory be used to provide that on particular facts a notice was always to be unilateral, but this is less likely.

[92] Cl 34(3)(a).

[93] Cl 34(3)(b).

[94] See Land Registration Act 1925, s 64(1).

[95] See Schedule 10, para 4; below, para 9.90.

6.24   The third situation will usually arise where the application for a notice is *not* in fact consensual. The registrar is to be able to enter an agreed notice where he is satisfied as to the validity of the applicant's claim.[96] If, for example, the applicant could establish to the registrar's satisfaction that a registered proprietor had granted him or her an option to purchase the land, the registrar could enter a notice in respect of that option, even if the registered proprietor had not agreed to the entry.

6.25   The third situation is likely to be important in at least one other context. As we have indicated above,[97] it is likely that rules will provide that, in relation to certain types of application, an agreed notice should be the only form of entry. Unlike unilateral notices, which we explain below,[98] there will be no procedure for the cancellation of such notices on application by the registered proprietor or some person who is entitled to be registered as proprietor. Under the present law, there are certain situations in which, for policy reasons, a notice can be entered on the register without the production of the proprietor's land certificate, instead of leaving the applicant to lodge a caution.[99] One example (by way of illustration) is a spouse's charge in respect of his or her matrimonial home rights under section 31(10) of the Family Law Act 1996.[100] We anticipate that those cases that can presently be protected by notice without the production of the proprietor's land certificate are likely to be protected by agreed notices under the Bill.

Unilateral notices

THE NATURE OF UNILATERAL NOTICES

6.26   Unilateral notices are intended as part of the replacement for cautions against dealings. As we have explained above, *all* notices, whether agreed or unilateral, will protect the priority of an interest, if valid, as against a subsequent registered disposition.[101] In this respect, unilateral notices are a very considerable improvement on cautions (which, as we have explained, confer no priority[102]). The essence of a unilateral notice is that it does not require the consent of the registered proprietor of the estate or charge to which it relates. It can be entered even though the applicant has not satisfied the registrar as to the validity of his or her claim. A unilateral notice must indicate that it is such a notice and identify who is the beneficiary of it.[103] It is unlikely that anything else will appear on the

---

[96]   Cl 34(3)(c).

[97]   See above, para 6.22.

[98]   See paras 6.26 and following.

[99]   See Land Registration Act 1925, s 64(1)(c), (5)—(7).

[100]   Land Registration Act 1925, s 64(5).

[101]   See para 6.6.

[102]   See above, para 6.2.

[103]   Cl 35(2). The beneficiary of such a notice may apply to the registrar at any time for the removal of the notice: Cl 35(3).

register.[104] This is a point of some importance. Under the present law, cautions are often lodged in respect of agreements in preference to a notice in order to protect their confidentiality. This is because the entry of the caution on the register gives no indication as to the matter that lies behind it. A number of those who responded to the Consultative Document were concerned that it should remain possible to preserve commercial confidentiality in the same way after cautions had been abolished.

PROTECTION AGAINST THE IMPROPER ENTRY OF A UNILATERAL NOTICE

6.27   Because a unilateral notice may be entered without the consent of the registered proprietor, it is necessary to provide safeguards for that proprietor. Under the Bill there are three principal safeguards.

6.28   First, a person must not exercise his or her right to apply for a notice without reasonable cause.[105] Any person who does apply for a notice without reasonable cause is in breach of this statutory duty and is liable in tort accordingly to any person who suffers damage in consequence of that breach.[106]

6.29   Secondly, where a unilateral notice is entered by the registrar, he must give notice of the entry to the proprietor of the registered estate or charge to which it relates and to such other persons as rules may provide.[107]

6.30   Thirdly, and following from this, the Bill makes provision for the cancellation of a unilateral notice. Both the registered proprietor of the estate or charge to which the notice relates and any person who is entitled to be registered as the proprietor of that estate or charge may apply to the registrar for the cancellation of a unilateral notice.[108] When such an application is made, the registrar must serve a notice on the person who is identified on the register as the beneficiary of the unilateral notice.[109] That notice must inform the beneficiary—

(1)   of the application; and

(2)   that if he or she fails to exercise his or her right to object before the end of the period specified in the notice, the registrar will cancel the notice.[110]

---

[104]   Cf Cl 39 (rules may make provision about the form and content of notices in the register); above, para 6.6.

[105]   Cl 77(1)(b). This applies to *all* notices. As we have indicated above, some agreed notices may in fact be entered without the agreement of the registered proprietor: see paras 6.24, 6.25.

[106]   Cl 77(2). Cf above, para 3.59; below, paras 6.55, 16.6.

[107]   Cl 35(1). The rules will be land registration rules and will be required to be laid before Parliament only. See Cls 125, 129(1). It is anticipated that rules may provide that notice be served (for example) on a liquidator of a company which was the registered proprietor.

[108]   Cl 36(1).

[109]   Cl 36(2), (4).

[110]   Cl 36(2), (3).

The right to object is the general right conferred by the Bill to object to an application to the registrar.[111] If the matter cannot be disposed of by agreement, it must be referred to the Adjudicator for resolution.[112]

6.31   There are a number of possible outcomes where an application is made for the cancellation of a unilateral notice.

   (1)   First, the notice may indeed be cancelled, either because the person who entered the notice does not contest the application or because it is determined that he or she had no interest that could be protected by a notice.

   (2)   Secondly, the Adjudicator[113] may determine that the person who had entered a unilateral notice was entitled to do so, and that the unilateral notice should therefore be replaced by an agreed notice (or perhaps some other form of entry, such as a registered charge).

   (3)   Thirdly, the Adjudicator[114] may determine that although the person who had entered a unilateral notice was not entitled to do so, he or she was entitled to enter a restriction on the register instead. The appropriate entry will then be made.

Abolition of inhibitions as a separate form of entry

6.32   Under the present law, an inhibition is an order made by the court or registrar that inhibits the registration or entry of any dealing in relation to any registered land or charge.[115] There is no separate category of entries corresponding to inhibitions in the Bill. This is because inhibitions are simply one form of restriction on the power of the registered proprietor (or other person) to make a disposition of registered land. As such, they are subsumed within restrictions, which we explain below.[116] This makes it unnecessary to include in the Bill any specific transitional provisions in relation to either inhibitions or restrictions entered under the Land Registration Act 1925. The provisions of the Bill on restrictions apply to such inhibitions and restrictions.[117]

---

[111]   Under Cl 73: see below, para 16.6.

[112]   See Cls 73(7); 106(1). For the Adjudicator and his jurisdiction, see below, paras 16.3 and following.

[113]   Or, if there is an appeal from his decision under Cl 109, the High Court (see below, para 16.24).

[114]   Or High Court.

[115]   See Land Registration Act 1925, s 57.

[116]   See paras 6.33 and following.

[117]   Schedule 12, para 2(2).

Restrictions

Introduction

6.33   The Bill makes provision as to the following matters—

(1)   the nature and effect of a restriction;

(2)   the purposes for, and the circumstances in which, a restriction may or must be entered on the register;

(3)   notifiable applications for a restriction; and

(4)   the withdrawal of restrictions.

These are explained below.

The nature and effect of a restriction

6.34   Under the Bill, a restriction is an entry in the register which regulates the circumstances in which a disposition of a registered estate or charge may be the subject of an entry in the register.[118] A restriction can be entered, therefore, only in respect of dispositions—

(1)   of a registered estate or charge; and

(2)   in relation to which *some* entry on the register may be made.

It follows that restrictions cannot be entered in relation to dealings with any unregistered interests.[119] Nor can a restriction prevent any disposition of registered land in relation to which no entry on the register is needed.[120] The way that a restriction operates is to restrict in some way the circumstances in which any entry may be made in the register.[121] The restriction is entered in relation to the registered estate or charge to which it relates.[122]

6.35   The Bill gives particular instances as to the form of restriction.[123] First, it may prohibit the making of any disposition or of a disposition of a kind specified in the

---

[118]   Cl 40(1).

[119]   For example, leases granted for 7 years or less normally take effect without registration as overriding interests: see below, paras 8.9, 8.50. They are not registered estates and have no title on the register. It would not be possible to enter any restriction against, say, the assignment of such a lease because there would be no title against which to enter it, nor would it be possible to make any form of entry in respect of any such assignment on the register.

[120]   As, for example, where a registered proprietor grants a lease for 3 years or less that takes effect without registration as an overriding interest. The restriction may reflect a prohibition on the creation of *any* interest, including an unregistrable interest, out of a registered estate.

[121]   See below, para 6.37.

[122]   Cl 40(4).

[123]   These are no more than instances. They do not qualify the generality of what may be done by restriction set out in Cl 40(1).

restriction.[124] For example, at one extreme it might "freeze" the register and prevent any disposition at all that might be the subject of an entry on the register.[125] Another case might be where a registered proprietor (typically a corporation or statutory body) has limited powers of disposition.[126] A restriction should then be entered to prevent the registration of any disposition that was outside those powers.

6.36   Secondly, a restriction may prohibit the making of an entry—

(1)   indefinitely;

(2)   for a period specified in the restriction; or

(3)   until the occurrence of a specified event.[127]

An indefinite restriction would be appropriate where the registered proprietor had limited powers. A restriction for a specified period might be appropriate where the proprietor had contracted not to make a disposition of the property for that period. As regards (3), the Bill gives examples of the kinds of events that might be specified, namely the giving of notice,[128] the obtaining of consent[129] and the making of an order by the court or registrar.[130] These are no more than examples, and there are many other forms which a restriction may take.

6.37   In general, where a restriction is entered on the register, no entry in respect of a disposition to which the restriction applies may be made in the register, except in accordance with the terms of the restriction.[131] This general principle is, however, subject to an exception. On the application of a person who appears to the registrar to have a sufficient interest in the restriction,[132] the registrar has power by order to disapply a restriction or provide that a restriction has effect with modifications in relation to either—

(1)   a disposition; or

---

[124]   Cl 40(2)(a).

[125]   Typically this might be to give effect to a "freezing injunction", restraining any disposition or dealing with a registered property. Under the present law, this would be achieved by the entry of an inhibition on the register.

[126]   For the powers of disposition of a registered proprietor, see above, paras 4.2—4.8.

[127]   Cl 40(2)(b).

[128]   In this way, a restriction can perform a function akin to a caution under the present law. It can be employed to warn an interested person of any impending disposition of the property.

[129]   An example would be in relation to a trust of land, where a beneficiary of full age who was entitled to an interest in possession could enter a restriction to ensure that the trustees consulted him or her before exercising any of their functions in relation to land subject to the trust: see Trusts of Land and Appointment of Trustees Act 1996, s 11(1).

[130]   Cl 40(3).

[131]   Cl 41(1).

[132]   See Cl 41(3).

106

(2) dispositions of a kind;

specified in the order.[133] The sort of case in which it would be appropriate for the registrar to exercise his power would be where a disposition of a registered estate could only be made with the consent of a named individual who had disappeared. But for this power, the applicant would be compelled to incur the expense of an application to the court. It should be noted that, in conferring this dispensing power, the Bill does no more than codify present practice. When a restriction is currently entered, it is always prefaced by the words "Except under an order of the registrar...".

When a restriction may or must be entered

INTRODUCTION

6.38   Under the present law,[134] a restriction is normally entered by the registrar on application either by the registered proprietor[135] or by certain other persons who, under rules,[136] may apply for such an entry. There are occasions on which the registrar must or may enter a restriction, whether under the Land Registration Act 1925,[137] the Land Registration Rules 1925,[138] or some other statute.[139] Inhibitions are entered either on the order of the court or by the registrar, on the application of any person interested. The Bill provides a more coherent framework as to when a restriction may or must be entered.

WHEN THE REGISTRAR MAY OR MUST ENTER A RESTRICTION

6.39   The Bill sets out the circumstances in which the registrar has—

(1) power; and

(2) a duty;

to enter a restriction in the register. We explain below when the registrar is under a *duty* to enter a restriction.[140] Under Clause 42(1) of the Bill, he has a *power* to do so if it appears to him that it is necessary or desirable to do so for any one of three purposes.

---

[133] Cl 41(2).

[134] See Law Com No 254, paras 6.28—6.36.

[135] See Land Registration Act 1925, s 58(1).

[136] Made pursuant to Land Registration Act 1925, s 58(5). See Land Registration Rules 1925, r 236.

[137] See s 58(3).

[138] See r 236A.

[139] See below, para 6.46.

[140] See paras 6.42, 6.46.

Where the registrar may enter a restriction

6.40 The first purpose is to prevent invalidity or unlawfulness in relation to dispositions of a registered estate or charge.[141] The following examples illustrate the kinds of circumstance in which such an entry might be made—

(1) Where the registered proprietor of an estate or charge is a corporation or statutory body that has limited powers. If a restriction were not entered to record that limitation, the proprietor's powers of disposition would, as regards any disponee, be taken to be free of any limitation affecting the validity of that disposition.[142]

(2) Where the registered proprietor has contracted with some third party that he or she will not make any disposition either at all or without the consent of that third party. An obvious example of this is a right of pre-emption,[143] but there are many other cases.[144] The unlawfulness which the restriction prevents is a breach of contract.

(3) Where trustees of land are required to obtain the consent of some person to a disposition.[145] The unlawfulness which the restriction prevents is a disposition in breach of trust.

6.41 The second purpose is to secure that interests which are capable of being overreached on a disposition of a registered estate or charge are overreached.[146]

---

[141] Cl 42(1)(a).

[142] See Cl 26(1); above, para 4.4; and Cl 52(1); below, para 7.7. This provision operates only to prevent the title of the disponee from being questioned. It does not affect the lawfulness of the disposition: see Cls 26(3); 52(2).

[143] The *priority* of a right of pre-emption can be protected by a notice. As we explain at para 6.43 below, a restriction cannot be *directly* employed to protect priority. However, a restriction can be entered as well as a notice, to ensure that the registered proprietor first offers to sell the land to the grantee of the right of pre-emption before he or she contracts to sell it to anybody else. In this way it can *indirectly* protect the priority of the right of pre-emption by prohibiting any disposition that would affect its priority.

[144] Three further examples may be given. The first is where, under a registered charge, the chargor agrees with the chargee to the exclusion of his or her statutory power of leasing under Law of Property Act 1925, s 99. The second is where a chargor contracts with a chargee that he or she will not further charge the registered estate, without the chargee's consent. On such agreements, see below, paras 7.26, 7.27. The third arises where there is a housing or industrial estate and each freeholder covenants with a management company (which owns the verges, roads, parks, etc) to pay service charges in respect of the amenities which it provides. As the burden of such positive covenants may not run (except perhaps through the rather uncertain doctrine of mutual benefit and burden), each freeholder also covenants with the management company that when he or she sells the land, he or she will take a covenant from the buyer by which that buyer undertakes to enter into a covenant with the management company to pay the service charges.

[145] That consent might be that of a third party who, under the terms of the trust, must consent to the disposition. However, in the case of a trust of land, it might also be the beneficiaries of full age who are beneficially entitled to an interest in possession in the land, whom the trustees should consult before exercising their functions under Trusts of Land and Appointment of Trustees Act 1996, s 11(1) (unless the trust instrument provides otherwise).

[146] Cl 42(1)(b).

This is directed primarily at trusts of land and at settlements under the Settled Land Act 1925.[147] Where there is a disposition by trustees of land or by the tenant for life under a settlement,[148] any capital moneys that arise must be paid to the trustees or to the trustees of the settlement, of whom (in either case) there must be at least two unless the trustee is a trust corporation.[149] If this requirement is not met, the beneficial interests under the trust of land or settlement will not be overreached.[150] To ensure that overreaching *does* take place, the registrar may enter a restriction to ensure that the proceeds of any disposition *are* paid to at least two trustees or to a trust corporation.

6.42 This power to enter a restriction is in fact supplemented in the Bill by a *duty* to do so in the specific case of legal co-ownership. When the registrar enters two or more persons in the register as the proprietor of a registered estate,[151] he must also enter in the register such restrictions as rules may provide for the purpose of securing that interests which are capable of being overreached on a disposition are overreached.[152]

6.43 The third purpose is to protect a right or claim in relation to a registered estate or charge.[153] For example, a restriction could be entered in relation to a claim by a person that he or she had a beneficial interest in a property under a resulting or constructive trust because he or she had contributed to the cost of its acquisition. The restriction might be that no disposition of the land should be registered without the consent of the person claiming the interest. The Bill specifically provides that a person who is entitled to the benefit of a charging order relating to an interest under a trust is, for these purposes, to be treated as having a right or claim in relation to the trust property.[154] This means that a restriction can be

---

[147] There are other situations in which overreaching can take place, such as a sale by a mortgagee pursuant to its paramount powers, which do not require the entry of any restriction on the register. Where the disposition is a registered disposition for valuable consideration, the disponee will take free of any interests under any settlement because there will be no restriction on the register to protect them and interests under a settlement cannot be overriding interests: see Schedule 3, para 2(1), see below, para 8.59. As regards a trust of land, the disponee will take free of any interests under the trust in the absence of any restriction unless a beneficiary under the trust is in actual occupation of the land. If so, he or she will have an overriding interest under Schedule 3, para 2(1); see below, para 8.54.

[148] Or person having the powers of the tenant for life under Settled Land Act 1925, s 20.

[149] Law of Property Act 1925, s 27(2); Settled Land Act 1925, s 94(1).

[150] If overreaching does not take place, the normal rules of priority apply to determine whether the disponee is or is not bound by the interests under the trust or settlement: see Cls 28—30; above, paras 5.5—5.6.

[151] So that there is, necessarily, a trust of land.

[152] Cl 44. The rules will be land registration rules and will be required to be laid before Parliament only. See Cls 125, 129(1).

[153] Cl 42(1)(c). This is an example of the use of a restriction in circumstances where, under the present law, a caution would commonly be entered.

[154] Cl 42(4).

entered in relation to that order.[155] Charging orders over beneficial interests under a trust of land are fairly common.[156] At present they are protected by the entry of a caution against dealings,[157] but this will cease to be possible under the Bill.[158] Because they relate to an overreachable interest under a trust, they cannot be protected by the entry of a notice either under the present law[159] or under the Bill.[160]

6.44   There is one limitation on the power explained in paragraph 6.43. In exercising it, the registrar may not enter any restriction to protect the priority of an interest that is or could be the subject of a notice.[161] In fact, it is contrary to the nature of a restriction that it should confer priority on an interest. A restriction is simply a means of preventing some entry on the register except to the extent (if any) that is permitted by the terms of the restriction.[162] As we have mentioned above, in the context of a right of pre-emption, both a notice and a restriction could be entered in relation to the same interest.[163] Each would serve a different function. The notice would protect the priority of the interest against a subsequent registered disposition and the restriction would ensure the compliance with certain conditions or requirements in relation to any disposition of the property by the registered proprietor.

6.45   Where the registrar exercises his power to enter a restriction under Clause 42(1),[164] he must give notice to the proprietor of the registered estate or charge concerned, except where the entry is made in pursuance of an application as explained below, at paragraph 6.47.[165] If the proprietor wishes to challenge the exercise of the registrar's power, he or she may do so by seeking a judicial review.[166]

---

[155]   The form of restriction is likely to provide that no disposition should be made of the registered estate held in trust without the prior notification of the person having the benefit of the charging order.

[156]   For charging orders over interests under a trust of land, see Charging Orders Act 1979, s 2(1)(a)(ii).

[157]   See Ruoff & Roper, *Registered Conveyancing*, 35-32; 36-08.

[158]   For the prospective abolition of cautions against dealings, see above, para 6.3.

[159]   *Ibid.*

[160]   See Cl 33(a); above, para 6.9.

[161]   Cl 42(2).

[162]   Of course a restriction may *indirectly* have the effect of protecting the priority of an interest. This is because it can prevent the registration of a disposition that *would* affect the priority of that interest.

[163]   See para 6.40(2).

[164]   See above paras 6.39 and following.

[165]   Cl 42(3).

[166]   The Adjudicator does not have jurisdiction in this case, because the entry of a restriction does not arise out of an application to which the registered proprietor may object: see Cls 73, 109; below, paras 16.6 and following. See too para 16.14.

Where the registrar must enter a restriction

6.46 We have mentioned above one case where the registrar is under a duty to enter a restriction to ensure that interests under a trust of land are overreached.[167] However, there are many other situations in which this is so. Thus a number of statutes require the registrar to enter a restriction in particular circumstances without application,[168] and the Bill provides for the form of those restrictions to be such as rules may provide.[169] In addition, there are a number of situations in which the Bill itself imposes a duty on the registrar to enter a restriction. One case has been mentioned above,[170] and the entry of a bankruptcy restriction is another.[171]

APPLICATIONS FOR THE ENTRY OF A RESTRICTION

6.47 The Bill permits a person to apply for the entry of a restriction if he or she—

(1) is either the registered proprietor or a person entitled to be registered as proprietor of the estate or charge to which the application relates;[172]

(2) has the consent of the registered proprietor or a person entitled to be registered as proprietor of the estate or charge to which the application relates;[173]

(3) has otherwise a sufficient interest in the making of an entry.[174]

6.48 There is a power to make rules that will *require* that an application be made in such circumstances and by such persons as may be prescribed.[175] Under the present law there are a number of situations in which there is a duty to apply for a restriction. For example, where the powers of trustees of land are limited by virtue of section 8 of the Trusts of Land and Appointment of Trustees Act 1996,[176] the

---

[167] Where the registrar enters two or more persons in the register as registered proprietors: see Cl 44; above, para 6.42.

[168] See, eg, Housing Act 1985, s 157(7); Schedule 9A, paras 4, 5(2); Housing Act 1988, ss 81(10), 133(9); Local Government and Housing Act 1989, s 37(8); Charities Act 1993, ss 37(8), 39(1B) (each as amended by Schedule 11 of the Bill). For the entry of a restriction on application, see below, para 6.47.

[169] Cl 44(2). The rules will be land registration rules and will be required to be laid before Parliament only. See Cls 125, 129(1).

[170] Para 6.42.

[171] Cl 86(2); below, para 11.40.

[172] Cl 43(1)(a), (4).

[173] Cl 43(1)(b), (4). The form of consent may be prescribed by rules: see Cl 43(2)(b).

[174] Cl 43(1)(c).

[175] Cl 43(2)(a). The rules will be land registration rules and will be required to be laid before Parliament only. See Cls 125, 129(1).

[176] The general powers of trustees and their powers to partition, conferred respectively by Trusts of Land and Appointment of Trustees Act 1996, ss 6 and 7, do not apply to a trust of land created by a disposition where the disposition makes provision to that effect: *ibid*, s 8(1). The disposition may also provide that powers conferred by ss 6 and 7 can only be exercised with consent: *ibid*, s 8(2).

trustees must apply for a restriction.[177] It is likely that in these and perhaps other cases, rules made under the Bill will require an application for a restriction.

6.49   Rules may also prescribe classes of person who are to be regarded as having a sufficient interest in the making of an entry of a restriction mentioned in paragraph 6.47(3) above.[178] These rules will not in any way detract from the generality of those who may apply under that category. They will simply specify the most important classes of such persons and might include—

(1)   a person having an interest in land that is capable of being protected by the entry of a restriction, such as a beneficiary under a trust of land;[179]

(2)   the donee of a special power of appointment in relation to registered land;[180]

(3)   the Charity Commission in relation to registered land held upon charitable trusts;

(4)   the Church Commissioners in respect of any registered land relating to or administered by them under any statute;[181] and

(5)   a receiver (whether or not appointed by the court), administrative receiver, or an administrator or a sequestrator appointed in respect of registered land or a registered charge.[182]

Where an applicant falls within one of the categories prescribed by rules, he or she will obviously not have to satisfy the registrar that he or she has a sufficient interest in the making of the entry. He or she will be regarded as doing so.[183]

6.50   Standard forms of restriction may be prescribed by rules.[184] If there is an application for the entry of a restriction that is not in one of the forms so prescribed, the registrar may only approve the application if it appears to him that the terms of the restriction are reasonable, and that applying the restriction would

[177]   Land Registration Rules 1925, rr 59A (duty on first registration), 106A(1) (duty on registration of a disposition of registered land in favour of the trustees). For other examples of a duty to apply for a restriction, see *ibid*, rr 124, 169A.

[178]   Cl 43(2)(c). The rules will be land registration rules and will be required to be laid before Parliament only. See Cls 125, 129(1).

[179]   Cf Land Registration Rules 1925, r 236.

[180]   A donee of a general power of appointment can always appoint to him or herself, and therefore falls within the category mentioned above, in para 6.47(1).

[181]   Cf Land Registration Rules 1925, r 238. See Ruoff & Roper, *Registered Conveyancing*, 10-21, where there is a discussion of the relevant statutes.

[182]   Such persons have no interest in any land or charge as such, but they may have a right or claim that can appropriately be protected by means of a restriction.

[183]   Under Cl 43(1)(c).

[184]   Cl 43(2)(d). The rules will be land registration rules and will be required to be laid before Parliament only. See Cls 125, 129(1).

be straightforward and would not place an unreasonable burden on him.[185] This power replicates the effect of one that is found in the Land Registration Act 1925.[186] There are from time to time applications for restrictions that the registrar has to refuse for one or more of the reasons set out above. For example, a restriction might provide for something to happen on the occurrence of some event, where it might be difficult for the registrar to determine whether or not that event had occurred.[187]

WHERE THE COURT MAY ORDER THE ENTRY OF A RESTRICTION

6.51 Under the Bill, if it appears to the court that it is necessary or desirable to do so for the purpose of protecting a right or claim in relation to a registered estate or charge, it may make an order requiring the registrar to enter a restriction in the register.[188] The cases in which the court is most likely to make such an order are in circumstances when, under the present law, it orders the entry of an inhibition.[189] However, whereas inhibitions prevent the entry of *any* dealing on the register, the jurisdiction of the court under the Bill is not so constrained. It could therefore order the entry of a restriction of a much more limited kind where that was necessary or desirable to protect the relevant right or claim.[190] What the court cannot do is to make an order for the purpose of protecting the priority of an interest which is, or could be, the subject of a notice,[191] any more than can the registrar when he exercises his power to enter a restriction.[192] However, as we explain in the next paragraph, an issue of priority can arise in a case where the court orders that a restriction be entered which prevents the registration of any disposition pending its further order.

6.52 As we explain more fully in Part IX of this Report, there are two situations under the Bill in which an entry on the register is protected if it is made within a priority period,[193] namely, where there is an official search and where an estate contract is protected by the entry of a notice.[194] Where an intending buyer has priority protection, and the court then orders that a restriction be entered that prevents the registration of any dealing with the registered estate, it needs to be clear

---

[185] Cl 43(3).

[186] See s 58(2). See too Land Registration Rules 1925, r 78.

[187] Such as a restriction that precluded any disposition until certain building works had been completed. It would be unreasonable to expect the registrar to have to ascertain whether those works had in fact been completed.

[188] Cl 46(1).

[189] In other words, where it is necessary to "freeze" the register and to prevent the registration of *any* dealing with or disposition of the estate or charge.

[190] For example, if it determined that a person was entitled to a beneficial interest under a resulting or constructive trust, it might also order the entry of a restriction to ensure that there was no disposition of the registered estate without the prior consent of the beneficiary.

[191] Cl 46(2).

[192] See above, para 6.44.

[193] Cl 72; below, para 9.67.

[194] Cl 72(6); below, para 9.68.

whether the restriction overrides the priority protection enjoyed by the intending buyer so as to prevent the registration of the subsequent transfer in his or her favour. Under the present law, the issue could arise where the court orders that an inhibition be entered on the register.[195] However, there is no reported instance in which the point has arisen. In the Consultative Document, we sought views as to whether, in ordering that a restriction be entered, the court should have power to direct that its order should have overriding priority.[196] The responses were almost evenly divided on the point, but with a slight preponderance in favour of such a power, provided that it was coupled with strict safeguards. The Bill reflects the view of the majority.

6.53 The effect of the Bill may be summarised as follows—

(1) in the absence of any order of the court, the priority protection given to an official search or the entry of a notice in respect of an estate contract would prevail over any order of the court that a restriction should be entered on the register;[197]

(2) the court would, however, have a power to include in its order a direction that the restriction should have overriding priority;[198]

(3) in exercising its power under (2), the court could impose such terms and conditions as it thought fit,[199] and would probably require an undertaking from the applicant that he or she should indemnify any person acting in good faith who had suffered loss as a result of the court's direction; and

(4) when a court made a direction under (2), the registrar would be required to make such entry in the register as rules might provide,[200] so as to ensure that it was apparent from the register that the restriction did indeed have overriding priority.

Notifiable applications for a restriction

6.54 Under the present law, unless the registered proprietor's land certificate is deposited with the registry, it normally has to be produced before a restriction can be entered.[201] As we have explained above, the role of land certificates under the Bill is greatly reduced from that which they presently have.[202] They will not have to be produced when an applicant seeks the entry of a restriction any more than

---

[195] See Law Com No 254, para 6.38.

[196] Law Com No 254, paras 6.60, 6.61. We made no recommendation on the point.

[197] This follows from Cl 72(2).

[198] Cl 46(3).

[199] Cl 46(5).

[200] Cl 46(4). The rules will be land registration rules and will be required to be laid before Parliament only. See Cls 125, 129(1).

[201] Land Registration Act 1925, s 64(1)(c).

[202] See para 6.23. See further below, paras 9.88, 9.90.

when he or she applies for the entry of a notice.[203] As with unilateral notices, there have to be safeguards therefore to protect a registered proprietor from the improper entry of restrictions.

6.55 First, as with applications for a notice,[204] a person must not exercise his or her right to apply for a restriction without reasonable cause.[205] As we have explained in the context of notices,[206] any person who does so without reasonable cause commits a breach of statutory duty and is liable accordingly to any person who suffers damage in consequence.[207]

6.56 Secondly, the Bill creates a procedure by which, where there is an application for the entry of a restriction, the registrar must give notice of it to both the proprietor of the registered estate or charge to which the application relates and such other persons as rules may provide (such as registered chargees and any other persons who may have a direct interest in any disposition of the property).[208] The registrar's obligation to serve notice of an application applies in all cases *except* where—

(1) the application is made by or with the consent of—

(a) the proprietor of the registered estate or charge to which the application relates; or

(b) a person who is entitled to be registered as the proprietor;[209]

(2) there is a duty under rules to apply for a restriction as explained above in paragraph 6.48;[210] and

(3) there is an application for the entry of a restriction that reflects a limitation under either—

(a) an order of the court or registrar; or

(b) an undertaking given in place of such an order.[211]

---

[203] Cf para 6.23.

[204] See above, para 6.28.

[205] Cl 77(1)(b).

[206] Above, para 6.28. See too above, para 3.59 (lodging a caution unreasonably); and below, para 16.6 (objecting to an application unreasonably).

[207] Cl 77(2).

[208] Cl 45(1). The rules will be land registration rules and will be required to be laid before Parliament only. See Cls 125, 129(1).

[209] Cl 45(3)(a).

[210] Cl 45(3)(b).

[211] Cl 45(3)(c).

In essence, therefore, the registrar will serve notice of an application of a restriction which is both voluntary (in the sense that it is not one that the applicant or registrar is or can be required to make) and unilateral (because it is not made with the concurrence of the registered proprietor).

6.57   Once notice of the application is given, the registered proprietor may object to it and the usual provisions of the Bill that relate to objections, explained in Part XVI of this Report, will apply.[212] If the objection cannot be resolved by agreement of the parties, it will be referred to the Adjudicator for his decision.[213]

Withdrawal of restrictions

6.58   The Bill makes provision by which an application may be made for the withdrawal of a restriction.[214] Both the persons who may apply for withdrawal and the circumstances in which such an application may be made will be prescribed by rules.[215] In general, this power is likely to be applicable primarily in respect of restrictions that were entered on application rather than those which were entered because there was a duty to do so, or because they were entered on the order of the court or by the registrar. However, even in respect of restrictions that were entered otherwise than on application, it may be appropriate for an interested person to apply for the withdrawal of a restriction, as where it is spent.

Pending land actions, writs, orders and deeds of arrangement

6.59   The Bill makes special provision as to how to protect the following matters—

(1)   a pending land action;[216]

(2)   a writ or order affecting land issued or made by any court for the purpose of enforcing a judgment or recognisance;[217]

(3)   an order appointing a receiver or a sequestrator of land;[218] and

(4)   a deed of arrangement within the meaning of the Deeds of Arrangement Act 1914.[219]

At present such matters are protected by the entry of a caution. It is therefore necessary to make alternative provision for them in the Bill, given the prospective abolition of cautions.[220]

---

[212]   See Cls 73; 106; below, paras 16.6 and following.

[213]   Cl 73(7); below, para 16.6.

[214]   Cl 47.

[215]   *Ibid.* The rules will be land registration rules and will be required to be laid before Parliament only. See Cls 125, 129(1).

[216]   See Land Charges Act 1972, s 5(1)(a).

[217]   See *ibid*, s 6(1)(a).

[218]   See *ibid*, s 6(1)(b).

[219]   See *ibid*, s 7(1). For the relevant deeds of arrangement, see Deeds of Arrangement Act 1914, s 1.

6.60   Under the Bill, all of these matters are treated as interests affecting an estate or charge.[221] Some entry is, therefore, required to protect them on the register.[222] The effect of the Bill is that the *only* entry that can be made in relation to an order appointing a receiver or a sequestrator of land and a deed of arrangement is a restriction.[223] The reasons for this are as follows—

(1)   An order appointing a receiver or sequestrator will sometimes be regarded as a proprietary right and sometimes it will not.[224] We were concerned that there should be one method for protecting all such orders without an inquiry as to which side of the line the order fell.

(2)   A deed of arrangement is registered to protect creditors during the interim between a debtor assigning his or her property to a trustee for his or her creditors' benefit and the trustee being registered as proprietor. They are, therefore, analogous to bankruptcy orders which, under the Bill, are protected by the entry of a restriction.[225]

Although, as we have explained, a restriction cannot be used to protect the priority of an interest that could be protected by a notice,[226] they can provide very effective protection for a right by preventing the registration of any dealing with the registered estate or charge affected.

6.61   As regards a pending land action or a writ or order affecting land issued or made by any court for the purpose of enforcing a judgment or recognisance, it will be possible to protect such an interest by the entry of a notice, a restriction or both. There is a power to modify the application of the Bill by rules in relation to any of the matters listed above in paragraph 6.59.[227] This is because there may be cases where such matters may not naturally fall within the wording of the provisions of the Bill, but where those provisions should, nonetheless, apply.[228]

---

[220] See above, para 6.3.

[221] Cl 87(1). In other words, they are "an adverse right affecting the title to the estate or charge": see Cl 129(3)(b).

[222] Such rights cannot be protected as overriding interests under either Schedule 1, para 2, or Schedule 3, para 2, where the person having the benefit of the interest is in actual occupation.

[223] The Bill achieves this in a negative way by providing that no notice may be entered in respect of such rights: see Cl 87(2).

[224] See *Clayhope Properties Ltd v Evans* [1986] 1 WLR 1223, 1228.

[225] Cl 86(4); below, para 11.40.

[226] Cl 42(2); above, para 6.44.

[227] Cl 87(4). Any rules will be land registration rules and will be required to be laid before Parliament only. See Cls 125, 129(1).

[228] For example, a restraint order under Criminal Justice Act 1988, s 77, takes effect as a pending land action. However, there might be a doubt as to whether a prosecutor who seeks a restraint order against a criminal's registered estate can be said to "be entitled to the benefit of an interest affecting a registered estate" within Cl 34(1) (above, para 6.22).

117

PART VII
CHARGES

INTRODUCTION

7.1 In this Part we explain the provisions of the Bill that govern charges of registered land. In a number of respects the Bill simplifies and in some cases changes the present law. The Bill makes provision as to the following matters—

(1) the power of a registered proprietor to charge his or her land and the powers of any registered chargee;

(2) sub-charges and the powers of the sub-chargee;

(3) the priority of competing charges; and

(4) three miscellaneous matters, namely—

    (a) the application of proceeds of sale;

    (b) consolidation; and

    (c) the power to give receipts where there are two or more proprietors of the registered charge.

We give particular weight to the priority of further advances, because this proved to be the most contentious issue that emerged in preparing Instructions for the Bill.

THE POWER TO CREATE CHARGES AND THE POWERS OF THE CHARGEE

Legal charges

The creation of charges and the powers of the chargee

7.2 Under the present law, a registered proprietor can by deed create a legal mortgage or charge[1] of registered land in any one of *three* ways—

(1) he or she may in the usual way create a charge expressed to be by way of legal mortgage;[2]

(2) he or she may charge the registered land with the payment of money and this will take effect as a charge by way of legal mortgage, even though not expressed to do so;[3] or

---

[1] "A mortgage is a conveyance of property subject to a right of redemption, whereas a charge conveys nothing and merely gives the chargee certain rights over the property as security for the loan": *Megarry & Wade's Law of Real Property* (6th ed 2000), 19-005.

[2] Cf Law of Property Act 1925, s 87(1).

[3] See *Cityland and Property (Holdings) Ltd v Dabrah* [1968] Ch 166, 171.

118

(3)   he or she may create a mortgage by demise or sub-demise but must do so expressly: the presumption is in favour of a charge by way of legal mortgage.

These three propositions state the combined effect of sections 25(1) and 27 of the Land Registration Act 1925. The reason for (2) is historical. Charges over registered land were introduced by the Land Transfer Act 1875.[4] They therefore pre-date by half a century the introduction of the charge expressed to be by way of legal mortgage in section 87 of the Law of Property Act 1925.[5] Mortgages by demise or sub-demise — (3) above — are in practice now obsolete because of the advantages offered by a charge. The main advantages of a charge are that—

(a)   freeholds and leaseholds can be the subject of a single charge rather then separate demises or sub-demises;

(b)   the grant of a charge over a lease is not thought to amount to a breach of the common-form covenant against subletting without the landlord's consent (such consent would be required to a mortgage by sub-demise); and

(c)   the form of legal charge is short and simple.[6]

It should be noted that the mortgage by demise or sub-demise was as much a creation of the Law of Property Act 1925 as was the charge expressed to be by way of legal mortgage. The charge over registered land for the payment of money — (2) above — is in fact the form of permitted legal mortgage or charge that has the longest pedigree.[7]

7.3   As we have explained in Part IV of this Report, the Bill implements a recommendation in the Consultative Document[8] that it should not be possible to create mortgages by demise or sub-demise in relation to registered land.[9] Under the Bill, a registered proprietor can create a legal mortgage in one of two ways—

---

[4]   "The charge of registered land under the Land Transfer Acts did not necessarily involve any conveyance of an estate, but merely conferred powers of realisation by entry, foreclosure or sale": *Brickdale & Stewart-Wallace's Land Registration Act, 1925* (4th ed 1939), p 118.

[5]   The reform of the manner in which unregistered land could be mortgaged by Law of Property Act 1925, ss 85—87 was a "compromise... whereby the two systems [that is the unregistered and the registered systems] have been harmonised with one another": *Brickdale & Stewart-Wallace's Land Registration Act, 1925* (4th ed 1939), p 118.

[6]   See *Megarry & Wade's Law of Real Property* (6th ed 2000), 19-034. See too Law Com No 254, para 9.4.

[7]   We make this point because, in response to the Consultative Document, the Bar Council expressed the view that the mortgage by demise or sub-demise was "still the paradigm". However, this overlooks the charge of registered land created by the Land Transfer Act 1875.

[8]   Law Com No 254, para 9.5.

[9]   See above, paras 4.6, 4.7.

(1)   by a charge expressed to be by way of legal mortgage;[10] or

(2)   by a charge to secure the payment of money.[11]

There will be no practical difference between these two methods any more than there is now. This is because, on completion of the relevant registration requirements,[12] a charge has effect "if it would not otherwise do so, as a charge by deed by way of legal mortgage",[13] with the concomitant powers. Those powers are, of course, those conferred on a legal mortgagee by the Law of Property Act 1925 (unless modified or excluded by the terms of the charge) together with any additional powers that may be conferred by the charge.

7.4   It should be noted that, although under the Land Registration Act 1925 a charge may be in any form,[14] there is a general power in the Bill to prescribe by rules the form and content of any registrable disposition of a registered estate or charge.[15] It will therefore be possible for the Lord Chancellor to prescribe the form of any registered charge. Furthermore, in relation to any charge in electronic form, a form of electronic document will in practice have to be prescribed.[16]

The definition of "charge"

7.5   In the Consultative Document we considered whether the present definition of "registered charge" was wide enough.[17] In particular, we were concerned that it should clearly include both charges to secure the discharge of some obligation and statutory charges.[18] The Bill meets these concerns by providing a wide definition of "charge" to mean "any mortgage, charge or lien for securing money or money's worth".[19] This will necessarily encompass both charges to secure the discharge of some obligation[20] and statutory charges.[21]

---

[10]   Cl 23(1)(a). See above, para 4.6.

[11]   Cl 23(1)(b). See above, para 4.6. For the necessary consequential amendments to Law of Property Act 1925, ss 85 and 86, see Schedule 11, para 2(6), (7).

[12]   The registered chargee must be registered as the proprietor of the charge and the charge must be entered in the register in relation to the registered estate on which it is a charge: see Cl 59(2).

[13]   Cl 51.

[14]   Subject to certain conditions: see s 25(2).

[15]   Cl 25(1).

[16]   See below, para 13.12.

[17]   See Law Com No 254, paras 9.2—9.3.

[18]   Such as one to pay a share of the profits of a business, as in *Santley v Wilde* [1899] 2 Ch 474.

[19]   Cl 129. A "registered charge" is, therefore, a "a charge to the title which is registered under this Act": *ibid.*

[20]   In relation to such charges, it is the financial liability arising from non-performance of the obligation that is secured.

[21]   It may be noted that, in Part 5 of the Bill, "Charges", there are two provisions that specifically concern statutory charges: see Cls 50, 55. These are explained below at paras 7.40, 7.42 respectively.

Powers of chargees and the need for a deed

7.6 Section 101 of the Law of Property Act 1925 confers a number of important powers on a mortgagee "where the mortgage is made by deed", including the power to sell and to appoint a receiver. In the Consultative Document,[22] we suggested that, even in advance of the introduction of electronic conveyancing, a deed should not be necessary for the creation of a registered charge but that the chargee should nonetheless have the powers conferred by section 101. Although that proposal was supported by most of those who responded, it has not been necessary to include any such provision in the Bill. There are two main factors that persuaded us of this. First, it is anticipated that one of the first types of disposition of registered land that it will be possible to effect in electronic form will be a charge over registered land. Secondly, under the Bill, electronic documents are made in the same way, whether they are required by law to be made by deed or merely in writing.[23] There seems little point in dispensing with the requirement of a deed in what is likely to be the comparatively short interim period between the implementation of the Bill and the time when all registered charges are effected electronically.

Dispositions made by chargees and the protection of disponees

7.7 As we have explained in Part IV of this Report,[24] it is intended that, if there are limitations of some kind on a registered proprietor's powers of disposition, that fact should be apparent from the register, usually from the entry of a restriction.[25] Clause 52(1) implements this objective in relation to dispositions by the proprietor of a registered charge. Under that Clause, subject to any entry in the register to the contrary, the registered proprietor of a charge is taken to have, in relation to the property subject to the charge, the powers of disposition conferred by law on a legal mortgagee.[26] The purpose of the Clause is to protect any disponee in the case where, for example, the chargee purports to exercise a power of disposition (typically a sale or the grant of a lease) in circumstances where either it had no such power at all[27] or that power had not become exercisable.[28] In the absence of some entry on the register (such as a restriction), the disponee's title cannot be questioned.[29] However, this will not affect the lawfulness of the

---

[22] Law Com No 254, para 9.6.

[23] See Cl 91; below, para 13.11.

[24] See above, para 4.4; and Cl 23.

[25] Or cautions that were lodged prior to the coming into force of the Bill.

[26] It should be emphasised that Cl 52(1) does not *define* the powers of a chargee (such powers follow from Cl 51, above, para 7.3, and from the fact that a charge is or, if in electronic form is deemed to be, made by deed), but merely protects disponees of charged property, as the marginal note suggests.

[27] As where the mortgagee's power of leasing under Law of Property Act 1925, s 99(2), had been excluded, but no restriction had been entered on the register to reflect this.

[28] Some of the powers conferred on a mortgagee by Law of Property Act 1925, s 101, become exercisable only "when the mortgage money has become due" — that is, after the legal date for redemption.

[29] Cl 52(2).

disposition.[30] It is open to the chargor to pursue any other remedies he or she may have, such as the right to sue the chargee for damages for an irregular exercise of the latter's powers.[31]

7.8 It should be noted that the Bill confers (and is intended to confer) greater protection on disponees than does the Law of Property Act 1925.

(1) First, although the Law of Property Act 1925 contains provisions that are intended to protect a buyer of land when the mortgagee's power of sale has arisen,[32] there are judicial statements that suggest that this protection will not avail a buyer who becomes aware of "any facts showing that the power of sale is not exercisable, or that there is some impropriety in the sale".[33] A disponee's title will not be impeachable on that ground under the Bill.

(2) Secondly, even if a chargee's power of disposition has not arisen at all — as where the legal date for redemption has been postponed for many years[34] — a disponee will obtain a good title in the absence of anything on the register to indicate some limitation on those powers. The rule that would otherwise apply is that the chargee could only transfer its charge. It could not sell the land free of the chargor's equity of redemption.[35] The legal date for redemption will commonly be six months after the date of the charge. However, it is not anticipated that chargors will feel it necessary to enter a restriction on the register to protect themselves from a possible improper disposition by the chargee in that short period. The risk of such a disposition is minimal, particularly where the chargor remains in possession. However, if the legal date for redemption were postponed for a substantial period, the entry of a restriction might then be considered an appropriate safeguard.[36] Similarly, if (say) the chargee's leasing powers were excluded, a restriction should be entered on the register to record this fact.

Equitable charges

7.9 The Bill has nothing specific to say about equitable charges. A registered proprietor may create them to the extent permitted by the general law under his

---

[30] *Ibid.*

[31] Law of Property Act 1925, s 104(2). There may be remedies against the disponee, perhaps for wrongful interference with a contract, as where he or she deliberately induced the chargor to sell to him or her when there was no ground for exercising the power of sale.

[32] See s 104(2), (3).

[33] *Lord Waring v London and Manchester Assurance Co Ltd* [1935] Ch 310, 318, *per* Crossman J.

[34] As in *Twentieth Century Banking Corporation v Wilkinson* [1977] Ch 99.

[35] See *Megarry & Wade's Law of Real Property* (6th ed 2000), 19-059.

[36] In such a case, the chargee can always seek a sale before the date for redemption by an application to the court under Law of Property Act 1925, s 91

or her owner's powers.[37] They may also arise in other ways, as where a creditor obtains a charging order over the land of a registered proprietor.[38]

7.10 The fact that the Bill says nothing about such charges is important for one specific reason. In the Consultative Document,[39] we recommended that the statutory power[40] to create a lien over registered land by depositing the land certificate as security should be abolished. Our reasoning was as follows. Such charges operated by analogy with the mortgage by deposit of title deeds in unregistered land. However, in *United Bank of Kuwait Plc v Sahib*,[41] the Court of Appeal held that the basis for mortgages by deposit of title deeds was the doctrine of part performance that had been abolished by the Law of Property (Miscellaneous Provisions) Act 1989.[42] Such mortgages were only valid if they complied with the formal requirements for contracts laid down in that Act. That decision rendered obsolete the power to create a lien by the deposit of a land certificate. All but one of those who responded to our recommendation in the Consultative Document to abolish such liens agreed with it. The Bill therefore contains nothing replicating the power.[43]

SUB-CHARGES AND THE POWERS OF THE SUB-CHARGEE

7.11 A sub-mortgage is a mortgage of a mortgage.[44] The effect of Clause 23(2) and (3) of the Bill is that there is only one way in which a registered chargee can create a legal sub-charge, namely the method specified in Clause 23(2)(b).[45] The chargee is thereby empowered "to charge at law with the payment of money indebtedness secured by the registered charge". In other words, what is actually charged is the indebtedness secured by the registered charge. This power, which is unique to registered land, is derived from the present provisions of the Land Registration Rules 1925 as to the creation of sub-charges.[46] A sub-chargee can, of course, further sub-charge the indebtedness which its sub-charge secures.

---

[37] Cl 23; above, para 4.6.

[38] Such a charge takes effect as "an equitable charge created by the debtor by writing under his hand": Charging Orders Act 1979, s 3(4).

[39] Law Com No 254, paras 9.8—9.11.

[40] Found in Land Registration Act 1925, s 66.

[41] [1997] Ch 107; explained in Law Com No 254, para 9.9.

[42] Section 2.

[43] The role of land certificates under Land Registration Act 1925 is very significantly reduced under the Bill: see above, paras 6.23, 6.54; below, paras 9.88—9.91.

[44] E L G Tyler, *Fisher & Lightwood's Law of Mortgage* (10th ed 1988), p 272.

[45] Cf the definition of "sub-charge" in Cl 129(1).

[46] See r 163(1) which provides that "The proprietor of a charge or incumbrance may at any time charge the mortgage debt with the payment of money in the same manner as the proprietor of land can charge the land; and such charges are in these rules referred to as sub-charges". This does of course echo the power of a proprietor of a registered estate to charge that estate with the payment of money at law which is, again, unique to registered land: see above, para 7.2.

7.12 Under the Bill, the registered proprietor of a sub-charge[47] has, in relation to the property subject to the principal charge or to any intermediate charge, the same powers as the sub-chargor.[48] This is also the position under the present law.[49]

PRIORITIES

Priority of registered charges

7.13 In making provision for the priority of competing registered charges in the Bill, we have attempted to meet three objectives—

(1)   the rule giving special effect to registered dispositions in relation to priority, explained in Part V of this Report,[50] should apply except as stated in (2);

(2)   where there is more than one registered charge, the proprietors of those charges should always be permitted to agree between themselves that the order of priority should be different from that which would arise from the application of the principle set out in (1);[51] and

(3)   the priority of competing registered charges should in any event be apparent from the register as it is now.[52]

7.14 The effect of (1), so far as is relevant here, is that on registration, a registered chargee will only take subject to a prior charge if it is either a registered charge or the subject of a notice on the register.[53] If, for example—

(1)   A contracts to lend money to B on the security of a charge over B's registered land and protects that estate contract by the entry of a notice on the register;

(2)   B then charges the land to C, who registers her charge;

(3)   pursuant to the earlier contract, B executes the charge in favour of A which is completed by registration;

---

[47]   The registered sub-chargee must be registered as the proprietor of the sub-charge and the sub-charge must be entered in the register: see Cl 59(3).

[48]   See Cl 53.

[49]   See Land Registration Rules 1925, r 163(2).

[50]   See Cl 29; above, para 5.6.

[51]   In the absence of a contractual agreement between the chargor and chargee, the former has no right to insist on the order as to which successive mortgage debts are satisfied. It is therefore open to chargees to alter the priorities *inter se* without the chargor's consent: *Cheah v Equiticorp Finance Group Ltd* [1992] 1 AC 472.

[52]   See Land Registration Act 1925, s 29, under which in the absence of any entry to the contrary on the register, the priority of registered charges is determined not by the order in which they are created but by the order in which they are registered.

[53]   Cl 29(2)(a)(i).

A's registered charge ought to take priority over C's, even though C's was registered before A's. A's charge gives effect to a contract that was binding on C.[54] However, notwithstanding that outcome, it follows from the principle stated in paragraph 7.13(2) above, that A and C should be free to agree that C's charge should in fact take priority over A's if they so wish.[55]

7.15 The Bill achieves the objectives set out in paragraph 7.13 by providing that registered charges on the same registered estate are to be taken to rank as between themselves in the order shown in the register.[56] The detail of how such priority should be shown in the register as well as how applications for registration of the priority of registered charges between themselves is left to be stipulated in rules.[57] Those rules must, however, reflect the legal rules set out above in paragraph 7.13(1) and (2). It should be noted that there are some statutory charges which can override prior charges. The Bill makes special provision for these and this is explained below.[58]

Registered sub-charges

7.16 The rules as to the priority of competing registered sub-charges are the same as those for competing registered charges. The rule giving special effect to registered dispositions of a registered charge in relation to priority[59] will apply, but it will be open to the sub-chargees to vary that priority by agreement. The principles applicable to the recording of that priority on the register are the same as those explained above in paragraph 7.15.[60]

Equitable charges

7.17 The Bill contains no specific provisions as to the priority of equitable charges. They are subject to the basic rule, explained in Part V, by which the priority of an interest affecting a registered estate or charge is not affected by a disposition of the estate or charge.[61] It follows that the priority of competing equitable charges will be determined by the date of their respective creations. As we explain in Part XIII,

---

[54] This is the same result as occurred in the analogous case with unregistered land: see *Williams v Burlington Investments Ltd* (1977) 121 SJ 424 (HL). We consider that the same result would probably be reached in registered land under the present law (because of the power to make an entry to the contrary under Land Registration Act 1925, s 29), though one very experienced respondent to the Consultative Document (who had been involved in the *Burlington* case) thought otherwise. The Bill places the matter beyond doubt.

[55] When electronic conveyancing is introduced, such agreements may have no effect unless registered: see Cl 93(6); below, para 13.83.

[56] Cl 48(1).

[57] Cl 48(2). The rules will be land registration rules and will be required to be laid before Parliament only. see Cls 125, 129(1).

[58] See para 7.39.

[59] See Cl 30; above, para 5.6.

[60] Cl 48 applies to the ranking of both registered charges on the same estate and registered charges on the same registered charge.

[61] Cl 28; above, para 5.5.

following the introduction of electronic conveyancing, rules will be made which will have the effect that most interests in registered land will not be capable of being created except by simultaneously registering them.[62] When that happens, the register will in fact be conclusive as to the priority of competing equitable charges. This is because the date of registration and the date of creation of a charge will necessarily coincide. This improvement is likely to be a particular advantage in relation to competing equitable charges, where issues of priority are not infrequent.

Tacking and further advances

Present law and practice

7.18 Under the doctrine of tacking, a mortgagee who has granted more than one mortgage to the borrower may sometimes gain the same priority for a later charge as it has for the earlier one, by effectively amalgamating them. The typical case of tacking is where a bank takes a charge to secure an overdraft as it stands from time to time. Every increase in that overdraft is a fresh advance by the bank and, in effect, a new charge for the additional sum advanced. The borrower may, of course, enter into other secured borrowing arrangements after the charge to the bank is executed. Ideally, the bank ("Lender 1") would wish its charge for further advances to have priority over any such second charge by Lender 2. However, the circumstances in which Lender 1 can achieve that are now comparatively limited, as we explain below. In general, what Lender 1 now wishes to ensure therefore, is that it is alerted to the creation of any second charge, because once registered, the second charge will normally take priority over any further advances made thereafter by Lender 1.

7.19 The fundamental rule in relation to tacking at common law is that a first mortgagee, whose mortgage covers both what is due and further advances, cannot claim priority for those further advances over the mortgage of a second mortgagee, of whose mortgage he has notice when he made the further advances.[63] As regards *unregistered* land, the Law of Property Act 1925 lays down the only permitted circumstances in which a right to make further advances ranks in priority to a subsequent mortgagee.[64] Except in these circumstances the right to tack further advances has been abolished.[65] These provisions do not apply to registered land,[66] and the Land Registration Act 1925 makes express provision in relation to tacking.[67] However, it does not abolish the common law rules. The ironic result is that the fundamental notice-based rule set out above continues to

---

[62] See Cl 93; below, paras 13.74 and following.

[63] *Hopkinson v Rolt* (1861) 9 HLC 514; 11 ER 829.

[64] Law of Property Act 1925, s 94(1) lists three: (a) by arrangement with subsequent mortgagees; (b) where the prior mortgagee had no notice of any subsequent mortgages at the time when the further advances were made by him; and (c) regardless of notice, where the mortgage imposes an obligation on the prior mortgagee to make such further advances.

[65] It is abolished by Law of Property Act 1925, s 94(3).

[66] Law of Property Act 1925, s 94(4).

[67] Section 30, explained below, paras 7.20 and following.

apply to registered land.[68] Furthermore, as we discovered from our inquiries, most chargees of registered land still operate on the basis of the common law rule (as they are entitled to do) rather than in accordance with the provisions of the Land Registration Act 1925.[69]

7.20 Section 30(1) of the Land Registration Act 1925 provides that—

> When a registered charge is made for securing further advances, the registrar shall, before making any entry on the register which would prejudicially affect the priority of any further charge thereunder, give to the proprietor of the charge at his registered address, notice by registered post of the intended entry, and the proprietor of the charge shall not, in respect of any further advance, be affected by such entry unless the advance is made after the date when the notice ought to have been received in due course of post.

The purpose of this provision is, therefore, to ensure that the lender is alerted to the intended charge and can decline to make further advances thereafter.

7.21 Section 30(1) does not depend upon Lender 1 actually having notice of the creation of charge in favour of Lender 2. It effectively deems him to know of that charge once he *ought* to have done so if the post had been delivered on time. It follows, therefore, that there may be cases in which Lender 1 may continue to make further advances oblivious of the existence of the charge in favour of Lender 2. In such circumstances, these advances will not have priority over but will be subject to the charge in favour of Lender 2. Accordingly, section 30(2) makes provision for the payment of indemnity where a notice under section 30(1) is not served properly as a result of some failure by the registrar or the post office, and Lender 1 suffers loss as a result.

7.22 It sometimes happens that a lender not only agrees to permit further borrowing by the borrower (as with an overdraft arrangement) but is contractually *obliged* to lend money to the borrower. For example, a bank might undertake to advance money in a series of instalments, secured on the borrower's land, to finance (say) some development. Section 30(3) of the Land Registration Act 1925 provides that—

> Where the proprietor of a charge is under an obligation, noted on the register, to make a further advance,[70] a subsequent registered charge shall take effect subject to any further advance made pursuant to the obligation.

---

[68] As we have explained above, in paragraphs 5.16 and following, notice is normally irrelevant to the priority of interest in registered land.

[69] See below, para 7.25.

[70] For the noting of the obligation, see Land Registration Rules 1925, r 139A.

There is one drawback with this provision. It appears only to protect Lender 1 against a subsequent *registered* charge and not, say, a later equitable charge.[71]

7.23 As we have indicated above,[72] these provisions are not much employed. Although at the time of the Consultative Document, we suspected this was the case, we were uncertain as to exactly what practice lenders were employing in relation to further advances secured on registered land. Our proposals in the Consultative Document were restricted to some suggestions for improvements in the drafting of the provisions.[73] In preparing Instructions for the present Bill, we explored some more radical options in relation to further advances. To test these, we had very informative and constructive discussions with representatives of the lending industry,[74] whose extensive and generous assistance we gratefully acknowledge.

7.24 They were able to inform us as to their current practice, which is generally as follows. Where there is a prior charge, Lender 2 sends written notice of its charge to Lender 1, and Lender 1 then treats that notice as determinative of priority. After receipt of that notice, Lender 1 will treat any further advances made by itself as subject to the charge of Lender 2, unless it is under an obligation to make that further advance. In this way, even if Lender 2 fails to submit its charge to HM Land Registry for registration,[75] it secures priority over any further advance by Lender 1.

7.25 It will be noted that it is Lender 2 — and not HM Land Registry under the provisions of section 30(1) of the Land Registration Act 1925[76] — that serves notice on Lender 1. The legal basis for the current practice would therefore appear to be the old common law principles on tacking further advances, which, as we have indicated, still apply to registered land.[77] There are sound practical reasons why lenders prefer to rely on the common law rather than on section 30(1) of the Land Registration Act 1925. As we have explained, under section 30(1), only the *registrar* can serve notice on the proprietor of the charge for securing further advances. This means that second chargees have no control over the date on which the statutory notice is issued by the registrar. In practice, HM Land Registry can only send a notice to Lender 1 when it has approved the making of the entry of the second charge on the register. There are cases when this approval cannot be given for some considerable time. Whilst this may arise

---

[71] See Law Com No 254, para 7.9, referring to Transfer of Land — Land Mortgages (1991) Law Com No 204, para 9.5.

[72] See para 7.19.

[73] Law Com No 254, paras 7.7—7.9.

[74] We particularly wish to record our thanks to Fiona Hoyle and Sharanjit Dosanjh of the Council of Mortgage Lenders, John Thirlwell of the British Bankers' Association, Hilary Plattern of the Finance & Leasing Association, Stephen Garratt-Frost of HSBC Holdings Plc, and David Bowden of The Woolwich. We also received helpful information from others in the lending industry.

[75] Whether as a registered charge (if legal) or by way of the entry of a notice (if equitable).

[76] See above, para 7.20.

[77] See above, para 7.19.

from shortcomings in the application for registration of the second charge, there are also cases where Lender 2 is in no way to blame for the delay. We have therefore concluded that little purpose would be served by the retention of section 30(1) of the Land Registration Act 1925 and that it seems preferable to give statutory form to the practice of lenders.

7.26 The representatives of the primary lenders — those that tend to lend on first mortgage — expressed themselves content with the present practice, set out above in paragraph 7.24, and agreed with the conclusion that it should be given statutory form. However, those who represented the secondary lending market, particularly those lenders who lent on the security of second or subsequent charges that were regulated by the Consumer Credit Act 1974, took a very different view. It transpired that the reason for their concern did not lie with the actual mechanism of notification that we explained in paragraph 7.24. It was because of a widespread practice of primary lenders by which a chargor is required to enter into a covenant with Lender 1 not to borrow further sums on the security of the property charged by the first charge without the prior consent of Lender 1. At present, such agreements are commonly protected by the entry of a restriction on the register on the application of the chargor. To the best of our knowledge, neither the efficacy nor the effect of such agreements has ever been tested in the courts. In particular it is unclear whether—

(1) they create proprietary rights and if so, of what kind;[78] and

(2) they are open to challenge on the grounds of their anti-competitive nature.[79]

7.27 It became apparent from our discussions with representatives of the lending industry that they were expecting us to resolve the conflict of opinion over the validity and effect of such agreements in the Bill. However, not only would this be inappropriate,[80] but it would lie outside the scope of a Land Registration Bill. The position of the Law Commission and HM Land Registry on this issue must be one of scrupulous neutrality as between the primary and secondary lenders. It will remain the practice of HM Land Registry to accept applications for the entry of restrictions in relation to such agreements unless and until their validity is

---

[78] There are circumstances in which it could be material whether any right created by such an agreement is proprietary or not, as where a second charge is created in ignorance of the restriction and is then not registered because of it. There is an argument that such an agreement might create a restrictive covenant by analogy with a tying covenant. It is well-established that a tying covenant by (for example) a mortgagor-publican not to buy beer other than from his or her mortgagee-brewer is a restrictive covenant capable of binding third parties: see *John Brothers Abergarw Brewery Co v Holmes* [1900] 1 Ch 188; *Regent Oil Co Ltd v Gregory (Hatch End) Ltd* [1966] Ch 402, 433. However, against this, there is a respectable argument that a covenant not to borrow without consent is not a restrictive covenant because it does not restrict the *user* of the land but merely its disposition.

[79] At first sight they would appear to be. However, we should record that we have received correspondence in which the contrary was strongly argued.

[80] It would not be a measure for the reform of property law as such and would undoubtedly raise difficult competitiveness issues that lie outside our expertise.

successfully challenged in the courts. As regards the Bill, we consider that we should adopt a similarly neutral approach to the tacking of further advances.

The provisions of the Bill

7.28   Clause 49 sets out four circumstances in which the proprietor of a registered charge may secure further advances so that they have priority over any subsequent charge of whatever kind.[81] No other means are permitted.[82] Of these four circumstances, only the last is novel.

FURTHER ADVANCES MADE WITH THE AGREEMENT OF SUBSEQUENT CHARGEES

7.29   First, the proprietor of a registered charge may make further advances on the security of its charge that will rank in priority to subsequent charges if the subsequent chargees agree.[83] That does no more than reflect the general rule that the priority of charges can always be adjusted by agreement between the parties.[84]

FURTHER ADVANCES WHERE THE PRIOR CHARGEE HAS NOT RECEIVED NOTICE OF THE SUBSEQUENT CHARGE

7.30   We have explained above that the present practice under section 30(1) of the Land Registration Act 1925, by which the registrar serves notice of the second charge on Lender 1, is not much used and is, in any event, unsatisfactory.[85] It is not therefore replicated in the Bill. Instead the Bill gives statutory effect to the present practice of lenders, that is based on the common law. It provides that the proprietor of a registered charge may make further advances on the security of its charge that will rank in priority to a subsequent charge if he has not received from Lender 2 notice of the creation of that subsequent charge.[86] The Bill also provides that notice of this kind is to be treated as received at the time when, in accordance with rules, it ought to have been received.[87] This means that provision can be made as to when notice served by (for example) first class post, by fax or by e-mail is to be taken to be received.[88] There will of course be no payment of indemnity if notice is not in fact received and a further advance is made in ignorance of the second charge. This is the position under the present law when

---

[81]   For the meaning of "charge" under the Bill, see Cl 129(1); above, para 7.5.

[82]   Cl 49(6).

[83]   *Ibid.*

[84]   See above, para 7.13(2). Cf Law of Property Act 1925, s 94(1)(a), which expressly so provides in relation to unregistered land. When electronic conveyancing is introduced, such agreements may have no effect unless registered: see Cl 93(6); below, para 13.83.

[85]   See para 7.25.

[86]   Cl 49(1).

[87]   Cl 49(2).

[88]   Cf Schedule 10, para 5; below, para 17.9, which provides that the form, content and service of notices which fall to be given under the Bill are a matter for rules, and makes provision about matters such as when service is to be regarded as having taken place.

Lender 2 notifies Lender 1 of its charge.[89] It is anticipated that, when electronic conveyancing is introduced, it may be possible for Lender 2 to notify Lender 1 simultaneously with the execution of the charge and its registration.

WHERE THERE IS AN OBLIGATION TO MAKE A FURTHER ADVANCE

7.31 Thirdly, the proprietor of a registered charge may make further advances on the security of its charge that will rank in priority to a subsequent charge if the advance was made in pursuance of an obligation and that obligation was entered in the register at the time of the creation of the subsequent charge in accordance with rules.[90] This replicates the effect of section 30(3) of the Land Registration Act 1925, except that it applies in respect of *any* subsequent charge and not merely a registered charge.[91]

FURTHER ADVANCES UP TO A MAXIMUM AMOUNT

7.32 The fourth means by which further advances may be secured is new.[92] The proprietor of a registered charge may make further advances on the security of its charge that will rank in priority to a subsequent charge if the parties to the charge have agreed a maximum amount for which the charge is security and, at the time of the creation of the subsequent charge, the agreement was entered in the register in accordance with rules.[93]

7.33 The manner in which this method will work can best be illustrated by an example.

> X charges her land to Y to secure an overdraft up to a maximum figure of £100,000. A note is made on the register to this effect. At a time when X is indebted to Y for £50,000, X creates a second charge in favour of Z for the sum of £50,000. X then borrows a further £20,000 from Y. As regards the sum of £20,000 borrowed by X from Y, Y's charge takes priority over Z's because it is within the maximum amount for which it is security.

7.34 The maximum sum is necessarily an inclusive sum that must include all principal, interests and costs due under the mortgage. It will not include the costs of enforcing the security which are additional but which the mortgagee is entitled nonetheless to deduct from the proceeds of sale.[94] Once the maximum sum was

---

[89] Under Land Registration Act 1925, s 30(2), it is only where the *registrar* fails to serve notice under s 30(1) or the notice is lost in the post, that there is any liability to pay indemnity to Lender 1, if it suffers loss in consequence.

[90] Cl 49(3).

[91] See above, para 7.28. For this shortcoming in Land Registration Act 1925, s 30(3), see above, para 7.22.

[92] Although we know of no authority in point, we have assumed that the result that it achieves cannot be achieved under the present law.

[93] Cl 49(4).

[94] Cf Law of Property Act 1925, s 105 (the mortgagee is entitled to apply the proceeds of sale in payment of costs, charges and expenses properly incurred as incident to the sale or attempted sale).

reached, in order to secure any advances above that ceiling, the parties would either have to create a new charge or increase the maximum sum for which the charge was security. If a further charge had been created and registered in the interim, it would necessarily take priority over the new charge or for the additional sums secured under the original charge.

7.35 The justification for having a charge that secures a maximum security sum is that any intending Lender 2 will know from the amount of the security sum what the maximum liability of the borrower will be under the charge (apart from the costs of enforcement, the likely magnitude of which lenders can generally assess). This enables Lender 2 to make a better evaluation as to whether the property is good security for the proposed second charge. This form of charge will therefore be advantageous to secondary lenders. Representatives of the primary lenders have objected to this new form of charge.[95] They point to the difficulty of fixing a maximum sum in advance to cover (for example) a charge to secure an overdrawn current account. Lenders would tend to fix the maximum sum at a much higher level than the likely borrowings might appear to warrant to be sure that they were adequately secured. However, while acknowledging these difficulties, there might be forms of lending for which this form of charge is ideal. An example might be where a development is to be funded by a series of agreed advances secured on the land to be developed. In such a case it might well be possible to calculate the maximum potential liabilities with some accuracy at the outset. We understand that this form of securing further advances is used in certain other countries, such as Sweden. We would stress that this fourth method of securing further advances is no more than an option. No lender is forced to adopt it and it has the considerable merit of simplicity.

7.36 There may be types of secured lending for which this new form of registered charge should not be available at all, or only subject to specified conditions.[96] Provision can be made to this effect by rules made under the Bill.[97]

Statutory charges

7.37 There are numerous charges that are imposed on land by statute. For the most part, no special rules are required to deal with the priority of such charges over registered land as against other charges. They are subject to the normal rules of priority *inter se*[98] and as to further advances that we have explained in this Part. In two cases, however, special provision is required. We explain these below.[99]

---

[95] The representatives of the secondary lending industry took the opposite view.

[96] One possible example — and it should be emphasised that this is only a possible example given by way of illustration — might be a regulated agreement secured by a land mortgage under the Consumer Credit Act 1974.

[97] Cl 49(5).

[98] Some statutory charges can be registered as registered charges. As such they are subject to the rules of priority explained above, paras 7.13 and following. Other charges are subject to the usual rule of priority that is determined by the date of their creation: see above, para 7.17.

[99] See paras 7.39 and 7.42 respectively.

Types of statutory charge

7.38 We have examined a number of provisions which permit or require the creation of statutory charges, though we would certainly not claim to have discovered all of them by any means. However, as might be expected, such charges fall into two main categories, namely—

(1) those which make express provision as to the priority of the charge in relation to any other charges, namely—

(a) those which provide that the statutory charge is to have priority over existing charges (though in practice this is not often insisted upon);[100] and

(b) those which state that the charge is to take subject to certain specified prior charges or have a particular priority;[101] and

(2) those which say nothing at all about such priority.[102]

By far the most important form of statutory charges in terms of the numbers that are made are charging orders,[103] which come within (2).

Overriding statutory charges

7.39 Where a statutory charge has, according to its terms, priority over any pre-existing charge or charges (the situation in paragraph 7.38(1)(a) above), it creates obvious risks for those pre-existing chargees. They may, for example, make further advances to the chargor, oblivious of the fact that the security for any such advance may have been eroded or extinguished because of the statutory charge. As that statutory charge has overriding priority, the chargee is under no obligation to notify existing chargees. The Bill includes two provisions that will go some way to alleviate this problem.

7.40 First, on the registration of a statutory charge that overrides an existing charge that is entered on the register or is protected by a restriction[104] or caution,[105] the

---

[100] The only two examples of which we are aware are Legal Aid Act 1988, s 16(6), and Access to Justice Act 1999, s 10(7) (which, when it is brought into force, will replace s 16(6) of the 1988 Act).

[101] Such as Housing Act 1985, ss 36, 156; Agricultural Holdings Act 1986, s 87(6); Housing Act 1988, Schedule 11, para 2; Housing Act 1996, s 12.

[102] Such as Landlord and Tenant Act 1927, Schedule 1; Health and Social Services and Social Security Adjudications Act 1983, s 22; Housing Act 1985, Schedule 10, para 7; Environmental Protection Act 1990, s 78P; Housing Grants, Construction and Regeneration Act 1996, s 88.

[103] Whether made under the Charging Orders Act 1979, or under other statutes that impose charging orders, such as Solicitors Act 1974, s 73; Highways Act 1980, s 212; Criminal Justice Act 1988, s 78; Child Support Act 1991, s 36; Local Government (Finance) Act 1992, Schedule 4, para 11; Drug Trafficking Act 1994, s 27.

[104] As in the case of a charging order over a beneficial interest under a trust of land affecting the property: see Cl 42(1)(c), (4); above, para 6.43.

registrar is under a duty to give notice about the creation of that charge to such persons as rules provide[106] — who will, of course, be those having some form of charge or sub-charge over the registered land. This is an important new duty and will, it is hoped, meet a concern that has been expressed to us by the lending industry. Secondly, indemnity is payable for any loss suffered as a result of a failure by the registrar to perform this duty.[107]

7.41 The effect of overriding statutory charges is by no means certain. In particular, it is unclear whether such charges do in fact take priority over existing charges.[108] This is recognised by the Land Registration Rules 1925, which deliberately leave the matter for determination on an *ad hoc* basis.[109] The resolution of these uncertainties necessarily lies outside the scope of the present Bill and restricts what can be done in relation to them. It is therefore likely that rules made under the Bill will follow the present model and will adopt a similar *ad hoc* approach, at least until such time as the status of such charges receives judicial clarification.

Charges which are local land charges

7.42 Local land charges take effect as overriding interests and are, therefore, binding on any disponee of registered land.[110] Such charges are normally registered in the local land charges register kept by the relevant local authority. Some local land charges are charges on land to secure the payment of money. These include—

(1) a charge by a street works authority for the cost of executing street works;[111] and

(2) a charge to recover expenses incurred by a local authority because of non-compliance with a repair notice.[112]

Although such charges are binding on disponees as overriding interests, they are not presently enforceable as charges unless registered as registered charges.[113] In

---

[105] Although cautions are prospectively abolished by the Bill, existing cautions will remain on the register: see Schedule 12, para 2(3).

[106] Cl 50.

[107] Schedule 8, para 1(1)(h); see below, para 10.38.

[108] If they do, questions may arise as to their compatibility with Article 1 of the First Protocol of the European Convention on Human Rights (protection of property). For Article 1 of the First Protocol, see below, para 8.89.

[109] See rr 157, 158. Under r 158, the issue of priority is to be resolved by the registrar "if and when it becomes important". In *Brickdale & Stewart-Wallace's Land Registration Act, 1925* (4th ed 1939), p 404, it is stated in relation to r 158, that "the reason for thus postponing the question of priority appears to be that the charges referred to are often of comparatively small importance, and are nearly always terminable, while the questions arising on the construction of the statutes present considerable difficulty". The same is true 62 years later.

[110] See Schedule 3, para 6; below, paras 8.29, 8.48.

[111] Highways Act 1980, s 212.

[112] Housing Act 1985, s 193; Schedule 10.

[113] See Land Registration Act 1925, s 70(1)(i).

the Consultative Document, we recommended that this rule should continue,[114] and most of those who responded on the point agreed. As we have explained above, the proprietor of a registered charge has the powers of a legal mortgagee.[115] In principle, under a land registration system, it is desirable that, if any person has dispositive powers over registered land, that fact should be apparent on the face of the register.[116] The Bill therefore provides that a charge over registered land which is a local land charge may only be realised if the title to the charge is registered.[117]

MISCELLANEOUS

Application of proceeds of sale

7.43   A mortgagee who exercises its power of sale holds the proceeds of sale in trust and is required to apply them in discharge of—

(1)   any incumbrance having priority over his charge;

(2)   the costs of the sale; and

(3)   the moneys due to him under the charge.[118]

The residue is held in trust for and must be paid to "the person entitled to the mortgaged property"[119] which may, of course, be a subsequent chargee. Where title is unregistered, it is clear that the mortgagee holds the surplus on trust for any subsequent mortgagee of whose mortgage it has notice, actual, constructive or imputed.[120] Puisne mortgages of unregistered land, although legal, are registrable as land charges.[121] As the registration of a land charge constitutes actual notice of that charge,[122] a mortgagee of unregistered land having a surplus in his hands will in practice search the land charges register to ascertain if there are any subsequent chargees. The position in relation to registered land is not presently so clear. Registration does not constitute notice and the chargee should presumably pay any surplus to the chargor unless it has been notified of the existence of a subsequent charge.[123] As we have explained,[124] one the goals of the Bill is to try to make the register as complete a record of title as possible. It is consistent with that

---

[114]   Law Com No 254, para 5.83.

[115]   See para 7.3.

[116]   See Law Com No 254, para 5.82.

[117]   Cl 55. See above, para 4.29.

[118]   Law of Property Act 1925, s 105.

[119]   *Ibid.* Interpreted literally, this would mean the buyer. The phrase does, of course, mean the person who was entitled to the mortgaged property immediately before it was sold. See *Megarry & Wade's Law of Real Property* (6th edition 2000), 19-063, n 49.

[120]   See, *eg, West London Commercial Bank v Reliance Permanent Building Society* (1885) 29 ChD 954.

[121]   Land Charges Act 1972, s 2(4)(i) (Class C(i) land charges).

[122]   Law of Property Act 1925, s 198(1).

[123]   See *Megarry & Wade's Law of Real Property* (6th edition 2000), 19-064.

[124]   See above, para 1.5.

goal that a chargee should look to the register to ascertain whether there are any other chargees before it pays over any surplus after sale to the chargor, particularly as a search of the register is a quick, simple and cheap procedure. The Bill therefore provides that as regards the chargee's duties in relation to the proceeds of sale of registered land, "a person shall be taken to have notice of anything in the register".[125] The chargee must, therefore, search the register before paying over any surplus in its hands.

Consolidation

7.44 Consolidation has been described as "the right of a person in whom two or more mortgages are vested to refuse to allow one mortgage to be redeemed unless the other or others are also redeemed".[126] The standard mortgage terms of many lending institutions make provision by which the chargor shall not be entitled to redeem a charge without at the same time redeeming every other security on any other property for the time being charged to the chargee.

7.45 Consolidation in relation to registered land is presently dealt with by rule 154 of the Land Registration Rules 1925. That provides a procedure by which the right to consolidate will, in certain circumstances, be noted against the titles affected.[127] Under the Bill, there is a rule-making power to make provision about entry in the register of a right of consolidation in relation to a registered charge.[128]

Power to give receipts

7.46 Clause 56 is concerned with the power to give a valid receipt for the money secured by a charge where that charge is registered in the names of two or more proprietors. It provides that a valid receipt may be given in such circumstances by—

   (1) the registered proprietors;

   (2) the survivor or survivors of the registered proprietors; or

   (3) the personal representatives of the last survivor of the registered proprietors.

This Clause replicates in rather simpler terms the effect of section 32 of the Land Registration Act 1925.[129]

---

[125] Cl 54.

[126] *Megarry & Wade's Law of Real Property* (6th edition 2000), 19-096.

[127] This presently requires the production to the registrar of the charge certificates of the titles affected. Charge certificates are abolished under the Bill: see below, para 9.89.

[128] Cl 57. The rules will be land registration rules and will be required to be laid before Parliament only. see Cls 125, 129(1).

[129] There is a good deal of learning behind Land Registration Act 1925, s 32, but it is unnecessary for present purposes to explain it.

PART VIII
OVERRIDING INTERESTS

INTRODUCTION

8.1 We have explained that one of the principal objectives of the Bill is to create a faster and simpler conveyancing system, electronically based, under which it is possible to investigate title to the land almost entirely on-line with the bare minimum of additional enquiries.[1] A major obstacle to achieving that goal is the existence of a category of interests in registered land that are not on the register but which will, nonetheless, bind any person who acquires an interest in the land.[2] These unregistered interests have been known as overriding interests since the enactment of the Land Registration Act 1925.[3] To achieve the objective mentioned at the beginning of this paragraph, the Bill seeks to minimise the circumstances in which new overriding interests can arise and also to provide mechanisms to ensure that existing overriding interests are brought on to the register wherever possible.

8.2 In this Part therefore, we explain the provisions of the Bill relating to overriding interests. We begin with an analysis of the nature of overriding interests.[4] Secondly, we examine the estates, rights and interests which, under the Bill, take effect as overriding interests and in what circumstances.[5] Thirdly, we explain how, as a result of the provisions of the Bill, the circumstances in which a proprietary right can exist as an overriding interest will be significantly reduced.[6] As regards this third point, it may assist readers if we summarise at the outset the main techniques that we have adopted to achieve this goal. This will enable them to understand better the approach that we have adopted in relation to individual categories of overriding interest.

   (1) Subject to transitional arrangements, certain overriding interests are not replicated but are dealt with in some other way under the Bill.

   (2) The scope of certain existing classes of overriding interests is substantially narrowed for the future.

---

[1] See above, para 1.5.

[2] Cf *Secretary of State for the Environment, Transport and the Regions v Baylis (Gloucester) Ltd* (2000) 80 P & CR 324, 338, where Kim Lewison QC (sitting as a Deputy High Court Judge) said, "[i]t is not in doubt that the purpose of a system of land registration is to promote certainty of title. To achieve that objective it is necessary to keep to a minimum the number of matters which may defeat the title of a registered proprietor".

[3] See particularly Land Registration Act 1925, ss 3(xvi) and 70. The term was not found in the Land Transfer Act 1875.

[4] See below, para 8.3.

[5] See below, para 8.6.

[6] See below, para 8.74.

(3) Some overriding interests will lose their overriding status after a period of 10 years, but those who have the benefit of such interests will be entitled to protect them on the register or the register of cautions without charge during that period.

(4) The introduction of electronic conveyancing will of itself reduce the circumstances in which overriding interests can arise. This is because the Bill makes specific provision by which dispositions of registered land may be required to be made in electronic form and to be registered simultaneously.[7] The consequence of that provision when it is brought into force will be that any express transfer or creation of an interest in registered land to which it applies will have to be registered in the appropriate manner. For the future, this is likely to be the most effective way of limiting the numbers of such interests.

THE NATURE OF OVERRIDING INTERESTS

8.3 Overriding interests are not different in their nature from any other unregistered interests that subsist in relation to registered land. However, for various reasons of policy, they are given a special status in two circumstances, namely—

(1) on first registration, when the estate is vested in the first registered proprietor subject to overriding interests but free from most other interests not entered on the register;[8] and

(2) where a registrable disposition for valuable consideration is completed by registration, when the disponee takes subject to overriding interests but free from most other unregistered interests.[9]

These two situations are intrinsically different. In general, first registration has no dispositionary effect because the first registered proprietor will already have the legal title vested in him or her.[10] Whether or not the first registered proprietor is bound by an interest that can be an overriding interest on first registration will have been determined prior to that date.[11] By contrast, where there is a registrable disposition for valuable consideration, the registration of that disposition is dispositionary and vests the legal title in the disponee. An issue of priority therefore arises at the time of the disposition and whether or not the disponee is

---

[7] Cl 93; below, paras 13.74 and following.

[8] See Cls 11(4)(b); 12(4)(c); above, paras 3.45 and following. For the other unregistered interests to which the registered proprietor takes subject, see above, paras 3.45, 3.51.

[9] See Cls 29(2)(a)(ii), 30(2)(a)(ii); above, para 5.11. For the other unregistered interests to which the registered disponee takes subject, see above, paras 5.11, 5.13.

[10] For a case where it does, see Cls 11(4)(c); 12(4)(d); above, paras 3.45, 3.46, 3.50.

[11] Where first registration is voluntary, the overriding interest may have arisen or been created after the first registered proprietor acquired the land, but before he or she applied for the registration of his or her title. Even where a disposition triggered compulsory first registration (under Cl 4; above, paras 3.22 and following) the interests to which the disponee took subject will have been determined according to the rules of unregistered conveyancing applicable to that disposition.

bound by an interest has to be determined then. This distinction has an effect in some cases on the substantive requirements for what amounts to an overriding interest. For example, the rights of persons in actual occupation constitute an overriding interest both under the present law[12] and under the Bill.[13] However, whether a disponee has made enquiries of a person in actual occupation is irrelevant on first registration because the issue of whether or not the first registered proprietor is bound by the rights of such an occupier will already have been decided.[14] By contrast it *is* material in relation to a registered disposition to decide whether registration vests the legal title in the disponee free of the rights of the occupier or not.[15] If the disponee has made appropriate enquiries prior to the disposition, the occupier is, in effect, estopped from asserting his or her interest.

8.4   The Bill explicitly recognises this distinction. It sets out those unregistered interests which override—

(1)   first registration;[16] and

(2)   registered dispositions.[17]

8.5   Overriding interests are interests which are not registered or protected on the register. Accordingly, they fall to be treated as unregistered land, except where the Bill provides otherwise.[18] It follows that they must be conveyed or disposed of as unregistered land. It also means that, for example, a contract to sell such an overriding interest that was a legal estate would be registrable as a land charge under the provisions of the Land Charges Act 1972,[19] a provision which obviously has no application to dealings with a registered estate. It should be noted that an interest may be overriding in relation to more than one registered estate that subsists simultaneously in the same parcel of land.[20]

UNREGISTERED INTERESTS WHICH MAY BE OVERRIDING: INTRODUCTION

8.6   It is the fact that overriding interests do not appear on the register, yet bind any person who acquires any interest in registered land, that makes them such an

[12]   See Land Registration Act 1925, s 70(1)(g).

[13]   See Schedules 1, para 2; 3, para 2.

[14]   See below, para 8.21.

[15]   See below, para 8.60.

[16]   Schedule 1.

[17]   Schedule 3.

[18]   As it does in relation to priorities: see above, paras 5.6; 5.15.

[19]   Section 2(4)(iv).

[20]   As, for example, where the land is subject to the burden of an easement acquired by prescription that is not noted on the register (and which is therefore an overriding interest), and both the freehold of that property and a 99-year lease of it are registered.

unsatisfactory feature of the system of registered conveyancing.[21] The existence of such rights means that inquiries as to title cannot be confined to a search of the register. We devoted a substantial part of the Consultative Document to a discussion of overriding interests and how their impact might be reduced without causing any disadvantage to those who have the benefit of them.[22] Our conclusion was that interests should *only* have overriding status where protection against buyers was needed, but where it was neither reasonable to expect nor sensible to require any entry on the register.[23] We suggested a number of strategies to ensure that the only overriding interests were those which met these criteria.[24] As we have explained above,[25] the introduction of electronic conveyancing will, of itself, substantially reduce the circumstances in which those criteria are met. As might be anticipated, our proposals attracted a good deal of interest and the responses were lively. However, for the most part they were supported. Where this was not so, or where better solutions were proposed, those contrary or better views have been adopted. In view of the extensive discussion of the issues in the Consultative Document, it is only necessary in the present Report to explain the provisions of the Bill and the thinking behind them.

8.7 We explain the categories of unregistered interests which, under the Bill, will override—

(1) first registration;[26] and

(2) registered dispositions.[27]

UNREGISTERED INTERESTS WHICH OVERRIDE FIRST REGISTRATION

Introduction

8.8 In Part III of this Report,[28] we explained that, under the Bill, when a person is registered as first registered proprietor, he or she takes the estate subject to certain interests, including "interests the burden of which is entered on the register" and "interests the burden of which is not so entered, but which fall within any of the paragraphs of Schedule 1".[29] Schedule 1 lists fourteen such overriding interests.

---

[21] As we explained in the Consultative Document, "[b]ecause such rights subsist and operate outside the register, they are an inevitable source of tension within the land registration system": Law Com No 254, para 4.1.

[22] See Law Com No 254, Parts IV, V.

[23] Law Com No 254, para 4.17.

[24] See Law Com No 254, paras 4.23—4.39.

[25] See para 8.2.

[26] See below, para 8.8.

[27] See below, para 8.47.

[28] See above, para 3.45.

[29] Cl 11(4)(a) and (b) respectively.

There is also a fifteenth, under Clause 90,[30] which takes effect as if it were included in Schedule 1. We explain each of the fifteen overriding interests in turn.

Short leases

8.9   Under the Bill, a leasehold estate granted for a term not exceeding seven years from the date of the grant, overrides first registration.[31] The principle that short leases (which under the present legislation means leases granted for 21 years or less) should take effect as overriding interests is presently embodied in section 70(1)(k) of the Land Registration Act 1925. Such leases are granted and assigned as unregistered interests in accordance with the principles of unregistered conveyancing. The policy behind this class of overriding interest has been to keep the register free of such leases because of their short duration and the risk that they would clutter the register. The introduction of electronic conveyancing will, however, make it possible to register shorter leases very easily and to ensure that they are removed on expiry. As we have explained,[32] it is likely that, once it is possible to grant and assign leases electronically, the Lord Chancellor may, in exercise of his powers, already described,[33] seek views on a further reduction of the period of seven years that will initially apply under the Bill.[34]

8.10   There are, however, three situations in which a lease cannot be an overriding interest even if it is granted for seven years or less.[35] In each case, the grant of such a lease is required to be completed by the registration of the estate with its own title.[36] They are as follows

(1)   a reversionary lease granted to take effect in possession more than three months after the date of the grant of the lease;

(2)   a lease granted out of an unregistered legal estate under the right to buy provisions of Part V of the Housing Act 1985;[37] and

(3)   a lease granted by a private sector landlord out of an unregistered legal estate to a person who was formerly a secure tenant and has a preserved right to buy.[38]

---

[30]   PPP leases relating to transport in London: see below, para 8.11.

[31]   Schedule 1, para 1.

[32]   See para 3.17.

[33]   See Cl 116(1); above, para 3.30.

[34]   The obvious period for registrable leases would be those exceeding 3 years, which are required to be made by deed: see Law of Property Act 1925, ss 52(1), (2)(d); 54(2).

[35]   Schedule 1, para 1.

[36]   See Clause 4(1)(d)—(f); above, paras 3.32—3.34. Where such a lease exists, a notice in respect of the burden of it should be entered on the register of the title out of which it has been granted, as and when that title itself comes to be registered.

[37]   For a secure tenant's right to buy, see Housing Act 1985, s 118. The tenant is entitled to a lease if the landlord does not own the freehold, or if the dwelling-house is a flat.

[38]   For the preserved right to buy, see Housing Act 1985, ss 171A—171H.

Only the first of these exceptions involves any change in the present law: the second and third already exist.[39] The reason for the first exception is, as we have explained, because reversionary leases may be very difficult to discover.[40]

PPP Leases

8.11 PPP leases will arise out of the arrangements for the future running of the London underground railway. Under the Greater London Authority Act 1999, provision is made for London Regional Transport, Transport for London or any of their subsidiaries to enter into public-private partnership agreements — "PPP agreements" — with a third party, for "the provision, construction, renewal, or improvement... of a railway or proposed railway" and for its maintenance.[41] The railways in question are the London underground network. The Act contains provisions that are intended to prevent the disposal of "key system assets" — those assets that are needed to run the railways.[42] Both the circumstances in which, and the persons to whom, such assets can be transferred, are severely limited.[43] The intention is that, when any such PPP agreement terminates, the assets that are required to run the particular railway line will be available to the relevant public authority, so that rail services are not disrupted. The 1999 Act makes provision for the grant of PPP leases of any real property that may be comprised in a PPP agreement.[44] These leases will include underground railway lines, stations and other installations. The normal rules that apply to protect tenants, such as the security of tenure given to business leases under Part II of the Landlord and Tenant Act 1954, are all disapplied, thereby ensuring that the land can be recovered as soon as any PPP lease determines.[45] It is envisaged that such leases will be granted for a period of 30 years.

8.12 The 1999 Act makes specific provision as to land registration and PPP leases.[46] The effect of these provisions is that PPP leases—

(1) do not trigger first registration when granted;[47]

(2) are not registrable dispositions but take effect as if they were;[48]

(3) take effect as overriding interests; and

---

[39] See Housing Act 1985, ss 154(6), (7); 171G; Schedule 9A, para 3. It is obviously sensible to set out the exceptions on the face of the Land Registration Bill, where they are likely to be more accessible.

[40] See above, para 3.32.

[41] Greater London Authority Act 1999, s 210.

[42] *Ibid*, ss 213, 214, 216.

[43] *Ibid*, s 217.

[44] *Ibid*, s 218.

[45] See *ibid*, s 218(4), (5).

[46] *Ibid*, s 219. The section amends the Land Registration Act 1925.

[47] See above, paras 3.13, 3.30.

[48] See above, para 4.22.

(4)   are incapable of substantive registration.[49]

Our present concern is with (3). The 1999 Act adds a new class of overriding interest by inserting a new section 70(1)(kk) into the Land Registration Act 1925 in respect of PPP leases.[50]

8.13   The reason for the overriding status of PPP leases is as follows. Such leases will be "key system assets" and, as such, will only be transferable within very narrow limits.[51] They are not, therefore, likely to be the subject of regular dealings. In practice, therefore, the principal justification for registering them would be to enable their existence and extent to be ascertained by any person dealing with land under which such lines and installations existed. However, that justification is outweighed by other factors. At present, some parts of the London underground railway network are registered, but other parts are not.

(1)   As regards those parts of the network that are unregistered, there would be serious practical difficulties in preparing the necessary maps for the purposes of registration.[52] The amount of work and the difficulties and disputes to which the process of registering such leases would be likely to give rise would be wholly out of proportion to the benefits to be conferred from so doing.

(2)   Even where a section of the network has been registered as a freehold estate, there could be considerable difficulties in identifying those parts that were to be leased. The patterns of registration will not coincide with the leasing arrangements.

(3)   It would not be practicable to register leases to the extent that the freehold title is registered. Leases will inevitably include a mix of land that is registered and unregistered. In the interests of uniformity, it is simplest that all leases should be treated in the same way and no entries made in respect of them in the register.

For these reasons, and with some reluctance on the part of the Law Commission, the Bill therefore preserves the overriding status of PPP leases.[53] It should, however, be stressed that such leases are of a wholly exceptional character. As will be apparent from what has been said above,[54] one of the principal aims of the Bill is to eliminate overriding interests as far as is possible. The creation of new categories of overriding interest is at variance with that aim and can only be justified in the most extreme cases.

---

[49]   See above, para 6.16.

[50]   Greater London Authority Act 1999, s 219(7)(a). This category of overriding interest had not been created at the time of the Consultative Document.

[51]   See above, para 8.11.

[52]   Compare rights to coal, below, para 8.32, where similar considerations apply.

[53]   Cl 90(5).

[54]   See paras 8.1, 8.2.

Interests of persons in actual occupation

8.14   The Bill provides that, subject to one exception, an interest belonging to a person in actual occupation, so far as relating to land of which he or she is in actual occupation, overrides first registration.[55] The exception is an interest under a settlement under the Settled Land Act 1925.[56] A person is only to be regarded as in actual occupation of land for these purposes if he or she, or his or her agent or employee, is physically present there.[57] As we explain below, this provision necessarily differs in a number of respects from the equivalent paragraph that applies in relation to registered dispositions.[58]

8.15   The comparable provision of the Land Registration Act 1925, the notorious and much-litigated section 70(1)(g), provides that—

> the rights of every person in actual occupation of the land or in receipt
> of the rents and profits thereof, save where enquiry is made of such
> person and the rights are not disclosed

are to take effect as overriding interests. In the Consultative Document, we acknowledged that "any proposal which we may make in relation to this paragraph will be controversial because it is a provision that has both strong supporters and equally vocal detractors".[59] In fact, most of the proposals that we made were supported on consultation. Only those recommendations that are relevant to the overriding status of occupiers' rights on first registration are discussed here. Those that apply exclusively to registered dispositions are explained in that context.[60]

8.16   First, we recommended the retention of the overriding status of occupiers' rights[61] and this was supported by all but one of those who responded to the proposal.[62] As we have explained above,[63] this is duly reflected in the Bill. The thinking behind our recommendation was set out in the Consultative Document,[64] but as it

[55]   Schedule 1, para 2(1).

[56]   *Ibid*, para 2(1). There are some additional exceptions under Cl 87(3). None of the following is capable of falling within Schedule 1, para 2: a pending land action, a writ or order affecting land issued or made by any court for the purpose of enforcing a judgment or recognisance, an order appointing a receiver or a sequestrator of land or a deed of arrangement. For these rights, see above, paras 6.59 and following. There is no authority of which we are aware as to whether any of these rights could be protected by actual occupation under the present law. However, given both the unusual nature of such rights and our objective of reducing the numbers of overriding interests, it seems in principle desirable that they should be protected in the appropriate way on the register.

[57]   Schedule 1, para 2(2).

[58]   See paras 8.54 and following.

[59]   Law Com No 254, para 5.56.

[60]   See below, paras 8.54 and following.

[61]   See Law Com No 254, paras 5.61, 5.62.

[62]   The dissentient was the Society of Public Teachers of Law.

[63]   See para 8.14.

[64]   Law Com No 254, para 5.61.

was primarily concerned with interests that override registered dispositions rather than first registration, we explain it in that context.[65] However, even in relation to first registration, there is a case for protecting the rights of those who are in actual occupation. Such persons will often not have appreciated the need to take further steps to protect their rights against buyers by lodging a caution against first registration. This is particularly so in relation to informally created rights.[66]

8.17 Secondly, we recommended that, where there was a settlement for the purposes of the Settled Land Act 1925, the rights of a beneficiary who was in actual occupation should be capable of being an overriding interest[67] and not, as now, merely a minor interest.[68] This was the one recommendation that we made in relation to this paragraph that was not supported on consultation. Very few readers responded to the point, but of those who did, a majority opposed the proposal. As a result of the Trusts of Land and Appointment of Trustees Act 1996, it ceased to be possible to create new settlements under the Settled Land Act 1925 after 1996.[69] This is, therefore, an issue of rapidly diminishing importance. Settlements of registered land that were expressly created before 1997 should have been protected by the entry of the prescribed restrictions on the register.[70] It is, therefore, unlikely that any substantial hardship will be caused by the abandonment of this recommendation. Accordingly, the Bill retains the present exception by which a beneficiary under a settlement cannot protect his or her interest by virtue of his or her actual occupation of the settled land.[71]

8.18 Thirdly, we recommended the removal of overriding status for the rights of persons who were not in actual occupation but were in receipt of the rents and profits of the land.[72] This proposal was, as we anticipated, somewhat contentious, but was still supported by a substantial majority of those who responded to the point on consultation. It is duly reflected in the Bill, which confines the protection of this class of overriding interest to those in actual occupation.[73] It should be noted that the first registration of a leasehold estate in circumstances where the superior titles are not themselves registered and were not deduced to the registrar

---

[65] See below, para 8.53.

[66] Where an occupier of unregistered land has an interest that can be protected by the entry of a land charge under the Land Charges Act 1972, it should be registered. He or she cannot protect that interest against a purchaser merely by virtue of his or her actual occupation of that land: see below, para 8.57.

[67] Law Com No 254, para 5.63.

[68] See Land Registration Act 1925, s 86(2). The rights of beneficiaries entitled under a trust of land can be protected as overriding interests under s 70(1)(g).

[69] Trusts of Land and Appointment of Trustees Act 1996, s 2(1). This is subject to a very limited exception contained in s 2(2).

[70] See Land Registration Rules 1925, rr 56—58.

[71] See above, para 8.14.

[72] Law Com No 254, paras 5.64—5.68. There were transitional recommendations in relation to existing overriding interests. These are not relevant to the position on first registration and are explained in the context of registered dispositions: see below, para 8.64.

[73] See above, para 8.14.

on that first registration, will be reflected in the class of title which the registrar gives to that leasehold estate.[74] Usually, the lease will be registered with good leasehold title.[75] This means that, in any subsequent dealings with that leasehold estate, any disponee will necessarily be alerted to the fact that there are one or more superior titles that are not registered.

8.19 Fourthly, we recommended that "where someone is in actual occupation of part of the land but they have rights over the whole of the land purchased, their rights protected by actual occupation should be confined to the part which they occupy".[76] This recommendation was accepted by all those who commented on it, with no objectors and, once again, it is reflected in the Bill.[77] We have more to say about this limitation on the rights of occupiers. However, as it arises in the context of overriding interests and registered dispositions, it is addressed there.[78]

8.20 There are three points about the provision in the Bill[79] that require explanation. First, it enables a person in actual occupation to protect an "interest" which that person had at the time of first registration. We explain elsewhere in this Report what constitutes an "interest" for these purposes.[80]

8.21 Secondly, the provision in the Bill does not replicate the words "save where enquiry is made of such person and the rights are not disclosed" that are found in section 70(1)(g) of the Land Registration Act 1925. This is because such words can have no relevance to overriding interests on first registration. As we have explained above,[81] the process of first registration normally has no effect on the priority of an overriding interest as against the first registered proprietor. There is, therefore, no occasion on which any inquiry of the occupier could be made and no issue of priority to which such an inquiry would be relevant.[82] For the same reason, there is no requirement that the person's occupation should be obvious on a reasonable inspection of the land, as there is under the Bill in relation to the rights of occupiers in relation to registered dispositions.[83]

8.22 Thirdly, the Bill provides some guidance as to the meaning of "actual occupation".[84] A person is only to be regarded as being in actual occupation of land if he or she, or his or her agent or employee, is physically present there. This

---

[74] See Cl 10; above, para 3.44.

[75] For the effect of registration with good leasehold title, see Cl 12(6); above, para 3.51.

[76] Law Com No 254, para 5.70.

[77] See above, para 8.14.

[78] See below, para 8.55.

[79] That is, Schedule 1, para 2.

[80] See Cl 129(3)(b); above, para 5.5.

[81] See para 8.3.

[82] This must be true in relation to Land Registration Act 1925, s 70(1)(g), but the point has never been articulated.

[83] See below, para 8.61.

[84] Schedule 1, para 2(2).

reflects the way in which the concept of "actual occupation" under section 70(1)(g) of the Land Registration Act 1925 has been judicially interpreted. The requirement of physical presence means that a mere legal entitlement to occupy will not suffice.[85] Thus, a person who has merely contracted to take a lease or licence of a property, but has not yet entered into possession of it, will not be in actual occupation. Obviously, as under the present law, what constitutes physical presence will depend upon "the nature and state of the property in question".[86] Actual occupation does not require residence,[87] and the nature of the property may indeed be such that residence is impossible.[88] In the absence of residence, a person having an interest in the property may establish physical presence by his or her user of the premises.[89] The Bill confirms the view that the physical presence can be that of an agent or employee rather than of the person having the interest.[90]

Legal easements and *profits à prendre*

8.23 Under the Bill, a *legal* easement or *profit à prendre* may override first registration.[91] The provisions that presently govern the overriding status of easements and *profits à prendre* are found in section 70(1)(a) of the Land Registration Act 1925 and rule 258 of the Land Registration Rules 1925. In the Consultative Document, we described these provisions as being "amongst the most unsatisfactory" in the legislation that governs land registration.[92] We therefore made a substantial number of recommendations that were intended to limit the circumstances in which easements and *profits à prendre* could be overriding interests.[93] These were supported by a substantial majority of those who responded to them on consultation.

8.24 One of these recommendations is relevant to the overriding status of such rights on first registration, namely that it should no longer be possible for *equitable* easements to take effect as overriding interests.[94] Under the present law, equitable easements that are openly exercised and enjoyed by the dominant owner as

---

[85] "…what is required is physical presence, not some entitlement at law": *Williams & Glyn's Bank Ltd v Boland* [1981] AC 487, 505, *per* Lord Wilberforce.

[86] *Lloyds Bank Plc v Rosset* [1989] Ch 350, 377, *per* Nicholls LJ.

[87] *Ibid.*

[88] As in *Kling v Keston Properties Ltd* (1983) 49 P & CR 212 (garage).

[89] *Ibid,* at 219. A person does not cease to be in actual occupation merely because he or she has been temporarily excluded, especially when that exclusion is wrongful: see *Chhokar v Chhokar* [1984] FLR 313.

[90] See *Lloyds Bank Plc v Rosset*, above.

[91] Schedule 1, para 3.

[92] Law Com No 254, para 5.2.

[93] See Law Com 254, paras 5.2—5.24.

[94] *Ibid*, para 5.18.

appurtenant to his or her land can take effect as overriding interests.[95] That will not be so under the Bill. We explained in the Consultative Document[96] that—

(1) equitable easements[97] over unregistered land should be protected by registering them as Class D(iii) land charges under the Land Charges Act 1972;[98]

(2) if they are not so protected, they are not binding on a purchaser of a legal estate in the servient land for money or money's worth;[99] and

(3) the position of such easements should not be improved on first registration by elevating their status to overriding interests that would bind any person who thereafter acquired the registered estate (as would appear to be the case under the present law).

8.25 Although legal easements and *profits à prendre* can take effect as overriding interests on first registration, it is hoped that in future few will. As we explain more fully below,[100] the Bill contains rule-making powers to ensure that, so far as possible, overriding interests are disclosed to the registrar on first registration so that they can be entered on the register.[101] The Bill also contains provisions that substantially restrict the circumstances in which unregistered easements and *profits à prendre* can override registered dispositions. These are explained below.[102]

Customary and public rights

8.26 Both customary and public rights are to remain overriding interests under the Bill.[103] They are presently overriding interests by virtue of section 70(1)(a) of the Land Registration Act 1925. We recommended their retention in the Consultative Document[104] and our proposals were unanimously supported on consultation. Such rights are comparatively common and, when they come to light on an application for first registration, they will continue to be noted on the register as they are now.

8.27 In relation to customary rights, we explained that the term had two meanings, namely—

---

[95] *Celsteel Ltd v Alton House Holdings Ltd* [1985] 1 WLR 204, 291—221; *Thatcher v Douglas* (1996) 146 NLJ 282.

[96] Law Com No 254, para 5.18.

[97] Which, for these purposes, includes equitable *profits à prendre*.

[98] Section 2(5)(iii).

[99] Land Charges Act 1972, s 4(6).

[100] See para 8.91.

[101] See Cl 71(a).

[102] See para 8.67.

[103] Schedule 1, paras 4, 5.

[104] See Law Com No 254, paras 5.25—5.31.

(1)   rights which had their origins in tenure and which were abolished as part of the 1925 property reforms; and

(2)   rights which were enjoyed by all or some of inhabitants of a particular locality, many of which still survive.[105]

The term "customary rights" in the Bill necessarily refers to the latter.

8.28   In the Consultative Document,[106] we noted that in *Overseas Investment Services Ltd v Simcobuild Construction Ltd*,[107] the Court of Appeal had accepted that, for the purposes of section 70(1)(a) of the Land Registration Act 1925, public rights were—

(1)   those which were "exercisable by anyone, whether he owns land or not, merely by virtue of the general law";[108] and

(2)   rights presently exercisable but not ones that might become exercisable in future.[109]

Although in the Consultative Document we proposed that the term "public rights" should be defined in the terms set out above, we have, on reflection, decided that it is unnecessary. The term is to have the meaning which the courts have now given it.[110]

Local land charges

8.29   A local land charge overrides first registration.[111] This replicates the effect of section 70(1)(i) of the Land Registration Act 1925 and implements proposals made in the Consultative Document.[112] The effect of local land charges is governed by the Local Land Charges Act 1975.[113] This Act makes provision—

---

[105]   Law Com No 254, paras 5.26, 5.27. As we explained in para 5.26, the wording of Land Registration Act 1925, s 70(1)(a) could be read to mean only the first of these, though it should plainly include the second.

[106]   Law Com No 254, para 5.30.

[107]   (1995) 70 P & CR 322.

[108]   For this definition, see *Megarry & Wade's Law of Real Property* (6th ed 2000), 18-064.

[109]   The trial judge, Judge Colyer QC, had taken a wider view, namely that public rights were rights of a public nature, and included not only present rights, but rights that would become exercisable in future.

[110]   The rights can be extensive and have been held to include a fee simple vested in a highway authority in respect of a dedicated highway: see *Secretary of State for the Environment, Transport and the Regions v Baylis (Gloucester) Ltd* (2000) 80 P & CR 324.

[111]   Schedule 1, para 6.

[112]   See Law Com No 254, paras 5.80—5.83. The proposals were supported by the great majority of those who responded.

[113]   What does and does not constitute a "local land charge" is defined by Local Land Charges Act 1975, ss 1, 2.

(1)   for the registration of local land charges by local authorities;[114]

(2)   for local land charges to be binding even if not so registered;[115] and

(3)   for compensation for any loss suffered by a person as a consequence of such non-registration.[116]

In other words, local land charges operate under a regime that is quite distinct from the system of land registration. The overriding status of local land charges recognises that they are governed by a parallel regime. It should be noted, however, that local land charge searches are being computerised, along with other local searches.[117] This development is taking place in tandem with the system of electronic conveyancing by which land can be transferred and rights in land created electronically.[118]

8.30   For reasons that we have explained in Part VII of this Report,[119] under the Bill,[120] as under the present law,[121] a local land charge that secures the payment of money cannot be realised unless it is registered as a registered charge.

Mines and minerals

8.31   The Bill preserves the overriding status of certain mineral rights that is presently found in section 70(1)(l) and (m) of the Land Registration Act 1925. These relate respectively to mineral rights in relation to land, the title to which was registered before 1926, and to interests and rights in coal.

Rights to coal

8.32   The Bill provides that an interest in any coal or coal mine, the rights attached to any such interest and certain other rights in relation to coal[122] all take effect as overriding interests on first registration.[123] As we explained in the Consultative Document,[124] the present provision — section 70(1)(m) of the Land Registration Act 1925 — was inserted by the Coal Industry Act 1994. The overriding status of

---

[114]   *Ibid*, ss 3—5.

[115]   *Ibid*, s 10.

[116]   *Ibid*.

[117]   As part of the National Land Information Service.

[118]   See above, para 2.41.

[119]   See above, para 7.42.

[120]   Cl 55.

[121]   See Land Registration Act 1925, s 70(1)(i).

[122]   Under the Coal Industry Act 1994, ss 38 (rights to withdraw support), 49 (rights to work coal in former copyhold land) and 51 (additional rights in relation to underground land).

[123]   Schedule 1, para 7. At present, the Land Registration Act 1925 defines this category of overriding interest by reference to the Coal Industry Act 1994. By contrast, the Bill defines it directly, with an appropriate consequential repeal in the Coal Industry Act 1994.

[124]   See Law Com No 254, para 5.98.

rights in coal had previously been laid down in a series of statutes on the coal industry.[125] The reason for the overriding status was that it was, in practice, impossible for such rights to or in coal to be registered, given both their extent and complexity.[126] It would, for example, be virtually impossible to prepare the maps that would be required for registration and the cost of so doing would be out of proportion to any possible benefits that might be obtained. In the Consultative Document we recommended the retention of this category of overriding interest[127] and this was unanimously supported by those who responded to the point on consultation. In practice, in present or former coal mining areas, a coal mining search will commonly be made of the Coal Authority using a standard search form.[128] That is likely to provide detailed information about coal mining activities on the land, whether past, present or proposed. It is anticipated that it will be possible to conduct such searches on-line through the National Land Information Service.

Certain mineral rights where the title was registered before 1926

8.33   The reason for the overriding status of certain mineral rights in relation to land where the title was registered prior to 1926 lies in the provisions of the legislation then governing land registration.[129] We explained in the Consultative Document that—

(1)   where land was registered before 1898, *all* mineral rights created before that date take effect as overriding interests because the existence of such rights was not usually recorded on the register; and

(2)   where land was registered after 1897 but before 1926, any mineral rights created before the land was registered take effect as overriding interests for the same reason.[130]

Unfortunately, it is impossible to identify those titles to land that were registered prior to 1926. There is, therefore, little option but to retain the overriding status of such rights and we so recommended in the Consultative Document.[131] This

---

[125]   *Ibid*, para 5.97.

[126]   *Ibid.*

[127]   *Ibid*, para 5.98.

[128]   Law Society Search Form Con29M.

[129]   As we explained in the Consultative Document, para 5.95, n 233, "The Land Transfer Act 1862..., s 9, provided that unless mineral rights were expressly mentioned as being within the description of the land to be registered, they were not included. The Land Transfer Act 1875, s 18(4), provided that transfers of registered land were subject to any third party rights to mines and minerals as what would now be called overriding interests. The Land Transfer Act 1897, Schedule 1, amended s 18(4) of the 1875 Act. Only mineral rights created prior to the registration of the land or the commencement of the 1897 Act (on January 1, 1898) took effect as overriding interests".

[130]   Law Com No 254, para 5.95.

[131]   *Ibid*, para 5.96.

proposal was supported by almost all of those who responded to the issue on consultation.

8.34 The Bill provides accordingly that—

(1) in the case of land the title to which was registered before 1898, the rights to mines and minerals (and incidental rights) created before 1898; and

(2) in the case of land the title to which was registered between 1898 and 1925 inclusive, rights to mines and minerals (and incidental rights) created before the date of registration of title;

take effect as overriding interests on first registration.[132]

Miscellaneous

Introduction

8.35 The Bill groups together five categories of overriding interests under the heading of "miscellaneous". All the rights in question take effect as overriding interests on first registration under the present law. What links them is that—

(1) they are of ancient origin;

(2) they are of an unusual character that a buyer would not normally expect to encounter;

(3) they can be very difficult to discover; and

(4) they may be exceptionally onerous.

8.36 The rights in question are—

(1) franchises;

(2) manorial rights;

(3) crown rents;

(4) certain rights in relation to embankments and sea walls; and

(5) what are commonly called "corn rents".[133]

8.37 Of these rights, (1) and (2) are the most commonly found and can be of considerable value for those who have the benefit of them. As regards the remainder, such rights do still exist but are rare or, in some cases, exceptionally rare. Because all of these five categories of rights still exist and are enforced, their overriding status cannot be abolished at once. In the Consultative Document we

---

[132] Schedule 1, paras 8, 9.

[133] See Land Registration Act 1925, s 70(1)(b)—(e), (j).

concluded that there was *some* risk — though perhaps not a very great one — that to do so might contravene the European Convention on Human Rights.[134]

8.38 As we explain more fully below, the retention of the overriding status of a number of these miscellaneous rights was the subject of adverse comment by a significant minority of those who responded to the relevant part of the Consultative Document.[135] In the light of these comments, we have concluded that they should be protected either on the register of cautions (where the land affected is not presently registered) or on the register of title (where the land is registered). Any intending buyer will be then made aware of them, and can decide whether to buy the land and if so, at what price. However, it is necessary to strike a fair balance between (i) the interests of buyers, and (ii) the interests of the persons having the benefit of such rights who have not had to take any steps to protect them hitherto. Therefore, as we explain below, the Bill makes provision by which—

(1) these rights will cease to have overriding status 10 years after the provisions of the Bill on overriding interests are brought into force; but

(2) those who have the benefit of such rights will be able to protect them—

(a) where the title to the land affected is not yet registered, by the entry of a caution against first registration; and

(b) where the title affected is registered, by an entry in the register;

without charge during that 10-year period.[136]

8.39 In the context of interests that override first registration, if no caution against first registration is entered against the title prior to first registration the position after the 10-year period will be as follows.

(1) Although immediately prior to first registration the legal owner will be bound by such rights because each of them is a legal estate,[137] he or she will hold the estate free of such rights on first registration.[138]

(2) In that case the person having the benefit of the right will be able to seek rectification of the register against the first registered proprietor because the omission from the register is a mistake.[139] However, it may not be possible to obtain rectification of the register if the first registered

---

[134] See Law Com No 254, paras 4.27—4.30. The Article of the Convention in issue is Article 1 of Protocol 1 (right to property). See below, para 8.82.

[135] The greatest criticism was levelled at a category of overriding interests that has since become unenforceable as a result of judicial decision, namely chancel repair liability. See below, para 8.75.

[136] See paras 8.81 and following; and Cl 115.

[137] Cf Law of Property Act 1925, s 1(4).

[138] This follows from Cl 11(4); above, para 3.45.

[139] See Schedule 4, paras 2(1)(a), 5(a); below, paras 10.10, 10.19.

proprietor is a proprietor who is in possession, because of the special protection given by the Bill to such persons.[140]

(3) If rectification is not sought, the right will be at risk as against any person who *subsequently* acquires the registered estate from the first registered proprietor because—

    (a) where that disponee acquired the estate for valuable consideration, he or she will take it free of the unregistered right;[141] and

    (b) where that disponee acquired the estate as a donee, it may not be possible for the person having the right to obtain rectification of the register if the disponee is a proprietor who is in possession, as explained in (2).

Franchises and manorial rights

8.40 The Bill provides that franchises and manorial rights can be overriding interests,[142] as indeed they are under section 70(1)(j) of the Land Registration Act 1925. In the Consultative Document, we recommended the retention of this category of overriding interests and this was supported by most of those who responded. However, we consider that it is reasonable that such rights should be protected on (and therefore apparent from) the register[143] for the following reasons—

(1) Those who enjoy such rights tend to know that they have them.

(2) Such rights can be very valuable and must therefore detract from the value of the land which is subject to them.

(3) Many manorial rights are of a kind that could have been the subject of an express grant, such as a right to fish, shoot or take minerals. It is not apparent to us why their manorial origin should give them a special status when it comes to the issue of whether or not they should be registered.

(4) Similarly, as we explain below,[144] franchises originate in a royal grant, actual or presumed. There is no reason why such rights should not be registered.

For these reasons, we have concluded that the overriding status of franchises and manorial rights should be phased out over a period of 10 years.[145]

8.41 As regards manorial rights, we explained in the Consultative Document that—

---

[140] See Schedule 4, paras 3(2), 6(2); below, paras 10.13—10.17.

[141] See Cl 29; above, para 5.6.

[142] Schedule 1, paras 10, 11.

[143] Cf, above, para 8.6.

[144] See para 8.42.

[145] See further, below, para 8.88.

(1)   the meaning of "manorial rights" was a precise one: the rights in question were listed in some detail in paragraphs 5 and 6 of Schedule 12 of the Law of Property Act 1922,[146] provisions that have since been repealed;[147]

(2)   such rights could no longer be created after 1925;[148] and

(3)   on first registration, the existence of such rights is normally apparent from the deeds so that the burden of them is noted on the register in most cases.[149]

8.42   Franchises arise by royal grant (actual or, in cases of prescription, presumed).[150] Indeed it would still be open to the Crown to grant new franchises.[151] Under the Bill, it will be possible for a franchise holder to apply for the voluntary registration of the franchise with its own title.[152] The grant or reservation by the Crown of a new franchise out of unregistered land is not, however, to be a trigger for compulsory registration.[153] Many existing franchises are of ancient origin. They are analogous to customary rights and some — particularly franchises of market — are of some economic importance. So far as we are aware, the overriding status of franchises has not been a cause of particular difficulty. However, given the potential value of such rights, we consider that they should be protected on the register, whether by registering them with their own titles[154] or by the entry of a notice on the register of the title affected.[155]

Crown rents

8.43   At present "crown rents" take effect as overriding interests under section 70(1)(b) of the Land Registration Act 1925. In the Consultative Document, we explained that we had had some difficulty in ascertaining precisely what Crown rents might be. We concluded that they were—

---

[146] In Law Com No 254, para 5.84, we summarised the main manorial rights as (1) the lord's sporting rights; (2) the lord's or tenant's rights to mines or minerals; (3) the lord's right to hold fairs and markets; (4) the tenant's rights of common; and (5) the lord's or tenant's liability for the construction, maintenance and repair of dykes, ditches, canals and other works.

[147] Because the provisions of the 1922 Act have been repealed, it has not been possible in the Bill to define "manorial rights" by reference to them. However, it may be taken that the list found in Schedule 12 of the 1922 Act is a comprehensive statement of these rights.

[148] Law Com No 254, para 4.7.

[149] *Ibid*, para 5.85.

[150] *Ibid*, para 5.86. Cf above, para 3.19.

[151] In this sense, franchises differ from manorial rights.

[152] See Cl 3(1)(c); above, para 3.19. This would be so in relation to an existing franchise or on the grant or reservation of a new one.

[153] Cf Cl 4(1); above, para 3.23. By contrast, the grant or reservation of a franchise out of registered land is a registrable disposition: see Cl 27(2)(d); above, para 4.24.

[154] See Cl 3(1); above, para 3.19.

[155] For notices, see above, paras 6.5 and following.

probably the rents payable on land held in ancient demesne, that is, land of the manor that belonged to the Crown at the time of the Norman Conquest and which was then granted by the Crown to a subject in return for the payment of a rent.[156]

On the evidence then available to us, we considered that such rights had probably been obsolete for many years and that their overriding status should, therefore, be abolished.[157] Although this recommendation was supported by almost all of those who responded to the point on consultation, we received further evidence from the Crown Estate which has prompted us to reconsider the position. This may be summarised as follows.

(1)   A "crown rent" might refer to—

    (a)   the rent payable to the Crown for freehold land in a manor of ancient demesne; or

    (b)   the rent reserved to the Crown under the grant of a freehold estate, whether or not that estate was situated in a manor of ancient demesne.

(2)   As regards (b), there were many examples of such rents in conveyances of the foreshore made by the Board of Trade up to 1949.

(3)   Even though the significance of such rents in monetary terms might not be substantial, the Crown could not say that they were obsolete, particularly as, in some cases, the Crown had sold on and was no longer the recipient of the rents.[158]

8.44   In the light of this, and with considerable reluctance, we have decided that crown rents should retain their overriding status for 10 years. The Bill therefore provides that a right to rent which was reserved to the Crown on the granting of any freehold estate (whether or not the right is still vested in the Crown), overrides first registration.[159]

Certain rights in respect of embankments and sea and river walls

8.45   Under section 70(1)(d) of the Land Registration Act 1925, liability in respect of embankments and sea and river walls is an overriding interest. In the Consultative

---

[156] Law Com No 254, para 5.35.

[157] *Ibid*, paras 5.35, 5.36.

[158] We take the view that crown rents are "rentcharges" for the purposes of the Rentcharges Act 1977, s 1. As such, they will be phased out in 2037: see s 3. It has been suggested to us that this is not so and that crown rents are excluded from the Act because they fall within the exception in s 1(a) of the Act, "rent reserved by a lease or tenancy". However, we consider that such words are intended to cover leases or non-feudal lease-like arrangements, such as tenancies at will. It is not a normal use of language to suggest that a tenancy includes a fee simple held of the Crown in feudal tenure.

[159] Schedule 1, para 12.

Document, we explained the nature of this rather esoteric form of liability.[160] It is a liability falling on a person whose property fronts on the sea or a river that has arisen by prescription, grant, a covenant supported by a rentcharge, custom or tenure. We were satisfied that such liability still existed and we recommended that it should remain an overriding interest. That view was supported by most of those who responded and the Bill preserves the overriding status of a non-statutory right in respect of an embankment or sea or river wall.[161] However, once again, that overriding status will cease after 10 years.[162]

A right to payment in lieu of tithe

8.46   The rarest and most obscure of the overriding interests found in the Land Registration Act 1925 is found in section 70(1)(e), namely—

> ...payments in lieu of tithe, and charges or annuities payable for the redemption of tithe rentcharges.

We explained in the Consultative Document[163] that—

(1)   there is in fact only one surviving class of right that now falls within this rubric, namely payments that are commonly called "corn rents";

(2)   not all "corn rents" are within this class of overriding interest: it is only where there is a liability to make payments by any Act of Parliament other than one of the Tithe Acts, out of or charged upon any land in commutation of tithes;[164]

(3)   the principal beneficiary of corn rents are the Church Commissioners, who no longer collect them because it is uneconomic to do so; and

(4)   corn rents are payable to persons other than the Church Commissioners and although the sums involved are normally negligible, we discovered one case where the sums were substantial.

In the light of this we recommended the retention of liability to pay corn rent (in the sense explained in (2) above) as an overriding interest. Our recommendation was supported, but there was dissent and a strong view expressed for the abolition or phasing out of this class of overriding interest. In the light of this, "a right to payment in lieu of tithe" remains an overriding interest under the Bill,[165] but it

---

[160]   Law Com No 254, paras 5.38—5.39.

[161]   Schedule 1, para 13. A statutory liability in respect of an embankment or sea wall cannot be an overriding interest. It is simply a liability under the general law.

[162]   Cl 115(1). See below, para 8.88.

[163]   See Law Com No 254, para 5.40.

[164]   Some corn rents are unrelated to tithes and are not, therefore, within Land Registration Act 1925, s 70(1)(e).

[165]   Schedule 1, para 14.

joins the list of those that are to lose their overriding status after 10 years after the Bill is brought into force.[166]

UNREGISTERED INTERESTS WHICH OVERRIDE REGISTERED DISPOSITIONS

Introduction

8.47　As we explained in Part V of this Report, under Clauses 29 and 30, a registered disposition for valuable consideration of a registered estate or a registered charge takes subject to those overriding interests affecting the estate or charge that are listed in Schedule 3.[167] These overriding interests are, therefore, relevant to priority, because any disponee of registered land will take subject to them.

Categories of overriding interest that are the same as those that apply on first registration

8.48　As with unregistered interests which override first registration, there are 15 unregistered interests which override registered dispositions, all but one of which are listed in Schedule 3.[168] Of these 15, 12 are identical to those which override first registration, and nothing more need be said of them—

　　(1)　a PPP lease;[169]

　　(2)　a customary right;[170]

　　(3)　a public right;[171]

　　(4)　a local land charge;[172]

　　(5)　certain rights to coal;[173]

　　(6)　where title to land was registered before 1898, rights to mines and minerals created before 1898;[174]

　　(7)　where title to land was registered between 1898 and 1925, rights to mines and minerals created before registration;[175]

　　(8)　a franchise;[176]

---

[166] Cl 115(1). See below, para 8.88.

[167] See above, para 5.11.

[168] The one exception is PPP lease: see below (1).

[169] Cl 90(5); cf above, para 8.11.

[170] Schedule 3, para 4; cf above, para 8.26.

[171] Schedule 3, para 5; cf above, para 8.26.

[172] Schedule 3, para 6; cf above, para 8.29.

[173] Schedule 3, para 7; cf above, para 8.32.

[174] Schedule 3, para 8; cf above, para 8.33.

[175] Schedule 3, para 9; cf above, para 8.33.

(9)   a manorial right;[177]

(10)   a crown rent;[178]

(11)   a non-statutory right in respect of an embankment or a river or sea wall;[179] and

(12)   a corn rent.[180]

Of these, those mentioned in (8) — (12) are to lose their overriding status after 10 years.[181] This is explained more fully below.[182]

Categories of overriding interest that differ from those that apply on first registration

8.49   Three categories of unregistered interest that override a registered disposition are in some way different from those that override first registration. These are—

(1)   short leases;

(2)   interests of persons in actual occupation; and

(3)   easements and *profits à prendre*.

We explain each of these in turn.

Short leases

8.50   Under the Bill, a leasehold estate granted for a term not exceeding seven years from the date of the grant, overrides a registered disposition,[183] just as it overrides first registration.[184] To this general principle there are eight exceptions. The first three are identical to those that apply in relation to first registration and have already been explained.[185] These are—

(1)   a reversionary lease granted out of unregistered land to take effect in possession more than three months after the date of the grant of the lease;

---

[176] Schedule 3, para 10; cf above, para 8.40.

[177] Schedule 3, para 11; cf above, para 8.40.

[178] Schedule 3, para 12; cf above, para 8.43.

[179] Schedule 3, para 13; cf above, para 8.45

[180] Schedule 3, para 14; cf above, para 8.46.

[181] Cf above, para 8.38.

[182] See paras 8.81 and following.

[183] Schedule 3, para 1.

[184] See above, para 8.9.

[185] See above, para 8.10.

(2)   a lease granted out of an unregistered legal estate under the right to buy provisions of Part V of the Housing Act 1985; and

(3)   a lease granted by a private sector landlord out of an unregistered legal estate to a person who was formerly a secure tenant and has a preserved right to buy.[186]

In these three cases, a lease granted out of an *unregistered* legal estate for a term of seven years or less is a disposition that is subject to the requirement of compulsory registration.[187] It is not, therefore, an overriding interest.

8.51   The five remaining exceptions[188] apply in respect of a lease granted by a proprietor of a registered estate or charge where that grant constituted a registrable disposition that was required to be completed by registration. Some leases which are granted out of a *registered* estate for a term of seven years or less are registrable dispositions and are not therefore overriding. These are—

(1)   a reversionary lease granted to take effect in possession more than three months after the date of the grant of the lease;[189]

(2)   a lease under which the right to possession is discontinuous;[190]

(3)   a lease granted in pursuance of the right to buy provisions of Part V of the Housing Act 1985;[191]

(4)   a lease granted by a private sector landlord to a person who was formerly a secure tenant and has a preserved right to buy;[192] and

(5)   a lease of a franchise or a manor.[193]

8.52   The Bill contains straightforward transitional arrangements for leases that were granted for a term of more than 7 but not more than 21 years. They remain overriding interests.[194] Those who hold under such leases will not, therefore, be prejudiced by the reduction in the length of leases that do not require legislation. However, any assignment of such leases will trigger compulsory registration if the term has more than 7 years to run at the time of assignment.[195]

---

[186] Schedule 3, para 1.

[187] See Cl 4(1)(d)—(f) respectively. See above, paras 3.32—3.34.

[188] Schedule 3, para 1.

[189] Cl 27(2)(b)(ii); above, para 4.20.

[190] Cl 27(2)(b)(iii); above, para 4.20.

[191] Cl 27(2)(b)(iv); above, para 4.20.

[192] Cl 27(2)(b)(v); above, para 4.20.

[193] Cl 27(2)(c); above, para 4.23.

[194] Schedule 12, para 12.

[195] Cl 4(1)(a), (2)(b); above, para 3.24.

Interests of persons in actual occupation

Introduction

8.53 As we have explained,[196] we recommended in the Consultative Document that the rights of persons in actual occupation should remain as a category of overriding interest. Our reasoning was as follows—

> ...it is unreasonable to expect all encumbrancers to register their rights, particularly where those rights arise informally, under (say) a constructive trust or by estoppel. The law pragmatically recognises that some rights can be created informally, and to require their registration would defeat the sound policy that underlies their recognition. Furthermore, when people occupy land they are often unlikely to appreciate the need to take the formal step of registering any rights that they have in it. They will probably regard their occupation as the only necessary protection. The retention of this category of overriding interest is justified... because this is a very clear case where protection against purchasers is needed but where it is "not reasonable to expect or not sensible to require any entry on the register".[197]

By contrast, it *is* in principle reasonable to expect that expressly created rights which are substantively registrable should be registered, and these should no longer enjoy the protection of this category of overriding interests. Although this goal will not be achieved at once, the introduction of electronic conveyancing will in time bring it about, because registration will become a necessary adjunct of the express creation of many rights.[198]

The general principle

8.54 An interest belonging at the time of the registered disposition to a person in actual occupation is an overriding interest, so far as it relates to land of which he or she is in actual occupation.[199] For these purposes, a person is to be regarded as in actual occupation of land if he or she, or his or her agent or employee, is physically present there.[200] As we have explained, this does no more than restate the present law.[201] To this general principle, there is one qualification and there are also four exceptions.

---

[196] See above, para 8.16.

[197] Law Com No 254, para 5.61. The quotation is from Law Com No 254, para 4.17. See above, para 8.6.

[198] See Cl 91, below, paras 13.74 and following.

[199] Schedule 3, para 2(1). Cf above, para 8.14. Under Cl 87(3), none of the following rights is capable of falling within Schedule 3, para 2: a pending land action, a writ or order affecting land issued or made by any court for the purpose of enforcing a judgment or recognisance, an order appointing a receiver or a sequestrator of land or a deed of arrangement. For the reasons for this, see above, para 8.14. For the rights in question and their protection, see above, paras 6.59 and following.

[200] Schedule 3, para 2(2).

[201] See above, para 8.22.

Qualification: Protection is restricted to the land in actual occupation

8.55   It will be noted that actual occupation only protects a person's interest so far as it relates to land of which he or she is in actual occupation. We have already explained that this limitation was one that was proposed in the Consultative Document and was supported by all those who responded to the point.[202] A person's actual occupation will not therefore protect his or her proprietary rights except in relation to the land that he or she actually occupies. So far as he or she has rights over other registered land, those rights will not be protected in the absence of an appropriate entry on the register.

8.56   At the time when we made the recommendation in the Consultative Document, it did no more than reflect the way in which section 70(1)(g) of the Land Registration Act 1925 had been interpreted by the Court of Appeal in *Ashburn Anstalt v Arnold*.[203] However, after the Consultative Document had been published, the Court of Appeal reconsidered the matter in *Ferrishurst Ltd v Wallcite Ltd*,[204] but without reference to the Consultative Document.[205] The Court declined to follow its earlier decision. In that case, Ferrishurst was in actual occupation of part of a registered leasehold title as an underlessee. It had an option to purchase the whole of the immediate leasehold title, but had not protected that option by a notice or caution on the register. It was held that this option was binding on a buyer of the leasehold title in respect of the whole title and not merely that part which Ferrishurst occupied.

8.57   This leads to a strange result. Under an ancient common law rule, a person in possession of *unregistered* land can protect some of his or her rights by virtue of that possession against a buyer.[206] This protection does not extend to rights which are registrable under the Land Charges Act 1972 but have not been so registered.[207] Nor has it ever been extended to protect any rights that the person might have over other land which was also acquired by a buyer. The effect of the *Ferrishurst* decision is that, in relation to land with registered title, "the burden on a purchaser to make inquiries is now heavier than before",[208] and considerably heavier than it is in relation to unregistered land. First, a person who is acquiring registered land other than with vacant possession (whether as purchaser or registered chargee) must ascertain who is in actual occupation of any part of the land that he or she is purchasing. Secondly, that buyer or chargee must then make

---

[202]   See above, para 8.19.

[203]   *Ashburn Anstalt v Arnold* [1989] Ch 1, 28, where Fox LJ, giving the judgment of the Court, commented that "[t]he overriding interest will relate to the land occupied but not anything further".

[204]   [1999] Ch 355.

[205]   In his judgment (at pp 368, 369), Robert Walker LJ referred to the Law Commission's Third Report on Land Registration (1987) Law Com No 158, para 2.55, but not to Law Com No 254, paras 5.70, 5.75.

[206]   See *Megarry & Wade's Law of Real Property* (6th ed 2000), 5-019, 5-020.

[207]   See, *eg, Midland Bank Trust Co Ltd v Green* [1981] AC 513. Cf *Megarry & Wade's Law of Real Property* (6th ed 2000), 5-121.

[208]   *Ferrishurst Ltd v Wallcite Ltd* [1999] Ch 355, 372, *per* Robert Walker LJ.

inquiries as to the extent of the occupier's rights, in relation not only to the land occupied but also to the entirety of the title to be acquired or charged. Where there is (say) a series of leases or underleases, such inquiries may be complex and onerous. If the disponee fails to make what a court may subsequently consider to be adequate inquiries, he or she may be held bound by some undiscovered right.[209]

8.58　The decision in the *Ferrishurst* case runs counter to two of the principal objectives of the present Bill. The first is the creation of a faster and simpler electronically based conveyancing system, where title can be investigated almost entirely on-line with only the minimum of additional enquiries.[210] The second objective is to lay to rest the notion, on which the decision in *Ferrishurst* is premised,[211] that it is somehow unreasonable to expect those who have rights over registered land to register them.[212] Protection of rights by registration is not difficult to accomplish. The move to electronic conveyancing will make it still easier and, indeed, as we explain elsewhere, it will in time become impossible to create or transfer many interests in registered land without simultaneously registering them.[213] The Bill therefore reverses the *Ferrishurst* decision and does so in furtherance of these two objectives.[214]

Exception 1: No protection for settled land

8.59　The first exception to the general proposition stated in paragraph 8.54 is the same as that which applies on first registration, namely where the person has an interest under a settlement under the Settled Land Act 1925.[215] This involves no change in the law and has already been explained.[216]

Exception 2: Rights not disclosed on reasonable inquiry

8.60　The second exception is a reformulation of one that presently applies.[217] An interest of a person of whom inquiry was made before the disposition and who failed to disclose the right when he or she could reasonably have been expected to do so will not be protected under the general principle stated above in paragraph 8.54.[218] This exception operates in effect as a form of estoppel. Our proposal to retain this exception in the Consultative Document[219] was supported by all of

---

[209] Cf below, para 8.60.

[210] See above, paras 1.5, 8.1.

[211] Cf [1999] Ch 355, 360H.

[212] See above, para 1.9.

[213] See below, paras 13.74 and following.

[214] Cf [1999] Ch 355, 372A, B.

[215] Schedule 3, para 2(1)(a).

[216] See above, para 8.17.

[217] Cf Land Registration Act 1925, s 70(1)(g), "...save where enquiry is made of such person and the rights are not disclosed".

[218] Schedule 3, para 2(1)(b).

[219] See Law Com No 254, para 5.69.

those who responded to the point. We have explained above that this exception cannot apply on first registration but only where there is a registered disposition.[220] It is only where there is a registered disposition that any issue of priority arises and where there is any occasion to make inquiry.

Exception 3: Rights of persons whose occupation is not apparent

8.61 The third exception is new and it derives from a recommendation in the Consultative Document.[221] An interest—

(1) which belongs to a person whose occupation would not have been obvious on a reasonably careful inspection of the land at the time of the disposition; and

(2) of which the person to whom the disposition is made does not have actual knowledge at that time;

will not be protected as an overriding interest under the general principle stated above in paragraph 8.54.

8.62 There are a number points to note about the exception in paragraph 8.61(1). It has obvious similarities with the rule of conveyancing law that a seller of land must disclose to an intending buyer prior to contract all latent defects in title (those that are not apparent on a reasonable inspection of the land) and which are not known to the buyer.[222] Three points should be noted about this exception—

(1) For the purposes of the Bill, it is not the *interest* that has to be apparent (as is the case in relation to contracts for the sale of land), but the *occupation* of the person having the interest.[223]

(2) The test is not one of constructive notice of the occupation. It is the less demanding one (derived from the test applicable to intending buyers of land) that it should be obvious on a reasonably careful inspection of the land.[224]

(3) Even if a person's occupation is not apparent, the exception does not apply where a buyer has actual knowledge of that occupation.

The object of this exception is, therefore, to protect buyers and other registered disponees for valuable consideration in cases where the fact of occupation is

---

[220] See para 8.21.

[221] See Law Com No 254, paras 5.71—5.73. Cf above, para 5.21.

[222] See *Megarry & Wade's Law of Real Property* (6th ed 2000), 12-068.

[223] We stress this point because although it was made in the Consultative Document (see Law Com No 254, para 5.73), one correspondent took the view that we had confused the two issues. We had not. We had earlier explained that the authorities were in some disarray as to whether the occupation had to be apparent or not: see Law Com No 254, para 5.58.

[224] See *Megarry & Wade's Law of Real Property* (6th ed 2000), 12-068; Law Com No 254, para 5.72.

neither subjectively known to them nor readily ascertainable. Once an intending buyer becomes aware of the occupation, he or she should make inquiry of the occupier because of the second exception mentioned above.[225] All of those who responded to the proposal in the Consultative Document that a person's actual occupation should be apparent supported it.[226]

Exception 4: Leases granted to take effect in possession more than three months after grant

8.63 The fourth exception is where a leasehold estate is granted to take effect in possession more than three months from the date of the grant and has not taken effect in possession at the time of the disposition. This exception is a necessary corollary of the provisions of the Bill that require the registration of reversionary leases that are to take effect in possession more than three months after their grant.[227] Such leases cannot be overriding interests under the provisions on short leases explained above.[228] This fourth exception will not often occur. It would only be relevant where—

(1) a reversionary lease had been granted to take effect in possession more than three months after the date of the grant but had not been registered; and

(2) the grantee was in actual occupation of the land to which the lease would relate, but at a time when the lease has necessarily not taken effect in possession.[229]

In those circumstances, the reversionary lease would not be binding on any person who acquired an interest in the land for valuable consideration under a registered disposition.

Transitional provisions

8.64 We have explained above, at paragraph 8.18, that the protection that is presently enjoyed by those who are not in actual occupation of land but are in receipt of the rents and profits of the land is not retained under the Bill. As will be apparent from the statement of the general proposition in paragraph 8.54, that change will apply as much where there is a registered disposition as it will on first registration. The Bill provides that an interest which, immediately before the coming into force of the Bill, was an overriding interest under section 70(1)(g) of the Land Registration Act 1925 by virtue of a person's receipt of rents and profits,

---

[225] See para 8.60.

[226] Some raised points or qualified their acceptance. We have given such points careful consideration.

[227] See Cl 4(1)(d) (compulsory first registration); Cl 27(2)(b)(ii) (registrable dispositions); see above, paras 3.32, 4.20.

[228] Schedule 3, para 1; above, paras 8.50(1), 8.51(1).

[229] This might happen where the grantee was already occupying the land under a pre-existing lease, or as a licensee or a tenant at will.

continues to be so for the purposes of Schedule 3.[230] However, that interest will cease to be overriding for these purposes, if at any time thereafter the person having the interest ceases to be in receipt of the rents and profits.[231] If, for example, X holds the residue of an unregistered 99-year lease and, before the Bill came into force granted an underlease to Y, X would continue to have an overriding interest for the purposes of the Bill. If, however, Y's underlease determined and X then granted a new underlease to Z, X would at that point cease to have an overriding interest.

Legal easements and *profits à prendre*

The problem

8.65   Some of the most far-reaching changes made by the Bill to the scope of overriding interests are in relation to easements and *profits à prendre*.[232] The concerns that we have attempted to address are as follows—

> (1)   It is in principle wrong that easements and profits that are expressly granted or reserved should take effect as overriding interests as at present they may.[233] Such a grant or reservation constitutes a registrable disposition and should therefore be completed by registration.[234]

> (2)   It is almost impossible to prove that an easement or profit once acquired has been abandoned. Mere non-user, even for many years, will not amount to abandonment.[235] Indeed this is part of a wider problem. Unless registered, it is often very difficult to discover the existence of easements and profits, particularly those that are either not used at all or only occasionally.[236]

As regards (2), a purchaser of registered land may be seriously disadvantaged given the wide range of easements and profits that can be overriding under the present law.[237]

8.66   Although each of those concerns was expressed in the Consultative Document, our ideas as to how to address them have developed considerably since its publication and the Bill reflects this development. The Bill limits the

---

[230] Schedule 3, para 2(1)(C)(i), inserted by Schedule 12, para 8.

[231] Schedule 3, para 2(1)(C)(ii).

[232] Their impact is, however, softened by the transitional provisions of the Bill: see below, para 8.73.

[233] See Law Com No 254, paras 5.6—5.9.

[234] See Law Com No 254, para 5.14.

[235] See Law Com No 254, para 5.21.

[236] See Law Com No 254, para 5.22. The law of prescription, as it presently stands, can lead to the assertion of rights even though they have not been exercised for many years: see Law Com No 254, para 10.86 (criticism of the doctrine of lost modern grant).

[237] There is no mechanism for the discharge or modification of easements and profits analogous to that which applies to restrictive covenants under Law of Property Act 1925, s 84.

circumstances in which an easement or profit can be an overriding interest more than did our proposals in the Consultative Document.[238] Although, as we have explained, we have decided at this stage not to take forward the recommendations in the Consultative Document on prescription,[239] the Bill has been influenced by some of our thinking in the Consultative Document on prescription.[240] The policy that we have adopted reflects one of the principal aims of the Bill, already mentioned, which is to ensure that it is possible to investigate title to the land almost entirely on-line with the minimum of additional enquiries.[241]

Only legal easements and profits may be overriding interests

8.67   As regards the first of the concerns explained in paragraph 8.65, the Bill provides that only a *legal* easement or *profit à prendre* can be overriding in relation to a registered disposition.[242] Any easement or profit that is expressly granted or reserved out of registered land will be a registrable disposition.[243] It will not take effect at law until it is registered.[244] It follows that it can never be an overriding interest under Schedule 3. As a result of this provision—

   (1)   no easements or profits that are expressly created after the Bill is brought into force will be able to take effect as overriding interests;

   (2)   no equitable easements or profits, however created, will be capable of overriding a registered disposition;

   (3)   the only legal easements and profits that will be capable of being overriding interests are—

        (a)   those already in existence at the time when the Bill is brought into force that have not been registered;[245]

        (b)   those arising by prescription; and

        (c)   those arising by implied grant or reservation.[246]

---

[238]   For those proposals, see Law Com No 254, para 5.24.

[239]   See above, para 1.19.

[240]   For the treatment of prescription in the Consultative Document, see Law Com No 254, paras 10.79—10.94.

[241]   See above, para 8.1.

[242]   Schedule 3, para 3(1).

[243]   Cl 27(2)(d); above, para 4.25.

[244]   Cl 27(1). For the registration requirements applicable to easements and profits, see Schedule 2, para 7; above, para 4.26.

[245]   There are also transitional provisions that relate to *any* easements and profits that were overriding prior to the coming into force of the Bill: see below, para 8.73.

[246]   Implied grant includes easements and profits arising through the operation of Law of Property Act 1925, s 62: see Cl 27(7); above, para 4.25.

Legal easements and profits that are not easily discoverable should not be overriding interests

8.68   However, to meet the second concern set out in paragraph 8.65, the Bill goes further by excluding certain categories of *legal* easements and profits from those that can be overriding. Under the Bill, the following legal easements and profits cannot be overriding interests unless they have either been registered under the Commons Registration Act 1965,[247] or have been exercised in the period of one year prior to the registered disposition in question,[248] namely—

(1)   those that are not within the actual knowledge of the person to whom the disposition was made; and

(2)   those that would not have been obvious on a reasonably careful inspection of the land over which the easement or profit is exercisable.[249]

8.69   The effect of this provision can be summarised as follows. Any person who acquires an interest for valuable consideration under a registered disposition will only be bound by an easement or profit that is an overriding interest if—

(1)   it is registered under the Commons Registration Act 1965;[250]

(2)   he or she actually knows of it;

(3)   it is patent: in other words, it is obvious on a reasonably careful inspection of the land over which the easement or profit is exercisable, so that no seller of land would be obliged to disclose it;[251] or

(4)   it has been exercised within the period of one year before the disposition.

8.70   The fourth case is important and is intended to cover, in particular, the numerous "invisible" easements such as rights of drainage or the right to run a water supply pipe over a neighbour's land. These rights have often existed for many years, but because they were commonly not the subject of any express arrangement between the parties are not recorded on the register. The selection of any period will necessarily be arbitrary. However, we consider that a period of one year is not unreasonable.[252]

---

[247]   See Schedule 3, para 3(1).

[248]   Schedule 3, para 3(2).

[249]   Schedule 3, para 3(1).

[250]   Cf Cl 27(2)(d); above, para 4.25, where the interrelationship between this Bill and the Commons Registration Act 1965 is explained.

[251]   See *Megarry & Wade's Law of Real Property* (6th ed 2000), 12-068.

[252]   For reasons that we explain in the next paragraph, the period is in practice likely to be longer than one year in most cases. The point has been made to us that some easements and profits might be seasonal in nature, as where a farmer uses a track for bringing in the harvest. Such seasonal activities will obviously not operate according to a strict calendar year.

8.71 What we wish to encourage is the creation of a straightforward system of standard inquiries as to easements and profits which will prompt sellers to disclose what they can reasonably be expected to know. This in turn will ensure that such rights are then registered.[253] We anticipate that, prior to contract, a seller would be expected to disclose any unregistered easements or profits affecting his or her property of which he or she was aware, at least to the extent that they were not obvious on a reasonably careful inspection of the land. In particular, he or she would be asked to disclose any easements or profits that had been exercised in the year preceding the inquiry.[254] The result of such inquiries is likely to be that the buyer will have actual knowledge of any unregistered legal easements and profits long before the transaction is completed.

8.72 As regards those who have the benefit of easements or profits that are overriding interests, particularly where their exercise has been intermittent or indeed non-existent for many years, the onus must be on them to register the rights or, where the title of the servient tenement is presently unregistered, to lodge a caution against its first registration. As we have indicated above, we do not consider that it is unreasonable to expect those who have rights over land to register them.[255] Nor, in the light of that, do we see why the risk of undiscoverable and unregistered rights should be imposed upon buyers of land.

Transitional arrangements

8.73 The Bill contains two significant transitional provisions.

(1) Where an easement or profit is an overriding interest at the time when the Bill comes into force, but would not be under the provisions of Schedule 3,[256] it will retain its overriding status. Those who have the benefit of such rights are not at risk of losing them, though for the future it is hoped that they will register them in any event.[257]

(2) For three years after the Bill is brought into force *any* legal easement or profit that is not registered will be an overriding interest.[258] However, apart from those easements and profits that fall within (1), that overriding status will cease three years after the date on which the Bill is brought into force.[259] There will, therefore, be a period of three years' grace before the

---

[253] See below, para 8.91.

[254] As the inquiry will necessarily precede the registered disposition, there will normally be a period of more than one year before the disposition within which any easement must have been exercised.

[255] See paras 1.9, 8.58.

[256] That is, para 3.

[257] Schedule 12, para 9.

[258] In practice, this will protect easements and profits that arise within the three year period by prescription, or by implied grant or reservation. Easements and profits that are expressly granted or reserved after the Bill comes into force will only be equitable unless and until they are registered.

[259] Schedule 12, para 10.

new arrangements take effect, except in relation to equitable easements and profits. Any equitable easements and profits created after the Bill is brought into force will need to be protected by registration.

These transitional arrangements will, we believe, achieve a fair balance between the interests of buyers and encumbrancers.

REDUCING THE IMPACT OF OVERRIDING INTERESTS

Introduction

8.74   In this final section we examine the ways in which the Bill will reduce the impact of overriding interests. One technique for achieving this goal will be evident from our explanation of the interests that will be overriding under the Bill. It is to narrow and clarify their scope, which we have done. The Bill adopts three other means to the same end.

(1)   One existing category of overriding interest will be abolished outright and another is to be dealt with in a different way.[260]

(2)   Certain categories of overriding interests that will initially exist when the Bill is brought into force, will be abolished after 10 years.[261]

(3)   There will be requirements to ensure that when overriding interests come to light they are, so far as possible, entered on the register.[262]

In addition to these techniques, as we have explained above,[263] and will explain more fully below,[264] the introduction of electronic conveyancing will in itself reduce the scope of certain categories of overriding interest. This is because, in time, it will become impossible to create most rights expressly except by registering them simultaneously. This means (for example) that the interests that can be protected by virtue of a person's actual occupation will be significantly reduced.

Categories of overriding interests that are to be abolished

Introduction

8.75   Three categories of overriding interests that exist under the Land Registration Act 1925 are not replicated under the Bill, namely—

(1)   "liability to repair the chancel of any church" (section 70(1)(c) of the 1925 Act);

---

[260] See below, para 8.75.

[261] See below, para 8.81.

[262] See below, para 8.90.

[263] See above, para 8.2.

[264] See below, paras 13.74 and following.

(2) "rights acquired or in course of being acquired under the Limitation Acts" (section 70(1)(f) of the 1925 Act); and

(3) "in the case of a possessory, qualified, or good leasehold title, all estates, rights, interests, and powers, excepted from the effect of registration" (section 70(1)(h) of the 1925 Act).

The first category is no longer enforceable. In a recent decision, the Court of Appeal has held that chancel repair liability contravenes the European Convention on Human Rights and is, therefore, unenforceable.[265] It is therefore unnecessary for us to say any more about this.[266] The second category is abolished by the Bill. The third category is dealt with in a different way under the Bill.

Squatters' rights

8.76 As we explain in Part XIV of this Report, the Bill introduces a completely new system of adverse possession in relation to registered estates. The circumstances in which a squatter becomes entitled to be registered as proprietor in place of an existing one will be considerably reduced. However—

(1) there will still be cases where there is such an entitlement to be registered;[267] and

(2) there will be cases where a person had become entitled to be registered before the Bill is brought into force.

8.77 In the Consultative Document, we recommended that section 70(1)(f) of the Land Registration Act 1925 should not be replicated.[268] We noted that—

(1) a squatter who had acquired a right to be registered as proprietor had a proprietary right that he or she could protect by actual occupation; but

(2) as the law stood, once a squatter was entitled to be registered, his or her rights constituted an overriding interest even if he or she thereafter ceased to be in actual occupation.

If a squatter ceased to occupy the land after he or she had become entitled to be registered as proprietor,[269] the following events might occur. The registered proprietor might resume possession of the land and then sell it to a buyer before the squatter's right to be registered was itself barred by the registered proprietor's own adverse possession. The buyer would then be bound by the squatter's overriding interest even though he or she had bought the land from a registered

---

[265] *Aston Cantlow Parochial Church Council v Wallbank* [2001] EWCA Civ 713; [2001] 21 EG 167 (CS); Morritt V-C, Robert Walker and Sedley LJJ.

[266] Cf Law Com No 254, para 5.37.

[267] See below, para 14.63.

[268] Law Com No 254, paras 5.49—5.55.

[269] See Land Registration Act 1925, s 75.

proprietor in possession. The buyer would not be entitled to any indemnity should the register be rectified in favour of the squatter, because he or she would not have suffered loss by reason of the rectification, but because he or she was subject to the squatter's overriding interest.[270]

8.78 Our recommendation to abolish this category of overriding interests was supported by 80 per cent of those who responded to the point on consultation and the Bill does not, therefore, replicate section 70(1)(f). However, the Bill does contain two provisions that relate to the rights of squatters. First, there are limited transitional provisions to protect vested rights. For three years after the Bill is brought into force a squatter, even if not in actual occupation, will have an overriding interest—

    (1)   on first registration, where he or she had extinguished the title of the person who is registered as first registered proprietor prior to the coming into force of the Bill;[271]

    (2)   in relation to any registered disposition, where he or she was entitled to be registered as proprietor of registered land prior to the coming into force of the Bill.[272]

These transitional provisions will provide a reasonable opportunity for any squatter who is no longer in actual occupation of the land which he or she claims, to register his or her rights.[273] Secondly, as we have explained in Part III of this Report, on first registration, the legal estate is vested in the first registered proprietor subject to interests acquired under the Limitation Act 1980 of which he or she has notice at the time of registration.[274] We consider that these provisions strike a fair balance between the vested rights of squatters and the need to protect innocent buyers who cannot discover the existence of those rights.

Rights excepted from the effect of registration

8.79 We explained in the Consultative Document that where land is registered with possessory, qualified or good leasehold title, we could not see why it was necessary

---

[270] See Law Com No 254, paras 5.46, 5.47.

[271] Schedule 12, para 7, inserting a para 15 into Schedule 1.

[272] Schedule 12, para 11, inserting a para 15 into Schedule 3.

[273] In the Consultative Document, we asked whether squatters who had become entitled to the land by reason of their adverse possession should be able to sue for damages in trespass a registered proprietor who sold the land in question: see Law Com No 254, para 5.53. We assumed that the squatter would have such an entitlement at common law. However, after examining such little analogous authority as there is, we are now rather less certain that that would be the case. In any event, the proposal was rejected by a majority of those who responded to the point on consultation. Accordingly, the Bill contains no provision. The matter will, therefore, be left for judicial determination in the event that it arises.

[274] Cls 11(4)(c); 12(4)(d); above, paras 3.43—3.48.

to retain the overriding status of rights excluded from the effect of registration.[275] We there explained that—

> On any disposition of property with such a title, the [Land Registration Act 1925] expressly provides that the transferee takes subject to these estates, rights and interests in any event.[276] They operate outside the register and it is unnecessary to confer upon them the status of overriding interests. Where the registrar amends the register to give effect to rights which are excluded from the effect of registration of land with a qualified or possessory title, this does not amount to "rectification" of the register, because it does not involve the correction of any error or omission. It follows that such an amendment to the register can never trigger the payment of an indemnity.[277]

8.80 The great majority of those who responded to the Consultative Document agreed with our recommendation. The Bill does not, therefore, replicate section 70(1)(h) of the Land Registration Act 1925. What it does instead is to make express provision—

(1) to protect the priority of an interest that appears from the register to be excepted from the effect of registration;[278] and

(2) for the court or registrar to alter the register to give effect to any estate, right or interest excepted from the effect of registration.[279]

Categories of overriding interests that are to be phased out

The principle of phasing out overriding status and the objections to it

8.81 In the Consultative Document, we considered whether certain rights should lose their overriding status.[280] Where such rights existed in significant numbers, we had reservations about so doing. Our reasons were two-fold. First, we had concerns as a matter of principle which we summarised as follows—

> First, many such persons would not appreciate the need to register their rights (though this difficulty could be minimised by consultation and publicity). Secondly, in order to register their rights they would have to pay for legal advice and the costs of registration (though it may be possible to meet this objection in part by transitional provisions). Thirdly, failure to register carries with it the risk that the right might

---

[275] For these gradations of title and their effect under the Bill, see Cls 9, 10, 11, 12; above, paras 3.42—3.44, 3.49—3.51. For the upgrading of such titles, see Cls 62, 63; below, paras 9.16—9.27.

[276] Land Registration Act 1925, ss 20(2), (3); 23(2), (3), (4).

[277] Law Com No 254, para 5.79.

[278] Cls 29(2)(a)(iii); 30(2)(a)(iii); above, para 5.11.

[279] Schedule 4, paras 2(1)(c), 5(c). There is no provision for the payment of indemnity in such a case.

[280] Law Com No 254, paras 4.25—4.31.

be lost. This would occur if the land affected by it was sold to a purchaser, who would necessarily take free of it as an unprotected minor interest. ...this might be regarded as tantamount to expropriation. Finally, experience of the workings of the one modern statute that has required the registration of existing property rights on a large scale — registration of rights of common under the Commons Registration Act 1965 — strongly suggests that it is an experiment not to be repeated.[281]

8.82   Secondly, the removal of overriding status without compensation carried with it *some* risk of contravening Article 1 of the First Protocol of the European Convention on Human Rights.[282] That Article provides—

> 1. Every natural or legal person is entitled to the peaceful enjoyment of his possessions. No one shall be deprived of his possessions except in the public interest and subject to the conditions provided for by law and by the general principles of international law.
>
> 2. The preceding provisions shall not, however, in any way impair the right of a State to enforce such laws as it deems necessary to control the use of property in accordance with the general interest or to secure the payment of taxes or other contributions or penalties.

8.83   As we explained in the Consultative Document—

> Article 1 has been held by the European Court of Human Rights in *Sporrong and Lönnroth v Sweden*[283] to comprise three distinct rules. The first "enounces the principle of peaceful enjoyment of property". The second "covers deprivation of possessions and subjects it to certain conditions". The third "recognises that States are entitled, amongst other things, to control the use of property in accordance with the general interest, by enforcing such laws as they deem necessary for the purpose".

The jurisprudence of the Court of Human Rights establishes that *deprivation* in the public interest without compensation "is treated as justifiable only in exceptional circumstances"[284] because it fails to meet the requirements of proportionality between the means employed and the aims that are sought to be realised. By contrast, in cases where the issue is one of *control*, "a right to

---

[281]   Law Com No 254, para 4.26.

[282]   Law Com No 254, para 4.30.

[283]   (1982) 5 EHRR 35, 50, para 61. This analysis has been applied by the Court in all subsequent cases.

[284]   *James v United Kingdom* (1986) 8 EHRR 123, 147, para 54.

compensation is not inherent",[285] though in some cases the necessary requirement of proportionality will not be met in the absence of such compensation.[286]

8.84 The cautious approach that we adopted in the Consultative Document towards the immediate abolition of the overriding status of certain rights was prompted by our uncertainty as to whether this would constitute a deprivation of rights of possession within Article 1 of the First Protocol or merely a control of them.[287]

The views expressed on consultation

8.85 It was clear from many of those who responded to the Consultative Document that they wished to see the abolition of a number of categories of overriding interests, given their troublesome nature. There was a strong feeling that, if it was not possible to do so immediately, we should at the very least consider the phasing out of these overriding interests over a period of years in the alternative. The reduction in the number of overriding interests would be a significant step towards a conveyancing environment in which title can be investigated on line with the minimum of additional inquiries.[288] We have therefore reconsidered the matter, having particular regard to the concerns listed above in paragraph 8.81 and the need to comply with the European Convention on Human Rights. In the light of this, the Bill makes provision to phase out five categories of overriding interests, in relation both to first registration and registered dispositions.[289]

The scheme adopted in the Bill

8.86 The essential features of this scheme are—

(1) the rights involved will remain overriding for 10 years;[290]

(2) those who have the benefit of such rights over *unregistered* land, which would, therefore, be overriding on first registration, will be able to lodge a caution against first registration without payment of any fee during that 10 year period;[291] and

(3) those who have the benefit of such rights over *registered* land, which would, therefore, be overriding on any registered disposition, will be able to

---

[285] *Banér v Sweden* No 11763/85, 60 DR 128, 142 (1989) (a decision of the European *Commission* of Human Rights, not the *Court*).

[286] Cf *Chassagnou v France*, Nos 25088/94; 28331/95; 28443/95; 29 April 1999, especially at paras 80—85.

[287] Cf Law Com No 254, para 4.30.

[288] See above, para 8.1.

[289] Cl 115. For the categories of overriding interests that are to be phased out, see below, para 8.88.

[290] Cl 115(1).

[291] Cl 115(2)(a).

register a notice in respect of such a right without payment of any fee during the 10 year period.[292]

8.87 We have given careful thought to the categories of overriding interests that should be phased out. In particular, we have had regard to our guiding principle that interests should only have overriding status where protection against buyers is needed, but where it is neither reasonable to expect nor sensible to require any entry on the register.[293]

8.88 We have identified four classes of overriding interests. We consider that the phasing out of overriding status is justified in relation to the fourth of these but not in relation to the first three. Our conclusions can be summarised as follows.

(1) There are good reasons why some interests are overriding and where it is either not feasible or indeed positively undesirable to remove their overriding status. We include in this category—

   (a) PPP leases;[294]

   (b) local land charges;[295] and

   (c) mines and minerals.[296]

(2) There are other overriding interests the scope of which is significantly reduced by the Bill, either with immediate effect or over a period of time. In relation to these, overriding status is justifiable in its restricted form. We include in this category—

   (a) short leases;[297]

   (b) the interests of persons in actual occupation;[298] and

   (c) legal easements and profits.[299]

(3) There are two categories of overriding interests which it might be desirable to eliminate but where, in practice, there is a significant risk that nobody would see fit to register them within any period of grace. These are—

   (a) customary rights;[300]

---

[292] Cl 115(2)(b).

[293] See above, para 8.6.

[294] See above, para 8.11.

[295] See above, para 8.29.

[296] See above, para 8.31.

[297] See above, paras 8.9, 8.50.

[298] See above, paras 8.14, 8.54.

[299] See above, paras 8.23, 8.65.

(b)   public rights.[301]

(4)   There are five miscellaneous overriding interests, whose shared characteristics have been described above at paragraph 8.35. All are relics from past times and are of an unusual character. Most of them can no longer be created. Those who have the benefit of such rights ought to be aware of them. These characteristics make them obvious and sensible candidates to be phased out. If such rights are to bind those who acquire registered land, they should be protected on the register. The rights in question are—

(a)   a franchise;[302]

(b)   a manorial right;[303]

(c)   a crown rent;[304]

(d)   a non-statutory right in respect of an embankment or a river or sea wall;[305] and

(e)   a corn rent.[306]

Under the Bill, these five rights will cease to be overriding interests both in relation to first registration and on a registered disposition 10 years after the Bill is brought into force.[307]

Human rights

8.89   We are satisfied that our proposals will comply with the requirements of Article 1 of the First Protocol of the European Convention on Human Rights.[308] First, there can be little doubt that the phasing out of overriding status over a period of 10 years with a view to encouraging the registration of such rights instead constitutes a "control" and not a "deprivation" of property rights. The removal of overriding status has no effect *per se* on the rights themselves. Secondly, a requirement for securing the registration of such rights of an unusual character is obviously a legitimate aim for a state to pursue and is "in accordance with the general interest" as that Article requires. Indeed, the Court of Human Rights has recently reiterated the need for rules of domestic law to be "sufficiently accessible, precise

---

[300]   See above, para 8.26.

[301]   See above, para 8.26.

[302]   See above, para 8.40.

[303]   See above, para 8.40.

[304]   See above, para 8.43.

[305]   See above, para 8.45.

[306]   See above, para 8.46.

[307]   Cl 115(1).

[308]   See above, para 8.82.

and foreseeable" in the context of the protection of possessions.[309] Thirdly, what is proposed is undoubtedly proportionate in terms of the end desired and the means to achieve it. The period of 10 years is generous. It gives more than adequate time both to publicise the need to register such rights and for those who have the benefit of them to ensure that they are registered. Furthermore, no fee is to be charged for the entry of such rights on either the register or the cautions register.

Ensuring that overriding interests are protected on the register when they come to light

8.90 The Bill contains three provisions that are intended to ensure that, when overriding interests come to light, they are protected on the register.

8.91 First, by Clause 71, there is a power to make provision by rules requiring a person who applies—

(1) for first registration[310] to provide to the registrar in specified circumstances specified information about overriding interests affecting the estate that fall within Schedule 1 and are of a kind specified in rules;[311] and

(2) to register a registrable disposition[312] to provide to the registrar in specified circumstances specified information about overriding interests affecting the estate that fall within Schedule 3 and are of a kind specified in rules.[313]

The purpose of these provisions is similar. In relation to both, the objective is to ensure that the applicant for registration discloses any overriding interests so that they can be entered on the register.[314] This is intended to ensure that such rights are, in consequence, registered. There will be cases where an applicant is aware of what might or might not be an overriding interest. The registrar will only wish to enter on the register such rights as are clear and undisputed.[315] The rules will therefore provide guidance as to when the buyer has to provide information and in relation to which overriding interests it is required. There will be no direct sanction for this obligation, at least when the Bill is first introduced. However, when electronic conveyancing becomes operative, those solicitors and licensed conveyancers who enter into network access agreements with the registrar are likely to be required to ensure compliance with this obligation under the network transaction rules.[316]

---

[309] See *Belvedere Alberghiera SRL v Italy* No 31524/96; 30 May 2000, para 57; *Carbonara and Ventura v Italy* No 24638/94; 30 May 2000, para 64.

[310] Under Chapter 1 of Part 1 of the Bill.

[311] Cl 71(a).

[312] Under Cl 27.

[313] Cl 71(b).

[314] Unless the overriding interest is one that cannot be noted on the register. For these, see below, para 8.93.

[315] See Law Com No 254, para 5.106.

[316] Cf Schedule 5, para 5(2)(b). See below, para 13.52.

8.92   Clause 71 implements a recommendation that was made in the Consultative Document.[317] It was supported by three-fifths of those who responded to it. It was clear that those who were opposed to it feared that it would impose a much higher burden on solicitors and licensed conveyancers than will in fact be the case. As we have indicated, that will not be so and rules will provide guidance as to when disclosure must be made to the registrar.

8.93   Secondly, by Clause 37, if it appears to the registrar that a registered estate is subject to an overriding interest that falls within Schedule 1, he may enter a notice in the register in respect of it, unless it is one of the following—

(1)   a lease that is granted for a term of 3 years or less from the date of the grant and is not required to be registered;[318]

(2)   a PPP lease;[319] or

(3)   any interest in any coal or coal mine and certain other rights in relation to coal.[320]

8.94   There are good reasons why these three categories of overriding interest cannot be noted on the register and the exceptions reflect the present law, except that the class of leases in respect of which a notice may not be entered is much narrower than at present for reasons that have been explained in Part VI of this Report.[321] Clause 37 replaces section 70(2), (3), (3A) and (4) of the Land Registration Act 1925, but it recasts the law in the manner proposed in the Consultative Document.[322]

8.95   Thirdly, once an overriding interest has been protected by the entry of a notice on the register, it can never again become an overriding interest, even if, say, the notice were removed in error from the register.[323] Any such error would be a matter for the payment of indemnity to any person who suffered loss as a result.[324]

---

[317]   See Law Com No 254, paras 5.104—5.107.

[318]   See Cl 33(b).

[319]   See Cl 90(4). For PPP leases, see above, paras 8.11 and following.

[320]   See Cl 33(e). For these rights, see above, para 8.32.

[321]   See paras 6.10—6.12.

[322]   See Law Com No 254, paras 5.99—5.103, where the existing provisions are criticised. The proposals were supported by all save one of those who responded to them.

[323]   This is the effect of Cls 29(3) and 30(3).

[324]   See Schedule 8, para 1(1)(b); see below, para 10.32.

PART IX
THE REGISTER AND REGISTRATION

INTRODUCTION

9.1 In this Part we consider a variety of matters that are concerned with the register and registration. These are, mainly but not exclusively, matters that are covered by Part 6 of the Bill and they are necessarily something of a miscellany. The matters covered are as follows—

(1) the register;

(2) the conclusiveness of registration;

(3) boundaries;

(4) quality of title;

(5) accessing information;

(6) priority protection;

(7) applications; and

(8) land certificates.

9.2 The following matters are not considered in this Part—

(1) the requirements for the registration of a registrable disposition,[1] which has already been explained in Part IV;[2]

(2) the duty to disclose overriding interests,[3] which has been explained in Part VIII;[4]

(3) the alteration of the register,[5] which is examined in its own right in Part X, below; and

(4) proceedings before the registrar,[6] which are addressed in relation to the judicial provisions of the Bill in Part XVI.[7]

---

[1] Cl 27(4); Schedule 2.

[2] See above, para 4.16.

[3] Cl 71.

[4] See above, para 8.91.

[5] See Cl 65; Schedule 4.

[6] Cls 75, 76.

[7] See para 16.11.

THE REGISTER

9.3 The Bill provides that the register of title shall continue to be kept.[8] There is a power, by rules, to make provision about how the register is to be kept.[9] In particular, such rules may make provision about the information that is to be included in the register, the form in which it is to be kept and its arrangement.[10] This approach allows for flexibility and means that changes in the way in which the register is kept will not require primary legislation.[11]

REGISTRATION AS PROPRIETOR

Conclusiveness

9.4 One of the most fundamental principles of registered conveyancing is that it is registration that vests the legal estate in the registered proprietor.[12] Clause 58(1) of the Bill provides accordingly that if, on the entry of a person in the register as the proprietor of a legal estate,[13] the legal estate would not otherwise be vested in him or her, it shall be deemed to be vested in him or her as a result of registration. Thus, for example, if a person is registered as proprietor on the strength of a forged transfer, the legal estate will vest in that transferee even though the transfer was a nullity.

9.5 In Part IV of this Report it was explained that the Bill lays down the registration requirements for registrable dispositions in Schedule 2.[14] It is therefore necessary for the purposes of the principle set out in paragraph 9.4 for the Bill to make provision for the case where some but not all of those registration requirements are met. It therefore provides that the principle stated in paragraph 9.4 does not apply where—

    (1)   there is a registrable disposition; and

    (2)   an entry is made in the register in respect of that disposition; but

    (3)   some further entry is required to meet the registration requirements in Schedule 2.[15]

---

[8] Cl 1(1). Cf Land Registration Act 1925, s 1(1).

[9] At present almost all titles on the register are kept in electronic form, though there are still a few that are held in documentary form.

[10] Cl 1(2). The rules will be land registration rules and will be required to be laid before Parliament only. See Cls 125, 129(1). For the present rules on the manner in which the register is arranged and its content, see Land Registration Rules 1925, Part 1.

[11] Land Registration Act 1925, s 1 had to be amended by Administration of Justice Act 1982, s 66 to make it clear that the register did not have to be kept in documentary form.

[12] Cf Land Registration Act 1925, s 69(1).

[13] "Legal estate" has the meaning given to it by Law of Property Act 1925, s 1(4): see Cl 129(1).

[14] See para 4.16.

[15] Cl 58(2).

But for this exception to the principle in paragraph 9.4, the provisions of Schedule 2 would not be registration *requirements* at all.

9.6 The following events will exemplify how the provision in paragraph 9.5 will operate. X applies to be registered as the grantee of a 99-year lease. The lease is registered with its own title. However, the registrar fails to enter a notice of the lease on the superior freehold title. The legal estate is not vested in X by virtue of Clause 58(1).[16]

Dependent entries

9.7 The Bill explains where entries on the register are to be made in relation to certain dispositions. First, if a legal estate subsists for the benefit of a registered estate, such as an easement or a *profit à prendre* appurtenant or appendant,[17] the entry of a person in the register as proprietor of that legal estate must be made in relation to the registered estate.[18] Secondly, where a person is registered as the proprietor of a registered charge, that entry must be made in relation to the registered estate subject to the charge.[19] Thirdly, where a person is registered as proprietor of a sub-charge,[20] that entry must be made in relation to the registered charge that is subject to the sub-charge.[21]

Effective date of registration

9.8 At present, the Land Registration Rules 1925 provide that registration is taken to be completed as of the day on which the application for first registration or for registration (as the case may be) is deemed under rules to have been delivered to the Registry.[22] The Bill makes provision as to the time from which registration has effect. In relation to both an application for first registration and an application to register a registrable disposition, it has effect from the time of the making of the application.[23] There are several points that should be noted about this provision. First, the fact that registration will take effect from the *time* of the making of the application is significant. The Land Registry has recently moved to a system of real time priority[24] under which the priority of an application is determined by the

---

[16] The grant will, however, be effective in equity.

[17] For profits appurtenant and appendant, see *Megarry & Wade's Law of Real Property* (6th ed 2000), 18-082, 18-083, respectively.

[18] Cl 59(1).

[19] Cl 59(2).

[20] For sub-charges, see above, para 7.11

[21] Cl 59(3).

[22] Land Registration Rules 1925, rr 24, 42, 83.

[23] Cl 74. For the rule-making power to provide when an application is taken to be made, see Schedule 10, para 6(c); below, para 9.77(3).

[24] As from 28 May 2001.

actual time at which it is entered on the day list.[25] Secondly, it is intended that, under the system of electronic conveyancing that it is proposed to introduce, the making of a disposition and its registration will in fact occur simultaneously.[26] The provision mentioned in this paragraph may therefore become obsolete in the comparatively near future.

BOUNDARIES

The general boundaries rule

9.9 In many countries, there is a *cadastre*,[27] which is a record of all land holding. This is commonly kept for fiscal purposes, and under such systems, boundaries are often surveyed and delimited with at least some degree of precision. No doubt because of a different approach to taxes on land ownership, this cadastral system has not been adopted in England and Wales. In general, in this country, the register is not conclusive as to boundaries. This is because of the so-called "general boundaries rule" that is presently contained in rule 278 of the Land Registration Rules 1925. This provides that—

> Except in cases in which it is noted in the Property Register that the boundaries have been fixed, the filed plan... shall be deemed to indicate the general boundaries only.[28]

9.10 Although there is a power to fix boundaries,[29] it has hitherto hardly ever been used for two main reasons.[30] The first is the expense of so doing, which, given the manner in which boundaries have been fixed hitherto, is considerable. The second is that the process of fixing of a boundary is all too likely to create a boundary dispute where none had existed hitherto. This is because it is necessary to investigate the titles of all adjoining landowners.[31]

9.11 The general boundaries rule is to be retained under the Bill. However, as we explain below, it is anticipated that fixed boundaries are likely to become more common for the future.[32] Given the importance of the rule, it is included in the Bill itself rather than, as now, in rules. The Bill provides accordingly that the

---

[25] See Land Registration Rules 1925, rr 24(2), 85(1). The day list is a record of pending applications for first registration and for making, rectifying or cancelling an entry on the register: *ibid*, r 7A.

[26] This is explained fully below, see paras 13.74 and following.

[27] Or whatever the local variant of that word may be.

[28] Land Registration Rules 1925, r 278(1).

[29] See Land Registration Rules 1925, r 278(2). Once so fixed, the boundary is guaranteed by the Registry.

[30] See Ruoff & Roper, *Registered Conveyancing*, 4-22.

[31] *Ibid*. In the Land Registry's *Practice Leaflet No 16: Boundaries in Land Registration*, para 1.2, it is stated that "in view of the need for the precise boundaries to be agreed between neighbouring parties, a fixed boundary registration is not the solution for solving a boundary dispute".

[32] See para 9.12.

boundary of a registered estate as shown for the purposes of the register is a general boundary, unless it is shown on the register as determined.[33] A general boundary does not determine the exact boundary.[34] Rules may, however, make provision which will enable or require the exact line of the boundary of a registered estate to be determined.[35] In particular, rules may make provision about—

(1) the circumstances in which the exact line of a boundary may or must be determined;

(2) how the exact line may be determined;

(3) the procedure in relation to applications for the determination of a fixed boundary; and

(4) the recording of the fact of determination in the register or in the parcels index (which is explained below[36]).

9.12 There are two points that emerge from this rule-making power. First, it will be open to the Lord Chancellor to prescribe a means of fixing boundaries that is less demanding than that which is presently employed. The development of modern mapping techniques is likely to make this possible. It is anticipated that, if this can be done, wider use may be made of voluntary fixing of boundaries, for example, when a development is laid out.

9.13 Secondly, there may be circumstances in which it will be possible to *require* that the boundary be fixed. One particular case arises in the context of adverse possession. We explain in Part XIV of this Report that the Bill introduces a new system of adverse possession in relation to registered estates. In general, a person who has been in adverse possession of a registered estate for at least 10 years will be able to apply to be registered as proprietor of it.[37] However, if the proprietor (or certain other interested persons) serves a counter-notice, the application will be rejected.[38] There are certain exceptions to this. In particular, where—

(1) an adjacent landowner has been in adverse possession; and

(2) for at least 10 years of that period of adverse possession, he, she or any predecessor in title has reasonably believed that the land to which the application relates belonged to him or her

---

[33] Cl 60(1)

[34] Cl 60(2).

[35] Cl 60(3). The rules will be land registration rules and will be required to be laid before Parliament only. see Cls 125, 129(1).

[36] See paras 9.54, 9.55.

[37] See Schedule 6, para 1; below, para 14.20.

[38] Schedule 6, paras 2, 3; below, paras 14.32—14.33, 14.35.

the applicant will be entitled to be registered.[39] The thinking behind this exception is that legal and physical boundaries do not always coincide, as where an estate is laid out and the fences are not where the plans on the register say that they are. If, in such circumstances, a neighbour has acted in the reasonable belief that he or she owned the land, his or her claim should succeed. The exception does not, however, apply where the boundary has been determined by rules under Clause 60(3).[40] Furthermore, rules under Clause 60(3) are likely to require that where an applicant *does* come within the exception and acquires title to the land, he or she will be required to have the boundary fixed when he or she is registered. This will ensure that he or she (or any successor in title) cannot ever invoke this exception again.

Accretion and diluvion

9.14 In *Southern Centre of Theosophy Inc v State of South Australia*,[41] in giving the opinion of the Privy Council, Lord Wilberforce explained the principles of accretion and diluvion as follows. The doctrine of accretion, he said gave recognition–

> to the fact that where land is bounded by water, the forces of nature are likely to cause changes in the boundary between the land and the water. Where these changes are gradual and imperceptible..., the law considers the title to the land as applicable to the land as it may be so changed from time to time. This may be said to be based on grounds of convenience and fairness. Except in cases where a substantial and recognisable change in boundary has suddenly taken place (to which the doctrine of accretion does not apply), it is manifestly convenient to continue to regard the boundary between land and water as being where it is from day to day or year to year. To do so is also fair. If part of an owner's land is taken from him by erosion, or diluvion (*ie* advance of the water) it would be most inconvenient to regard the boundary as extending into the water: the landowner is treated as losing a portion of his land. So, if an addition is made to the land from what was previously water, it is only fair that the landowner's title should extend to it. The doctrine of accretion, in other words, is one which arises from the nature of land ownership from, in fact, the long-term ownership of property inherently subject to the gradual processes of change. When land is conveyed, it is conveyed subject to and with the benefit of such subtractions and additions (within the limits of the doctrine) as may take place over the years. It may of course be excluded in any particular case, if such is the intention of the parties. But if a rule so firmly founded in justice and convenience is to be excluded, it is to be expected that the intention to do so should be plainly shown. The authorities... have firmly laid down that where land is granted with a water boundary, the title of the grantee extends

---

[39] Schedule 6, para 5(4); below, paras 14.44—14.52.

[40] Schedule 6, para 5(4)(b); below, para 14.49. This in itself may encourage landowners to have their boundaries determined where the boundaries do not coincide with the physical layout of the land.

[41] [1982] AC 706, 716.

to that land, as added to or detracted from by accretion, or diluvion, and that this is so, whether or not the grant is accompanied by a map showing the boundary, or contains a parcels clause stating the area of the land, and whether or not the original boundary can be identified.

9.15 The Bill gives effect to these principles. First, it provides that the fact that a registered estate is shown as having a particular boundary does not affect the operation of accretion or diluvion.[42] The doctrines of accretion and diluvion will apply therefore, whether the general boundaries rule applies[43] or whether the exact line of the boundary has been determined under the principles explained above.[44] Secondly, if the parties enter into an agreement about the operation of the doctrine of accretion or diluvion in relation to a registered estate, it has effect only if registered in accordance with rules.[45] If, for example, the boundary of two registered estates is a stream, and the respective owners agree that the boundary shall be in a particular place notwithstanding any changes that might otherwise be made by movement of the stream, that agreement will only be effective if it is recorded on the register in accordance with rules.

QUALITY OF TITLE

Introduction

9.16 In Part III of this Report we have explained that, on first registration, the registrar may not always register the proprietor with an absolute title.[46] He or she may, instead, be registered with a good leasehold title, a possessory title or a qualified title.[47] The Land Registration Act 1925 contains provisions which, in their present form date from 1986, for the upgrading of titles.[48] Clause 62 of the Bill replicates those provisions with some amendments. In essence, what it does is to empower the registrar to upgrade a title if certain conditions are met. The rules can be summarised as follows.

When title can be upgraded

Upgrading freehold title which has possessory title

9.17 Where a freehold estate is registered with a possessory title, the registrar may enter it as absolute in two cases.

    (1)   The first is if he is satisfied as to the title to the estate.[49] It sometimes happens that a person is registered as proprietor with possessory title not

---

[42] Cl 61(1).

[43] See above, paras 9.9, 9.11.

[44] See paras 9.11, 9.12.

[45] Cl 61(2).

[46] See above, paras 3.43, 3.44, and Cls 9, 10.

[47] For the effect of registration with the different grades of title, see Cls 11, 12; above, paras 3.45—3.51.

[48] See s 77, substituted by Land Registration Act 1986, s 1(1).

[49] Cl 62(1).

because his or her title is based upon adverse possession, but because he or she is unable to prove title for the statutory period.[50] This may happen because documents of title have been lost or destroyed. If, for example, some missing evidence of title subsequently came to light, the registrar could then upgrade the title. In determining whether he is satisfied as to the title for any of the purposes of Clause 62, the registrar must apply the same standards as he would on an application for first registration.[51]

(2) The second is if the title has been registered as possessory for 12 years and he is satisfied that the proprietor is in possession of the land.[52] If the proprietor has been in possession for 12 years after first registration, the likelihood of any adverse rights being successfully asserted is significantly reduced. Even if they were not barred by adverse possession at the time of first registration,[53] it is likely that they will be 12 years later. The Bill defines when a proprietor is to be regarded as being in possession.[54] This definition is explained fully in Part X, in the context of rectification of the register.[55] There is a power for the Lord Chancellor by order to change the period of 12 years to some other period.[56] Thus, if there were (for example) a reduction in the limitation period applicable to actions for the recovery of unregistered land from 12 to 10 years,[57] the period of 12 years might be reduced to 10.

Upgrading freehold title which has qualified title

9.18 Where a freehold estate is registered with a qualified title, the registrar may enter it as absolute if he is satisfied as to the title to the estate.[58] A person will be registered with a qualified title only where the registrar considers that his or her title can only be established for a limited period or subject to certain reservations that may disturb the holding under that title.[59] Before he could upgrade the title under this power, the registrar would have to be satisfied that the cause of his original objections no longer threatened the holding under that title.

---

[50] Which is for at least 15 years: see Law of Property Act 1925, s 44(1) (as amended).

[51] Cl 62(8).

[52] Cl 62(4).

[53] Where the application for first registration is based upon adverse possession, the applicant will have to satisfy the registrar that he or she has been in adverse possession for at least 12 years *before* he or she can be registered as proprietor.

[54] See Cl 128.

[55] See below, para 10.17. The concept of when a proprietor is in possession is very wide under the Bill.

[56] Cl 62(9). Any such order must be made by statutory instrument and would be subject to annulment in pursuance of a resolution of either House of Parliament: Cl 125(4).

[57] As the Law Commission has recommended: see Limitation of Actions (2001) Law Com No 270.

[58] Cl 62(1).

[59] Cl 9(4); above, para 3.43.

Upgrading leasehold title which has a good leasehold title

9.19 A leasehold estate will be registered with good leasehold title because the registrar has not been able to satisfy himself as to the superior title. As and when he is able to do so, he may upgrade the title to an absolute one.[60] The obvious case would be where the superior title was itself registered for the first time.

Upgrading leasehold title which has a possessory title

9.20 Where the title to a leasehold estate is possessory, the registrar may upgrade it from possessory to—

(1) good leasehold, if—

(a) he is satisfied as to the title to the estate;[61] or

(b) the title has been registered as possessory for 12 years and he is satisfied that the proprietor is in possession of the land;[62] and

(2) absolute, if he is satisfied both as to the title to the estate and as to the superior title.[63]

Upgrading leasehold title which has a qualified title

9.21 Where the title to a leasehold estate is qualified, the registrar may upgrade it from possessory to—

(1) good leasehold, if he is satisfied as to the title to the estate;[64] and

(2) absolute, if he is satisfied both as to the title to the estate and as to the superior title.[65]

No power to upgrade where there is an outstanding adverse claim

9.22 None of the powers conferred by the Bill to upgrade a title may be exercised by the registrar if there is outstanding any claim adverse to the title of the registered proprietor which is made by virtue of an estate, right or interest whose enforceability is preserved by virtue of the existing entry about the class of title.[66] This provision reproduces the effect of the present law,[67] and it is intended to

---

[60] Cl 62(2).

[61] Cl 62(3)(a).

[62] Cl 62(5). Once again, as to when the proprietor will be regarded as being in possession, see Cl 128; below, para 10.17.

[63] Cl 62(3)(b).

[64] Cl 62(3)(a).

[65] Cl 62(3)(b).

[66] Cl 62(6).

[67] See Land Registration Act 1925, s 77(4).

ensure that, if there are any such adverse claims outstanding, they are resolved before any application to upgrade the title is made.

Who may apply for the upgrading of a title

9.23 At present, it is apparently only the registered proprietor who can apply to have his or her title upgraded.[68] However, the registered proprietor may not be the only person who has an interest in the class of title with which a property is registered. For example—

(1) a mortgagee in possession might wish to apply for the upgrading of a title if it was minded to exercise its power of sale, not least because it is under a duty to obtain the best price reasonably obtainable on any sale;[69] and

(2) a person who is not registered as proprietor, but is entitled to be so registered,[70] might wish to secure the upgrading of the title of that registered estate in order (say) to sell the property at a higher price.

9.24 The Bill therefore widens the categories of persons who can apply to have the title upgraded. They are—

(1) the proprietor of the estate to which the application relates;

(2) a person entitled to be registered as the proprietor of that estate;

(3) the proprietor of a registered charge affecting that estate;

(4) a person interested in a registered estate which derives from that estate.[71]

As now, there will be nothing to stop a person who is interested in some other way in a registered estate from *requesting* the registrar to exercise his power to upgrade a title, even though they have no right to apply to him to do so and he would, therefore, be under no obligation to consider his or her request.

Effect of upgrading title

9.25 The Land Registration Act 1925 does not set out the effect of upgrading title. It is left to be inferred. By contrast, the Bill does set it out in order to make the process of upgrading title easier to understand.[72]

9.26 First, the Bill provides that where a registered freehold or leasehold title is upgraded to absolute title, the proprietor ceases to hold the estate subject to any

---

[68] Land Registration Act 1925, s 77 refers only to the registrar acting on his own initiative or "on application by the proprietor". The registrar can act on his own initiative so that, even under the present law, some other interested person could draw the matter to his attention.

[69] Cf *Cuckmere Brick Co Ltd v Mutual Finance Ltd* [1971] Ch 949.

[70] Such as an executor in respect of the testator's registered estate.

[71] Cl 62(7).

[72] Cl 63.

estate, right or interest whose enforceability was preserved by virtue of the previous entry about the class of title.[73]

9.27 Secondly, where a leasehold title is upgraded from a possessory or qualified title to a good leasehold title, the proprietor also ceases to hold the estate subject to any estate, right or interest whose enforceability was preserved by virtue of the previous entry about the class of title. However, the upgrading of the title does not affect or prejudice the enforcement of any estate, right or interest affecting, or in derogation of, the title of the lessor to grant the lease.[74]

Indemnity

9.28 A point that emerges very clearly from the provisions explained in paragraphs 9.26 and 9.27 is that, on the upgrading of a title, there is some risk that an estate, right or interest may thereby be defeated. The person who had previously had the benefit of that estate, right or interest may therefore suffer loss. We explain in Part X of this Report[75] that, where a person suffers loss by reason of the change of title under Clause 62, he or she is to be regarded as having suffered loss by reason of the rectification of the register.[76] As such, he or she is entitled to be indemnified for that loss.[77]

Use of register to record defects in title

9.29 Clause 64 of the Bill creates a new power, and the background to it requires some explanation. One of the principal objectives of the Bill is to create a conveyancing system in which title can, so far as possible, be investigated on line by computer.[78] It follows that every effort should be made to make the register as conclusive as to title as it is practically possible to make it.

9.30 Matters that can make a title defective come in several forms and the Bill deals with them in different ways.

(1) *The person who appears to be owner may not be.* The fact that a person is entered in the register as proprietor of a legal estate is itself proof that that legal estate is vested in him or her, even if, but for the fact of registration, it would not be.[79]

(2) *The owner may have limited powers and may make a disposition that he or she had no power to make.* As regards any disponee, the proprietor of a registered estate or charge is taken to have unlimited powers of disposition

---

[73] Cl 63(1).

[74] Cl 63(2).

[75] See below, para 10.31.

[76] Schedule 8, para 1(2)(a).

[77] Schedule 8, para 1(1)(a).

[78] See above, paras 1.5, 2.1(1).

[79] See Cl 58; above, para 9.4.

in the absence of any entry to the contrary on the register.[80] This protects disponees against dispositions that might otherwise be open to challenge as being *ultra vires*.

(3) *The property may be subject to incumbrances.* We have explained in Part V of this Report how a disponee under a registered disposition takes his or her interest subject only to—

(a) entries on the register;

(b) overriding interests;

(c) matters excepted from the effect of registration; and

(d) in the case of a disposition of a leasehold estate, the burden of any interest that is incident to the estate (such as a restrictive covenant contained in the lease).[81]

9.31 There is, however, another kind of defect in title. It is one for which the land registration system does not presently cater. It can only be investigated by forms of inquiry outside the registration system. This is where something occurs in the course of the ownership of property that itself makes the title bad. The obvious cases are where either a lease is subject to a right of re-entry for breach of covenant and the tenant commits a breach of covenant, or where a freehold is subject to a rentcharge, the rentcharge is supported by a right of re-entry, and the freeholder has failed to pay the rentcharge. However, it is only a few such situations that are a cause of concern and it is these that Clause 64 is intended to meet.

9.32 In many of the most obvious situations in which an occurrence of itself invalidates the title, there are already simple and well-developed practices for meeting the problem. These practices are unlikely to impede speedy conveyancing and do not require extensive inquiries "off line". The obvious example is that of an assignment of a lease or under-lease, where the assignor is in breach of covenant. Where a landlord accepts rent from a tenant whom he or she knows to be in breach of covenant, he or she will be taken to have waived the breach of covenant.[82] Conveyancers take advantage of this and require the assignor of a lease to produce the last receipt for rent prior to the assignment. This creates a rebuttable presumption that all the covenants and provisions of the lease have been duly performed.[83] This is a comparatively simple matter and it is performed as a matter of course. No change in the law or in practice is needed so long as waiver continues to have this potent effect.

---

[80] See Cl 26; above, para 4.8; Cl 52; above, para 7.7.

[81] See Cls 29, 30; above, Part V.

[82] See *Megarry & Wade's Law of Real Property* (6th ed 2000), 14-125, 14-126.

[83] See Law of Property Act 1925, s 45(2), (3).

9.33   There are however situations which are not satisfactorily met at present and where it would be desirable to have a means of entering on the register a defect in title that could cause the registered estate to be terminated. There is one case, in particular, that concerns us. It is, we suspect, fairly common, and it can best be explained by an example. X purchases a registered freehold estate from Y which is subject to a rentcharge in favour of Z. Z has a right of re-entry in the event of the non-payment of the rentcharge. In the course of undertaking the conveyancing work, X's solicitor discovers that the rentcharge has not been paid by Y for some years. X is prepared to take the risk of acquiring the land nonetheless. X's title is, in law, a bad one. If X decides to sell the land, an intending buyer may not enquire as to whether the rentcharge has been paid until after he or she has expended money in relation to the purchase, perhaps having made local searches or engaged a surveyor. There will be nothing on the register to indicate the defect in the title.

9.34   Clause 64(1) provides that, if it appears to the registrar that the right to determine a registered estate in land has become exercisable, he may enter the fact on the register. There is a rule-making power in relation to entries made under Clause 64(1). Such rules may, in particular, make provision about—

(1)   the circumstances in which there is a duty to exercise the power conferred by that subsection;

(2)   how entries under that subsection may be made; and

(3)   the removal of such entries.[84]

As regards the first of these matters, it is likely that the duty will be confined to cases, such as that explained above in paragraph 9.33, where there is no well established procedure for dealing with the problem.

9.35   An obvious objection to this new duty is that it will not be easy to enforce. A solicitor or licensed conveyancer will be very reluctant to inform the Registry of a defect in his or her client's title, particularly where it is one that could lead to the determination of that client's estate. However, as we explain in Part XIII of this Report, the move to electronic conveyancing will provide a means of enforcing such obligations via network access agreements.[85] Under the system of electronic conveyancing that is to be created under the Bill, it will be solicitors or licensed conveyancers acting for buyers who will actually carry out the process of registration. They will do so in accordance with the terms of a network access agreement with the Registry that may require them to disclose specified information.[86] They are likely to know far more about the conveyancing transaction than the Registry does at present when documents are submitted for registration. They may therefore know the facts that make a title bad, even though

---

[84]   Cl 64(2).

[85]   See below, para 13.52.

[86]   See below, paras 13.36 and following.

these will not necessarily appear from the conveyancing documents that, under present arrangements, would be sent to the Registry for registration.

ACCESSING INFORMATION

Introduction

9.36 The ability to obtain information from the registers of title and cautions is an essential feature of the system of conveyancing that the Bill seeks to create. Easy and open access to information held by the Registry are the keys to speedier conveyancing. The Bill contains a number of provisions which relate to the access of information from the registers. Some of the provisions are new or are an extension of existing ones.

Open registers and their inspection

The significance of the open register

9.37 One of the most important provisions of the Land Registration Act 1925 is section 112, as substituted by the Land Registration Act 1988.[87] It created the open register.[88] Prior to the substitution of the new section 112, the register could only be inspected by the registered proprietor or by an authorised person. Those constraints were removed by the new section. Section 112 has fundamentally changed both the perception and the potential of land registration. First, it has provided the necessary springboard for the development of electronic conveyancing. An open register is essential to a system of conveyancing in which inquiries on title can be made on line by direct access without requiring the consent of the registered proprietor. Secondly, the section has changed the perception of the register itself. Its contents are no longer regarded as a private matter relevant only to the parties to a conveyancing transaction, but as a source of public information about land that can be used for many purposes unconnected with conveyancing.

The rights conferred by the Bill

9.38 Clause 66 of the Bill replaces section 112 and in some respects extends it. It provides that a person may inspect and make copies of, or of any part of—

(1) the register of title;

(2) any document kept by the registrar[89] which is referred to in the register of title;

---

[87] The Land Registration Act 1988 implemented the recommendations of the Law Commission in its Second Report on Land Registration (1985) Law Com No 148.

[88] For the rules governing the operation of the open register, see Land Registration (Open Register) Rules 1991; Ruoff & Roper, *Registered Conveyancing*, B-404.

[89] In practice such documents will, increasingly, be held in electronic form. With the introduction of electronic conveyancing, all conveyancing documents thereafter created will be held in electronic form. Furthermore, the Registry is embarked on a programme of scanning existing documents so that they can be kept in dematerialised form.

(3) any other document kept by the registrar which relates to an application to him; or

(4) the register of cautions against first registration.[90]

As we explain below,[91] this is not in all respects an unfettered right.

9.39 The right conferred by Clause 66(1) goes beyond what can be done under section 112 of the Land Registration Act 1925 in the following respects.

9.40 First, there is a right to inspect and copy *any* document that is kept by the registrar. There is no exception, as there is now, for leases or charges (or copies of leases or charges).[92] However, that right is subject to rules, as explained below[93] and it will be necessary to place some restrictions on the right of access to protect private information. Furthermore, the Registry does not necessarily have copies of all leases.[94] The present practice is as follows[95]—

> it is seldom that a copy of a lease, which is noted as an incumbrance on first registration of the title of the reversion, is supplied so that it can be filed in the Land Registry. Again, when an assignee of a lease applies for the first registration of his title, he is required to supply a certified copy of the assignment but he may not supply a copy of the lease itself. However, when an original lessee applies for first registration, he must furnish a certified copy of his lease.[96]

9.41 Secondly, there is a right to inspect and copy any document kept by the registrar which relates to an application to him but is not referred to in the register. At present, such documents can only be inspected at the discretion of the registrar.[97] However, once again, this right is likely to be qualified by rules, as explained below.[98]

9.42 Thirdly, the formal establishment of the register of cautions against first registration is of course new to the Bill.[99] Like the register of title, it is to be an open register. This is not in fact a novelty. At present, cautions against first

---

[90] Cl 66(1).

[91] See para 9.43.

[92] See Land Registration Act 1925, s 112(1)(b). The registrar has a discretion to issue office copies of such documents under *ibid*, s 112(2)(b).

[93] See para 9.43.

[94] It does have copies of all charges created over registered land: see Land Registration Rules 1925, r 139.

[95] Ruoff & Roper, *Registered Conveyancing*, 21-22.

[96] Land Registration Rules 1925, r 21.

[97] There is an exception for criminal investigations if the applicant falls within one of the categories specified in Land Registration (Open Register) Rules 1991, Schedule 2. In such cases and for the purposes there specified, the applicant has a right of inspection.

[98] See para 9.43.

[99] See Cl 19; above, para 3.65.

registration are recorded in the Index Map[100] and there is a right to search the Index Map and also to obtain copies of a caution title.[101]

The limitations on the rights to inspect and copy

9.43   Clause 66(2) provides that the right to inspect and copy conferred by Clause 66(1)[102] is subject to rules. These rules may, in particular, provide for exceptions to the right and impose conditions on its exercise, including conditions requiring the payment of fees. It is likely that rules will restrict access to documents that may be of a sensitive nature to those who have a good reason to see them.[103] In particular, it is important to protect commercially sensitive information and the rules are likely to ensure that this can be done.[104]

Official copies

9.44   Under section 113 of the Land Registration Act 1925 —

> Office copies of and extracts from the register and of and from documents ... filed in the registry shall be admissible in evidence in all actions and matters, and between all persons or parties, to the same extent as the originals would be admissible...

The mysterious term "office copy" is not defined and what distinguishes it from any other copy is not prescribed by the present legislation. However, in practice, office copies are made on paper bearing the Land Registry watermark and an official label describing the document as an official copy. It is therefore, by necessary inference, an official copy issued by the Land Registry and one which is, by statute, certified to be accurate.

9.45   The Bill abandons the language of "office copies" and employs instead the term "official copy", which gives a clearer idea of the concept. It provides that an official copy of, or of a part of—

(1)   the register of title;

(2)   any document kept by the registrar which is referred to in the register of title;

(3)   any other document kept by the registrar which relates to an application to him; or

(4)   the register of cautions against first registration

---

[100] See Land Registration Rules 1925, r 8.

[101] See Land Registration (Open Register) Rules 1991, rr 9 and 8, respectively.

[102] See above, para 9.38.

[103] One of the most sensitive pieces of information — the amount secured by a charge over registered land — is in fact seldom apparent from the documents kept by the Registry.

[104] The rules will follow the scheme laid down in the Freedom of Information Act 2000.

is admissible in evidence to the same extent as the original.[105] The matters in respect of which an official copy can be obtained do of course mirror the matters listed in Clause 66, in respect of, and to the extent to which, there is a right to inspect and to make copies.[106]

9.46 As might be expected, there is a power for rules to make provision about—

(1) the form of official copies;

(2) who may issue official copies;[107]

(3) applications for official copies;[108] and

(4) the conditions to be met by applicants for official copies, including conditions requiring the payment of fees.[109]

9.47 The Bill provides that a person who relies on an official copy in which there is a mistake is not liable for the loss suffered by another by reason of that mistake.[110] However, as we explain in Part X of this Report, a person who suffers loss by reason of a mistake in an official copy is entitled to be indemnified.[111]

Conclusiveness of filed copies

Introduction

9.48 Although it is not contained in Part 6 of the Bill, Clause 118 may be considered in the present context. Under the present law, section 110(4) of the Land Registration Act 1925 has the effect of making the register conclusive in relation to the abstracts and extracts from documents that that are referred to in it. So far as material, section 110(4) provides as follows—

> Where the register refers to a filed abstract or copy of or extract from a deed or other document such abstract or extract shall as between vendor and purchaser be assumed to be correct, and to contain all material portions of the original, and no person dealing with any registered land or charge shall have a right to require production of

---

[105] Cl 67(1).

[106] See above, paras 9.38 and 9.43.

[107] In this context it may be noted that, when electronic conveyancing is introduced, there will be power to authorise persons such as solicitors and licensed conveyancers to issue official copies pursuant to a network access agreement: see Schedule 5, para 1(2)(d); below, para 13.37.

[108] Such applications can already be made electronically by means of the Direct Access system: see Directions of the Chief Land Registrar, 12 May, 1997, Ruoff & Roper, *Registered Conveyancing*, F-12.

[109] Cl 67(3). Such rules will be land registration rules and will be laid before Parliament only: Cls 125(3), 129(1).

[110] Cl 67(2), replicating in part Land Registration Act 1925, s 113.

[111] Schedule 8, para 1(1)(d); below, para 10.34.

the original, or be affected in any way by any provisions of the said document other than those appearing in such abstract, copy or extract...

9.49 Clause 118 attempts to serve the same purpose as section 110(4) of the Land Registration Act 1925. However, in making adjustments to take account of the open register, it goes considerably further than section 110(4).

The preconditions

9.50 Clause 118 applies where two pre-conditions are met. First, there must be a disposition "that relates to land to which a registered estate relates".[112] This expression requires explanation. It will include not only dispositions that require registration, but some dealings which do not. One consequence of the open register[113] is that it may be relied upon not only by those who are parties to dispositions of, or out of, a registered estate that are capable of being protected on the register, but also by—

(1) those who are granted interests out of a registered estate that are not registrable; and

(2) those who are parties to any subsequent dealings with such unregistered interests.

The obvious case is where a registered freeholder grants a lease for seven years or less. That lease will commonly take effect without registration as an overriding interest[114] and, as such, will not be the subject of any entry on the register. However, the grantee of that lease may search and rely upon the extracts from documents referred to in the register of the freehold title in ascertaining what incumbrances (if any) affect it. Similarly, should that lessee come to assign that lease, the intending assignee might search and similarly rely upon the register of the freehold title out of which the lease had been granted. The presumption of conclusiveness in Clause 118 applies to such dealings.[115] Indeed there might be difficulties if it did not. If the Clause were limited to those who were parties to registrable dealings with registered land, it might create a paradox. Although such parties would be unable to go behind the extracts from the documents referred to in the register, those who were parties to dealings with unregistered interests derived out of a registered estate might claim to be able to do so.

9.51 The second pre-condition to the operation of Clause 118 is that there is an entry in the register relating to a registered estate that refers to a document kept by the registrar which is not an original.[116] As we have explained above, where the register

---

[112] Cl 118(1)(a).

[113] See above, para 9.37.

[114] See Schedule 3, para 1; see above, para 8.50. A lease granted for more than three years may be protected by the entry of a notice: see Cl 33(b); above, paras 6.10—6.12.

[115] Land Registration Act 1925, s 110(4), only applies as between a seller and buyer under a disposition of registered land other than a lease or a charge.

[116] Cl 118(1)(b).

refers to an original document that is kept by the registrar, any person may inspect and copy it, except to the extent that rules may provide otherwise.[117] There is, therefore, no need for any provision as to the conclusiveness of the document. Like section 110(4) of the 1925 Act, the sort of cases that Clause 118 is intended to meet is where the register refers to an abstract, copy or extract from a document but where the registrar no longer retains the original. It should be noted that, in relation to some classes of documents, notably leases, the registrar has hitherto only kept copies and not the originals.

Conclusiveness

9.52 The Bill contains three provisions as to conclusiveness of the documents mentioned in paragraph 9.51. It provides that—

(1) as between the parties to a disposition, the document kept by the registrar is to be taken to be correct and to contain all the material parts of the original document;[118]

(2) no party to the disposition may require production of the original document;[119] and

(3) no party to the disposition is to be affected by any provision of the original document which is not contained in the document kept by the registrar.[120]

9.53 In this way, the register is made a barrier to further enquiry in relation to the documents referred to in it. We explain in Part X of this Report that, as now, a person who suffers loss by reason of a mistake in a document kept by the registrar which is not an original and is referred to in the register, is entitled to be indemnified.[121]

Index

9.54 Under rule 8 of the Land Registration Rules 1925—

> The Registrar shall keep an Index Map from which it is possible, in relation to any parcel of land, to ascertain whether that land is registered or affected by a caution against first registration and, if so, the title number or numbers under which the land is registered or the distinguishing number of every caution against first registration that affects it.

Despite the practical importance of this Index Map, it has been created under the rule-making powers in the Land Registration Act 1925 and not by the Act itself. The Bill places the Index where it belongs, in primary legislation.

---

[117] Cl 66; above, paras 9.38 and following.

[118] Cl 118(2).

[119] Cl 118(3).

[120] Cl 118(4).

[121] Schedule 8, para 1(1)(e); below, para 10.35.

9.55   Clause 68(1) provides that the registrar must keep an index for enabling certain matters to be ascertained in relation to any parcel of land in England and Wales, whether registered or unregistered. The matters are—

(1)   whether any registered estate relates to the land;

(2)   how any registered estate which relates to the land is identified for the purposes of the register;

(3)   whether the land is affected by any, and, if so what, caution against first registration;[122] and

(4)   such other matters as may be prescribed by rules.

9.56   It will be noted that the Index is not specifically tied to a map as such. As information is, increasingly, held in dematerialised form, it was not thought to be desirable to tie the Index to any specific format. What is required is that the information set out in Clause 68(1) should be ascertainable from it.

9.57   There is a power for rules[123] to make provision about the following matters—

(1)   how the Index is to be kept, and in particular—

(a)   the information to be included in it;[124]

(b)   the form in which such information is to be kept;[125] and

(c)   the arrangement of that information;

(2)   official searches of the Index.[126]

Historical information

9.58   The register of title only provides details of the title as it stands at any given moment. It is a snapshot not a chronology of the title. It does not provide any details of the historical devolution of that title as do the title deeds on a conveyance of unregistered land, at least to some extent.[127] However, there may be

---

[122]   Under the Bill there is a separate register of cautions against first registration: see Cl 19; above, para 3.65.

[123]   Such rules will be land registration rules and will be laid before Parliament only: Cls 125(3), 129(1).

[124]   This might be wider than it is at present and might, for example, include land use.

[125]   This would include the medium in which the Index would be kept and would, in particular, enable it to be kept in electronic form.

[126]   Cl 68(2). For official searches of the register of title, see below, para 9.61. Official searches of the index map can already be made electronically through Direct Access: see Direction of the Chief Land Registrar, 12 May 1997, Ruoff & Roper, *Registered Conveyancing*, F-12.

[127]   The title which a seller of unregistered land has to deduce is fairly limited in point of time. His or her obligation to a buyer is to deduce title from the first good root of title that is more

occasions when a person has a reason for wishing to know the historical devolution of a registered title, as the following examples indicate—

(1) an issue might arise as to whether a former owner is liable on the covenants for title which were implied on an earlier transfer;[128]

(2) it may be necessary to discover more about the ownership of land at the time when a restrictive covenant was entered into in order to determine the extent of the land that it was intended to benefit; or

(3) there might be an issue whether certain freeholds had at some stage been in common ownership so as to extinguish by unity of seisin various easements or restrictive covenants.

9.59 We were repeatedly told by respondents to the Consultative Document that the inability to trace the historical devolution of a registered title caused practical difficulties. HM Land Registry does in fact keep on computer an historical record of registered titles for its own purposes, though it is not necessarily complete. Although there is no right for any person to inspect that record, the registrar does sometimes provide information as to the devolution of a registered title if the applicant can show a good reason for wishing to see it. However, there is presently no statutory basis for this.

9.60 In response to the many representations that we received, the Bill remedies this shortcoming. Clause 69(1) provides that the registrar may on application provide information about the history of a registered title. Rules may make provision about applications to the registrar for the exercise of this power.[129] It will be necessary to place some restrictions on the exercise of this power. An examination of the history of a title will inevitably add to the time and expense of the conveyancing process and it should only be made where there is a sound conveyancing reason to do so. It should *never* be a routine inquiry that a buyer's solicitor or licensed conveyancer feels that he or she is bound to make. It should also be stressed that the Bill imposes no obligation on the Registry to keep a complete historical record of every title, nor to keep any record of a title for an unlimited period. The historical record that the registrar may disclose under the power contained in Clause 69(1) is such as the Registry happens to have.

Official searches

9.61 Official searches were first introduced by rules in 1930 under a rule-making power contained in the Land Registration Act 1925.[130] What are now the Land

than 15 years old: see Law of Property Act 1925, s 44(1) (as amended). Problems about tracing the history of a title can therefore arise even where it is unregistered.

[128] The benefit of such covenants is annexed to the land benefited and runs with it: see Law of Property (Miscellaneous Provisions) Act 1994, s 7 (a provision introduced by an amendment tabled by Lord Brightman during the passage of the Act through Parliament).

[129] Cl 69(2). The rules will be land registration rules and will be laid before Parliament only: Cls 125(3), 129(1).

[130] Section 144(1)(ix); see below, para 9.66.

Registration (Official Searches) Rules 1993, make provision for official searches of the register. The Bill confers an express rule-making power to make provision for official searches of the register, including searches of pending applications for first registration.[131] It is provided that rules may, in particular, make provision about the following matters—

(1) the form of applications for searches;

(2) the manner in which such applications may be made;[132]

(3) the form of official search certificates;

(4) the manner in which such certificates may be issued.[133]

PRIORITY PROTECTION

The present law

9.62 It is not enough that an intending buyer of registered land should be able to search the register and obtain an official copy of the register of title and of any documents extracted in it. That copy is a statement of the title to the land on the date on which the search is made. Between the date on which the intending buyer obtains that copy and completion, third party rights might supervene. As a result, the buyer might—

(1) complete and find him or herself bound by such rights; or

(2) conduct a search just before completion, discover the existence of such rights and either—

(a) not complete at all; or

(b) complete only when the defect in title has been removed.

9.63 To obviate this problem, a buyer may make an official search with priority[134] under the Land Registration (Official Searches) Rules 1993.[135] The official certificate of the result of that search then confers priority on him or her. What this means is that—

---

[131] Cl 70. The rules will be land registration rules and will be laid before Parliament only: Cls 125(3), 129(1).

[132] Such applications can already be made electronically by means of the Direct Access system: see Notice of the Chief Land Registrar, 12 May 1997, Ruoff & Roper, *Registered Conveyancing*, F-14.

[133] When electronic conveyancing is introduced, persons such as solicitors and licensed conveyancers may be authorised to issue official search certificates pursuant to a network access agreement: see Schedule 5, para 1(2)(c); below, para 13.37.

[134] It is also possible to search without priority: see Land Registration (Official Searches) Rules 1993, rr 9, 10.

[135] See Ruoff & Roper, *Registered Conveyancing*, B-429 and following.

any entry which is made in that register during the priority period relating to that search shall be postponed to a subsequent application to register the instrument effecting the purchase...[136]

The "priority period" is 30 days.[137] Priority protection is only available to a "purchaser", namely—

any person (including a lessee or chargee) who in good faith and for valuable consideration acquires or intends to acquire a legal estate in land...[138]

Although this summary greatly over-simplifies the position, it does, we hope, identify the essential elements of an official search with priority.[139]

9.64 At present, official searches can be made in any of the following ways—

(1)   by post;[140]

(2)   by telephone or personal attendance at a district land registry;[141]

(3)   by fax;[142] and

(4)   by direct access.[143]

9.65 Three developments should be noted.

(1)   The system of priority searches has been extended to protect a buyer of unregistered land who has applied for first registration of his or her title.[144] Where an application has been made for first registration by a buyer, but the registration has not yet been completed,[145] the intending buyer from the applicant can make an application for a priority search. This will

---

[136] Land Registration (Official Searches) Rules 1993, r 6.

[137] See Land Registration (Official Searches) Rules 1993, r 2(1), where the matter is more precisely defined. The rules are likely to change because of the move to "real time priority". In other words, priority is determined by the actual time that an application or search is entered on the day list at the Registry. See below, para 9.79.

[138] Land Registration (Official Searches) Rules 1993, r 2(1). See Ruoff & Roper, *Registered Conveyancing*, 30-08.

[139] For an account of the present law, see Ruoff & Roper, *Registered Conveyancing*, Chapter 30.

[140] *Ibid*, 30-03.

[141] *Ibid*, 30-04.

[142] *Ibid*, 30-05.

[143] *Ibid*, 30-06.

[144] *Ibid*, 30-07. What underlies this is the fact that a first registration is completed on the date on which the application for first registration is made (even though in practice the registration will not in fact be made until the application has been processed, which may take some considerable time in some cases): see Land Registration Rules 1925, rr 24, 42.

[145] Cf Land Registration (Official Searches) Rules 1993, r 2(1).

ensure that his or her application for registration will take priority over any subsequent application for any entry in the register of title to that land.[146]

(2) Since the introduction of real time priority, the priority of all searches and applications is determined by the time at which they are entered on the day list.[147] This does not apply, however, to those applications that have been protected by a priority search and which take their priority accordingly.

(3) It will be apparent from what has been said above, in paragraph 9.63, that there are many applications to the Registry that cannot be protected by a priority search. A limited form of protection has recently been introduced for such applications concurrently with the introduction of real time priority. It is now possible to make an outline application to reserve a short period of priority for interests that cannot be protected by an official search with priority.[148]

9.66 The priority protection accorded by a certificate issued in response to a search is a matter of considerable practical importance in the conduct of conveyancing. It will remain so, even after the introduction of electronic conveyancing. As now, intending buyers will wish to protect themselves from supervening third party rights between contract and completion. The only basis for the present practice in primary legislation is found in section 144(1)(ix) of the Land Registration Act 1925, which gives the Lord Chancellor power to make rules "[f]or the conduct of official searches".

Priority protection under the Bill

9.67 The Bill makes express provision for priority protection and extends the circumstances in which it can be obtained.[149]

The circumstances in which priority protection will be available

9.68 Under the Bill, there is a power for rules to make provision for priority periods in connection with—

(1) official searches of the register, including searches of pending applications for first registration; or

(2) the noting in the register of a contract for the making of a registrable disposition of a registered estate or charge.[150]

---

[146] See Land Registration (Official Searches) Rules 1993, r 7.

[147] See above, para 9.8.

[148] See Land Registration Rules 1925, r 83A. Under r 83A(8), the reserved period "means the period ending at 12 noon on the third day following the day that notice of an outline application was deemed... to be delivered" (which normally means from the time that the application is entered in the day list).

[149] Cl 72.

We say more about the power to make rules below.[151] The first of these two cases replicates the circumstances in which priority protection can already be obtained. The second is new and it has been included in the Bill with the introduction of electronic conveyancing in mind.

9.69 The reasoning behind the second is as follows. One of the goals of the Bill is that, once electronic conveyancing is in place—

(1) any disposition of a registered estate or charge,[152] or a contract to make such a disposition, will only take effect when it is registered; but

(2) the making of that disposition or contract will occur simultaneously with its registration.[153]

It follows, therefore, that it will be necessary to enter a notice in the register in respect of any estate contract. It is at present unusual to enter a notice in respect of an estate contract. The entry of such a notice protects an interest against a subsequent registered disposition. It is, in practice, only needed therefore where that contract may have an extended lifespan, as may be the case, for example, with a conditional contract. Given that it will become necessary to enter a notice for any contract to be valid, it is reasonable that that entry should confer the additional advantage of priority protection. We give an example below to demonstrate the advantage of that protection.[154]

The meaning of priority protection

9.70 An application for an entry in the register will be protected if it is one to which a priority period relates — in other words it falls within one of the two cases explained above at paragraph 9.68 — and it is made before the end of that period.[155] Except in two cases explained below,[156] where an application for an entry in the register is protected in this way, any entry made in the register during the period relating to the application, is postponed to any entry that is made in pursuance to that entry.[157]

9.71 An example may be given to demonstrate the efficacy of the priority protection in relation to land of which X is the registered proprietor.

(1) On 1 March Z obtains a charging order over X's land.

---

[150] Cl 72(6)(a). The rules will be land registration rules and will be laid before Parliament only: Cls 125(3), 129(1).

[151] See para 9.73.

[152] Or indeed of an interest which is the subject of a notice in the register.

[153] Cl 93; below, paras 13.74 and following.

[154] See para 9.71.

[155] Cl 72(1).

[156] See para 9.72.

[157] Cl 72(2).

(2) On 1 April, X contracts to sell his land to Y. Y's estate contract is protected by a notice and the entry of that notice also confers priority protection for the priority period which is, say, 30 days.

(3) On 7 April, Z applies for the entry of a notice on the register in respect of her charging order.[158]

(4) On 21 April, X executes a transfer on sale of the land to Y, Y applies to register that transfer and is then registered.

In these circumstances, Y will take free of Z's charging order. Even though Z's charging order had priority over Y's estate contract (because it pre-dated that contract[159]), Y will take free of it because it was not protected on the register at the time of the transfer.[160] But for the priority protection which was triggered by the entry of the notice in relation to Y's estate contract Z's application for a notice would have been effective, and her charging order would have bound Y on registration. In other words, the priority protection given to the estate contract prevents the entry on the register of a prior interest which, if it were entered on the register prior to the registration of the disposition that gives effect to the estate contract, would have priority over that disposition.

9.72 As we have mentioned, the principle that where an application for an entry in the register is protected, any entry made in the register during the period relating to the application, is postponed to any entry that is made in pursuance to that entry,[161] is subject to two exceptions.

(1) The first case is if the earlier entry was itself made in pursuance of a protected application and the priority period relating to that application itself ranked ahead of the one relating to the application for the other entry.[162] In other words, if A had made an official search with priority on 1 April, and B then made an official search with priority on 10 April, A's application to register a transfer in her favour would not be postponed to, but would take priority over, B's application.

(2) The second case is where the court, in exercise of powers explained in Part VI of this Report,[163] orders that a restriction be entered and directs that it is to have overriding priority.[164] Once again, this overrides the priority that the application would otherwise have.[165]

---

[158] Cf Cl 87(1)(b); above, para 6.61; Charging Orders Act 1979, s 3(2).

[159] Cf Cl 28; above, para 5.5.

[160] Cl 29; above, para 5.6.

[161] Above, para 9.70.

[162] Cl 72(3).

[163] See paras 6.52, 6.53.

[164] Cl 46(3).

[165] Cl 72(4).

Rules

9.73 As we have indicated above, the power to make provision for the two cases in which priority protection would be given is subject to rules.[166] Those rules may, in particular, make provisions as to the following matters—

(1) the commencement and length of the priority period;

(2) the applications for registration to which such a period relates;

(3) the order in which competing priority periods rank; and

(4) the application of the priority principle explained in paragraph 9.70 and the exception to it set out in paragraph 9.72(1) in cases where more than one priority period relates to the same application.[167]

9.74 Two of those cases require some explanation. As regards (2), this can best be explained by an example. A buyer will commonly be buying the land with the aid of a mortgage. It is not only his or her application to register the transfer, but also the charge, that will require priority protection. The reason for (4) lies in the possibility that a person might, say, make an official search with priority before he or she contracts to buy certain land. A further period of priority protection might then be obtained when he or she either enters into the contract or makes a second official search with priority. There need to be rules (as there are now) about how the two periods interrelate, especially if a third party makes a priority search in between the two events.[168]

9.75 Under the Bill rules may also make provision for the keeping of records in relation to priority periods and the inspection of such records.[169] In other words, it will be possible, as it is now,[170] to discover whether there is any priority period in place in respect of another application.

APPLICATIONS

The form and content of applications

9.76 There are many circumstances in which, under the provisions of the Bill, a person may apply to the registrar. The applications that can be made include the following—

---

[166] See para 9.68.

[167] Cl 72(7). The rules will be land registration rules and will be laid before Parliament only: Cls 125(3), 129(1).

[168] For the present rules about concurrent applications for official searches with priority: see Land Registration (Official Searches) Rules 1993, rr 8, 9.

[169] Cl 72(6)(b). The rules will be land registration rules and will be laid before Parliament only: Cls 125(3), 129(1).

[170] See Land Registration (Official Searches) Rules 1993, r 5.

(1) for first registration;[171]

(2) to lodge or cancel a caution against first registration;[172]

(3) to register a registrable disposition;[173]

(4) to enter, remove or cancel a notice;[174]

(5) to enter or withdraw a restriction;[175]

(6) to register the priority of registered charges;[176]

(7) to determine the exact line of a boundary;[177]

(8) to upgrade title;[178]

(9) to obtain an official copy;[179]

(10) to obtain an official search;[180]

(11) to enter into a network access agreement;[181]

(12) by a squatter to be registered as proprietor;[182] and

(13) for the Adjudicator to rectify or set aside a document.[183]

9.77 Although in certain cases there are, necessarily, specific rules about particular kinds of application,[184] the Bill also contains a general power to make rules to make provision—

(1) about the form and content of applications under the Bill;

---

[171] Cls 3, 4.

[172] Cls 15, 18

[173] Cl 27.

[174] Cls 34, 35, 36.

[175] Cls 43, 47.

[176] Cl 48.

[177] Cl 60.

[178] Cl 62.

[179] Cl 67.

[180] Cl 70.

[181] Schedule 5, para 1.

[182] Schedule 6, paras 1, 6.

[183] Cl 106(2).

[184] See, eg, Cl 14 (rules about first registration); Schedule 6, para 15 (procedure on applications by an adverse possessor).

(2)   requiring applications under the Bill to be supported by such evidence as rules may prescribe;

(3)   when an application under the Bill is to be taken as made;

(4)   about the order in which competing applications are to be taken to rank; and

(5)   for an alteration made by the registrar for the purpose of correcting a mistake in an application or accompanying document to have effect in such circumstances as the rules may provide as if made by the applicant or other interested party or parties.[185]

A number of these powers require comment.

9.78   As regards (1), it will be possible under the Bill to require all applications to be in prescribed form. Indeed it is likely that all applications in electronic form will in fact be prescribed to ensure the effective working of the system.[186]

9.79   One of the reasons for the provision in paragraph 9.77(3) and (4), is to ensure that there is a power to allocate priority to competing applications that come into the Registry. As has been explained, HM Land Registry is moving from a system whereby the priority of applications is determined according to a formula set out in rules,[187] to one of "real time priority", by which priority is determined by the time at which the application is entered on the day list at the Registry.[188] In relation to electronic conveyancing, there will, in any event, have to be a system of real time priority because it is envisaged that the making of a disposition and its registration will occur simultaneously.[189]

9.80   The purpose of the power in paragraph 9.77(5) is to enable the registrar to correct what are purely clerical errors without the need to obtain the consent of the applicant. This power, which corresponds to that which presently exists under rule 13 of the Land Registration Rules 1925, is explained in Part X of this Report.[190]

Registered charges and company charges

9.81   Where a company creates a registered charge over its property, that charge will not only be registrable under the Bill, but it will also be required to be registered

---

[185]   Schedule 10, para 6. The rules will be land registration rules and will be laid before Parliament only: Cls 123, 125(3), 129(1).

[186]   Cf below, para 13.12 (in relation to applications to register dispositions).

[187]   See Land Registration Rules 1925, rr 24, 84, 85.

[188]   See above, para 9.8.

[189]   See Cl 93; below, paras 13.74 and following.

[190]   See para 10.28.

under the Companies Act 1985.[191] Registration in the Companies Register under the Companies Act 1985 fulfils a wholly different function from registration on the register of title. It does not affect the priority of competing charges over a company's property. Its intended purpose is to protect actual or potential creditors by making the liabilities of a company apparent on the face of the register. Notwithstanding these differences of function and the fact that, at present, the applications for registration are very different in form, it is highly desirable that it should be possible to make a combined application to the Land Registry to register the charge on the register and for that application then to be forwarded to Companies House for registration in the Companies Register. It is anticipated that this will apply primarily to applications in electronic form. The power, explained above,[192] for rules to make provision about the form and content of applications under the Bill,[193] means that it will be possible to prescribe a combined form of application for this purpose. HM Land Registry is discussing with Companies House ways in which the two systems may be linked.[194]

9.82 Clause 119 of the Bill therefore provides for rules to make provision about the transmission by the registrar to the registrar of companies of applications to register company charges where those charges are submitted for registration at the Land Registry.[195]

LAND CERTIFICATES

The nature of a land or charge certificate under the present law

9.83 The nature of a land or charge certificate appears from section 63(1) of the Land Registration Act 1925, which provides that—

> On the first registration of a freehold or leasehold interest in land, and on the registration of a charge, a land certificate, or charge certificate, as the case may be, shall be prepared in the prescribed form: it shall state whether the title is absolute, good leasehold, qualified or possessory, and it shall be delivered to the proprietor or deposited at the registry as the proprietor may prefer.[196]

---

[191] Under either Part 12 of that Act (registration of charges) or Chapter 3 of Part 23 (corresponding provision for oversea companies).

[192] See para 9.77.

[193] Schedule 10, para 6(a).

[194] Certain technical difficulties have to be overcome.

[195] The rules will be laid before Parliament only: Cl 125(3); but will not be land registration rules: Cl 129(1). There is no reason why rules on the transmission of information from one Government department to another should have to be considered by the Rules Committee under Cl 124.

[196] But see below, para 9.85.

There is also provision for the issue of a land or charge certificate on the completion of the registration of a transfer or grant of any registered land or charge.[197]

9.84 The form of the certificate is prescribed by rules.[198] The certificate contains a copy of the register with a note of the date on which it was examined, and there is provision for the certificate to be endorsed from time to time with subsequent entries in the register.[199] The certificate is admissible as evidence "of the several matters therein contained".[200] There is power for the registrar to issue a new certificate in place of one which is produced to him,[201] and in certain other cases, as where a certificate has been lost or destroyed.[202]

9.85 A certificate is "outstanding" for the purposes of the Land Registration Act 1925, when it is retained by the proprietor and not deposited at the Registry.[203] When a charge is registered, the land certificate has to be deposited at the Registry until the charge or mortgage is cancelled.[204] This provision, which was at one time literally observed, is now a fiction. In practice, where a property is subject to a registered charge, the registry does not issue a land certificate until such time as the charge is redeemed.

Present practice

9.86 Where the land or charge certificate is outstanding, it must be produced to the registrar—

(1)   on an entry made in relation to a registered disposition;

(2)   on every registered transmission;[205] and

(3)   on the entry of a notice or restriction.[206]

This requirement is subject to certain exceptions. First, in certain specified cases a notice may be entered without the production of the certificate.[207] Secondly, where the certificate is deposited in the Registry, it obviously cannot be produced in relation to the transactions listed in (1)—(3) above. However, because all of those

---

[197] Land Registration Act 1925, s 64(3).

[198] See Land Registration Rules 1925, rr 261—264; Schedule 2, Form 78.

[199] Land Registration Act 1925, s 63(2).

[200] *Ibid*, s 68.

[201] *Ibid*, s 67(1).

[202] *Ibid*, s 67(2); Land Registration Rules 1925, r 271.

[203] See Land Registration Act 1925, s 64(1).

[204] *Ibid*, s 65. The reference to mortgage cautions in that section refers to a type of entry that is now obsolete, having been abolished by Administration of Justice Act 1977.

[205] That is, transmissions on death or bankruptcy.

[206] Land Registration Act 1925, s 64(1).

[207] See *ibid*, s 64(5)—(7) (as inserted).

transactions require either the consent of the registered proprietor or an order of the court before they can be effected, the registry does in practice notify the registered proprietor before making any such entry.

9.87   When the Land Registration Act 1925 was first enacted, land and charge certificates were regarded as being much more important than they are now. In a commentary published in 1939, the then Chief Land Registrar commented that "the Land Certificate (or, in the case of a mortgage, the charge certificate) takes the place of the title deeds for almost all purposes".[208] This is reflected in the now-obsolete provision which sanctioned the creation of a lien by deposit of a land or charge certificate to secure indebtedness.[209]

The impact of the Bill

9.88   It will be apparent from what has been said in Parts IV and VI of this Report, that the role of land certificates is to be reduced considerably under the Bill. There will be no requirement that they should be produced on a disposition of a registered estate.[210] Nor will they have to be produced to secure the entry on the register of either a notice or a restriction.[211] Instead, as we have explained, there will be procedures that will enable the registered proprietor to secure the cancellation of a notice[212] and object to the entry of a restriction.[213] Furthermore, a person who applies for the entry of a notice or restriction without reasonable cause commits a breach of statutory duty that is actionable in damages.[214] Perhaps the most important factor, however, is that any requirement to submit a land or charge certificate to the registrar on registration is not readily compatible with the system of electronic conveyancing that the Bill is intended to introduce.

Abolition of charge certificates

9.89   The first steps in the process of introducing electronic conveyancing are likely to be in relation to registered charges. It is already possible to discharge a registered charge electronically,[215] and it is likely that the creation of registered charges will be the first forms of disposition of registered land that can be effected electronically. We can see no useful purpose in retaining charge certificates. There is therefore no provision in the Bill either to authorise the issue of charge certificates, or in relation to those already in existence. Charge certificates will be abolished once the Bill is brought into force.

---

[208]   Brickdale and Stewart-Wallace, *The Land Registration Act, 1925* (4th ed), p 176.

[209]   Land Registration Act 1925, s 66; see above, para 7.10.

[210]   See above, para 4.31.

[211]   See above, paras 6.23, 6.54.

[212]   See Cl 36; above, para 6.30.

[213]   See Cl 45; above, para 6.56.

[214]   Cls 77(1)(b) and 77(2); above, paras 6.28, 6.55.

[215]   See Land Registration Rules 1925, r 151A.

Land certificates

9.90 There is very little in the Bill about land certificates. The only provision is a power by rules to make provision about—

    (1)   when a certificate of registration of title may be issued;

    (2)   the form and content of such a certificate; and

    (3)   when such a certificate must be produced or surrendered to the registrar.[216]

9.91 It is envisaged that a land certificate will be a document certifying that the registration of a registered estate has taken place and that a named person is the registered proprietor. It will, in short, be an indicium of title. It is possible that it may no longer even contain a copy of the register as it does now because that can be misleading. This is because the register alone is conclusive as to the state of the title to a registered estate at any given time. Given that a land certificate will be no more than an indicium of title, its most important function for the future may have no connection with the conveyancing process. It will, for example, alert an executor to the fact that the deceased was the registered proprietor of a property, which might not otherwise be apparent to him or her.

---

[216] Schedule 10, para 4. The rules will be land registration rules and will be laid before Parliament only: Cls 123, 125(3), 129(1).

PART X
ALTERATION, RECTIFICATION AND INDEMNITY

INTRODUCTION

10.1 In this Part we explain the provisions of the draft Bill that govern the alteration of the register and the payment of indemnity. The Land Registration Act 1925 makes detailed provision for one particular type of alteration to the register, namely rectification. There are presently ten grounds on which rectification may be ordered under the Land Registration Act 1925 or the Land Registration Rules 1925.[1] These can be broadly summarised as follows—

(1) Where a court either makes an order which gives effect to an established property right or interest, or orders the removal from the register of an entry in respect of a right which has not been established.[2]

(2) Where the court or the registrar decides that the register is incorrect in some way.[3]

(3) Where the registrar decides that a clerical error needs to be corrected.[4]

Under that Act, rectification is always discretionary.[5] However, in practice, it is only where rectification is concerned with the correction of some mistake in the register — the cases summarised in (2) and (3) above — that the discretion is normally exercised. In cases where a court has concluded that a person is entitled to a right or interest in the land, rectification will usually, though not invariably, be ordered.[6] Indeed, it would be strange if it were otherwise. Where a person establishes his or her entitlement to some such right or interest, there will not often be any reason why a court should refuse to give effect to it, as this would leave the successful claimant with a mere right to indemnity.

---

[1] See Law Com No 254, paras 2.37—2.39; summary, paras 8.6—8.22 (where the provisions are analysed in detail).

[2] Land Registration Act 1925, s 82(1)(a), (b).

[3] *Ibid*, s 82(1)(d)—(h). There is also a power to rectify where all interested persons consent: *ibid*, s 82(1)(c).

[4] Land Registration Rules 1925, rr 13, 14.

[5] See Law Com No 254, para 8.5.

[6] See *Norwich & Peterborough Building Society v Steed* [1993] Ch 116, 139; Law Com No 254, paras 8.12—8.13. However, see now *Kingsalton Ltd v Thames Water Developments Ltd* [2001] EWCA Civ 20; [2001] EGCS 12 where rectification was refused in a case that was held to fall within Land Registration Act 1925, s 82(1)(a) (though in reality, on the facts, it appears to have been a case involving a mistake that fell within s 82(1)(g), that is "where the legal estate has been registered in the name of a person who if the land had not been registered would not have been the estate owner"). On the power of the court to refuse rectification when s 82(1)(a) applied, see in particular the comments of Arden LJ at [2001] EWCA Civ 20, [39].

10.2 Where the register is changed for some reason other than one of the statutory grounds for rectification, as where the registrar removes an entry on the register that is spent because the interest to which it relates has terminated, that alteration is not "rectification" for the purposes of the Act. Indeed, the Act has no specific name for it. It is simply part of the process of ensuring that the register is kept up to date. Although this distinction between rectification of the register and its alteration is implicit in the Land Registration Act 1925, it is not spelt out explicitly.[7]

10.3 Indemnity is, in some senses, the correlative of rectification. It is payable where a person suffers loss as a result of an error or omission in the register, whether or not the register is rectified, and in certain other circumstances.[8] The availability of indemnity is of great importance to the system of land registration. It is the basis of the so-called "State guarantee of title" which registration confers.[9]

10.4 In the Consultative Document, we explained that the practice that has developed both in the courts and in the Land Registry in relation to the rectification of the register was largely sound and that the deficiencies lay in the way in which the legislation was drafted.[10] The provisions of the Land Registration Act 1925 tend to obscure the real nature of rectification and the manner in which it operates. We considered that the main task of any new legislation should be to recast the legislation in a much more transparent form. However, we did make a number of recommendations to change the law where it was either unsatisfactory or could be improved.[11] We did not propose any substantive changes to the law governing indemnity because the subject had been considered recently by the Joint Working Group[12] and its recommendations had been implemented by the Land Registration Act 1997.[13] The recommendations in the Consultative Document on rectification, amendment and indemnity were strongly supported on consultation.

THE EFFECT OF THE BILL: ALTERATION

Introduction

10.5 In considering the effect of the Bill, we explain first the provisions governing alteration before examining those which deal with indemnity. The Bill makes separate provision for alterations to the register of title[14] and to the register of

---

[7]   Compare, for example, Land Registration Act 1925, ss 35 (discharge of charges), 46 (determination of leases and other registered estates), 50(3) (discharge of restrictive covenants), 75 (registration of adverse possessor) on the one hand with s 82 (rectification) on the other.

[8]   See Land Registration Act 1925, s 83 (as substituted by Land Registration Act 1997, s 2).

[9]   On this, see Ruoff & Roper, *Registered Conveyancing*, 2-10; 2-13; 40-02.

[10]   See Law Com No 254, para 8.1.

[11]   *Ibid*, paras 8.40—8.55.

[12]   See (1995) Law Com No 235, Part IV.

[13]   See s 2.

[14]   Cl 65; Schedule 4.

cautions.[15] The latter provisions are new, and reflect the fact that the register of cautions is to be placed on a clear statutory footing.[16]

The circumstances in which the register may be altered

The meaning of alteration and rectification

10.6 The provisions of the Bill which govern the alteration of the register of title bear no resemblance to their equivalents in the Land Registration Act 1925. In accordance with the recommendations in the Consultative Document, they have been recast to reflect the present practice in relation to rectification and amendment of the register.[17] The basic concept that the Bill employs is that of *alteration* of the register[18] and the circumstances in which such an alteration can be made are explained below.[19] The Bill makes it clear that rectification is just one particular form of alteration, and it is defined as one which—

(1) involves the correction of a mistake; *and*

(2) prejudicially affects the title of a registered proprietor.[20]

The latter requirement is directly linked to the circumstances in which an indemnity is payable. This is explained below.[21] As a result of this latter requirement, the concept of "rectification" as it is used in the Bill is narrower than it is under the Land Registration Act 1925.

10.7 The principal differences may be summarised as follows—

(1) Rectification is confined to cases where a mistake is to be corrected. This will not include every case which is at present treated as rectification. It will not therefore cover cases where the register is altered to give effect to rights that have been acquired over the land since it was registered,[22] or where the register was originally correct, but subsequent events have made it incorrect.[23] In such cases the court will no longer have any discretion (albeit one that has seldom been exercised[24]) whether or not to give effect to the right so established.

---

[15] Cls 20—21.

[16] For the register of cautions, see above, para 3.65; and Cl 19.

[17] See above, para 10.4.

[18] Schedule 4, paras 2(1), 5.

[19] See paras 10.10 (alteration ordered by the court), 10.19 (alteration by the registrar).

[20] Schedule 4, para 1.

[21] See para 10.30.

[22] As where a court determines that X has acquired an easement by prescription over Y's land subsequent to Y's acquisition of that land as registered proprietor.

[23] As where A was registered as proprietor, but B subsequently obtains an order setting aside the transfer to A on the grounds that A procured it by fraud on B.

[24] See above, para 10.1.

(2)   Not every correction of a mistake will constitute rectification. The correction must be one which prejudicially affects the title of a registered proprietor. Under the 1925 Act, if, in order to correct a mistake, the register is altered to give effect to an overriding interest, that is regarded as rectification.[25] However, no indemnity will be payable because the proprietor will suffer no loss in consequence. He or she had taken the land subject to any overriding interests.[26] Rectification in such a case therefore does no more than update the title and the registered proprietor is in no worse position than he or she was before.[27] In other words, there can be rectification under the present law even where an alteration to the register does *not* prejudicially affect the title of the registered proprietor. That will cease to be so under the Bill. The circumstances in which the register is rectified and those in which the proprietor will be entitled to an indemnity will coincide.

10.8   The Bill makes it clear that—

(1)   rectification of the register, whether by order of the court or by the register can (as now[28]) affect derivative interests; but

(2)   any such changes are prospective only,[29] which accords with the manner in which the analogous provisions of the Land Registration Act 1925 have been interpreted.[30]

Powers of alteration

10.9   Under the Bill, powers are conferred on—

(1)   the court to order the alteration of the register;[31] and

(2)   the registrar to alter the register.[32]

THE POWERS OF THE COURT

The circumstances in which the court may order the alteration of the register

10.10   The court may order the alteration of the register in three cases.[33]

---

[25]   See *Chowood Ltd v Lyall (No 2)* [1930] 2 Ch 156. In that case the mistake was to register X as proprietor of land when Y had already acquired title to it by adverse possession: see *ibid*, at p 168.

[26]   See Land Registration Act 1925, ss 20(1), 23(1).

[27]   *Re Chowood's Registered Land* [1933] Ch 574, 582.

[28]   See Land Registration Act 1925, s 82(2).

[29]   See Schedule 4, para 8.

[30]   The Land Registration Act 1925 is not explicit on this point: see *Freer v Unwins Ltd* [1976] Ch 288, 296.

[31]   Schedule 4, paras 2—4.

[32]   Schedule 4, paras 5—7.

(1)   The first is for the purpose of correcting a mistake. As we have indicated above—

      (a)   under the Land Registration Act 1925 all such cases are treated as rectification of the register;[34] but

      (b)   under the Bill this will cease to be so: the correction of a mistake will amount to rectification only if it prejudicially affects the title of a registered proprietor.[35]

(2)   The second is for the purpose of bringing the register up to date. If, for example, a court decided that a claimant in proceedings had established his or her entitlement to an easement by prescription over a parcel of registered land, it could[36] order that the benefit and burden of the easement be recorded on the registers of the dominant and servient titles respectively. Similarly, if a court ordered the forfeiture of a registered leasehold title for breach of covenant, it could also order that the title to the lease be deleted from the register.

(3)   The third is to give effect to any estate, right or interest excepted from the effect of registration. Under the Land Registration Act 1925, where land is registered with good leasehold, possessory or qualified title, the rights excepted from the effect of registration have the status of overriding interests.[37] It follows that, if the register is rectified to give effect to any such right, no indemnity will be payable, because the registered proprietor will not have suffered loss by reason of the rectification.[38] We have explained elsewhere that we do not consider that the rights excepted from the effect of registration need to have the status of overriding interests.[39] This is because, under both the Land Registration Act 1925[40] and the Bill,[41] any registered disposition will take effect subject to such rights. The inclusion in the Bill of an express power for the court to order the alteration of the register to give effect to such excepted rights merely reflects this change. It is a necessary consequence of this power that such an alteration will not amount to rectification. Nor will it give rise to a claim for indemnity.[42]

---

[33]   Schedule 4, para 2(1).

[34]   See above, para 10.1.

[35]   See above, paras 10.6, 10.7.

[36]   Cf below, para 10.12.

[37]   Land Registration Act 1925, s 70(1)(h).

[38]   Cf above, para 10.7(2).

[39]   See above, paras 8.81—8.84.

[40]   Sections 20(2), (3), 23(2), (3), (4).

[41]   See Cls 29(2)(a)(iii), 30(2)(a)(iii); above, para 5.11.

[42]   For the grounds on which indemnity is payable, see below, paras 10.30 and following.

10.11 Where the court does order the alteration of the register under the powers explained in paragraph 7.10, the registrar is under a duty to give effect to the order once it has been served on him.[43] This is similar to, but wider than, the equivalent provision in the Land Registration Act 1925, which applies only in relation to an order of the court to *rectify* the register.

10.12 Normally, where a court determines that there is ground for the alteration of the register, it will order the registrar to make that alteration unless it amounts to rectification of the register,[44] to which special rules, explained below, will apply.[45] Under the Bill, the Lord Chancellor may make rules as to when a court must exercise its power to alter the register in cases which do not amount to rectification.[46] These rules are likely to restrict the court's *duty* to order an alteration to cases where it has made a determination in proceedings.[47] It is unlikely to extend to a case where the court incidentally discovers in the course of such proceedings that some entry on the register is incorrect or has ceased to have effect, but where that fact is not relevant to the outcome of the proceedings before it.[48]

Qualified indefeasibility: the protection for the proprietor who is in possession

10.13 Section 82(3) of the Land Registration Act 1925 embodies what we described in the Consultative Document as a principle of qualified indefeasibility.[49] It restricts the circumstances in which it is possible to rectify the register so as to affect the title of a "proprietor who is in possession" to four named circumstances, namely—

(1) for the purpose of giving effect to an overriding interest;

(2) for the purpose of giving effect to an order of the court;

(3) where "the proprietor has caused or substantially contributed to the error or omission by fraud or lack of proper care"; and

(4) where "for any other reason, in any particular case, it is considered that it would be unjust not to rectify the register" against the proprietor.

---

[43] Schedule 4, para 2(2). There is a power to make rules both as to the form of the court's order and as to its service on the registrar: see *ibid*, para 4(b), (c). Such rules will be land registration rules and will be laid before Parliament only: Cls 125(3), 129(1).

[44] See above, para 10.6.

[45] See paras 10.15 and following.

[46] Schedule 4, para 4(a). Such rules will be land registration rules and will be laid before Parliament only: Cls 125(3), 129(1).

[47] Though it would be free to order an alteration in other cases if it considered it to be appropriate.

[48] The rules which impose a duty on the registrar to alter the register are likely to be much more sweeping: see below, para 10.20.

[49] See para 8.23.

The thinking behind the protection of a proprietor in possession is obvious enough. When a person is registered as proprietor of a parcel of land *and* is in possession of it, there should be a presumption against rectifying the register against him or her. Thus, in the case where, by mistake, two neighbouring landowners are both registered as proprietors of a strip of land on their common boundary, the register should (in general) be rectified against the one who is *not* in possession of the strip. The registered titles thereby come to reflect the practical reality of the situation.

10.14   We explained in detail the shortcomings of section 82(3) of the Land Registration Act 1925 in the Consultative Document.[50] We sought views on whether it should (as we thought) have an equivalent in any new legislation and if so, how wide the scope of that equivalent should be.[51] The Bill reflects the outcome of that consultation.[52] The great majority of those who responded to this point favoured a provision which gave a wide meaning as to who was a proprietor in possession. This enhances the conclusive nature of the register by restricting the circumstances in which it can be rectified. However, it should be noted that—

(1)   rectification has a narrower meaning under the Bill than it does under the Land Registration Act 1925;[53] and

(2)   the principle of qualified indefeasibility contained in the Bill does not affect the circumstances in which the register can be altered in cases not amounting to rectification.

10.15   The Bill precludes an order for the alteration of the register that amounts to rectification[54] without the proprietor's consent[55] if it affects the title of a registered estate in land[56] that is in the possession of the proprietor except in two cases.[57] Those are—

(1)   where the proprietor has by fraud or lack of proper care caused or substantially contributed to the mistake; or

(2)   it would for any other reason be unjust for the alteration not to be made.

These two exceptions to indefeasibility replicate those that are presently found in section 82(3)(a) and (c) of the Land Registration Act 1925 respectively.

---

[50]   See paras 8.23—8.31.

[51]   See Law Com No 254, paras 8.47—8.53. We deliberately did not express any provisional view on the width of the provision.

[52]   See Schedule 4, paras 3, 6; Cl 128.

[53]   See above, para 10.7.

[54]   Cf Schedule 4, paras 1, 2(a).

[55]   The proprietor commonly does consent in practice.

[56]   Including for these purposes the benefit of any registered estate, such as an easement, that subsists for the benefit of that title: Schedule 4, para 3(4).

[57]   Schedule 4, para 3(1), (2).

10.16 It will be noted that the Bill does not replicate the other two exceptions that are currently found in the opening words of section 82(3) of the 1925 Act, namely rectification to give effect to an overriding interest or to an order of the court.[58] Neither is needed for the following reasons.

(1) Under the Bill, if the register is altered to give effect to an overriding interest it will never amount to *rectification*. This is because the alteration does not prejudicially affect the title of the registered proprietor as the Bill's definition of rectification requires.[59] He or she already holds the land subject to the overriding interest and the alteration merely updates the register to record the true position.

(2) We explained in the Consultative Document that the obscure exception for orders of the court—

> appears to have been intended to ensure that there were no restrictions on the powers of the court to order rectification... where the order gives effect to the substantive rights and entitlements of the parties.[60]

Under the Bill, an order by the court to give effect to such rights will no longer amount to rectification, either because the order will not involve the correction of any mistake,[61] or if it does, because the alteration does not prejudicially affect the title of the registered proprietor.

10.17 In the Consultative Document, we explained that there is some uncertainty as to who is a "proprietor who is in possession" for the purposes of section 82(3) of the Land Registration Act 1925.[62] We were particularly concerned to remove that uncertainty for the future. Under the Bill,[63] a proprietor will be a proprietor in possession of land for the purposes of the provision explained in paragraph 10.15 above, in the following circumstances —

(1) The first is where the land is physically in his or her possession.[64] This codifies the present law.[65]

(2) The second is where the land is physically in the possession of a person who is entitled to be registered as proprietor.[66] There is no obvious reason

---

[58] For these, see above, para 10.13.

[59] Schedule 4, para 1(b); above, para 10.6.

[60] Law Com No 254, para 8.29.

[61] As where events subsequent to the acquisition of the land by the registered proprietor mean that the register no longer accurately records the true state of the title. Cf above, para 10.7(1).

[62] *Ibid*, paras 8.24—8.26.

[63] Cl 128.

[64] Cl 128(1).

[65] See *Chowood Ltd v Lyall (No 2)* [1930] 2 Ch 156, 166, 167; *Epps v Esso Petroleum Co Ltd* [1973] 1 WLR 1071, 1078.

for differentiating this case from (1). There will be some cases where a person entitled to be registered as proprietor has the legal estate in the land vested in him or her by operation of law,[67] such as a proprietor's trustee in bankruptcy or a deceased proprietor's personal representatives.[68] In other cases, the land may be in the possession of a person entitled to be registered who has only an equitable interest. An example would be where a beneficiary under a bare trust was in physical possession of land and the registered proprietor was his or her nominee. A squatter who is entitled to be registered as proprietor under the provisions of Schedule 6 of the Bill[69] is *not*, for these purposes, a person entitled to be registered.[70] There is no obvious reason for extending the protection given to a proprietor in physical possession to a person whose claim to the land is essentially unlawful, being founded on trespass.[71]

(3)   The third circumstance is in relation to specified relationships where the possession of another person is attributed to the registered proprietor.[72] This will be the case where—

   (a)   the registered proprietor is the landlord and the person in possession is a tenant;

   (b)   the registered proprietor is a mortgagor and the person in possession is the mortgagee;[73]

   (c)   the registered proprietor is a licensor and the person in possession is a licensee; and

   (d)   the registered proprietor is a trustee and the person in possession is a beneficiary under the trust.[74]

---

[66]   Cl 128(1).

[67]   See Cl 27(5). Normally, as that subclause makes apparent, where there is a vesting by operation of law, the legal estate does *not* vest until the transferee is registered as the new proprietor. See above, paras 4.16—4.20.

[68]   It is very common for personal representatives *not* to have themselves registered as proprietor.

[69]   See Part XIV of this Report.

[70]   Cl 128(3).

[71]   Adverse possession has been described as "possession as of wrong": see *Buckinghamshire County Council v Moran* [1990] Ch 623, 644, *per* Nourse LJ; *Sze To Chun Keung v Kung Kwok Wai David* [1997] 1 WLR 1232, 1233, *per* Lord Hoffmann.

[72]   Cl 128(2).

[73]   This reverses the present law. It has been held that a mortgagee in possession is *not* a proprietor who is in possession for the purposes of Land Registration Act 1925, s 82(3): see *Hayes v Nwajiaku* [1994] EGCS 106.

[74]   Normally, where land is settled, the registered proprietor will be the tenant for life. He or she will then be a proprietor in possession within Cl 128(1). However, there may be some cases where settled land is vested in statutory owners and where the beneficiaries under the trust

In fact the protection is wider than this. It applies not only where the second-named person is actually in possession, but where he or she is *treated* as being in possession.[75] This would cover the cases where (for example) a tenant had sublet, or a mortgagee in possession had exercised its power of leasing.[76]

10.18 Under the present law, where a proprietor is *not* in possession of the registered land in question (so that section 82(3) of the Land Registration Act 1925 is inapplicable), and a ground exists for rectification, "the court will normally grant rectification".[77] However, the matter remains discretionary and "there may still be circumstances which defeat a claim for rectification".[78] That principle is codified in the Bill. Where the court can order rectification of the register and the land is not in the possession of the proprietor (as defined),[79] "it must make an order... unless it considers that there are exceptional circumstances which justify its not doing so".[80]

THE POWERS OF THE REGISTRAR

The circumstances in which the registrar may alter the register

10.19 Most alterations to the register are made by the registrar rather than in response to an order of the court. His powers of amendment are therefore of considerable importance. Under the Bill, the registrar will be able to alter the register in the same three circumstances as those in which the court may order its alteration,[81] namely to correct a mistake, to bring the register up to date[82] and to give effect to an estate, right or interest excepted from the effect of registration.[83] In addition, he will also be able to alter the register in order to remove any superfluous entry.[84] This would, for example, cover cases where—

---

are in possession. This might happen if, for example, the person entitled to a life interest were a minor. See Settled Land Act 1925, s 23.

[75] Cl 128(2).

[76] See Law of Property Act 1925, s 99(2).

[77] *Epps v Esso Petroleum Co Ltd* [1973] 1 WLR 1071, 1078, *per* Templeman J.

[78] *Ibid*, at p 1079, *per* Templeman J.

[79] Or is in the possession of the proprietor, but in circumstances where rectification can nonethless be ordered: see above, para 10.15.

[80] Schedule 4, para 3(3).

[81] See above, para 10.10, where these are explained.

[82] An example might be where a registered proprietor had died or become insolvent and his personal representatives or trustee in bankruptcy respectively applied to be registered as proprietor of his or her registered estate. In each case, the title to the registered estate would have vested in the applicant by operation of law: see above, para 4.19.

[83] Schedule 4, para 5(a)—(c).

[84] Schedule 4, para 5(d). There is obviously some overlap with para 5(b) (alteration to bring the register up to date).

(1) a restriction had been entered on the register to freeze all dealings with a registered estate,[85] but the circumstances which made that precaution necessary had subsequently passed;

(2) an interest protected on the register by one entry was adequately protected by another; or

(3) a restriction on the powers of a registered proprietor had ceased to apply.

The registrar's power to remove spent entries is likely to become increasingly important with the advent of electronic conveyancing. Authorised practitioners will be able to register dispositions of, and the creation of rights and interests in or over, registered land.[86] However, the registrar will have an important role in policing the register to ensure that it is not cluttered with entries that are no longer operative.[87]

10.20 The Bill contains a power by which the Lord Chancellor may make rules which regulate the alteration of the register.[88] First, there is a power to specify when the registrar is under a *duty* to alter the register other than in cases of rectification.[89] In practice this will be an important power. It is likely that, subject to necessary qualifications, the registrar will be subject to a duty to alter the register whenever he discovers grounds for doing so (save in cases of rectification) regardless of the circumstances under which those grounds came to light.[90] Secondly, rules may be made dealing with the manner in which the registrar should exercise the power, applications for alteration of the register and the procedure for exercising the power of alteration, whether on application or not.[91] As we have mentioned in paragraph 10.19, it is envisaged that the registrar will be authorised to undertake periodic "audits" of registered titles. This is to ensure that the entries on the register are still current and to remove any that, on inquiry, are not. This is in accordance with one of the main objectives of the Bill, namely to ensure that the register should at all times be an accurate reflection of the true state of the title.

---

[85] See above, para 6.51.

[86] See Part XIII.

[87] For the power to make rules which will authorise the registrar to contract-out the making of alterations to the register, see below, para 10.23.

[88] See Schedule 4, para 7. Such rules will be land registration rules and will be laid before Parliament only: Cls 125(3), 129(1).

[89] Schedule 4, para 7(a).

[90] Compare the position that is likely to apply to the court: above, para 10.12. There may be cases where the registrar *cannot* alter the register, because it is, in practice, impossible for him to discover in whom the land is now vested. For example, there are still some parcels of land which are registered in the name of "London County Council". There have been a succession of statutory vestings since the dissolution of the London County Council, and it is often very difficult to ascertain the body in which the land is now vested. For an illustration, see *Prudential Assurance Co Ltd v Eden Restaurants (Holborn) Ltd* [2001] L & TR 480.

[91] Schedule 4, para 7(b)—(d).

10.21 Where a person applies to the registrar to rectify the register, and the registered proprietor objects, and it is not possible to dispose of the matter by agreement, the registrar must refer the matter to the Adjudicator.[92] Any contested application for the rectification of the register will, therefore, be resolved by the Adjudicator.[93] The office of Adjudicator to HM Land Registry is a new one that will be created by the Bill,[94] and an explanation of his functions is given in Part XVI of this Report.[95]

Qualified indefeasibility: the protection for the proprietor who is in possession

10.22 We have explained above the provisions which restrict the circumstances in which the register may be rectified against a proprietor of a registered estate in land who is in possession of land (in the extended meaning which that phrase has under the Bill) except where he or she consents.[96] These apply as much where the power to rectify is exercised by the Adjudicator as they do in proceedings before the court.[97] Similarly, where grounds for rectification of the register exist and the land is *not* in the possession of the proprietor, the Adjudicator must rectify the register — much as the court must order its rectification[98] — unless he considers that there are exceptional circumstances which justify his not doing so.[99]

Alteration under network access agreements

10.23 We explain in Part XIII of this Report how electronic conveyancing is intended to operate. The registration of many dispositions of registered land will no longer be conducted by the registrar directly, but will be initiated by solicitors or licensed conveyancers, who are authorised to do so under a network access agreement.[100] However, it will not merely be the process of registration of dispositions that can be delegated in this way. Under such a contract, a person may be authorised to initiate alterations to the register of title or to the cautions register.[101] This power to initiate alterations is an essential concomitant of the power to authorise practitioners to make dispositions that will change the register. Commonly, on a sale of land, a charge may be discharged on completion. Electronic conveyancing would be impossible if a practitioner could bring about the registration of the transfer but not initiate the removal of the discharged mortgage. However, the authority to alter the register is likely to be extended more widely. When a practitioner is examining a title in relation to a proposed disposition, he or she

---

[92] Cl 73; see below, para 16.6.

[93] Cf Cl 106(1); below, para 16.7.

[94] See Cl 105; Schedule 7; below, para 16.3.

[95] See below, paras 16.6 and following.

[96] See paras 10.15—10.17.

[97] See Schedule 4, para 6.

[98] See above, para 10.18.

[99] Schedule 4, para 6(3).

[100] See below, para 13.36.

[101] Schedule5, para 1(2)(b).

may (for example) discover spent entries on the register. The powers that the Bill are likely to give will enable him or her to set in train the removal of such entries.[102]

Costs in non-rectification cases

10.24 Under the Bill, where the register is altered by the registrar, whether of his own initiative or to give effect to a court order, and the case is not one of rectification, he may pay such amount as he thinks fit in respect of any costs or expenses reasonably incurred by a person in connection with the alteration.[103] The power may always be exercised by the registrar where the costs or expenses were incurred with his consent. Even where the registrar did not give his prior consent, he may pay costs and expenses where—

(1)   it appears to him that they had to be incurred urgently and that it was not reasonably practicable to apply for his consent in advance; or

(2)   he has subsequently approved their incurrence.[104]

10.25 This is a new power. Under the present law, the registrar may pay *indemnity* in respect of costs in cases of *rectification* where those costs have been either approved by him[105] or incurred in proceedings to determine the amount of any indemnity.[106] There is, however, no power to pay a party's costs in relation to any alteration that does not amount to rectification of the register.[107] The Bill therefore remedies this deficiency.[108]

The circumstances in which the register of cautions may be altered

10.26 We have explained the nature of the register of cautions against first registration in Part III of this Report.[109] This register does, of course, relate to an *unregistered* legal estate[110] and not to a registered estate. Its purpose is to provide a mechanism by which a person having the requisite interest in the land[111] may require to be notified of an application for the first registration of that land. Any such application cannot be approved until the cautioner has been given an opportunity

---

[102]   See below, para 13.39.

[103]   Schedule 4, para 9(1).

[104]   *Ibid*, para 9(2).

[105]   See Land Registration Act 1925, s 83(9).

[106]   See Land Registration and Land Charges Act 1971, s 2.

[107]   It is easy to see how such costs might be incurred, as where the registrar seeks to verify whether certain entries on the register are spent, and the registered proprietor has to incur expense in taking legal advice to resolve the matter.

[108]   For the registrar's power under the Bill to pay indemnity in respect of costs incurred in relation to a claim for rectification, see below, para 10.45.

[109]   See above, para 3.65.

[110]   Cl 15(1).

[111]   See Cl 15(1), (2); above, para 3.56.

to object within a specified period.[112] There may be circumstances in which it is necessary to alter the register of cautions, whether for the purpose of correcting a mistake or of bringing it up to date. Although these situations will not be common, the Bill makes provision for such alteration.[113] The register may be altered either by an order of the court,[114] or by the registrar,[115] for the purpose of correcting a mistake or bringing the register up to date. Thus, for example—

(1) if the court decides that a cautioner lacks the requisite interest to lodge a caution, it may order that it be cancelled;

(2) if the cautioner dies and her successor in title applies to the the registrar to be registered in her place, he may register that successor.

Where the registrar alters the register, he may pay such amount as he thinks fit in respect of any costs reasonably incurred by a person in connection with the alteration.[116] There are rule-making powers[117] under which (for example) provision may be made as to when there is a duty to alter the register.[118] As noted above, when electronic conveyancing is introduced, a practitioner may be authorised to initiate the alteration of the cautions register under a network access contract.[119]

Alteration of documents

10.27 Under rule 13 of the Land Registration Rules 1925, the registrar has a power to correct "any clerical error or error of like nature" in the register or any plan or document to which it refers. This power may only be exercised where the correction can be made "without any detriment to any registered interest". In practice, the registrar will either—

(1) secure the consent of the registered proprietor affected to the correction; or (in the rare cases where such consent cannot be obtained)

(2) serve notice on him or her that he intends to correct the mistake unless he or she objects.

It will be noted that this power — which is widely used — does not just apply to the correction of errors *in the register*, but to mistakes in documents to which the register refers as well. A typical case might be where a lease is lodged with the

---

[112] Cl 16.

[113] Cls 20; 21.

[114] Cl 20(1). The order has effect when served on the registrar. He is under a duty to give effect to it: Cl 20(2).

[115] Cl 21(1).

[116] Cl 21(3). When the court orders an alteration, it can award costs under the general rules found in CPR r 44.

[117] Cl 20(3) (orders of the court); Cl 21(2) (alteration by the registrar). Such rules will be land registration rules and will be laid before Parliament only: Cls 125(3), 129(1).

[118] Cl 20(3)(a) (orders of the court); Cl 21(2)(a) (alteration by the registrar).

[119] See para 10.23; Schedule 5, para 1(2)(b).

registry and, either before or after it is registered, it becomes apparent that there is a mistake in the reddendum so that the annual rental appears as £6,050, when it is in fact £6,500. The registrar will correct the mistake unless there is an objection from either party to the lease.

10.28 In the Consultative Document, we provisionally recommended that the power contained in rule 13 was sufficiently important that it should be in primary legislation.[120] This view was supported on consultation and the Bill provides accordingly. It contains a specific rule-making power to make provision that will enable the registrar to correct a mistake in an application or accompanying document. In the circumstances prescribed in such rules, the correction will have the same effect as if made by the parties.[121] In other words, the registrar will, as now, be able to serve notice on interested parties of his intention to correct a mistake in a particular document and then make such a correction in the absence of any objection.

THE EFFECT OF THE BILL: INDEMNITY

Introduction

10.29 As we have explained above,[122] the provisions of section 83 of the Land Registration Act 1925, which govern the payment of indemnity, were amended by section 2 of the Land Registration Act 1997. For that reason, we did not make any recommendations for reform in the Consultative Document, although we did anticipate that there might be minor amendments to the law to reflect more clearly the current practice in relation to the payment of indemnity.[123] In the event, the provisions[124] have been completely recast in accordance with the style of the present Bill. The substance of them has not, however, been altered in any significant way.

The grounds on which indemnity is payable

10.30 The Bill sets out eight circumstances in which a person who suffers loss is entitled to be indemnified.[125] It should be noted that, under this provision, a claimant can recover any loss that flows from the particular ground, whether that loss is direct or consequential. A number of the grounds for indemnity arise out of a mistake of some description. A "mistake" in something is taken to include anything mistakenly omitted from it as well as anything mistakenly included in it.[126]

---

[120] Law Com No 254, para 8.43.

[121] Schedule 10, para 6(e). See above, para 9.80. Such rules will be land registration rules and will be laid before Parliament only: Cls 123, 125(3), 129(1).

[122] See para 10.4.

[123] Law Com No 254, para 8.2.

[124] See Cl 102; Schedule 8.

[125] Schedule 8, para 1(1).

[126] *Ibid*, para 11(1).

Loss by reason of rectification

10.31 There is an entitlement to indemnity where a person suffers loss by reason of rectification of the register.[127] This replicates the effect of section 83(1)(a) of the Land Registration Act 1925 and it is a common reason for the payment of indemnity. In two specific cases, both of which are carried forward from the Land Registration Act 1925,[128] a person is treated as if he or she has suffered loss by reason of rectification, even though, but for the provision this might not have been so.[129]

(1) The first is where he or she suffers loss by reason of the change of title resulting from the exercise by the registrar of his power to upgrade the title under Clause 62 of the Bill.[130] The purpose of this provision is to remove any doubt as to whether the registrar can be said to have made a mistake when he has upgraded a title, but where, under the Bill, he is not required to be satisfied as to that title.[131]

(2) The second case is where the register is rectified in relation to a proprietor of a registered estate or charge claiming in good faith under a forged disposition. That proprietor is treated as having suffered loss by reason of that rectification as if the disposition had not been forged. The reason for this provision is to reverse one effect of a case decided under the Land Transfer Acts 1875 and 1897, *Re Odell*.[132] The Court of Appeal there held that an innocent purchaser of a registered charge who was registered as proprietor of it on the basis of a transfer that turned out to be forgery, was not entitled to any indemnity. Because the transfer was a forgery and therefore of no effect, he was not regarded as suffering any loss, even though he had been registered.[133]

Loss by reason of a mistake

10.32 A person is entitled to an indemnity if he or she suffers loss by reason of a mistake, whose correction would involve rectification of the register.[134] No

---

[127] *Ibid*, para 1(1)(a). For the meaning of rectification, see *ibid*, para 11(2); and para 10.6, above.

[128] Sections 77(5) and 83(4) respectively.

[129] See Schedule 8, para 1(2).

[130] See above, paras 9.16 and following.

[131] An example might be where a possessory title was upgraded to an absolute one after 12 years under the power conferred by Cl 62(5). A person under a disability, whose rights had not been extinguished after 12 years, might be able to establish a claim that, by granting an absolute title, the registrar had deprived him of the power to challenge the validity of the original registration with possessory title.

[132] [1906] 2 Ch 47.

[133] Under the legislation then current, registration was merely a ministerial act by the registrar. It did not confer on the transferee any estate or right that he or she did not have before the registration. That principle was itself changed by the Land Registration Act 1925: see s 69(1). Its effect is replicated in Cl 58 of the Bill. See above, para 9.4.

[134] Schedule 8, para 1(1)(b).

indemnity is payable, however, until a decision has been made about whether or not to alter the register. The loss suffered by reason of the mistake will be determined in the light of that decision.[135] It follows that this entitlement does in fact encompass two distinct situations.

(1)   The first, presently covered by section 83(2) of the Land Registration Act 1925, is where, notwithstanding the mistake, the register is not rectified.[136]

(2)   The second is where the register *is* rectified, but the person in whose favour rectification is granted still suffers loss as a result of the mistake. This can happen, because rectification has prospective and not retrospective effect. A person may suffer loss in the period between the occurrence of the mistake and its rectification.[137] To that extent the mistake is not corrected[138] and, for the loss so attributable, indemnity is therefore payable. This second situation did not give rise to a claim for indemnity until the Land Registration Act 1997 remedied the shortcoming[139] and provided for it in what is presently section 83(1)(b) of the Land Registration Act 1925.

Mistake in an official search

10.33   If there is a mistake in an official search and a person suffers loss as a result, he or she is entitled to be indemnified for that loss.[140] This is a necessary corollary of the provisions of the Bill governing official searches and the rules to be made under them,[141] and it replicates part of the provisions of section 83(3) of the Land Registration Act 1925.

Mistake in an official copy

10.34   Indemnity is payable where loss is suffered by reason of a mistake in an official copy.[142] This replicates in part the effect of section 113 of the Land Registration Act 1925. As we explain elsewhere,[143] the Bill makes provision both for the issue of official copies and their legal effect.[144] The terminology of section 113 of the Land

---

[135]   *Ibid*, para 1(3).

[136]   As where there is a "proprietor in possession", and neither of the circumstances in which the register can be rectified against such a proprietor is applicable: see above, paras 10.15, 10.17.

[137]   See *Freer v Unwins Ltd* [1976] Ch 288.

[138]   See Schedule 8, para 1(3).

[139]   See s 2 of that Act, substituting a new s 83 in the Land Registration Act 1925.

[140]   Schedule 8, para 1(1)(c). In relation to land with registered title, the register is necessarily conclusive and prevails over the contents of any certificate of search.

[141]   See Cl 70; above, para 9.61.

[142]   Schedule 8, para 1(1)(d).

[143]   See below, para 9.45.

[144]   See Cl 67. Cl 67(2) provides expressly that a person who relies on an official copy in which there is a mistake is not liable for loss suffered by another by reason of that mistake. That other party will be entitled instead to indemnity under Schedule 8, para 1(1)(d).

Registration Act 1925, which refers rather Delphically to "office copies" has been abandoned in favour of the more comprehensible "official copies".[145]

Mistake in a document kept by the registrar which is not an original

10.35   Indemnity is to be payable if a person suffers loss by reason of a mistake in a document kept by the registrar, which is not an original and is referred to in the register of title.[146] The register may refer to extracts from or abstracts of conveyancing documents that the registrar does not retain. Furthermore, in relation to many conveyancing documents referred to in the register, such as leases, the registrar does not keep the original but only a copy. However, the Bill creates a presumption by which, where there is an entry in the register to a registered estate which refers to a document kept by the registrar that is not an original, the document kept by the registrar is to be taken as correct and to contain all the material parts of the original document.[147] As we explain elsewhere,[148] this presumption applies as between the parties to a disposition of or out of the registered estate in question, and also to dealings with interests in the registered land which are not themselves registered, such as leases granted for 7 years or less. The right to indemnity is a necessary concomitant of this presumption.

Loss or destruction of a document lodged at the registry

10.36   Following the provisions of the Land Registration Act 1925,[149] indemnity will be paid to a person if he or she suffers loss by reason of the loss or destruction of a document lodged at the registry for inspection or safe custody.[150] It is intended that the terms "loss or destruction" should be widely understood. It would include a case where the material part of a written document became illegible for some reason, as where it was damaged by water or smoke. As the provision will apply to documents in electronic form,[151] "loss or destruction" would encompass cases where an electronic file was mistakenly deleted or where it became corrupted and unreadable.

Mistake in the register of cautions against first registration

10.37   The Bill confers a right to indemnity where a person suffers loss by reason of a mistake in the register of cautions against first registration.[152] This right is new. It is a necessary concomitant of the formal establishment of the register of cautions

---

[145]   See above, para 9.45

[146]   Schedule 8, para 1(1)(e).

[147]   Cl 118; above, paras 9.48 and following. This provision is based upon, but substantially extends the scope of, Land Registration Act 1925, s 110(4).

[148]   See above, para 9.50.

[149]   Section 83(3).

[150]   Schedule 8, para 1(1)(f).

[151]   Cf Cl 91.

[152]   Schedule 8, para 1(1)(g).

against first registration under the Bill,[153] and of the provisions about the alterations of that register.[154]

Failure to notify a chargee of an overriding statutory charge

10.38   We have explained in Part VII of this Report, that when the registrar registers a person as proprietor of a statutory charge that has priority over a prior charge that is entered on the register,[155] he must notify the prior chargee of that statutory charge.[156] If he fails to do so, he is liable to pay the prior chargee indemnity for any loss that it may suffer in consequence.[157] The prior chargee is most likely to suffer loss if it makes a further advance to the registered proprietor in ignorance of the fact that there is an overriding statutory charge, and the security then proves to be insufficient to meet the advance.

Mines and minerals

10.39   There is one qualification to the rights to indemnity explained above. The Bill provides that no indemnity is payable on account of any mines or minerals or the existence of any right to work or get mines or minerals, unless it is noted on the register of title that the title to the registered estate includes the mines or minerals.[158] This replicates section 83(5)(b) of the Land Registration Act 1925. Registration of title to land under the Bill (as under the Land Registration Act 1925) includes mines and minerals, unless there is any entry to the contrary in the register.[159] However, the policy that is embodied in the Bill (as it is in section 83(5)(b) of the 1925 Act), is that the guarantee of title to registered land should not extend in all cases to mines and minerals in or under the land. To do so would expose the registry to a substantial risk of liability to pay indemnity. This is because of the difficulty of ascertaining on first registration—

(1)   whether or not there has been some prior unrecorded severance of the mines and minerals; or

(2)   whether the land was formerly copyhold and the lord of the manor's right to mines and minerals was preserved on enfranchisement, so that they are not in fact included in the title.

For this reason, indemnity is only to be available in those cases where the registrar is satisfied, after careful investigation, that the mines and minerals are included in

---

[153]   See Cl 19(1); see above, paras 3.65, 3.66.

[154]   Cls 20, 21; above, para 10.26.

[155]   Such as a Community Legal Service charge under Access to Justice Act 1999, s 10(7).

[156]   Cl 50; above, para 7.40. This is a new duty: it has no parallel in the Land Registration Act 1925.

[157]   Schedule 8, para 1(1)(h).

[158]   Schedule 8, para 2.

[159]   This follows from Cls 11(3), 12(3) (effects of first registration); and 129 (definition of "land").

the title and has made an entry in the register to that effect. That will not often be the case.

The measure of indemnity

Introduction

10.40   The function of indemnity is to make good the loss suffered by the person who is entitled to be indemnified. The Bill makes provision in relation to the following matters—

(1)   the elements that are taken into account in assessing indemnity;

(2)   factors that will bar a claim for indemnity or reduce the amount that can be recovered; and

(3)   the mechanisms for the making of the assessment.

We describe each of these in turn.

Elements to be taken into account in assessing indemnity

GENERAL

10.41   As we have explained, a person is entitled to be indemnified by the registrar if he or she suffers loss "by reason of" one of the circumstances listed above in paragraphs 10.31— 10.38.[160] The Bill contains no restriction on the type of loss that is recoverable. It follows, therefore, that a claimant can recover *any* loss that flows from the particular circumstance, whether that loss is direct[161] or consequential.[162] However, where his or her loss includes or consists entirely of costs and expenses incurred in relation to the matter,[163] it will be recoverable by him or her as indemnity only if he or she meets certain requirements explained below.[164]

VALUING THE LOSS OF AN ESTATE, INTEREST OR CHARGE

10.42   Where the party is seeking indemnity for the loss of an estate, interest or charge, the Bill states what the maximum value of that estate, interest or charge is to be taken to be for the purposes of that indemnity.[165] Where indemnity is payable

---

[160]   Schedule 8, para 1(1).

[161]   Direct loss would include (for example) the value of the land of which the claimant for indemnity had been deprived.

[162]   As, for example, where a valuable contract to sell the land was lost as a result of one of the grounds that gives rise to indemnity.

[163]   That is, one of the circumstances listed above in paragraphs 10.31—10.38.

[164]   See Schedule 8, para 3; explained at para 10.45.

[165]   Schedule 8, para 6. Compare Land Registration Act 1925, s 83(8), from which this provision derives. Cf *Kingsalton Ltd v Thames Water Developments Ltd* [2001] EWCA Civ 20, [45], where Arden LJ held that the court's power to decline rectification did not contravene Article 1 of the First Protocol of the European Convention on Human Rights because of the power to pay compensation under s 83(8).

because the claimant has suffered the loss by reason of rectification,[166] it is the value of the estate, charge or interest immediately before rectification of the register of title, but as if there were to be no rectification.[167] By contrast, where the claimant has suffered the loss because of a mistake but where the register was not rectified, it is the value of the estate, interest or charge at the time when the mistake which caused the loss was made.[168]

10.43   A number of points about this provision should be noted.

(1)   First, it merely states what the maximum value of the estate, interest or charge is taken to be for the purposes of assessing indemnity. It does not limit the entire claim to indemnity to that sum. For example, the claimant can recover additionally any consequential loss that he or she may have suffered.

(2)   Secondly, where the register is not rectified, it has been the practice of the Land Registry in such cases to pay interest on the sum from the date of the mistake.[169] Express provision is made for the payment of interest in the Bill so that this practice can be placed on a more formal and transparent basis by rules made under the Bill.[170]

(3)   Thirdly, there has been some criticism of the fact that, where the register is not rectified, the value of the estate, interest or charge is assessed at the time of the mistake.[171] However, there could be considerable difficulties if indemnity were to be assessed at the date on which any claim for rectification were refused. In the period between the making of the mistake and any such refusal, the character of the land could have changed fundamentally. This might be perhaps because substantial building work had been carried out by the registered proprietor, thereby considerably enhancing the value of the land, or it could be the converse, as where the registered proprietor had caused environmental damage to the land, thereby diminishing its value. As the claimant is entitled to an indemnity, he or she should be neither overcompensated nor penalised as a result of the acts of an independent third party which have affected the value of the land since the mistake. The two-fold strategy adopted by the Bill[172] of valuing the claimant's estate, interest or charge at the date of the mistake

---

[166]   Under Schedule 8, para 1(1)(a).

[167]   Schedule 8, para 6(a).

[168]   *Ibid*, para 6(b).

[169]   The basis for this practice is to be found in Land Registration and Land Charges Act 1971, s 2(5), which permits the registrar to settle by agreement claims for indemnity. That subsection will be repealed by the Bill.

[170]   Schedule 8, para 9; below, para 10.44.

[171]   See, *eg*, Roger J Smith, *Property Law* (3rd ed 2000), p 244.

[172]   Reflecting what has been the long-standing practice of the Registry.

and then paying interest on that sum until the claim for indemnity is settled, overcomes this difficulty in a straightforward manner.[173]

INTEREST

10.44 The Bill makes provision — not found expressly in the present legislation on land registration — for the payment of interest on an indemnity.[174] The circumstances in which, the periods for, and rates at which interest is to be payable are to be prescribed by rules.[175] It can, however, be anticipated that those rules are likely to make provision for the case mentioned above in paragraph 10.43(2).

COSTS

10.45 The general principle under the Bill[176] is that a claimant is entitled to recover as indemnity costs or expenses in relation to the matter only if they were reasonably incurred by him or her with the consent of the registrar.[177] As we explained in an earlier Report, "this accords with the principle that an insurer should not be expected to settle a claim for costs incurred without his prior consent".[178] This general principle is subject to three exceptions.

(1) The first is where—

(a) the costs or expenses were incurred by the claimant urgently; and

(b) it was not reasonably practicable for him or her to apply for the registrar's consent in advance.[179]

(2) The second is where the registrar subsequently approves the costs or expenses. These are treated as having been incurred with his consent.[180]

(3) The third arises where a person has applied to the court to determine whether he or she is entitled to an indemnity at all, or to determine the amount of any indemnity.[181] The applicant does not need the prior consent

---

[173] It is true that, if the rate of increase in the price of land is greater than interest rates, the claimant will not be fully compensated. But that should be set against the possibility — which has occurred in comparatively recent memory — that land prices may fall, or may increase at a rate that is lower than interest rates.

[174] Schedule 8, para 9.

[175] Such rules will be land registration rules and will be laid before Parliament only: Cls 125(3), 129(1).

[176] Replicating the effect of provisions of the Land Registration Act 1925, s 83(5)(c), (9).

[177] Schedule 8, para 3(1).

[178] Transfer of Land: Land Registration (1995) Law Com No 235, para 4.12.

[179] Schedule 8, para 3(2).

[180] Schedule 8, para 3(3).

[181] See *ibid*, para 7; below, para 10.50.

of the registrar in relation to the costs of the application.[182] The right of indemnity claimants to go to court would otherwise be compromised.

10.46　The Bill makes new provision for a case not presently covered by the Land Registration Act 1925. It sometimes happens that a person incurs expenses in determining whether or not he or she has a claim to indemnity, as where it appears that there may have been a mistake by the registrar but, on further investigation, this proves not to be the case. The Bill gives the registrar discretion to pay the claimant's costs or expenses provided that they were incurred both reasonably and with the consent of the registrar.[183] Once again, where the registrar's prior consent was not obtained, he may nonetheless exercise his power to pay indemnity where—

(1)　it appears to him either that the costs or expenses were incurred by the claimant urgently or that it was not reasonably practicable for him or her to apply for the registrar's consent in advance; or

(2)　he, the registrar, has subsequently approved the costs or expenses.[184]

Factors that will bar a claim for indemnity or reduce the amount that can be recovered

WHEN A CLAIM WILL BE BARRED

10.47　There are three circumstances in which a claim for indemnity will fail. The provisions in question are not new but replicate those found in section 83 of the Land Registration Act 1925.[185]

(1)　The first is where the claim is barred by lapse of time.[186] For the purposes of the Limitation Act 1980, the liability to pay indemnity is a simple contract debt.[187] It will therefore be barred six years after the cause of action arose.[188] The cause of action arises at the time when the claimant knew, or but for his or her own default might have known, of the existence of his or her claim.[189]

(2)　The second is where the loss suffered by the claimant is wholly or partly the result of his or her own fraud.[190] It is plainly right that a claimant whose

---

[182]　Schedule 8, para 7(2). This provision replicates in part the effect of s 2(2) of the Land Registration and Land Charges Act 1971 (which is repealed by the Bill).

[183]　Schedule 8, para 4(1).

[184]　*Ibid*, para 4(2).

[185]　As substituted by Land Registration Act 1997, s 2.

[186]　Schedule 8, para 8, replicating the effect of Land Registration Act 1925, s 83(12).

[187]　Schedule 8, para 8(a).

[188]　Limitation Act 1980, s 5.

[189]　Schedule 8, para 8(b).

[190]　*Ibid*, para 5(1)(a); replicating in part the effect of Land Registration Act 1925, s 83(5)(a).

conduct is tainted by fraud should recover nothing for any loss he or she suffers in consequence.

(3)   The third is where the loss suffered by the claimant is wholly the result of his or her own lack of proper care.[191] The registrar should not be required to indemnify a person who is entirely the author of his or her own misfortune.

As regards situations (2) and (3), the bar on recovering indemnity extends beyond the case where the claimant was fraudulent or negligent. It also applies to any person who derives title from such a person, unless the disposition to him or her was for valuable consideration and his or her title was either registered or protected on the register.[192]

WHEN A CLAIM WILL BE REDUCED

10.48   Under the Land Registration Act 1925, in the form in which it stood prior to the Land Registration Act 1997, no indemnity was ever payable to an applicant who had caused or substantially contributed to the loss that he or she had suffered by his or her lack of proper care.[193] As a result of the Land Registration Act 1997, a principle of contributory negligence was introduced,[194] which the Bill replicates. Where any loss is suffered by a claimant partly as a result of his or her own lack of proper care, any indemnity payable to him or her is to be reduced "to such extent as is fair having regard to his share in the responsibility for the loss".[195]

The mechanism for determining indemnity

10.49   The Bill makes it clear that a person who suffers loss falling within one of the situations explained above in paragraphs 10.31—10.38, is entitled to be indemnified *by the registrar*.[196] In many cases a claim to indemnity will arise out of an application for the rectification of the register. In such a case, the application for rectification will be made to the registrar and will be in the form (if any) that is

---

[191]   Schedule 8, para 5(1)(b); replicating in part the effect of Land Registration Act 1925, s 83(5)(a). In determining whether the loss suffered by the claimant was wholly the result of his or her own lack of proper care, it is not appropriate to apply a "but for" test. If there are in fact several causes of the loss, even though all or some of them would not have occurred but for something done by the claimant, this provision will not bar his or her claim: see *Dean v Dean* (2000) 80 P & CR 457.

[192]   Schedule 8, para 5(3); replicating the effect of Land Registration Act 1925, s 83(7).

[193]   See Land Registration Act 1925, s 83(5)(a), as amended by Land Registration and Land Charges Act 1971, s 3(1).

[194]   See Land Registration Act 1925, s 83(6) (as substituted by Land Registration Act 1997, s 2).

[195]   Schedule 8, para 5(2). Land Registration Act 1925, s 83(6) employed the phrase "to such extent as is *just and equitable* having regard to his share in the responsibility for the loss", echoing the words of Law Reform (Contributory Negligence) Act 1945, s 1(1). The substitution of "fair" for "just and equitable" in the Bill is not intended to change the law, but is merely a simplification and modernisation of the language.

[196]   Schedule 8, para 1(1).

prescribed in rules made under Schedule 4, paragraph 7(c).[197] If there is an objection to that application that cannot be disposed of by agreement and which the registrar does not consider to be groundless, it must be referred to the Adjudicator.[198] He will also deal with any questions of indemnity arising from such applications. However, as will be apparent from the circumstances in which there is an entitlement to indemnity, not every case in which there is a claim for indemnity will arise out of an application for the rectification of the register.[199] In these other cases, subject to what is said in paragraph 10.50 below, application for indemnity will be made to the registrar.[200]

10.50 Under the Bill, a person is entitled to apply to the court for a determination of any question as to whether he or she is entitled to an indemnity, or, if he or she is, the amount of that indemnity.[201] This provision replicates the effect of section 2(1) of the Land Registration and Land Charges Act 1971.[202] There is no requirement that the person should have made any application to the registrar for indemnity. He or she can, if so minded, go to the court at the outset, though such applications are, in practice, rare.[203]

Rights of recourse

10.51 The Bill replicates the effect of the provisions of the Land Registration Act 1925 which enable the registrar, in certain circumstances, to recover from a third party the amount of any indemnity that he has paid to a claimant.[204] Where the registrar has paid an indemnity[205] to a claimant in respect of any loss, he is given three distinct rights of recourse.[206]

---

[197] See above, para 10.20.

[198] Cl 73; below, para 16.6. Cf above, para 10.21.

[199] See above, paras 10.33—10.38.

[200] Cf Schedule 8, para 1(1) ("a person is entitled to be indemnified *by the registrar...*").

[201] Schedule 8, para 7(1). Cf above, para 10.45.

[202] Which is to be repealed.

[203] Land Registration and Land Charges Act 1971, s 2(3), presently provides that, on an application under s 2(1), the court shall not order the applicant, even if unsuccessful, to pay costs except his or her own unless it considers that the application was unreasonable. This provision is not replicated in the Bill because it has tended to encourage hopeless appeals to the court to contest awards of (or a refusal to award) indemnity.

[204] See Land Registration Act 1925, s 83(10), (11). These provisions were introduced by the Land Registration Act 1997, with the intention of clarifying and strengthening the Registry's rights of recourse: see Transfer of Land: Land Registration (1995) Law Com No 235, paras 4.10, 4.11. Prior to the 1997 Act, the Registry's rights of recourse were much more limited: see Land Registration Act 1925, s 83(9) as originally enacted. These new rights of recourse are being enforced by the Land Registry: see HM Land Registry, *Annual Report and Accounts 1999 — 2000*, p 25, showing that the Registry recovered nearly one-fifth of the sum paid out in indemnity during that financial year.

[205] Including any interest paid on an indemnity: see Schedule 8, para 10(3).

[206] These are conferred without prejudice to any other rights of recourse that he may have: *ibid*, para 10(1). For examples of such other rights, see Housing Act 1985, s 154(5); s 171G; Sched 9A, para 9(2); s 547; Sched 20, para 17(2); Housing Act ss 81(9)(c), 133(8)(c).

(1) First, he is entitled to recover the amount paid from any person who caused or substantially contributed to that loss by fraud.[207]

(2) Secondly, he is entitled to enforce any right of action (of whatever nature and however arising) which the claimant would have been entitled to enforce had the indemnity not been paid.[208] This is akin to an insurer's right of subrogation.

(3) Thirdly, where the register has been rectified, the registrar is entitled to enforce any right of action (of whatever nature and however arising) which the person in whose favour the register is rectified would have been entitled to enforce had it not been rectified.[209]

10.52 The third right of recourse goes beyond an insurer's rights of subrogation. It is intended to cover the following type of case:

(1) Rectification is ordered in favour of X because of a mistake caused by the negligence of X's solicitor.

(2) As a result of the rectification, Y suffers loss for which the registrar duly indemnifies her.

(3) The registrar can recover from X's solicitor the amount of the indemnity he has had to pay Y. This is so, even though at common law, X's solicitor might not have owed any duty of care to Y.

As the registrar has had to meet the cost of X's solicitor's negligence, it does, in principle, seem right that he should have a right of recoupment against that solicitor.

---

[207] Schedule 8, para 10(1)(a). In cases of fraud, there is no requirement that the recipient of any indemnity could have sued the perpetrator of the fraud if indemnity had not been paid, though there will be few cases where he or she could not have done.

[208] Schedule 8, paras 10(1)(b), 10(2)(a). An example would be where the error in the register was brought about because of the negligence of the solicitor or licensed conveyancer who was acting for the party who suffered the loss indemnified by the Registry.

[209] Schedule 8, paras 10(1)(b), 10(2)(b).

PART XI
SPECIAL CASES

INTRODUCTION

11.1 Part 7 of the Bill is concerned with a number of special cases. Some of these are addressed elsewhere in the Report.[1] Our main concern is with the Crown and with bankruptcy, but we also mention settlements briefly.

THE CROWN

Acknowledgements

11.2 Due to the complex and arcane nature of the law that governs the land holding of the Crown and the Royal Duchies of Cornwall and Lancaster, the preparation of the relevant provisions of the Bill proved to be particularly difficult. However, we received considerable assistance in this task from those who were much more familiar with these mysteries than ourselves. We are very grateful to all involved. We would in particular wish to record our thanks to Mr Henry Boyd-Carpenter, CVO, and Mr Christopher Jessel,[2] both of Farrer & Co, Sir Anthony Hammond, KCB, QC, the then Treasury Solicitor, and Mr David Harris, Solicitor and Legal Advisor to the Crown Estate Commissioners.

Crown land

11.3 The main categories of Crown land are as follows—

(1)   Land belonging to Government Departments. Much of this land is "in the name of" the Minister of the Crown, such as the Ministry of Defence, but there may be some properties (such as ancient defence installations in particular) which are "in the name of" the Queen. There may also be other "semi-Government property", such as old lighthouses, some of which date back to the sixteenth century. Much of such property is governed by specific legislation, such as the Defence Act 1842 (and later legislation dealing with land acquired for the purposes of defence). Where there is no such legislation, it is thought that the Crown Lands Act 1702 applies.

---

[1]   For pending land actions, etc (Cl 87), see above, paras 6.59, 8.14, 8.54. For PPP leases (Cl 90), see above, paras 3.13, 3.30, 4.22, 6.16, 8.11—8.13, 8.48(1).

[2]   Mr Jessel is the author of the section on Crown Property in *Halsbury's Laws of England* (4th ed), vol 12(1). For other accounts of the law governing Crown land that we have consulted, see Joseph Chitty, *A Treatise on the Law of the Prerogatives of the* Crown (1820), 226—236; C Sweet, *Challis's Law of Real Property* (3rd ed 1911), Chapters 1, 2 and 6; T Cyprian Williams, "The Fundamental Principles of the Present Law of Ownership of Land" (1931) 75 SJ 843.

(2) Land under the management of the Crown Estate Commissioners, which is known as the Crown Estate. This comprises land held by the monarch in right of the Crown in her political capacity.[3]

(3) The Crown's Private Estate, which comprises land which is owned by the monarch in her private capacity.[4] These lands are subject to the Crown Private Estates Acts 1800, 1862 and 1873. The best known of the estates is the Sandringham Estate.

(4) The two Royal Duchies of Cornwall and Lancaster.[5]

(5) A residual category of land which is subject to the Crown Lands Act 1702.[6] This category includes the royal palaces and parks,[7] together with any other Crown land not falling under any other arrangement. These lands are inalienable, and the maximum length of lease that may granted of them is 31 years.[8]

These categories of Crown land are not discrete. Thus surplus Government land may sometimes come under the management of the Crown Estate. Furthermore, it is provided by statute that land may pass between categories (5) and (2).[9]

The issues addressed by the Bill

11.4 The Bill addresses the following issues in relation to Crown land—

(1) registration of title to Crown land that is held by the monarch in demesne;

(2) escheat of registered land;

(3) representation in relation to Crown and Duchy land; and

(4) the disapplication of certain requirements relating to Duchy land.

There are certain matters that are addressed in the Land Registration Act 1925 which have no equivalent in the Bill and we explain why this is so.

---

[3] See *Halsbury's Laws of England* (4th ed), vol 12(1), para 278.

[4] See *Halsbury's Laws of England* (4th ed), vol 12(1), paras 354 and following.

[5] References in this Part to "Duchy land" are to the land that is vested in the Crown in right of the Duchy of Lancaster and the land belonging to the Duchy of Cornwall.

[6] See *Halsbury's Laws of England* (4th ed), vol 12(1), paras 364 and following.

[7] These may also be subject to the provisions of the Crown Lands Act 1851: see s 22 of that Act.

[8] Crown Lands Act 1702, s 5. See *Halsbury's Laws of England* (4th ed), vol 12(1), para 205.

[9] See Crown Lands Act 1927, s 13; Crown Estate Act 1961, s 5(5).

Registration of land held in demesne

The present law

11.5 Most land in England and Wales is held by a landowner for a legal estate in fee simple. The only exception is the land held by the Crown in demesne, for "no subject in England can hold lands allodially".[10] Demesne lands are those held by the Crown as sovereign or lord paramount.[11] The Crown has the power to grant an estate in fee simple by infeudation out of land held in demesne. Indeed it is the only way in which it can create such a freehold estate.[12] No other landowner has a power to subinfeudate,[13] as it is prohibited by Statute *Quia Emptores* 1290.[14] A landowner who has an estate in fee simple can only transfer title to it by making a substitutionary grant.[15] There is a strong presumption that a freeholder holds directly of the Crown and not of some mesne lord.[16] As a result, when a fee simple determines, as it does in certain circumstances that we explain below,[17] the land "escheats" to the Crown, and the Crown as paramount lord becomes entitled to the land in demesne.[18]

11.6 The essentials of land held in demesne are that the Crown —

(1) has dominion over that land as lord paramount; and

---

[10] J Burke, *Jowitt's Dictionary of English Law* (2nd ed 1977), p 89. See to like effect, *Coke on Littleton*, 65a.

[11] Cf *Coke on Littleton*, 65a.

[12] Such grants are made in socage tenure by virtue of the Tenures Abolition Act 1660, s 4.

[13] The Crown as paramount feudal lord "infeudates". Prior to Statute *Quia Emptores* 1290, mesne (or intermediate) lords holding of the Crown could "*sub*infeudate" by making a feudal grant out of their land. We have had some discussions with those representing the Crown as to whether the Royal Duchies can subinfeudate. Whatever the answer to this question may be in theory, the Duchies in practice make substitutionary grants. We have examined a number of conveyances in relation to the Poundbury Estate in Dorset that were granted by HRH the Duke of Cornwall, which confirm this.

[14] Section 1. The Statute only applies to land held in fee simple (*ibid*, s 3), and is inapplicable to the Crown, as indeed it has to be. Were it otherwise, the Crown would be unable to make any grant of land which it held in demesne. It could hardly transfer its position as lord paramount.

[15] Statute *Quia Emptores* 1290, s 1.

[16] See *Re Lowe's WT* [1973] 1 WLR 882, 886 ("the theoretical possibility of escheat to some mesne lord... is one that is so remote that it may be wholly ignored": per Russell LJ). See too *Re Holliday* [1922] 2 Ch 698, 713. This has long been the case: see Real Property Commissioners, *Third Report on Real Property* (1832), p 3. We note that one respondent to the Consultative Document had rather different views.

[17] See para 11.23.

[18] If the land is in either the Duchy of Cornwall or the Duchy of Lancaster, the land escheats to the respective duchy. This is escheat to a mesne freehold and not to the Crown as paramount lord. What actually happens is that the landowner's fee simple is destroyed, but that of the mesne lord is not. The escheated land therefore remains freehold land, albeit that it is a *different* freehold that subsists. This should be contrasted with cases where land passes to the Crown as bona vacantia, where the fee simple is not destroyed but is transferred to the Crown: see *Halsbury's Laws of England* (4th ed), vol 12(1), para 236.

241

(2)   has no estate in that land.

11.7   The demesne lands of the Crown are very substantial and include—

(1)   the foreshore around England and Wales except where it has been granted away or is in some other way vested in a private owner;

(2)   land which has escheated to the Crown; and

(3)   the ancient lands of the Crown which it has never granted away in fee.

11.8   As the law stands, the Crown cannot register the title to land held in demesne under the Land Registration Act 1925. That Act provides that "estates capable of subsisting as legal estates shall be the only interests in land in respect of which a proprietor can be registered".[19] As the Crown has no estate in its demesne land it cannot register the title. This has been described as "a major, but unremarked, lacuna in the system of land registration in England and Wales".[20]

11.9   We have explained above the strong presumption that the owner of a fee simple holds it directly of the Crown and not of some mesne lord.[21] However, the theoretical possibility of the existence of a mesne lord may explain why the Crown can own a freehold estate in land as well as having its paramount lordship. The freehold does not merge in the Crown's higher right.[22] However, it is very questionable whether the Crown could make an infeudatory grant to itself in fee simple out of its paramount lordship. We cannot see how the Crown, one and indivisible as it is, can hold land of itself as tenant-in-chief.[23]

11.10   The fact that the Crown cannot register the title to land that it holds in demesne is unsatisfactory, particularly given the substantial extent of those lands.[24] It is a significant barrier to the goal of total registration that we have explained in Part II of this Report.[25] Furthermore, the Crown Estate wishes to be able to register such lands, particularly the foreshore.[26]

---

[19]   Land Registration Act 1925, s 2(1).

[20]   *Scmlla Properties Ltd v Gesso Properties (BVI) Ltd* [1995] BCC 793, 798, *per* Stanley Burnton QC (sitting as a Deputy High Court Judge). See above, para 2.33.

[21]   See para 11.5.

[22]   At least not normally. We have been told of instances where such merger has been assumed, and we have had some interesting correspondence as to whether Buckingham Palace is held by the Crown in demesne or (as we think) in fee simple.

[23]   Cf *Scmlla Properties Ltd v Gesso Properties (BVI) Ltd* [1995] BCC 793, 801H.

[24]   See above, para 11.7.

[25]   See above, para 2.9.

[26]   This would bring with it a greater protection from encroachment than presently exists because of the provisions of the Bill on adverse possession: see below Part XIV.

Voluntary registration under the Bill

11.11 The Bill addresses the problem explained above. It provides that Her Majesty may grant an estate in fee simple absolute in possession out of demesne land to Herself.[27] That grant will, however, be treated as not having been made, unless an application for the voluntary first registration under Clause 3[28] is made within 2 months of the grant.[29] That period may be extended by the registrar to such later period as he may specify on application by Her Majesty, if he is satisfied that there is a good reason for doing so.[30] If the registrar makes an order extending the period after the 2 month period has elapsed, the grant will not be treated as having been invalidated by the failure to register it within the 2 month period.[31] These provisions may at first sight seem odd in the context of *voluntary* registration, as they resemble the sanctions that apply in relation to dispositions that are subject to *compulsory* first registration.[32] However, the thinking behind them is to ensure that the power to grant a fee simple can *only* be employed to secure the registration of the title to the land. This ensures that the Crown does not inadvertently create a fee simple in its own favour if, for some reason, the grant is made but no registration then takes place.[33]

11.12 Demesne land is defined as land belonging to Her Majesty in right of the Crown which is not held for an estate in fee simple absolute in possession.[34] That does no more than state the position at common law. However, as we explain below, for the purposes of the Bill, that definition is qualified in cases where a freehold estate has determined.[35]

Compulsory registration under the Bill

11.13 Under the present law, the provisions on compulsory first registration apply to an infeudatory grant by the Crown of a freehold estate for valuable or other consideration, by way of gift or pursuant to a court order. This is because such a grant is a "qualifying conveyance" for the purpose of section 123 of the Land Registration Act 1925,[36] which specifies the dispositions that are subject to the requirement of compulsory registration. However, the compulsory registration provisions of the Bill are couched in terms of a "transfer of a qualifying estate".[37]

---

[27] Cl 79(1).

[28] See above, para 3.6.

[29] Cl 79(2), (3).

[30] Cl 79(3), (4).

[31] Cl 79(5).

[32] See Cl 6; above, paras 3.38—3.41.

[33] This could be important if the Crown subsequently wished to make an infeudatory grant of the land to some person. The Crown could be confident that it was making a grant out of the demesne.

[34] Cl 129(1).

[35] See Cl 129(2); below, para 11.28.

[36] As substituted by Land Registration Act 1997, s 1.

[37] Cl 4(1)(a), (2)(a); above, paras 3.24 and following.

Plainly an infeudatory grant of a freehold is not a "transfer" which can only apply to a substitutionary disposition. The Bill therefore makes specific provision to bring such grants within the ambit of its provisions on compulsory first registration.

11.14   The compulsory registration provisions of the Bill, found in Clauses 4 and 6—8, that have been explained in Part III of this Report,[38] are applied by Clause 80 to the following grants by Her Majesty out of demesne land—

(1)   the grant of an estate in fee simple absolute in possession, other than a voluntary grant to Herself, under the power explained above in paragraph 11.11;

(2)   the grant of a term of years absolute of more than seven years from the date of the grant that is made for valuable or other consideration, by way of gift[39] or in pursuance of an order of the court.[40]

11.15   These provisions do not apply to the grant of mines and minerals held apart from the surface for reasons that have been explained in Part III.[41] There is a power for the Lord Chancellor, by order, to add to the events relating to demesne land that trigger compulsory registration.[42]

11.16   As the requirement of compulsory registration applies, any grant must be registered within two months of its being made or such longer period as the registrar may have provided.[43] If the grant is not registered within that period, it takes effect as a contract made for valuable consideration to grant the legal estate concerned.[44]

Cautions against the first registration of demesne land

11.17   The provisions of the Bill concerning cautions against first registration have been explained in Part III of this Report.[45] Those provisions, which allow for such a caution to be lodged in relation to an unregistered legal estate,[46] cannot apply to

---

[38]   See above, paras 3.22 and following.

[39]   A grant by way of gift includes a grant for the purpose of constituting a trust under which Her Majesty does not retain the whole of the beneficial interest: Cl 80(2). Cf above, para 3.27(1).

[40]   Cl 80(1).

[41]   Cl 80(3); cf above, para 3.23.

[42]   Cl 80(4). He may also make such consequential amendments as he thinks fit: *ibid*. The power is exercisable by statutory instrument that is subject to annulment in pursuance of the resolution of either House of Parliament: Cl 125(2), (4). Cf Cl 5; above, para 3.37.

[43]   Cf Cl 6(4), (5); above, para 3.39.

[44]   Cl 80(5). Cf above, para 3.40.

[45]   See above, paras 3.56 and following.

[46]   Cl 15; above, para 3.56.

land held in demesne, because the Crown has no estate in land.[47] However, the Bill provides for their application as if demesne land were held by Her Majesty for an unregistered estate in fee simple absolute in possession.[48] They take effect subject to such modifications as rules may provide.[49]

11.18 In one respect the provisions on cautions against the first registration of demesne land differ from those applicable to cautions against the first registration of an estate. We have explained in Part III of this Report that, two years after the Bill is brought into force, it will cease to be possible for a person who owns either a freehold estate or leasehold estate that is capable of being registered with its own title, to lodge a caution against the first registration of that title.[50] This is because the lodging of a caution against first registration of a legal estate is not intended to be a substitute for its registration.[51] In relation to the Crown, it is necessary to make special provision in this regard. As we have explained above,[52] the Crown cannot at present register land which it holds in demesne, though the Bill makes provision for it to do so. It will plainly take some considerable time for the Crown to register all of the land that it holds in demesne, which, as we have explained, is extensive.[53] In the interim it may wish to protect that land by lodging a caution against first registration to alert it to any unauthorised application by a third party. The Bill therefore permits the Crown to lodge cautions against the first registration of any demesne land for 10 years after it comes into force, or such longer period as rules may provide.[54] It is almost certain that the 10-year period will in fact be extended by rules, given the magnitude of the task of registering all demesne land. The purpose of stipulating a period is to ensure that the process of registration is kept under review, having regard to the goal of total registration that is explained in Part II of this Report.[55] Once the time needed for registration has

---

[47] There is arguably a doubt about whether the present provisions on cautions against first registration apply to demesne land. Land Registration Act 1925, s 53 permits a person claiming "an interest in land" to lodge a caution. Land is defined as "land of any tenure": *ibid*, s 3(ix). Although we think that land held in demesne is "land of any tenure", the matter is not completely beyond doubt. The registrar has in practice been willing to accept the lodgement of "Crown cautions" against the first registration of demesne land.

[48] Cl 81(1).

[49] Cl 81(2). The rules will be land registration rules and will be required to be laid before Parliament only. See Cls 125, 129(1).

[50] Cl 15(3); Schedule 12, para 14(1); above, para 3.58.

[51] See above, para 3.58.

[52] See para 11.8.

[53] See above, para 11.7.

[54] Schedule 12, para 15(1). The rules will be land registration rules and will be required to be laid before Parliament only. See Cls 125, 129(1).

[55] See above, paras 2.9, 2.13.

become clearer, the period within which the Crown can lodge and retain cautions against first registration in the register of cautions can be adjusted accordingly.[56]

11.19 It should be noted that persons other than the Crown may wish to lodge cautions against the first registration of demesne land and the Bill permits this. As we explain below, when a freehold estate escheats either to the Crown or to one of the Royal Duchies, that does not extinguish any incumbrances to which that estate is subject.[57] A person having the benefit of any such an incumbrance may wish to ensure that, as and when either the Crown grants, or the Duchy transfers, such land to some person, the incumbrance is appropriately protected on the register.[58]

Escheat

The nature of escheat

11.20 Escheat occurs where a freehold estate determines. The effect is that the lord of whom that estate was held becomes entitled to the land by his or her own right.[59] If the land was held of a mesne lord (such as one of the Royal Duchies), this will be by virtue of that lord's own estate in fee simple. If, as will usually be the case, the land is held directly of the Crown, it will be because the Crown is entitled to the land in demesne. In either eventuality, the lord takes the land subject to any charges or other incumbrances created by the tenant.[60] Although it is "difficult to understand how a subordinate interest, created out of a freehold, can survive the termination of the freehold interest, any more than a sublease can survive the determination of a head lease",[61] it is, nevertheless, well-established by authority that it does.[62]

11.21 The manner in which escheat operates is not altogether straightforward. Although it occurs automatically on the determination of an estate,[63] escheat is only completed when the lord to whom the land reverts takes possession or control of

---

[56] Once the 10-year or extended period has come to an end, any caution will be spent, except where an application to register the title to the land affected has been made before the end of the period: Schedule 12, para 15(2).

[57] See para 11.20.

[58] The grant or transfer will trigger compulsory registration.

[59] As Earl of Selborne explained in *Attorney-General of Ontario v Mercer* (1883) 8 App Cas 767, 772, "when there is no longer any tenant, the land returns, by reason of tenure, to the lord by whom, or by whose predecessors in title, the tenure was created".

[60] *Scmlla Properties Ltd v Gesso Properties (BVI) Ltd* [1995] BCC 793, 806—808 (where the authorities are reviewed).

[61] *Scmlla Properties Ltd v Gesso Properties (BVI) Ltd*, above, at p 806, *per* Burnton QC.

[62] See, *eg*, *Attorney-General of Ontario v Mercer* (1883) 8 App Cas 767, 772, where Earl of Selborne commented that "[t]he tenant's estate (subject to any charges upon it which he may have created) has come to an end, and the lord is in by his own right". There is, perhaps, an analogy with a squatter who acquires title to land by adverse possession under the Limitation Act 1980, ss 15, 17. Even though he or she extinguishes the estate of the paper owner, the squatter takes subject to the incumbrances on the estate that are not barred by his or her adverse possession: see *Re Nisbet & Potts' Contract* [1906] 1 Ch 386.

[63] *Scmlla Properties Ltd v Gesso Properties (BVI) Ltd* [1995] BCC 793, 802—806.

it or takes proceedings for its recovery.[64] At one time it was necessary for there to be an inquisition before an escheat could take place.[65] Such inquisitions have long been obsolete[66] and were formally abolished in 1961.[67] The need for some step to complete the escheat means that although the lord's seignory "is no longer encumbered by the freehold estate",[68] he does not automatically become subject to the liabilities that affect the land, such as the burden of a landlord's covenants where the land is subject to a subsisting tenancy. As we explain below this is a matter of some practical importance.[69]

11.22 At first sight, escheat might seem to be a quaint feudal relic of little if any relevance to an overhaul of the legislation on the registration of title. However, as we have indicated in Part II of this Report, something like 500 freehold estates escheat every year.[70] When a registered estate escheats, the title has to be removed from the register because the estate no longer exists. If, as usual, the land passes to the Crown, it will be held in demesne and (as the law stands) cannot be registered.[71] If it passes to one of the Royal Duchies, that Duchy will hold the land by virtue of its own unregistered fee simple as mesne lord. While it could, in theory, choose to register the title to the land voluntarily, it is very unlikely in practice that it will do so, for reasons that are explained below.[72] Given the goal of total registration,[73] our concern has been to try to find a way by which, where title to land has once been registered, it does not have to be removed from the register due to escheat. We explain below how the Bill achieves this objective.[74] However, it is necessary first to outline the principal circumstances in which an escheat may occur.

---

[64] See *Blackstone's Commentaries*, Vol 2, p 245.

[65] Indeed the Crown employed an "escheator" in every county to enforce its rights. For the development of the office of escheator, see J M W Bean, *The Decline of English Feudalism 1215 – 1540* (1968), pp 17 *et seq*.

[66] Procedure was rationalised by the Escheat (Procedure) Act 1887, but it was apparently inoperative even then.

[67] See Crown Estate Act 1961, s 8(3).

[68] *Scmlla Properties Ltd v Gesso Properties (BVI) Ltd* [1995] BCC 793, 804, *per* Burnton QC.

[69] See para 11.25.

[70] See above, para 2.35.

[71] See above, para 11.8. Although, as we have explained above, at para 11.11, the Bill confers a power for Her Majesty to grant Herself a fee simple out of demesne land for the purpose of registering it, it is unlikely that this power would be used in relation to land that had escheated. In most cases of escheat, the Crown does not wish to become responsible for the land that has escheated because of its invariably onerous nature: see below, para 11.24.

[72] See para 11.25.

[73] See above, paras 2.9, 2.13.

[74] See para 11.28.

The circumstances in which escheat occurs

11.23   As we have indicated above,[75] escheat occurs whenever an estate in fee simple determines. The circumstances in which this can happen are now much more limited than was formerly the case.[76] Whilst it is not possible to set out all the situations in which a fee simple might determine, they include the following—

(1)   where the freehold is disclaimed in cases that normally involve insolvency: this is the usual case and it is more fully explained below;[77]

(2)   where the Crown makes an infeudatory grant subject to restrictions on the user of the land that is enforceable by a right of entry, and that right is exercised;[78] and

(3)   where a settlement is created which includes an entail, the right of reverter is in the Crown, and the entailed interest determines.[79]

11.24   As we have indicated above, by far the commonest circumstance in which escheat occurs is where a freehold estate is disclaimed.[80] There are three situations in which this may happen—

(1)   First, a trustee in bankruptcy may disclaim onerous property under section 315 of the Insolvency Act 1986. Onerous property is defined as "any unprofitable contract" and "any other property comprised in the bankrupt's estate which is unsaleable or not readily saleable, or is such that it may give rise to a liability to pay money or perform any other onerous act".[81] A freehold might be onerous if (for example) it were subject to charges or other liabilities that exceeded its value.[82]

(2)   Secondly, there is an analogous provision in section 178 of the Insolvency Act 1986, by which a liquidator of a company that is being wound up may

---

[75]   See para 11.20.

[76]   Escheat for the commission of a felony (other than treason) was abolished by the Forfeiture Act 1870. Escheat on intestacy was abolished by Administration of Estates Act 1925, s 45(1)(d). When treason was committed, the land did not escheat to the traitor's immediate feudal lord but was forfeited to the Crown. Forfeiture for treason was also abolished by the Forfeiture Act 1870.

[77]   See para 11.24.

[78]   See Crown Estate Act 1961, s 3(8), which permits such grants. The right of entry is exercisable in perpetuity under that subsection ("...the restrictions may, notwithstanding any enactment or rule of law relating to perpetuities, be made enforceable by a right of entry exercisable on behalf of Her Majesty on a breach of the restrictions occurring at any distance of time"). We were given sight of such a grant made in 1870.

[79]   See Settled Land Act 1925, ss 1(5), 20(1).

[80]   When a lease is disclaimed, it terminates, and no question of escheat therefore arises. For the effects of disclaimer in relation to a lease, see *Megarry & Wade's Law of Real Property* (6th ed 2000), 14-182—14-185.

[81]   Section 315(2).

[82]   Cf *Hackney London Borough Council v Crown Estate Commissioners* (1995) 72 P & CR 233.

disclaim onerous property.[83] Onerous property is defined in the same way as in (1).[84]

(3)   Thirdly, under section 654 of the Companies Act 1985, when a company is dissolved, all its property vests either in the Crown or in one of the Royal Duchies as bona vacantia. However, section 656 of that Act permits the Crown, by means of a notice issued by the Treasury Solicitor (or relevant Duchy official) within 12 months of the date on which the company's property vested in it, to disclaim any such property. In practice, if the property is onerous (as it commonly is), the Treasury Solicitor disclaims for reasons that we explain below.[85] The effect of this is that, in the case of freehold land, the estate determines and therefore escheats to the Crown or one of the Duchies. It follows that, what the Crown disclaims as bona vacantia, it receives in a different capacity by way of escheat.

11.25   It is this third case that accounts for the great majority of escheats and the reasons for it require some explanation.[86] Sections 654 and 656 of the Companies Act 1985 are not new. The former was first introduced by the Companies Act 1928,[87] the latter by the Companies Act 1948.[88] These provisions have puzzled both academic commentators[89] and the judiciary.[90] We have examined their legislative history[91] and it is clear that there are in fact very good reasons for them. It was appreciated shortly after the enactment of the Companies Act 1929 that the Crown was potentially at risk in relation to real property that passed to it as bona vacantia. The legal estate in such property vests in the Crown and there was a fear that the Crown might find itself subject to the liabilities attaching to the property if it was of an onerous character.[92] The Companies Act 1948 introduced a number

---

[83]   The leading modern authority on escheat, *Scmlla Properties Ltd v Gesso Properties (BVI) Ltd* [1995] BCC 793, arose out of a disclaimer by a liquidator under Insolvency Act 1986, s 178.

[84]   Section 178(3).

[85]   See para 11.25.

[86]   There is an irony in this. For nearly 500 years, on the basis of a passage in *Coke on Littleton*, 23b, it was thought that the doctrine of escheat did not apply to a corporation. If a corporation was dissolved, any lands which it held reverted to the grantor: "the law doth annex a condition to every such grant, that if the corporation be dissolved, the grantor shall have the lands again, because the cause of the grant faileth": *Blackstone's Commentaries*, Vol 1, p 472. This view must have been based on the sort of charitable and eleemosynary corporations that Coke would have known in the early seventeenth century, because it seems oddly inappropriate in relation to joint stock companies. It was finally rejected by the Court of Appeal in a bona vacantia case, *Re Wells* [1933] Ch 29.

[87]   Section 71. Cf *Re C W Dixon Ltd* [1947] Ch 251.

[88]   Section 355.

[89]   See D W Elliott, "Land Without an Owner" (1954) 70 LQR 25.

[90]   *Scmlla Properties Ltd v Gesso Properties (BVI) Ltd* [1995] BCC 793, 805, where Burnton QC remarked that "it was difficult to see the object of these provisions in so far as they concern freeholds".

[91]   From the correspondence files at the Office of Parliamentary Counsel.

[92]   As, for example, where it was a reversion on a lease and the landlord was subject to substantial liabilities under the repairing covenants in the lease.

of provisions to protect the Crown from this risk,[93] of which what is now section 654 of the Companies Act 1985 is just one.[94] It cannot be regarded as finally settled whether the Crown does in fact become subject to the liabilities affecting property which it receives by way of bona vacantia. Although it was conceded that it was in one decision,[95] there are powerful arguments against this view.[96] However, if the Treasury Solicitor disclaims a freehold and the land thereby escheats to the Crown Estate, it is well settled that the Crown *can* protect itself against liability. As we have explained above, although escheat occurs automatically, it requires some act to complete it.[97] If, therefore, the Crown does not take possession or perform any acts of management in relation to such land, it will not become subject to the liabilities of the freeholder.[98] What in practice happens is that the Crown Estate takes no action in relation to onerous land disclaimed by the Treasury Solicitor until such time as some interested person agrees to acquire the property and assume such liabilities as may still affect it.[99] The land can then be granted to that person.[100]

The treatment of escheat in the Bill

11.26　It scarcely needs to be said after this account that the present law is indefensible. It also has unfortunate practical implications. Bona vacantia is administered by the Treasury Solicitor, whereas escheated property is a matter for the Crown Estate.[101] Those who have an interest in such property and wish to take steps in

---

[93]　See Companies Act 1948, ss 352—355.

[94]　See too Insolvency Act 1986, ss 178—180 (replacing provisions that were formerly in Companies Act 1985). Correspondence in the Office of Parliamentary Counsel from 1947 shows that there was close co-ordination between those instructing upon and drafting the Companies Bill and the draftsman of the Crown Proceedings Bill.

[95]　*Toff v McDowell* (1993) 69 P & CR 535; where it was assumed without argument that, where a freehold reversion on a lease vested in the Crown as bona vacantia, the Crown became subject to the burden of the covenants of that lease.

[96]　It would provide a ready means for a person to escape his or her liabilities for onerous property which he or she owned by transferring it to a company set up for the purpose and then arranging for its dissolution. Compare the comments of Earl Jowitt in *Attorney-General v Parsons* [1956] AC 421, 435, in the analogous context of the now-repealed mortmain legislation.

[97]　See above, para 11.21.

[98]　See *Scmlla Properties Ltd v Gesso Properties (BVI) Ltd* [1995] BCC 793, 804, 805, where the authorities are reviewed. Cf Crown Proceedings Act 1947, s 40(4), which protects the Crown from tort claims in relation to land which vests in the Crown "by virtue of any rule of law which operates independently of the acts or the intentions of the Crown" unless and until the Crown takes possession or control of such property, or enters into occupation of it. The Crown was not liable to tort claims prior to the 1947 Act.

[99]　For an interesting illustrative decision, see *Hackney London Borough Council v Crown Estate Commissioners* (1995) 72 P & CR 233.

[100]　It is because the Crown is at risk in relation to escheated land that it is most unlikely that it would exercise its power under the Bill, explained above at para 11.11, to grant itself a fee simple in the land in order to register it. Cf above, para 11.22.

[101]　Except where the property escheats to one of the Royal Duchies.

relation to it, are often bewildered because they do not know with which organ of state they have to deal.

11.27   We had extended discussions with both the Crown Estate and the then Treasury Solicitor to see if a more rational system could be constructed, at least for registered land (we were constrained by the scope of the Bill). We explored a possible solution, but in the end it foundered because of the uncertainty of the present law. Given that uncertainty there was a risk that in solving one set of problems, we might have created new ones. What is needed is a fundamental reform of the law governing both ownerless property, and the Crown's responsibilities in relation to it.

11.28   What the Bill does, therefore, is to provide what can only be a stop-gap solution to the specific problem of how to prevent a registered estate that has escheated from having to be removed from the register. What we wish to achieve, is that where a registered freehold estate escheats, its title should not be closed. Instead, it is anticipated that either the Treasury Solicitor (if he or she disclaims) or the Crown Estate[102] (in other cases) will apply for the entry of a restriction in the register.[103] This is likely to provide that no disposition is to be made of the estate except by order of the court or by or on the direction of the Crown Estate.[104] When such a disposition is eventually made, it will necessarily create a new fee simple and it will be registered with a new title number. The old title will then be closed. Any encumbrances to which the former title was subject and which still subsist in relation to the new estate will be entered in the register of the new title. In this context, it should be noted that, for the purposes of the Bill, land in which a freehold estate has determined is not regarded as "demesne land" unless there has been some act of entry or management by the Crown.[105] In other words, where an escheat has occurred but has not been completed,[106] the land in question is not treated as demesne land under the Bill. This reflects the rule, explained above,[107] that the Crown incurs no responsibility for land that has escheated unless and until it takes possession of the land or undertakes some act of management in relation to it.[108]

11.29   Clause 82 contains a series of rule-making powers to enable the objectives set out in paragraph 11.28 to be achieved. Rules[109] may make provision about—

[102]   Or, where relevant, Royal Duchy.

[103]   For restrictions under the Bill, see above, paras 6.33 and following.

[104]   Or, where relevant, Royal Duchy.

[105]   Cl 129(2). For the definition of "demesne land" that otherwise applies, see Cl 129(1); above, para 11.12.

[106]   See above, para 11.21.

[107]   See para 11.25.

[108]   See *Halsbury's Laws of England* (4th ed), vol 12(1), para 234.

[109]   These rules will be land registration rules and will be required to be laid before Parliament only. See Cls 125, 129(1).

(1)   the determination of a registered freehold estate in land; and

(2)   the registration of an unregistered freehold legal estate in land in respect of land to which a former registered freehold estate in land related.[110]

11.30   Clause 82(2) gives specific guidance as to some of the rules that may be made under this power. Rules may make provision for the effect of the determination of a registered estate to be dependent on compliance with specified registration requirements. In this way, it will be possible to require (for example) that appropriate restrictions are entered in the register when a disclaimer occurs. Rules may provide for entries relating to an estate to continue notwithstanding that it has determined for such period as may be specified. This ensures that the register records the encumbrances to which the determined estate was subject and to which the land therefore remains subject.[111] Provision may be made as to the entries that may be made in the register of the former registered estate. It is likely to be necessary to have some entry on the register that will indicate that escheat has taken place. This will ensure that when a new estate is eventually granted, the old title can be closed and the entries of any subsisting encumbrances carried across to the new title.[112] Rules may also impose requirements that have to be met in connection with an application for the registration of any new estate granted out of the land in relation to which the escheat had occurred. It might be necessary (for example) to refer to the number of the former title in the application.

Crown and Duchy land: representation

11.31   Clause 83 of the Bill performs the same function that section 96 of the Land Registration Act 1925 does under the present law, and little needs to be said about it. In relation to a Crown or Duchy interest,[113] it explains—

(1)   who may represent the owner of that interest for all purposes of the Bill;

(2)   who is entitled to receive such notice as the owner of that interest is entitled to receive under the Bill; and

(3)   who may make such applications and do such other acts that the owner of that interest is entitled to make or do under the Bill.[114]

---

[110]   Cl 82(1).

[111]   See above, para 11.20.

[112]   Some entries may be cleared from the title by court order, or they may have become unenforceable.

[113]   A Crown interest is an estate, interest or charge in or over land and any right or claim in relation to land belonging to Her Majesty in right of the Crown, or belonging to a government department, or held in trust for Her Majesty for the purposes of a government department: Cl 83(2). A Duchy interest means an estate, interest or charge in or over land and any right or claim in relation to land belonging to Her Majesty in right of the Duchy of Lancaster, or belonging to the Duchy of Cornwall: *ibid*.

[114]   Cl 83(1).

11.32 Thus, for example, in relation to an interest belonging to Her Majesty that forms part of the Crown Estate, the appropriate authority for the three purposes listed above is the Crown Estate Commissioners.[115]

The disapplication of certain requirements in relation to Duchy land

Introduction

11.33 There are no special requirements applicable to the manner in which the Crown Estate Commissioners make dispositions of Crown land.[116] They may be made in the same way as if the Commissioners were acting on behalf of a subject and are similarly registrable.[117] Although the Commissioners must act in accordance with the directions of the Chancellor of the Exchequer and the Secretary of State, this is not a matter that need concern any disponee.[118] In relation to dispositions by the two Royal Duchies of Cornwall and Lancaster, there are no equivalent provisions. The legal position in relation to both Duchies is in fact arcane and complex.

The present law

THE DUCHY OF CORNWALL

11.34 The Duchy of Cornwall's powers in relation to the sale and acquisition of land are governed by the Duchy of Cornwall Management Acts 1863 to 1982,[119] of which the 1863 Act is the principal Act. The relevant provisions of the 1863 Act may be summarised as follows[120]—

(1) where the Duchy makes a sale or disposal within its powers,[121] any capital money arising has to be paid into the Bank of England (or other authorised institution) and a receipt given by one of the cashiers;[122]

(2) the "grant or assurance" by which the sale or other disposal is made must be made by deed under the seal of the Duchy and a memorandum must be endorsed on the deed, signed by the auditor of the Duchy acknowledging that the amount has been paid into the Bank of England or other authorised institution in the manner directed by the Act, and specifying the date of payment;[123]

---

[115] Cl 83(2).

[116] For the Crown Estate Commissioners, see Crown Estate Act 1961, s 1(1).

[117] *Ibid*, s 1(6).

[118] *Ibid*, s 1(4), (5).

[119] See *Halsbury's Laws of England* (4th ed), vol 12(1), para 319.

[120] See *Halsbury's Laws of England* (4th ed), vol 12(1), paras 342 and following.

[121] Duchy of Cornwall Management Act 1863, s 3 (as amended).

[122] *Ibid*, s 4.

[123] *Ibid*, s 5.

(3)   every deed or instrument by which any land is acquired, sold or disposed of by the Duchy is required to be enrolled in the Duchy office within 6 months after it is made;[124]

(4)   a deed or instrument enrolled in the Duchy Office has the same force and effect as if it had been enrolled or registered at the High Court;[125]

(5)   once enrolled, the deed or instrument is valid and effectual against the Duke of Cornwall;[126] and

(6)   no person claiming under any deed, instrument or assurance that is made or purports to be made under the powers given by the Act is bound to enquire whether the provisions of the Act have been complied with, or that the transaction was in fact authorised.[127]

11.35   The provisions on enrolment reflect the uncertainties of conveyancing in the mid-19th century and were intended to provide some degree of certainty in transactions that is now much more effectively achieved by registration of title under the Land Registration Act 1925. Indeed, it is not at first easy to see how the provisions of the 1863 Act on enrolment can be reconciled with the fundamental principle of registered conveyancing by which it is registration that confers legal title on the proprietor, though in practice a mechanism exists by which both elements are satisfied.[128] In addition to this general point, our attention has been drawn to a number of practical difficulties that apply in relation to these provisions.[129]

THE DUCHY OF LANCASTER

11.36   The position of the Duchy of Lancaster is similar to but not the same as the Duchy of Cornwall. The Chancellor and Council of the Duchy of Lancaster have powers both to sell and convey land forming part of the possessions of the

---

[124] *Ibid*, s 30. The Keeper of the Records is directed to make the enrolment: *ibid*, s 31. There are provisions by which an enrolment may be made out of time: *ibid*, s 33.

[125] *Ibid*, s 32. For enrolment in the High Court, see Supreme Court Act 1981, s 133; CPR PD5, 6.1.

[126] Duchy of Cornwall Management Act 1863, s 19.

[127] *Ibid*.

[128] See Land Registration Act 1925, s 69(1). The transaction is not binding on the Duke of Cornwall until it is enrolled. That takes place within 6 months of the transaction or some extended period. What happens at present is, we are informed, as follows. Following completion of a sale or lease, the transfer or lease is not immediately returned to the transferee or grantee but is retained by the Duchy for enrolment. In practice this is done within the 30 days which are allowed for stamping the instrument and usually within the priority period allowed for by the Land Registration (Official Searches) Rules 1993. The latter is not regarded as important because it is extremely unlikely that the Duchy would enter into any other transaction in relation to the same land. There is, however, the risk that some third party might, say, enter a caution.

[129] In particular, the giving of receipts on a sale of Duchy land where the consideration is paid in instalments and the title is registered.

Duchy[130] and to lease it on such terms as they think fit.[131] There are also elaborate provisions for the exchange of Duchy land for other land and for the payment of any money necessary for equality of exchange.[132] The Chancellor and Council of the Duchy are also empowered to purchase land. Such land is conveyed to and assured to the use of Her Majesty in right of the Duchy.[133] There are similar enrolment provisions applicable to such dispositions as those which apply in relation to the Duchy of Cornwall.[134]

The provisions of the Bill

11.37 It will be obvious from the account of the law given above, that the law which governs dispositions of land to or by the Royal Duchies is hopelessly out of date, difficult to operate, and badly in need of a fundamental review. The scope of the Bill necessarily limits what can be done to cut through this legislative thicket in relation to dispositions of registered land to or by the Duchies. The Bill does, however, provide that nothing in any enactment relating to the Duchy of Lancaster or the Duchy of Cornwall shall have effect to impose any requirement with respect to formalities or enrolment in relation to a disposition by a registered proprietor.[135] The effect of this provision is, therefore, that a disposition of a registered estate or charge by or to either the Duchy of Cornwall or the Duchy of Lancaster can be made in the usual way, regardless of the requirements that would otherwise apply under the legislation governing the Duchies.

Matters for which the Bill makes no provision

11.38 There are at least two matters presently found in the Land Registration Act 1925 relating to the Crown that are not replicated in the Bill. First, there is no provision directly equivalent to section 80 of the 1925 Act saving the right of Her Majesty in relation to bona vacantia.[136] No provision is needed because there is nothing in the Bill that would affect its operation. However, the Bill does contain a power to make rules making provision about how the passing of a registered estate or charge is to be dealt with for the purposes of the Bill.[137] Secondly, the Land Registration Act 1925 requires the registrar to notify the Crown Estate Commissioners or the relevant Royal Duchy if there is an application to register

---

[130] Duchy of Lancaster Lands Act 1855, s 1.

[131] Duchy of Lancaster Act 1988, s 1.

[132] See Duchy of Lancaster Act 1808, ss 28, 29.

[133] Duchy of Lancaster Lands Act 1855, s 3.

[134] This is brought about by a very circuitous legislative route. See Duchy of Lancaster Lands Act 1855, s 1; Duchy of Cornwall Act 1844 (7 & 8 Vict, c 65, *not* c 105), ss 30, 31; Assessionable Manors Award Act 1848, s 14; and *Halsbury's Laws of England* (4th ed), vol 12(1), para 316.

[135] Cl 84.

[136] Cf Land Registration Act 1925, s 80.

[137] See Cl 85.

land that includes foreshore.[138] He may not register the estate until one month after giving such notice. The Bill does not replicate this provision because it belongs more properly in the rules that will govern applications for first registration.[139]

BANKRUPTCY

Introduction

11.39 Clause 86 of the Bill makes special provision for the effect of bankruptcy. This is necessary to reflect the provisions of the Insolvency Act 1986. The provisions in the Bill differ somewhat from those found in the Land Registration Act 1925[140] because of the prospective abolition of inhibitions that has been explained in Part VI of the Report.[141]

Procedure in relation to bankruptcy petitions

11.40 When a petition in bankruptcy is filed against a debtor, the relevant court official[142] must apply to register the petition as a land charge in the register of pending actions.[143] Where the debtor is the registered proprietor of any land or charge, this can have no direct effect, because registration of a land charge does not affect registered land.[144] However, this registration serves to trigger a procedure for ensuring that an appropriate entry is made on the register of title. The Chief Land Registrar maintains both the land charges register and the register of title. Using the index of proprietor's names,[145] he will attempt to ascertain whether the debtor is the registered proprietor of any land or charge on the register. If he thinks that he is, he must then register a creditor's notice against the title of any land or charge that *appears* to him to be affected.[146] Clause 86(2) of the Bill replicates this procedure. The registrar must enter a notice of the pending action.[147] That entry must remain in the register until either a restriction is entered

---

[138] Land Registration Act 1925, s 97(1). The section does not apply to the registration of an estate with a possessory or good leasehold title: *ibid*, s 97(2).

[139] See Cl 14; above, para 3.53.

[140] Section 61.

[141] See above, para 6.32.

[142] A registrar in bankruptcy of the High Court or the registrar of the county court.

[143] Under Land Charges Act 1972, s 5(1)(b). The obligation to apply for registration is imposed by the Insolvency Rules 1986: see Ruoff & Roper, *Registered Conveyancing*, 28-07.

[144] Under Cl 86(7), a person to whom a registrable disposition is made is not required to make a search under Land Charges Act 1972. Cf Land Registration Act 1925, s 61(6), which is to like effect under the present law.

[145] For this index, see Land Registration Rules 1925, r 9.

[146] Land Registration Act 1925, s 61(1). With a common name, there can be considerable difficulties in identifying the land in question: see Ruoff & Roper, *Registered Conveyancing*, 28-08.

[147] For notices in relation to pending land actions, see Cl 87; above, paras 6.59—6.61.

in the manner explained below in paragraph 11.41, or the trustee in bankruptcy is registered as proprietor.[148]

Procedure in relation to bankruptcy orders

11.41   A similar procedure applies when a person is adjudicated bankrupt and a bankruptcy order is made against him or her. The order is registered by the relevant court official[149] as a land charge under the Land Charges Act 1972.[150] At present, the Chief Land Registrar is then required to enter a bankruptcy inhibition.[151] Under the Bill, because inhibitions are prospectively abolished,[152] the registrar is required to protect a bankruptcy order by the entry of a restriction.[153] That restriction must reflect the limitation under section 284 of the Insolvency Act 1986, by which a disposition by a bankrupt is void, except to the extent that it is either made with the consent of the court or is subsequently ratified by the court.[154]

Protection for disponees in good faith

11.42   As we have explained in Part V of this Report—

(1)   neither a petition in bankruptcy nor a bankruptcy order is, for the purposes of the Bill, an interest affecting an estate or charge;[155] and

(2)   the Bill makes express provision for the protection of disponees in relation to such petitions and orders.[156]

In this, we follow the model of both the Land Registration Act 1925[157] and the Insolvency Act 1986.[158]

11.43   Clause 86(5) provides that, where the proprietor of a registered estate or charge is adjudged bankrupt, the title of his or her trustee in bankruptcy is void against a disponee to whom a registrable disposition has been made and where the

---

[148]   Cl 86(3). Cf Land Registration Act 1925, s 61(1).

[149]   See above, para 11.40.

[150]   Section 6(1)(c).

[151]   Land Registration Act 1925, s 61(3).

[152]   See above, para 6.32.

[153]   Cl 86(4).

[154]   *Ibid.*

[155]   Cl 86(1).

[156]   See Cl 86(5) above, para 5.20.

[157]   Section 61(6).

[158]   Section 284(4).

registration requirements have been met, provided certain conditions are satisfied.[159] Those conditions are as follows[160]—

(1)   the disposition was made for valuable consideration;

(2)   the disponee acted in good faith;

(3)   at the time of the disposition—

    (a)   there was no notice or restriction entered under Clause 86;[161] and

    (b)   the disponee had no notice of the bankruptcy petition or the adjudication.

11.44   As we have explained in Part V of this Report, questions of notice are almost always irrelevant to issues of priority under the Bill.[162] However, in relation to bankruptcy petitions and orders, we have felt obliged to follow the approach adopted in the Insolvency Act 1986 which protects a bona fide purchaser for value without notice.

SETTLEMENTS

11.45   The Land Registration Act 1925 contains detailed provisions about its application to settlements under the Settled Land Act 1925.[163] The Bill does not replicate these. It provides instead that rules may make provision for its purposes in relation to the application to registered land[164] of those various enactments[165] relating to settlements under the Settled Land Act 1925.[166] We believe that it is now more appropriate to deal with settled land in rules. It ceased to be possible to create new settlements under the Settled Land Act 1925 after 1996.[167] Settlements were not very common even before 1997, and they will, in time, disappear. It would be unfortunate to encumber the Bill with provisions that would rapidly become obsolete.

---

[159]   Cl 86(5), (6). For the registration requirements, see Cl 27(4); Schedule 2; above, paras 4.16 and following.

[160]   See Cl 86(5).

[161]   See above, paras 11.40 (notice of pending action) and 11.41 (bankruptcy restriction).

[162]   See above, para 5.16.

[163]   See Land Registration Act 1925, ss 86—92.

[164]   Which, for these purposes, means an interest the title to which is, or is required to be, registered: Cl 89(3).

[165]   Which include, eg, Trustee Act 1925 and Administration of Estates Act 1925.

[166]   Cl 89(1). These rules will be land registration rules and will be required to be laid before Parliament only. See Cls 125, 129(1). They may include provision modifying any of the enactments referred to in Cl 89(1) in its application to registered land: Cl 89(2).

[167]   Trusts of Land and Appointment of Trustees Act 1996, s 2.

PART XII
CONVEYANCING 1: GENERAL PROVISIONS

INTRODUCTION

12.1 A number of issues that are relevant to the conveyancing process have already been explained in Part IX of this Report in the context of the register and registration. Electronic conveyancing is addressed in Part XIII. In this Part we are concerned with—

(1) the proof of title —

    (a) to registered land; and

    (b) where there is a contract to grant a lease out of unregistered land that will trigger the requirement of compulsory registration; and

(2) covenants for title in relation to dispositions of registered estates.

PROOF OF TITLE

Introduction

12.2 In the Consultative Document,[1] we summarised the three obligations of a seller of land to a buyer, namely—

(1) to disclose latent defects in title prior to contracting;[2]

(2) to convey to the buyer on completion a title to the land that is in accordance with the contract;[3] and

(3) to prove that title.[4]

We emphasised that (2) and (3) were distinct obligations, and this has indeed been reiterated by the Court of Appeal.[5] We made no recommendations in relation to (1) and (2), as the principles appeared to us to be sound and to require no change. As regards (3) however, we considered that changes were needed.

---

[1] Law Com No 254, para 11.30.

[2] See *ibid*, paras 11.32—11.33.

[3] See *ibid*, para 11.34.

[4] See *ibid*, paras 11.35 and following.

[5] *Barclays Bank Plc v Weeks Legg & Dean* [1999] QB 309, 324.

12.3 A seller's obligations as to proof of title are presently governed by section 110 of the Land Registration Act 1925.[6] We commented in detail on these provisions in the Consultative Document.[7] In essence, they require the seller to produce—

(1) copies of subsisting entries on the register;

(2) copies of filed plans;

(3) copies or abstracts of documents noted on the register so far as they affect the property and will not be discharged or overridden on completion;[8] and

(4) copies, abstracts and evidence in respect of subsisting rights and interests which are either appurtenant to the registered land or are matters excepted from the effect of registration.[9]

The seller's obligations in relation to the first three of these matters cannot be altered by contrary stipulation,[10] whereas in relation to the fourth they can.[11]

What proof of title must a seller deduce?

12.4 Section 110 also makes provision for the case where a seller of land is not in fact registered as proprietor of the land.[12] In this case, at the request of the buyer, the seller must, at his or her own expense, either—

(1) procure his or her registration as proprietor; or

(2) procure a disposition from the proprietor to him or herself.[13]

This subsection applies notwithstanding any stipulation to the contrary.[14]

---

[6] See s 110(1)—(3), (5). The section applies "on a sale or other disposition of registered land to a purchaser other than a lessee or a chargee".

[7] Law Com No 254, paras 11.35—11.43.

[8] Land Registration Act 1925, s 110(1).

[9] Land Registration Act 1925, s 110(2).

[10] Land Registration Act 1925, s 110(1).

[11] Land Registration Act 1925, s 110(2).

[12] In the absence of a special condition this will only arise where the seller is entitled to be registered, as where he or she is the executor of a deceased registered proprietor or the registered proprietor holds the registered estate or charge on trust for the seller.

[13] Land Registration Act 1925, s 110(5).

[14] This subsection was first enacted as Land Transfer Act 1897, s 16(2). However, by Law of Property Act 1925, s 42(3) (a provision first introduced in 1925), "[a] stipulation contained in any contract for sale or exchange of land made after the commencement of this Act, to the effect that an outstanding legal estate is to be traced or got in at the expense of a purchaser or that no objection is to be taken on account of an outstanding legal estate, shall be void". This subsection places a significant restriction on what an unscrupulous seller of land can foist on a purchaser, and greatly weakens the need for a provision equivalent to Land Registration Act 1925, s 110(5).

12.5   When section 110 was first enacted, there were no postal searches — they were not introduced until 1930. It was necessary to attend in person at the Land Registry in London to undertake a search of the register.[15] Although there was statutory provision for the creation of district land registries,[16] none had been created outside London prior to the Second World War.[17] Against that background, the prescriptive nature of section 110 is comprehensible. When the Land Registration Act 1925 was first enacted, searching the register and obtaining office copies were expensive matters.

12.6   The contrast with the position today could not be more striking.

(1)   The register is now open, and it is no longer necessary for an intending buyer to obtain the consent of the seller to search the register, or to obtain copies of documents referred to in the register.[18]

(2)   The system of searching the register has become very much simpler and cheaper than was formerly the case. A direct access official search by computer costs £2 and an official search in any other way costs £4. An office copy obtained by direct access costs £2 and one obtained by some other means £4.[19]

(3)   Registered conveyancing is now the normal method of conveyancing, with unregistered conveyancing applicable only to dealings with leases granted for 21 years or less and dispositions of unregistered freeholds that trigger first registration.

12.7   In the light of these fundamental changes, the present rules that govern proof of title look very prescriptive and heavy-handed. They are certainly badly out of date. In the Consultative Document,[20] we recommended that—

(1)   the provisions of section 110 of the Land Registration Act 1925, explained above, should not be replicated in the Bill;

(2)   in principle, parties should be left to make their own contractual arrangements as to how title should be deduced;

(3)   there should be a safeguard in case this freedom is abused;[21]

---

[15]   See *Brickdale & Stuart Wallace's Land Registration Act, 1925* (4th ed 1939), p 493.

[16]   See Land Registration Act 1925, s 132.

[17]   *Brickdale & Stuart Wallace's Land Registration Act, 1925* (4th ed 1939), p 283.

[18]   See above, para 9.37.

[19]   See Land Registration Fees Order 2001, Schedule 3.

[20]   Law Com No 254, paras 11.47, 11.48.

[21]   As by buyers making excessive requests for evidence of title, or by sellers who impose terms which unreasonably preclude inquiries on matters upon which the register is not conclusive.

(4)   this should be in the form of a rule-making power to make rules as to the proof of title that a buyer might require; and

(5)   such rules would override any contractual term that conflicted with them.

On consultation, some four-fifths of those who responded on this point supported our recommendations.

12.8   The Bill accordingly provides a rule-making power to make provision about the obligations with respect to—

(1)   proof of title; or

(2)   perfection of title

of a seller under a contract for the transfer or other disposition for valuable consideration of a registered estate or charge.[22] The reference to provision about perfection of title is to cover the case of the seller who is not the registered proprietor.[23] Any rules that may be made under this power may be expressed to have effect notwithstanding any stipulation to the contrary.[24] If any such rules are made, they will be land registration rules, and will be laid before Parliament only.[25]

What title is a buyer entitled to see?

12.9   The Bill makes one other change in relation to the proof of title. This arises, in part at least, as a consequence of the fact, mentioned above,[26] that the register is now open, and an intending buyer no longer requires the seller's consent to search the register. Section 44 of the Law of Property Act 1925 prescribes the statutory commencement of title. Thus, for example, the period of commencement of title is 15 years,[27] and there are a series of rules as to the title that an intending lessee or sub-lessee or an intending assignee of a lease or sub-lease is entitled to see under a contract to grant or assign a lease.[28] As regards the latter, an intending tenant or assignee may always inspect any lease under which the other contracting party holds, but there is no right to inspect the title to the freehold.[29]

---

[22]   Schedule 10, para 2(1).

[23]   Cf above, para 12.4.

[24]   Schedule 10, para 2(2). This leaves open the possibility of making rules that are *not* overriding, for example, by way of guidance as to what might be considered to be good practice. These would then apply unless the parties stipulated to the contrary.

[25]   See Cls 125(3); 129(1); below, para 17.5.

[26]   See para 12.6(1).

[27]   Law of Property Act 1925, s 44(1) (as amended by Law of Property Act 1969, s 23).

[28]   Law of Property Act 1925, s 44(2)—(5).

[29]   *Megarry and Wade's Law of Real Property* (6th ed 2000), 14-295.

12.10   The rules found in section 44 are default rules and can be ousted by express provision to the contrary in the contract,[30] and in practice, often are. Thus, under condition 8.2.4 of the Standard Conditions of Sale,[31] on the grant of a new lease—

> If the term of the new lease will exceed 21 years, the seller[32] is to deduce a title which will enable the buyer[33] to register the lease at HM Land Registry with an absolute title.

12.11   Neither the rules on the commencement of title, nor those which apply to the grant of leases, have any practical effect as to the proof of title to the transfer of a registered estate or the grant of a lease out of such a registered estate. This is because the register itself is proof of a registered estate and any transferee or grantee can inspect the title of the estate that is to be transferred or out of which the grant is to be made.[34] The Bill therefore disapplies section 44 of the Law of Property Act 1925 in relation to registered land or to a lease derived out of registered land.[35]

12.12   The Bill goes further than that however and introduces provisions in relation to any contract to grant a lease out of an unregistered estate where that lease will be subject to the requirement of compulsory registration.[36] Wherever possible, we are anxious to ensure that such leases can be registered with absolute and not merely good leasehold title. This is in accordance with what is now common practice, as the condition of sale quoted in paragraph 12.10 above demonstrates. The Bill therefore disapplies the relevant provisions of section 44 of the Law of Property Act 1925[37] in relation to contracts to grant leases that trigger compulsory first registration under Clause 4.[38] As a result, where the owner of an unregistered freehold contracts to grant a lease that will be subject to the requirement of compulsory registration, he or she will have to deduce his or her title for the statutory period[39] unless the parties agree to the contrary. In most cases, the lessee will then be registered with an absolute title.

12.13   Section 44 of the Law of Property Act 1925 only applies to *contracts* to grant or transfer estates. It is of course common for leases to be granted without any prior contract. Nevertheless, the changes that the Bill makes in the default position

---

[30]   Law of Property Act 1925, s 44(11).

[31]   3rd ed 1995.

[32]   That is, the landlord: Standard Conditions of Sale, c 8.2.2.

[33]   That is, the tenant: Standard Conditions of Sale, c 8.2.2.

[34]   See above, para 9.37.

[35]   Law of Property Act 1925, s 44(12), inserted by Schedule 11, para 2(4).

[36]   For the requirement of compulsory registration, see Cl 4; above, paras 3.22 and following.

[37]   Namely s 44(2) and (4).

[38]   Law of Property Act 1925, s 44(4A), inserted by Schedule 11, para 2(2).

[39]   That is, for at least 15 years: Law of Property Act 1925, s 44(1), above, para 12.9. The commencement of title would be the first instrument that could be a good root of title that was more than 15 years old.

contained in section 44 will, it is hoped, also establish the default position in relation to the title to be deduced when making grants of leases that are not preceded by a contract.

COVENANTS FOR TITLE

Introduction

12.14 The obligation of a seller of land to deduce a title in accordance with the terms of the contract of sale,[40] like most other obligations under the contract, is merged in the deed of conveyance under the doctrine of merger, and no action lies for its breach thereafter.[41] As the seller's obligations in relation to his or her title cease to be enforceable on completion, it has long been customary for a seller to provide some kind of warranty as to his title in the conveyance. Such covenants for title are covenants which may be given either by a seller of freehold or leasehold land or, on or after 1 July 1995, by the grantor of a lease.[42] Such covenants are the principal, and indeed often the only, remedy that a grantee or transferee of land may have for any defects in title that emerge after completion.

12.15 Covenants for title have been implied since the Conveyancing Act 1881 by the use of certain words in a conveyance. The use of the appropriate words carried with it the implication of certain covenants. Prior to July 1, 1995, the relevant words were "as beneficial owner", "as settlor", "as trustee", "as mortgagee", "as personal representative of X deceased" or "under an order of the court".[43] After June 1995, as part of a major reform of the law governing such covenants,[44] the relevant words are "with full guarantee" or "with limited guarantee".[45] The Bill does not materially change the substance of the present law as to the implication of covenants for title on the transfer of a registered estate.[46] It does, however, create a more coherent framework for it.

---

[40] See above, para 12.2.

[41] See generally *Knight Sugar Co Ltd v The Alberta Railway & Irrigation Co* [1938] 1 All ER 266, 269. Where title is unregistered, merger operates on the execution of the conveyance. Although merger does apply to registered land, it is not settled whether it occurs on the execution of the transfer or on registration. The former seems preferable: see D G Barnsley, "Completion of a Contract for the Sale and Purchase of Land" [1991] Conv 15, 24.

[42] There were no covenants for title implied on the grant of leases prior to that date.

[43] See Law of Property Act 1925, s 76(1). This section is repealed as regards dispositions made on or after July 1, 1995: see Law of Property (Miscellaneous Provisions) Act 1994, s 10.

[44] Brought about by Law of Property (Miscellaneous Provisions) Act 1994, which implemented (with amendments) the recommendations of the Law Commission in Transfer of Land: Implied Covenants for Title (1988) Law Com No 199.

[45] Law of Property (Miscellaneous Provisions) Act 1994, s 1. The Welsh language equivalents which may be used (see s 8(4)) are, respectively, "gyda gwarant teitl llawn" and "gyda gwarant teitl cyfyngedig".

[46] There are some marginal changes: cf below paras 12.18, 12.19.

No liability for matters on the register

12.16 Where a covenant is implied under the Law of Property (Miscellaneous Provisions) Act 1994 and the disposition of property is a registered disposition under the Land Registration Act 1925, rule 77A(2) of the Land Registration Rules 1925 presently provides that *any* covenant implied by virtue of Part I of the 1994 Act "shall take effect as if the disposition had been expressly made subject to—

> (a) all charges and other interests appearing or protected on the register at the time of the execution of the disposition and affecting the title of the registered proprietor;

> (b) any overriding interest of which the person to whom the disposition is made has notice and which will affect the estate created or disposed of when the disposition is registered."

12.17 Section 6 of the Law of Property (Miscellaneous Provisions) Act 1994 provides that there is no liability in relation to *some* of the covenants implied by Part I of that Act[47] in certain circumstances. In particular, under section 6(2), the person making the disposition is not liable under any of the relevant covenants for anything that is either within the actual knowledge or is a necessary consequence of facts that are within the actual knowledge of the person to whom the disposition is made.

12.18 To deal with the matters that are presently covered by rule 77A(2) of the Land Registration Rules 1925, the Bill inserts a new subsection (4) into section 6 of the Law of Property (Miscellaneous Provisions) Act 1994.[48] It provides that where the disposition is of an interest, the title to which is registered under the Bill, the covenantor is not liable for anything which was at the time of the disposition entered in relation to that interest in the register of title under the Bill. It will be noted that there is nothing that corresponds to rule 77A(2)(b)[49] in relation to overriding interests. However, section 6(2) of the 1994 Act would appear to make that provision unnecessary.[50]

---

[47] Namely the covenants that the person making the disposition has the right to dispose of the property (Law of Property (Miscellaneous Provisions) Act 1994, s 2(1)(a)), that he or she is disposing of the property free from charges, incumbrances and third party rights (*ibid*, s 3), and that where the disposition is of leasehold land, the lease is valid (*ibid*, s 4).

[48] Schedule 11, para 31(2).

[49] Overriding interests of which the disponee had notice.

[50] Rule 77A(2)(b) speaks of an overriding interest of which the disponee "has notice", whereas under Law of Property (Miscellaneous Provisions) Act 1994, the covenant does not extend to matters that are either within the disponee's "actual knowledge" or are a "necessary consequence of facts" that are within his or her actual knowledge. A disponee is not therefore affected by matters of which he or she merely has *constructive notice* under section 6(2). In Ruoff & Roper, *Registered Conveyancing*, 16-11, it is stated that "notice" in r 77A(2)(b) does in fact have the same meaning as Law of Property (Miscellaneous Provisions) Act 1994, s 6(2), and does *not* include overriding interests of which the disponee merely has constructive notice.

12.19   This new provision does not precisely replicate the effect of rule 77A(2) of the Land Registration Rules 1925. This is because rule 77A(2) applies in relation to *all* the covenants implied under Part I of the Law of Property (Miscellaneous Provisions) Act 1994, and not merely those listed in section 6. However, this change is unlikely to be material. The effect of the change is to make the law clearer, more coherent and more accessible. The relevant exceptions to the application of the implied covenants will all be found in one statutory provision and apply to the same covenants.

Rules

12.20   The Land Registration Act 1925 contains a rule-making power "prescribing the effect" of covenants for title implied under the Law of Property Act 1925 and Part I of the Law of Property (Miscellaneous Provisions) Act 1994.[51] The rule-making powers in relation to covenants for title that are contained in the Bill are more precisely focused.[52]

(1)   First, there is a power for rules to make provision about the form of provisions that extend or limit any covenant that is implied by virtue of Part I of the Law of Property (Miscellaneous Provisions) Act 1994.[53] There are certain rules in the Land Registration Rules 1925 that have this effect[54] and the power under the Bill will enable similar provisions to be made.

(2)   Secondly, there is a power for rules to make provision about the application of section 77 of the Law of Property Act 1925 to transfers of registered estates.[55] Section 77, which applies to transfers of registered land, is concerned with the covenants that are to be implied on a conveyance of land subject to a rentcharge.[56] Many rentcharges will be phased out in 2037 under the Rentcharges Act 1977, and the circumstances in which new ones can be created under that Act are very limited. To the extent that the rules may be needed, they may be employed (for example) to enable the implication of the covenants to be modified or negatived.[57]

(3)   Thirdly, there is a power for rules to make provision about reference in the register to implied covenants, including provision for the state of the

---

[51]   See s 38(2).

[52]   See Schedule 10, para 3.

[53]   Schedule 10, para 3(a).

[54]   See Land Registration Rules 1925, rr 76A(5), 77A(3).

[55]   Schedule 10, para 3(b).

[56]   At present, Land Registration Rules 1925, r 109, makes provision for the application of the implied covenants to registered land and (somewhat curiously) replicates for registered land certain provisions found in Law of Property Act 1925, s 77, which would in any event apply.

[57]   Cf Land Registration Rules 1925, r 109(6).

register to be conclusive in relation to whether covenants have been implied.[58]

Covenants implied on the assignment of a lease prior to 1996

12.21 In relation to leases granted prior to 1996, a tenant who assigns a lease remains liable to the landlord on the covenants in that lease for its entire duration notwithstanding any assignment by him or her of that lease. Such "first tenant liability" has been abolished for leases granted after 1995 by the Landlord and Tenant (Covenants) Act 1995. However, leases granted prior to 1996 will continue in existence for many years. As regards such leases, section 24(1)(b) and (2) of the Land Registration Act 1925 made provision for implied indemnity covenants on the part of the transferee in favour of the transferor, and, in relation to a transfer of part, an implied indemnity covenant on the part of the *transferor* in favour of the *transferee*. Section 24(1)(b) and (2) of the Land Registration Act 1925 were repealed prospectively by the Landlord and Tenant (Covenants) Act 1995,[59] but only in respect of "new tenancies" — in essence those granted after the Act was brought into force.[60] The Bill replicates in more comprehensible form the effect of section 24(1)(b) and (2) in relation to the assignment of leases which are not "new tenancies" for the purposes of the 1995 Act.[61]

---

[58] Schedule 10, para 3(c). At present, under Land Registration Rules 1925, r 76A(4), *no* reference is to be made in the register to any covenant implied by Part 1 of Law of Property (Miscellaneous Provisions) Act 1994, subject to one exception.

[59] Sections 14(b), 30(3).

[60] See *ibid*, s 1.

[61] Schedule 12, para 20.

PART XIII
CONVEYANCING 2: ELECTRONIC CONVEYANCING

INTRODUCTION

13.1   The most important single function of the Land Registration Bill is to create the necessary legal framework for the introduction of electronic conveyancing. In Part II of this Report we have explained how it is envisaged that electronic conveyancing is likely to operate. In this Part we explain in detail the provisions of the Bill on electronic conveyancing. These provisions are contained in Part VIII and Schedule 5 of the Bill and fall into three parts—

   (1)   the formal requirements for electronic dispositions;

   (2)   the provisions governing the land registry network; and

   (3)   the power to require both the use of electronic conveyancing and that electronic dispositions be simultaneously registered.

13.2   It will be recalled from Part II[1] that the main features of the proposed system of electronic conveyancing are as follows—

   (1)   the system will be operated through a secure electronic communications network;

   (2)   HM Land Registry will authorise access to that electronic communications network by contract with the users, such as solicitors and licensed conveyancers;

   (3)   that electronic communications network will be employed to conduct all the stages of a transaction in electronic form;

   (4)   the electronic communications network may be used to manage chain transactions, at least in relation to residential properties;

   (5)   the process of registering dispositions will be conducted by persons authorised by the terms of their access to the electronic communications network, and it will take place at the same moment as the disposition;

   (6)   there will be power to make electronic conveyancing compulsory; and

   (7)   there will be provision to enable persons who wish to undertake their own conveyancing to take advantage of electronic conveyancing.

13.3   The issue of electronic conveyancing was one of the main issues addressed in the Consultative Document.[2] Nearly 80 per cent of those who responded to the issue

---

[1]   See above, paras 2.52 and following.

were in favour of the principle of electronic conveyancing. There was, however, a widely expressed view that there should be full public consultation over the details of electronic conveyancing and that interested parties should work with HM Land Registry in developing electronic conveyancing. We agree with that view. Indeed, we consider that it would be impossible to establish an effective system of electronic conveyancing without such consultation and the advantage of informed expert comment that it would bring, particularly from those who will have to operate the system. An inter-governmental working party was set up in 2000 to ensure co-ordination within government and this has met a number of times. In preparing the first stage of the introduction of electronic conveyancing by an order under the Electronic Communications Act 2000, which is explained below,[3] the Lord Chancellor's Department set up a steering group to advise it, consisting of representatives from the bodies most likely to be affected. Furthermore, both HM Land Registry and the Law Commission have engaged in extensive informal consultation since the publication of the Consultative Document in 1998, particularly with conveyancing practitioners. The outcome is a legislative framework that differs in a number of respects from that which was visualised in the Consultative Document.

13.4   We now examine in detail the provisions of the Bill on electronic conveyancing.

FORMAL REQUIREMENTS FOR ELECTRONIC DISPOSITIONS

Introduction

13.5   In the Consultative Document, we explained that, because any system of electronic conveyancing would necessarily be paperless, something would have to be done in relation to the existing formal requirements that apply to most dispositions of land and to contracts for the sale or other disposition of land.[4] Those provisions can be summarised as follows—

(1)   It is normally necessary to use signed writing to create or dispose of any interest in land, whether legal or equitable.[5]

(2)   Most conveyances of a legal estate in land have to be made not only in writing but also by deed.[6] There are some exceptions to this,[7] such as

---

[2]   See Law Com No 254, Part XI.

[3]   See paras 13.7 and following.

[4]   Law Com No 254, para 11.21.

[5]   Law of Property Act 1925, s 53(1)(a).

[6]   Law of Property Act 1925, s 52(1). A deed must make it clear on its face that it is a deed and must be validly executed: see Law of Property (Miscellaneous Provisions) Act 1989, s 1(2). The requirements for execution vary according to the person or body making the deed. However some form of subscription is required, as is delivery of the deed.

[7]   See Law of Property Act 1925, s 52(2).

assents by personal representatives, where the conveyance of a legal estate can be made instead by signed writing.[8]

(3) Most contracts for the sale or other disposition of land can only be made by signed writing and must meet certain other conditions.[9]

13.6 Our provisional view in the Consultative Document was that there should be a power in the Bill to disapply or modify these provisions, and that this power should be exercisable by statutory instrument.[10] Subsequent events have led to the adoption of a somewhat different solution to this problem. The existence of these formal provisions is the immediate impediment to the introduction of any form of electronic conveyancing. If this impediment were removed, it would be possible to take the first steps towards the introduction of electronic conveyancing even in advance of the enactment of the present Bill. There are reasons why this should happen. HM Land Registry is keen to begin the introduction of some aspects of electronic conveyancing as soon as possible. These include—

(1) the creation of registered charges; and

(2) the making of applications for entries on the register, such as cautions, notices and restrictions;

in electronic form. The Electronic Communications Act 2000 has provided a means of achieving this.[11]

THE DRAFT LAW OF PROPERTY (ELECTRONIC COMMUNICATIONS) ORDER

13.7 Part II of the Electronic Communications Act 2000 contains provisions to facilitate the use of electronic communications and electronic data storage. So far as relevant, section 8 of the Act gives the appropriate Minister[12] power to modify by order made by statutory instrument the provisions of any enactment in such manner as he may think fit for the purpose of authorising or facilitating the use of electronic communications or electronic storage (instead of other forms of communication or storage).[13] Two of the purposes for which such an order may be made are where legislative provisions—

---

[8] See Law of Property Act 1925, s 52(2)(a); Administration of Estates Act 1925, s 36(4).

[9] Law of Property (Miscellaneous Provisions) Act 1989, s 2. For those contracts that are not required to meet the requirements of s 2, see s 2(5).

[10] Law Com No 254, paras 11.22, 11.23.

[11] Even before the Consultative Document had been published, the Law Commission and HM Land Registry were in discussions with the Department of Trade and Industry about the possibility of using powers under the proposed Electronic Communications Bill to overcome the formal requirements for dealings with land. The Electronic Communications Bill was in fact amended during its passage through Parliament to ensure that it could be employed for this purpose.

[12] In this case, the Lord Chancellor.

[13] Electronic Communications Act 2000, s 8(1).

(1)   require or permit something to be done or evidenced in writing using a document, notice or instrument;[14] and

(2)   require or authorise something to be signed or sealed by a person, delivered as a deed or witnessed.[15]

13.8   It should be noted that the powers under this Act permit the modification of "any enactment".[16] There is no power to amend any formal requirements that exist at common law.[17]

13.9   In March of this year, the Lord Chancellor's Department issued for consultation a draft Order to be made under section 8 of the Electronic Communications Act 2000.[18] This draft Order and the accompanying consultation paper were prepared in conjunction with HM Land Registry and the Law Commission. The draft Law of Property (Electronic Communications) Order 2001 contains three main provisions.

(1)   First, it inserts a new section 144A into the Land Registration Act 1925.[19] This prescribes the formalities required for dispositions in electronic form of—

(a)   registered land; and

(b)   unregistered land that trigger compulsory first registration.

(2)   Secondly, it confers additional rule-making powers in the Land Registration Act 1925 in relation to—

(a)   various applications to the registrar in electronic form; and

(b)   the storage of documents in electronic form.[20]

(3)   Thirdly, it inserts a new section 2A into the Law of Property (Miscellaneous Provisions) Act 1989.[21] This lays down the formalities required to make a contract for the sale of an interest in land in electronic form. The new section will apply whether the title to the land is registered or unregistered.

---

[14]   *Ibid*, s 8(2)(a).

[15]   *Ibid*, s 8(2)(c).

[16]   *Ibid*, s 8(1)(a).

[17]   Cf below, para 13.10.

[18]   Electronic Conveyancing: A draft order under section 8 of the Electronic Communications Act 2000; CP: 5/2001.

[19]   Article 3.

[20]   Article 2.

[21]   Article 4.

13.10 The present Bill will repeal the Land Registration Act 1925.[22] It necessarily contains provisions that replicate the effect of the first two elements of the draft Law of Property (Electronic Communications) Order 2001.[23] In fact, the provisions of the Bill go further than does the Order. There are two significant limits on what can be done by an order under section 8 of the Electronic Communications Act 2000. First, as we have mentioned above,[24] there is no power to amend any formal requirements at common law, but only those that are statutory. Secondly, by section 8(6)(a) of the Electronic Communications Act 2000, it is not possible to *require* that electronic communications or storage should be used. As we explain below, the Bill departs from both of these principles.[25]

THE PROVISIONS OF THE BILL

Introduction

13.11 Clause 91 of the Bill derives from the proposed section 144A of the Land Registration Act 1925 that is to be inserted by the draft Law of Property (Electronic Communications) Order. It enables certain dispositions to be effected electronically when they would otherwise have to be made in writing or by deed. It provides that, by meeting the requirements specified in the section, the parties to an electronic document are taken to have complied with the requirements for a written document or a deed. In some cases this will be for the purposes of any enactment[26] and in other cases for the purposes of the common law as well.[27] It should be noted that Clause 91 lays down a uniform requirement for making any electronic document, whether that document does the work of a deed or of signed writing. This is a striking development, though it is one that had been anticipated by the Law Commission in 1998.[28]

The applicability of Clause 91

13.12 For Clause 91 of the Bill to apply, the following requirements must be met.

(1) First, there must be a document made in electronic form that purports to effect a disposition.[29]

(2) Secondly, that disposition must be —

---

[22] See Cl 132; and Schedule 13.

[23] See respectively, Cls 91 (below, para 13.11); and 94 (below, para 13.32). The third element of the draft Order could not be included in the Land Registration Bill because of its application to unregistered land. It therefore goes beyond the scope of the Bill.

[24] See para 13.8.

[25] See paras 13.30, 13.74.

[26] Cl 91(5)—(7).

[27] Cl 91(4).

[28] See The Execution of Deeds and Documents by and on behalf of Bodies Corporate (1998) Law Com No 253, paras 1.14, 9.9.

[29] Cl 91(1)(a).

(a)   of a registered estate or charge;[30]

(b)   of an interest which is the subject of a notice in the register, such as an equitable charge or an option;[31] or

(c)   one which triggers the requirement of compulsory registration under Clause 4 of the Bill.[32]

(3)   Thirdly, the disposition must be of a kind for which the Lord Chancellor has prescribed a form of electronic disposition.[33] It is intended that, in due course, a form will be prescribed for *all* dispositions that could be made in electronic form under the section. These forms are likely to be similar to those that have been successfully employed in paper form since 1997 in relation to applications for registration.[34]

(4)   Fourthly, a document in electronic form must satisfy the four conditions that are laid down in Clause 91(3). These are explained below.

The four conditions

13.13   First, the document must make provision for the time and date when it takes effect.[35] At present, it is the usual practice for conveyancing documents to be signed and otherwise executed by the parties to them, but not dated. The instrument takes effect at the time when the conveyancers are ready for it to do so and it is dated shortly in advance. Where the document is a deed, this will be signified when it is delivered. The concept of delivery will not apply to documents in electronic form. An electronic document will not in fact *be* a deed, but is merely to be regarded as one for the purposes of any enactment.[36] It follows, therefore, that the concept of delivery is inapplicable. Clearly there has to be another means of fixing the operative moment of a document in electronic form. The requirement that an electronic document must make provision for the time and date when it takes effect achieves that. It will also enable the continuation of the present practice of completing when all parties are ready to do so. The time and date are likely to be inserted shortly before the document is to take effect.

---

[30]   Cl 91(2)(a).

[31]   Cl 91(2)(b). This goes beyond the Law of Property (Electronic Communications) Order. It is envisaged that it will become possible to transfer electronically certain legal and equitable interests that are protected by a notice on the register but are not registered estates or charges. See below, paras 13.22, 13.81.

[32]   Cl 91(2)(c). For dispositions that trigger the requirement of compulsory registration under Cl 4, see above, paras 3.23 and following.

[33]   See Cl 91(2).

[34]   See Land Registration Rules 1925, Schedule 1 (which was inserted by Land Registration Rules 1997, r 2(2)). Whereas approximately 50% of all applications to HM Land Registry are in some way defective, so that the registrar is obliged to raise requisitions upon them, the number of errors in relation to the new forms of application is much less.

[35]   Cl 91(3)(a).

[36]   See Cl 91(5), below, para 13.19.

13.14   Secondly, the document must have the electronic signature of each person by whom it purports to be authenticated.[37] An electronic signature is not a "signature" in the ordinarily accepted sense. It is a means by which an electronic document can be authenticated as that of the party making it.[38] There are several ways in which this can be done.[39] One method that is employed commercially is "public" or "dual" "key cryptography".[40] In the barest outline, the way in which this might work in electronic conveyancing is as follows. One party to a disposition, typically a seller or mortgagor of registered land, will send to the other party, the buyer or mortgagee (and HM Land Registry), some text which the sender will have encrypted using a "private key".[41] The recipient will be able to decode the text by means of a "public key", which will normally be obtained from the certification authority. That authority will have supplied the sender with his or her private key and the public key will only decipher the encoded text if it was indeed encoded by that private key. The recipient can tell whether there has been any interference with the message by, say, a hacker. It should be noted that although dual key cryptography is a common form of electronic signature, there will be no restriction on the types of electronic signature that will be permitted, provided that they meet the necessary security requirements. It is important that the legislation is flexible enough to allow for further developments.

13.15   Normally it will only be the disponor[42] whose electronic signature will be required. However, Clause 91(3)(b) specifies that the electronic signature is needed "of each person by whom it purports to be authenticated". This is because a disponee may sometimes need to be a party to the document. In particular, where there is a disposition of registered land and the disponees are to be joint proprietors, both the disponor and the disponees[43] should execute the transfer or application.[44] This

---

[37]   Cl 91(3)(b).

[38]   References in Cl 91 to an electronic signature are to be read in accordance with Electronic Communications Act 2000, s 7(2): see Cl 91(10). Section 7(2) provides that for the purposes of that section, an electronic signature "is so much of anything in electronic form as—

   (a) is incorporated into or logically associated with any electronic communication or electronic data; and

   (b) purports to be incorporated or associated for the purpose of being used in establishing the authenticity of the communication or data, the integrity of the communication or data, or both".

[39]   On electronic signatures generally, see *Digital Signature Guidelines*, which was produced for the Judicial Studies Board by a working group chaired by Lord Saville of Newdigate. It is published by the Judicial Studies Board in electronic form and is available from the websites of both the Judicial Studies Board (**www.jsboard.co.uk**) and the Law Commission (**www.lawcom.gov.uk**). The Law Commission was represented on the working group by Judge Diana Faber, who was then a Commissioner.

[40]   This is explained in some detail in *Digital Signature Guidelines*, above, paras 18—26.

[41]   Which can be made available on a smart card. There are strict safeguards employed in relation to the use of such smart cards.

[42]   Or the disponor's agent.

[43]   Or their agents.

274

is because the transfer form sets out the trusts upon which the land is to be held and, in this way, there will always be written evidence of the trust to satisfy the requirements of section 53(1)(b) of the Law of Property Act 1925. That provides that "a declaration of trust respecting any land or any interest therein must be manifested and proved by some writing signed by some person who is able to declare such trust...".[45]

13.16   Thirdly, each electronic signature must be certified.[46] Certification is the mechanism by which an electronic signature is authenticated. By way of example,[47] in relation to dual key cryptography, the "private key", mentioned above,[48] can be linked to a particular individual who signs a document electronically.[49] A private key will be issued to an individual by a certifying authority, which will have satisfied itself as to his or her identity, and will take appropriate steps to ensure that it is not employed by anyone else. The private key will commonly be incorporated in a smart card issued to the individual, which will also contain an electronic certificate from the certifying authority. The certificate will, therefore be sent electronically by the person signing the electronic document together with the document that he has just signed.

13.17   Fourthly, there must be compliance with such other conditions as may be prescribed by rules.[50] The purpose of this fourth requirement is to provide some flexibility in relation to the creation of dispositions in electronic form. It is possible that, with experience of electronic documents, it may be thought advisable to add further requirements, having regard (in particular) to the need for the security of transactions. For example, there are various levels of assurance that can be achieved in relation to the security of electronic signatures, and it might be appropriate to require compliance with a specified standard.

---

[44]   See, for example, under the present law, Land Registration Rules 1925, Schedule 1, Form TR1. In practice, this is not always done.

[45]   See too below, para 13.19.

[46]   Cl 91(3)(c).

[47]   It should be stressed that this is only by way of example and that dual key cryptography is just one form of electronic signature.

[48]   See para 13.14.

[49]   For the purposes of Cl 91, references to the certification of an electronic signature are to be read in accordance with Electronic Communications Act 2000, s 7(3): see Cl 91(10). Section 7(3) provides that "an electronic signature incorporated into or associated with a particular electronic communication or particular electronic data is certified by any person if that person (whether before or after the making of the communication) has made a statement confirming that—

(a) the signature,

(b) a means of producing, communicating or verifying the signature, or

(c) a procedure applied to the signature,

is (either alone or in combination with other factors) a valid means of establishing the authenticity of the communication or data, the integrity of the communication or data, or both".

[50]   Cl 91(3)(d).

Deemed execution

13.18 Clause 91 depends for its operation on subsection (4). An electronic document that meets the requirements that have been explained in paragraphs 13.12—13.17, above, is to be regarded as a document which is (a) in writing and (b) is signed by each individual, and sealed by each corporation,[51] whose electronic signature it has. In other words, the Bill does not disapply the relevant formal provisions,[52] but instead deems compliance with them if the requirements for an electronic document laid down in Clause 91 are met. This provision goes further than its equivalent in the draft Law of Property (Electronic Communications) Order.[53] It not only deems the document to comply with any *statutory* requirements of formality,[54] but also with those that apply *at common law*. This is important in the context of those corporations that have no statutory powers of execution.[55] At common law, any instrument that effects a disposition of property by a corporation must be executed under that corporation's seal.[56]

Deeds

13.19 Clause 91(5) is a similar deeming provision and is important for exactly the same reasons. It provides that any document to which Clause 91 applies is to be regarded as a deed for the purposes of any enactment. One result of this should be mentioned. Where the electronic document is signed electronically by joint disponees or by their agent, the fact that the document is to be regarded as a deed will mean that it necessarily satisfies the requirements for a valid declaration of trust under section 53(1)(b) of the Law of Property Act 1925. These requirements have been explained in paragraph 13.15, above.

Execution by agents

13.20 It will be possible for an agent to sign a document in electronic form on behalf of his or her principal. This may be of some importance. It is likely that, at least in the initial stages of electronic conveyancing, solicitors, licensed conveyancers and other authorised practitioners will sign electronic documents on behalf of their clients.[57] Although at common law an agent cannot execute a deed unless he or

---

[51] For the means by which a corporation can execute a document in electronic form, see below, paras 13.24 and following.

[52] As was provisionally proposed in the Consultative Document: see above, para 13.6.

[53] See the suggested Land Registration Act 1925, s 144A(4).

[54] Which is all that the draft Order can do, given the terms of Electronic Communications Act 2000, s 8: see above, para 13.8.

[55] The corporations in question are those to which neither the provisions of the Companies Act 1985 nor any other statute governing the execution of documents by particular corporations or classes of corporation apply.

[56] See further below, para 13.30.

[57] This gives rise to certain problems as to an agent's authority to make contracts and other dispositions on behalf of his or her clients. These are, however, addressed by the Bill: see below, para 13.60.

she is authorised to do so by a deed,[58] this rule will be inapplicable to execution of an electronic document that takes effect as a deed. This is because the document is not in fact a deed, but is only to be "regarded as a deed for the purposes of any enactment".[59]

13.21 Clause 91(6) contains a further deeming provision, which relates to agents. It provides that where an electronic disposition to which the Clause applies is authenticated by an individual as agent, it is to be regarded for the purposes of any enactment as authenticated by him or her under the written authority of his or her principal. By statute, some dispositions can only be made by an agent on behalf of his or her principal if he or she is authorised to do so in writing.[60] The result of Clause 91(6) is that where an agent makes an electronic disposition, it will not be possible to raise any question as to whether the agent did in fact have *written* authority to make it.

Notice of assignments

13.22 It is envisaged under the Bill, that—

(1) it will become possible to assign electronically certain legal and equitable interests in registered land that are not registered estates or charges, but are merely protected by the entry of a notice; and

(2) that assignment will not take effect unless there is a change in the terms of the notice.[61]

13.23 This is something of a novelty. At present only the transfer of registered estates and charges is effected by registration. However, as we explain below, under the Bill there will be power to *require* that an assignment of an interest protected by a notice[62] is made in electronic form and registered simultaneously with the assignment.[63] In relation to any such interest that is a debt or legal chose in action — such as the benefit of an option or other estate contract — it is necessary to give "express notice *in writing*" of the assignment to the debtor or other contracting party.[64] Clause 91(7) provides that if notice of an assignment made by means of a document to which the Clause applies is given in electronic form in

---

[58] *Steiglitz v Eggington* (1815) Holt 141; 171 ER 193; *Powell v London and Provincial Bank* [1893] 2 Ch 555, 563.

[59] Cl 91(5); above, para 13.19.

[60] Notably Law of Property Act 1925, s 53(1)(a), which provides that "no interest in land can be created or disposed of except by writing signed by the person creating or conveying the same, *or by his agent thereunto lawfully authorised in writing…*".

[61] See Cls 91(2)(b) (above, para 13.12); 93 (below, para 13.81).

[62] This could include both *legal estates* (such as a *profit à prendre* in gross or a franchise, which was not registered with its own title) and *equitable interests* (such as the benefit of an option or other estate contract or an equitable charge).

[63] Cl 93; below, para 13.74.

[64] Law of Property Act 1925, s 136.

accordance with rules, it is to be regarded for the purposes of any enactment as given in writing.

Execution by corporations

13.24 There are a number of ways in which a corporation (whether aggregate or sole) may execute a disposition of its land. We explain what these are and how it will be possible for a corporation to execute a document in electronic form under Clause 91.

Execution by corporations which are companies for the purposes of the Companies Act 1985

13.25 The provisions of the Companies Act 1985, which govern the execution of documents, apply to the following types of corporation—

(1) corporations that are companies for the purposes of the Companies Act 1985;[65]

(2) unregistered companies for the purposes of the Companies Act 1985;[66] and

(3) foreign companies for the purposes of the Foreign Companies (Execution of Documents) Regulations 1994.[67]

There are two relevant provisions of the Companies Act 1985 as to execution, namely section 36A(2) and (4).

13.26 Section 36A(2) provides that "a document is executed by a company by the affixing of its common seal". We can see no reason why a company itself should not have an electronic signature and this is recognised in Clause 91(4)(b).[68] It would no doubt be the case that that signature could only be incorporated into or otherwise logically associated with an electronic document[69] at the direction of one or more authorised officers of the company. However, were that done, a document would then take effect as if it had been sealed by the company.[70]

13.27 A company does not, however, have to have a common seal.[71] Where it does not, it must execute instruments in some other way. It may appoint an agent to act on its behalf, whether under a power of attorney[72] or otherwise. Alternatively, section

---

[65] Companies Act 1985, s 735(1).

[66] Companies Act 1985, s 718 and Schedule 22.

[67] SI 1994 No 950 (as amended).

[68] See above, para 13.18.

[69] This is the language employed by Electronic Communications Act 2000, s 7(1).

[70] Cl 91(4); above, para 13.18.

[71] Companies Act 1985, s 36A.

[72] See Powers of Attorney 1971, s 7, which provides that a donee of a power of attorney who is an individual may execute any instrument with the authority of the donor of the power which

36A(4) of the Companies Act 1985 provides that "a document signed by a director and the secretary of a company, or by two directors of a company, and expressed (in whatever form) to be executed by the company has the same effect as if it were executed under the common seal of the company". Where a document is in electronic form and is signed electronically by the relevant company officers, section 36A(4) will apply.[73]

13.28 Where an electronic document has apparently been executed in accordance with section 36A(4) of the Companies Act 1985, section 36A(6) of the Companies Act 1985 may be relevant. Section 36A(6) provides that "in favour of a purchaser[74] a document shall be deemed to have been duly executed by a company if it purports to be signed by a director and the secretary of the company, or by two directors of the company...".[75] Although the provisions of Part III of the Companies Act 1985 provide a significant measure of protection for those dealing with a company in respect of acts which it lacked the capacity to do under its constitution,[76] that protection is not complete. It does not apply in relation to—

(1) the unauthorised acts of individual directors;

(2) the acts of directors acting otherwise than as a board of directors;[77] or

(3) the acts of persons who have ceased to be office-holders but whose resignation had not yet been filed with the Register of Companies.[78]

13.29 However, the presumption of due execution under section 36A(6) *will* apply in such cases to protect a purchaser because it applies to a document that *purports* to be signed by the relevant officers of the company. Clause 91(9) makes it clear that section 36A(6) applies to a document that has been signed electronically. It provides that, if section 36A(4) of the Companies Act 1985[79] applies to a document because of Clause 91(4), section 36A(6) shall have effect in relation to

---

is as effective as if it were done in the name of that donor. It is expressly provided that this power can be exercised on behalf of *any* corporation sole or aggregate to make a conveyance of its land: see *ibid*, s 7(2); Law of Property Act 1925, s 74(3).

[73] Again, this follows from Cl 91(4); above, para 13.18.

[74] Defined by the subsection as "a purchaser in good faith for valuable consideration and includes a lessee, mortgagee or other person who for valuable consideration acquires an interest in property".

[75] The subsection also creates a presumption of delivery in relation to a deed. That is irrelevant to electronic documents: see above, para 13.13.

[76] See especially Companies Act 1985, ss 35, 35A, 35B.

[77] Cf Companies Act 1985, s 35A (which deals only with the power of the *board of directors* to bind the company).

[78] Cf The Execution of Deeds and Documents by and on behalf of Bodies Corporate (1998) Law Com No 253, para 5.35.

[79] See above, para 13.27.

the document with the substitution of "authenticated" for "signed".[80] This reflects the requirement contained in Clause 91(3)(b) that an electronic document must have the electronic signature of each person by whom it purports to be authenticated.[81]

Execution by other corporations

13.30 There are many significant categories of corporation[82] that cannot avail themselves of the provisions of the Companies Act 1985 that relate to the execution of documents. Some such corporations have express statutory powers that are similar to those found in the Companies Act 1985 in that they make provision for the signature of an instrument by specified persons.[83] Other corporations have no statutory powers of execution and in relation to these the common law rules apply. At common law, any instrument that effects a disposition of property by a corporation must be executed under that corporation's seal. However, as we have explained, under the Bill, *all* corporations can sign an electronic document,[84] and in this respect the Bill goes further than the draft Law of Property (Electronic Communications) Order.[85] In any event, any corporation could appoint an agent to execute an electronic document on its behalf, whether under a power of attorney or otherwise.

Rights of a purchaser as to execution

13.31 Under section 75(1) of the Law of Property Act 1925,[86] a purchaser is "entitled to have, at his own cost, the execution of the conveyance [to him] attested by some person appointed by him, who may, if he thinks fit, be his solicitor". Attestation is not appropriate to forms of electronic disposition and the right to such attestation (which we suspect is little used in practice) is therefore abrogated for such dispositions by Clause 91(8).

Supplementary rule-making powers

13.32 We have explained elsewhere the provisions of the Bill that govern applications for registration.[87] It is unnecessary to have specific rule-making powers in relation to

---

[80] While an electronic document can be regarded as having been signed under Cl 91(4), but for Cl 91(9), it would not be obvious that this would include a purported signature for the purposes of Companies Act 1985, s 36A(6).

[81] See above, para 13.14.

[82] Including local authorities, building societies, industrial and provident societies and corporations sole. The Secretary of State is a corporation sole.

[83] As in relation to charities (see Charities Act 1993, s 60) and friendly societies (see Friendly Societies Act 1992, Schedule 6, para 2).

[84] Cl 91(4).

[85] This is because only *statutory* requirements can be altered under the Order: see above, para 13.8.

[86] The section was intended to reverse the effect of a number of rather troublesome judicial decisions as to what was to happen on the completion of a conveyance.

[87] See Schedule 10, para 6; above, para 9.77.

applications for registration in electronic form, because the general rule-making power in relation to applications is wide enough to authorise the making of such rules. However, there are certain matters for which specific rule-making powers are required, and the Bill provides for the making of rules about—

(1) the communication of documents in electronic form to the registrar; and

(2) the electronic storage of documents communicated to the registrar in electronic form.[88]

13.33 Rules made under the latter power are likely to include not only the manner in which such electronic documents are stored but, in relation to certain entries, such as estate contracts, the length of time that the document is kept.[89]

PROVISIONS GOVERNING THE LAND REGISTRY NETWORK

Introduction

13.34 In Part II of this Report, we have given an account of how it is visualised that electronic conveyancing is likely to operate,[90] and a brief summary of its main aspects is given above at paragraph 13.2. The second element of the Bill is intended to provide for that operation. It concerns the provision of an electronic communications network and the rules that govern its use. These provisions are of the greatest practical importance because they provide the necessary framework for the development and operation of electronic conveyancing. Under the Bill,[91] the registrar is given power either himself to provide an electronic communications network or to arrange for its provision.[92] This network, which is called in the Bill "a land registry network", is to be used for such purposes as the registrar thinks fit "relating to registration or the carrying on of transactions which—

(1) involve registration, and

(2) are capable of being effected electronically".[93]

13.35 Those purposes will, therefore, include—

(1) the provision of information to the registrar or to any party to a transaction or proposed transaction that will involve—

---

[88] Cl 94.

[89] Many estate contracts by their nature have a comparatively short life. While not all contractual obligations are merged in the subsequent transfer, most are. It is therefore unlikely that it will be necessary for the Registry to retain a copy of such contracts for very long.

[90] See paras 2.52—2.58.

[91] Cl 92(1).

[92] The network may well be provided by a private sector partner.

[93] Cl 92(1).

(a) some disposition of registered land or of an interest in registered land; or

(b) a disposition of unregistered land that will trigger compulsory first registration;

(2) the preparation of conveyancing documents in electronic form in relation to (1)(a) or (b) above; and

(3) the registration of any disposition.

The Bill makes detailed provision in relation to this land registry network.[94]

Access to the network

Network access agreements

13.36 In Part II, we explained that the introduction of electronic conveyancing would bring about a fundamental change in the way in which registered conveyancing is conducted. Instead of the registrar registering dispositions on application, solicitors and licensed conveyancers will register dispositions at the same time as they are made.[95] This is the only practicable way in which one of the main goals of the Bill can be achieved, namely, that dispositions and their registration should take place simultaneously.[96] The Bill therefore creates the necessary framework for this to happen. At the core of that framework is the mechanism that will give access to the land registry network.

13.37 A person who is not a member of HM Land Registry will only have access to a land registry network if he or she is authorised by means of an agreement with the registrar.[97] A "network access agreement"[98] of this kind will necessarily be a contract and enforceable as such.[99] This agreement may authorise access for any one or more of the following purposes—

(a) the communication, posting or retrieval of information;

(b) the making of electronic dispositions and applications which will result in changes to the register of title[100] or to the cautions register;[101]

---

[94] See Cl 92(2); Schedule 5.

[95] See paras 2.51, 2.57.

[96] See below, para 13.74.

[97] Schedule 5, para 1(1).

[98] Schedule 5, para 1(2).

[99] There will be an exception to this in relation to other emanations of the Crown (such as the Crown Estate) which cannot contract with HM Land Registry (the Crown cannot contract with itself). In relation to any such bodies, there will simply be an agreement in exactly the same terms.

[100] See above, Part X.

(c)   the issue of official search certificates;[102]

(d)   the issue of official copies;[103] or

(e)   such other conveyancing purposes as the registrar thinks fit.[104]

There are three significant points about this provision.

THE LEVEL OF ACCESS WILL BE VARIABLE

13.38   First, it permits the level of access to be varied according to the purposes for which it is required. Access will not be restricted to solicitors and licensed conveyancers, but may include, for example, estate agents and mortgage lenders. A solicitor or licensed conveyancer who is authorised to conduct electronic conveyancing may be granted access for all or at least most of the purposes listed in paragraph 13.37 above. However, an estate agent might only be authorised to have access for the first of them, and a mortgage lender might have access for, say, the first three, and then only in relation to a charge in its favour over a registered estate.

AUTHORITY MAY BE GIVEN TO PERFORM REGISTRAR'S FUNCTIONS

13.39   Secondly, there is a rule-making power by which network access agreements may confer authority to carry out functions of the registrar.[105] Plainly, the functions listed above in paragraph 13.37, (b)—(d), and no doubt at least some of those that may be specified in (e), will be functions of the registrar. A solicitor or licensed conveyancer who is appropriately authorised will, within the limits of that authority, be able to carry out functions that are conferred by the Bill on the registrar. Obviously the principal function that is essential to the operation of electronic conveyancing is that such solicitor or licensed conveyancer should be able to register dispositions and make other entries on the register.[106] However, the powers need to go beyond that and include, for example, the ability to remove spent entries on the register, as where, on the completion of a disposition, a registered charge is redeemed. It is also necessary that authorised solicitors and licensed conveyancers should have power to carry out the various ancillary matters that will or may arise in the course of a conveyancing transaction, such as the issue of official search certificates or official copies.

CRITERIA FOR ENTRY INTO A NETWORK ACCESS AGREEMENT

13.40   Thirdly, the registrar *must*, on application, enter into a network access agreement with an applicant if it appears to him that he or she meets such criteria as rules

---

[101]   See above, para 10.26.

[102]   See above, para 9.61.

[103]   See above, para 9.45.

[104]   Schedule 5, para 1(2).

[105]   Schedule 5, para 1(3).

[106]   Such as entering restrictions.

may provide.[107] In other words, if the pre-conditions are met, the applicant has a right to enter into a network access agreement. Before the Lord Chancellor can make any such rules, he must consult such persons as he considers appropriate.[108] Given the great importance of these rules, he is likely to consult very widely, not only with the professions but also with other interested bodies. The rules must be fair and reasonable to those who wish to conduct conveyancing, while at the same time providing proper safeguards for the integrity of the register. In making such rules, the Lord Chancellor is to have particular regard to the need to secure certain objectives, namely—

(1)   the confidentiality of private information kept on the network;

(2)   competence in relation to the use of the network (in particular for the making of changes); and

(3)   the adequate insurance of potential liabilities in connection with the use of the network.[109]

These are important provisions, and the thinking behind them requires explanation. It should be noted that the competence envisaged in (2) applies not just to the likely ability of the person entering into the agreement to be able to operate a system of electronic conveyancing. It also applies much more importantly to that person's competence as a conveyancer. He or she must have a proven record of competent conveyancing.

13.41   First, registered dispositions are guaranteed by virtue of the provisions of the Bill on indemnity.[110] If mistakes are made, the registrar must pay indemnity in respect of any loss suffered in consequence. Although solicitors and licensed conveyancers will perform many of the registrar's functions, his liability for mistakes remains, and it is essential, therefore, that he is able to ensure the integrity of the register.

13.42   Secondly, it is an explicit aim of the Bill to improve the quality of conveyancing services available to the public and to maintain that higher quality. This is because the standard of a significant proportion of conveyancing work nowadays is regrettably poor.[111] This has been a matter of concern for some considerable time both to the Registry and to the many solicitors and licensed conveyancers whose

---

[107]   Schedule 5, para 1(4).

[108]   Schedule 5, para 11(1), (2).

[109]   Schedule 5, para 11(3).

[110]   See Schedule 8; explained above, paras 10.29 and following.

[111]   It is well known that one of the main reasons for the demise of the Solicitors' Indemnity Fund was the number of claims for negligent conveyancing. As we have explained above, at para 13.12, approximately 50% of all applications to HM Land Registry are in some way defective.

work is exemplary.[112] Furthermore, Mr Andrew Edwards CB, in the course of his recent Quinquennial Review of HM Land Registry, has also specifically raised it.

13.43 Thirdly, the quality or otherwise of conveyancing work has no necessary correlation with the size of the firm of practitioners. Many small firms deliver work of very high quality. Equally, we are aware of regular complaints about the standard of the work of some of the large "conveyancing factories".

13.44 As a result of these concerns, it is essential that those who are authorised to undertake electronic conveyancing should meet specific criteria to protect the integrity of the register. In the end, it will be the users of the register who will have to pay for the cost of indemnity claims. Every effort must therefore be made to keep such claims down to no more than present levels.[113] The specific criteria must be such as not to discriminate in any way against either small or large firms. The most important factor must, however, be a proven record of conveyancing competence.[114] Indeed fairness demands that this should be so. Precisely how that will be judged has not yet been settled and must be a matter for discussions with the professions and interested bodies.[115] It should be noted that the criteria are, in any event, likely to differ according to the level of access that the applicant seeks under the network access agreement.[116]

13.45 We are acutely aware that, if a firm of solicitors or licensed conveyancers is not permitted to enter into a network access agreement, it will, for practical purposes, be excluded from the conduct of conveyancing. This is because electronic conveyancing seems certain to become the only form of dealing with registered land within a comparatively short time. However, although this is unquestionably a serious matter, there can be little sympathy for those practitioners who cannot establish the necessary record of competence to meet the criteria.

13.46 Even when a person has entered into a network access agreement, he or she will be required to continue to meet its terms. As we explain below, a failure to do so may result in the termination of the network access agreement.[117] As a means of

---

[112] We have had a number of discussions with well-known firms of solicitors over the last two years. We have been repeatedly told that, where such a firm is acting in a conveyancing transaction, the firm acting for the other party often fails to do the work properly and simply relies upon the better-known firm to make good its shortcomings. There is entirely justified resentment of such practice.

[113] The amount currently paid out on indemnity claims is remarkably low given the volume of business that HM Land Registry transacts. For example, in the financial year 1999 — 2000, despite millions of transactions handled by the Registry, there were only 703 claims for indemnity, and the net amount paid was £891,504. Some 98.66% of applications in that period were processed free of error. These figures are taken from HM Land Registry's *Annual Report and Accounts 1999 — 2000*.

[114] Cf above, para 13.40.

[115] We note that some years ago, The Law Society considered the introduction of a conveyancing "chartermark" for conveyancing solicitors who met specified standards. However, nothing came of that proposal. It may now perhaps merit reconsideration.

[116] Cf above, para 13.38.

[117] See below, para 13.55.

assisting those who have entered into such agreements to continue to meet the requirements, the Bill empowers the registrar to provide education and training in relation to the use of a land registry network.[118] It is likely that—

(1)   on-line training and education programmes will be provided by the registrar; and

(2)   participation in such programmes will be a condition of a network access contract.[119]

Terms of access

13.47   Under the Bill, the terms on which access to a land registry network is authorised will, as a general principle, be such as the registrar thinks fit, and may, in particular, include charges for access.[120] That principle is, however, qualified in a number of ways.

THE PURPOSES FOR WHICH THE POWER TO AUTHORISE MAY BE USED

13.48   The power to authorise access to the land registry network on terms may be used not only for regulating the use of that network but also for three other purposes.

To require transactions to be conducted electronically

13.49   The terms may require that the person authorised should *have* to use the network to carry on such transactions as may be specified that involve registration and are capable of being effected electronically.[121] It would not, therefore, be open to the person authorised to conduct such transactions in paper form. In this way, the registrar can ensure that those who use the network must carry out all (or all specified) registrable transactions electronically. This is part of the Bill's strategy of ensuring a speedy transition from a paper-based system of conveyancing to an electronic one. Although there is a power under the Bill to require that dispositions be made in electronic form,[122] this power is unlikely to be exercised until electronic conveyancing has become the norm.[123]

To regulate ancillary purposes

13.50   The terms on which the registrar may grant access to a land registry network may include such other purpose relating to the carrying on of qualifying transactions as

---

[118]   Schedule 5, para 10.

[119]   Cf Schedule 5, para 2(4); below, para 13.54.

[120]   Schedule 5, para 2(1). Those who have direct access to the register of title by means of Land Registry Direct (see above, para 2.41), already pay a fee for such access.

[121]   Schedule 5, paras 2(2)(a), 11.

[122]   See Cl 93; below, para 13.74.

[123]   Cf above, paras 2.59—2.61

rules may provide.[124] This power might be used for a variety of purposes, such as to require the person authorised to issue official search certificates or official copies when requested.[125]

To enable transactions to be monitored

13.51 The terms may be used to enable network transactions to be monitored.[126] We explain the monitoring of network transactions below.[127]

THE OBLIGATION TO COMPLY WITH NETWORK TRANSACTION RULES

13.52 Where a network access agreement grants a person access to the network to carry on transactions that involve registration and are capable of being effected electronically, it will be a condition of that agreement, that he or she will comply with any network transaction rules that are for the time being in force.[128] The network transaction rules will be of the greatest practical importance, as they will be the rules which specify how electronic conveyancing is to be conducted. The power conferred on the Lord Chancellor[129] is to make provision by such rules "about how to go about network transactions".[130] These rules may, in particular, make provision about dealings with the Land Registry, including provision about the procedure to be followed, and the supply of information.[131] The rules are likely to require an authorised solicitor or licensed conveyancer to provide specified information about any dealing and, in particular, information about overriding interests.[132] This is a significant requirement. It will for example provide a means of enforcing the obligation on persons applying for registration to disclose overriding interests affecting the estate to which the application relates.[133] This has been explained in Part VIII of this Report.[134] The rules are likely to require the disclosure of other information that a registered proprietor might not wish to have disclosed, such as the fact that a right to determine a registered estate in land has become exercisable.[135]

---

[124] Schedule 5, para 2(2)(b). Qualifying transactions are those that involve registration and are capable of being effected electronically: Schedule 5, para 12. The rules will be made by the Lord Chancellor.

[125] Cf above, para 13.37.

[126] Schedule 5, para 2(2)(c).

[127] See para 13.64.

[128] Schedule 5, para 2(3). These rules may vary during the period of a network access agreement. The obligation will be to comply with the rules as they stand at any given time.

[129] With the advice of the Rule Committee: see Cl 124; below, para 17.5.

[130] Schedule 5, para 5(1).

[131] Schedule 5, para 5(2).

[132] *Ibid.*

[133] Cl 71.

[134] See para 8.91.

[135] See Cl 64; above, paras 9.29 and following.

13.53 Another important function which these rules will almost certainly perform is to require that the making of a disposition or the entering into a contract and its registration shall occur simultaneously. As we have mentioned[136] and will explain more fully below,[137] this is probably the single most important technical principle in the Bill. Although there will be a power to make this principle compulsory,[138] it can at least be introduced without the exercise of that power by means of the network transaction rules.

THE POWER TO REGULATE TERMS OF ACCESS BY RULES

13.54 The terms on which access to a land registry network is authorised may be regulated by rules.[139] It is likely that rules will specify terms that should be included in any network access agreement. These terms will almost certainly vary according to the level of access that any such agreement gives.[140]

Termination of access

13.55 The Bill makes provision for the termination of network access agreements. The right to terminate is exercisable by giving notice of the termination of the agreement to the other party to it. However, the circumstances in which the parties are permitted to terminate the agreement are not the same. A person who is granted access may terminate the agreement at any time.[141] By contrast, the registrar's powers of termination are more limited and will be defined in rules. The Bill confers a power for rules to make provision about the termination of a network access agreement, and in particular—

(1) the grounds of termination;

(2) the procedure to be followed in relation to termination; and

(3) the suspension of termination pending appeal.[142]

In particular, rules may make provision that authorises the registrar to terminate a network access agreement if the party granted access—

(a) fails to comply with the terms of the agreement;[143]

---

[136] See above, paras 2.1(2), 2.17, 2.26, 2.56, 2.59, 2.60.

[137] See para 13.74.

[138] Under Cl 93; below, para 13.74. We explain at para 13.79, that there are reasons why that power may *have* to be exercised, to ensure that the principle of making a disposition or a contract and simultaneously registering it is effective.

[139] Schedule 5, para 2(4). The rules will be made by the Lord Chancellor, and he will be under an obligation to consult before making them: *ibid*, para 11(1), (2).

[140] Cf above, para 13.38.

[141] Schedule 5, para 3(1).

[142] Schedule 5, para 3(2). The rules will be made by the Lord Chancellor, who must consult such persons as he considers appropriate before he does so: *ibid*, para 11(1), (2). The rules must be made by statutory instrument that is subject to annulment in pursuance of a resolution of either House of Parliament: Cl 125(4).

(b)   ceases to be a person with whom the registrar would be required to enter into a network access agreement conferring the authority which the agreement confers;[144] or

(c)   does not meet such conditions as rules may provide.[145]

13.56   It should be stressed that the termination of a network access agreement is likely to be a remedy of absolute last resort. Because the agreement will normally be a contract, the registrar will have contractual remedies against a party to such an agreement that will stop short of termination.[146]

Appeals

13.57   There will, inevitably, be disputes as to whether the registrar has acted properly in either rejecting an application to enter into a network access agreement or in terminating such an agreement. For any practitioner involved, the refusal of an application for a network access agreement or the termination of an existing access agreement is likely to be a very serious matter that may cause the loss of his or her livelihood.[147] The Bill therefore confers a right of appeal to the Adjudicator.[148] This has two significant advantages over the alternative of leaving the aggrieved person to seek judicial review. First, it will be both quicker and substantially cheaper. Secondly, it will not be confined to a *review* of the registrar's decision. The Adjudicator will be able to reconsider the matter himself and substitute his own decision for that of the registrar's. He may then give such directions as he considers appropriate to give effect to his determination.[149] There will be a further right of appeal from the Adjudicator's decision to the High Court, but as this is a second appeal, only on a point of law.[150]

Overriding nature of network access obligations

13.58   The requirements of a network access agreement may be such as to create conflicts of interest. If, say, a solicitor or licensed conveyancer has entered into a

---

[143] A person in whose favour a network access agreement has been made, must comply with the relevant conditions of access as they stand at any given time. If, for example, the network transaction rules are changed, he or she must comply with the revised rules.

[144] As we have explained above, para 13.38, there will be different levels of access, and what may suffice for one may not suffice for another.

[145] Schedule 5, para 3. The rules referred to in (c) are those specifically made under Schedule 5, para 3.

[146] What these may be will depend upon the terms of the agreement. Those terms cannot be a matter for legislation.

[147] As we have explained above, in para 13.55, where an existing agreement is terminated, rules may provide for the suspension of termination pending an appeal.

[148] Schedule 5, para 4(1). This does not displace any contractual remedy that a person may have if it transpires that his or her network access agreement was wrongly terminated.

[149] Schedule 5, para 4(2). Rules may make provision about such appeals: *ibid*, para 4(3). Such rules will be land registration rules which will be required to be laid before Parliament only: Cls 125(3); 129(1).

[150] Cl 109(2); see below, para 16.23.

network access agreement, she may find herself in a position where she is required to act contrary to the wishes of her client. For example—

(1) she might have to register an overriding interest affecting the property that her client is purchasing which he would prefer to keep off the title; or

(2) where the transaction is part of a chain, she might have to disclose information about it that her client regards as confidential.[151]

13.59 Where such conflicting obligations do arise, the Bill provides that the obligation under the network access agreement prevails and discharges the other obligation to the extent that the two conflict.[152] Such a provision appears to us to be necessary to ensure that the aims of the Bill can be properly implemented.

Presumption of authority

13.60 As we have indicated, it is likely that, at least in the early days of electronic conveyancing, solicitors and licensed conveyancers may wish to sign documents in electronic form on behalf of their clients.[153] There are, however, a number of problems that arise in this context because of certain limitations on an agent's implied authority to conclude transactions. In particular, a solicitor (and therefore, presumably, a licensed conveyancer) has no *implied* authority to sign a contract for the sale or purchase of an interest in land on behalf of his or her client.[154] He or she can only conclude such a contract if he or she has *actual* authority. We anticipate that it would in practice be very unusual for a solicitor, licensed conveyancer or authorised practitioner to conclude a contract in electronic form without such authority. However, because of the absence of any implied authority, a solicitor, licensed conveyancer or authorised practitioner acting for one party to a conveyancing transaction would be entitled to see the written authority from the other party to his or her solicitor or licensed conveyancer and *vice versa*. It rather defeats the point of electronic conveyancing if such paper-based written authorities have to be exchanged before contracts can be concluded electronically.

13.61 The Bill therefore makes provision to meet the point.[155] It applies where a person who is authorised under a network access agreement to use the network to make either a disposition or contract, purports to do so as agent. In favour of any other party, that person will be deemed to be acting with the authority of his or her

---

[151] Cf below, para 13.64.

[152] Schedule 5, para 6.

[153] See above, para 13.20. For electronic signatures, see above, para 13.14.

[154] *Smith v Webster* (1876) 3 ChD 49; *H Clark (Doncaster) Ltd v Wilkinson* [1965] Ch 694, 702. There are related questions in relation to a solicitor's authority to execute a deed and to sign a declaration of a trust of land on behalf of his or her client. In the course of preparing the Bill we have addressed those situations in detail. We do not consider that it is necessary to discuss them here.

[155] Schedule 5, para 8.

principal if the document which purports to effect the disposition or to be a contract—

> (1) purports to be authenticated by him or her as agent; and
>
> (2) contains a statement to the effect that he or she is acting under the authority of his or her principal.

13.62   It is intended that, under the network transaction rules,[156] there will be a standard form of authority which a practitioner will be required to use to obtain his or her client's authority where he or she is to execute an electronic instrument as agent for that client.[157]

Managing network transactions

13.63   It is intended that the registrar (or such person as he may delegate) shall have power to monitor certain types of transaction in order to facilitate them. In particular, we have explained in Part II of this Report, it is anticipated that chains of sales, at least of residential properties, are likely to be managed in order to expedite them and reduce the risk of any break in them.[158] This is an intrusive power and should only be employed sparingly in those situations where the benefits that it offers outweigh the drawbacks.[159] It is, however, a very important power and one that has the potential to eliminate much of the stress and uncertainty that presently arises in chain transactions. The Bill therefore makes provision to enable network transactions to be managed.

13.64   First, as we have mentioned, the terms of a network access agreement may require the person granted such access to provide monitoring information.[160] In relation to a transaction that was part of a chain, this would probably require the solicitor or licensed conveyancer who had been granted access to provide the registrar[161] with information such as the following as soon as it became available—

> (1) that his or her client was proposing to enter into a transaction that appeared to be part of a chain;[162] and
>
> (2) that he or she had performed a specified conveyancing step, such as having completed local searches or that his or her client had received a mortgage offer.

---

[156]   See above, para 13.52.

[157]   A failure to obtain the authority in the prescribed form would be a breach of the rules, but would not invalidate the disposition or contract.

[158]   See above, para 2.52.

[159]   It may not be required in relation to chains of commercial transactions, particularly as there may be issues of commercial confidentiality involved.

[160]   Schedule 5, para 2(2)(c); above, para 13.51.

[161]   Or his delegate: see below, para 13.65.

[162]   Rules will no doubt define what constitutes a chain for these purposes.

13.65 Secondly, the registrar, or the person to whom he has delegated his "chain management" functions,[163] may use monitoring information[164] for the purpose of managing network transactions.[165] In particular, he may disclose such information to persons authorised to use the network, and may authorise further disclosure, if he considers it necessary or desirable to do so.[166] Typically, this will mean that the registrar (or his delegate as "chain manager") can disclose to other parties in the chain the state of progress of the other transactions in the chain. Although the "chain manager" will not have any direct coercive powers (indeed it is not easy to see what effective powers there could be), he will be able to identify the link in the chain that is causing the delay. He will then be able to encourage that party to proceed with due despatch.

Rules

Introduction

13.66 It will be apparent from this survey of the provisions that what the Bill does is to create a framework for electronic conveyancing. The detail has to be filled in by rules. There are two aspects of this that require comment. The first is to explain why this approach has to be adopted. The second is to summarise the safeguards that have been built in to ensure that any proposed rules are subject to proper scrutiny.

Why a rules-based approach is necessary

13.67 As a general principle, the Bill follows the model of the Land Registration Act 1925, in that the primary legislation is intended to contain the governing principles, leaving the technical details for rules.[167] The move from a paper-based system of conveyancing to one that is completely dematerialised will inevitably take some years. It is likely to be introduced in stages, starting with the simplest matters and gradually progressing to the most complex transactions.[168] The electronic and paper-based systems will necessarily co-exist during that transitional period.

13.68 At this stage, the precise form that electronic conveyancing will take has not yet been settled, though HM Land Registry intends to demonstrate a proposed model in the autumn. In any event, it is certain that electronic conveyancing will evolve

---

[163] Schedule 5, para 9(2). It is not yet certain whether HM Land Registry will be responsible for these functions or whether they will be contracted out. The Bill permits such contracting out.

[164] That is the information provided in pursuance of a network access agreement included under Schedule 5, para 2(2)(c): *ibid*, para 9(3). See above, paras 13.51, 13.64.

[165] Schedule 5, para 9(1). A network transaction is a transaction carried on by means of a land registry network: *ibid*, para 12.

[166] Schedule 5, para 9(1).

[167] As we explain below, para 17.2, the 1925 legislation does in fact leaves something to be desired in this regard. It is often quite arbitrary whether a matter is in the Land Registration Act 1925 or the Land Registration Rules 1925.

[168] It will almost certainly be necessary to conduct pilot schemes in particular areas to test the proposed systems.

and change, just as has been the case in relation to paper-based conveyancing.[169] It is therefore necessary to have a framework that is flexible enough to allow for this development. The Bill seeks to do that by providing a structure within which electronic conveyancing can operate, leaving the exact manner of its operation to be laid down from time to time in rules.

13.69 It is the considered view of both HM Land Registry and the Law Commission that it would be impossible to introduce electronic conveyancing in any other manner than that which the Bill adopts. It is the only way that enables the legislative framework to be in place in time and at the same time to offer sufficient flexibility for future developments.

Safeguards

13.70 As we explain in Part XVII, most of the powers to make rules under the Bill are powers to make "land registration rules". These will be made according to long-established procedures that were created under the 1925 Act.[170] However, subject to certain exceptions, for network transaction rules,[171] the rules applicable to electronic conveyancing are *not* land registration rules[172] and are deliberately subject to a higher level of scrutiny. First, before the Lord Chancellor can make any relevant rules,[173] he must consult such persons as he considers appropriate.[174] Secondly, whereas land registration rules merely have to be laid before Parliament,[175] the rules under discussion here are subject to annulment in pursuance of a resolution of either House of Parliament.[176]

13.71 It should be added that, although network transaction rules will be land registration rules and not therefore subject to any *formal* requirement of prior public consultation, it is inconceivable that any such rules would be introduced

---

[169] In 1990 alone, 9 sets of land registration rules were issued, with a further 38 sets since then.

[170] See para 17.5. Land registration rules are subject to scrutiny by a technical committee, the Rule Committee: see Cl 124. This Committee has operated very effectively for more than 75 years: cf Land Registration Act 1925, s 144(1).

[171] In particular, network transaction rules under Schedule 5, para 5; above, para 13.52. These are technical rules that make provision "about how to go about network transactions" and should therefore be land registration rules just as are the equivalent rules in relation to paper-based conveyancing at present.

[172] See the definition of "land registration rules" in Cl 129(1).

[173] That is the rules under Schedule 5, paras 1, 2 and 3, above, paras 13.39, 13.50, 13.54, 13.55.

[174] See Schedule 5, para 11(1), (2). The words "consult such persons as he considers appropriate" in para 11(2) are the ones commonly employed in a statute when it is intended that there should be public consultation.

[175] Cl 125(3).

[176] Cl 125(4)(a).

without such consultation, at least until electronic conveyancing is firmly established.[177]

Do-it-yourself conveyancing

13.72 Although the number of persons who conduct their own registered conveyancing is very small — it is understood to be less than 1 per cent of transactions — it is plainly important that they should still be able to do so, even when all registered conveyancing has become paperless. We mentioned the issue of "do-it-yourself conveyancers" in the Consultative Document. Our provisional view was that such persons would have to lodge the relevant documents with a district land registry, which would, as now, register the transaction.[178] This approach would deny do-it-yourself conveyancers the opportunity to take advantage of electronic conveyancing. It could also have deleterious effects if, say, such a person was involved in a chain of other transactions. We have therefore reconsidered the matter and the Bill adopts a different approach.

13.73 Once there is a land registry network, the registrar is to be under a duty to provide such assistance as he thinks appropriate for the purpose of enabling persons engaged in qualifying transactions[179] who wish to do their own conveyancing by means of the land registry network.[180] The duty does not, however, extend to the provision of legal advice.[181] It is envisaged that the way in which this will operate is that a person who is undertaking his or her own conveyancing, will be able to go to a district land registry for this service. The registrar will carry out the necessary transactions in electronic form on his or her instructions. Obviously that person will be required to pay an appropriate fee for the service that will reflect the costs involved to the Registry.

THE POWER TO MAKE ELECTRONIC CONVEYANCING COMPULSORY AND TO REQUIRE THAT ELECTRONIC DISPOSITIONS SHOULD BE SIMULTANEOUSLY REGISTERED

The objective of the power

13.74 We have briefly explained in Part II of this Report why the Bill contains and needs to contain a power by which, in due course, the use of electronic conveyancing could be made compulsory.[182] In particular, we explained that it might be

---

[177] When HM Land Registry was planning to introduce new forms in 1997, it consulted widely on its proposals before the rules were laid.

[178] See Law Com No 254, para 11.11(2). In other words, there would, in such cases, have continued to be a "registration gap".

[179] That is, those which involve registration and are capable of being effected electronically: see Schedule 5, para 12.

[180] Schedule 5, para 7(1).

[181] Schedule 5, para 7(2). It would be wholly inappropriate for the Registry, in effect, to be in competition with conveyancing practitioners. The Registry has neither the wish nor the resources to do so.

[182] See above, paras 2.59—2.61.

necessary to require at least some transactions to be effected electronically because otherwise the benefits of electronic conveyancing could be lost. We also explained that the power of compulsion was linked to the single most important technical aim of the Bill.[183] That is to bring about the situation in which many transactions involving registered land will have no effect unless registered. Much of the thinking underlying this Bill rests on that principle. However, it can only happen if the making of the transaction and its registration are simultaneous and that in turn is possible only if both can be effected electronically.

13.75 The power to make electronic conveyancing compulsory is found in Clause 93 and, as the comments in the last paragraph suggest, it has twin objectives. If the power is exercised, it will require, in relation to any disposition or contract to make such a disposition that is specified in rules, that—

(1) the transaction shall only take effect if it is electronically communicated to the registrar; *and*

(2) the relevant registration requirements are met.[184]

13.76 In other words, it will be possible to require not only that a particular disposition (or contract to make a disposition) should be effected in electronic form, but that it should only have effect when it is entered on the register in the appropriate way. Those two elements will occur simultaneously. This double effect of the power is essential to an understanding of its purpose. The objective is to link inextricably the elements of making a contract or disposition electronically and the registration of that contract or disposition. Although there will be no contract or no disposition at all unless and until registration occurs, an electronic system means that these two steps can be made to coincide. There will no longer be any registration gap because it will no longer be possible to create or dispose of rights and interests off the register (as it is at present). This is the goal that all registration systems have so long sought to attain. Its benefits are considerable.

13.77 The absence of any period of time between the transaction and its registration eliminates any risk of the creation of third party interests in the interim. It also means that there is no risk that the transferor may destroy the interest after its transfer but before its registration, as where X Plc assigns its lease to Y Ltd and X Plc surrenders the lease to its landlord after assigning it but before the assignment is registered.[185]

13.78 At present the priority of an interest in registered land, other than a registrable disposition that has been registered, depends upon the date of its creation, not the date on which it is entered on the register.[186] That will remain so under the Bill.[187]

---

[183] See above, para 2.60.

[184] Cl 93(2).

[185] Cf *Brown & Root Technology Ltd v Sun Alliance and London Assurance Co* [2000] 2 WLR 566; above, para 1.20.

[186] See Law Com No 254, para 7.17, where the authorities are explained.

[187] See Cl 28, above, para 5.5.

However, the exercise of the power under Clause 93 will mean that a transaction and its registration must coincide. In this way, the register will become conclusive as to the priority of many interests in registered land, because the date of registration and the date of disposition or contract will be one and the same.

13.79 Quite apart from the reasons already given why electronic conveyancing might be made compulsory in relation to at least some transactions,[188] there is, therefore, also an important legal goal to be achieved by doing so. It is to make an inextricable link as a matter of law between the making of a transaction and its registration. It is true that network transaction rules[189] can achieve the effect that a transaction and its registration coincide. But if by some mischance in a particular case that did not happen, a transaction might still have some effect between the parties (as it would now) if it were not registered. There is a risk that the mere fact that this could happen might undermine one of the goals of ensuring simultaneity of transaction and registration, namely that a person could rely on the register as being conclusive as to priority. It is therefore necessary to have statutory provision to ensure the linkage between a transaction and its registration.

The application of the power

13.80 The power in Clause 93 will apply to a disposition of—

(1) a registered estate or charge; or

(2) an interest which is the subject of a notice in the register;

where the disposition is one specified by rules.[190] The scope of the power will, therefore, be determined by rules. This means that the power can (and doubtless will) be exercised progressively. As the use of electronic conveyancing becomes the norm in relation to particular transactions, the power to require them to be made electronically and simultaneously registered could then be exercised. Given the considerable importance of this power, the Lord Chancellor is required to consult before he makes any rules under it.[191] There are two points that should be noted about the power.

13.81 The first is of some general importance. The power conferred by the Bill would mean that it was possible to require a disposition of an interest protected by a notice to be made electronically and registered. This is something new under the Bill. It is not at present possible to register transfers of such interests. The types of interest to which this power is likely to be applied include—

---

[188] See above, paras 2.60, 2.61, 13.74.

[189] Schedule 5, para 5, above, para 13.52.

[190] Cl 93(1).

[191] Cl 93(5).

(1)   a *profit à prendre* in gross that has not been registered with its own title;[192]

(2)   a franchise that has not been registered with its own title;[193]

(3)   an equitable charge;

(4)   the benefit of an option or right of pre-emption.

13.82   The extension of the system of title registration to interests that were protected by notice and not registered with their own titles was canvassed in the Consultative Document,[194] and we have already explained how the system of priority searches could, under the Bill, be extended to such interests.[195]

13.83   The second point is more technical. For the purposes of Clause 93, a "disposition", in relation to a registered charge, includes postponement.[196] We have explained in Part VII of this Report that registered charges are to be taken to rank as between themselves in the order shown in the register.[197] If, say, by agreement between two chargees, charge A is to be postponed to charge B over which it would otherwise have priority, the communication and the necessary entry in the register could be required to be made electronically and would only be effective when registered. This is in accordance with one of the main aims of introducing electronic conveyancing, which is to make the register conclusive as to the state of title. This can only happen if transactions that affect priorities are required to be registered in order to have effect.

Registration requirements

13.84   As we have explained, when exercised, the power under Clause 93 will mean that a specified disposition or contract that is electronically communicated to the registrar will only take effect when the relevant registration requirements are met.[198] The Bill explains what is meant by the relevant registration requirements for these purposes.[199] First, as regards registrable dispositions, they are the requirements set out in Schedule 2. These have been explained in Part IV of this Report.[200] Secondly, as regards any other disposition, or a contract, the requirements are such as will be set out in rules.[201] When Clause 93 is applicable,

---

[192] For the power to register such interests with their own titles under the Bill, see Cl 3; above, para 3.20.

[193] For the power to register such interests with their own titles under the Bill, see Cl 3; above, para 3.19.

[194] See Law Com No 254, Part VII.

[195] See Cl 72; above, para 9.68.

[196] Cl 93(6).

[197] Cl 48; above, para 7.15.

[198] Cl 93(2), above, para 13.75.

[199] Cl 93(3).

[200] See paras 4.16 and following.

[201] In the case of a contract, the requirement is likely to be the entry of a notice.

Clause 27(1), which provides that a registrable disposition does not operate at law until the registration requirements are met, is disapplied.[202] The reason for this is that under Clause 93, a disposition has *no* effect whether at law or in equity, until the registration requirements are met.

Rules

13.85 Under Clause 93, the dispositions (and, therefore, also contracts to make such dispositions[203]) that will be subject to the requirement that they be made in electronic form and simultaneously registered will be specified in rules.[204] Such rules will be made by the Lord Chancellor by statutory instrument and will be subject to annulment in pursuance of a resolution of either House of Parliament.[205]

---

[202] Cl 93(4).

[203] See Cl 93(2).

[204] Cl 93(1).

[205] See Cl 125(1), (2), (4).

PART XIV
ADVERSE POSSESSION

INTRODUCTION

14.1   In the recent decision in *J A Pye (Oxford) Holdings Ltd v Graham*,[1] Neuberger J, having reluctantly given judgment in favour of a claim by squatters to be entitled to some 25 hectares of land in Berkshire (a decision since reversed by the Court of Appeal on an interpretation of the inferences to be drawn from the facts[2]), commented that—

> the right to acquire title to land by adverse possession is often explained by reference to the uncertainties which sometimes arise in relation to the ownership of land, but it appears to me that, with one or two exceptions those uncertainties are very unlikely to arise in the context of a system of land ownership involving compulsory registration; the owner of the land is readily identifiable, by inspecting the proprietorship register of the relevant title at the Land Registry. In the days when land was unregistered, one can well understand that uncertainties could arise where the owner was seeking to rely upon an old conveyance; the person in possession might claim to have lost the documents which established his title, and the legislature may have concluded that arguments about what happened long ago should be avoided, and that this should be achieved by depriving the person with apparently good if somewhat ancient paper title of his ownership if the squatter could establish more than 12 years uninterrupted possession of the land. I accept that even with registered land a problem can arise over strips of land near to boundaries, as the Land Registry plans normally show general boundaries only. In this connection I welcome the joint recommendations of the Law Commission and the Land Registry (1998) (Law Com No 254, Pt X)...
>
> A frequent justification for limitation periods generally is that people should not be able to sit on their rights indefinitely, and that is a proposition to which, at least in general, nobody could take exception. However, if as in the present case the owner of land has no immediate use for it and is content to let another person trespass on the land for the time being, it is hard to see what principle of justice entitles the trespasser to acquire the land for nothing from the owner simply because he has been permitted to remain there for 12 years. To say that in such circumstances the owner who has sat on his rights should therefore be deprived of his land appears to me to be illogical and disproportionate. Illogical because the only reason that the owner can be said to have sat on his rights is because of the existence of the 12-year limitation period in the first place; if no limitation period existed,

---

[1]   [2000] Ch 676.

[2]   [2001] EWCA Civ 117; [2001] 2 WLR 1293. The case is of some significance for another reason. The Court of Appeal rejected the view, canvassed by some writers, that the law of adverse possession contravened Article 1 of the First Protocol of the European Convention on Human Rights (right to enjoyment of possessions).

he would be entitled to claim possession whenever he wanted the land... I believe that the result is disproportionate, because... it does seem draconian to the owner, and a windfall for the squatter that, just because the owner has taken no steps to evict a squatter for 12 years, the owner should lose 25 hectares of land to the squatter with no compensation whatsoever.[3]

14.2 We have quoted these remarks at length, because they encapsulate the concerns that prompted the Law Commission and HM Land Registry to recommend in the Consultative Document that there should be a wholly new system of adverse possession to be applicable to registered land.[4] In that Consultative Document we explained the justifications for adverse possession.[5] The most important reason for it is in relation to unregistered land, where title is relative and rests ultimately on possession. We explained that—

> [t]he fact that adverse possession can extinguish earlier rights to possess facilitates and cheapens the investigation of title to *unregistered* land. The length of title that a vendor is required to deduce is and always has been closely linked to the limitation period. Indeed, the principal reason for having limitation statutes in relation to real property appears to have been to facilitate conveyancing.[6]

It is noteworthy that, on at least one occasion, where the courts had developed a doctrine that significantly curtailed the circumstances in which title could be acquired by adverse possession, Parliament intervened to reverse the errant doctrine.[7] If the requirements for adverse possession of unregistered land are made too demanding, it weakens the security of title to that land. Gaps in a paper title are not infrequently cured by showing possession of the land for the limitation period.

14.3 None of these considerations apply where title is registered. As we explained in the Consultative Document—

> Where title is registered, the basis of title is primarily the fact of registration rather than possession. Registration confers title because the registration of a person as proprietor of land of itself vests in him or her the relevant legal estate (whether freehold or leasehold).[8] The

---

[3] [2000] Ch 676, 709, 710.

[4] See Law Com No 254, Part X.

[5] See *ibid*, paras 10.5—10.10. See further below, para 14.54.

[6] Law Com No 254, para 10.9.

[7] See what is now Limitation Act 1980, Schedule 1, para 8(4), which reversed decisions such as *Wallis's Cayton Bay Holiday Camp Ltd v Shell-Mex and BP Ltd* [1975] QB 94, and was enacted to give effect to the recommendations of the Law Reform Committee in its 21st Report: Final report on limitation of actions (1977) Cmnd 6923, paras 3.47—3.52.

[8] See Land Registration Act 1925, s 69(1).

ownership of the land is therefore apparent from the register. Only a change in the register can take that title away...[9]

Indeed, the doctrine of adverse possession runs counter to the fundamental concept of indefeasibility of title that is a feature of registered title.[10] It is only where the register is not conclusive — as is the case, for example, in relation to boundaries[11] and short leases that are not registrable[12] — that the conveyancing justification for adverse possession[13] is the same as it is in relation to unregistered land. We noted in the Consultative Document that many other common law jurisdictions which have systems of title registration have either abolished the doctrine of adverse possession completely or have substantially restricted its effects.[14] In adopting a system of adverse possession that is specific to registered land, English law will, therefore, be following a well-worn path.

14.4 The new system of adverse possession proposed in the Consultative Document was intended both to reflect the logic of title registration and to strike a more appropriate balance between landowner and squatter. It was supported in principle by 60% of those who responded on the issue.[15] It attracted some attention in the press.[16] *J A Pye (Oxford) Holdings Ltd v Graham*[17] was just one of a number of recent, much-publicised cases in which squatters have claimed title to land of great value by virtue of 12 years' adverse possession. Some of these involved land owned by local authorities, so that the loss resulting from a successful claim has fallen on the public purse. If the reports in the press are any kind of barometer, there would appear to be considerable public disquiet with the way that the law on adverse possession presently operates. We have therefore decided to proceed with the essentials of the scheme that we proposed. Details of that scheme have been amended to take account of both the responses to the

---

[9] Law Com No 254, para 10.11.

[10] *Ibid.* That indefeasibility is qualified because the register can be rectified or amended. However, as we have explained, the circumstances in which that can happen are limited: see above, paras 10.13—10.18.

[11] See below, paras 14.7, 14.44.

[12] See below, para 14.10(1).

[13] See above, para 14.2.

[14] See Law Com No 254, para 10.17.

[15] Including the Bar Council, Bristol Law Society, the Crown Estate, Country Landowners' Association (now the Country Land and Business Association), British Property Federation, City of London Law Society, Ministry of Defence, National Farmers' Union, Roger Smith, Warwickshire Law Society and the Woolwich Building Society. There was also strong support from litigators both from the Bar (seminars held at Falcon Chambers and the Chancery Bar Association) and amongst the solicitors' profession (seminar with the Property Litigation Association). Those opposed to the proposal included Professor Graham Barnsley, Ian Leeming QC, and the Advisory Service for Squatters.

[16] For example, the headline in the Daily Mail on 2 September 1998 was "Swat the squatters. Owners to be protected from home hijackers".

[17] [2000] Ch 676 (as we have explained above, at para 14.1, the decision was reversed on its facts by the Court of Appeal).

Consultative Document and issues that were thrown up during the drafting of the Bill.

14.5   The essence of the scheme is that—

(1)   adverse possession of itself, for however long, will not bar the owner's title to a registered estate;

(2)   a squatter will be entitled to apply to be registered as proprietor after 10 years' adverse possession, and the registered proprietor, any registered chargee, and certain other persons interested in the land will be notified of the application;

(3)   if the application is not opposed by any of those notified the squatter will be registered as proprietor of the land;

(4)   if any of those notified oppose the application it will be refused, unless the adverse possessor can bring him or herself within one of three limited exceptions;[18]

(5)   if the application for registration is refused but the squatter remains in adverse possession for a further two years,[19] he or she will be entitled to apply once again to be registered and will this time be registered as proprietor whether or not the registered proprietor objects;

(6)   where the registered proprietor brings proceedings to recover possession from a squatter, the action will succeed unless the squatter can establish certain limited exceptions which are consistent with those in (4) above.

There are certain particular rules for special cases and there are transitional provisions to protect the rights of squatters who had barred the rights of the registered proprietor prior to the coming into force of the legislation.

14.6   The aims of the scheme are as follows.

(1)   Registration should of itself provide a means of protection against adverse possession, though it should not be unlimited protection. Title to registered land is not possession-based as is title to unregistered land. It is registration that vests the legal estate in the owner and that person's ownership is apparent from the register. The registered proprietor and other interested persons, such as the proprietor of a registered charge, are therefore given the opportunity to oppose an application by a squatter to be registered as proprietor.

---

[18]   Explained below, paras 14.36—14.52

[19]   Which might happen if no steps were taken to evict the squatter, or to regularise his or her possession so that it would no longer be adverse, as where the squatter agreed to be the tenant or licensee of the registered proprietor.

(2) If the application is not opposed, however, whether because the registered proprietor has disappeared or is unwilling to take steps to evict the squatter, the squatter will be registered as proprietor instead. This ensures that land which has (say) been abandoned by the proprietor, or which he or she does not consider to be worth the price of possession proceedings, will remain in commerce.

(3) If the registered proprietor (or other interested person) opposes the registration, then it is incumbent on him or her to ensure that the squatter is either evicted or his or her position regularised[20] within two years. If the squatter remains in adverse possession for two years after such objection has been made, he or she will be entitled to apply once again to be registered, and this time the registered proprietor will not be able to object. In other words, the scheme provides a registered proprietor with one chance, but only one chance, to prevent a squatter from acquiring title to his or her land. The proprietor who fails to take appropriate action following his or her objection will lose the land to the squatter.

(4) Consistently with the approach set out above, a registered proprietor who takes possession proceedings against a squatter will succeed, unless the squatter can bring him or herself within some very limited exceptions.

It will be apparent from this summary that one of the essential features of the scheme is that it must produce a decisive result. Either the squatter is evicted or otherwise ceases to be in *adverse* possession, or he or she is registered as proprietor of the land.

14.7 As we have mentioned above, there are certain very limited cases in which either—

(1) a squatter's application to be registered will be successful notwithstanding the registered proprietor's objections; or

(2) he or she may successfully resist possession proceedings brought by the proprietor.

This will be so where the squatter —

(a) was otherwise entitled to the land, as for example—

(i) where he or she was a purchaser in possession who had paid the whole of the contract price; or

(ii) by application of the principles of proprietary estoppel; or

(b) had been in adverse possession of land adjacent to his or her own under the mistaken but reasonable belief that he or she was the owner of it.

---

[20] In other words, where the squatter agrees to become the tenant or licensee of the registered proprietor.

The situation in (a) is self-evident, but that in (b) needs explanation. As mentioned above, the register is not normally conclusive as to boundaries.[21] Furthermore, cases often occur where the physical boundaries of the land and the legal boundaries as they appear from the register do not coincide. A common case is where a developer lays out an estate and constructs the fences between properties otherwise than in accordance with the boundaries as they are set out on the plan on the register. In these cases, we think that the squatter, whose conduct has been perfectly reasonable, should prevail over the registered proprietor.

14.8 In the remainder of this Part, we set out in more detail the effect of the main provisions of the Bill in relation to adverse possession. The following issues are examined—

(1) the underlying principle that adverse possession does not extinguish the title to a registered estate;[22]

(2) the right to apply for registration after 10 years' adverse possession and the circumstances in which such an application may or must succeed and when it will be rejected;[23]

(3) the right to make a further application for registration after two more years' adverse possession where the application for registration was initially refused;[24]

(4) the status of an indefeasible right for the squatter to be registered;[25]

(5) the effect of the registration of a squatter in place of the registered proprietor;[26]

(6) possession proceedings: when they will succeed and the defences that the squatter may raise;[27]

(7) cases for which special provision has to be made, namely adverse possession of rentcharges, land held in trust and Crown foreshore;[28] and

(8) transitional provisions.[29]

---

[21] See above, para 14.1; and see paras 9.9 and following.

[22] See paras 14.9—14.18.

[23] See paras 14.19—14.52.

[24] See paras 14.53—14.62.

[25] See paras 14.63—14.64.

[26] See paras 14.65—14.81.

[27] See paras 14.82—14.87.

[28] See paras 14.88—14.100.

[29] See paras 14.101—14.105.

THE EFFECT OF THE BILL

Adverse possession shall not extinguish the title to a registered estate

The governing principle

14.9   Clause 95 of the Bill gives effect to the fundamental principle of the new scheme. In relation to a registered estate in land or registered rentcharge, no period of limitation runs in relation to —

(1)   actions for the recovery of land[30] except in favour of a chargee;[31] and

(2)   actions for redemption.[32]

As a necessary consequence, the Bill provides that title to such an estate or rentcharge cannot be extinguished under section 17 of the Limitation Act 1980.[33] There are a number of points implicit in the fundamental principle that require explanation.

The principle applies only in relation to registered estates and rentcharges

14.10   The rationale of the new scheme is that the registration of an estate or rentcharge protects the proprietor, because the register is conclusive as to the ownership of the land. The disapplication of the limitation periods for actions to recover land is therefore confined to *registered estates in land* and *registered rentcharges*.[34] It follows that the Limitation Act 1980 will continue to apply in certain situations where there has been adverse possession of registered land.

(1)   The first is where there has been adverse possession against a leasehold estate, where the lease was granted for a term of 21 years or less prior to the coming into force of the Bill, and which therefore took effect as an overriding interest.[35] Such a lease is not a registered estate and is treated in most (but not all) respects in the same way as unregistered land. In particular, on any assignment of such a lease, title to it is deduced in the same way as if it were unregistered.[36] This class of case will necessarily disappear within 21 years of the Bill coming into force. This is because, under the Bill, the only leases that will take effect as overriding interests

---

[30]   Limitation Act 1980, s 15.

[31]   Cl 95(1). For the reason why Limitation Act 1980, s 15, continues to apply to an action by a chargee for possession or foreclosure, see below, para 14.12.

[32]   Cl 95(2). For the reasons why Limitation Act 1980, s 16, is disapplied, see below, paras 14.15 and following.

[33]   Cl 95(3).

[34]   See Cl 95(1).

[35]   See Land Registration Act 1925, s 70(1)(k).

[36]   See above, para 8.9; and see para 14.2.

are those granted for a term of seven years or less.[37] The title to leases of such short duration cannot be barred by adverse possession.

(2)   The second concerns claims brought by licensees and tenants at will. Possession is protected against all save those who have a better right to possess.[38] It follows that licensees[39] and tenants at will can take proceedings to recover possession from a squatter. Once again, as such persons are not registered proprietors, the new scheme will not apply to them, and such proceedings may therefore become time-barred under the Limitation Act 1980.

(3)   Thirdly, a lease may become liable to forfeiture for breach of some condition or covenant in the lease, or a right of re-entry may become exercisable in respect of a fee simple for breach of condition or on the occurrence of some event.[40] If the right of re-entry is not exercised within 12 years of the breach or other event, the right to do so will be lost in respect of that breach or event.[41] This right of re-entry is not an estate in land and the disapplication of section 15 of the Limitation Act 1980 does not therefore apply to it.[42] This situation is not, in truth, one of adverse possession at all. It is simply a case where the landlord or other person having a right of re-entry has a right to determine an estate. As such it is outside our scheme and will continue to be subject to the Limitation Act 1980.

Provisions of the Limitation Act 1980 which depend on the accrual of a cause of action or the limitation period will not apply

14.11   Because the scheme that we propose breaks away from the concept of an accrual of a cause of action or the period of limitation, certain provisions of the Limitation Act 1980 which depend upon this concept will also be inapplicable under it. In particular, certain provisions in Part II of that Act (which are concerned with the extension or exclusion of ordinary time limits) will not apply.[43] The nature of our

---

[37]   See Cls 3(3), 4(1); Schedules 1, para 1; 3, para 1; above, paras 8.9, 8.50.

[38]   *Asher v Whitlock* (1865) LR 1 QB 1, 5; *Hunter v Canary Wharf Ltd* [1997] AC 655, 703.

[39]   Including it seems not just those in possession, but those who have a contractual right to possession: see *Manchester Airport Plc v Dutton* [2000] 1 QB 133. But see *Hunter v Canary Wharf Ltd*, above, at p 703, where Lord Hoffmann explained that it was *exclusive possession* that distinguished an occupier who might in due course acquire a title under the Limitation Act 1980 by adverse possession from a mere trespasser. A person who merely has a right to possession does not have exclusive possession. Lord Hoffmann's remarks were not cited in *Dutton*.

[40]   As where the fee simple owner fails to pay rent due under a rentcharge and the rentcharge owner thereupon becomes entitled to exercise a right of re-entry.

[41]   See Limitation Act 1980, Schedule 1, para 7.

[42]   Cf Cl 95(1).

[43]   See Limitation Act 1980, ss 29 (fresh accrual on acknowledgment or part payment), 30 (formal provisions as to acknowledgment and part payments), 31 (effect of acknowledgment or part payment on persons other than the maker or recipient), 32 (postponement of limitation period in case of fraud, concealment or mistake).

scheme, under which the registered proprietor (and others) may object to a squatter's application to be registered, makes these provisions unnecessary.

Mortgagors in possession

14.12   Where a mortgagor is in possession, the rights of the mortgagee[44] to recover possession or to foreclose remain subject to the provisions of the Limitation Act 1980. The reason for this is simple. A mortgagee has two sets of remedies, its personal remedies against the mortgagor for the moneys due under the mortgage, and its remedies against the property to enforce its security.[45] In essence, the assertion of the mortgagee's proprietary rights is linked to its personal remedies to recover the moneys that are secured by the charge. Once the latter are barred then so too are the former. As a mortgage is no more than a security for moneys owed, it would be very strange if, after the mortgagee's direct rights of enforcement were time-barred, it could still enforce them against the property.[46] The present law achieves the necessary linkage between the mortgagee's personal and proprietary rights and may be summarised as follows.

14.13   Under the Limitation Act 1980, a 12 year limitation period applies to the mortgagee's rights to recover the moneys due under the mortgage, to possession and to foreclose. The right of action accrues—

(1)   as regards the right to possession, on the date of the mortgage;[47]

(2)   as regards the rights to recover the moneys due under the mortgage[48] and to foreclose,[49] on the date when the right to receive the money accrued, which will be the legal date for redemption.[50]

However, in relation to each of these limitation periods, if (as normally happens) the mortgagor pays any instalments under the mortgage, the 12 year period runs afresh from that payment.[51] It follows that, in the typical case where the mortgagor

---

[44]   Strictly a chargee under the Bill. See above, para 7.5.

[45]   See *Kibble v Fairthorne* [1895] 1 Ch 219, 224.

[46]   However, just such a strange result occurred in Hong Kong recently: see the decision of the Court of Final Appeal in *Common Luck Investment Ltd v Cheung Kam Chuen* (1999) 2 HKCFAR 229; [1999] 2 HKLRD 417. The decision does, with respect, seem wrong in principle.

[47]   Limitation Act 1980, s 15(1). The mortgagee has a right to possession from the date of the mortgage: *Four-Maids Ltd v Dudley Marshall (Properties) Ltd* [1957] Ch 317, 320. If, therefore, the mortgagor fails to make any payment, the right to recover possession is time barred 12 years from the date of the mortgage.

[48]   Limitation Act 1980, s 20(1).

[49]   *Ibid*, ss 15, 20(4).

[50]   The legal date for redemption is normally six months after the date of the mortgage. In theory, therefore, a mortgagee may be able to foreclose even after its right to possession is barred.

[51]   See Limitation Act 1980, s 29(3) (fresh accrual by part payment). The mortgagor is in adverse possession for the purposes of the Limitation Act 1980, because the land subject to the charge is in the possession of "some person in whose favour the period of limitation can

307

pays instalments, the limitation period will run from the date of the last instalment that he or she has paid.

14.14 We can see no reason to depart from these principles. If our scheme were to apply to a mortgagor in possession, it would lead to the result that a mortgagee's remedies to recover its security would never be extinguished,[52] even though its rights to recover the moneys secured by the charge were time-barred. Under the Bill, the Limitation Act 1980 therefore continues to apply to claims by a mortgagee against a mortgagor in possession.[53]

Mortgagees in possession

14.15 The position in relation to a *mortgagee* in possession is very different. Under section 16 of the Limitation Act 1980, once a mortgagee has been in possession of land for 12 years, the mortgagor loses his or her right to redeem the mortgage,[54] his or her title is extinguished,[55] and, in consequence, the mortgagee becomes the owner of the land. We consider this rule to be wrong in principle and the Bill therefore disapplies section 16 in relation to an estate in land or a rentcharge which is registered under the Bill.[56] Our principal — but not exclusive — reasons for this are set out below.

14.16 First, it is strange that, where a mortgagee exercises its power to take possession of land, it should be treated in the same way as if it were in adverse possession. The mortgagee's possession is plainly not adverse. A mortgagee is either a tenant under a long lease (in the case of a mortgage by demise or sub-demise),[57] or has the same rights as if it were (in the usual case of a charge by way of legal mortgage).[58] A tenant can never adversely possess against his or her landlord while the lease subsists, because his or her possession is not *adverse*, but is attributable to the tenancy.[59]

---

run": see Schedule 1, Part 1, para 8(1). The mortgagor does not in any sense have to be a "trespasser" for these purposes. It was this point that was overlooked in *Common Luck Investment Ltd v Cheung Kam Chuen* (1999) 2 HKCFAR 229; [1999] 2 HKLRD 417.

[52] Because no period of limitation under Limitation Act 1980 would run: see Cl 95(1).

[53] Cl 95(1); above, para 14.9.

[54] Limitation Act 1980, s 16.

[55] *Ibid*, s 17.

[56] Cl 95(2).

[57] See Law of Property Act 1925, ss 85, 86.

[58] See Law of Property Act 1925, s 87.

[59] See *Megarry & Wade's Law of Real Property* (6th ed 2000), 21-027.

14.17 Secondly, section 16 is a relic from the days when the nature of a mortgage was very different from what it is today. Since it was first enacted in 1832,[60] the following significant changes have occurred:

(1) Mortgages are no longer made by an outright transfer of the mortgagor's legal estate to the mortgagee, with a proviso for reconveyance on redemption.[61] The mortgagor remains the owner of the legal estate, and the mortgage is perceived to be what it is: a charge on the land as security for a loan of money.

(2) Foreclosure – the remedy by which a mortgagee can extinguish the mortgagor's equity of redemption and become absolute owner of the land — has become virtually obsolete.[62] One reason for this is that, since 1852, there has been a statutory power to order sale in lieu of foreclosure.[63] Any such sale will necessarily be fairer to the mortgagor and to any other mortgagees if the property is worth more than the sum owed to the first mortgagee, because it means that the surplus will be available to the mortgagor or to any subsequent mortgagees. Section 16 of the Limitation Act 1980, operates almost as a form of statutory foreclosure, but without any possibility of a sale in lieu.

(3) A legal mortgagee has had a statutory power of sale since 1860.[64] Indeed, a mortgagee will invariably be able to realise its security if the mortgagor is in default under the mortgage.[65] Even in those rare cases when the power of sale is in some way excluded or deferred, it can still seek sale under the power, explained above in (2), for the court to order sale in lieu of foreclosure.[66]

(4) Where the mortgagee does exercise its power of sale, it holds any surplus after discharge of the mortgage and any prior encumbrances and the payment of the expenses of sale, on trust for the person entitled to the mortgaged property.[67] Claims to recover trust property are never time-

---

[60] By the Real Property Limitation Act 1832, s 28. It was re-enacted in the Real Property Limitation Act 1874, s 7 and the Limitation Act 1939, s 12. The precise wording of the provision has changed over time, but the substance has not.

[61] See Law of Property Act 1925, ss 85, 86.

[62] See *Palk v Mortgage Services Funding Plc* [1993] Ch 330, 336.

[63] See Law of Property Act 1925, s 91(2) for the present power. It was first introduced by Chancery Procedure Act 1852, s 48.

[64] Lord Cranworth's Act, 23 & 24 Vict c 145, s 32. The present provisions are found in the Law of Property Act 1925, ss 101(1), 103.

[65] See Law of Property Act 1925, s 103.

[66] Law of Property Act 1925, s 91(2); see *Twentieth Century Banking Corporation v Wilkinson* [1977] Ch 99.

[67] Law of Property Act 1925, s 105, re-enacting Conveyancing and Law of Property Act 1881, s 21(3). This was, it seems, no more than a codification of the common law. A mortgagee who sold under an express power of sale in the mortgage deed was "a trustee for the mortgagor of any surplus": see *Matthison v Clarke* (1854) 3 Drew 3, 4; 61 ER 801, *per*

barred.[68] This leads to the paradox under the present law that, if the mortgagee simply remains in possession, it can acquire title to the mortgaged property, but if it sells the land, it will remain accountable to the mortgagor indefinitely for any surplus in the proceeds of sale.

14.18 Finally, it is not easy to see how any equivalent of section 16 could be retained under our scheme. As we have explained above,[69] the essence of it is that the registered proprietor is given notice of the squatter's application to be registered, to which he or she may then object. That notice will be sent to the registered proprietor's address for service, which will usually be that of the property mortgaged. Where a mortgagee takes possession, the last thing that the mortgagor is likely to have on his or her mind is the need to change the address for service at the Land Registry. In practice, therefore, any notice would be served on the mortgaged premises and would, in consequence, probably never come to the attention of the registered proprietor. As a result, he or she would never have an opportunity to object to the application for registration.

The right to apply for registration after ten years' adverse possession

The prerequisites for an application: the general position

14.19 The present limitation period applicable to actions for the recovery of land is normally (but not invariably[70]) 12 years.[71] However, in both its Consultation Paper and subsequent Report on Limitation of Actions, the Law Commission has recommended that the period be reduced to 10 years.[72] Although that recommendation will not apply to the adverse possession of a registered estate or rentcharge (because the present scheme will apply instead), the Law Commission and HM Land Registry considered that it should adopt the same 10 year period of adverse possession as the trigger for its new scheme.[73]

14.20 Under the Bill and subject to what is said below at paragraph 14.24, a person may apply to be registered as the proprietor of a registered estate if he or she has been in adverse possession of that estate for the period of 10 years ending on the date of the application.[74] As is presently the case with an application to register under section 75 of the Land Registration Act 1925, the squatter will have to prove to

Kindersley V-C. For the effect of the Bill on Law of Property Act 1925, s 105, see Cl 54; above, para 7.43.

[68] Limitation Act 1980, s 21(1).

[69] See para 14.5.

[70] See *Megarry & Wade's Law of Real Property* (6th ed 2000), 21-004—21-011.

[71] Limitation Act 1980, s 15(1).

[72] See respectively Consultation Paper No 151 (1998) and (2001) Law Com No 270. The Consultation Paper preceded (1998) Law Com No 254, in which the proposals for a wholly new system of adverse possession for registered land were first made.

[73] See (1998) Law Com No 254, para 10.46.

[74] Schedule 6, para 1(1). Because the claimant must have been in *adverse* possession, a mortgagee in possession will never be able to apply to be registered. Cf Cl 95(2); above, para 14.9 and see above, para 14.16.

the registrar that he or she[75] has been in adverse possession for the relevant period.[76] The estate need not have been registered throughout the period of adverse possession.[77] If, say, a squatter went into adverse possession when the title to it was unregistered, but four years later, the owner voluntarily registered it, the squatter would be able to apply to be registered after six more years of adverse possession.[78] For these purposes,[79] and subject to what is said in paragraph 14.23 below, adverse possession has the same meaning as it does under the Limitation Act 1980: the Bill provides that a person is in adverse possession of an estate in land, if but for Clause 95,[80] a period of limitation under section 15 of the Limitation Act[81] would run in his or her favour in relation to the estate.[82] However, to satisfy the requirement of 10 years' adverse possession, the applicant, X, does not in fact have to show that she has herself been in adverse possession for that period.[83] Under the Bill it will suffice that—

(1) X is the successor in title of an earlier squatter from whom she acquired the land, and, taken together, the two periods of adverse possession amount to 10 years;

(2) X has been in adverse possession, has herself been dispossessed by a second squatter Y, and has then recovered the land from Y. In these circumstances, she can add Y's period of adverse possession to her own to make up the necessary 10 year period.

14.21 By contrast, where squatter Y, has evicted a prior squatter, X, Y cannot add X's period of adverse possession to his own to make up the necessary 10 year period. Y is not X's successor in title, but has a freehold estate of his own by virtue of his adverse possession.[84] He will be unable to apply to be registered until he can show 10 years' adverse possession of his own. This is a necessary concomitant of the scheme which we propose. An example will demonstrate the problems which would otherwise result.

> X has been in adverse possession for 9 years. Y, a second squatter, dispossesses her. If Y could add X's adverse possession to his own, he would be entitled to apply to be registered as proprietor after 1 year. If

[75] Or those through whom he or she claims: see below.

[76] Whenever under Schedule 6 a squatter has to establish a period of adverse possession, he or she will have to prove that adverse possession to the registrar. It will not be presumed.

[77] Schedule 6, para 1(4).

[78] But see Schedule 6, para 5(4)(d); below, para 14.45.

[79] That is, for the purposes of the scheme contained in Schedule 6.

[80] See above, para 14.9.

[81] Time limit for actions to recover land.

[82] See Schedule 6, para 11(1).

[83] See *ibid*, para 11(2).

[84] As we explain more fully below, para 14.66, every squatter acquires an independent fee simple from the moment that he or she commences adverse possession.

his application were successful (as it might be), it would then be necessary to make some provision by which X could recover the land from Y, notwithstanding that Y had been registered as proprietor.

Under what we propose, taken together with the proposed reduction in the limitation period contained in the Law Commission's Report on Limitation of Actions,[85] Y would not be able to apply to be registered as proprietor until he had been in adverse possession for 10 years. At the very moment that Y could first apply to be registered as proprietor,[86] X's right to recover the land from Y would be time-barred.[87]

14.22 The ten year period of adverse possession must be unbroken. If X, a squatter, were to abandon land after she had been in adverse possession for 7 years, and then, some time later, Y were to take adverse possession, Y could not add X's period of adverse possession to his own. Adverse possession would start afresh when Y took possession of the land. However, once a squatter has been in adverse possession for ten years, the right to apply to be registered will not necessarily be lost if he or she is subsequently evicted by the registered proprietor other than pursuant to a judgment for possession. The squatter will still be able to apply to be registered, provided that he or she does so within six months of being evicted.[88] We consider that it would be wrong in principle for a registered proprietor to be able to deny the squatter his or her right to apply to be registered by having resort to self-help. This is because, as we explain below, there are certain limited circumstances in which a squatter will have a right to be registered, even if the registered proprietor objects to his or application to be registered.[89] Furthermore, in those same limited circumstances, a squatter will also have a defence to any proceedings brought to recover possession of the land.[90]

14.23 The Bill qualifies in two respects the principle[91] that adverse possession has the same meaning as it does for the purposes of section 15 of the Limitation Act 1980. The first way in which it does so is to disapply a technical rule about the adverse possession of a reversion[92] which is not needed under the scheme which the Bill introduces.[93] The second way is more significant. In determining whether

---

[85] (2001) Law Com No 270; see above, para 14.19.

[86] Because Y does not have a *registered* estate, Cl 95 does not apply to it.

[87] If the Land Registration Bill is enacted before the Limitation Bill, there will be a minor anomaly. Y would be able to apply to be registered 10 years after he had dispossessed X, whereas under the Limitation Act 1980, s 15(1), X would have 12 years to recover the land from Y. However, if Y were registered after 10 years, that would necessarily defeat any claim that X might bring. This is because, as we explain below, para 14.71, Y will be registered as the successor in title of the former registered proprietor and he will thereby acquire an unassailable title. In practice, any case of this kind is likely to be very rare indeed.

[88] Schedule 6, para 1(2).

[89] See below, paras 14.36—14.52.

[90] See Cl 97; below, paras 14.85—14.87.

[91] See above, para 14.20.

[92] See Limitation Act 1980, Schedule 1, para 6.

[93] Schedule 6, para 11(3)(b).

a period of limitation would run for the purposes of section 15 of the Limitation Act 1980, the commencement of proceedings which involve asserting a right to possession of land is to be disregarded.[94] Under the present law, as we explain below,[95] the commencement of proceedings stops time running under the Limitation Act 1980 for the purposes of that particular action. This principle has no relevance to our scheme, because a right of recovery is never barred by lapse of time alone.[96]

Where no valid application to be registered can be made

14.24 Under the Bill there are four situations in which a squatter cannot make a valid application to be registered even though he or she may have been in adverse possession for 10 years. The first two are related and can be considered together.

WHERE THERE ARE POSSESSION PROCEEDINGS AGAINST THE SQUATTER THAT ARE STILL CURRENT

14.25 A squatter may not apply to be registered—

(1) at any time when he or she is a defendant in proceedings which involve asserting a right to possession of the land; or

(2) if in any such proceedings judgment for possession is given against him or her, for two years from the date of judgment.[97]

14.26 The effect of these provisions is to prevent a squatter, who has been in adverse possession for more than 10 years, from applying to be registered as proprietor while there are current proceedings against him or her in which the registered proprietor[98] could obtain possession of the land. That will be so in the following circumstances—

(1) at any time after proceedings been commenced and have not been struck out or discontinued; or

(2) for two years after any judgment has been obtained against the squatter in such proceedings.

As regards (2), as we explain below, any judgment obtained against a squatter who had been in adverse possession for 10 years at the time when proceedings were commenced, ceases to be enforceable after two years.[99]

---

[94] Schedule 6, para 11(3)(b).

[95] See para 14.27.

[96] See Cl 95; above, para 14.9.

[97] Schedule 6, para 1(3).

[98] Or other person entitled to bring proceedings, such as a registered chargee: see below, para 14.33(2).

[99] Cl 97(2); below, para 14.59.

14.27 Under the present law, the commencement of proceedings against a squatter prevents time running against that squatter for the purposes of that action.[100] The function of the two exceptions set out in paragraph 14.25 is plainly not identical, but it is somewhat similar. The effect of the exceptions is that the registered proprietor can take proceedings against the squatter without the risk that he or she might also have to fend off an application for registration by the squatter at the same time.

WHERE THE PROPRIETOR IS AN ENEMY OR HELD IN ENEMY TERRITORY

14.28 No application can be made during, or before the end of twelve months after the end of, any period in which the existing registered proprietor is for the purposes of the Limitation (Enemies and War Prisoners) Act 1945[101] either an enemy or detained in enemy territory.[102] This provision is designed to ensure that the protection conferred by the 1945 Act[103] is carried through to the present Bill.

WHERE THE PROPRIETOR IS SUFFERING FROM MENTAL DISABILITY OR PHYSICAL IMPAIRMENT

14.29 The final case is more important than the previous one and it provides protection in some cases where a registered proprietor is suffering from mental disability or physical impairment. Under the Bill no application can be made by a squatter to be registered as proprietor during any period in which the existing registered proprietor is either—

(1) unable because of mental disability[104] to make decisions about issues of the kind to which such an application for registration would give rise; or

(2) unable to communicate such decisions because of mental disability or physical impairment.[105]

The mischief that this provision is intended to meet is an obvious one. Where a registered proprietor is under a disability covered by this provision, someone may be looking after his or her affairs, either under an enduring power of attorney or because the court has appointed a receiver under section 99 of the Mental Health

---

[100] *Markfield Investments Ltd v Evans* [2001] 2 All ER 238. In that case, the proceedings had been dismissed for want of prosecution. It was held that although the commencement of proceedings had prevented the running of time in relation to that first action, it did not have that effect as regards a second action that was unsuccessfully brought by the former owner. In other words, the period of time that that squatter had remained in possession during the currency of the first proceedings were relevant to the running of the limitation period in relation to the second action.

[101] See s 2(1) of that Act for the relevant definitions.

[102] Schedule 6, para 8(1).

[103] See s 1 of that Act.

[104] Defined by the Bill to mean "a disability or disorder of the mind or brain, whether permanent or temporary, which results in an impairment or disturbance of mental functioning": Schedule 6, para 8(3).

[105] Schedule 6, para 8(2).

Act 1983. That person may have taken steps to ensure that he or she receives any notices served on the proprietor under a disability. But in some cases that will not be the case. There is, therefore, a danger that the application to register may be successful because no one responds when the registrar serves notice under the provisions of the Bill,[106] and the registrar is therefore obliged to register the applicant.[107] The Bill addresses that concern and it does so whether or not some person is looking after the affairs of the person under a disability.

14.30   The protection afforded by this provision goes beyond that which applies to a person under a disability under the Limitation Act 1980.[108] First, the time at which the person has to be suffering the disability is when squatter applies to be registered and when the registered proprietor therefore needs to be able to act to protect his or her position. It is not (as is the case under the Limitation Act 1980), the time when the cause of action accrued (in other words, when adverse possession commenced).[109] Secondly, it protects not only those suffering from a mental disability,[110] but also those who are so physically impaired that they cannot communicate their decisions.

14.31   There is a power for the registrar to enter a note on the register to indicate that a registered proprietor falls within the Limitation (Enemies and War Prisoners) Act 1945 or is suffering from the requisite disability or physical impairment.[111]

Notification of the registered proprietor and others

14.32   Under the Bill, once a valid application to be registered has been made by a squatter who has been in adverse possession for 10 years,[112] the registrar must serve notice of that application on all the persons listed below in paragraph 14.33 (in essence those who would be prejudiced if the squatter's application were successful).[113] That notice must inform the person—

    (1)   of the application for registration;[114]

---

[106] See below, para 14.32.

[107] See below, para 14.34.

[108] See s 28 of that Act which extends the limitation period when a cause of action accrues to a person under a disability.

[109] See Limitation Act 1980, s 28(1).

[110] See Limitation Act 1980, s 38(2)—(4).

[111] Schedule 6, para 8(4). In practice, the registrar will probably be unaware of the proprietor's position, so that no note will be made on the register. It follows that, in such circumstances, the registrar is likely to register the squatter applicant as proprietor. That will be a mistake. It will therefore be open to the proprietor (or those representing his or her affairs) to seek rectification of the register in the usual way: see Schedule 4, paras 2, 5; above, paras 10.10, 10.19. If rectification is refused because the new proprietor is a proprietor who is in possession within Cl 128 (above, para 10.17), the registrar will be obliged to pay indemnity.

[112] That is, under Schedule 6, para 1.

[113] Schedule 6, para 2(1).

[114] Schedule 6, para 2(1).

(2)   that he or she may serve a counter-notice on the registrar within a period prescribed by rules[115] requiring him to reject the application unless the squatter can satisfy one of the three conditions, explained below,[116] which will entitle him or her to be registered;[117] and

(3)   that if such a counter-notice is not served by at least one of those notified of the application, the registrar must enter the applicant as the new proprietor of the estate.[118]

In other words, the recipient of the registrar's notice can require that the application for registration be rejected unless the squatter can bring him or herself within one of the special cases where the squatter is entitled to be registered.

14.33   The persons on whom the registrar must serve notice are—

(1)   The registered proprietor.[119] He or she is the person most likely to oppose the registration, and obviously has the power either to take possession proceedings against the squatter or to negotiate the grant of a lease or licence to the squatter.[120]

(2)   The proprietor of any registered charge.[121] The chargee has a right to possession of the land[122] and can, therefore, take possession proceedings against any squatter should the registered proprietor fail to do so.[123] As we explain below, under the Bill, the registered chargee will have a powerful incentive to act to protect its security in this way.[124]

---

[115]   The length of the period of notice is considered to be a matter for rules rather than for the Bill. In Law Com No 254, a period of 2 months was suggested as being the appropriate period. A number of respondents considered that the period was too short. The period is likely to be 3 months, at least initially. However, when there has been some experience of how the procedure works in practice, the length of the period can be reviewed if need be.

[116]   See paras 14.36—14.52.

[117]   This states the effect of Schedule 6, paras 3, 4.

[118]   Schedule 6, paras 2(2), 4.

[119]   Schedule 6, para 2(1)(a).

[120]   This is important: see below, para 14.56.

[121]   Schedule 6, para 2(1)(b).

[122]   In *Four-Maids Ltd v Dudley Marshall (Properties) Ltd* [1957] Ch 317, 320, Harman J explained that "the right of the mortgagee to possession in the absence of some contract has nothing to do with default on the part of the mortgagor. The mortgagee may go into possession before the ink is dry on the mortgage unless there is something in the contract, express or by implication, whereby he has contracted himself out of that right. He has that right because he has a legal term of years in the property or its statutory equivalent".

[123]   It is perhaps noteworthy that Law of Property Act 1925, s 98, makes express provision that a *mortgagor* can take proceedings for possession in his own name without joining the mortgagee as a party.

[124]   See para 14.74.

316

(3) Where the squatter applies to be registered as proprietor of a leasehold estate, the proprietor of any superior registered estate.[125] In practice, few landlords will wish to find themselves with a squatter as tenant.[126] Although such landlords have no right to take possession proceedings against the squatter directly, many are likely to take steps to ensure that the tenant evicts the squatter.

(4) Any person who, on application to the registrar, is registered in accordance with rules as a person who is to be notified.[127] This category is likely to comprise those who can satisfy the registrar that they have some estate, right or interest in the land that would or might be prejudicially affected if a squatter were to acquire it. Such persons might include an equitable chargee (perhaps having the benefit of a charging order) or a rentcharge owner. Once again, such persons have no right to take possession proceedings against the squatter themselves, but they may be in a position to take steps to encourage the registered proprietor to do so.

(5) Such other persons as rules may provide.[128] There are certain bodies or persons who should be notified of an application by a squatter to be registered even though they have not registered any interest under (4) above. Indeed, the sort of persons or bodies we have in mind may have a supervisory role in relation to the property, rather than necessarily having any interest in it as such. These might include the Charity Commission in relation to land held in charitable trusts, the Church Commissioners as regards benefices, and trustees in bankruptcy in respect of land registered in the bankrupt's name.[129] If such bodies or persons are notified of and object to the squatter's application, they can either take steps to ensure that he or she is evicted, or, where they have standing to do so, take proceedings for the recovery of the land in their own right.

---

[125] Schedule 6, para 2(1)(c).

[126] In relation to commercial leasehold property, most assignments require the landlord's consent, and the assignor will commonly have to enter into some form of financial guarantee in relation to the assignee's performance of the covenants. In relation to leases granted after 1995, this will take the form of an authorised guarantee agreement under the Landlord and Tenant (Covenants) Act 1995, s 16. Where a lease is assigned by operation of law, as will be the case where a squatter is registered (see below, para 14.73), the former tenant remains liable on the covenants in the lease (see, *eg*, in relation to leases granted after 1995, Landlord and Tenant (Covenants) Act 1995, s 11). However, having a squatter as tenant may affect the value both of the premises and of the landlord's reversion.

[127] Schedule 6, para 2(1)(d).

[128] Schedule 6, para 2(1)(e).

[129] A trustee in bankruptcy does have an interest in the property. The legal title vests in him by operation of law: see Insolvency Act 1986, s 306. However, until the trustee is registered as proprietor the bankrupt remains on the register as registered proprietor, though a notice or a restriction should be entered to prevent any disposal by him of the land: see Cl 86. See above, paras 11.40, 11.41.

Registration where no counter-notice is served

14.34 Where a notice is served by the registrar (as explained in paragraph 14.32) and no counter-notice is served on him within the time prescribed, the registrar *must* approve the squatter's application to be registered as proprietor of the land in place of the existing proprietor.[130] We explain the effect of such registration below, at paragraph 14.71. One point does need to be emphasised as a result of this provision. It will be particularly important that the registered proprietor and any registered chargee should keep up to date his or her address for service.[131]

No registration where a counter-notice is served

14.35 By contrast, where a counter-notice is served on the registrar, he must reject the application for registration by the squatter, unless he or she can establish any one of three conditions, described in the following paragraphs, which will entitle him or her to be registered.[132] Even if the application is rejected, it is not necessarily the end of the matter, because, as we explain below, the squatter is entitled to re-apply to be registered if he or she remains in adverse possession for a further two years.[133]

Special cases: registration even where a counter-notice is served

GENERAL SUMMARY

14.36 Even if a recipient of the notice of application for registration by the squatter serves a counter-notice on the registrar, he must approve the squatter's application in three situations. Those situations are—

(1) where, under the principles of proprietary estoppel, it would be unconscionable for the registered proprietor to object to the squatter's application to be registered;

(2) where the squatter was otherwise entitled to the land; or

(3) where the squatter is the owner of adjacent property and has been in adverse possession of the land in question under the mistaken but reasonable belief that he or she was the owner of it.

As we have already indicated,[134] in these situations, we consider that the balance of fairness plainly lies with the squatter, and he or she should prevail.

14.37 As regards the first two grounds, there is nothing whatever to prevent the squatter from taking court proceedings to establish his or her rights to the land, regardless of how long or short a period he or she has been in adverse possession. However,

---

[130] Schedule 6, para 4.

[131] Cf Schedule 10, para 5(2).

[132] Schedule 6, para 5(1).

[133] See para 14.57.

[134] See above, para 14.7.

under the present law, where such a person has been in adverse possession of the land claimed for 12 years, he or she is entitled to be registered on the ground of adverse possession alone without the need to establish in what may be costly court proceedings his or her rights on the basis of estoppel or some other ground. In other words, the claimant can take advantage of his or her adverse possession and the comparatively simple administrative procedure of an application to register under section 75 of the Land Registration Act 1925. We did not wish to deprive such persons of a cheap and simple avenue to registration, especially as the parcels of land in dispute are often small.[135] However, under our scheme, in addition to showing 10 years' adverse possession, it will be necessary to establish the necessary elements of estoppel or other ground in making the application for registration. That is not so under the present law: the claimant need satisfy the registrar only that he or she was in adverse possession for 12 years.

14.38 Under the judicial provisions of the Bill, which we explain more fully in Part XVI of this Report, the registrar will no longer be able to determine an application if there has been an objection to it and it is not possible to dispose of it by agreement. He must instead refer the matter to the Adjudicator.[136] Therefore, unless the registered proprietor and any chargee agree that the squatter is entitled to be registered because he or she falls within one of the three exceptional cases mentioned in paragraph 14.36, the matter will be resolved by the Adjudicator.

ESTOPPEL

The principle

14.39 To fall within this exception the squatter applicant will have to show two distinct matters—

(1) that it is unconscionable to dispossess him or her; and

(2) that the circumstances are such that he or she ought to be registered as the proprietor.[137]

14.40 Although these principles are stated in statutory form, they are intended to embody the equitable principles of proprietary estoppel as these have developed.[138] The applicant will therefore have to establish that an "equity" has arisen in his or her favour. To this end, he or she will have to show that—

(1) in some way, the registered proprietor encouraged or allowed the applicant to believe that he or she owned the parcel of land in question;

---

[135] Under the Bill, the procedure will not be the same as it is now: see below, para 14.38.

[136] See Cls 73(1), (7); 106; below, paras 16.6; 16.7. For the new office of Adjudicator to HM Land Registry, see Cl 105; below, para 16.3.

[137] Schedule 6, para 5(2).

[138] For an account of these principles, see *Megarry & Wade's Law of Real Property* (6th ed 2000), Chapter 13.

(2)   in this belief, he or she acted to his or her detriment to the knowledge of the proprietor; and

(3)   it would be unconscionable for the proprietor to deny the applicant the rights which he or she believed that he or she had.

When a claimant establishes an equity, that is no more than an inchoate right. It is not a defined property right, but merely gives the claimant a right to go to court to seek relief. The court has a discretion as to how to give effect to that equity, and it will ascertain what constitutes "the minimum equity" to do justice to the claimant.[139] There is a wide range of relief which it may give.[140] At one extreme it may order the landowner to convey the freehold to or grant some right over his or her land to the claimant.[141] At the other, it may order the landowner to compensate the claimant for the detriment which he or she has suffered,[142] or merely restrain the owner from enforcing his or her strict legal rights against the claimant.[143]

14.41   As we have explained above,[144] it will almost always fall to the Adjudicator to resolve a claim by a squatter that he or she is entitled to be registered because an equity by estoppel has arisen in his or her favour. Because the Adjudicator must give the applicant no more than the minimum necessary to do justice,[145] there will inevitably be cases where the Adjudicator considers that, although the squatter has established an equity, it would be over-generous to grant him or her the registered estate.[146] Under his powers of determination,[147] he will then decide how effect should be given to that equity and he is expressly empowered to grant the applicant some less extensive form of relief.[148] The Bill provides that if, on any appeal from the Adjudicator's decision,[149] in a case arising out of an application by a squatter to be registered as proprietor,[150] the court determines that it would be unconscionable for the registered proprietor to seek to dispossess the applicant,

---

[139]   *Crabb v Arun DC* [1976] Ch 179, 198, *per* Scarman LJ.

[140]   For a discussion, see Simon Gardner, "The Remedial Discretion in Proprietary Estoppel" (1999) 115 LQR 438.

[141]   As in *Pascoe v Turner* [1979] 1 WLR 431; *Voyce v Voyce* (1991) 62 P & CR 290 (transfer of the freehold); *Crabb v Arun DC* [1976] Ch 179 (grant of an easement).

[142]   As in *Dodsworth v Dodsworth* (1973) 228 EG 1115; *Baker v Baker* [1993] 2 FLR 247.

[143]   As in *Maharaj v Chand* [1986] AC 898.

[144]   See para 14.38.

[145]   See above, para 14.40.

[146]   In other words, where although Schedule 6, para 5(2)(a) is satisfied, para 5(2)(b) is *not*. We give some examples below, in para 14.42, where it *would* often be appropriate for the applicant to be registered with the registered estate. For the Adjudicator's power to determine how the equity should be satisfied in such a case, see Cl 108(4).

[147]   See Cl 106(1); below, para 16.7.

[148]   Cl 108(4); below, para 16.8.

[149]   For the right of appeal from the Adjudicator's decisions, see Cl 109; below, para 16.23.

[150]   That is, an application under Schedule 6, para 1.

but the circumstances are not such that the applicant ought to be registered as proprietor, it must determine how best to satisfy the applicant's equity.[151]

Examples

14.42 It may be helpful to give examples of the typical kinds of case in which this exception is likely to be in issue.

(1) Where the squatter has built on the registered proprietor's land in the mistaken belief that he or she was the owner of it, and the proprietor has knowingly acquiesced in his or her mistake. The squatter eventually discovers the true facts and applies to be registered after 10 years.

(2) Where neighbours have entered into an informal sale agreement for valuable consideration by which one agrees to sell the land to the other. The "buyer" pays the price, takes possession of the land and treats it as his own. No steps are taken to perfect his or her title. There is no binding contract either because the agreement does not comply with the formal requirements for such a contract,[152] or, once electronic conveyancing is fully operative, because the agreement has not been protected on the register by means of a notice.[153] The "buyer" discovers that he or she has no title to the land. If he or she been in possession of it for 10 years he or she can apply to be registered as proprietor.

In each of these cases, an equity arises by estoppel, and it would be just to give effect to that equity by registering the squatter as owner of the registered estate in place of the existing proprietor.

SOME OTHER RIGHT TO THE LAND

14.43 This exception[154] is more straightforward. From time to time there may be cases where the squatter has some other right to the land that would entitle him or her to be registered as proprietor irrespective of any period of adverse possession. Two examples may be given by way of illustration.

(1) The claimant is entitled to the land under the will or intestacy of the deceased proprietor.

(2) The claimant contracted to buy the land and paid the purchase price, but the legal estate was never transferred to him or her. In a case of this kind, the squatter-buyer is a beneficiary under a bare trust, and, as such, can be in adverse possession.[155]

---

[151] Cl 109(3).

[152] See Law of Property (Miscellaneous Provisions) Act 1989, s 2.

[153] See above, para 13.76.

[154] See Schedule 6, para 5(3).

[155] See *Bridges v Mees* [1957] Ch 475. A buyer who has not paid the whole of the purchase price will not be in adverse possession. His or her possession is under the contract. Were it not so,

In such cases, the Adjudicator will be entitled to order that the claimant be registered as proprietor even though the existing registered proprietor objects.

REASONABLE MISTAKE AS TO BOUNDARY

The principle

14.44 The third exception[156] has proved to be the most difficult to define.[157] It will apply only where the land which is claimed by the squatter is adjacent to land which he or she owns[158] and the boundary between the two properties is a general boundary[159] and has not been fixed.[160] To fall within the exception the squatter will have to prove that—

(1)   there has been a period of adverse possession of at least 10 years[161] by the applicant or his or her predecessor in title ending on the date of the application;

(2)   for at least 10 years of that period, the applicant or his or her predecessor in title reasonably believed that the land to which the application relates belonged to him or her;[162] and

(3)   the estate to which the land relates was registered more than one year prior to the date of the application.[163]

At some point prior to making the application to be registered, the squatter will have become aware that he or she is not in fact the owner of the land in issue. It is likely to be this realisation that prompts the application. It follows that the period of adverse possession that will be needed will, in practice, be more (even if only marginally) than 10 years.

14.45 The reason for the requirement in paragraph 14.44(3), above, is as follows. As the law stands, title to *unregistered* land can normally be acquired by 12 years' adverse

---

the validity of agreements for leases would be undermined: see Law Com No 254, para 10.53.

[156]   See Schedule 6, para 5(4).

[157]   The final version of this exception differs in a number of respects from what we proposed in Law Com No 254, paras 10.54—10.57, 10.66(4)(c). This exception was the subject of a good deal of comment both in response to Law Com No 254, and in our discussions with property litigators (both barristers and solicitors).

[158]   Schedule 6, para 5(4)(a).

[159]   See Cl 60(1), (2); above, para 9.11.

[160]   Schedule 6, para 5(4)(b). For the power to make rules as to the circumstances in which the exact line of the boundary can be fixed, see Cl 60(3); above, paras 9.11, 9.12.

[161]   In practice it will have to be longer because of the requirement in (2): see below.

[162]   Schedule 6, para 5(4)(c).

[163]   Schedule 6, para 5(4)(d).

possession.[164] Under this third exception in the Bill, title to *registered* land may, however, be acquired after 10 years' adverse possession. There might be a case where—

(1) a squatter had been in adverse possession of a parcel of unregistered land for more than 10 but less than 12 years;

(2) the title to the land was then registered; and

(3) the requirements of this third "reasonable mistake as to boundary" exception were otherwise met.

The squatter would not have barred the title of the landowner prior to the registration of the title, but, if no special provision were made, would be entitled to apply to be registered as proprietor under this third exception as soon as the owner registered his or her title. In other words, the owner would have no opportunity to evict the squatter. The requirement that the estate to which the land relates was registered more than one year prior to the date of the application[165] overcomes this difficulty. If the limitation period for unregistered land is reduced from 12 years to 10 years as the Law Commission has recommended,[166] the requirement in paragraph 14.44(3) would no longer be needed and could be repealed. It should be noted that the problem explained in this paragraph is confined to the "reasonable mistake as to boundary" exception and does not apply to the other two special situations where a squatter is entitled to be registered as proprietor even though the registered proprietor objects.[167] This is because, in those other two situations, the squatter is entitled to be registered as proprietor of the land, regardless of his or her adverse possession.

When will this exception be invoked?

14.46 Before explaining the various elements set out in paragraph 14.44, it is necessary to illustrate the types of case which this exception is intended to meet.

(1) The first is where the boundaries as they appear on the ground and as they are according to the register do not coincide. This may happen because—

(a) the physical features (such as the position of trees or other landmarks) suggest that the boundary is in one place but where in fact, according to the plan on the register, it is in another;

---

[164] Limitation Act 1980, s 15(1). This will change if the Law Commission's proposals on limitation of actions are carried forward, and the limitation period is reduced to 10 years. See above, para 14.19.

[165] Schedule 6, para 5(4)(d). If the squatter had barred the rights of the owner *prior* to first registration, that squatter might apply to have the register rectified to give effect to his or her rights. See Schedule 4, paras 2, 5, above, para 10.10, 10.19. But cf Cl 11(4)(c); above, paras 3.46, 3.47.

[166] See above, para 14.19.

[167] See para 14.36, above.

(b) when an estate was laid down, the dividing fences or walls were erected in the wrong place and not in accordance with the plan lodged at the Registry.

(2) The second is where the registered proprietor leads the squatter to believe that he or she is the owner of certain land on the boundary when in fact it belongs to the registered proprietor. Where the squatter has acted to his or her detriment in reliance upon the proprietor's representation, he or she may be able to rely upon the estoppel exception explained above.[168] However, there will be cases where there is no such detrimental reliance, and the applicant will, therefore, have to rely on this third exception.

14.47 The existence of this third exception is likely to make it easier to define the boundaries between properties. This could be relevant where there is an application to fix a boundary[169] or indeed whenever and for whatever reason, it becomes desirable to locate the line of the boundary more precisely. If it is known that X has been in possession of a parcel of land on a boundary for at least 10 years and reasonably believed him or herself to be the owner of that land, X can safely be assumed to be the owner of the land. The elements that have to be established to fall within the exception follow from this.

What has to be established to fall within the exception — factual elements

14.48 The factual elements of this third exception that have to be established are twofold. First, the land which is claimed must be adjacent to land which belongs to the squatter applicant.[170] It follows that, if a person entered into adverse possession of another's land under the mistaken belief that he or she owned it, this exception could not be invoked unless the squatter owned the adjoining land.[171]

14.49 Secondly, the line of the boundary must be one which has not been exactly determined.[172] Rules will be made under Clause 60(3) to allow for such a determination. As we have explained earlier,[173] it is possible to have boundaries fixed under the present law,[174] though it is extremely rare for it to happen and the process can be very costly. It is anticipated, however, that with improved mapping techniques, such determinations may become much more common. Where a landowner has gone to the trouble of having a boundary fixed under this

---

[168] See para 14.39.

[169] Under Cl 60; above, paras 9.11, 9.12.

[170] Schedule 6, para 5(4)(a).

[171] If the applicant was the tenant of the registered proprietor of the land in dispute, his or her claim would necessarily fail. A tenant cannot adversely possess against his or her landlord: *Megarry & Wade's Law of Real Property* (6th ed 2000), 21-027.

[172] Schedule 6, para 5(4)(b).

[173] See above, para 9.10.

[174] See Land Registration Rules 1925, r 276. The fact of such a fixed boundary is noted on the Property Register of the title: *ibid*, r 277. It is anticipated that the same will be true under rules made pursuant to Cl 60(3)(d) of the Bill.

procedure, then the register *is* conclusive as to the boundary and the justification for the third exception is, therefore, absent. One very good reason why a registered proprietor might wish to have the boundary exactly determined would be where the legal boundary of the land and its apparent physical boundaries did not coincide.

What has to be established to fall within the exception — the mental element

14.50 To fall within the third exception, the squatter will have to demonstrate that, for a period of 10 years, either he or she or his or her predecessor in title reasonably believed that the land to which the application relates belonged to him or her.[175] At first sight this may seem to be a very demanding requirement. In practice, it is unlikely to be.

14.51 Under the present law and under the Bill,[176] any squatter will have to show the necessary *animus possidendi* to establish that he or she was in adverse possession. The *animus* that is required is "an intention for the time being to possess the land to the exclusion of all other persons, including the owner with the paper title".[177] If a person is in adverse possession of land under the mistaken belief that he or she owns it, that necessarily satisfies the *animus possidendi* for adverse possession.[178] In other words, the *animus* that will be required to establish the third exception is no more than one specific form of the *animus possidendi* that is needed to satisfy the requirements of adverse possession.

14.52 If X has been in possession of a parcel of land for 10 years or more in circumstances where the physical boundaries of the land suggest that it belongs to X, that fact of itself will, in practice, raise a rebuttable presumption that X had the *animus* needed to establish the third exception. It will then be incumbent on the registered proprietor to show that X knew or ought to have known that the parcel of land did not belong to him or her.[179]

The right to make a further application for registration after two more years' adverse possession

Introduction

14.53 As we have explained above,[180] the essence of the scheme which we propose is that it should produce a decisive result. It is therefore necessary to make provision as to what is to happen after a squatter has applied to be registered as proprietor and his or her application has been rejected because the proprietor or other interested

---

[175] Schedule 6, para 5(4)(c).

[176] See above, para 14.20.

[177] *Buckinghamshire County Council v Moran* [1990] Ch 623, 643, *per* Slade LJ. This test has been repeatedly applied since, see, *eg, J A Pye (Oxford) Holdings Ltd v Graham* [2001] EWCA Civ 117; [2001] 2 WLR 1293, 1299, [10].

[178] See, *eg, Prudential Assurance Co Ltd v Waterloo Real Estate Inc* [1999] 2 EGLR 85.

[179] As by showing that he or she had told X that the land did not belong to X.

[180] See para 14.6.

person served a counter-notice and none of the special exceptions was applicable. The following matters therefore need to be apparent—

(1) whether the squatter can re-apply to be registered if his or her adverse possession continues and if so when; and

(2) what steps should be taken by the registered proprietor (or other interested person, particularly a registered chargee) after serving a counter-notice.

14.54 In the Consultative Document,[181] we identified the most important reasons why English law has a doctrine of adverse possession. The most important of these reasons — that it facilitates *unregistered* conveyancing, where title is relative and ultimately rests on possession[182] — does not apply to registered land. Indeed, it was for that reason that we devised a new system of adverse possession which was compatible with the principles of registration. However, there are other justifications for adverse possession that *do* apply to registered land. In particular—

(1) adverse possession is one facet of the law of limitation, the policy of which is to protect defendants from stale claims and to encourage claimants not to sleep on their rights;[183] and

(2) if possession and ownership become wholly out of kilter, it renders land unmarketable.[184]

14.55 The essence of our scheme is that registration should protect a registered proprietor of an estate or charge against an application for registration by a squatter in the sense that it gives him or her the chance to stop that application and then to take steps to terminate that squatter's adverse possession. However, if the registered proprietor of the estate or of a charge over that estate fails to take steps to do this within a reasonable period, the other policy objectives outlined in paragraph 14.54 come into play. As we explained in the Consultative Document—

> It is important that the marketability of land should be upheld, and if a registered proprietor fails to take steps to vindicate his or her title within two years of being given a clear warning to do so, we consider that it should be extinguished and that the squatter should obtain the land. Were this not so, possession and title could remain permanently out of kilter.[185]

---

[181] Law Com No 254, paras 10.6—10.10.

[182] *Ibid*, para 10.9. See above, para 14.2.

[183] Law Com No 254, para 10.6. However, as we pointed out there, that principle cannot be pressed too far. See too, above, para 2.71.

[184] Law Com No 254, para 10.7.

[185] *Ibid*, para 10.59.

14.56 Two years is a reasonable period to enable the registered proprietor or registered chargee[186] to take steps either to evict the squatter (or at least to start proceedings to do so) or to regularise his or her possession by negotiating a bilateral agreement under which he or she can stay as the proprietor's tenant or licensee.[187] It is possible that even where a squatter's possession ceases to be adverse because he or she becomes the tenant or licensee of the registered proprietor, it may, once again, become adverse at some future date.[188] If so, there is no reason why the squatter should not apply to be registered as proprietor once ten years' adverse possession have elapsed.

The right to make a further application to be registered

14.57 The Bill makes provision by which, where the registrar has rejected an application[189] by a squatter to be registered as proprietor, the squatter may re-apply in the three situations explained in the following paragraphs. In each case, the registrar *must* register the applicant as proprietor in place of the existing proprietor if he or she establishes those circumstances.[190]

WHERE THE SQUATTER REMAINS IN ADVERSE POSSESSION TWO YEARS AFTER THE REJECTION OF HIS APPLICATION TO BE REGISTERED

14.58 The first is if the squatter was in adverse possession from the date of his or her application to be registered until the end of the period of two years from the date on which his or her application was rejected.[191] This is likely to be the commonest situation. The registered proprietor[192] having objected to the squatter's application

---

[186] As we have explained above, a registered chargee, as mortgagee, has a right to possession and can therefore bring possession proceedings against a squatter: see para 14.33(2).

[187] There is one decision in the Court of Appeal that appears to hold that a landowner, X, can make a squatter, Y, his licensee unilaterally, simply by writing to Y and informing her that she is his licensee. Provided that Y does not write back to X to say that she is not his licensee, then she is: see *BP Properties Ltd v Buckler* (1987) 55 P & CR 337, 345 — 347. This decision has been criticised, rightly in our view: see Herbert Wallace "Limitation, Prescription and Unsolicited Permission" [1994] Conv 196. It appears to rest on the assumption (see 55 P & CR at 346), since discredited, that the paper owner's intentions can be relevant to whether a squatter's possession is adverse. However, it is now firmly settled that "it is the intention of the squatter that is decisive": *Buckinghamshire County Council v Moran* [1990] Ch 623, 644, *per* Nourse LJ. It is also difficult to reconcile with the subsequent decision of the Court of Appeal in *Mount Carmel Investments Ltd v Peter Thurlow Ltd* [1988] 1 WLR 1078. In that case, a letter sent by the paper owners to the squatters demanding that they vacate the premises by a specified date did not determine the squatter's adverse possession. Cf *Markfield Investments Ltd v Evans* [2001] 2 All ER 238, 241, [12], where Simon Brown LJ assumed the correctness of *BP Properties Ltd v Buckler* on this point. That assumption was, however, unnecessary for the decision in the case.

[188] Compare para 14.11 above. As we explain there, matters which would either postpone the limitation period (such as fraud, concealment or mistake) or cause it to run afresh (as with a written acknowledgment) have no application to our scheme.

[189] Under Schedule 6, para 1; above, para 14.20.

[190] Schedule 6, para 7.

[191] *Ibid*, para 6(1).

[192] Or other interested person.

for registration, fails thereafter to take any steps either to evict the squatter (by commencing possession proceedings) or otherwise to regularise his or her possession so that it is no longer adverse. This situation will also cover the case where the registered proprietor has commenced proceedings which have been discontinued or struck out,[193] all within the two year period.[194]

WHERE THE PROPRIETOR OBTAINS A JUDGMENT AGAINST THE SQUATTER BUT FAILS TO ENFORCE IT WITHIN TWO YEARS

14.59　The second situation in which the squatter is entitled to be registered is where the registered proprietor of the estate or some charge *does* commence possession proceedings against the squatter within two years of the rejection of the squatter's application, but then fails to take any steps to enforce the judgment within two years of obtaining it.[195] To establish this situation, the squatter will have to satisfy the registrar that—

(1)　he or she has been in adverse possession since the date of his or her application to be registered;[196]

(2)　the registered proprietor of the estate or of a charge over it has obtained judgment for possession against the squatter;

(3)　a further two years have elapsed since the date of that judgment; and

(4)　the judgment has not been enforced against the squatter.[197]

The Bill provides that, in those circumstances the judgment for possession ceases to be enforceable.[198]

14.60　The reasons for this second situation are fairly obvious. If the procedure is to bring about a decisive result,[199] it must not be possible to circumvent it by the simple expedient of bringing an action for possession and then not troubling to enforce it.[200] It should be noted that, but for these provisions, the registered proprietor of the estate or charge would have six years either to bring an action on the judgment for possession[201] or to execute the judgment without the leave of the

---

[193]　See below, para 14.62.

[194]　For the purposes of Schedule 6, the commencement of possession proceedings is disregarded in determining whether a period of limitation would run in the squatter's favour: Schedule 6, para 11(3)(b); above, para 14.23.

[195]　Cf Cl 97(4).

[196]　Which is unaffected by the commencement of the proceedings for these purposes: see Schedule 6, para 11(3)(b); above, para 14.23.

[197]　Schedule 6, para 6(2).

[198]　Cl 97(2), (4).

[199]　See above, para 14.6.

[200]　Were it to be otherwise, the squatter would be left in a legal limbo.

[201]　Limitation Act 1980, s 24(1); *Lowsley v Forbes* [1999] 1 AC 329 (the case was concerned with a charging order and garnishee proceedings, not possession proceedings).

court.[202] There is, therefore, an incentive for the registered proprietor of the estate or charge to ensure that any judgment for possession is enforced promptly.

WHERE PROCEEDINGS ARE DISCONTINUED OR STRUCK OUT MORE THAN TWO YEARS AFTER THE SQUATTER'S APPLICATION WAS REJECTED

14.61 The need to bring about a decisive result also underlies the third situation. This time, the registered proprietor of the estate or charge—

(1) commences proceedings against the squatter within two years of the rejection of the squatter's application for registration; but

(2) they are discontinued or struck out after the two year period referred to in (1) has elapsed.

In these circumstances, if the squatter has remained in adverse possession since he or she first applied to be registered as proprietor, he or she is entitled to apply once again to be registered.[203]

14.62 Under the Civil Procedure Rules—

(1) discontinuance is a formal step by which an action is brought to an end;[204] and

(2) the court has an unqualified discretion to strike out a case where there is a failure to comply with the time limits laid down by those Rules.[205]

As regards (2), the court's case management powers should mean that the long delays that occurred prior to the introduction of the Rules should be far less frequent. Occasions in which it will be appropriate to strike out for delay should therefore be less common.[206] Nevertheless, we anticipate that, in cases where a squatter's application to be registered has been rejected, a court would be likely to take a strict view of the need to comply with time limits laid down in the Civil Procedure Rules in any possession proceedings then brought by the registered proprietor or chargee. The purpose of our scheme is to bring about a decisive

---

[202] Under CPR, Schedule 1, R46.2(a); Schedule 2, C26.5.1(a), the leave of the court is needed to execute a judgment more than six years after it is given. As *Lowsley v Forbes* demonstrates, such leave may be given even though an action on the judgment would have been time-barred. However, the court will "not, in general, extend time beyond the six years save where it is demonstrably just to do so", and the onus of so proving rests on the party seeking to enforce the judgment: see *Duer v Frazer* [2001] 1 All ER 249, 255, *per* Evans-Lombe J.

[203] This follows from Schedule 6, para 6(2). Cf *ibid*, para 11(3)(b); above, para 14.23.

[204] See CPR, Part 38.

[205] See *Biguzzi v Rank Leisure Plc* [1999] 1 WLR 1926, 1932 and following.

[206] But they may occur: see *UCB Corporate Services Ltd v Halifax (SW) Ltd*, *The Times* 23 December 1999.

resolution as to the ownership of the land in dispute.[207] In fairness to the squatter, that resolution should also be expeditious.[208]

The status of a right to be registered

14.63 There are a number of situations under the Bill where a squatter acquires an indefeasible statutory right to be registered as proprietor in place of the registered proprietor. Some of these have been mentioned above, and others are explained below in relation to possession proceedings. The situations that have already been explained are where—

(1) no counter-notice is served in response to a squatter's application to be registered as proprietor;[209]

(2) the squatter establishes any one of the three exceptional cases in which he or she is entitled to be registered even though the registered proprietor (or other person) serves a counter-notice;[210]

(3) the squatter becomes entitled to re-apply to be registered as proprietor, even though his initial application was rejected.[211]

There will also be an entitlement to be registered where the squatter has a defence to any possession proceedings that are brought against him or her, or where the squatter barred the rights of the registered proprietor prior to the coming into force of the Act. These are explained below.[212]

14.64 The squatter's statutory right to be registered is, necessarily, a proprietary right. This is because it is a right to have a legal estate vested in him or her. Not only can it be asserted by the squatter against the registered proprietor, but if that proprietor transfers the registered estate to, or creates proprietary rights in favour of, a third party, it may be binding on that person as well. This will be the case where the squatter remains in actual occupation of the land and therefore has an overriding interest.[213]

---

[207] See above, para 14.6.

[208] This is why (for example) the registered proprietor will only have two years in which to enforce any judgment that he or she may obtain for possession: see above, para 14.59.

[209] Above, para 14.34.

[210] Above, para 14.36.

[211] Above, paras 14.57 and following.

[212] See paras 14.84 and following; and para 14.105.

[213] See Schedule 3, para 2; above, para 8.54. As we explain below, at para 14.66, a squatter has an independent fee simple from the moment that he or she enters into adverse possession. This fee simple, when coupled with the squatter's actual occupation, will constitute an overriding interest that could, therefore, bind any disponee of the land. However, such an overriding interest will be of little value to a squatter if the registered proprietor can terminate his or her adverse possession. That will be the case except where the squatter has a right to be registered.

330

The effect of registration

Introduction

14.65 A squatter may be registered as proprietor in place of the registered proprietor because—

    (1)   no counter-notice has been served on the registrar in response to his or her application to be registered;[214]

    (2)   there has been such a counter-notice, but the squatter—

        (a)   falls within one of the three exceptional cases which entitle him or her to be registered notwithstanding;[215] or

        (b)   is able to re-apply to be registered, because he or she has remained in adverse possession for the relevant period since the unsuccessful application for registration was made.[216]

To appreciate the effect of the registration of a squatter under the Bill, it is necessary to explain the legal background. Transitional provisions for cases where a squatter had barred the rights of the registered proprietor prior to the coming into force of the Bill are explained below.[217]

The legal background

14.66 Where title to land is unregistered, and the owner's title is extinguished by a squatter's adverse possession,[218] the squatter has the land not by any "Parliamentary conveyance" of the paper owner's legal estate,[219] but by virtue of the independent fee simple which every squatter has from the moment that he or she enters into adverse possession.[220] This is so, even though the title barred by such adverse possession is merely a leasehold estate.[221] The results of this are entirely logical, but their effect can appear strange. If a squatter has barred the estate of a leaseholder, the lease still remains in some kind of notional existence until it expires, is forfeited by the landlord for breach of covenant or is surrendered by the tenant whose rights the squatter has extinguished.[222] Although

---

[214] Schedule 6, para 4.

[215] *Ibid*, para 5. For those exceptions, see above, paras 14.36 and following.

[216] Schedule 6, para 7. For these situations, see above, paras 14.57 and following.

[217] See para 14.101.

[218] Under Limitation Act 1980, s 17.

[219] See *Tichborne v Weir* (1892) 67 LT 735.

[220] See *Rosenberg v Cook* (1881) 8 QBD 162, 165; *Central London Commercial Estates Ltd v Kato Kagaku Co Ltd* [1998] 4 All ER 948, 950.

[221] *Central London Commercial Estates Ltd v Kato Kagaku Co Ltd*, above, at p 950.

[222] For the right of the tenant to surrender the lease, even though his or her title has been extinguished by the squatter, see *Fairweather v St Marylebone Property Co Ltd* [1963] AC 510, a decision that remains controversial.

the squatter is neither bound by nor able to enforce the covenants contained in that lease, he or she must, in practice, submit to its obligations.[223] If he or she does not, the landlord may forfeit the lease[224] and can then recover the land from the squatter. This is because the estate against which the squatter had adversely possessed has terminated and the landlord is therefore entitled to immediate possession.

14.67   Where title is registered, the matter is very different. If a squatter has been in adverse possession for the limitation period, the Limitation Act 1980 cannot operate in the same way as it does where title is unregistered, and extinguish the proprietor's legal title.[225] While a person is the registered proprietor the legal estate necessarily remains vested in him or her. What happens instead is that the registered proprietor holds the estate on a bare trust for the squatter.[226] What the incidents of this trusteeship might be "are far from clear" and have yet to be judicially explored.[227] It has now been decided that the squatter is entitled to be registered as proprietor in place of and as successor in title to the registered proprietor.[228] The registration does, in other words, operate as a "Parliamentary conveyance". It appears that the independent fee simple that the squatter had by virtue of his or her adverse possession is in some way "nullified".[229] Because the squatter is successor in title to the former registered proprietor, it means (for example) that where the registered estate is leasehold, the benefit and burden of the covenants in the lease will pass. The squatter will therefore be directly subject to the burdens of the covenant but will, equally, be able to enforce covenants against the landlord.

The recommendations in the Consultative Document and the response on consultation

14.68   In the Consultative Document,[230] we proposed the following changes in the law—

---

[223] Such as paying the rent, or observing any repairing covenants.

[224] Assuming that it contains a right of re-entry as it almost certainly will.

[225] Cf Limitation Act 1980, s 17.

[226] Under Land Registration Act 1925, s 75.

[227] *Central London Commercial Estates Ltd v Kato Kagaku Co Ltd*, above, at p 959, *per* Sedley J. We are very grateful to Mr Edward Nugee QC, who, in correspondence with us, drew our attention to the considerable difficulties to which this trust could give rise.

[228] *Central London Commercial Estates Ltd v Kato Kagaku Co Ltd*, above. This has important implications, *eg* in relation to the transmission of covenants where the registered estate is leasehold.

[229] See *Central London Commercial Estates Ltd v Kato Kagaku Co Ltd*, above, at p 958, *per* Sedley J. At p 954, Sedley J commented that "a squatter on registered land is deprived by s 75(1) [of the Land Registration Act 1925] of his own prescriptive title... and is furnished instead with the right to acquire and register as his own the usurped leasehold title" [it was a leasehold title in that case]. This is no more than an inference from s 75: the section says nothing directly to this effect.

[230] See Law Com No 254, paras 10.70—10.76, 10.78.

(1) the trust should no longer be used as a means of giving effect to the rights of an adverse possessor who had barred the estate of the registered proprietor;

(2) where an adverse possessor was entitled to be registered as proprietor, he or she should be registered with an absolute, possessory or qualified title;

(3) where the title barred was that of a tenant under a lease—

  (a) the adverse possessor should normally be registered with a qualified freehold title;

  (b) the qualification should be that he or she took subject to the estate or interest of any person or persons entitled on the termination of the lease; and

(4) where the title barred was that of a tenant under a lease, the freehold (or other) title of any person entitled to the reversion on that or any superior lease should not be closed or otherwise affected by registration of the adverse possessor with a freehold title.

14.69 The effect of these recommendations would have been to bring the effect of adverse possession in registered land in line with those applicable to unregistered land. However, our recommendations were finalised before the judgment in *Central London Commercial Estates Ltd v Kato Kagaku Co Ltd*[231] had been given: the case came out as we were about to go to press. We did not, therefore, have time to give full consideration to its effects. It was clear from the responses to consultation, that although the logic of what we proposed was understood,[232] the result in the *Kato* decision was widely supported. The reason for this was that the decision accorded with expectations and produced an outcome that was neither artificial nor technical.[233] Thus, for example, if a person adversely possesses against a leaseholder, he or she expects to acquire that person's lease with the rights and burdens that go with it. In the light of this, we reconsidered our recommendations and took the decision in *Kato* as our guide.

---

[231] [1998] 4 All ER 948.

[232] Of those who responded in writing, a small majority supported our view. However, we were persuaded that we were wrong by the opposition to the proposals that were voiced by The Law Society, by members of the Association of Property Litigators and by many members of the Bar.

[233] The sort of objection that we received to our proposals was along the lines of "your client has barred the right of a leaseholder by adverse possession. You tell her that she actually has a freehold and not a leasehold title, but that if she does not observe the covenants (which do not bind her) in the lease (which she does not have), the landlord can evict her. You also have to explain that although she has a freehold title, when the lease terminates, the landlord can recover the land from her".

The provisions in the Bill

NO TRUST

14.70 The Bill abandons the device of the trust that is employed in the Land Registration Act 1925[234] as a means of giving effect to the rights of squatters, even under the transitional provisions.[235] We criticised the device of the trust in the Consultative Document as being unnecessary.[236] On consultation, not only was our view unanimously endorsed, but we also received some very helpful comments from senior members of the Chancery Bar about the problems to which the trust could give rise. As we have explained, the circumstances in which a squatter will be *entitled* to be registered as proprietor under the Bill will be very limited.[237] Where there is such a right, the squatter will be adequately protected against third parties provided that he or she is in actual occupation of the land in question. His or her proprietary rights[238] will then constitute an overriding interest.[239]

THE SQUATTER IS SUCCESSOR IN TITLE TO THE PREVIOUS PROPRIETOR

14.71 When a squatter's application for registration is successful for any of the reasons explained above,[240] the registrar will register him or her as the new proprietor of the estate against which he or she adversely possessed.[241] The squatter will, therefore, be the successor in title to the previous registered proprietor.[242] The fee simple absolute in possession which the squatter has hitherto had by virtue of his or her adverse possession will be expressly extinguished.[243]

14.72 Registration of the squatter as proprietor will carry with it the extinction of any claims that the former registered proprietor might have had against the squatter for damages for trespass or to recover rent. This is by analogy with the rule[244] applicable to cases where title to land is extinguished by adverse possession under section 17 of the Limitation Act 1980—

---

[234] Section 75.

[235] See below, para 14.105.

[236] See Law Com No 254, paras 10.40 and following.

[237] See above, para 14.65.

[238] Namely, the fee simple absolute in possession which the squatter has by virtue of his or her adverse possession, and his or her right to be registered as proprietor to which the existing registered proprietor cannot object.

[239] See Schedule 3, para 2; above, para 8.54.

[240] See para 14.65.

[241] See Schedule 6, paras 1(1), 4, 7.

[242] Where the property is a lease which was granted after 1995, the registration of the squatter as the new proprietor will operate as an "excluded assignment" under the Landlord and Tenant (Covenants) Act 1995, s 11. This is one case under that Act where the former tenant will remain liable on the covenants of the lease.

[243] Schedule 6, para 9(1).

[244] Laid down in *Re Jolly* [1900] 2 Ch 616.

When title to land is extinguished by the statute, the rights which that title carried must also be extinguished.[245]

The claim to mesne profits or rent is dependent on the claimant showing that he or she was entitled to possession as against the squatter. Once the squatter has been registered, the former registered proprietor is unable to do that.[246]

14.73 As a general principle,[247] the registration of the squatter as proprietor will not affect the priority of any interest affecting the registered estate.[248] He or she will, therefore, take the land subject to the same estates, rights and interests that bound the previous proprietor.

REGISTRATION OF THE SQUATTER AND THE EFFECT ON REGISTERED CHARGES

14.74 To this general principle there is one significant exception. We have explained above that, where a squatter applies to be registered, not only the registered proprietor but also any registered chargee will be given the opportunity to object.[249] Furthermore, if objection is made, a registered chargee is entitled to take possession proceedings against the squatter to recover the land (even if the proprietor of the registered estate does not) because, as mortgagee, it has a right to possession of the land.[250] Given that the registered chargee has the same opportunity and right as the registered proprietor to prevent the squatter from acquiring title to the land by adverse possession, any squatter who is registered under the relevant provisions of the Bill[251] should take the land free from the charge. The Bill so provides.[252] The registered chargee will not lose its charge if the squatter's application to be registered succeeds notwithstanding the objection by the registered proprietor or the registered chargee. This will be the case where the squatter shows that he or she falls within one of the three exceptional situations, explained above,[253] where this may happen.[254]

14.75 The policies that underlie this exception are twofold. First, as is mentioned in paragraph 14.74, a registered chargee is as well placed as the registered proprietor to stop the squatter from acquiring title to the registered estate. It would be illogical if the registered proprietor lost his or her estate, but the registered chargee could continue to be able to assert its charge against the squatter.

---

[245] *Mount Carmel Investments Ltd v Peter Thurlow Ltd* [1988] 1 WLR 1078, 1089, *per* Nicholls LJ.

[246] *Ibid.*

[247] But see below, para 14.74.

[248] Schedule 6, para 9(2).

[249] See para 14.33.

[250] See above, para 14.56.

[251] Namely, Schedule 6, paras 4 or 7.

[252] Schedule 6, para 9(3).

[253] See paras 14.36—14.52.

[254] For the position where the squatter is registered subject to the charge, see below, paras 14.76 and following.

Secondly, it means that there is a "clean break". The squatter acquires the land unencumbered by any registered charge. This will necessarily facilitate any dealings which he or she may wish to make with the land, and so promote one of our aims,[255] namely, that the land should remain in commerce,[256] whether the title to the land is retained by the registered proprietor or is acquired by the squatter.

WHERE THE SQUATTER WILL BE BOUND BY CHARGES

14.76　There will be rare cases, however, where a squatter *is* bound by a charge over land. That will be so in two situations. The first is where the squatter is registered as proprietor notwithstanding that the registered proprietor or chargee has objected, because the facts fall within one of the three exceptions explained above.[257] Even in some of these cases, the squatter's independent right that justifies his or her registration as proprietor will take priority over the registered charge so that he or she will in fact take free of it.[258] The second situation is where the charge is not a registered charge, but is (for example) a charging order. Once again, such a charge will not necessarily bind the squatter: his or her independent right may precede and therefore take priority over it.[259] Where a squatter is bound by a charge, a practical problem can arise, and we have concluded that the law should be changed to deal with it as set out in the following paragraphs.

APPORTIONMENT

14.77　Under the present law, where there is a charge over a parcel of land, part of which has been acquired by a squatter by adverse possession, that charge will be binding on the squatter.[260] However, if the squatter wants to redeem that mortgage in order, say, to sell the land, he or she will have to pay the full amount of the debt. This is because—

---

[255]　See para 14.6(2).

[256]　Cf para 14.78, below. It is the practice of the Land Registry when a squatter applies to be registered as proprietor under Land Registration Act 1925, s 75, to approach any registered chargee to enquire whether it will release any charge affecting the land. In many cases the chargee agrees to such a release.

[257]　See paras 14.36—14.52.

[258]　This will generally be so if that right was created before the charge and the squatter was in actual occupation of the land at the time when the registered charge was created, so that his or her rights took effect as an overriding interest: see Schedule 3, para 2; above, para 8.54.

[259]　Cf Cl 28; above, para 5.5.

[260]　See Land Registration Act 1925, s 75(3). As we have explained, where a squatter is registered, any registered chargee is normally contacted by HM Land Registry to see whether it will release its charge as against the squatter. Although the squatter is bound by the charge over the land, he or she does not become subject to the personal covenant in the mortgage by which the mortgagor undertakes to repay the mortgage debt.

the general rule applies that anyone entitled to redeem even if in right of part of the mortgaged property, can do so only upon payment of the full amount of the debt and the interest secured.[261]

14.78 The squatter who pays the charge on the whole will be subrogated to the mortgage in so far as it relates to the other land of the mortgagor. This is on the principle that "where a third party pays off a mortgage he is presumed, unless the contrary appears, to intend that the mortgage shall be kept alive for his own benefit".[262] However, that right of subrogation is likely to be of little practical assistance to a squatter who has, say, acquired title by adverse possession to a small portion of a large estate[263] that is mortgaged for a substantial sum. It will mean that the portion acquired by adverse possession will in practice be unsaleable. This conflicts with our aim of seeking to ensure that land remains in commerce. If, under our scheme, a squatter does manage to acquire title to the land (which is not likely to be very often), we wish to ensure that he or she is in a position to dispose of the land freely.

14.79 To meet this concern, the Bill makes provision by which, where a squatter is registered as proprietor under our scheme, but the land in question is subject to a charge that is binding on him or her,[264] he or she may require the chargee to apportion the charge.[265] Apportionment is to be on the basis of—

   (1) the respective values of the parcels of land subject to the charge; and

   (2) the amount of the mortgage debt at the time when the squatter requires the chargee to make the apportionment.[266]

14.80 There is, inevitably, a somewhat arbitrary element in this approach. The amount of the debt may fluctuate if, for example, the mortgage secures an overdraft on a running account. There will, in such a case, be an element of fortuity as to the date when the squatter applies for an apportionment, particularly as he or she is unlikely to be aware of the state of accounts between the mortgagee and the

---

[261] *Carroll v Manek* (1999) 79 P & CR 173, 188, *per* Judge Hicks, QC, citing *Hall v Heward* (1886) 32 ChD 430 for the general rule. In that latter case, Cotton LJ explained at pp 434—435 that "[t]he owner of the equity of redemption in one of two estates comprised in the same mortgage cannot claim to redeem that estate alone. The mortgagee might refuse to allow him to do so. So on the other hand, the mortgagee cannot compel him to redeem that estate alone — he is entitled to redeem the whole, reserving the equities between him and the other part owner".

[262] *Ghana Commercial Bank v Chandiram* [1960] AC 732, 745, *per* Lord Jenkins.

[263] The common case will be where the squatter owns the adjoining land and encroaches on part of his or her neighbour's land, incorporating it into his or her own title. The squatter then seeks to sell his or her own land, together with the parcel acquired by adverse possession.

[264] Whether that charge is a registered charge or merely a minor interest.

[265] Schedule 6, para 10.

[266] *Ibid*, para 10(1).

mortgagor. However, it is not easy to see on what other basis any apportionment could be made.

14.81 The person who requires the apportionment is entitled to have his or her estate discharged from the charge if he or she pays the amount apportioned to that estate together with the chargee's costs in making the apportionment.[267] On payment, the liability of the mortgagor to the mortgagee will be reduced accordingly.[268]

Possession proceedings

Introduction

14.82 In many cases, the issue of whether a squatter has acquired title to registered land by adverse possession does not arise on application by that squatter to be registered as proprietor. It is raised instead in possession proceedings brought by the registered proprietor (or by a registered chargee[269]) to recover the land. It is therefore necessary to ensure that, in relation to such proceedings, the position of a squatter mirrors that which applies in relation to an application for registration.

The general rule: the registered proprietor is entitled to possession as against the squatter

14.83 The general rule is, therefore, that if the registered proprietor or registered chargee brings proceedings for the recovery of land in the possession of a squatter, those proceedings will succeed, regardless of how long the squatter has been in adverse possession. Under our scheme, as we have explained, the rights of the registered proprietor are not barred by lapse of time.[270] To this general rule there are, necessarily, exceptions.

Exceptions: defences to possession proceedings

DEFENCES WHICH ARE UNCONNECTED WITH THE SQUATTER'S ADVERSE POSSESSION

14.84 In any possession proceedings, a squatter who has a defence to the action that is unconnected with his or her adverse possession, will be able to rely upon it just as he or she can now.[271] In other words, if the squatter has some independent right to possession of the land, he or she is entitled to raise it by way of defence. If, for example, he or she had entered into possession under a contract to purchase the land and had paid the purchase price, so that the registered proprietor held the land on a bare trust for him or her, that would, as now, be a defence to possession

---

[267] *Ibid*, para 10(2).

[268] *Ibid*, para 10(3). It is anticipated that the *mortgagor* will be entitled to be reimbursed by the squatter for any costs that he or she incurs in the course of the making of the apportionment, because rules may be made to this effect: *ibid*, para 10(4)(d).

[269] See above, para 14.33(2).

[270] Cl 95; above, para 14.9.

[271] Cl 97(6). Cf Schedule 6, para 5(3); above, para 14.43.

proceedings brought by the proprietor.[272] Similarly, if the squatter had an equity arising in his or her favour by proprietary estoppel, he or she could raise that equity as a defence in possession proceedings.[273]

OTHER DEFENCES

14.85 The squatter will have certain new defences under the Bill that *are* connected with his or her adverse possession. These mirror the grounds on which he or she will be entitled to be registered as proprietor.

Reasonable mistake as to boundary

14.86 First, it is to be a defence to possession proceedings that the squatter had been in adverse possession of land adjacent to his or her own for 10 years under the mistaken but reasonable belief that he or she was the owner of it, and was entitled to be registered as proprietor of it under Schedule 6, paragraph 5(4).[274]

Where the squatter has become entitled to be registered even though his or her application to be registered was rejected

14.87 Secondly, as we have explained, there will be situations where a squatter, who had been in adverse possession for 10 years and whose application to be registered as proprietor under Schedule 6, paragraph 1, has been rejected, nonetheless becomes entitled to be registered because—

(1) neither the registered proprietor nor the registered chargee took steps to terminate the squatter's adverse possession within two years of that rejection and during that period he or she remained in adverse possession;[275]

(2) although the proprietor or chargee obtained a judgment against the squatter he or she failed to enforce it within two years;[276]

(3) although the proprietor or chargee brought possession proceedings, these were discontinued or struck out more than two years after the squatter's application had been rejected.[277]

If, in any of these situations, the registered proprietor or a registered chargee were to bring proceedings (or, as the case may be, fresh proceedings) for possession, the squatter would have a defence to them.[278] In such circumstances, the court would

---

[272] Cf *Bridges v Mees* [1957] Ch 475, where, in the face of a claim to possession by the registered proprietor, the squatter-buyer sought a declaration that he was entitled to the land.

[273] There is, therefore, no need for any equivalent to Schedule 6, para 5(2); above, para 14.39.

[274] Cl 97(1). See above, paras 14.44—14.52.

[275] See above, para 14.58.

[276] See above, para 14.59.

[277] See above, para 14.61.

[278] Cl 97(3).

be required to order the registrar to register the squatter as proprietor of the estate in respect of which he or she has been in adverse possession.[279] Furthermore, as regards situation (2) above, the Bill renders any judgment unenforceable two years after it was obtained.[280]

Special cases

14.88 There are three special cases of adverse possession for which the Bill makes provision, namely rentcharges, trusts and Crown foreshore.

Rentcharges

14.89 Under the provisions of the Limitation Act 1980,[281] the rights of an owner of a rentcharge[282] are barred in two cases[283]—

(1) *Where no rent is paid for 12 years.* The consequence of this is that the rentcharge is then extinguished.

(2) *Where the rent is paid to a third party for 12 years.*[284] In such a case, the rentcharge can still be enforced against the land. However, the previous owner's title to the rentcharge is extinguished and the third party becomes entitled to it instead.

14.90 Under the Bill, it is intended to make provision by rule which will apply to rentcharges the scheme that has been explained in this Part, with such modifications and exceptions as those rules may provide.[285] This is considered to be the most appropriate way of dealing with rentcharges for the following reasons. First, the necessary provisions are likely to be technical and of a length that is disproportionate to their comparative unimportance. Secondly, the incidence of rentcharges tends to be rather localised.[286] Thirdly, most rentcharges will terminate in 2037,[287] which, given the infrequency with which statutes on property law tend to be revisited, may occur within the lifetime of the present Bill.

---

[279] Cl 97(5)(a). The effects of such registration have already been explained: see above, paras 14.70 and following.

[280] Cl 97(4). But for this provision, the judgment would be enforceable for six years: see above, para 14.60.

[281] The relevant provisions are section 38(8) and Schedule 1, Part 1, para 8(3)(a).

[282] See Limitation Act 1980, s 38(1), for the definition of "rentcharge".

[283] See *Megarry & Wade's Law of Real Property* (6th ed 2000), 21-034.

[284] Which will, no doubt, occur because the person paying the charge was under the mistaken belief that the payee was entitled to the rent when he or she was not.

[285] Cl 97(7); Schedule 6, para 14.

[286] They are most common in Greater Manchester, Lancashire, Sunderland and Bristol.

[287] See the Rentcharges Act 1977, ss 2, 3.

Trusts

ADVERSE POSSESSION BY A STRANGER OF LAND HELD IN TRUST

14.91 The application of the new scheme to land held in trust[288] has caused us some difficulty.[289] Under the present law, *equitable* interests under trusts as well as legal estates may be barred by adverse possession.[290] However, the *legal* estate of the tenant for life or the trustees of land (as the case may be) is not extinguished by adverse possession until all the equitable interests under the trust have been successively barred.[291] Where there are successive interests under the settlement or trust, the squatter must therefore bar each equitable interest *seriatim* before he or she can claim the legal estate. In accordance with this rule, the registrar will not register as proprietor[292] a squatter who has adversely possessed against a tenant for life under the Settled Land Act 1925.[293] It is only where the registrar is satisfied that *all* beneficial interests under the settlement have been barred that the squatter will be so registered.

14.92 The manner in which the Bill deals with the adverse possession of registered land that is held in trust is necessarily different from the approach adopted in the Limitation Act 1980 because it rests on different principles.

(1) The essence of the new scheme of adverse possession in the Bill is that a squatter can apply to be registered as proprietor of a *registered estate* in place of the existing registered proprietor, and will be registered in the limited circumstances that have been described in this Part.

(2) Because the effluxion of time does not of itself have any effect, there can be no concept in our scheme of the barring of the rights of those with merely *equitable* interests in land.

(3) Where a squatter *is* registered as proprietor under the scheme, it is with the same estate as, and as successor in title to, the previous registered proprietor.[294]

However, the solution adopted in the Bill shares the same objective as the provisions of the Limitation Act 1980, namely, that where there are successive

---

[288] Whether there is a trust of land or a settlement made under the Settled Land Act 1925.

[289] Cf Law Com No 254, para 10.77.

[290] Limitation Act 1980, s 18(1).

[291] Cf Law Com No 254, para 10.26, where the detailed rules laid down in Limitation Act 1980, s 18, are explained.

[292] Under Land Registration Act 1925, s 75.

[293] The tenant for life is the registered proprietor: see Land Registration Act 1925, s 86(1).

[294] As we have explained above, at paras 14.68—14.69, this marks a departure from what we proposed in Law Com No 254 as to effect of registering the squatter as proprietor. Our proposals in relation to adverse possession of land held in trust for successive interests in the Consultative Document (see Law Com No 254, paras 10.77—10.78) were premised on what we recommended in Law Com No 254 as to the effect of registration. We have therefore had to abandon them and devise a scheme that accords with our revised policy.

interests, adverse possession by a squatter should not prejudice the rights of beneficiaries who are not yet entitled in possession.

14.93 Under the Bill, for the purposes of our scheme on adverse possession,[295] a squatter will not be regarded as being in adverse possession at any time when a registered estate is held in trust, as long as there are successive interests in the land. It is only where the interest of each of the beneficiaries in the estate is an interest in possession that a squatter can commence such adverse possession.[296] The operation of this provision can best be illustrated by an example.

> Land is held on a trust of land for A for life, thereafter for B for life, thereafter for C absolutely. S, a squatter goes into adverse possession of the land during A's lifetime and remains there. For as long as either A or B are alive, S will be unable to apply to be registered as proprietor of the land under Schedule 6, paragraph 1.[297] Indeed, it is only 10 years after C's interest has fallen into possession[298] that S can make such an application. This is because S is not regarded as being in adverse possession for the purposes of Schedule 6 until C, the remainderman, becomes entitled to the land. It follows that S will have no defence under the Bill[299] to any possession proceedings brought by the trustees during the lifetimes of A and B, or ten years thereafter.

14.94 The approach adopted in the Bill will make it very difficult for a squatter to acquire title to land held on trust for successive interests. However, it is not easy under the present law. The effect of the provisions of the Limitation Act 1980 is that although S might bar A's equitable interest after 12 years' adverse possession, B's would not be barred until 12 years after S took adverse possession against A or six years after B's interest fell into possession on A's death, whichever was later.[300] Similarly, C's interest — and the trustees' legal estate[301] — would not be extinguished until 12 years after S took adverse possession against B[302] or six years after C's interest fell into possession on B's death, whichever was later. The difficulty which the squatter faces under both the Limitation Act 1980 and the Bill is an inevitable consequence of the need to protect those with future interests against squatters.

ADVERSE POSSESSION BY A TRUSTEE OR BENEFICIARY OF LAND HELD IN TRUST

14.95 Under the Limitation Act 1980—

---

[295] Summarised above, in para 14.5.

[296] Schedule 6, para 12.

[297] See above, para 14.20.

[298] On the death of A or B, whichever is the last to die.

[299] S can raise any defence that he or she may have that is unconnected with his or her adverse possession.

[300] See Limitation Act 1980, s 15(2).

[301] See Limitation Act 1980, s 18.

[302] Which, in our example, would be on the date on which A died.

(1) there is no limitation period applicable to claims by a beneficiary to recover trust property from a trustee;[303] and

(2) the possession of a beneficiary under a trust of land or settlement is—

    (a) never adverse to that of the trustee or trustees[304] unless and until he is absolutely entitled to the land under the trust; and

    (b) never adverse to that of any other beneficiary under the trust.[305]

14.96 The practical effect of these provisions is transposed into the scheme of the Bill. In other words, neither a trustee nor a beneficiary (other than a beneficiary who is absolutely entitled) will ever be able to—

(1) apply to be registered as proprietor under Schedule 6, paragraph 1; or

(2) resist proceedings to recover possession.

This is because neither would be in adverse possession for the purposes of Schedule 6 of the Bill.[306]

Crown foreshore

14.97 It is necessary in the Bill to make special provision for the foreshore which belongs to the Crown.[307] This may seem puzzling because, at present, little if any such land is likely to be registered land. Most of the foreshore is held by the Crown in demesne, in other words in its capacity as paramount feudal lord[308] and not for an estate in fee simple. We explain more fully elsewhere in this Report that—

(1) because only an estate can be registered, the Crown cannot be registered as proprietor of land that it holds in demesne;[309] but

(2) the Bill makes provision by which the Crown may grant to itself a fee simple out of land held in demesne in order to register it.[310]

In this way it will become possible for the Crown to register Crown foreshore. We understand from our discussions with the Crown Estate that it is likely to avail

---

[303] See s 21(1)(b).

[304] There may be a single trustee of the legal estate where the land is settled land, namely the life tenant. He will be the registered proprietor: see Land Registration Act 1925, s 86(1).

[305] Limitation Act 1980, Schedule 1, para 9.

[306] This follows from Schedule 6, para 11(1).

[307] "Foreshore" is defined by Schedule 6, para 13(3) to mean "the shore and bed of the sea and of any tidal water, below the line of the medium high tide between the spring and neap tides". For the application of the Bill to land covered by internal waters, see Cl 127; above, para 3.5.

[308] What Coke called "*dominium directum*": see *Coke on Littleton*, 1a.

[309] See para 11.8.

[310] See para 11.11

itself of these provisions so as to protect vulnerable areas of the foreshore from the encroachments of squatters.[311] There is, therefore, a real prospect that there may in time be substantial areas of Crown foreshore that are registered land.

14.98   Under the Limitation Act 1980, the limitation period for the recovery of foreshore by the Crown[312] is 60 years or, where land has ceased to be foreshore but remains in the ownership of the Crown,[313] either 60 years from the date of the accrual of the cause of action, or 30 years from the date on which the land ceased to be foreshore, whichever period expires first.[314] The practical problem in relation to adverse possession of the foreshore is that it is very difficult for the Crown to monitor the very substantial areas of foreshore which it holds, to ensure that there are no persons in adverse possession of it. The present 60-year limitation period reflects this difficulty.

14.99   One of the commonest situations in which adverse possession of the foreshore takes place is where the adjoining landowner encroaches on it, as by building a jetty or slipway on the foreshore. Under the scheme explained in this Part, a registered proprietor will usually be in a position to prevent a squatter from acquiring title to his or her registered estate. However, one situation in which that will not be the case is in relation to land which is adjacent to the squatter's and where the squatter reasonably believed that the land belonged to him or her.[315] There is, therefore, a risk that an owner of land adjoining foreshore the title to which has been registered by the Crown, might sometimes be able to acquire title to that foreshore under this exception, notwithstanding the Crown's objection.

14.100   The Bill meets this point by requiring that a squatter be in adverse possession for 60 years instead of 10 years before he or she can apply to be registered in place of the Crown as proprietor of any foreshore under the scheme explained in this Part.[316] Where land ceases to be foreshore, the squatter may apply to be registered after he or she has been in adverse possession for a period of either—

(1)   60 years; or

(2)   10 years from the time when the land ceased to be foreshore;

---

[311]   Which are regrettably common.

[312]   Or Her Majesty in right of the Duchy of Lancaster, or the Duchy of Cornwall.

[313]   Normally land ceases to be foreshore by reason of accretion. If that is so, ownership of the accretion usually passes to the person who owns the land to which the accretion took place. If, therefore, the Crown owns the adjoining land, it will generally acquire the accretion, but not otherwise. For the law on accretion, see generally *Southern Centre of Theosophy Inc v State of Australia* [1982] AC 706; above, para 9.14.

[314]   Schedule 1, Part 2, para 11.

[315]   See Schedule 6, para 5(4); above, paras 14.44—14.52.

[316]   Schedule 6, para 13(1).

whichever is the shorter.[317] This approach ensures that land which ceases to be foreshore is treated in the same way as any other registered estate.

Transitional provisions

14.101 It is necessary to make transitional provisions to accommodate the very substantial changes to the law that the Bill will make, and to ensure that vested rights are preserved.

Introducing the new system

14.102 The provisions of the Bill involve a transition from a world in which there is a 12 year limitation period to one in which there is no limitation period as such, but where it is possible for a squatter to be registered as proprietor after 10 years' adverse possession. In most cases, the fact that the squatter might acquire title after only 10 years rather than 12 does not matter. The registered proprietor can stop the squatter from acquiring title by objecting to his or her application for registration. In the exceptional cases where the squatter relies upon an equity arising by proprietary estoppel or has some independent right to be registered, so that the registered proprietor's objection will not prevent the squatter from being registered, that proprietor is in the same position under the Bill as he or she is under the present law. The squatter had a right to be registered apart from his or her adverse possession. In one case, however, the provisions of the Bill could prejudice the rights of the registered proprietor. This is in relation to the case where a squatter is entitled to be registered because he or she reasonably but mistakenly believed him or herself to be the owner of the land under Schedule 6, paragraph 5(4). A squatter might find that he or she was entitled to be registered as proprietor of the land on this basis on the day that the legislation is brought into force, even though he or she had only been in adverse possession after 10 years and, the day before, the registered proprietor could have successfully initiated possession proceedings against him. It is therefore necessary to make transitional provision to cover this one case.

14.103 The provisions of the Bill are to be brought into force by order.[318] What it is proposed to do is to bring Schedule 6, paragraph 5(4), into force one year after the rest of Schedule 6. This means that registered proprietors will have one year from the coming into force of the rest of the Bill to take proceedings against any squatter who might fall within paragraph 5(4) or otherwise regularise his or her position so that he or she is no longer in adverse possession. It follows from this that there are no provisions as such in the Bill to deal with this problem.

Preserving vested rights

14.104 The Bill necessarily contains provisions to protect the rights of squatters who, prior to the coming into force of the Bill, had become entitled to be registered as proprietor of an estate under the provisions of section 75 of the Land Registration Act 1925, but who had not been registered. Immediately prior to the coming into

---

[317] This states the effect of Schedule 6, para 13(2).

[318] See Cl 133(2).

force of the Bill, the registered proprietor will hold the registered estate on a bare trust for the squatter under section 75. We have explained above[319] that the incidents of this trust are far from clear, and that it could give rise to considerable difficulties. The Bill therefore adopts a double strategy. It preserves the rights of those who are entitled to be registered prior to its coming into force, but it also abolishes the trust in their favour.

14.105 The trust is abolished by the repeal without replication of section 75 of the Land Registration Act 1925. Instead, the Bill confers on a squatter who is a beneficiary under a trust under section 75 immediately before it comes into force an entitlement to be registered.[320] That entitlement will necessarily be a proprietary right,[321] so that the squatter will be able to protect it against third parties as an overriding interest, provided that he or she is in actual occupation.[322] It will also constitute a defence to any proceedings for possession.[323] If a squatter does establish this defence in such proceedings, the court must order the registrar to register him or her as proprietor of the estate to which his or her entitlement relates.[324]

---

[319] See para 14.67.

[320] Schedule 12, para 18(1). Transitional provisions for rentcharges held in trust under Land Registration Act 1925, s 75, will be made by rules: see Schedule 12, para 18(4).

[321] See above, para 14.64.

[322] See Schedule 3, para 2; above, para 8.54.

[323] Schedule 12, para 18(2).

[324] Schedule 12, para 18(3).

PART XV
THE LAND REGISTRY

INTRODUCTION

15.1 The provisions of the Bill relating to HM Land Registry itself are to be found in Part 10 and Schedule 7 of the Bill. Except in relation to judicial matters, which are explained in Part XVI of this Report, the position of the Registry is not changed in any very material respect by the Bill.

THE LAND REGISTRY

15.2 The Bill makes provision for the continuance of the HM Land Registry which is to deal with the business of registration under the Bill.[1] The land registry is to consist of the Chief Land Registrar ("the registrar" for the purposes of the Bill[2]), who is its head, and the staff of the registry who are to be appointed by him[3] on such terms and conditions as he, with the approval of the Minister for the Civil Service, thinks fit.[4] The Chief Land Registrar is himself to be appointed by the Lord Chancellor,[5] and the Bill makes provision dealing with the Chief Land Registrar's resignation, removal, re-appointment and remuneration.[6]

15.3 At present, the office of Chief Land Registrar is not a disqualifying office for the purpose of membership of the House of Commons or the Northern Ireland Assembly. This is considered to be inappropriate, and the Bill amends the House of Commons Disqualification Act 1975 and the Northern Ireland Assembly Disqualification Act 1975 accordingly.[7]

15.4 Following the model of the Land Registration Act 1925,[8] the Bill protects any member of the land registry from a claim in damages for any act or omission in the discharge or purported discharge of any function relating to land registration, unless it is shown that the act or omission was in bad faith.[9]

---

[1] Cl 98(1). Cf Land Registration Act 1925, s 127(1). The registry is to continue to have a seal and any document purporting to be sealed with it is to be admissible in evidence without any further proof: Schedule 7, para 5. This replicates the effect of Land Registration Act 1925, s 126(7).

[2] See Cl 129(1).

[3] Cl 98(2).

[4] Schedule 7, para 3.

[5] Cl 98(3).

[6] Cl 98(4); Schedule 7, paras 1, 2.

[7] Schedule 7, para 7.

[8] See s 131.

[9] Schedule 7, para 4.

CONDUCT OF BUSINESS

15.5   Any function of the Chief Land Registrar may be carried out by any member of the land registry who is authorised for the purpose by the registrar.[10] There is power for the Lord Chancellor by regulations to make provision about the carrying out of the registrar's functions during any vacancy in the office.[11]

15.6   The land registry operates through a series of district registries.[12] There is power for the Lord Chancellor by order to designate a particular office of the land registry as the proper office for the receipt of applications or a specified description of applications.[13] This means that a particular district land registry can be designated to receive applications from particular areas of England and Wales (as happens now), or indeed a specific type of application. It would (for example) be possible to designate one particular registry to deal with applications by the Crown to register its demesne land under Clause 79.[14]

15.7   The registrar is empowered to prepare and publish such forms and directions as he considers necessary or desirable for facilitating the conduct of the business of registration under the Bill.[15] This replicates an existing power[16] which has been used for a variety of matters, such as giving guidance as to how to conduct official searches of the register by fax and telephone, and prescribing the conditions of use of the registry's direct access service.[17] The Bill makes provision so that such forms and directions are admissible in evidence under the Documentary Evidence Act 1868.[18]

ANNUAL REPORT

15.8   The Bill requires the registrar to publish an annual report on the business of the land registry to the Lord Chancellor,[19] who must in turn lay copies of each of them before Parliament.[20]

[10]   Cl 99(1).

[11]   Cl 99(2). This replicates the effect of Land Registration Act 1925, s 126(6). For the present regulations, see Ruoff & Roper, *Registered Conveyancing*, E-01—E-03.

[12]   There are presently 24. For the administrative area covered by each district land registry, see Land Registration (District Registries) Order 2000; Ruoff & Roper, *Registered Conveyancing*, E-41—E-43.

[13]   Cl 99(3). Cf Land Registration Act 1925, s 132 (which presently governs district land registries). The order is required to be made by statutory instrument, to be laid before Parliament only: see Cl 125(3)(d).

[14]   See above, para 11.11.

[15]   Cl 99(4).

[16]   See Land Registration Act 1925, s 127.

[17]   The relevant directions are collected in Ruoff & Roper, *Registered Conveyancing*, Appendix F.

[18]   Schedule 7, para 6.

[19]   Cl 100(1).

[20]   Cl 100(3).

FEES

15.9 The Bill replaces the existing powers to charge fees[21] with a simpler provision. The Bill provides[22] that the Lord Chancellor may, by order, with the advice and assistance of the Rule Committee,[23] and the consent of the Treasury—

(1) prescribe fees to be paid in respect of dealings with the land registry (subject to one exception explained below[24]); and

(2) make provision about the payment of prescribed fees.[25]

Furthermore, the power to make a fee order includes the power to make different provision for different cases under the general provision of the Bill.[26]

15.10 Unlike the present provisions, the Bill does not prescribe the method for assessing fees.[27] It is in fact likely that the method of assessment may change from its present basis.

MISCELLANEOUS FUNCTIONS

Power to publish information about land

15.11 The registrar is empowered by the Bill to publish information about land in England and Wales if it appears to him to be information in which there is a legitimate public interest.[28] The registrar already publishes data about changes in property prices on a quarterly basis, and these are widely used. Because all sales of freehold land are required to be registered the Registry's figures are the most accurate available. It will doubtless become possible to publish further information that can be ascertained either from the register itself or from applications for registration.

Consultancy and advisory services

15.12 The registrar is given power by the Bill to provide consultancy or advisory services about the registration of land in England and Wales or elsewhere. The terms on which he provides such services, including in particular the terms of payment, are such as the registrar thinks fit.[29] The registrar will, in other words, have a free hand

---

[21] See Land Registration Act 1925, s 145; Land Registration Act 1936, s 7.

[22] See Cl 101.

[23] For the Rule Committee and its functions, see Cl 124; below, paras 17.6—17.8.

[24] See Cl 104; below, para 15.12.

[25] As now, an order prescribing fees is not made by statutory instrument: see Cl 101(b).

[26] See Cl 125(1). This, in the context of fee orders, replicates the effect of Land Registration Act 1925, s 145(3A) (which was inserted by Land Registration Act 1997, s 3).

[27] Which, as regards the registration of an estate, is presently determined by the value of the land registered rather than by the amount of work that the transaction entails: see Land Registration Act 1925, s 145(1).

[28] Cl 103.

[29] Cl 104.

to negotiate such fees as the amount of such charges will not be prescribed by fee order.[30] This power will enable the registrar to offer consultancy services both within England and Wales and elsewhere. In particular, it is likely that his expertise may be in demand in relation to the development of electronic registration systems in other countries.

---

[30] See Cl 101(a); above, para 15.9.

PART XVI
JUDICIAL PROVISIONS

INTRODUCTION

16.1 In this Part we explain the judicial provisions contained in the Bill. These differ in a number of respects from the present law and practice. In particular, the Bill creates a new office, that of Adjudicator to HM Land Registry, that is independent of the Registry. The function of the Adjudicator is to determine any contested application to the registrar that cannot be disposed of by agreement between the parties.[1] At present, this function is performed by the Solicitor to HM Land Registry, who is the senior lawyer in the Registry. Notwithstanding that he adjudicates only in disputes between parties and not those involving the Registry, issues can still arise in such cases which involve the decisions of officials of the Registry. There could therefore be a perception that he is not sufficiently independent.[2] As a matter of principle, it is desirable to create a completely independent office for adjudication. The great merits of the present system of determinations by the Solicitor are that they are cheap, swift and a great deal more informal than a hearing before a court. In practice, remarkably few decisions have been appealed and virtually none of those successfully. It is intended that the practice of the Adjudicator should offer a similar service and thereby obviate the need for, and expense of, court proceedings.

16.2 In this Part, we explain the following matters—

    (1)   the office of Adjudicator;

    (2)   proceedings in land registration matters and the roles in relation to them of—

        (a)   the registrar;

        (b)   the Adjudicator;

        (c)   the court; and

    (3)   criminal offences.

Most of these matters are covered by Part XI and Schedule 9 of the Bill. However, proceedings before the registrar fall within Part VI of the Bill, and offences are found in Part XII.

---

[1]   See below, para 16.6.

[2]   Cf Article 6.1 of the European Convention on Human Rights, which provides, so far as presently material, that "In the determination of his civil rights and obligations… everyone is entitled to a fair and public hearing within a reasonable time by an independent and impartial tribunal established by law".

THE ADJUDICATOR

The office of Adjudicator

16.3 Under Clause 105(1) of the Bill, the Lord Chancellor is required to appoint a person to be the Adjudicator to HM Land Registry. To be qualified for appointment, that person must have a 10 year general qualification within the meaning of section 71 of the Courts and Legal Services Act 1990.[3] The Bill makes provision dealing with the Adjudicator's resignation, his removal by the Lord Chancellor, his re-appointment on ceasing to hold office, and his remuneration.[4] The office is to be a disqualifying office for the purpose of membership of the House of Commons or the Northern Ireland Assembly.[5]

16.4 The volume of judicial business that is currently handled by the Solicitor to HM Land Registry and those to whom he delegates his functions strongly suggests that the Adjudicator will not only need a secretariat to assist him, but that he is unlikely to be able to determine all cases himself. He will therefore require the assistance of a number of appropriately qualified lawyers to determine those cases that he cannot deal with himself. The Bill therefore provides that—

(1) the Adjudicator may appoint such staff on such terms as he thinks fit and on such conditions as he, with the approval of the Minister for the Civil Service, thinks fit;[6] and

(2) any function of the Adjudicator may be carried out by any member of his staff who is authorised by him for the purpose.[7]

However, as regards (2), the Adjudicator may only delegate functions that are not of an administrative character to a member of his staff who himself has 10 year general qualification within the meaning of section 71 of the Courts and Legal Services Act 1990.[8] There is a power for the Lord Chancellor by regulations to make provision about the carrying out of any functions during any vacancy in the office of Adjudicator.[9] The Adjudicator is to be under the supervision of the Council on Tribunals.[10] At present, the Solicitor to HM Land Registry is not. This

---

[3] Cl 105(2). Under Courts and Legal Services Act 1990, s 71(3)(c), a person has a "general qualification" if "he has a right of audience in relation to any class of proceedings in any part of the Supreme Court, or all proceedings in county courts or magistrates' courts".

[4] Schedule 9, paras 1, 2.

[5] Schedule 9, para 9.

[6] Schedule 9, para 3.

[7] Schedule 9, para 4(1).

[8] Schedule 9, para 4(2). For the meaning of a 10 year general qualification, see above, para 16.3.

[9] Schedule 9, para 5. Such regulations must be made by statutory instrument to be laid before Parliament only: Cl 125(3).

[10] Schedule 9, para 8.

means that the Adjudicator will have to satisfy the various requirements laid down for tribunals subject to the Council in the Tribunals and Inquiries Act 1992.[11]

16.5 The Lord Chancellor will meet the costs of the office of the Adjudicator,[12] but he may require the Chief Land Registrar to contribute towards those expenses.[13]

Jurisdiction

The general right to object to an application to the registrar and the registrar's duty to refer contested applications to the Adjudicator

16.6 To understand the Adjudicator's jurisdiction, it is necessary to explain the fundamental principle upon which it primarily rests. As we have explained elsewhere, the Bill makes provision for the making of applications in many circumstances.[14] There must therefore be some mechanism by which the making of an application can be challenged. Clause 73 of the Bill therefore creates what is referred to as a "right to object".[15] Subject to two exceptions, anyone may object to an application to the registrar.[16] The two exceptions to this are—

(1) on an application for the cancellation of a caution against first registration under Clause 18, where only the person who lodged the caution or his or her personal representative may object;[17] and

(2) on an application for the cancellation of a unilateral notice under Clause 36, where only the person shown in the register as the beneficiary of the notice may object.[18]

Where an objection is made, then unless the registrar is satisfied that it is groundless, he must give notice of it to the applicant and may not determine the application until the objection has been disposed of.[19] If it is not possible to dispose of the objection by agreement, Clause 73(7) requires the registrar to refer the matter to the Adjudicator.[20] It may not be the entire application that is referred to the Adjudicator, but merely one or more of the issues raised by it. It

---

[11] Such as the obligation to give reasons for his decision if requested, as required by s 10 of that Act, which in practice the Solicitor already does.

[12] Schedule 9, para 6.

[13] Schedule 9, para 7.

[14] See above, para 9.76.

[15] See Cl 129(3)(c). The right to object is subject to rules: see Cl 73(4). Such rules are land registration rules to be laid before Parliament only: Cl 125(3), 129(1).

[16] This principle is presently found in rules: see Land Registration Rules 1925, r 298(1). Although that rule was only substituted in 2000, it does no more than reflect what has in fact been the practice for many years.

[17] Cl 73(2); see above, para 3.63.

[18] Cl 73(3); see above, para 6.30.

[19] Cl 73(5), (6).

[20] There is a power to make provision about such references by rules: Cl 73(8). Such rules are land registration rules to be laid before Parliament only: Cl 125(3), 129(1).

should be noted that a person may not exercise his or her right to object to an application to the registrar without reasonable cause.[21] A breach of this statutory duty is actionable in damages at the behest of any person who suffers loss in consequence.[22]

16.7   Clause 106(1) sets out the Adjudicator's two principal functions.

(1)   The first is to determine matters referred to him under Clause 73(7).[23] This function is confined to disputes between a person who has made an application to the registrar and some other person.

(2)   The second, which has already been explained, is the power to hear appeals by a person who is aggrieved by a decision of the registrar with respect to entry into, or termination of, a network access agreement.[24]

It should be noted that, apart from (2), the Adjudicator has no jurisdiction in relation to any dispute that an applicant may have with the registrar.[25]

Other matters

16.8   The Bill confers jurisdiction on the Adjudicator in certain other matters. One of these situations has already been explained in the context of the provisions on adverse possession.[26] However, the most significant is the Adjudicator's power, exercisable on an application to him, to rectify or set aside a document.[27] The power may only be exercised in relation to a document which does any one of the following:[28]

(1)   Where it effects a disposition of a registered estate or charge where that disposition is either a registrable disposition or one which creates an interest which may be protected by the entry of a notice. This will therefore include documents such as a transfer or grant of a legal estate and an instrument creating a restrictive covenant.

(2)   Where the document is a contract to make a disposition that falls within (1).

(3)   Where the instrument effects the transfer of an interest which is the subject of a notice in the register. An example, might be where there was a

---

[21]   Cl 77(1)(c). Cf above, paras 3.57, 6.28, 6.55.

[22]   Cl 77(2).

[23]   Cl 106(1)(a).

[24]   Cl 106(1)(b). See above, para 13.

[25]   For challenges to decisions of the registrar, see below, para 16.14.

[26]   See Cl 108(4); above, para 14.41 (giving effect to an equity by estoppel on a squatter's application to be registered as proprietor).

[27]   Cl 106(2).

[28]   *Ibid.*

conveyance of a *profit à prendre* that was noted on the register but not registered with its own title, and there was an error in that conveyance.[29]

16.9   Under the present law, the registrar has no power to rectify or set aside a document. On occasions this has meant that he has had to refer a matter to the High Court that he could otherwise have resolved. To avoid the cost and delay that such a reference is likely to entail, it was considered appropriate that the Adjudicator should have a limited power to rectify and set aside conveyancing (but not other) documents. This power is a free-standing one. The Adjudicator's jurisdiction is not tied to some disputed application to the registrar. Application is therefore to be made directly to the Adjudicator and not on a reference from the registrar.

16.10   Under the Bill, the general law about the effect of an order of the High Court for the rectification or setting aside of a document applies to an order made under this power.[30] This means (for example) that—

(1)   rectification relates back to the time when the instrument was executed;[31] and

(2)   after rectification the instrument is to be read as if it had been drawn up in its rectified form[32].

PROCEEDINGS

Proceedings before the registrar

16.11   We have explained above how, where there is a contested application to the registrar that cannot be resolved by agreement, he must refer the matter to the Adjudicator.[33] However, there will be many cases where a matter arises before the registrar, whether on application or otherwise, that will be determined by him. For example, an issue might arise—

(1)   where there has been an application for first registration and the registrar is examining the applicant's title; and

---

[29]   As we have explained, it is anticipated that it will become possible to transfer electronically certain interests in registered land that do not have their own titles, such as options and equitable charges, and to complete those transfers by an entry in the register: see Cl 93(1)(b), above, paras 13.80—13.83. The registrar would be able to rectify or set aside such documents in electronic form under this power.

[30]   Cl 106(4).

[31]   *Earl of Malmsbury v Countess of Malmsbury* (1862) 31 Beav 407, 418; 54 ER 1196, 1200.

[32]   *Craddock Bros v Hunt* [1923] 2 Ch 136, 151. See also *Re Slocock's Will Trusts* [1979] 1 All ER 358, 363.

[33]   See above, para 16.6.

(2) where the registrar is exercising his powers to alter the register, whether on application or on his own volition, perhaps to bring it up to date or to remove a spent entry.[34]

16.12 The Bill gives the registrar specific powers in relation to two matters.[35]

(1) It provides that, subject to rules,[36] he may require a person to produce a document for the purposes of the proceedings before him.[37]

(2) It empowers him to make orders about costs in relation to proceedings before him.[38] This power is subject to rules.[39] These may, in particular, make provision about whose costs and the kind of costs that a person may be required to pay, and also the assessment of such costs.[40] The rules may include provision about costs incurred by the registrar and liability for costs thrown away as the result of neglect or delay by a legal representative of a party to proceedings.[41]

16.13 Where the registrar either requires the production of a document or makes an order for the payment of costs—

(1) the requirement or order is enforceable as an order of the court;[42] and

(2) a person who is aggrieved by it, has a right to appeal to a county court, which may make any order which appears appropriate.[43]

16.14 The only rights of appeal from the registrar are those mentioned above in paragraphs 16.7 and 16.13(2). A person who wishes to challenge any other decision of the registrar must seek judicial review of it. This so whether the challenge arises out of an uncontested application to the registrar or from some

---

[34] See Schedule 4, para 5(b); above, para 10.19.

[35] For the analogous powers under the present legislation, see Land Registration Act 1925, s 128.

[36] Cl 75(2). Such rules are to be made by the Lord Chancellor: Cl 112 and are to be made by statutory instrument that is to be laid before Parliament only: Cl 125(3). Such rules — like all the rules made under powers conferred in Part 11 of the Bill — are not land registration rules: Cl 129(1). They will *not* be made with the advice and assistance of the Rule Committee under Cl 124. See below, paras 17.6—17.8.

[37] Cl 75(1).

[38] Cl 76(1).

[39] Cl 76(2). Such rules are to be made by the Lord Chancellor: Cl 112 and are to be made by statutory instrument that is to be laid before Parliament only: Cl 125(3).

[40] Cl 76(2).

[41] Cl 76(3). This is, in effect, the equivalent of a "wasted costs order". Cf Supreme Court Act 1981, s 51(6); CPR r 48.7.

[42] Cls 75(3), 76(4).

[43] Cls 75(4), 76(5).

exercise by him of his powers on his own initiative or under some requirement of the Bill.[44]

Proceedings before the Adjudicator

16.15   When a matter is referred to the Adjudicator under Clause 73(7),[45] or an application is made to him for the rectification or setting aside of a document,[46] he may either—

(1)   determine the matters on the papers submitted to him by the parties; or

(2)   hold a hearing.[47]

When he has made a determination, whether on the papers or at a hearing, anything that he requires of any party is enforceable as an order of the court.[48]

16.16   The Bill makes provision as to the procedure at hearings before the Adjudicator.[49] Hearings are to be held in public except where the Adjudicator is satisfied that it is just and reasonable to exclude the public.[50] It is provided that, as regards—

(1)   the practice and procedure to be followed with respect to proceedings before the Adjudicator; and

(2)   any matters that are incidental to or consequential upon such proceedings;

may be the subject of rules.[51]

16.17   The Bill lists the matters in relation to which, in particular, rules may make provision.[52] These are—

(1)   when hearings are to be held;

---

[44]   An example would be where there was a challenge to the registrar's decision to enter (or not to enter) a restriction under Cl 42. Cf above, paras 6.40—6.46.

[45]   See above, paras 16.6—16.7.

[46]   See above, para 16.8.

[47]   Although the Bill makes express provision for hearings (see below, para 16.16), there is no necessity for the Adjudicator to hold a hearing unless one or both of the parties wish to have one. This is the case now in relation to a determination by the registrar.

[48]   Cl 110.

[49]   Cl 107. For the present rules governing hearings before the registrar, see Land Registration Rules 1925; r 299; Land Registration (Hearings Procedure) Rules 2000.

[50]   Cl 107(1). This is the present rule in hearings before the registrar: see Land Registration (Hearings Procedure) Rules 2000, r 15.

[51]   Cl 107(2). Such rules are to be made by the Lord Chancellor: Cl 112 and are to be made by statutory instrument that is to be laid before Parliament only: Cl 125(3).

[52]   Cl 107(3). Most of the matters listed in that sub-clause are all ones that are presently covered by Land Registration (Hearings Procedure) Rules 2000 in relation to hearings before the registrar. It is likely that any rules that are made will also take account of the Council of Tribunals Model Rules of Procedure.

(2)	requiring that persons attend hearings to give evidence or produce documents;

(3)	the form in which any decision of the Adjudicator is to be given;

(4)	the payment by one party to the proceedings of the costs of the other; and

(5)	liability for costs thrown away as the result of neglect or delay by a legal representative of a party to proceedings.[53]

16.18	We have mentioned above that the reference to the Adjudicator under Clause 73(7) may not be of the entire application to the registrar, but merely of some issue or issues raised by it.[54] Provision is therefore needed to explain what the Adjudicator may do on any reference to him. The matter is in fact one for which provision may be made by rules under the Bill.[55] Those rules may, in particular, make provision enabling the Adjudicator to determine or to make directions about the determination of—

(1)	the application to which the reference relates; or

(2)	such other present or future applications as the rules may provide.[56]

The principal reason for (2) is that where the Adjudicator decides a particular point, rules may enable him to give specific directions in related applications. However, the power is wide enough that rules might empower him to give general directions that could apply to pending and future applications that were quite unconnected with the case before him. This would of course obviate the need for further references to him on the same point and would provide guidance to the registrar as to what he is to do in future in a similar case.

16.19	The Lord Chancellor is given power by order both to prescribe fees to be paid in respect of proceedings before the Adjudicator, and to make provision about the payment of prescribed fees.[57]

Power for the Adjudicator to direct a hearing before the court

16.20	In proceedings on a reference to the Adjudicator under Clause 73(7),[58] he may, instead of deciding a matter himself, direct a party to the proceedings before him to commence proceedings in the court[59] within a specified time in order to obtain

---

[53]	Once again, this is the equivalent of a "wasted costs order". Cf above, para 16.12(2).

[54]	See above, para 16.6.

[55]	Cl 108(3). The rules are to be made by the Lord Chancellor by statutory instrument that is to be laid before Parliament only: Cls 112, 125(3).

[56]	Cl 108(3).

[57]	Cl 111. The power is exercisable by statutory instrument: see Cl 125(2).

[58]	Above, paras 16.6, 16.7.

[59]	For the meaning of "the court", see Cl 129(3)(a); below, para 16.25.

the court's decision on the matter.[60] This may be appropriate where, for example—

    (1)   the application raises an important or difficult point of law;

    (2)   there are substantial or complex disputes of fact that are more appropriate for a court hearing;

    (3)   there are other issues between the parties already before the court (such as matrimonial proceedings); or

    (4)   the court has powers not available to the Adjudicator, as for example, the power to award damages for lodging a caution, applying for the entry of a notice or restriction, or objecting to an application without reasonable cause.[61]

16.21   It should be emphasised that the Adjudicator may direct a reference to the court of either—

    (1)   the entirety of the proceedings before him; or

    (2)   one or more specific issues in those proceedings (such as a preliminary point of law).

16.22   Rules may make provision about references to the court.[62] In particular, they may make provision about the adjournment of the proceedings before the Adjudicator pending the outcome of the proceedings before the court.[63] They may also specify what the powers of the Adjudicator are to be in the event that a party fails to comply with a direction to commence proceedings in court. Thus, for example, if the defaulting party is the applicant, rules might empower the Adjudicator to dismiss his or her application in whole or part. Conversely, if the party in default was the person who had objected to the application, rules might authorise the Adjudicator to give effect to the application in whole or part and disregard the objection.[64]

---

[60]   Cl 108(1). Cf Land Registration Rules 1925, r 299(3) (which confers an equivalent power on the registrar).

[61]   See Cl 77; above paras 3.59, 6.28, 6.55, 16.6. Another example might be where a person has entered a restriction to prevent a transfer from executors to a devisee under a will, the executors challenge that application under Cl 45 (above, para 6.56), and the applicant alleges that the will should be set aside because it was induced by undue influence. The Adjudicator has no power to set aside a will and so the matter must be referred to the court.

[62]   Cl 108(2). The rules are to be made by the Lord Chancellor by statutory instrument that is to be laid before Parliament only: Cls 112, 125(3).

[63]   If, for example, the Adjudicator directed that a point of law raised by the application be determined by the court, the matter before him could be adjourned pending that application, he could then make his determination and direct what was required to be done.

[64]   Cf Land Registration Rules 1925, r 299(4) (which is the equivalent provision at present in relation to a direction by the registrar).

Right of appeal

16.23 A person aggrieved by a decision of the Adjudicator is given a right to appeal to the High Court.[65]

(1) As regards the matters set out in paragraph 16.7(1) (that is, to determine matters arising out of a disputed application that is referred to him under Clause 73(7)), that right is unqualified and is, therefore, a right to appeal on a point either of law or of fact.[66] However, it is subject to the power, contained in section 54 of the Access to Justice Act 1999, to provide by rules of court that any right of appeal may be exercised only with permission. These rights of appeal may have to be reconsidered in the light of any recommendations that may be made by Sir Andrew Leggatt in his forthcoming Review of Tribunals.

(2) As regards the matters set out in paragraph 16.7(2) (that is to hear appeals by a person who is aggrieved by a decision of the registrar with respect to entry into, or termination of, a network access agreement), it is a right of appeal on a point of law only.[67] This is because it is a second appeal, and it is not considered to be appropriate to permit unlimited rights to make a second appeal.

THE ROLE OF THE COURT

16.24 It will be apparent from what has been said in this Part that—

(1) the county court alone may hear appeals by a person aggrieved by an order of the registrar requiring the production of a document or to pay costs;[68]

(2) any other decision of the registrar may only be challenged in proceedings in the High Court for judicial review;[69] and

(3) the High Court alone may hear an appeal from the decision of the Adjudicator, whether on an issue of fact or law.[70]

16.25 However, in addition to these matters, the Bill makes a number of specific references to the powers of "the court" which, for the purposes of the Bill, means

---

[65] Cl 109(1). For one specific power relating to appeals from the Adjudicator in adverse possession cases, see Cl 109(3); above, para 14.41.

[66] Cf Tribunals and Inquiries Act 1992, s 11, which confers a right to appeal merely on a point of law (and not on a point of fact) from certain tribunals.

[67] Cl 109(2).

[68] Cls 75(4), 76(5); above, para 16.13.

[69] See above, para 16.14.

[70] Cl 109(1); above, para 16.23.

either the High Court or the county court.[71] What links these provisions is that they confer jurisdiction on "the court" in relation to the particular matter.[72]

OFFENCES

The present law

16.26 The Land Registration Act 1925 creates three offences. These are concerned with—

(1) the suppression of documents and facts relating to title in proceedings before the registrar or the court;[73]

(2) the fraudulent procurement of changes to the register or to any land or charge certificate;[74] and

(3) the refusal by a witness to attend before the registrar in obedience to a summons, produce documents or answer a question put to him or her on oath.[75]

16.27 The Bill creates three new offences to replace the first two of these. There is no equivalent of the third offence. It is not needed because all of the following are enforceable as an order of the court—

(1) a requirement of the registrar that a person should produce a document;[76]

(2) a requirement of the Adjudicator that a person should attend hearings to—

(a) give evidence; or

(b) produce documents.[77]

Non-compliance can, therefore, be dealt with by a court as contempt.

---

[71] Cl 129(3)(a). Where a provision of the Bill which does not confer jurisdiction is concerned, the Bill refers to "a court", rather than "the court", see, *eg*, Cl 97(5) (circumstances in which a court must order the registrar to register a squatter as proprietor, above, para 14.87) and Schedule 12, para 18(3) (transitional provisions about adverse possession).

[72] They include Cl 20 (alteration of the register of cautions; above, para 3.66); Cl 40(3)(c) (restriction to prohibit entry until the making of an order by the court; above, para 6.36); Cl 45(3)(c) (certain applications for restrictions not notifiable; above, para 6.56.); Cl 46 (power of the court to order the entry of a restriction; above, para 6.51); Cl 108(1) (power for the Adjudicator to direct proceedings; above, para 16.20); Cl 108(4) (power of the Adjudicator in giving effect to an equity; above, para 14.41); Cl 110 (enforceability of any requirement of the Adjudicator; above, para 16.15); Schedule 4, para 2(1) (alteration of the register; above, para 10. 10); Schedule 8, para 7(1) (determination of indemnity, above, para 10.50).

[73] Land Registration Act 1925, s 115. For the punishment, see *ibid*, s 117.

[74] *Ibid*, s 116. For the punishment, see *ibid*, s 117.

[75] *Ibid*, s 128(3).

[76] Cl 75; above, paras 16.12, 16.13.

[77] Cls 107(3)(b), 110; above, paras 16.15, 16.17.

The offences under the Bill

Suppression of information

16.28   The first new offence[78] is committed where, in the course of proceedings relating to registration under the Bill, a person suppresses information. "Proceedings" is to be widely understood. For example, it includes not only proceedings of a judicial character before the Adjudicator, but any procedure in connection with an application to the registrar under the Bill. To be guilty of the offence, the person must act with the intention of either concealing a person's right or claim or substantiating a false claim.[79] The offence may be tried on indictment or summarily.[80] In accordance with the Law Commission's normal practice, the Bill does not specify the maximum period of imprisonment, which is a matter for consultation with the Home Office. Any fine will be unlimited on indictment and will not exceed the statutory maximum on summary conviction.[81]

Improper alteration of the registers

16.29   The second and third of the new offences[82] are both concerned with improper alterations to the register. These offences may acquire added significance in the move to electronic conveyancing. This is because, as we have explained, persons other than the registrar will be given authority to change the register.[83] There is, therefore, a greater risk that an improper alteration could be made. The two offences are as follows.

DISHONESTLY INDUCING ANOTHER TO CHANGE OR AUTHORISE A CHANGE TO THE REGISTER

16.30   The second of the new offences is committed where a person dishonestly induces another—

   (1)   to change the register of title or the cautions register; or

   (2)   to authorise the making of such a change.[84]

For these purposes, a change to the register includes a change to a document referred to on it.[85]

16.31   The offence in paragraph 16.30(1) is, in essence, a re-enactment of the offence summarised in paragraph 16.26(2) above.[86] It would cover the case (for example) where a person deliberately makes a false statement in an application for

---

[78]   Which replaces the offence under Land Registration Act 1925, s 115; above, para 16.26(1).

[79]   Cl 120(1).

[80]   Cl 120(2).

[81]   *Ibid.* For the maximum fine that can be imposed on summary conviction, see Magistrates' Courts Act 1980, s 32(2), (9).

[82]   Which replace the offence under Land Registration Act 1925, s 116; above, para 16.26(2).

[83]   See above, paras 2.51 and following, and below, paras 13.36 and following.

[84]   Cl 121(1).

[85]   Cl 121(4).

[86]   See Land Registration Act 1925, s 116.

registration. As regards the offence in paragraph 16.30(2), we have explained above that, under the system of electronic conveyancing that the Bill is intended to create, those who enter into network access agreements may be authorised to change the register.[87] However, any changes to the register will have to be approved in advance by the registrar.[88] The offence in paragraph 16.30(2) will therefore cover the case of a party to a network access agreement who dishonestly induces the Registry to agree to a particular change in the register that he or she then makes. The position in relation to penalties is as set out above in paragraph 16.28.

INTENTIONALLY OR RECKLESSLY MAKING AN UNAUTHORISED CHANGE IN A REGISTER

16.32   The third of the new offences is committed where a person intentionally or recklessly makes an unauthorised change in the register of title or the cautions register.[89] This offence does in fact cover two distinct situations.

(1)   Where a person who is not authorised to change the register does so, knowing that he or she is not authorised to do so, or reckless as to that fact.

(2)   Where a person who has authority to make a particular change to the register intentionally or recklessly makes some other change that he or she is not authorised to make.

Once again, for the purposes of this provision, a change to the register includes a change to a document referred to on it.[90] The position in relation to penalties is as set out above in paragraph 16.28.

Privilege against self-incrimination

16.33   Clause 122(1) of the Bill replicates the effect of section 119(2) of the Land Registration Act 1925. It provides that the privilege against self-incrimination, so far as relating to offences under the Bill, does not entitle a person to refuse to answer any question or produce any document or thing in any legal proceedings other than criminal proceedings. However, no evidence so obtained is admissible in any criminal proceedings under the Bill against either the person from whom it was obtained or his or her spouse.[91] This particular approach is now a familiar one having been adopted in a number of statutes.[92]

---

[87]   See above, paras 13.36 and following.

[88]   See above, paras 2.53 and 2.55.

[89]   Cl 121(2).

[90]   Cl 121(4).

[91]   Cl 122(2).

[92]   See, *eg*, Theft Act 1968, s 31; Civil Evidence Act 1968, s 16; Supreme Court Act 1981, s 72.

PART XVII
RULES AND ORDERS

INTRODUCTION

17.1 It will be apparent from one glance at the Bill, that it confers extensive rule-making powers on the Lord Chancellor. In any modern legislation, rule-making powers are rightly the subject of close Parliamentary scrutiny and require justification.[1] It is for this reason that we devote a whole Part of this Report to the Bill's rule-making powers. The Bill also confers a very limited number of powers by which the Lord Chancellor may make orders. When any of these powers is exercised, it will result in a change in the substantive law. In relation to some of them, the Lord Chancellor must consult on the proposed change before he exercises the power.[2] *All* rules, regulations or orders under the Bill that are made by the Lord Chancellor have to be made by statutory instrument.[3]

RULES

The present law

17.2 In Parts II and XIII of this Report, we explained the importance of rules to the operation of the Land Registration Act 1925, and why an extensive network of rules was essential to the continuing development of land registration.[4] Indeed, we suggested not only that that the present system of land registration could not have been developed as it has been without the flexibility of wide rule-making powers,[5] but also that the development of electronic conveyancing over the next few years could not occur without a similar flexibility.[6] However, we also noted that the present law left something to be desired.[7] In particular, we commented on the absence of any principled demarcation between what is in the Act and what is in the rules made under it.[8] There are indeed some remarkably important matters

---

[1] Such powers are examined by the Delegated Powers Scrutiny Committee of the House of Lords (which was set up in 1992—93, "to report whether the provisions of any bill inappropriately delegate legislative power; or whether they subject the exercise of legislative power to an inappropriate degree of Parliamentary scrutiny"). Furthermore, in our experience, delegated powers are not infrequently the subject of comment in one or other House during the passage of a Bill.

[2] There are good reasons why there is no obligation to consult in relation to some of these powers.

[3] Cl 125(2). The Bill confers on the registrar the power to make orders, as in Cl 41; above, para 6.37. These orders are not made by statutory instrument.

[4] See above, paras 2.76—2.78; 13.66—13.71. The principal rules made under the Land Registration Act 1925 are the Land Registration Rules 1925. See above, para 2.76. As we there explained, there are presently more than 300 rules.

[5] In the period 1990—2001, there have been no less than 46 sets of rules or orders made under the Land Registration Act 1925.

[6] See above, paras 2.76, 13.69.

[7] See above, para 276.

[8] *Ibid.*

that are addressed in the rules rather than in the Act.[9] There is a lingering suspicion that this may not have been entirely accidental. Rules made under the Land Registration Act 1925 have "the same force and effect as if enacted in [that] Act",[10] a provision that has no counterpart in the Bill.

17.3 The rule-making powers are presently found in section 144 of the Land Registration Act 1925. However, although that subsection lists some 31 rule-making powers, almost all the rules have been made under the last of them. Section 144(1)(xxxi) permits rules to be made—

> For regulating any matter to be prescribed or in respect of which rules are to be made under this Act and any other matter or thing, whether similar or not to those above mentioned, in respect of which it may be expedient to make rules for the purpose of carrying this Act into execution.

The approach to rule-making powers adopted in the Bill

17.4 The approach of the Bill to rules is rather different to that adopted in the Land Registration Act 1925. First, the Bill attempts to make a more rational division between primary and secondary legislation. Secondly, although there is a residual rule-making power, similar to section 144(1)(xxxi) of the Land Registration Act 1925[11] it is, quite explicitly a *residual* power. Thirdly, the rule-making powers are not collected in one place, but are, in general, set out in the context in which they arise.[12] This is likely to make the legislation more comprehensible. It seems likely that many of the rules made under the Bill will be similar to those that have been made under the 1925 Act.

The rule-making powers under the Bill

Land registration rules

17.5 All rules under the Bill are designated "land registration rules" except[13]—

(1) those made under Clause 93, which require specified dispositions to be made electronically and simultaneously registered;[14]

(2) those made under Part 11 (the provisions dealing with adjudication);[15]

(3) those relating to the forwarding of applications relating to certain registered charges to the registrar of companies;[16] and

---

[9] The system of priority searches of the register is a case in point: see above, paras 9.62—9.66.

[10] Land Registration Act 1925, s 144(2).

[11] Schedule 10, para 8.

[12] There are also some general rule-making powers that are collected in Schedule 10.

[13] See the definition of "land registration rules" in Cl 129(1).

[14] See above, para 13.80.

[15] See above, Part XVI.

(4)   some of those made in relation to the Land Registry Network under Schedule 5.[17]

The reasons for the exclusions are explained below.[18] The role of land registration rules is to explain the detail of how land registration is to be conducted, matters such as the manner in which applications are to be made to the registrar, how notices are to be served, and the like. The power to make land registration rules is, as now, exercisable—

(a)   by the Lord Chancellor with the advice and assistance of a body called the Rule Committee;[19]

(b)   by statutory instrument to be laid before Parliament.[20]

17.6   The Rule Committee exists under the Land Registration Act 1925,[21] and presently consists of—

(1)   a judge of the Chancery Division of the High Court as Chairman (nominated by the Lord Chancellor);[22]

(2)   the Chief Land Registrar;

(3)   a person nominated by the General Council of the Bar;

(4)   a person nominated by the Council of the Law Society; and

(5)   a person nominated by the Minister of Agriculture Fisheries and Food.

The intention is that the Committee should comprise persons with a particular expertise in conveyancing matters. In its 76 years it has proved its worth repeatedly and subjects draft rules to intensive scrutiny.

17.7   Under the Bill the composition of the Rule Committee will change in two respects. First, at its own request, the Ministry of Agriculture Fisheries and Food will cease to be represented on it. In its place, the Council of Mortgage Lenders will nominate a member.[23] Given the great importance of secured lending on land which has developed since 1925, this is an obvious change. Secondly, the Lord Chancellor is to have power to nominate to be a member of the Rule Committee any person who appears to him to have qualifications or experience which would

---

[16]   Cl 119; above, para 9.81.

[17]   See Schedule 5, paras 1, 2, 3, 11.

[18]   See para 17.8.

[19]   Cl 124(1).

[20]   Cl 125(3).

[21]   Section 144(1).

[22]   Mr Justice Blackburne is currently the Chairman.

[23]   Cl 124(2).

be of value to the committee in considering any matter with which it is concerned.[24]

17.8 The reason why the four matters mentioned above, in paragraph 17.5, are not included within the definition of land registration rules is as follows. The first relates to a matter of importance both to the public and to those who conduct conveyancing. It would be inappropriate to make such a change without full consultation.[25] As regards the second and third, they are matters in which the Rule Committee could have no possible interest because they are not concerned with the conduct of the conveyancing process. As regards the fourth, the rules in question relate to network access agreements, and once again, these are of such importance that the Bill requires the Lord Chancellor to consult before he makes them.[26]

17.9 Many of the land registration rules arise out of specific provisions of the Bill and have been the subject of comment in the context of those provisions. However, Schedule 10[27] contains a series of miscellaneous and general powers. Although some of these have already been considered,[28] the matters explained in the following paragraphs have not.

(1) There is a power to make rules applying the Bill to a pre-registration dealing with a registrable legal estate[29] as if the dealing had taken place after the date of the first registration of the estate, and about the date on which registration of the dealing is effective.[30] This replicates a power under the present legislation.[31] The rules made under that power have provided that the provisions of the Land Registration Act 1925 apply to

---

[24] Cl 124(3).

[25] Though the views of the Rule Committee would, no doubt, be sought by the Lord Chancellor as part of that process of consultation.

[26] See Schedule 5, para 11. The rules relate to the terms of network access agreements, the terms of access to the Land Registry Network, and the termination of network access agreements: see Schedule 5, paras 1—3, above, paras 13.36—13.56. By contrast, the network transaction rules made under Schedule 5, para 5 *will* be land registration rules. These rules are concerned with the manner in which network transactions are conducted. That is plainly a matter of interest to the Rule Committee.

[27] See Cl 123.

[28] In relation to Schedule 10 para 2 (regulation of matters between sellers and buyer), see above, para 12.8; *ibid,* para 3 (implied covenants), see above, para 12.20; *ibid,* para 4 (land certificates), see above, para 9.90; *ibid,* para 6 (applications), see above, para 9.77; *ibid,* para 8 (residual power), above, para 17.4.

[29] That is, a legal estate that a person must register under Cl 6: Schedule 10, para 1(2)(a). For Cl 6, see above, paras 3.38, 3.39.

[30] Schedule 10, para 1(1). Cf above, paras 3.23—3.41. A pre-registration dealing is one that takes place before the application to register the registrable dealing with the legal estate: Schedule 10, para 1(2)(b).

[31] See Land Registration Act 1925, s 123A(10)(a).

such pre-registration dealings as if they had taken place after the date of first registration.[32]

(2) There is a power for rules to make provision about the form, content and service of any notice under the Bill.[33] As might be expected, the power enables rules to make provision for matters such as—

    (a) requiring that an address for service be supplied;

    (b) the entry of addresses for service in the register;

    (c) the time for service of notices;

    (d) the mode of service; and

    (e) when service is to be regarded as having taken place.[34]

(3) A number of statutes require that an instrument which makes a disposition must contain certain particulars. This is so (for example) in relation to certain dispositions by charities,[35] and in relation to vesting deeds which convey the legal estate to the tenant for life of a settlement under the Settled Land Act 1925.[36] Under the Bill, rules may make provision about the form of any statement required under an enactment to be included in an instrument effecting a registrable disposition or a disposition which triggers the requirement of compulsory registration.[37]

Other rules and regulations

17.10 The Bill contains certain other miscellaneous powers to make rules and regulations by statutory instrument that are required merely to be laid before Parliament, but which are not land registration rules. Some of these have already been mentioned above,[38] but they also include regulations made under the Bill.[39]

---

[32] Land Registration Rules 1925, r 73.

[33] Schedule 10, para 5. Again this replicates the effect of provisions found in the Land Registration Act 1925: see s 79; and Land Registration Rules 1925, rr 311—315.

[34] Schedule 10, para 5(2).

[35] See Charities Act 1993, ss 37, 39.

[36] See Settled Land Act 1925, s 5.

[37] Schedule 10, para 7.

[38] See para 17.5.

[39] Cl 125(3)(c). See, *eg*, Cl 99(2) (regulations about the carrying out of functions of the registrar during any vacancy in that office); see above, para 15.5 ; Schedule 9, para 5 (regulations about the carrying out of functions of the adjudicator during any vacancy in that office); see above, para 16.4.

17.11 There are certain rules that are required to be made by a statutory instrument that is subject to annulment in pursuance of a resolution of either House of Parliament and, indeed, only after prior consultation by the Lord Chancellor. These powers relate to network access agreements,[40] and have been mentioned above.[41]

ORDERS

17.12 The Bill contains a number of powers for the Lord Chancellor to make orders. These fall into three classes.

17.13 First, there are orders which can be made by the Lord Chancellor by a statutory instrument that does not require to be laid before Parliament.[42] None of these is in any way unconventional. They are—

(1) a fee order under Clause 101: this replicates the present position;[43]

(2) an order prescribing any fees that are to be paid in proceedings before the Adjudicator;[44]

(3) an order making any transitional provisions and savings in connection with the bringing into force of the Bill;[45] and

(4) a commencement order.[46]

17.14 Secondly, there is one class of order that has to be made by statutory instrument that is laid before Parliament after it is made. This is an order under Clause 99(3), designating a particular office of the Land Registry as the proper office for the receipt of specified applications or kinds of application.[47]

17.15 Thirdly, there is a limited class of orders that must be made by a statutory instrument that is subject to annulment in pursuance of a resolution of either House of Parliament.[48] As we have mentioned above,[49] what characterises an order of this kind, if made, is that it will change the substantive law. Some such orders

---

[40] See Cl 125(4)(a); Schedule 5, paras 1—3; above, paras 13.36—13.56.

[41] See para 17.8.

[42] See the matters excluded by Cl 125(4)(b).

[43] For fee orders, see above, para 15.9. Such fee orders are made at least once a year and sometimes more often.

[44] See above, para 16.19.

[45] Cl 131.

[46] Cl 133(2).

[47] Cl 125(3)(d). See above, para 15.6.

[48] Cl 125(4)(b).

[49] See para 17.1.

can be made without prior consultation,[50] but such is the importance of the others that they can only be made after consultation by the Lord Chancellor.[51]

LAW COMMISSION

ROBERT CARNWATH, *Chairman*
HUGH BEALE
CHARLES HARPUM
MARTIN PARTINGTON
ALAN WILKIE

MICHAEL SAYERS, *Secretary*

31 May 2001

HM LAND REGISTRY

PETER COLLIS, *Chief Land Registrar*
CHRISTOPHER WEST, *Solicitor*

---

[50] See Cl 62(9) (changing the number of years required to upgrade a possessory title); above, para 9.17(2); Cl 80(4) (extending events that trigger compulsory registration of demesne land); above, para 11.15. Although the latter power can be exercised without prior consultation, it is inconceivable that the Lord Chancellor would in practice exercise it without prior discussion with the Crown.

[51] See Cl 5 (power to extend triggers to compulsory registration); above, para 3.37; Cl 116 (power to reduce the length of lease that is registrable); above, para 3.17.

APPENDIX A
Draft Land Registration Bill

The draft Land Registration Bill begins on the next page. The Explanatory Notes begin on page 463.

Land Registration Bill

CONTENTS

PART 1

PRELIMINARY

1   Register of title
2   Scope of title registration

PART 2

FIRST REGISTRATION OF TITLE

CHAPTER 1

FIRST REGISTRATION

Voluntary registration

3   When title may be registered

Compulsory registration

4   When title must be registered
5   Power to extend section 4
6   Duty to apply for registration of title
7   Effect of non-compliance with section 6
8   Liability for making good void transfers etc

Classes of title

9   Titles to freehold estates
10   Titles to leasehold estates

Effect of first registration

11   Freehold estates
12   Leasehold estates

Dependent estates

13 Appurtenant rights and charges

Supplementary

14 Rules about first registration

CHAPTER 2

CAUTIONS AGAINST FIRST REGISTRATION

15 Right to lodge
16 Effect
17 Withdrawal
18 Cancellation
19 Cautions register
20 Alteration of register by court
21 Alteration of register by registrar
22 Supplementary

PART 3

DISPOSITIONS OF REGISTERED LAND

Powers of disposition

23 Owner's powers
24 Right to exercise owner's powers
25 Mode of exercise
26 Protection of disponees

Registrable dispositions

27 Dispositions required to be registered

Effect of dispositions on priority

28 Basic rule
29 Effect of registered dispositions: estates
30 Effect of registered dispositions: charges
31 Inland Revenue charges

PART 4

NOTICES AND RESTRICTIONS

Notices

32 Nature and effect
33 Excluded interests
34 Entry on application
35 Unilateral notices
36 Cancellation of unilateral notices
37 Unregistered interests

38   Registrable dispositions
39   Supplementary

Restrictions

40   Nature
41   Effect
42   Power of registrar to enter
43   Applications
44   Obligatory restrictions
45   Notifiable applications
46   Power of court to order entry
47   Withdrawal

PART 5

CHARGES

Relative priority

48   Registered charges
49   Tacking and further advances
50   Overriding statutory charges: duty of notification

Powers as chargee

51   Effect of completion by registration
52   Protection of disponees
53   Powers as sub-chargee

Realisation of security

54   Proceeds of sale: chargee's duty
55   Local land charges

Miscellaneous

56   Receipt in case of joint proprietors
57   Entry of right of consolidation

PART 6

REGISTRATION: GENERAL

Registration as proprietor

58   Conclusiveness
59   Dependent estates

Boundaries

60   Boundaries
61   Accretion and diluvion

Quality of title

62   Power to upgrade title
63   Effect of upgrading title
64   Use of register to record defects in title

Alteration of register

65   Alteration of register

Information etc.

66   Inspection of the registers etc
67   Official copies of the registers etc
68   Index
69   Historical information
70   Official searches

Applications

71   Duty to disclose unregistered interests
72   Priority protection
73   Objections
74   Effective date of registration

Proceedings before the registrar

75   Production of documents
76   Costs

Miscellaneous

77   Duty to act reasonably
78   Notice of trust not to affect registrar

PART 7

SPECIAL CASES

The Crown

79   Voluntary registration of demesne land
80   Compulsory registration of grants out of demesne land
81   Demesne land: cautions against first registration
82   Escheat etc
83   Crown and Duchy land: representation
84   Disapplication of requirements relating to Duchy land
85   Bona vacantia

Pending actions etc.

86   Bankruptcy
87   Pending land actions, writs, orders and deeds of arrangement

Miscellaneous

88 Incorporeal hereditaments
89 Settlements
90 PPP leases relating to transport in London

PART 8

ELECTRONIC CONVEYANCING

91 Electronic dispositions: formalities
92 Land registry network
93 Power to require simultaneous registration
94 Supplementary

PART 9

ADVERSE POSSESSION

95 Disapplication of periods of limitation
96 Registration of adverse possessor
97 Defences

PART 10

LAND REGISTRY

Administration

98   The land registry
99   Conduct of business
100 Annual report

Fees and indemnities

101 Fee orders
102 Indemnities

Miscellaneous

103 General information about land
104 Consultancy and advisory services

PART 11

ADJUDICATION

105 The adjudicator
106 Jurisdiction
107 Procedure
108 Functions in relation to disputes
109 Appeals
110 Enforcement of orders etc
111 Fees
112 Supplementary

PART 12

MISCELLANEOUS AND GENERAL

Miscellaneous

113 Rights of pre-emption
114 Proprietary estoppel and mere equities
115 Reduction in unregistered interests with automatic protection
116 Power to reduce qualifying term
117 Power to deregister manors
118 Conclusiveness of filed copies etc
119 Forwarding of applications to registrar of companies

Offences etc.

120 Suppression of information
121 Improper alteration of the registers
122 Privilege against self-incrimination

Land registration rules

123 Miscellaneous and general powers
124 Exercise of powers

Supplementary

125 Rules, regulations and orders
126 Crown application
127 Application to internal waters
128 "Proprietor in possession"
129 General interpretation

Final provisions

130 Minor and consequential amendments
131 Transition
132 Repeals
133 Short title, commencement and extent

Schedule 1 — Unregistered interests which override first registration
Schedule 2 — Registrable dispositions: registration requirements
  Part 1 — Registered estates
  Part 2 — Registered charges
Schedule 3 — Unregistered interests which override registered dispositions
Schedule 4 — Alteration of the register
Schedule 5 — Land registry network
Schedule 6 — Registration of adverse possessor
Schedule 7 — The land registry
Schedule 8 — Indemnities
Schedule 9 — The adjudicator

Schedule 10 — Miscellaneous and general powers
    Part 1 — Miscellaneous
    Part 2 — General
Schedule 11 — Minor and consequential amendments
Schedule 12 — Transition
Schedule 13 — Repeals

A

BILL

TO

Make provision about land registration; and for connected purposes.

B E IT ENACTED by the Queen's most Excellent Majesty, by and with the advice and consent of the Lords Spiritual and Temporal, and Commons, in this present Parliament assembled, and by the authority of the same, as follows:—

PART 1

PRELIMINARY

1   Register of title

(1)   There is to continue to be a register of title kept by the registrar.

(2)   Rules may make provision about how the register is to be kept and may, in particular, make provision about—
   (a)   the information to be included in the register,
   (b)   the form in which information included in the register is to be kept, and
   (c)   the arrangement of that information.

2   Scope of title registration

This Act makes provision about the registration of title to—
   (a)   unregistered legal estates which are interests of any of the following kinds—
        (i)   an estate in land,
        (ii)   a rentcharge,
        (iii)   a franchise,
        (iv)   a profit a prendre in gross, and
        (v)   any other interest or charge which subsists for the benefit of, or is a charge on, an interest the title to which is registered; and
   (b)   interests capable of subsisting at law which are created by a disposition of an interest the title to which is registered.

PART 2

FIRST REGISTRATION OF TITLE

CHAPTER 1

FIRST REGISTRATION

Voluntary registration

3   When title may be registered

(1)   This section applies to any unregistered legal estate which is an interest of any of the following kinds —
    (a)   an estate in land,
    (b)   a rentcharge,
    (c)   a franchise, and
    (d)   a profit a prendre in gross.

(2)   Subject to the following provisions, a person may apply to the registrar to be registered as the proprietor of an unregistered legal estate to which this section applies if —
    (a)   the estate is vested in him, or
    (b)   he is entitled to require the estate to be vested in him.

(3)   Subject to subsection (4), an application under subsection (2) in respect of a leasehold estate may only be made if the estate was granted for a term of which more than seven years are unexpired.

(4)   In the case of an estate in land, subsection (3) does not apply if the right to possession under the lease is discontinuous.

(5)   A person may not make an application under subsection (2)(a) in respect of a leasehold estate vested in him as a mortgagee where there is a subsisting right of redemption.

(6)   A person may not make an application under subsection (2)(b) if his entitlement is as a person who has contracted to buy under a contract.

(7)   If a person holds in the same right both —
    (a)   a lease in possession, and
    (b)   a lease to take effect in possession on, or within a month of, the end of the lease in possession,
then, to the extent that they relate to the same land, they are to be treated for the purposes of this section as creating one continuous term.

Compulsory registration

4   When title must be registered

(1)   The requirement of registration applies on the occurrence of any of the following events —
    (a)   the transfer of a qualifying estate —

        (i)   for valuable or other consideration, by way of gift or in pursuance of an order of any court, or

        (ii)   by means of an assent (including a vesting assent);

   (b)   the transfer of an unregistered legal estate in land in circumstances where section 171A of the Housing Act 1985 (c. 68) applies (disposal by landlord which leads to a person no longer being a secure tenant);

   (c)   the grant out of a qualifying estate of an estate in land —

        (i)   for a term of years absolute of more than seven years from the date of the grant, and

        (ii)   for valuable or other consideration, by way of gift or in pursuance of an order of any court;

   (d)   the grant out of a qualifying estate of an estate in land for a term of years absolute to take effect in possession after the end of the period of three months beginning with the date of the grant;

   (e)   the grant of a lease in pursuance of Part 5 of the Housing Act 1985 (the right to buy) out of an unregistered legal estate in land;

   (f)   the grant of a lease out of an unregistered legal estate in land in such circumstances as are mentioned in paragraph (b);

   (g)   the creation of a protected first legal mortgage of a qualifying estate.

(2)   For the purposes of subsection (1), a qualifying estate is an unregistered legal estate which is —

   (a)   a freehold estate in land, or

   (b)   a leasehold estate in land held for a term which, at the time of the transfer, grant or creation, has more than seven years to run.

(3)   In subsection (1)(a), the reference to transfer does not include transfer by operation of law.

(4)   Subsection (1)(a) does not apply to —

   (a)   the assignment of a mortgage term, or

   (b)   the assignment or surrender of a lease to the owner of the immediate reversion where the term is to merge in that reversion.

(5)   Subsection (1)(c) does not apply to the grant of an estate to a person as a mortgagee.

(6)   For the purposes of subsection (1)(a) and (c), if the estate transferred or granted has a negative value, it is to be regarded as transferred or granted for valuable or other consideration.

(7)   In subsection (1)(a) and (c), references to transfer or grant by way of gift include transfer or grant for the purpose of —

   (a)   constituting a trust under which the settlor does not retain the whole of the beneficial interest, or

   (b)   uniting the bare legal title and the beneficial interest in property held under a trust under which the settlor did not, on constitution, retain the whole of the beneficial interest.

(8)   For the purposes of subsection (1)(g) —

   (a)   a legal mortgage is protected if it takes effect on its creation as a mortgage to be protected by the deposit of documents relating to the mortgaged estate, and

   (b)   a first legal mortgage is one which, on its creation, ranks in priority ahead of any other mortgages then affecting the mortgaged estate.

(9) In this section—

> "land" does not include mines and minerals held apart from the surface;
>
> "vesting assent" has the same meaning as in the Settled Land Act 1925 (c. 18).

5   Power to extend section 4

(1) The Lord Chancellor may by order—

  (a) amend section 4 so as to add to the events on the occurrence of which the requirement of registration applies such relevant event as he may specify in the order, and

  (b) make such consequential amendments of any provision of, or having effect under, any Act as he thinks appropriate.

(2) For the purposes of subsection (1)(a), a relevant event is an event relating to an unregistered legal estate which is an interest of any of the following kinds—

  (a) an estate in land,

  (b) a rentcharge,

  (c) a franchise, and

  (d) a profit a prendre in gross.

(3) The power conferred by subsection (1) may not be exercised so as to require the title to an estate granted to a person as a mortgagee to be registered.

(4) Before making an order under this section the Lord Chancellor must consult such persons as he considers appropriate.

6   Duty to apply for registration of title

(1) If the requirement of registration applies, the responsible estate owner, or his successor in title, must, before the end of the period for registration, apply to the registrar to be registered as the proprietor of the registrable estate.

(2) If the requirement of registration applies because of section 4(1)(g)—

  (a) the registrable estate is the estate charged by the mortgage, and

  (b) the responsible estate owner is the owner of that estate.

(3) If the requirement of registration applies otherwise than because of section 4(1)(g)—

  (a) the registrable estate is the estate which is transferred or granted, and

  (b) the responsible estate owner is the transferee or grantee of that estate.

(4) The period for registration is 2 months beginning with the date on which the relevant event occurs, or such longer period as the registrar may provide under subsection (5).

(5) If on the application of any interested person the registrar is satisfied that there is good reason for doing so, he may by order provide that the period for registration ends on such later date as he may specify in the order.

(6) Rules may make provision enabling the mortgagee under any mortgage falling within section 4(1)(g) to require the estate charged by the mortgage to be registered whether or not the mortgagor consents.

7   Effect of non-compliance with section 6

(1) If the requirement of registration is not complied with, the transfer, grant or creation becomes void as regards the transfer, grant or creation of a legal estate.

(2) On the application of subsection (1) —
   (a) in a case falling within section 4(1)(a) or (b), the title to the legal estate reverts to the transferor who holds it on a bare trust for the transferee, and
   (b) in a case falling within section 4(1)(c) to (g), the grant or creation has effect as a contract made for valuable consideration to grant or create the legal estate concerned.

(3) If an order under section 6(5) is made in a case where subsection (1) has already applied, that application of the subsection is to be treated as not having occurred.

(4) The possibility of reverter under subsection (1) is to be disregarded for the purposes of determining whether a fee simple is a fee simple absolute.

8   Liability for making good void transfers etc

If a legal estate is retransferred, regranted or recreated because of a failure to comply with the requirement of registration, the transferee, grantee or, as the case may be, the mortgagor —
   (a) is liable to the other party for all the proper costs of and incidental to the retransfer, regrant or recreation of the legal estate, and
   (b) is liable to indemnify the other party in respect of any other liability reasonably incurred by him because of the failure to comply with the requirement of registration.

Classes of title

9   Titles to freehold estates

(1) In the case of an application for registration under this Chapter of a freehold estate, the classes of title with which the applicant may be registered as proprietor are —
   (a) absolute title,
   (b) qualified title, and
   (c) possessory title;
and the following provisions deal with when each of the classes of title is available.

(2) A person may be registered with absolute title if the registrar is of the opinion that the person's title to the estate is such as a willing buyer could properly be advised by a competent professional adviser to accept.

(3) In applying subsection (2), the registrar may disregard the fact that a person's title appears to him to be open to objection if he is of the opinion that the defect will not cause the holding under the title to be disturbed.

(4) A person may be registered with qualified title if the registrar is of the opinion that the person's title to the estate has been established only for a limited

period or subject to certain reservations which cannot be disregarded under subsection (3).

(5) A person may be registered with possessory title if the registrar is of the opinion—

  (a) that the person is in actual possession of the land, or in receipt of the rents and profits of the land, by virtue of the estate, and

  (b) that there is no other class of title with which he may be registered.

10 Titles to leasehold estates

(1) In the case of an application for registration under this Chapter of a leasehold estate, the classes of title with which the applicant may be registered as proprietor are—

  (a) absolute title,

  (b) good leasehold title,

  (c) qualified title, and

  (d) possessory title;

and the following provisions deal with when each of the classes of title is available.

(2) A person may be registered with absolute title if—

  (a) the registrar is of the opinion that the person's title to the estate is such as a willing buyer could properly be advised by a competent professional adviser to accept, and

  (b) the registrar approves the lessor's title to grant the lease.

(3) A person may be registered with good leasehold title if the registrar is of the opinion that the person's title to the estate is such as a willing buyer could properly be advised by a competent professional adviser to accept.

(4) In applying subsection (2) or (3), the registrar may disregard the fact that a person's title appears to him to be open to objection if he is of the opinion that the defect will not cause the holding under the title to be disturbed.

(5) A person may be registered with qualified title if the registrar is of the opinion that the person's title to the estate, or the lessor's title to the reversion, has been established only for a limited period or subject to certain reservations which cannot be disregarded under subsection (4).

(6) A person may be registered with possessory title if the registrar is of the opinion—

  (a) that the person is in actual possession of the land, or in receipt of the rents and profits of the land, by virtue of the estate, and

  (b) that there is no other class of title with which he may be registered.

Effect of first registration

11 Freehold estates

(1) This section is concerned with the registration of a person under this Chapter as the proprietor of a freehold estate.

(2) Registration with absolute title has the effect described in subsections (3) to (5).

(3)   The estate is vested in the proprietor together with all interests subsisting for the benefit of the estate.

(4)   The estate is vested in the proprietor subject only to the following interests affecting the estate at the time of registration—

    (a)   interests which are the subject of an entry in the register in relation to the estate,

    (b)   unregistered interests which fall within any of the paragraphs of Schedule 1, and

    (c)   interests acquired under the Limitation Act 1980 (c. 58) of which the proprietor has notice.

(5)   If the proprietor is not entitled to the estate for his own benefit, or not entitled solely for his own benefit, then, as between himself and the persons beneficially entitled to the estate, the estate is vested in him subject to such of their interests as he has notice of.

(6)   Registration with qualified title has the same effect as registration with absolute title, except that it does not affect the enforcement of any estate, right or interest which appears from the register to be excepted from the effect of registration.

(7)   Registration with possessory title has the same effect as registration with absolute title, except that it does not affect the enforcement of any estate, right or interest adverse to, or in derogation of, the proprietor's title subsisting at the time of registration or then capable of arising.

12   Leasehold estates

(1)   This section is concerned with the registration of a person under this Chapter as the proprietor of a leasehold estate.

(2)   Registration with absolute title has the effect described in subsections (3) to (5).

(3)   The estate is vested in the proprietor together with all interests subsisting for the benefit of the estate.

(4)   The estate is vested subject only to the following interests affecting the estate at the time of registration—

    (a)   implied and express covenants, obligations and liabilities incident to the estate,

    (b)   interests which are the subject of an entry in the register in relation to the estate,

    (c)   unregistered interests which fall within any of the paragraphs of Schedule 1, and

    (d)   interests acquired under the Limitation Act 1980 of which the proprietor has notice.

(5)   If the proprietor is not entitled to the estate for his own benefit, or not entitled solely for his own benefit, then, as between himself and the persons beneficially entitled to the estate, the estate is vested in him subject to such of their interests as he has notice of.

(6)   Registration with good leasehold title has the same effect as registration with absolute title, except that it does not affect the enforcement of any estate, right or interest affecting, or in derogation of, the title of the lessor to grant the lease.

(7) Registration with qualified title has the same effect as registration with absolute title except that it does not affect the enforcement of any estate, right or interest which appears from the register to be excepted from the effect of registration.

(8) Registration with possessory title has the same effect as registration with absolute title, except that it does not affect the enforcement of any estate, right or interest adverse to, or in derogation of, the proprietor's title subsisting at the time of registration or then capable of arising.

Dependent estates

13   Appurtenant rights and charges

Rules may —

(a) make provision for the registration of the proprietor of a registered estate as the proprietor of an unregistered legal estate which subsists for the benefit of the registered estate;

(b) make provision for the registration of a person as the proprietor of an unregistered legal estate which is a charge on a registered estate.

Supplementary

14   Rules about first registration

Rules may —

(a) make provision about the making of applications for registration under this Chapter;

(b) make provision about the functions of the registrar following the making of such an application, including provision about —

    (i) the examination of title, and

    (ii) the entries to be made in the register where such an application is approved;

(c) make provision about the effect of any entry made in the register in pursuance of such an application.

CHAPTER 2

CAUTIONS AGAINST FIRST REGISTRATION

15   Right to lodge

(1) Subject to subsection (3), a person may lodge a caution against the registration of title to an unregistered legal estate if he claims to be —

(a) the owner of a qualifying estate, or

(b) entitled to an interest affecting a qualifying estate.

(2) For the purposes of subsection (1), a qualifying estate is a legal estate which —

(a) relates to land to which the caution relates, and

(b) is an interest of any of the following kinds —

    (i) an estate in land,

    (ii) a rentcharge,

Land Registration Bill
Part 2 — First registration of title
Chapter 2 — Cautions against first registration

     (iii) a franchise, and

     (iv) a profit a prendre in gross.

(3) No caution may be lodged under subsection (1)—

  (a) in the case of paragraph (a), by virtue of ownership of—

    (i) a freehold estate in land, or

    (ii) a leasehold estate in land granted for a term of which more than seven years are unexpired;

  (b) in the case of paragraph (b), by virtue of entitlement to such a leasehold estate as is mentioned in paragraph (a)(ii) of this subsection.

(4) The right under subsection (1) is exercisable by application to the registrar.

16 Effect

(1) Where an application for registration under this Part relates to a legal estate which is the subject of a caution against first registration, the registrar must give the cautioner notice of the application and of his right to object to it.

(2) The registrar may not determine an application to which subsection (1) applies before the end of such period as rules may provide, unless the cautioner has exercised his right to object to the application or given the registrar notice that he does not intend to do so.

(3) Except as provided by this section, a caution against first registration has no effect and, in particular, has no effect on the validity or priority of any interest of the cautioner in the legal estate to which the caution relates.

(4) For the purposes of subsection (1), notice given by a person acting on behalf of an applicant for registration under this Part is to be treated as given by the registrar if—

  (a) the person is of a description provided by rules, and

  (b) notice is given in such circumstances as rules may provide.

17 Withdrawal

The cautioner may withdraw a caution against first registration by application to the registrar.

18 Cancellation

(1) A person may apply to the registrar for cancellation of a caution against first registration if he is—

  (a) the owner of the legal estate to which the caution relates, or

  (b) a person of such other description as rules may provide.

(2) Subject to rules, no application under subsection (1)(a) may be made by a person who—

  (a) consented in such manner as rules may provide to the lodging of the caution, or

  (b) derives title to the legal estate by operation of law from a person who did so.

(3) Where an application is made under subsection (1), the registrar must give the cautioner notice of the application and of the effect of subsection (4).

Land Registration Bill
Part 2 — First registration of title
Chapter 2 — Cautions against first registration

(4) If the cautioner does not exercise his right to object to the application before the end of such period as rules may provide, the registrar must cancel the caution.

19 Cautions register

(1) The registrar must keep a register of cautions against first registration.

(2) Rules may make provision about how the cautions register is to be kept and may, in particular, make provision about—
   (a) the information to be included in the register,
   (b) the form in which information included in the register is to be kept, and
   (c) the arrangement of that information.

20 Alteration of register by court

(1) The court may make an order for alteration of the cautions register for the purpose of—
   (a) correcting a mistake, or
   (b) bringing the register up to date.

(2) An order under subsection (1) has effect when served on the registrar to impose a duty on him to give effect to it.

(3) Rules may make provision about—
   (a) the circumstances in which there is a duty to exercise the power under subsection (1),
   (b) the form of an order under that subsection, and
   (c) service of such an order.

21 Alteration of register by registrar

(1) The registrar may alter the cautions register for the purpose of—
   (a) correcting a mistake, or
   (b) bringing the register up to date.

(2) Rules may make provision about—
   (a) the circumstances in which there is a duty to exercise the power under subsection (1),
   (b) how the cautions register is to be altered in exercise of that power,
   (c) applications for the exercise of that power, and
   (d) procedure in relation to the exercise of that power, whether on application or otherwise.

(3) Where an alteration is made under this section, the registrar may pay such amount as he thinks fit in respect of any costs reasonably incurred by a person in connection with the alteration.

22 Supplementary

In this Chapter, "the cautioner", in relation to a caution against first registration, means the person who lodged the caution, or his personal representative.

PART 3

DISPOSITIONS OF REGISTERED LAND

Powers of disposition

23 Owner's powers

(1) Owner's powers in relation to a registered estate consist of—
   (a) power to make a disposition of any kind permitted by the general law in relation to an interest of that description, other than a mortgage by demise or sub-demise, and
   (b) power to charge the estate at law with the payment of money.

(2) Owner's powers in relation to a registered charge consist of—
   (a) power to make a disposition of any kind permitted by the general law in relation to an interest of that description, other than a legal sub-mortgage, and
   (b) power to charge at law with the payment of money indebtedness secured by the registered charge.

(3) In subsection (2)(a), "legal sub-mortgage" means—
   (a) a transfer by way of mortgage,
   (b) a sub-mortgage by sub-demise, and
   (c) a charge by way of legal mortgage.

24 Right to exercise owner's powers

(1) A person is entitled to exercise owner's powers in relation to a registered estate or charge if he is—
   (a) the registered proprietor, or
   (b) entitled to be registered as the proprietor.

(2) The right conferred by subsection (1)(b) is subject to rules.

25 Mode of exercise

(1) A registrable disposition of a registered estate or charge only has effect if it complies with such requirements as to form and content as rules may provide.

(2) Rules may apply subsection (1) to any other kind of disposition which depends for its effect on registration.

26 Protection of disponees

(1) Subject to subsection (2), a person's right to exercise owner's powers in relation to a registered estate or charge is to be taken to be free from any limitation affecting the validity of a disposition.

(2) Subsection (1) does not apply to a limitation—
   (a) reflected by an entry in the register, or
   (b) imposed by, or under, this Act.

(3)   This section has effect only for the purpose of preventing the title of a disponee being questioned (and so does not affect the lawfulness of a disposition).

Registrable dispositions

27   Dispositions required to be registered

(1)   If a disposition of a registered estate or registered charge is required to be completed by registration, it does not operate at law until the relevant registration requirements are met.

(2)   In the case of a registered estate, the following are the dispositions which are required to be completed by registration—

   (a)   a transfer,

   (b)   where the registered estate is an estate in land, the grant of a term of years absolute—

      (i)   for a term of more than seven years from the date of the grant,

      (ii)   to take effect in possession after the end of the period of three months beginning with the date of the grant,

      (iii)   under which the right to possession is discontinuous,

      (iv)   in pursuance of Part 5 of the Housing Act 1985 (c. 68) (the right to buy), or

      (v)   in circumstances where section 171A of that Act applies (disposal by landlord which leads to a person no longer being a secure tenant),

   (c)   where the registered estate is a franchise or manor, the grant of a lease,

   (d)   the express grant or reservation of an interest of a kind falling within section 1(2)(a) of the Law of Property Act 1925 (c. 20), other than one which is capable of being registered under the Commons Registration Act 1965 (c. 64),

   (e)   the express grant or reservation of an interest of a kind falling within section 1(2)(b) or (e) of the Law of Property Act 1925, and

   (f)   the grant of a legal charge.

(3)   In the case of a registered charge, the following are the dispositions which are required to be completed by registration—

   (a)   a transfer, and

   (b)   the grant of a sub-charge.

(4)   Schedule 2 to this Act (which deals with the relevant registration requirements) has effect.

(5)   This section applies to dispositions by operation of law as it applies to other dispositions, but with the exception of the following—

   (a)   a transfer on the death or bankruptcy of an individual proprietor,

   (b)   a transfer on the dissolution of a corporate proprietor, and

   (c)   the creation of a legal charge which is a local land charge.

(6)   Rules may make provision about applications to the registrar for the purpose of meeting registration requirements under this section.

(7)   In subsection (2)(d), the reference to express grant does not include grant as a result of the operation of section 62 of the Law of Property Act 1925.

Effect of dispositions on priority

28 Basic rule

(1) Except as provided by sections 29 and 30, the priority of an interest affecting a registered estate or charge is not affected by a disposition of the estate or charge.

(2) It makes no difference for the purposes of this section whether the interest or disposition is registered.

29 Effect of registered dispositions: estates

(1) If a registrable disposition of a registered estate is made for valuable consideration, completion of the disposition by registration has the effect of postponing to the interest under the disposition any interest affecting the estate immediately before the disposition whose priority is not protected at the time of registration.

(2) For the purposes of subsection (1), the priority of an interest is protected —
  (a) in any case, if the interest —
    (i) is a registered charge or the subject of a notice in the register,
    (ii) falls within any of the paragraphs of Schedule 3, or
    (iii) appears from the register to be excepted from the effect of registration, and
  (b) in the case of a disposition of a leasehold estate, if the burden of the interest is incident to the estate.

(3) Subsection (2)(a)(ii) does not apply to an interest which has been the subject of a notice in the register at any time since the coming into force of this section.

(4) Where the grant of a leasehold estate in land out of a registered estate does not involve a registrable disposition, this section has effect as if —
  (a) the grant involved such a disposition, and
  (b) the disposition were registered at the time of the grant.

30 Effect of registered dispositions: charges

(1) If a registrable disposition of a registered charge is made for valuable consideration, completion of the disposition by registration has the effect of postponing to the interest under the disposition any interest affecting the charge immediately before the disposition whose priority is not protected at the time of registration.

(2) For the purposes of subsection (1), the priority of an interest is protected —
  (a) in any case, if the interest —
    (i) is a registered charge or the subject of a notice in the register,
    (ii) falls within any of the paragraphs of Schedule 3, or
    (iii) appears from the register to be excepted from the effect of registration, and
  (b) in the case of a disposition of a charge which relates to a leasehold estate, if the burden of the interest is incident to the estate.

(3) Subsection (2)(a)(ii) does not apply to an interest which has been the subject of a notice in the register at any time since the coming into force of this section.

31   Inland Revenue charges

The effect of a disposition of a registered estate or charge on a charge under section 237 of the Inheritance Tax Act 1984 (c. 51) (charge for unpaid tax) is to be determined, not in accordance with sections 28 to 30 above, but in accordance with sections 237(6) and 238 of that Act (under which a purchaser in good faith for money or money's worth takes free from the charge in the absence of registration).

PART 4

NOTICES AND RESTRICTIONS

Notices

32   Nature and effect

(1)   A notice is an entry in the register in respect of the burden of an interest affecting a registered estate or charge.

(2)   The entry of a notice is to be made in relation to the registered estate or charge affected by the interest concerned.

(3)   The fact that an interest is the subject of a notice does not necessarily mean that the interest is valid, but does mean that the priority of the interest, if valid, is protected for the purposes of sections 29 and 30.

33   Excluded interests

No notice may be entered in the register in respect of any of the following —
- (a)   an interest under —
    - (i)   a trust of land, or
    - (ii)   a settlement under the Settled Land Act 1925 (c. 18),
- (b)   a leasehold estate in land which —
    - (i)   is granted for a term of years of three years or less from the date of the grant, and
    - (ii)   is not required to be registered,
- (c)   a restrictive covenant made between a lessor and lessee, so far as relating to the demised premises,
- (d)   an interest which is capable of being registered under the Commons Registration Act 1965 (c. 64), and
- (e)   an interest in any coal or coal mine, the rights attached to any such interest and the rights of any person under section 38, 49 or 51 of the Coal Industry Act 1994 (c. 21).

34   Entry on application

(1)   A person who claims to be entitled to the benefit of an interest affecting a registered estate or charge may, if the interest is not excluded by section 33, apply to the registrar for the entry in the register of a notice in respect of the interest.

(2)   Subject to rules, an application under this section may be for —
- (a)   an agreed notice, or

(b)   a unilateral notice.

(3)   The registrar may only approve an application for an agreed notice if—

(a)   the applicant is the relevant registered proprietor, or a person entitled to be registered as such proprietor,

(b)   the relevant registered proprietor, or a person entitled to be registered as such proprietor, consents to the entry of the notice, or

(c)   the registrar is satisfied as to the validity of the applicant's claim.

(4)   In subsection (3), references to the relevant registered proprietor are to the proprietor of the registered estate or charge affected by the interest to which the application relates.

35   Unilateral notices

(1)   If the registrar enters a notice in the register in pursuance of an application under section 34(2)(b) ("a unilateral notice"), he must give notice of the entry to—

(a)   the proprietor of the registered estate or charge to which it relates, and

(b)   such other persons as rules may provide.

(2)   A unilateral notice must—

(a)   indicate that it is such a notice, and

(b)   identify who is the beneficiary of the notice.

(3)   The person shown in the register as the beneficiary of a unilateral notice may apply to the registrar for the removal of the notice from the register.

36   Cancellation of unilateral notices

(1)   A person may apply to the registrar for the cancellation of a unilateral notice if he is—

(a)   the registered proprietor of the estate or charge to which the notice relates, or

(b)   a person entitled to be registered as the proprietor of that estate or charge.

(2)   Where an application is made under subsection (1), the registrar must give the beneficiary of the notice notice of the application and of the effect of subsection (3).

(3)   If the beneficiary of the notice does not exercise his right to object to the application before the end of such period as rules may provide, the registrar must cancel the notice.

(4)   In this section—

"beneficiary", in relation to a unilateral notice, means the person shown in the register as the beneficiary of the notice;

"unilateral notice" means a notice entered in the register in pursuance of an application under section 34(2)(b).

37   Unregistered interests

If it appears to the registrar that a registered estate is subject to an unregistered interest which—

    (a)   falls within any of the paragraphs of Schedule 1, and

    (b)   is not excluded by section 33,

he may enter a notice in the register in respect of the interest.

38   Registrable dispositions

Where a person is entered in the register as the proprietor of an interest under a disposition falling within section 27(2)(b) to (e), the registrar must also enter a notice in the register in respect of that interest.

39   Supplementary

Rules may make provision about the form and content of notices in the register.

Restrictions

40   Nature

(1)   A restriction is an entry in the register regulating the circumstances in which a disposition of a registered estate or charge may be the subject of an entry in the register.

(2)   A restriction may, in particular —

    (a)   prohibit the making of an entry in respect of any disposition, or a disposition of a kind specified in the restriction;

    (b)   prohibit the making of an entry —

        (i)   indefinitely,

        (ii)   for a period specified in the restriction, or

        (iii)   until the occurrence of an event so specified.

(3)   Without prejudice to the generality of subsection (2)(b)(iii), the events which may be specified include —

    (a)   the giving of notice,

    (b)   the obtaining of consent, and

    (c)   the making of an order by the court or registrar.

(4)   The entry of a restriction is to be made in relation to the registered estate or charge to which it relates.

41   Effect

(1)   Where a restriction is entered in the register, no entry in respect of a disposition to which the restriction applies may be made in the register otherwise than in accordance with the terms of the restriction, subject to any order under subsection (2).

(2)   The registrar may by order —

    (a)   disapply a restriction in relation to a disposition specified in the order or dispositions of a kind so specified, or

    (b)   provide that a restriction has effect, in relation to a disposition specified in the order or dispositions of a kind so specified, with modifications so specified.

(3) The power under subsection (2) is exercisable only on the application of a person who appears to the registrar to have a sufficient interest in the restriction.

42   Power of registrar to enter

(1) The registrar may enter a restriction in the register if it appears to him that it is necessary or desirable to do so for the purpose of—

    (a) preventing invalidity or unlawfulness in relation to dispositions of a registered estate or charge,

    (b) securing that interests which are capable of being overreached on a disposition of a registered estate or charge are overreached, or

    (c) protecting a right or claim in relation to a registered estate or charge.

(2) No restriction may be entered under subsection (1)(c) for the purpose of protecting the priority of an interest which is, or could be, the subject of a notice.

(3) The registrar must give notice of any entry made under this section to the proprietor of the registered estate or charge concerned, except where the entry is made in pursuance of an application under section 43.

(4) For the purposes of subsection (1)(c), a person entitled to the benefit of a charging order relating to an interest under a trust shall be treated as having a right or claim in relation to the trust property.

43   Applications

(1) A person may apply to the registrar for the entry of a restriction under section 42(1) if—

    (a) he is the relevant registered proprietor, or a person entitled to be registered as such proprietor,

    (b) the relevant registered proprietor, or a person entitled to be registered as such proprietor, consents to the application, or

    (c) he otherwise has a sufficient interest in the making of the entry.

(2) Rules may—

    (a) require the making of an application under subsection (1) in such circumstances, and by such person, as the rules may provide;

    (b) make provision about the form of consent for the purposes of subsection (1) (b);

    (c) provide for classes of person to be regarded as included in subsection (1)(c);

    (d) specify standard forms of restriction.

(3) If an application under subsection (1) is made for the entry of a restriction which is not in a form specified under subsection (2)(d), the registrar may only approve the application if it appears to him—

    (a) that the terms of the proposed restriction are reasonable, and

    (b) that applying the proposed restriction would—

        (i) be straightforward, and

        (ii) not place an unreasonable burden on him.

(4)   In subsection (1), references to the relevant registered proprietor are to the proprietor of the registered estate or charge to which the application relates.

44   Obligatory restrictions

(1)   If the registrar enters two or more persons in the register as the proprietor of a registered estate in land, he must also enter in the register such restrictions as rules may provide for the purpose of securing that interests which are capable of being overreached on a disposition of the estate are overreached.

(2)   Where under any enactment the registrar is required to enter a restriction without application, the form of the restriction shall be such as rules may provide.

45   Notifiable applications

(1)   Where an application under section 43(1) is notifiable, the registrar must give notice of the application, and of the right to object to it, to—
  (a)   the proprietor of the registered estate or charge to which it relates, and
  (b)   such other persons as rules may provide.

(2)   The registrar may not determine an application to which subsection (1) applies before the end of such period as rules may provide, unless the person, or each of the persons, notified under that subsection has exercised his right to object to the application or given the registrar notice that he does not intend to do so.

(3)   For the purposes of this section, an application under section 43(1) is notifiable unless it is—
  (a)   made by or with the consent of the proprietor of the registered estate or charge to which the application relates, or a person entitled to be registered as such proprietor,
  (b)   made in pursuance of rules under section 43(2)(a), or
  (c)   an application for the entry of a restriction reflecting a limitation under an order of the court or registrar, or an undertaking given in place of such an order.

46   Power of court to order entry

(1)   If it appears to the court that it is necessary or desirable to do so for the purpose of protecting a right or claim in relation to a registered estate or charge, it may make an order requiring the registrar to enter a restriction in the register.

(2)   No order under this section may be made for the purpose of protecting the priority of an interest which is, or could be, the subject of a notice.

(3)   The court may include in an order under this section a direction that an entry made in pursuance of the order is to have overriding priority.

(4)   If an order under this section includes a direction under subsection (3), the registrar must make such entry in the register as rules may provide.

(5)   The court may make the exercise of its power under subsection (3) subject to such terms and conditions as it thinks fit.

47   Withdrawal

A person may apply to the registrar for the withdrawal of a restriction if —

(a)   the restriction was entered in such circumstances as rules may provide, and

(b)   he is of such a description as rules may provide.

PART 5

CHARGES

Relative priority

48   Registered charges

(1)   Registered charges on the same registered estate, or on the same registered charge, are to be taken to rank as between themselves in the order shown in the register.

(2)   Rules may make provision about —

(a)   how the priority of registered charges as between themselves is to be shown in the register, and

(b)   applications for registration of the priority of registered charges as between themselves.

49   Tacking and further advances

(1)   The proprietor of a registered charge may make a further advance on the security of the charge ranking in priority to a subsequent charge if he has not received from the subsequent chargee notice of the creation of the subsequent charge.

(2)   Notice given for the purposes of subsection (1) shall be treated as received at the time when, in accordance with rules, it ought to have been received.

(3)   The proprietor of a registered charge may also make a further advance on the security of the charge ranking in priority to a subsequent charge if —

(a)   the advance is made in pursuance of an obligation, and

(b)   at the time of the creation of the subsequent charge the obligation was entered in the register in accordance with rules.

(4)   The proprietor of a registered charge may also make a further advance on the security of the charge ranking in priority to a subsequent charge if —

(a)   the parties to the prior charge have agreed a maximum amount for which the charge is security, and

(b)   at the time of the creation of the subsequent charge the agreement was entered in the register in accordance with rules.

(5)   Rules may —

(a)   disapply subsection (4) in relation to charges of a description specified in the rules, or

(b)   provide for the application of that subsection to be subject, in the case of charges of a description so specified, to compliance with such conditions as may be so specified.

(6) Except as provided by this section, tacking in relation to a charge over registered land is only possible with the agreement of the subsequent chargee.

50 Overriding statutory charges: duty of notification

If the registrar enters a person in the register as the proprietor of a charge which—

(a) is created by or under an enactment, and

(b) has effect to postpone a charge which at the time of registration of the statutory charge is—

(i) entered in the register, or

(ii) the basis for an entry in the register,

he must in accordance with rules give notice of the creation of the statutory charge to such person as rules may provide.

Powers as chargee

51 Effect of completion by registration

On completion of the relevant registration requirements, a charge created by means of a registrable disposition of a registered estate has effect, if it would not otherwise do so, as a charge by deed by way of legal mortgage.

52 Protection of disponees

(1) Subject to any entry in the register to the contrary, the proprietor of a registered charge is to be taken to have, in relation to the property subject to the charge, the powers of disposition conferred by law on the owner of a legal mortgage.

(2) Subsection (1) has effect only for the purpose of preventing the title of a disponee being questioned (and so does not affect the lawfulness of a disposition).

53 Powers as sub-chargee

The registered proprietor of a sub-charge has, in relation to the property subject to the principal charge or any intermediate charge, the same powers as the sub-chargor.

Realisation of security

54 Proceeds of sale: chargee's duty

For the purposes of section 105 of the Law of Property Act 1925 (c. 20) (mortgagee's duties in relation to application of proceeds of sale), in its application to the proceeds of sale of registered land, a person shall be taken to have notice of anything in the register.

55 Local land charges

A charge over registered land which is a local land charge may only be realised if the title to the charge is registered.

Miscellaneous

56 Receipt in case of joint proprietors

Where a charge is registered in the name of two or more proprietors, a valid receipt for the money secured by the charge may be given by —

    (a)   the registered proprietors,

    (b)   the survivors or survivor of the registered proprietors, or

    (c)   the personal representative of the last survivor of the registered proprietors.

57 Entry of right of consolidation

Rules may make provision about entry in the register of a right of consolidation in relation to a registered charge.

PART 6

REGISTRATION: GENERAL

Registration as proprietor

58 Conclusiveness

(1)   If, on the entry of a person in the register as the proprietor of a legal estate, the legal estate would not otherwise be vested in him, it shall be deemed to be vested in him as a result of the registration.

(2)   Subsection (1) does not apply where the entry is made in pursuance of a registrable disposition in relation to which some other registration requirement remains to be met.

59 Dependent estates

(1)   The entry of a person in the register as the proprietor of a legal estate which subsists for the benefit of a registered estate must be made in relation to that estate.

(2)   The entry of a person in the register as the proprietor of a charge on a registered estate must be made in relation to that estate.

(3)   The entry of a person in the register as the proprietor of a sub-charge on a registered charge must be made in relation to that charge.

Boundaries

60 Boundaries

(1)   The boundary of a registered estate as shown for the purposes of the register is a general boundary, unless shown as determined under this section.

(2)   A general boundary does not determine the exact line of the boundary.

(3) Rules may make provision enabling or requiring the exact line of the boundary of a registered estate to be determined and may, in particular, make provision about—

    (a) the circumstances in which the exact line of a boundary may or must be determined,

    (b) how the exact line of a boundary may be determined,

    (c) procedure in relation to applications for determination, and

    (d) the recording of the fact of determination in the register or the index maintained under section 68.

61 Accretion and diluvion

(1) The fact that a registered estate in land is shown in the register as having a particular boundary does not affect the operation of accretion or diluvion.

(2) An agreement about the operation of accretion or diluvion in relation to a registered estate in land has effect only if registered in accordance with rules.

Quality of title

62 Power to upgrade title

(1) Where the title to a freehold estate is entered in the register as possessory or qualified, the registrar may enter it as absolute if he is satisfied as to the title to the estate.

(2) Where the title to a leasehold estate is entered in the register as good leasehold, the registrar may enter it as absolute if he is satisfied as to the superior title.

(3) Where the title to a leasehold estate is entered in the register as possessory or qualified the registrar may—

    (a) enter it as good leasehold if he is satisfied as to the title to the estate, and

    (b) enter it as absolute if he is satisfied both as to the title to the estate and as to the superior title.

(4) Where the title to a freehold estate in land has been entered in the register as possessory for at least twelve years, the registrar may enter it as absolute if he is satisfied that the proprietor is in possession of the land.

(5) Where the title to a leasehold estate in land has been entered in the register as possessory for at least twelve years, the registrar may enter it as good leasehold if he is satisfied that the proprietor is in possession of the land.

(6) None of the powers under subsections (1) to (5) is exercisable if there is outstanding any claim adverse to the title of the registered proprietor which is made by virtue of an estate, right or interest whose enforceability is preserved by virtue of the existing entry about the class of title.

(7) The only persons who may apply to the registrar for the exercise of any of the powers under subsections (1) to (5) are—

    (a) the proprietor of the estate to which the application relates,

    (b) a person entitled to be registered as the proprietor of that estate,

    (c) the proprietor of a registered charge affecting that estate, and

    (d) a person interested in a registered estate which derives from that estate.

(8)   In determining for the purposes of this section whether he is satisfied as to any title, the registrar is to apply the same standards as those which apply under section 9 or 10 to first registration of title.

(9)   The Lord Chancellor may by order amend subsection (4) or (5) by substituting for the number of years for the time being specified in that subsection such number of years as the order may provide.

63   Effect of upgrading title

(1)   On the title to a registered freehold or leasehold estate being entered under section 62 as absolute, the proprietor ceases to hold the estate subject to any estate, right or interest whose enforceability was preserved by virtue of the previous entry about the class of title.

(2)   Subsection (1) also applies on the title to a registered leasehold estate being entered under section 62 as good leasehold, except that the entry does not affect or prejudice the enforcement of any estate, right or interest affecting, or in derogation of, the title of the lessor to grant the lease.

64   Use of register to record defects in title

(1)   If it appears to the registrar that a right to determine a registered estate in land has become exercisable, he may enter the fact in the register.

(2)   Rules may make provision about entries under subsection (1) and may, in particular, make provision about—
   (a)   the circumstances in which there is a duty to exercise the power conferred by that subsection,
   (b)   how entries under that subsection are to be made, and
   (c)   the removal of such entries.

Alteration of register

65   Alteration of register

Schedule 4 (which makes provision about alteration of the register) has effect.

Information etc.

66   Inspection of the registers etc

(1)   Any person may inspect and make copies of, or of any part of—
   (a)   the register of title,
   (b)   any document kept by the registrar which is referred to in the register of title,
   (c)   any other document kept by the registrar which relates to an application to him, or
   (d)   the register of cautions against first registration.

(2)   The right under subsection (1) is subject to rules which may, in particular—
   (a)   provide for exceptions to the right, and

    (b)   impose conditions on its exercise, including conditions requiring the payment of fees.

67   Official copies of the registers etc

(1)   An official copy of, or of a part of —

    (a)   the register of title,

    (b)   any document which is referred to in the register of title and kept by the registrar,

    (c)   any other document kept by the registrar which relates to an application to him, or

    (d)   the register of cautions against first registration,

is admissible in evidence to the same extent as the original.

(2)   A person who relies on an official copy in which there is a mistake is not liable for loss suffered by another by reason of the mistake.

(3)   Rules may make provision for the issue of official copies and may, in particular, make provision about —

    (a)   the form of official copies,

    (b)   who may issue official copies,

    (c)   applications for official copies, and

    (d)   the conditions to be met by applicants for official copies, including conditions requiring the payment of fees.

68   Index

(1)   The registrar must keep an index for the purpose of enabling the following matters to be ascertained in relation to any parcel of land —

    (a)   whether any registered estate relates to the land,

    (b)   how any registered estate which relates to the land is identified for the purposes of the register,

    (c)   whether the land is affected by any, and, if so what, caution against first registration, and

    (d)   such other matters as rules may provide.

(2)   Rules may —

    (a)   make provision about how the index is to be kept and may, in particular, make provision about —

        (i)   the information to be included in the index,

        (ii)   the form in which information included in the index is to be kept, and

        (iii)   the arrangement of that information;

    (b)   make provision about official searches of the index.

69   Historical information

(1)   The registrar may on application provide information about the history of a registered title.

(2)   Rules may make provision about applications for the exercise of the power conferred by subsection (1).

70   Official searches

Rules may make provision for official searches of the register, including searches of pending applications for first registration, and may, in particular, make provision about—

(a)   the form of applications for searches,

(b)   the manner in which such applications may be made,

(c)   the form of official search certificates, and

(d)   the manner in which such certificates may be issued.

Applications

71   Duty to disclose unregistered interests

Where rules so provide—

(a)   a person applying for registration under Chapter 1 of Part 1 must provide to the registrar such information as the rules may provide about any interest affecting the estate to which the application relates which—

  (i)   falls within any of the paragraphs of Schedule 1, and

  (ii)   is of a description specified by the rules;

(b)   a person applying to register a registrable disposition of a registered estate must provide to the registrar such information as the rules may provide about any unregistered interest affecting the estate which—

  (i)   falls within any of the paragraphs of Schedule 3, and

  (ii)   is of description specified by the rules.

72   Priority protection

(1)   For the purposes of this section, an application for an entry in the register is protected if—

(a)   it is one to which a priority period relates, and

(b)   it is made before the end of that period.

(2)   Where an application for an entry in the register is protected, any entry made in the register during the priority period relating to the application is postponed to any entry made in pursuance of it.

(3)   Subsection (2) does not apply if—

(a)   the earlier entry was made in pursuance of a protected application, and

(b)   the priority period relating to that application ranks ahead of the one relating to the application for the other entry.

(4)   Subsection (2) does not apply if the earlier entry is one to which a direction under section 46(3) applies.

(5)   The registrar may defer dealing with an application for an entry in the register if it appears to him that subsection (2) might apply to the entry were he to make it.

(6)   Rules may—

(a)   make provision for priority periods in connection with—

  (i)   official searches of the register, including searches of pending applications for first registration, or

(ii) the noting in the register of a contract for the making of a registrable disposition of a registered estate or charge;

(b) make provision for the keeping of records in relation to priority periods and the inspection of such records.

(7) Rules under subsection (6)(a) may, in particular, make provision about—

(a) the commencement and length of a priority period,

(b) the applications for registration to which such a period relates,

(c) the order in which competing priority periods rank, and

(d) the application of subsections (2) and (3) in cases where more than one priority period relates to the same application.

73 Objections

(1) Subject to subsections (2) and (3), anyone may object to an application to the registrar.

(2) In the case of an application under section 18, only the person who lodged the caution to which the application relates, or his personal representative, may object.

(3) In the case of an application under section 36, only the person shown in the register as the beneficiary of the notice to which the application relates may object.

(4) The right to object under this section is subject to rules.

(5) Where an objection is made under this section, the registrar—

(a) must give notice of the objection to the applicant, and

(b) may not determine the application until the objection has been disposed of.

(6) Subsection (5) does not apply if the objection is one which the registrar is satisfied is groundless.

(7) If it is not possible to dispose by agreement of an objection to which subsection (5) applies, the registrar must refer the matter to the adjudicator.

(8) Rules may make provision about references under subsection (7).

74 Effective date of registration

An entry made in the register in pursuance of—

(a) an application for registration of an unregistered legal estate, or

(b) an application for registration in relation to a disposition required to be completed by registration,

has effect from the time of the making of the application.

Proceedings before the registrar

75 Production of documents

(1) The registrar may require a person to produce a document for the purposes of proceedings before him.

(2) The power under subsection (1) is subject to rules.

(3) A requirement under subsection (1) shall be enforceable as an order of the court.

(4) A person aggrieved by a requirement under subsection (1) may appeal to a county court, which may make any order which appears appropriate.

76 Costs

(1) The registrar may make orders about costs in relation to proceedings before him.

(2) The power under subsection (1) is subject to rules which may, in particular, make provision about—
    (a) who may be required to pay costs,
    (b) whose costs a person may be required to pay,
    (c) the kind of costs which a person may be required to pay, and
    (d) the assessment of costs.

(3) Without prejudice to the generality of subsection (2), rules under that subsection may include provision about—
    (a) costs of the registrar, and
    (b) liability for costs thrown away as the result of neglect or delay by a legal representative of a party to proceedings.

(4) An order under subsection (1) shall be enforceable as an order of the court.

(5) A person aggrieved by an order under subsection (1) may appeal to a county court, which may make any order which appears appropriate.

Miscellaneous

77 Duty to act reasonably

(1) A person must not exercise any of the following rights without reasonable cause—
    (a) the right to lodge a caution under section 15,
    (b) the right to apply for the entry of a notice or restriction, and
    (c) the right to object to an application to the registrar.

(2) The duty under this section is owed to any person who suffers damage in consequence of its breach.

78 Notice of trust not to affect registrar

The registrar shall not be affected with notice of a trust.

PART 7

SPECIAL CASES

The Crown

79 Voluntary registration of demesne land

(1) Her Majesty may grant an estate in fee simple absolute in possession out of demesne land to Herself.

(2) The grant of an estate under subsection (1) is to be regarded as not having been made unless an application under section 3 is made in respect of the estate before the end of the period for registration.

(3) The period for registration is two months beginning with the date of the grant, or such longer period as the registrar may provide under subsection (4).

(4) If on the application of Her Majesty the registrar is satisfied that there is a good reason for doing so, he may by order provide that the period for registration ends on such later date as he may specify in the order.

(5) If an order under subsection (4) is made in a case where subsection (2) has already applied, that application of the subsection is to be treated as not having occurred.

80 Compulsory registration of grants out of demesne land

(1) Section 4(1) shall apply as if the following were included among the events listed —
   (a) the grant by Her Majesty out of demesne land of an estate in fee simple absolute in possession, otherwise than under section 79;
   (b) the grant by Her Majesty out of demesne land of an estate in land —
      (i) for a term of years absolute of more than seven years from the date of the grant, and
      (ii) for valuable or other consideration, by way of gift or in pursuance of an order of any court.

(2) In subsection (1)(b)(ii), the reference to grant by way of gift includes grant for the purpose of constituting a trust under which Her Majesty does not retain the whole of the beneficial interest.

(3) Subsection (1) does not apply to the grant of an estate in mines and minerals held apart from the surface.

(4) The Lord Chancellor may by order —
   (a) amend this section so as to add to the events in subsection (1) such events relating to demesne land as he may specify in the order, and
   (b) make such consequential amendments of any provision of, or having effect under, any Act as he thinks appropriate.

(5) In its application by virtue of subsection (1), section 7 has effect with the substitution for subsection (2) of —

   "(2) On the application of subsection (1), the grant has effect as a contract made for valuable consideration to grant the legal estate concerned".

81 Demesne land: cautions against first registration

(1) Section 15 shall apply as if demesne land were held by Her Majesty for an unregistered estate in fee simple absolute in possession.

(2) The provisions of this Act relating to cautions against first registration shall, in relation to cautions lodged by virtue of subsection (1), have effect subject to such modifications as rules may provide.

82 Escheat etc

(1) Rules may make provision about—
   (a) the determination of a registered freehold estate in land, and
   (b) the registration of an unregistered freehold legal estate in land in respect of land to which a former registered freehold estate in land related.

(2) Rules under this section may, in particular—
   (a) make provision for the effect of determination to be dependent on the meeting of such registration requirements as the rules may specify;
   (b) make provision for entries relating to a freehold estate in land to continue in the register, notwithstanding determination, for such time as the rules may provide;
   (c) make provision for the making in the register in relation to a former freehold estate in land of such entries as the rules may provide;
   (d) make provision imposing requirements to be met in connection with an application for the registration of such an unregistered estate as is mentioned in subsection (1)(b).

83 Crown and Duchy land: representation

(1) With respect to a Crown or Duchy interest, the appropriate authority—
   (a) may represent the owner of the interest for all purposes of this Act,
   (b) is entitled to receive such notice as that person is entitled to receive under this Act, and
   (c) may make such applications and do such other acts as that person is entitled to make or do under this Act.

(2) In this section—
   "the appropriate authority" means—
   (a) in relation to an interest belonging to Her Majesty in right of the Crown and forming part of the Crown Estate, the Crown Estate Commissioners;
   (b) in relation to any other interest belonging to Her Majesty in right of the Crown, the government department having the management of the interest or, if there is no such department, such person as Her Majesty may appoint in writing under the Royal Sign Manual;
   (c) in relation to an interest belonging to Her Majesty in right of the Duchy of Lancaster, the Chancellor of the Duchy;
   (d) in relation to an interest belonging to the Duchy of Cornwall, such person as the Duke of Cornwall, or the possessor for the time being of the Duchy of Cornwall, appoints;

> (e) in relation to an interest belonging to a government department, or held in trust for Her Majesty for the purposes of a government department, that department;

"Crown interest" means an interest belonging to Her Majesty in right of the Crown, or belonging to a government department, or held in trust for Her Majesty for the purposes of a government department;

"Duchy interest" means an interest belonging to Her Majesty in right of the Duchy of Lancaster, or belonging to the Duchy of Cornwall;

"interest" means any estate, interest or charge in or over land and any right or claim in relation to land.

84   Disapplication of requirements relating to Duchy land

Nothing in any enactment relating to the Duchy of Lancaster or the Duchy of Cornwall shall have effect to impose any requirement with respect to formalities or enrolment in relation to a disposition by a registered proprietor.

85   Bona vacantia

Rules may make provision about how the passing of a registered estate or charge as bona vacantia is to be dealt with for the purposes of this Act.

Pending actions etc.

86   Bankruptcy

(1)   In this Act, references to an interest affecting an estate or charge do not include a petition in bankruptcy or bankruptcy order.

(2)   As soon as practicable after registration of a petition in bankruptcy as a pending action under the Land Charges Act 1972 (c. 61), the registrar must enter in the register in relation to any registered estate or charge which appears to him to be affected a notice in respect of the pending action.

(3)   Unless cancelled by the registrar in such manner as rules may provide, a notice entered under subsection (2) continues in force until—
> (a)   a restriction is entered in the register under subsection (4), or
> (b)   the trustee in bankruptcy is registered as proprietor.

(4)   As soon as practicable after registration of a bankruptcy order under the Land Charges Act 1972, the registrar must, in relation to any registered estate or charge which appears to him to be affected by the order, enter in the register a restriction reflecting the limitation under section 284 of the Insolvency Act 1986 (c. 45) (disposition by bankrupt void unless made with the consent of, or subsequently ratified by, the court).

(5)   Where the proprietor of a registered estate or charge is adjudged bankrupt, the title of his trustee in bankruptcy is void as against a person to whom a registrable disposition of the estate or charge is made if—
> (a)   the disposition is made for valuable consideration,
> (b)   the person to whom the disposition is made acts in good faith, and
> (c)   at the time of the disposition—
>> (i)   no notice or restriction is entered under this section in relation to the registered estate or charge, and

        (ii)   the person to whom the disposition is made has no notice of the bankruptcy petition or the adjudication.

(6)   Subsection (5) only applies if the relevant registration requirements are met in relation to the disposition, but, when they are met, has effect as from the date of the disposition.

(7)   Nothing in this section requires a person to whom a registrable disposition is made to make any search under the Land Charges Act 1972 (c. 61).

87 Pending land actions, writs, orders and deeds of arrangement

(1)   Subject to the following provisions, references in this Act to an interest affecting an estate or charge include—
    (a)   a pending land action within the meaning of the Land Charges Act 1972,
    (b)   a writ or order of the kind mentioned in section 6(1)(a) of that Act (writ or order affecting land issued or made by any court for the purposes of enforcing a judgment or recognisance),
    (c)   an order appointing a receiver or sequestrator, and
    (d)   a deed of arrangement.

(2)   No notice may be entered in the register in respect of—
    (a)   an order appointing a receiver or sequestrator, or
    (b)   a deed of arrangement.

(3)   None of the matters mentioned in subsection (1) shall be capable of falling within paragraph 2 of Schedule 1 or 3.

(4)   In its application to any of the matters mentioned in subsection (1), this Act shall have effect subject to such modifications as rules may provide.

(5)   In this section, "deed of arrangement" has the same meaning as in the Deeds of Arrangement Act 1914 (c. 47).

Miscellaneous

88 Incorporeal hereditaments

In its application to—
    (a)   rentcharges,
    (b)   franchises,
    (c)   profits a prendre in gross, or
    (d)   manors,
this Act shall have effect subject to such modification as rules may provide.

89 Settlements

(1)   Rules may make provision for the purposes of this Act in relation to the application to registered land of the enactments relating to settlements under the Settled Land Act 1925 (c. 18).

(2)   Rules under this section may include provision modifying any of those enactments in its application to registered land.

(3) In this section, "registered land" means an interest the title to which is, or is required to be, registered.

90 PPP leases relating to transport in London

(1) No application for registration under section 3 may be made in respect of a leasehold estate in land under a PPP lease.

(2) The requirement of registration does not apply on the grant or transfer of a leasehold estate in land under a PPP lease.

(3) For the purposes of section 27, the following are not dispositions requiring to be completed by registration—
    (a) the grant of a term of years absolute under a PPP lease;
    (b) the express grant of an interest falling within section 1(2) of the Law of Property Act 1925 (c. 20), where the interest is created for the benefit of a leasehold estate in land under a PPP lease.

(4) No notice may be entered in the register in respect of an interest under a PPP lease.

(5) Schedules 1 and 3 have effect as if they included a paragraph referring to a PPP lease.

(6) In this section, "PPP lease" has the meaning given by section 218 of the Greater London Authority Act 1999 (c. 29) (which makes provision about leases created for public-private partnerships relating to transport in London).

PART 8

ELECTRONIC CONVEYANCING

91 Electronic dispositions: formalities

(1) This section applies to a document in electronic form where—
    (a) the document purports to effect a disposition which falls within subsection (2), and
    (b) the conditions in subsection (3) are met.

(2) A disposition falls within this subsection if it is—
    (a) a disposition of a registered estate or charge,
    (b) a disposition of an interest which is the subject of a notice in the register, or
    (c) a disposition which triggers the requirement of registration,
which is of a kind specified by rules.

(3) The conditions referred to above are that—
    (a) the document makes provision for the time and date when it takes effect,
    (b) the document has the electronic signature of each person by whom it purports to be authenticated,
    (c) each electronic signature is certified, and
    (d) such other conditions as rules may provide are met.

(4) A document to which this section applies is to be regarded as—

(a) in writing, and

(b) signed by each individual, and sealed by each corporation, whose electronic signature it has.

(5) A document to which this section applies is to be regarded for the purposes of any enactment as a deed.

(6) If a document to which this section applies is authenticated by an individual as agent, it is to be regarded for the purposes of any enactment as authenticated by him under the written authority of his principal.

(7) If notice of an assignment made by means of a document to which this section applies is given in electronic form in accordance with rules, it is to be regarded for the purposes of any enactment as given in writing.

(8) The right conferred by section 75 of the Law of Property Act 1925 (c. 20) (purchaser's right to have the execution of a conveyance attested) does not apply to a document to which this section applies.

(9) If subsection (4) of section 36A of the Companies Act 1985 (c. 6) (execution of documents) applies to a document because of subsection (4) above, subsection (6) of that section (presumption of due execution) shall have effect in relation to the document with the substitution of "authenticated" for "signed".

(10) In this section, references to an electronic signature and to the certification of such a signature are to be read in accordance with section 7(2) and (3) of the Electronic Communications Act 2000 (c. 7).

92 Land registry network

(1) The registrar may provide, or arrange for the provision of, an electronic communications network for use for such purposes as he thinks fit relating to registration or the carrying on of transactions which—

(a) involve registration, and

(b) are capable of being effected electronically.

(2) Schedule 5 (which makes provision in connection with a network provided under subsection (1) and transactions carried on by means of such a network) has effect.

93 Power to require simultaneous registration

(1) This section applies to a disposition of—

(a) a registered estate or charge, or

(b) an interest which is the subject of a notice in the register,

where the disposition is of a description specified by rules.

(2) A disposition to which this section applies, or a contract to make such a disposition, only has effect if it is made by means of a document in electronic form and if, when the document purports to take effect—

(a) it is electronically communicated to the registrar, and

(b) the relevant registration requirements are met.

(3) For the purposes of subsection (2)(b), the relevant registration requirements are—

    (a)   in the case of a registrable disposition, the requirements under Schedule 2, and

    (b)   in the case of any other disposition, or a contract, such requirements as rules may provide.

(4)   Section 27(1) does not apply to a disposition to which this section applies.

(5)   Before making rules under this section the Lord Chancellor must consult such persons as he considers appropriate.

(6)   In this section, "disposition", in relation to a registered charge, includes postponement.

94 Supplementary

Rules may—

    (a)   make provision about the communication of documents in electronic form to the registrar;

    (b)   make provision about the electronic storage of documents communicated to the registrar in electronic form.

PART 9

ADVERSE POSSESSION

95 Disapplication of periods of limitation

(1)   No period of limitation under section 15 of the Limitation Act 1980 (c. 58) (time limits in relation to recovery of land) shall run against any person, other than a chargee, in relation to an estate in land or rentcharge the title to which is registered.

(2)   No period of limitation under section 16 of that Act (time limits in relation to redemption of land) shall run against any person in relation to such an estate in land or rentcharge.

(3)   Accordingly, section 17 of that Act (extinction of title on expiry of time limit) does not operate to extinguish the title of any person where, by virtue of this section, a period of limitation does not run against him.

96 Registration of adverse possessor

Schedule 6 (which makes provision about the registration of an adverse possessor of an estate in land or rentcharge) has effect.

97 Defences

(1)   A person has a defence to an action for possession of land if—

    (a)   on the day immediately preceding that on which the action was brought he was entitled to make an application under paragraph 1 of Schedule 6 to be registered as the proprietor of an estate in the land, and

    (b)   had he made such an application on that day, the condition in paragraph 5(4) of that Schedule would have been satisfied.

(2)   A judgment for possession of land ceases to be enforceable at the end of the period of two years beginning with the date of the judgment if the proceedings

in which the judgment is given were commenced against a person who was at that time entitled to make an application under paragraph 1 of Schedule 6.

(3)   A person has a defence to an action for possession of land if on the day immediately preceding that on which the action was brought he was entitled to make an application under paragraph 6 of Schedule 6 to be registered as the proprietor of an estate in the land.

(4)   A judgment for possession of land ceases to be enforceable at the end of the period of two years beginning with the date of the judgment if, at the end of that period, the person against whom the judgment was given is entitled to make an application under paragraph 6 of Schedule 6 to be registered as the proprietor of an estate in the land.

(5)   Where in any proceedings a court determines that—

    (a)   a person is entitled to a defence under this section, or

    (b)   a judgment for possession has ceased to be enforceable against a person by virtue of subsection (4),

the court must order the registrar to register him as the proprietor of the estate in relation to which he is entitled to make an application under Schedule 6.

(6)   The defences under this section are additional to any other defences a person may have.

(7)   Rules may make provision to prohibit the recovery of rent due under a rentcharge from a person who has been in adverse possession of the rentcharge.

PART 10

LAND REGISTRY

Administration

98   The land registry

(1)   There is to continue to be an office called Her Majesty's Land Registry which is to deal with the business of registration under this Act.

(2)   The land registry is to consist of—

    (a)   the Chief Land Registrar, who is its head, and

    (b)   the staff appointed by him;

and references in this Act to a member of the land registry are to be read accordingly.

(3)   The Lord Chancellor shall appoint a person to be the Chief Land Registrar.

(4)   Schedule 7 (which makes further provision about the land registry) has effect.

99   Conduct of business

(1)   Any function of the registrar may be carried out by any member of the land registry who is authorised for the purpose by the registrar.

(2)   The Lord Chancellor may by regulations make provision about the carrying out of functions during any vacancy in the office of registrar.

(3) The Lord Chancellor may by order designate a particular office of the land registry as the proper office for the receipt of applications or a specified description of application.

(4) The registrar may prepare and publish such forms and directions as he considers necessary or desirable for facilitating the conduct of the business of registration under this Act.

100 Annual report

(1) The registrar must make an annual report on the business of the land registry to the Lord Chancellor.

(2) The registrar must publish every report under this section in such manner as he thinks fit.

(3) The Lord Chancellor must lay copies of every report under this section before Parliament.

Fees and indemnities

101 Fee orders

The Lord Chancellor may with the advice and assistance of the body referred to in section 124(2) (the Rule Committee), and the consent of the Treasury, by order —

(a) prescribe fees to be paid in respect of dealings with the land registry, except under section 104;

(b) make provision about the payment of prescribed fees.

102 Indemnities

Schedule 8 (which makes provision for the payment of indemnities by the registrar) has effect.

Miscellaneous

103 General information about land

The registrar may publish information about land in England and Wales if it appears to him to be information in which there is legitimate public interest.

104 Consultancy and advisory services

(1) The registrar may provide consultancy or advisory services about the registration of land in England and Wales or elsewhere.

(2) The terms on which services are provided under this section, in particular terms as to payment, shall be such as the registrar thinks fit.

PART 11

ADJUDICATION

105 The adjudicator

(1) The Lord Chancellor shall appoint a person to be the Adjudicator to Her Majesty's Land Registry.

(2) To be qualified for appointment under subsection (1), a person must have a 10 year general qualification (within the meaning of section 71 of the Courts and Legal Services Act 1990 (c. 41)).

(3) Schedule 9 (which makes further provision about the adjudicator) has effect.

106 Jurisdiction

(1) The adjudicator has the following functions —
    (a) determining matters referred to him under section 73(7), and
    (b) determining appeals under paragraph 4 of Schedule 5.

(2) Also, the adjudicator may, on application, make any order which the High Court could make for the rectification or setting aside of a document which —
    (a) effects a qualifying disposition of a registered estate or charge,
    (b) is a contract to make such a disposition, or
    (c) effects a transfer of an interest which is the subject of a notice in the register.

(3) For the purposes of subsection (2)(a), a qualifying disposition is —
    (a) a registrable disposition, or
    (b) a disposition which creates an interest which may be the subject of a notice in the register.

(4) The general law about the effect of an order of the High Court for the rectification or setting aside of a document shall apply to an order under this section.

107 Procedure

(1) Hearings before the adjudicator shall be held in public, except where he is satisfied that exclusion of the public is just and reasonable.

(2) Subject to that, rules may regulate the practice and procedure to be followed with respect to proceedings before the adjudicator and matters incidental to or consequential on such proceedings.

(3) Rules under subsection (2) may, in particular, make provision about —
    (a) when hearings are to be held,
    (b) requiring persons to attend hearings to give evidence or to produce documents,
    (c) the form in which any decision of the adjudicator is to be given,
    (d) payment of costs of a party to proceedings by another party to the proceedings, and
    (e) liability for costs thrown away as the result of neglect or delay by a legal representative of a party to proceedings.

108   Functions in relation to disputes

(1)   In proceedings on a reference under section 73(7), the adjudicator may, instead of deciding a matter himself, direct a party to the proceedings to commence proceedings within a specified time in the court for the purpose of obtaining the court's decision on the matter.

(2)   Rules may make provision about the reference under subsection (1) of matters to the court and may, in particular, make provision about—

   (a)   adjournment of the proceedings before the adjudicator pending the outcome of the proceedings before the court, and

   (b)   the powers of the adjudicator in the event of failure to comply with a direction under subsection (1).

(3)   Rules may make provision about the functions of the adjudicator in consequence of a decision on a reference under section 73(7) and may, in particular, make provision enabling the adjudicator to determine, or give directions about the determination of—

   (a)   the application to which the reference relates, or

   (b)   such other present or future application to the registrar as the rules may provide.

(4)   If, in the case of a reference under section 73(7) relating to an application under paragraph 1 of Schedule 6, the adjudicator determines that it would be unconscionable for the registered proprietor to seek to dispossess the applicant, but that the circumstances are not such that the applicant ought to be registered as proprietor, the adjudicator—

   (a)   must determine how the equity due to the applicant is to be satisfied, and

   (b)   may for that purpose make any order that the High Court could make in the exercise of its equitable jurisdiction.

109   Appeals

(1)   Subject to subsection (2), a person aggrieved by a decision of the adjudicator may appeal to the High Court.

(2)   In the case of a decision on an appeal under paragraph 4 of Schedule 5, only appeal on a point of law is possible.

(3)   If on an appeal under this section relating to an application under paragraph 1 of Schedule 6 the court determines that it would be unconscionable for the registered proprietor to seek to dispossess the applicant, but that the circumstances are not such that the applicant ought to be registered as proprietor, the court must determine how the equity due to the applicant is to be satisfied.

110   Enforcement of orders etc

A requirement of the adjudicator shall be enforceable as an order of the court.

111   Fees

The Lord Chancellor may by order—

    (a)   prescribe fees to be paid in respect of proceedings before the adjudicator;

    (b)   make provision about the payment of prescribed fees.

112   Supplementary

Power to make rules under this Part is exercisable by the Lord Chancellor.

PART 12

MISCELLANEOUS AND GENERAL

Miscellaneous

113   Rights of pre-emption

(1)   A right of pre-emption in relation to registered land has effect from the time of creation as an interest capable of binding successors in title (subject to the rules about the effect of dispositions on priority).

(2)   This section has effect in relation to rights of pre-emption created on or after the day on which this section comes into force.

114   Proprietary estoppel and mere equities

It is hereby declared for the avoidance of doubt that, in relation to registered land, each of the following —

    (a)   an equity by estoppel, and

    (b)   a mere equity,

has effect from the time the equity arises as an interest capable of binding successors in title (subject to the rules about the effect of dispositions on priority).

115   Reduction in unregistered interests with automatic protection

(1)   Paragraphs 10 to 14 of Schedules 1 and 3 shall cease to have effect at the end of the period of ten years beginning with the day on which those Schedules come into force.

(2)   If made before the end of the period mentioned in subsection (1), no fee may be charged for —

    (a)   an application to lodge a caution against first registration by virtue of an interest falling within any of paragraphs 10 to 14 of Schedule 1, or

    (b)   an application for the entry in the register of a notice in respect of an interest falling within any of paragraphs 10 to 14 of Schedule 3.

116   Power to reduce qualifying term

(1)   The Lord Chancellor may by order substitute for the term specified in any of the following provisions —

    (a)   section 3(3),

    (b)   section 4(1)(c)(i) and (2)(b),

    (c)   section 15(3)(a)(ii),

      (d)   section 27(2)(b)(i),

      (e)   section 80(1)(b)(i),

      (f)   paragraph 1 of Schedule 1,

      (g)   paragraphs 4(1), 5(1) and 6(1) of Schedule 2, and

      (h)   paragraph 1 of Schedule 3,

such shorter term as he thinks fit.

(2)   An order under this section may contain such transitional provision as the Lord Chancellor thinks fit.

(3)   Before making an order under this section, the Lord Chancellor must consult such persons as he considers appropriate.

117 Power to deregister manors

On the application of the proprietor of a registered manor, the registrar may remove the title to the manor from the register.

118 Conclusiveness of filed copies etc

(1)   This section applies where—

      (a)   a disposition relates to land to which a registered estate relates, and

      (b)   an entry in the register relating to the registered estate refers to a document kept by the registrar which is not an original.

(2)   As between the parties to the disposition, the document kept by the registrar is to be taken—

      (a)   to be correct, and

      (b)   to contain all the material parts of the original document.

(3)   No party to the disposition may require production of the original document.

(4)   No party to the disposition is to be affected by any provision of the original document which is not contained in the document kept by the registrar.

119 Forwarding of applications to registrar of companies

The Lord Chancellor may by rules make provision about the transmission by the registrar to the registrar of companies (within the meaning of the Companies Act 1985 (c. 6)) of applications under—

      (a)   Part 12 of that Act (registration of charges), or

      (b)   Chapter 3 of Part 23 of that Act (corresponding provision for oversea companies).

Offences etc.

120 Suppression of information

(1)   A person commits an offence if in the course of proceedings relating to registration under this Act he suppresses information with the intention of—

      (a)   concealing a person's right or claim, or

      (b)   substantiating a false claim.

(2)   A person guilty of an offence under this section is liable—

    (a)   on conviction on indictment, to imprisonment for a term not exceeding two years or to a fine;

    (b)   on summary conviction, to imprisonment for a term not exceeding six months or to a fine not exceeding the statutory maximum, or to both.

121   Improper alteration of the registers

(1)   A person commits an offence if he dishonestly induces another—

    (a)   to change the register of title or cautions register, or

    (b)   to authorise the making of such a change.

(2)   A person commits an offence if he intentionally or recklessly makes an unauthorised change in the register of title or cautions register.

(3)   A person guilty of an offence under this section is liable—

    (a)   on conviction on indictment, to imprisonment for a term not exceeding 2 years or to a fine;

    (b)   on summary conviction, to imprisonment for a term not exceeding six months or to a fine not exceeding the statutory maximum, or to both.

(4)   In this section, references to changing the register of title include changing a document referred to in it.

122   Privilege against self-incrimination

(1)   The privilege against self-incrimination, so far as relating to offences under this Act, shall not entitle a person to refuse to answer any question or produce any document or thing in any legal proceedings other than criminal proceedings.

(2)   No evidence obtained under subsection (1) shall be admissible in any criminal proceedings under this Act against the person from whom it was obtained or that person's spouse.

Land registration rules

123   Miscellaneous and general powers

Schedule 10 (which contains miscellaneous and general land registration rule-making powers) has effect.

124   Exercise of powers

(1)   Power to make land registration rules is exercisable by the Lord Chancellor with the advice and assistance of the Rule Committee.

(2)   The Rule Committee is a body consisting of—

    (a)   a judge of the Chancery Division of the High Court nominated by the Lord Chancellor,

    (b)   the registrar,

    (c)   a person nominated by the General Council of the Bar,

    (d)   a person nominated by the Council of the Law Society,

    (e)   a person nominated by the Council of Mortgage Lenders,

    (f)   a person nominated by the Council of Licensed Conveyancers, and

    (g)   any person nominated under subsection (3).

(3) The Lord Chancellor may nominate to be a member of the Rule Committee any person who appears to him to have qualifications or experience which would be of value to the committee in considering any matter with which it is concerned.

Supplementary

125 Rules, regulations and orders

(1) Any power of the Lord Chancellor to make rules, regulations or orders under this Act includes power to make different provision for different cases.

(2) Any power of the Lord Chancellor to make rules, regulations or orders under this Act is exercisable by statutory instrument.

(3) A statutory instrument containing —
   (a) land registration rules,
   (b) rules under Part 11 or section 119,
   (c) regulations under this Act, or
   (d) an order under section 99,

   is to be laid before Parliament after being made.

(4) A statutory instrument containing —
   (a) rules under section 93 or paragraph 1, 2 or 3 of Schedule 5, or
   (b) an order under any provision of this Act other than section 99, 101, 111, 131 or 133,

   is subject to annulment in pursuance of a resolution of either House of Parliament.

126 Crown application

This Act binds the Crown.

127 Application to internal waters

This Act applies to land covered by internal waters of the United Kingdom which are —
   (a) within England or Wales, or
   (b) adjacent to England or Wales and specified for the purposes of this section by order made by the Lord Chancellor.

128 "Proprietor in possession"

(1) For the purposes of this Act, land is in the possession of the proprietor of a registered estate in land if it is physically in his possession, or in that of a person who is entitled to be registered as the proprietor of the registered estate.

(2) In the case of the following relationships, land which is (or is treated as being) in the possession of the second-mentioned person is to be treated for the purposes of subsection (1) as in the possession of the first-mentioned person —
   (a) landlord and tenant;
   (b) mortgagor and mortgagee;
   (c) licensor and licensee;

    (d)   trustee and beneficiary.

(3)   In subsection (1), the reference to entitlement does not include entitlement under Schedule 6.

129 General interpretation

(1)   In this Act—

"adjudicator" means the Adjudicator to Her Majesty's Land Registry;

"caution against first registration" means a caution lodged under section 15;

"cautions register" means the register kept under section 19(1);

"charge" means any mortgage, charge or lien for securing money or money's worth;

"demesne land" means land belonging to Her Majesty in right of the Crown which is not held for an estate in fee simple absolute in possession;

"land" includes—

    (a)   buildings and other structures,

    (b)   land covered with water, and

    (c)   mines and minerals, whether or not held with the surface;

"land registration rules" means any rules under this Act, other than rules under section 93, Part 11, section 119 or paragraph 1, 2 or 3 of Schedule 5;

"legal estate" has the same meaning as in the Law of Property Act 1925 (c. 20);

"legal mortgage" has the same meaning as in the Law of Property Act 1925;

"mines and minerals" includes any strata or seam of minerals or substances in or under any land, and powers of working and getting any such minerals or substances;

"registrar" means the Chief Land Registrar;

"register" means the register of title, except in the context of cautions against first registration;

"registered" means entered in the register;

"registered charge" means a charge the title to which is entered in the register;

"registered estate" means a legal estate the title to which is entered in the register, other than a registered charge;

"registered land" means a registered estate or registered charge;

"registrable disposition" means a disposition which is required to be completed by registration under section 27;

"requirement of registration" means the requirement of registration under section 4;

"sub-charge" means a charge under section 23(2)(b);

"term of years absolute" has the same meaning as in the Law of Property Act 1925;

"valuable consideration" does not include marriage consideration or a nominal consideration in money.

(2)   In subsection (1), in the definition of "demesne land", the reference to land belonging to Her Majesty does not include land in relation to which a freehold

estate in land has determined, but in relation to which there has been no act of entry or management by the Crown.

(3) In this Act—

    (a) references to the court are to the High Court or a county court,

    (b) references to an interest affecting an estate or charge are to an adverse right affecting the title to the estate or charge, and

    (c) references to the right to object to an application to the registrar are to the right under section 73.

Final provisions

130 Minor and consequential amendments

Schedule 11 (which makes minor and consequential amendments) has effect.

131 Transition

(1) The Lord Chancellor may by order make such transitional provisions and savings as he thinks fit in connection with the coming into force of any of the provisions of this Act.

(2) Schedule 12 (which makes transitional provisions and savings) has effect.

(3) Nothing in Schedule 12 affects the power to make transitional provisions and savings under subsection (1); and an order under that subsection may modify any provision made by that Schedule.

132 Repeals

The enactments specified in Schedule 13 (which include certain provisions which are already spent) are hereby repealed to the extent specified there.

133 Short title, commencement and extent

(1) This Act may be cited as the Land Registration Act 2001.

(2) This Act shall come into force on such day as the Lord Chancellor may by order appoint, and different days may be so appointed for different purposes.

(3) Subject to subsection (4), this Act extends to England and Wales only.

(4) Any amendment or repeal by this Act of an existing enactment, other than—

    (a) section 37 of the Requisitioned Land and War Works Act 1945 (c. 43), and

    (b) Schedule 2A to the Building Societies Act 1986 (c. 53),

has the same extent as the enactment amended or repealed.

SCHEDULES

SCHEDULE 1

Sections 11 and 12.

UNREGISTERED INTERESTS WHICH OVERRIDE FIRST REGISTRATION

Leasehold estates in land

1   A leasehold estate in land granted for a term not exceeding seven years from the date of the grant, except for a lease the grant of which falls within section 4(1) (d), (e) or (f).

Interests of persons in actual occupation

2   (1) An interest belonging to a person in actual occupation, so far as relating to land of which he is in actual occupation, except for an interest under a settlement under the Settled Land Act 1925 (c. 18).

     (2) For the purposes of this paragraph, a person is only to be regarded as in actual occupation of land if he, or his agent or employee, is physically present there.

Easements and profits a prendre

3   A legal easement or profit a prendre.

Customary and public rights

4   A customary right.

5   A public right.

Local land charges

6   A local land charge.

Mines and minerals

7   An interest in any coal or coal mine, the rights attached to any such interest and the rights of any person under section 38, 49 or 51 of the Coal Industry Act 1994 (c. 21).

8   In the case of land to which title was registered before 1898, rights to mines and minerals (and incidental rights) created before 1898.

9   In the case of land to which title was registered between 1898 and 1925 inclusive, rights to mines and minerals (and incidental rights) created before the date of registration of the title.

Miscellaneous

10   A franchise.

11   A manorial right.

12   A right to rent which was reserved to the Crown on the granting of any freehold estate (whether or not the right is still vested in the Crown).

13   A non-statutory right in respect of an embankment or sea or river wall.

14   A right to payment in lieu of tithe.

SCHEDULE 2   Section 27.

REGISTRABLE DISPOSITIONS: REGISTRATION REQUIREMENTS

PART 1

REGISTERED ESTATES

Introductory

1   This Part deals with the registration requirements relating to those dispositions of registered estates which are required to be completed by registration.

Transfer

2   (1) In the case of a transfer of whole or part, the transferee, or his successor in title, must be entered in the register as the proprietor.

      (2) In the case of a transfer of part, such details of the transfer as rules may provide must be entered in the register in relation to the registered estate out of which the transfer is made.

Lease of estate in land

3   (1) This paragraph applies to a disposition consisting of the grant out of an estate in land of a term of years absolute.

      (2) In the case of a disposition to which this paragraph applies—
          (a) the grantee, or his successor in title, must be entered in the register as the proprietor of the lease, and
          (b) a notice in respect of the lease must be entered in the register.

Lease of franchise or manor

4   (1) This paragraph applies to a disposition consisting of the grant out of a franchise or manor of a lease for a term of more than seven years from the date of the grant.

      (2) In the case of a disposition to which this paragraph applies—
          (a) the grantee, or his successor in title, must be entered in the register as the proprietor of the lease, and

        (b)   a notice in respect of the lease must be entered in the register.

5   (1) This paragraph applies to a disposition consisting of the grant out of a franchise or manor of a lease for a term not exceeding seven years from the date of the grant.

    (2) In the case of a disposition to which this paragraph applies, a notice in respect of the lease must be entered in the register.

Creation of independently registrable legal interest

6   (1) This paragraph applies to a disposition consisting of the creation of a legal rentcharge or profit a prendre in gross, other than one created for, or for an interest equivalent to, a term of years absolute not exceeding seven years from the date of creation.

    (2) In the case of a disposition to which this paragraph applies—

        (a)   the grantee, or his successor in title, must be entered in the register as the proprietor of the interest created, and

        (b)   a notice in respect of the interest created must be entered in the register.

    (3) In sub-paragraph (1), the reference to a legal rentcharge or profit a prendre in gross is to one falling within section 1(2) of the Law of Property Act 1925 (c. 20).

Creation of other legal interest

7   (1) This paragraph applies to a disposition which—

        (a)   consists of the creation of an interest of a kind falling within section 1(2)(a), (b) or (e) of the Law of Property Act 1925, and

        (b)   is not a disposition to which paragraph 4, 5 or 6 applies.

    (2) In the case of a disposition to which this paragraph applies—

        (a)   a notice in respect of the interest created must be entered in the register, and

        (b)   if the interest is created for the benefit of a registered estate, the proprietor of the registered estate must be entered in the register as its proprietor.

    (3) Rules may provide for sub-paragraph (2) to have effect with modifications in relation to a right of entry over or in respect of a term of years absolute.

Creation of legal charge

8   In the case of the creation of a charge, the chargee, or his successor in title, must be entered in the register as the proprietor of the charge.

PART 2

REGISTERED CHARGES

Introductory

9   This Part deals with the registration requirements relating to those dispositions of registered charges which are required to be completed by registration.

Transfer

10   In the case of a transfer, the transferee, or his successor in title, must be entered in the register as the proprietor.

Creation of sub-charge

11   In the case of the creation of a sub-charge, the sub-chargee, or his successor in title, must be entered in the register as the proprietor of the sub-charge.

SCHEDULE 3   Sections 29 and 30.

UNREGISTERED INTERESTS WHICH OVERRIDE REGISTERED DISPOSITIONS

Leasehold estates in land

1   A leasehold estate in land granted for a term not exceeding seven years from the date of the grant, except for—

     (a)   a lease the grant of which falls within section 4(1)(d), (e) or (f);

     (b)   a lease the grant of which constitutes a registrable disposition.

Interests of persons in actual occupation

2   (1)   An interest belonging at the time of the disposition to a person in actual occupation, so far as relating to land of which he is in actual occupation, except for—

     (a)   an interest under a settlement under the Settled Land Act 1925 (c. 18);

     (b)   an interest of a person of whom inquiry was made before the disposition and who failed to disclose the right when he could reasonably have been expected to do so;

     (c)   an interest—

         (i)   which belongs to a person whose occupation would not have been obvious on a reasonably careful inspection of the land at the time of the disposition, and

         (ii)   of which the person to whom the disposition is made does not have actual knowledge at that time;

     (d)   a leasehold estate in land granted to take effect in possession after the end of the period of three months beginning with the date of the grant and which has not taken effect in possession at the time of the disposition.

   (2)   For the purposes of this paragraph, a person is only to be regarded as in actual occupation of land if he, or his agent or employee, is physically present there.

Easements and profits a prendre

3   (1)   A legal easement or profit a prendre, except for an easement, or a profit a prendre which is not registered under the Commons Registration Act 1965 (c. 64), which at the time of the disposition—

(a) is not within the actual knowledge of the person to whom the disposition is made, and

(b) would not have been obvious on a reasonably careful inspection of the land over which the easement or profit is exercisable.

(2) The exception in sub-paragraph (1) does not apply if the person entitled to the easement of profit proves that it has been exercised in the period of one year ending with the day of the disposition.

Customary and public rights

4   A customary right.

5   A public right.

Local land charges

6   A local land charge.

Mines and minerals

7   An interest in any coal or coal mine, the rights attached to any such interest and the rights of any person under section 38, 49 or 51 of the Coal Industry Act 1994 (c. 21).

8   In the case of land to which title was registered before 1898, rights to mines and minerals (and incidental rights) created before 1898.

9   In the case of land to which title was registered between 1898 and 1925 inclusive, rights to mines and minerals (and incidental rights) created before the date of registration of the title.

Miscellaneous

10   A franchise.

11   A manorial right.

12   A right to rent which was reserved to the Crown on the granting of any freehold estate (whether or not the right is still vested in the Crown).

13   A non-statutory right in respect of an embankment or sea or river wall.

14   A right to payment in lieu of tithe.

SCHEDULE 4   Section 65.

ALTERATION OF THE REGISTER

Introductory

1   In this Schedule, references to rectification, in relation to alteration of the register, are to alteration which—

(a) involves the correction of a mistake, and

(b) prejudicially affects the title of a registered proprietor.

Alteration pursuant to a court order

2   (1)   The court may make an order for alteration of the register for the purpose of —
  (a)   correcting a mistake,
  (b)   bringing the register up to date, or
  (c)   giving effect to any estate, right or interest excepted from the effect of registration.

  (2)   An order under this paragraph has effect when served on the registrar to impose a duty on him to give effect to it.

3   (1)   This paragraph applies to the power under paragraph 2, so far as relating to rectification.

  (2)   If alteration affects the title of the proprietor of a registered estate in land, no order may be made under paragraph 2 without the proprietor's consent in relation to land in his possession unless —
  (a)   he has by fraud or lack of proper care caused or substantially contributed to the mistake, or
  (b)   it would for any other reason be unjust for the alteration not to be made.

  (3)   If in any proceedings the court has power to make an order under paragraph 2, it must do so, unless there are exceptional circumstances which justify its not doing so.

  (4)   In sub-paragraph (2), the reference to the title of the proprietor of a registered estate in land includes his title to any registered estate which subsists for the benefit of the estate in land.

4   Rules may —
  (a)   make provision about the circumstances in which there is a duty to exercise the power under paragraph 2, so far as not relating to rectification;
  (b)   make provision about the form of an order under paragraph 2;
  (c)   make provision about service of such an order.

Alteration otherwise than pursuant to a court order

5   The registrar may alter the register for the purpose of —
  (a)   correcting a mistake,
  (b)   bringing the register up to date,
  (c)   giving effect to any estate, right or interest excepted from the effect of registration, or
  (d)   removing a superfluous entry.

6   (1)   This paragraph applies to the power under paragraph 5, so far as relating to rectification.

  (2)   No alteration affecting the title of the proprietor of a registered estate in land may be made under paragraph 5 without the proprietor's consent in relation to land in his possession unless —

(a) he has by fraud or lack of proper care caused or substantially contributed to the mistake, or

(b) it would for any other reason be unjust for the alteration not to be made.

(3) If on an application for alteration under paragraph 5 the registrar has power to make the alteration, the application must be approved, unless there are exceptional circumstances which justify not making the alteration.

(4) In sub-paragraph (2), the reference to the title of the proprietor of a registered estate in land includes his title to any registered estate which subsists for the benefit of the estate in land.

7   Rules may —

(a) make provision about the circumstances in which there is a duty to exercise the power under paragraph 5, so far as not relating to rectification;

(b) make provision about how the register is to be altered in exercise of that power;

(c) make provision about applications for alteration under that paragraph, including provision requiring the making of such applications;

(d) make provision about procedure in relation to the exercise of that power, whether on application or otherwise.

Rectification and derivative interests

8   The powers under this Schedule to alter the register, so far as relating to rectification, extend to changing for the future the priority of any interest affecting the registered estate or charge concerned.

Costs in non-rectification cases

9   (1) If the register is altered under this Schedule in a case not involving rectification, the registrar may pay such amount as he thinks fit in respect of any costs or expenses reasonably incurred by a person in connection with the alteration which have been incurred with the consent of the registrar.

(2) The registrar may make a payment under sub-paragraph (1) notwithstanding the absence of consent if —

(a) it appears to him —

   (i) that the costs or expenses had to be incurred urgently, and

   (ii) that it was not reasonably practicable to apply for his consent, or

(b) he has subsequently approved the incurring of the costs or expenses.

SCHEDULE 5   Section 92.

LAND REGISTRY NETWORK

Access to network

1   (1)   A person who is not a member of the land registry may only have access to a land registry network under authority conferred by means of an agreement with the registrar.

(2)   An agreement for the purposes of sub-paragraph (1) ("network access agreement") may authorise access for —

(a)   the communication, posting or retrieval of information,

(b)   the making of changes to the register of title or cautions register,

(c)   the issue of official search certificates,

(d)   the issue of official copies, or

(e)   such other conveyancing purposes as the registrar thinks fit.

(3)   Rules may regulate the use of network access agreements to confer authority to carry out functions of the registrar.

(4)   The registrar must, on application, enter into a network access agreement with the applicant if the applicant meets such criteria as rules may provide.

Terms of access

2   (1)   The terms on which access to a land registry network is authorised shall be such as the registrar thinks fit, subject to sub-paragraphs (3) and (4), and may, in particular, include charges for access.

(2)   The power under sub-paragraph (1) may be used, not only for the purpose of regulating the use of the network, but also for —

(a)   securing that the person granted access uses the network to carry on such qualifying transactions as may be specified in, or under, the agreement,

(b)   such other purpose relating to the carrying on of qualifying transactions as rules may provide, or

(c)   enabling network transactions to be monitored.

(3)   It shall be a condition of a network access agreement which enables the person granted access to use the network to carry on qualifying transactions that he must comply with any rules for the time being in force under paragraph 5.

(4)   Rules may regulate the terms on which access to a land registry network is authorised.

Termination of access

3   (1)   The person granted access by a network access agreement may terminate the agreement at any time by notice to the registrar.

(2)   Rules may make provision about the termination of a network access agreement by the registrar and may, in particular, make provision about —

(a)   the grounds of termination,

(b)   the procedure to be followed in relation to termination, and

    (c)   the suspension of termination pending appeal.

  (3) Without prejudice to the generality of sub-paragraph (2)(a), rules under that provision may authorise the registrar to terminate a network access agreement if the person granted access—

    (a)   fails to comply with the terms of the agreement,

    (b)   ceases to be a person with whom the registrar would be required to enter into a network access agreement conferring the authority which the agreement confers, or

    (c)   does not meet such conditions as the rules may provide.

Appeals

4   (1) A person who is aggrieved by a decision of the registrar with respect to entry into, or termination of, a network access agreement may appeal against the decision to the adjudicator.

  (2) On determining an appeal under this paragraph, the adjudicator may give such directions as he considers appropriate to give effect to his determination.

  (3) Rules may make provision about appeals under this paragraph.

Network transaction rules

5   (1) Rules may make provision about how to go about network transactions.

  (2) Rules under sub-paragraph (1) may, in particular, make provision about dealings with the land registry, including provision about—

    (a)   the procedure to be followed, and

    (b)   the supply of information (including information about unregistered interests).

Overriding nature of network access obligations

6   To the extent that an obligation not owed under a network access agreement conflicts with an obligation owed under such an agreement by the person granted access, the obligation not owed under the agreement is discharged.

Do-it-yourself conveyancing

7   (1) If there is a land registry network, the registrar has a duty to provide such assistance as he thinks appropriate for the purpose of enabling persons engaged in qualifying transactions who wish to do their own conveyancing to do so by means of the network.

  (2) The duty under sub-paragraph (1) does not extend to the provision of legal advice.

Presumption of authority

8   Where—

    (a)   a person who is authorised under a network access agreement to do so uses the network for the making of a disposition or contract, and

    (b)   the document which purports to effect the disposition or to be the contract—

    (i)   purports to be authenticated by him as agent, and

    (ii) contains a statement to the effect that he is acting under the authority of his principal,

he shall be deemed, in favour of any other party, to be so acting.

Management of network transactions

9   (1) The registrar may use monitoring information for the purpose of managing network transactions and may, in particular, disclose such information to persons authorised to use the network, and authorise the further disclosure of information so disclosed, if he considers it is necessary or desirable to do so.

    (2) The registrar may delegate his functions under sub-paragraph (1), subject to such conditions as he thinks fit.

    (3) In sub-paragraph (1), "monitoring information" means information provided in pursuance of provision in a network access agreement included under paragraph 2(2)(c).

Supplementary

10   The registrar may provide education and training in relation to the use of a land registry network.

11   (1) Power to make rules under paragraph 1, 2 or 3 is exercisable by the Lord Chancellor.

    (2) Before making such rules, the Lord Chancellor must consult such persons as he considers appropriate.

    (3) In making rules under paragraph 1 or 3(2)(a), the Lord Chancellor must have regard, in particular, to the need to secure—

        (a) the confidentiality of private information kept on the network,

        (b) competence in relation to the use of the network (in particular for the purpose of making changes), and

        (c) the adequate insurance of potential liabilities in connection with use of the network.

12   In this Schedule—

        "land registry network" means a network provided under section 92(1);

        "network access agreement" has the meaning given by paragraph 1(2);

        "network transaction" means a transaction carried on by means of a land registry network;

        "qualifying transaction" means a transaction which—

           (a) involves registration, and

           (b) is capable of being effected electronically.

SCHEDULE 6

Section 96.

REGISTRATION OF ADVERSE POSSESSOR

Right to apply for registration

1 (1) A person may apply to be registered as the proprietor of a registered estate in land if he has been in adverse possession of the estate for the period of ten years ending on the date of the application.

   (2) A person may also apply to be registered as the proprietor of a registered estate in land if—

      (a) he has in the period of six months ending on the date of the application ceased to be in adverse possession of the estate because of eviction by the registered proprietor, or a person claiming under the registered proprietor,

      (b) on the day before his eviction he was entitled to make an application under sub-paragraph (1), and

      (c) the eviction was not pursuant to a judgment for possession.

   (3) However, a person may not make an application under this paragraph if—

      (a) he is a defendant in proceedings which involve asserting a right to possession of the land, or

      (b) judgment for possession of the land has been given against him in the last two years.

   (4) For the purposes of sub-paragraph (1), the estate need not have been registered throughout the period of adverse possession.

Notification of application

2 (1) The registrar must give notice of an application under paragraph 1 to—

      (a) the proprietor of the estate to which the application relates,

      (b) the proprietor of any registered charge on the estate,

      (c) where the estate is leasehold, the proprietor of any superior registered estate,

      (d) any person who is registered in accordance with rules as a person to be notified under this paragraph, and

      (e) such other persons as rules may provide.

   (2) Notice under this paragraph shall include notice of the effect of paragraph 4.

Treatment of application

3 (1) A person given notice under paragraph 2 may require that the application to which the notice relates be dealt with under paragraph 5.

   (2) The right under this paragraph is exercisable by notice to the registrar given before the end of such period as rules may provide.

4   If an application under paragraph 1 is not required to be dealt with under paragraph 5, the applicant is entitled to be entered in the register as the new proprietor of the estate.

5   (1) If an application under paragraph 1 is required to be dealt with under this paragraph, the applicant is only entitled to be registered as the new proprietor of the estate if any of the following conditions is met.

    (2) The first condition is that—

        (a) it would be unconscionable for the registered proprietor to seek to dispossess the applicant, and

        (b) the circumstances are such that the applicant ought to be registered as the proprietor.

    (3) The second condition is that the applicant is for some other reason entitled to be registered as the proprietor of the estate.

    (4) The third condition is that—

        (a) the land to which the application relates is adjacent to land belonging to the applicant,

        (b) the exact line of the boundary between the two has not been determined under rules under section 60,

        (c) for at least ten years of the period of adverse possession ending on the date of the application, the applicant (or any predecessor in title) reasonably believed that the land to which the application relates belonged to him, and

        (d) the estate to which the application relates was registered more than one year prior to the date of the application.

    (5) In relation to an application under paragraph 1(2), this paragraph has effect as if the reference in sub-paragraph (4)(c) to the date of the application were to the day before the date of the applicant's eviction.

Right to make further application for registration

6   (1) Where a person's application under paragraph 1 is rejected, he may make a further application to be registered as the proprietor of the estate if he is in adverse possession of the estate from the date of the application until the last day of the period of two years beginning with the date of its rejection.

    (2) However, a person may not make an application under this paragraph if—

        (a) he is a defendant in proceedings which involve asserting a right to possession of the land,

        (b) judgment for possession of the land has been given against him in the last two years, or

        (c) he has been evicted from the land pursuance to a judgement for possession.

7   If a person makes an application under paragraph 6, he is entitled to be entered in the register as the new proprietor of the estate.

Restriction on applications

8   (1) No one may apply under this Schedule to be registered as the proprietor of an estate in land during, or before the end of twelve months after the end of, any period in which the existing registered proprietor is for the purposes of the Limitation (Enemies and War Prisoners) Act 1945 (8 & 9 Geo. 6 c. 16)—

        (a) an enemy, or

        (b) detained in enemy territory.

(2) No-one may apply under this Schedule to be registered as the proprietor of an estate in land during any period in which the existing registered proprietor is—

    (a) unable because of mental disability to make decisions about issues of the kind to which such an application would give rise, or

    (b) unable to communicate such decisions because of mental disability or physical impairment.

(3) For the purposes of sub-paragraph (2), "mental disability" means a disability or disorder of the mind or brain, whether permanent or temporary, which results in an impairment or disturbance of mental functioning.

(4) Where it appears to the registrar that sub-paragraph (1) or (2) applies in relation to an estate in land, he may include a note to that effect in the register.

Effect of registration

9 (1) Where a person is registered as the proprietor of an estate in land in pursuance of an application under this Schedule, the title by virtue of adverse possession which he had at the time of the application is extinguished.

(2) Subject to sub-paragraph (3), the registration of a person under this Schedule as the proprietor of an estate in land does not affect the priority of any interest affecting the estate.

(3) Subject to sub-paragraph (4), where a person is registered under this Schedule as the proprietor of an estate, the estate is vested in him free of any registered charge affecting the estate immediately before his registration.

(4) Sub-paragraph (3) does not apply where registration as proprietor is in pursuance of an application determined by reference to whether any of the conditions in paragraph 5 applies.

Apportionment and discharge of charges

10 (1) Where—

    (a) a registered estate continues to be subject to a charge notwithstanding the registration of a person under this Schedule as the proprietor, and

    (b) the charge affects property other than the estate,

the proprietor of the estate may require the chargee to apportion the amount secured by the charge at that time between the estate and the other property on the basis of their respective values.

(2) The person requiring the apportionment is entitled to a discharge of his estate from the charge on payment of—

    (a) the amount apportioned to the estate, and

    (b) the costs incurred by the chargee as a result of the apportionment.

(3) On a discharge under this paragraph, the liability of the chargor to the chargee is reduced by the amount apportioned to the estate.

(4) Rules may make provision about apportionment under this paragraph, in particular, provision about—

    (a) procedure,

       (b)   valuation,

       (c)   calculation of costs payable under sub-paragraph (2)(b), and

       (d)   payment of the costs of the chargor.

Meaning of "adverse possession"

11   (1) A person is in adverse possession of an estate in land for the purposes of this Schedule if, but for section 95, a period of limitation under section 15 of the Limitation Act 1980 (c. 58) would run in his favour in relation to the estate.

   (2) A person is also to be regarded for those purposes as having been in adverse possession of an estate in land —

       (a)   where he is the successor in title to an estate in the land, during any period of adverse possession by a predecessor in title to that estate, or

       (b)   during any period of adverse possession by another person which comes between, and is continuous with, periods of adverse possession of his own.

   (3) In determining whether for the purposes of this paragraph a period of limitation would run under section 15 of the Limitation Act 1980, there are to be disregarded —

       (a)   the commencement of any legal proceedings, and

       (b)   paragraph 6 of Schedule 1 to that Act.

Trusts

12   A person is not to be regarded as being in adverse possession of an estate for the purposes of this Schedule at any time when the estate is subject to a trust, unless the interest of each of the beneficiaries in the estate is an interest in possession.

Crown foreshore

13   (1) Where —

       (a)   a person is in adverse possession of an estate in land,

       (b)   the estate belongs to Her Majesty in right of the Crown or the Duchy of Lancaster or to the Duchy of Cornwall, and

       (c)   the land consists of foreshore,

    paragraph 1(1) is to have effect as if the reference to ten years were to sixty years.

   (2) For the purposes of sub-paragraph (1), land is to be treated as foreshore if it has been foreshore at any time in the previous ten years.

   (3) In this paragraph, "foreshore" means the shore and bed of the sea and of any tidal water, below the line of the medium high tide between the spring and neap tides.

Rentcharges

14   Rules must make provision to apply the preceding provisions of this Schedule to registered rentcharges, subject to such modifications and exceptions as the rules may provide.

Procedure

15   Rules may make provision about the procedure to be followed pursuant to an application under this Schedule.

SCHEDULE 7

Section 98.

THE LAND REGISTRY

Holding of office by Chief Land Registrar

1   (1)   The registrar may at any time resign his office by written notice to the Lord Chancellor.

     (2)   The Lord Chancellor may remove the registrar from office if he is unable or unfit to discharge the functions of office.

     (3)   Subject to the above, a person appointed to be the registrar is to hold and vacate office in accordance with the terms of his appointment and, on ceasing to hold office, is eligible for reappointment.

Remuneration etc. of Chief Land Registrar

2   (1)   The Lord Chancellor shall pay the registrar such remuneration, and such travelling and other allowances, as the Lord Chancellor may determine.

     (2)   The Lord Chancellor shall—
           (a)   pay such pension, allowances or gratuities as he may determine to or in respect of a person who is or has been the registrar, or
           (b)   make such payments as he may determine towards provision for the payment of a pension, allowances or gratuities to or in respect of such a person.

     (3)   If, when a person ceases to be the registrar, the Lord Chancellor determines that there are special circumstances which make it right that the person should receive compensation, the Lord Chancellor may pay to the person by way of compensation a sum of such amount as he may determine.

Staff

3   (1)   The registrar may appoint such staff as he thinks fit.

     (2)   The terms and conditions of appointments under this paragraph shall be such as the registrar, with the approval of the Minister for the Civil Service, thinks fit.

Indemnity for members

4   No member of the land registry is to be liable in damages for anything done or omitted in the discharge or purported discharge of any function relating to land registration, unless it is shown that the act or omission was in bad faith.

Seal

5   The land registry is to continue to have a seal and any document purporting to be sealed with it is to be admissible in evidence without any further or other proof.

Documentary evidence

6   The Documentary Evidence Act 1868 (c. 37) has effect as if—

    (a)   the registrar were included in the first column of the Schedule to that Act,

    (b)   the registrar and any person authorised to act on his behalf were mentioned in the second column of that Schedule, and

    (c)   the regulations referred to in that Act included any form or direction issued by the registrar or by any such person.

Parliamentary disqualification

7   In Part 3 of Schedule 1 to the House of Commons Disqualification Act 1975 (c. 24) (other disqualifying offices), there is inserted at the appropriate place—

"Chief Land Registrar.";

and a corresponding amendment is made in Part 3 of Schedule 1 to the Northern Ireland Assembly Disqualification Act 1975 (c. 25).

SCHEDULE 8   Section 102.

INDEMNITIES

Entitlement

1   (1)   A person is entitled to be indemnified by the registrar if he suffers loss by reason of—

    (a)   rectification of the register,

    (b)   a mistake whose correction would involve rectification of the register,

    (c)   a mistake in an official search,

    (d)   a mistake in an official copy,

    (e)   a mistake in a document kept by the registrar which is not an original and is referred to in the register,

    (f)   the loss or destruction of a document lodged at the registry for inspection or safe custody,

    (g)   a mistake in the cautions register, or

    (h)   failure by the registrar to perform his duty under section 50.

    (2)   For the purposes of sub-paragraph (1)(a)—

    (a)   any person who suffers loss by reason of the change of title under section 62 is to be regarded as having suffered loss by reason of rectification of the register, and

     (b)   the proprietor of a registered estate or charge claiming in good faith under a forged disposition is, where the register is rectified, to be regarded as having suffered loss by reason of such rectification as if the disposition had not been forged.

(3) No indemnity under sub-paragraph (1)(b) is payable until a decision has been made about whether to alter the register for the purpose of correcting the mistake; and the loss suffered by reason of the mistake is to be determined in the light of that decision.

Mines and minerals

2   No indemnity is payable under this Schedule on account of —

     (a)   any mines or minerals, or

     (b)   the existence of any right to work or get mines or minerals,

unless it is noted in the register that the title to the registered estate concerned includes the mines or minerals.

Costs

3   (1) In respect of loss consisting of costs or expenses incurred by the claimant in relation to the matter, an indemnity under this Schedule is payable only on account of costs or expenses reasonably incurred by the claimant with the consent of the registrar.

(2) The requirement of consent does not apply where —

     (a)   the costs or expenses must be incurred by the claimant urgently, and

     (b)   it is not reasonably practicable to apply for the registrar's consent.

(3) If the registrar approves the incurring of costs or expenses after they have been incurred, they shall be treated for the purposes of this paragraph as having been incurred with his consent.

4   (1) If no indemnity is payable to a claimant under this Schedule, the registrar may pay such amount as he thinks fit in respect of any costs or expenses reasonably incurred by the claimant in connection with the claim which have been incurred with the consent of the registrar.

(2) The registrar may make a payment under sub-paragraph (1) notwithstanding the absence of consent if —

     (a)   it appears to him —

         (i)   that the costs or expenses had to be incurred urgently, and

         (ii) that it was not reasonably practicable to apply for his consent, or

     (b)   he has subsequently approved the incurring of the costs or expenses.

Claimant's fraud or lack of care

5   (1) No indemnity is payable under this Schedule on account of any loss suffered by a claimant —

     (a)   wholly or partly as a result of his own fraud, or

     (b)   wholly as a result of his own lack of proper care.

(2) Where any loss is suffered by a claimant partly as a result of his own lack of proper care, any indemnity payable to him is to be reduced to such extent as is fair having regard to his share in the responsibility for the loss.

(3) For the purposes of this paragraph any fraud or lack of care on the part of a person from whom the claimant derives title (otherwise than under a disposition for valuable consideration which is registered or protected by an entry in the register) is to be treated as if it were fraud or lack of care on the part of the claimant.

Valuation of estates etc.

6   Where an indemnity is payable in respect of the loss of an estate, interest or charge, the value of the estate, interest or charge for the purposes of the indemnity is to be regarded as not exceeding —

(a) in the case of an indemnity under paragraph 1(1)(a), its value immediately before rectification of the register (but as if there were to be no rectification), and

(b) in the case of an indemnity under paragraph 1(1)(b), its value at the time when the mistake which caused the loss was made.

Determination of indemnity by court

7   (1) A person may apply to the court for the determination of any question as to —

(a) whether he is entitled to an indemnity under this Schedule, or

(b) the amount of such an indemnity.

(2) Paragraph 3(1) does not apply to the costs of an application to the court under this paragraph or of any legal proceedings arising out of such an application.

Time limits

8   For the purposes of the Limitation Act 1980 (c. 58) —

(a) a liability to pay an indemnity under this Schedule is a simple contract debt, and

(b) the cause of action arises at the time when the claimant knows, or but for his own default might have known, of the existence of his claim.

Interest

9   Rules may make provision about the payment of interest on an indemnity under this Schedule, including —

(a) the circumstances in which interest is payable, and

(b) the periods for and rates at which it is payable.

Recovery of indemnity by registrar

10   (1) Where an indemnity under this Schedule is paid to a claimant in respect of any loss, the registrar is entitled (without prejudice to any other rights he may have) —

(a) to recover the amount paid from any person who caused or substantially contributed to the loss by his fraud, or

(b) for the purpose of recovering the amount paid, to enforce the rights of action referred to in sub-paragraph (2).

(2) Those rights of action are —

      (a)   any right of action (of whatever nature and however arising) which the claimant would have been entitled to enforce had the indemnity not been paid, and

      (b)   where the register has been rectified, any right of action (of whatever nature and however arising) which the person in whose favour the register has been rectified would have been entitled to enforce had it not been rectified.

  (3) References in this paragraph to an indemnity include interest paid on an indemnity under rules under paragraph 9.

Interpretation

11   (1) For the purposes of this Schedule, references to a mistake in something include anything mistakenly omitted from it as well as anything mistakenly included in it.

   (2) In this Schedule, references to rectification of the register are to alteration of the register which—

      (a)   involves the correction of a mistake, and

      (b)   prejudicially affects the title of a registered proprietor.

SCHEDULE 9

Section 105.

THE ADJUDICATOR

Holding of office

1   (1) The adjudicator may at any time resign his office by written notice to the Lord Chancellor.

   (2) The Lord Chancellor may remove the adjudicator from office on the ground of incapacity or misbehaviour.

   (3) Section 26 of the Judicial Pensions and Retirement Act 1993 (c. 8) (compulsory retirement at 70, subject to the possibility of annual extension up to 75) applies to the adjudicator.

   (4) Subject to the above, a person appointed to be the adjudicator is to hold and vacate office in accordance with the terms of his appointment and, on ceasing to hold office, is eligible for reappointment.

Remuneration

2   (1) The Lord Chancellor shall pay the adjudicator such remuneration, and such other allowances, as the Lord Chancellor may determine.

   (2) The Lord Chancellor shall—

      (a)   pay such pension, allowances or gratuities as he may determine to or in respect of a person who is or has been the adjudicator, or

      (b)   make such payments as he may determine towards provision for the payment of a pension, allowances or gratuities to or in respect of such a person.

(3) Sub-paragraph (2) does not apply if the office of adjudicator is a qualifying judicial office within the meaning of the Judicial Pensions and Retirement Act 1993 (c. 8).

(4) If, when a person ceases to be the adjudicator, the Lord Chancellor determines that there are special circumstances which make it right that the person should receive compensation, the Lord Chancellor may pay to the person by way of compensation a sum of such amount as he may determine.

Staff

3 (1) The adjudicator may appoint such staff as he thinks fit.

(2) The terms and conditions of appointments under this paragraph shall be such as the adjudicator, with the approval of the Minister for the Civil Service, thinks fit.

Conduct of business

4 (1) Subject to sub-paragraph (2), any function of the adjudicator may be carried out by any member of his staff who is authorised by him for the purpose.

(2) In the case of functions which are not of an administrative character, sub-paragraph (1) only applies if the member of staff has a 10 year general qualification (within the meaning of section 71 of the Courts and Legal Services Act 1990 (c. 41)).

5 The Lord Chancellor may by regulations make provision about the carrying out of functions during any vacancy in the office of adjudicator.

Finances

6 The Lord Chancellor shall be liable to reimburse expenditure incurred by the adjudicator in the discharge of his functions.

7 The Lord Chancellor may require the registrar to make payments towards expenses of the Lord Chancellor under this Schedule.

Application of Tribunals and Inquiries Act 1992

8 In Schedule 1 to the Tribunal and Inquiries Act 1992 (c. 53) (tribunals under the supervision of the Council on Tribunals), after paragraph 27 there is inserted—

"Land Registration	27B. The Adjudicator to Her Majesty's Land Registry."

Parliamentary disqualification

9 In Part 1 of Schedule 1 to the House of Commons Disqualification Act 1975 (c. 24) (judicial offices), there is inserted at the end—

"Adjudicator to Her Majesty's Land Registry.";
and a corresponding amendment is made in Part 1 of Schedule 1 to the Northern Ireland Assembly Disqualification Act 1975 (c. 25).

SCHEDULE 10

Section 123.

MISCELLANEOUS AND GENERAL POWERS

PART 1

MISCELLANEOUS

Dealings with estates subject to compulsory first registration

1   (1) Rules may make provision—
     (a) applying this Act to a pre-registration dealing with a registrable legal estate as if the dealing had taken place after the date of first registration of the estate, and
     (b) about the date on which registration of the dealing is effective.

     (2) For the purposes of sub-paragraph (1)—
     (a) a legal estate is registrable if a person is subject to a duty under section 6 to make an application to be registered as the proprietor of it, and
     (b) a pre-registration dealing is one which takes place before the making of such an application.

Regulation of title matters between sellers and buyers

2   (1) Rules may make provision about the obligations with respect to—
     (a) proof of title, or
     (b) perfection of title,
     of the seller under a contract for the transfer, or other disposition, for valuable consideration of a registered estate or charge.

     (2) Rules under this paragraph may be expressed to have effect notwithstanding any stipulation to the contrary.

Implied covenants

3   Rules may—
     (a) make provision about the form of provisions extending or limiting any covenant implied by virtue of Part 1 of the Law of Property (Miscellaneous Provisions) Act 1994 (c. 36) (implied covenants for title) on a registrable disposition;
     (b) make provision about the application of section 77 of the Law of Property Act 1925 (c. 20) (implied covenants in conveyance subject to rents) to transfers of registered estates;
     (c) make provision about reference in the register to implied covenants, including provision for the state of the register to be conclusive in relation to whether covenants have been implied.

Land certificates

4   Rules may make provision about—
     (a) when a certificate of registration of title to a legal estate may be issued,

443

(b)   the form and content of such a certificate, and

(c)   when such a certificate must be produced or surrendered to the registrar.

PART 2

GENERAL

Notice

5   (1)   Rules may make provision about the form, content and service of notice under this Act.

(2)   Rules under this paragraph about the service of notice may, in particular —

(a)   make provision requiring the supply of an address for service and about the entry of addresses for service in the register;

(b)   make provision about —

(i)   the time for service,

(ii)   the mode of service, and

(iii)   when service is to be regarded as having taken place.

Applications

6   Rules may —

(a)   make provision about the form and content of applications under this Act;

(b)   make provision requiring applications under this Act to be supported by such evidence as the rules may provide;

(c)   make provision about when an application under this Act is to be taken as made;

(d)   make provision about the order in which competing applications are to be taken to rank;

(e)   may make provision for an alteration made by the registrar for the purpose of correcting a mistake in an application or accompanying document to have effect in such circumstances as the rules may provide as if made by the applicant or other interested party or parties.

Statutory statements

7   Rules may make provision about the form of any statement required under an enactment to be included in an instrument effecting a registrable disposition or a disposition which triggers the requirement of registration.

Residual power

8   Rules may make any other provision which it is expedient to make for the purposes of carrying this Act into effect, whether similar or not to any provision which may be made under the other powers to make land registration rules.

SCHEDULE 11

Section 130.

MINOR AND CONSEQUENTIAL AMENDMENTS

Settled Land Act 1925 (c. 18)

1   Section 119(3) of the Settled Land Act 1925 ceases to have effect.

Law of Property Act 1925 (c. 20)

2   (1) The Law of Property Act 1925 is amended as follows.

     (2) In section 44, after subsection (4) there is inserted —

         "(4A)   Subsections (2) and (4) of this section do not apply to a contract to grant a term of years if the grant will be an event within section 4(1) of the Land Registration Act 2001 (events which trigger compulsory first registration of title)."

     (3) In that section, in subsection (5), for "the last three preceding subsections" there is substituted "subsections (2) to (4) of this section".

     (4) In that section, at the end there is inserted —

         "(12)   Nothing in this section applies in relation to registered land or to a term of years to be derived out of registered land."

     (5) In section 84(8), the words from ", but" to the end are omitted.

     (6) In section 85(3), for the words from the beginning to the second "or" there is substituted "Subsection (2) does not apply to registered land, but, subject to that, this section applies whether or not the land is registered land and whether or not".

     (7) In section 86(3), for the words from the beginning to the second "or" there is substituted "Subsection (2) does not apply to registered land, but, subject to that, this section applies whether or not the land is registered land and whether or not".

     (8) In section 94(4), for the words from "registered" to the end there is substituted "on registered land".

     (9) In section 97, for "Land Registration Act 1925" there is substituted "Land Registration Act 2001".

     (10) In section 115(10), for the words from "charge" to the end there is substituted "registered charge (within the meaning of the Land Registration Act 2001)".

     (11) In section 125(2), for the words from "(not being" to "1925)" there is substituted "(not being registered land)".

     (12) In section 205(1)(xxii) —
         (a)   for "Land Registration Act 1925" there is substituted "Land Registration Act 2001;", and
         (b)   the words from ", and" to the end are omitted.

Administration of Estates Act 1925 (c. 23)

3   In section 43(2) of the Administration of Estates Act 1925, for "Land Registration Act 1925" there is substituted "Land Registration Act 2001".

Requisitioned Land and War Works Act 1945 (c. 43)

4   (1) Section 37 of the Requisitioned Land and War Works Act 1945 is amended as follows.

   (2) In subsection (2), for "Land Registration Act 1925" there is substituted "Land Registration Act 2001".

   (3) Subsection (3) ceases to have effect.

Law of Property (Joint Tenants) Act 1964 (c. 63)

5   In section 3 of the Law of Property (Joint Tenants) Act 1964, for the words from "any land" to the end there is substituted "registered land".

Gas Act 1965 (c. 36)

6   (1) The Gas Act 1965 is amended as follows.

   (2) In section 12(3), for "Land Registration Act 1925" there is substituted "Land Registration Act 2001".

   (3) In sections 12(4) and 13(6), for the words from "be deemed" to the end there is substituted —
- (a) for the purposes of the Land Charges Act 1925, be deemed to be a charge affecting land falling within Class D(iii), and
- (b) for the purposes of the Land Registration Act 2001, be deemed to be an equitable easement."

Commons Registration Act 1965 (c. 64)

7   (1) The Commons Registration Act 1965 is amended as follows.

   (2) In sections 1(1), (2) and (3), 4(3) and 8(1), for "under the Land Registration Acts 1925 and 1936" there is substituted "in the register of title".

   (3) In section 9, for "the Land Registration Acts 1925 and 1936" there is substituted "in the register of title".

   (4) In section 12 (in both places), for "under the Land Registration Acts 1925 and 1936" there is substituted "in the register of title".

   (5) In section 22, in subsection (1), there is inserted at the appropriate place —

""register of title" means the register kept under section 1 of the Land Registration Act 2001;".

   (6) In that section, in subsection (2), for "under the Land Registration Acts 1925 and 1936" there is substituted "in the register of title".

Leasehold Reform Act 1967 (c. 88)

8   (1) The Leasehold Reform Act 1967 is amended as follows.

   (2) In section 5(5) —
- (a) for "an overriding interest within the meaning of the Land Registration Act 1925" there is substituted "regarded for the purposes of the Land Registration Act 2001 as an interest falling within any of the paragraphs of Schedule 1 or 3 to that Act", and

        (b)   for "or caution under the Land Registration Act 1925" there is substituted "under the Land Registration Act 2001".

   (3) In Schedule 4, in paragraph 1(3) –

        (a)   for paragraph (a) there is substituted –

> "(a)   the covenant may be the subject of a notice in the register of title kept under the Land Registration Act 2001, if apart from this subsection it would not be capable of being the subject of such a notice; and", and

        (b)   in paragraph (b), for "notice of the covenant has been so registered, the covenant" there is substituted "a notice in respect of the covenant has been entered in that register, it".

Law of Property Act 1969 (c. 59)

9   In section 24(1) of the Law of Property Act 1969, for "Land Registration Act 1925" there is substituted "Land Registration Act 2001".

Land Charges Act 1972 (c. 61)

10   (1) The Land Charges Act 1972 is amended as follows.

   (2) In section 14(1), for the words from "Land Registration" to the end there is substituted "Land Registration Act 2001".

   (3) In section 14(3) –

        (a)   for the words from "section 123A" to "register)" there is substituted "section 7 of the Land Registration Act 2001 (effect of failure to comply with requirement of registration)", and

        (b)   for "that section" there is substituted "section 6 of that Act".

   (4) In section 17(1), in the definition of "registered land", for "Land Registration Act 1925" there is substituted "Land Registration Act 2001".

Consumer Credit Act 1974 (c. 39)

11   In section 177(1) and (6) of the Consumer Credit Act 1974, for "Land Registration Act 1925" there is substituted "Land Registration Act 2001".

Solicitors Act 1974 (c. 47)

12   (1) The Solicitors Act 1974 is amended as follows.

   (2) In sections 22(1) and 56(1)(f), for "Land Registration Act 1925" there is substituted "Land Registration Act 2001".

   (3) Section 75(b) ceases to have effect.

Local Land Charges Act 1975 (c. 76)

13   In section 10(3)(b)(ii) of the Local Land Charges Act 1975, for "under the Land Registration Act 1925" there is substituted "in the register of title kept under the Land Registration Act 2001".

Rent Act 1977 (c. 42)

14   In section 136(b) of the Rent Act 1977, for the words from "charge" to the end there is substituted "registered charge (within the meaning of the Land Registration Act 2001)".

Charging Orders Act 1979 (c. 53)

15   In section 3(2) and (6) of the Charging Orders Act 1979, for "Land Registration Act 1925" there is substituted "Land Registration Act 2001".

Highways Act 1980 (c. 66)

16   Section 251(5) of the Highways Act 1980 ceases to have effect.

Inheritance Tax Act 1984 (c. 51)

17   In section 238(3) of the Inheritance Tax Act 1984, for paragraph (a) there is substituted —

    "(a)   in relation to registered land —

       (i)   if the disposition is required to be completed by registration, the time of registration, and

      (ii)   otherwise, the time of completion,".

Housing Act 1985 (c. 68)

18 (1) The Housing Act 1985 is amended as follows.

    (2) In section 37(5), for the words from "and" to the end there is substituted —

    "(5A) Where the Chief Land Registrar approves an application for registration of —

      (a)   a disposition of registered land, or

      (b)   the disponee's title under a disposition of unregistered land,

    and the instrument effecting the disposition contains a covenant of the kind mentioned in subsection (1), he must enter in the register a restriction reflecting the limitation imposed by the covenant".

    (3) In section 154(5), for "Land Registration Acts 1925 to 1971" there is substituted "Land Registration Act 2001".

    (4) In section 157(7), for the words from "the appropriate" to the end there is substituted "a restriction in the register of title reflecting the limitation".

    (5) In section 165(6), for "section 83 of the Land Registration Act 1925" there is substituted "Schedule 8 of the Land Registration Act 2001".

    (6) In Schedule 9A, in paragraph 2(2), for the words from the beginning to "the disponor" there is substituted "Where on a qualifying disposal the disponor's title to the dwelling-house is not registered, the disponor".

    (7) In that Schedule, for paragraph 4 there is substituted —

    "4   (1) This paragraph applies where the Chief Land Registrar approves an application for registration of —

      (a)   a disposition of registered land, or

        (b)   the disponee's title under a disposition of unregistered land,

and the instrument effecting the disposition contains the statement required by paragraph 1.

(2) The Chief Land Registrar must enter in the register —

        (a)   a notice in respect of the rights of qualifying persons under this Part in relation to dwelling-houses comprised in the disposal, and

        (b)   a restriction reflecting the limitation under section 171D(2) on subsequent disposal."

  (8) In that Schedule, for paragraph 5(2) there is substituted —

    "(2) If the landlord's title is registered, the landlord shall apply for the entry in the register of —

        (a)   a notice in respect of the rights of the qualifying person or persons under the provisions of this Part, and

        (b)   a restriction reflecting the limitation under section 171D(2) on subsequent disposal."

  (9) In that Schedule, paragraph 5(3) ceases to have effect.

 (10) In that Schedule, in paragraph 6, for sub-paragraph (1) there is substituted —

    "(1) The rights of a qualifying person under this Part in relation to the qualifying dwelling house shall not be regarded as falling within Schedule 3 to the Land Registration Act 2001 (and so are liable to be postponed under section 29 of that Act, unless protected by means of a notice in the register)."

 (11) In that Schedule, in paragraph 9(2), for "Land Registration Acts 1925 to 1986" there is substituted "Land Registration Act 2001".

 (12) In Schedule 17, in paragraph 2(2), for "Land Registration Acts 1925 to 1971" there is substituted "Land Registration Act 2001".

 (13) In Schedule 20, in paragraph 17(2), for "Land Registration Acts 1925 to 1986" there is substituted "Land Registration Act 2001".

Building Societies Act 1986 (c. 53)

19   (1) In Schedule 2A to the Building Societies Act 1986, paragraph 1 is amended as follows.

    (2) In sub-paragraph (2), for "charge or incumbrance registered under the Land Registration Act 1925" there is substituted "registered charge (within the meaning of the Land Registration Act 2001)".

    (3) Sub-paragraph (4) ceases to have effect.

    (4) In sub-paragraph (5), the definition of "registered land" and the preceding "and" cease to have effect.

Landlord and Tenant Act 1987 (c. 31)

20   In sections 24(8) and (9), 28(5), 30(6) and 34(9) of the Landlord and Tenant Act 1987, for "Land Registration Act 1925" there is substituted "Land Registration Act 2001".

Diplomatic and Consular Premises Act 1987 (c. 46)

21　(1)　The Diplomatic and Consular Premises Act 1987 is amended as follows.

　　(2)　In section 5, after the definition of the expression "diplomatic premises" there is inserted —

　　　　""land" includes buildings and other structure, land covered with water and any estate, interest, easement, servitude or right in or over land,".

　　(3)　In Schedule 1, in paragraph 1 —

　　　　(a)　before the definition of the expression "the registrar" there is inserted —

　　　　　　""registered land" has the same meaning as in the Land Registration Act 2001;", and

　　　　(b)　the words from "and expressions" to the end are omitted.

Criminal Justice Act 1988 (c. 33)

22　(1)　The Criminal Justice Act 1988 is amended as follows.

　　(2)　In section 77(12), for "Land Registration Act 1925" there is substituted "Land Registration Act 2001".

　　(3)　In section 79(1) and (4), for "Land Registration Act 1925" there is substituted "Land Registration Act 2001".

Housing Act 1988 (c. 50)

23　(1)　The Housing Act 1988 is amended as follows.

　　(2)　In section 81, in subsection (9)(c), for "Land Registration Acts 1925 to 1986" there is substituted "Land Registration Act 2001".

　　(3)　In that section, for subsection (10) there is substituted —

　　　　"(10)　Where the Chief Land Registrar approves an application for registration of —

　　　　　　(a)　a disposition of registered land, or

　　　　　　(b)　the approved person's title under a disposition of unregistered land,

　　　　and the instrument effecting the disposition contains the statement required by subsection (1) above, he shall enter in the register a restriction reflecting the limitation under this section on subsequent disposal."

　　(4)　In section 90(4), for "Land Registration Act 1925" there is substituted "Land Registration Act 2001".

　　(5)　In section 133, in subsection (8) —

　　　　(a)　for the words "conveyance, grant or assignment" there is substituted "transfer or grant",

　　　　(b)　for the words "section 123 of the Land Registration Act 1925" there is substituted "section 4 of the Land Registration Act 2001", and

　　　　(c)　in paragraph (c), for "Land Registration Acts 1925 to 1986" there is substituted "Land Registration Act 2001".

　　(6)　In that section, for subsection (9) there is substituted —

"(9) Where the Chief Land Registrar approves an application for registration of —
  (a) a disposition of registered land, or
  (b) a person's title under a disposition of unregistered land,
and the instrument effecting the original disposal contains the statement required by subsection (3)(d) above, he shall enter in the register a restriction reflecting the limitation under this section on subsequent disposal."

Local Government and Housing Act 1989 (c. 42)

24 (1) Section 173 of the Local Government and Housing Act 1989 is amended as follows.

(2) In subsection (8) —
  (a) for the words "conveyance, grant or assignment" there is substituted "transfer or grant",
  (b) for the words "section 123 of the Land Registration Act 1925" there is substituted "section 4 of the Land Registration Act 2001", and
  (c) in paragraph (c), for "Land Registration Acts 1925 to 1986" there is substituted "Land Registration Act 2001".

(3) For subsection (9) there is substituted —

"(9) Where the Chief Land Registrar approves an application for registration of —
  (a) a disposition of registered land, or
  (b) a person's title under a disposition of unregistered land,
and the instrument effecting the initial transfer contains the statement required by subsection (3) above, he shall enter in the register a restriction reflecting the limitation under this section on subsequent disposal."

Water Resources Act 1991 (c. 57)

25 (1) Section 158 of the Water Resources Act 1991 is amended as follows.

(2) In subsection (5) —
  (a) for paragraphs (a) and (b) there is substituted —
      "(a) the agreement may be the subject of a notice in the register of title under the Land Registration Act 2001 as if it were an interest affecting the registered land;
      (b) the provisions of sections 28 to 30 of that Act (effect of dispositions of registered land on priority of adverse interests) shall apply as if the agreement were such an interest;", and
  (b) in paragraph (c), for "where notice of the agreement has been so registered," there is substituted "subject to the provisions of those sections,".

(3) In subsection (6), for "Land Registration Act 1925" there is substituted "Land Registration Act 2001".

Access to Neighbouring Land Act 1992 (c. 4)

26 (1) The Access to Neighbouring Land Act 1992 is amended as follows.

(2) In section 4(1), for "Land Registration Act 1925" there is substituted "Land Registration Act 2001".

(3) In section 5, in subsection (4) —

(a) in paragraph (b), for "notice or caution under the Land Registration Act 1925" there is substituted "notice under the Land Registration Act 2001", and

(b) for "entry, notice or caution" there is substituted "entry or notice".

(4) In that section, for subsection (5) there is substituted —

"(5) The rights conferred on a person by or under an access order shall not be capable of falling within paragraph 2 of Schedule 1 or 3 to the Land Registration Act 2001 (overriding status of interest of person in actual occupation)."

(5) In that section, in subsection (6), for "Land Registration Act 1925" there is substituted "Land Registration Act 2001".

Further and Higher Education Act 1992 (c. 13)

27   In Schedule 5 to the Further and Higher Education Act 1992, in paragraph 6(1) —

(a) for "Land Registration Acts 1925 to 1986" there is substituted "Land Registration Act 2001", and

(b) for "those Acts" there is substituted "that Act".

Judicial Pensions and Retirement Act 1993 (c. 8)

28   In Schedule 5 to the Judicial Pensions and Retirement Act 1993, there is inserted at the end —

"Adjudicator to Her Majesty's Land Registry"

Charities Act 1993 (c. 10)

29 (1) The Charities Act 1993 is amended as follows.

(2) In section 37, for subsections (7) and (8) there is substituted —

"(7) Where the disposition to be effected by any such instrument as is mentioned in subsection (1)(b) or (5)(b) above will be —
(a) a registrable disposition, or
(b) a disposition which triggers the requirement of registration,
the statement which, by virtue of subsection (1) or (5) above, is to be contained in the instrument shall be in such form as may be prescribed by land registration rules.

(8) Where the registrar approves an application for registration of —
(a) a disposition of registered land, or
(b) a person's title under a disposition of unregistered land,
and the instrument effecting the disposition contains a statement complying with subsections (5) and (7) above, he shall enter in the

register a restriction reflecting the limitation under section 36 above on subsequent disposal."

(3) In that section, in subsection (9) —

    (a) for "the restriction to be withdrawn" there is substituted "the removal of the entry", and

    (b) for "withdraw the restriction" there is substituted "remove the entry".

(4) In that section, in subsection (11), for "Land Registration Act 1925" there is substituted "Land Registration Act 2001".

(5) In section 39, in subsection (1), at the end there is inserted "by land registration rules".

(6) In that section, for subsections (1A) and (1B) there is substituted —

"(1A)   Where any such mortgage will be one to which section 4(1)(g) of the Land Registration Act 2001 applies —

    (a) the statement required by subsection (1) above shall be in such form as may be prescribed by land registration rules; and

    (b) if the charity is not an exempt charity, the mortgage shall also contain a statement, in such form as may be prescribed by land registration rules, that the restrictions on disposition imposed by section 36 above apply to the land (subject to subsection (9) of that section).

(1B)   Where —

    (a) the registrar approves an application for registration of a person's title to land in connection with such a mortgage as is mentioned in subsection (1A) above,

    (b) the mortgage contains statements complying with subsections (1) and (1A) above, and

    (c) the charity is not an exempt charity,

the registrar shall enter in the register a restriction reflecting the limitation under section 36 above on subsequent disposal.

(1C)   Section 37(9) above shall apply in relation to any restriction entered under subsection (1B) as it applies in relation to any restriction entered under section 37(8)."

(7) In that section, in subsection (6), for the words from "and subsections" to the end there is substituted "and subsections (1) to (1B) above shall be construed as one with the Land Registration Act 2001".

Leasehold Reform, Housing and Urban Development Act 1993 (c. 28)

30   (1) The Leasehold Reform, Housing and Urban Development Act 1993 is amended as follows.

(2) In sections 34(10) and 57(11), for the words from "rules" to the end there is substituted "land registration rules under the Land Registration Act 2001".

(3) In section 97, in subsection (1) —

    (a) for "an overriding interest within the meaning of the Land Registration Act 1925" there is substituted "capable of falling within paragraph 2 of Schedule 1 or 3 to the Land Registration Act 2001", and

    (b)   for "or caution under the Land Registration Act 1925" there is substituted "under the Land Registration Act 2001".

(4) In that section, in subsection (2), for "Land Registration Act 1925" there is substituted "Land Registration Act 2001".

Law of Property (Miscellaneous Provisions) Act 1994 (c. 36)

31 (1) The Law of Property (Miscellaneous Provisions) Act 1994 is amended as follows.

(2) In section 6 (cases in which there is no liability under covenants implied by virtue of Part 1 of that Act), at the end there is inserted —

    "(4) Moreover, where the disposition is of an interest the title to which is registered under the Land Registration Act 2001, that person is not liable under any of those covenants for anything (not falling within subsection (1) or (2)) which at the time of the disposition was entered in relation to that interest in the register of title under that Act."

(3) In section 17(3) —

    (a)   in paragraph (c), for the words from "any" to the end there is substituted "the Adjudicator to Her Majesty's Land Registry", and

    (b)   for "section 144 of the Land Registration Act 1925" there is substituted "the Land Registration Act 2001".

Drug Trafficking Act 1994 (c. 37)

32 (1) The Drug Trafficking Act 1994 is amended as follows.

(2) In section 26(12), for "Land Registration Act 1925" there is substituted "Land Registration Act 2001".

(3) In section 28(1) and (4), for "Land Registration Act 1925" there is substituted "Land Registration Act 2001".

Landlord and Tenant (Covenants) Act 1995 (c. 30)

33 (1) The Landlord and Tenant (Covenants) Act 1995 is amended as follows.

(2) In sections 3(6) and 15(5)(b), for "Land Registration Act 1925" there is substituted "Land Registration Act 2001".

(3) In section 20, in subsection (2), for the words from "rules" to the end there is substituted "land registration rules under the Land Registration Act 2001".

(4) In that section, in subsection (6) —

    (a)   for "an overriding interest within the meaning of the Land Registration Act 1925" there is substituted "capable of falling within paragraph 2 of Schedule 1 or 3 to the Land Registration Act 2001", and

    (b)   for "or caution under the Land Registration Act 1925" there is substituted "under the Land Registration Act 2001".

Family Law Act 1996 (c. 27)

34   (1) The Family Law Act 1996 is amended as follows.

       (2) In section 31(10) –

          (a) for "Land Registration Act 1925" there is substituted "Land Registration Act 2001", and

          (b) for paragraph (b) there is substituted –

              "(b) a spouse's matrimonial home rights are not to be capable of falling within paragraph 2 of Schedule 1 or 3 to that Act."

       (3) In Schedule 4, in paragraph 4(6), for "section 144 of the Land Registration Act 1925" there is substituted "by land registration rules under the Land Registration Act 2001".

Housing Act 1996 (c. 52)

35   In section 13(5) of the Housing Act 1996, for the words from "if" to the end there is substituted "if the first disposal involves registration under the Land Registration Act 2001, the Chief Land Registrar shall enter in the register of title a restriction reflecting the limitation".

Education Act 1996 (c. 56)

36   In Schedule 7 to the Education Act 1996, in paragraph 11 –

          (a) in sub-paragraph (a), for "Land Registration Acts 1925 to 1986" there is substituted "Land Registration Act 2001", and

          (b) in sub-paragraphs (b) and (c), for "those Acts" there is substituted "that Act".

School Standards and Framework Act 1998 (c. 31)

37   In Schedule 22 to the School Standards and Framework Act 1998, in paragraph 9(1) –

          (a) in paragraph (a), for "Land Registration Acts 1925 to 1986" there is substituted "Land Registration Act 2001", and

          (b) in paragraphs (b) and (c), for "those Acts" there is substituted "that Act".

Terrorism Act 2000 (c. 11)

38   In Schedule 4 to the Terrorism Act 2000, in paragraph 8(1), for "Land Registration Act 1925" there is substituted "Land Registration Act 2001".

Finance Act 2000 (c. 17)

39   In section 128 of the Finance Act 2000 –

          (a) in subsection (2), for the words from "rule" to the end there is substituted "land registration rules under the Land Registration Act 2001", and

          (b) in subsection (8)(a), for "Land Registration Act 1925" there is substituted "Land Registration Act 2001".

International Criminal Court Act 2001 (c. 17)

40   In Schedule 6 to the International Criminal Court Act 2001, in paragraph 7(1), for "Land Registration Act 1925" there is substituted "Land Registration Act 2001".

SCHEDULE 12   Section 131.

TRANSITION

Existing entries in the register

1   Nothing in the repeals made by this Act affects the validity of any entry in the register.

2   (1) This Act applies to notices entered under the Land Registration Act 1925 (c. 21) as it applies to notices entered in pursuance of an application under section 34(2)(a).

        (2) This Act applies to restrictions and inhibitions entered under the Land Registration Act 1925 as it applies to restrictions entered under this Act.

        (3) Notwithstanding their repeal by this Act, sections 55 and 56 of the Land Registration Act 1925 shall continue to have effect so far as relating to cautions lodged under section 54 of that Act (cautions against dealings).

        (4) Rules may make provision about cautions entered in the register under section 54 of the Land Registration Act 1925.

        (5) In this paragraph, references to the Land Registration Act 1925 include a reference to any enactment replaced (directly or indirectly) by that Act.

3   An entry in the register which, immediately before the repeal of section 144(1)(xi) of the Land Registration Act 1925, operated by virtue of rule 239 of the Land Registration Rules (S.I. 1925/1093) as a caution under section 54 of that Act shall continue to operate as such a caution.

Existing cautions against first registration

4   (1) Notwithstanding the repeal of section 56(3) of the Land Registration Act 1925, that provision shall continue to have effect in relation to cautions lodged under section 53 of that Act (cautions against first registration).

        (2) In this paragraph, the reference to the Land Registration Act 1925 includes a reference to any enactment replaced (directly or indirectly) by that Act.

Pending applications

5   Notwithstanding the repeal of the Land Registration Act 1925, that Act shall continue to have effect in relation to an application for the entry in the register of a notice, restriction, inhibition or caution against dealings which is pending immediately before the repeal of the provision under which the application is made.

6   Notwithstanding the repeal of section 53 of the Land Registration Act 1925, subsections (1) and (2) of that section shall continue to have effect in relation

456

to an application to lodge a caution against first registration which is pending immediately before the repeal of those provisions.

Former overriding interests

7   For the period of three years beginning with the day on which Schedule 1 comes into force, it has effect with the insertion after paragraph 14 of—

"15. A right acquired under the Limitation Act 1980 before the coming into force of this Schedule."

8   Schedule 3 has effect with the insertion after paragraph 2 of—

"2A (1) An interest which, immediately before the coming into force of this Schedule, was an overriding interest under section 70(1)(g) of the Land Registration Act 1925 (c. 21) by virtue of a person's receipt of rents and profits, except for an interest of a person of whom inquiry was made before the disposition and who failed to disclose the right when he could reasonably have been expected to do so.

(2) Sub-paragraph (1) does not apply to an interest if at any time since the coming into force of this Schedule it has been an interest which, had the Land Registration Act 1925 continued in force, would not have been an overriding interest under section 70(1)(g) of that Act by virtue of a person's receipt of rents and profits."

9   (1) This paragraph applies to an easement or profit a prendre which was an overriding interest in relation to a registered estate immediately before the coming into force of Schedule 3, but which would not fall within paragraph 3 of that Schedule if created after the coming into force of that Schedule.

(2) In relation to an interest to which this paragraph applies, Schedule 3 has effect as if the interest were not excluded from paragraph 3.

10   For the period of three years beginning with the day on which Schedule 3 comes into force, paragraph 3 of the Schedule has effect with the omission of the exception.

11   For the period of three years beginning with the day on which Schedule 3 comes into force, it has effect with the insertion after paragraph 14 of—

"15. A right under paragraph 18(1) of Schedule 12."

12   Paragraph 1 of each of Schedules 1 and 3 shall be taken to include an interest which immediately before the coming into force of the Schedule was an overriding interest under section 70(1)(k) of the Land Registration Act 1925.

13   Paragraph 6 of each of Schedules 1 and 3 shall be taken to include an interest which immediately before the coming into force of the Schedule was an overriding interest under section 70(1)(i) of the Land Registration Act 1925 and whose status as such was preserved by section 19(3) of the Local Land Charges Act 1975 (c. 76) (transitional provision in relation to change in definition of "local land charge").

Cautions against first registration

14   (1) For the period of two years beginning with the day on which section 15 comes into force, it has effect with the following omissions—

(a) in subsection (1), the words "Subject to subsection (3),", and

(b) subsection (3).

(2) Any caution lodged by virtue of sub-paragraph (1) which is in force immediately before the end of the period mentioned in that sub-paragraph shall cease to have effect at the end of that period, except in relation to applications for registration made before the end of that period.

(3) This paragraph does not apply to section 15 as applied by section 81.

15 (1) As applied by section 81, section 15 has effect for the period of ten years beginning with the day on which it comes into force, or such longer period as rules may provide, with the omission of subsection (3)(a)(i).

(2) Any caution lodged by virtue of sub-paragraph (1) which is in force immediately before the end of the period mentioned in that sub-paragraph shall cease to have effect at the end of that period, except in relation to applications for registration made before the end of that period.

16 This Act shall apply as if the definition of "caution against first registration" in section 129 included cautions lodged under section 53 of the Land Registration Act 1925 (c. 21).

Applications under section 34 or 43 by cautioners

17 Where a caution under section 54 of the Land Registration Act 1925 is lodged in respect of a person's estate, right, interest or claim, he may only make an application under section 34 or 43 above in respect of that estate, right, interest or claim if he also applies to the registrar for the withdrawal of the caution.

Adverse possession

18 (1) Where a registered estate in land is held in trust for a person by virtue of section 75(1) of the Land Registration Act 1925 immediately before the coming into force of section 96, he is entitled to be registered as the proprietor of the estate.

(2) A person has a defence to any action for the possession of land (in addition to any other defence he may have) if he is entitled under this paragraph to be registered as the proprietor of an estate in the land.

(3) Where in an action for possession of land a court determines that a person is entitled to a defence under this section, the court must order the registrar to register him as the proprietor of the estate in relation to which he is entitled under this paragraph to be registered.

(4) Entitlement under this paragraph shall be disregarded for the purposes of section 128(1).

(5) Rules may make transitional provision for cases where a rentcharge is held in trust under section 75(1) of the Land Registration Act 1925 immediately before the coming into force of section 96.

Indemnities

19 (1) Schedule 8 applies in relation to claims made before the commencement of this section which have not been settled by agreement or finally determined

by that time (as well as to claims for indemnity made after the commencement of that Schedule).

(2) But paragraph 3(1) of that Schedule does not apply in relation to costs and expenses incurred in respect of proceedings, negotiations or other matters begun before 27 April 1997.

Implied indemnity covenants on transfers of pre-1996 leases

20 (1) On a disposition of a registered leasehold estate by way of transfer, the following covenants are implied in the instrument effecting the disposition, unless the contrary intention is expressed —

    (a) in the case of a transfer of the whole of the land comprised in the registered lease, the covenant in sub-paragraph (2), and

    (b) in the case of a transfer of part of the land comprised in the lease —

        (i) the covenant in sub-paragraph (3), and

        (ii) where the transferor continues to hold land under the lease, the covenant in sub-paragraph (4).

(2) The transferee covenants with the transferor that during the residue of the term granted by the registered lease the transferee and the persons deriving title under him will —

    (a) pay the rent reserved by the lease,

    (b) comply with the covenants and conditions contained in the lease, and

    (c) keep the transferor and the persons deriving title under him indemnified against all actions, expenses and claims on account of any failure to comply with paragraphs (a) and (b).

(3) The transferee covenants with the transferor that during the residue of the term granted by the registered lease the transferee and the persons deriving title under him will —

    (a) where the rent reserved by the lease is apportioned, pay the rent apportioned to the part transferred,

    (b) comply with the covenants and conditions contained in the lease so far as affecting the part transferred, and

    (c) keep the transferor and the persons deriving title under him indemnified against all actions, expenses and claims on account of any failure to comply with paragraphs (a) and (b).

(4) The transferor covenants with the transferee that during the residue of the term granted by the registered lease the transferor and the persons deriving title under him will —

    (a) where the rent reserved by the lease is apportioned, pay the rent apportioned to the part retained,

    (b) comply with the covenants and conditions contained in the lease so far as affecting the part retained, and

    (c) keep the transferee and the persons deriving title under him indemnified against all actions, expenses and claims on account of any failure to comply with paragraphs (a) and (b).

(5) This paragraph does not apply to a lease which is a new tenancy for the purposes of section 1 of the Landlord and Tenant (Covenants) Act 1995 (c. 30).

SCHEDULE 13   Section 132.

REPEALS

Short title and chapter	Extent of repeal
The Settled Land Act 1925 c. 18.	Section 119(3).
The Law of Property Act 1925 c. 20.	In section 84(8), the words from ", but" to the end. In section 205(1)(xxii), the words from ", and" to the end.
The Land Registration Act 1925 c. 21.	The whole Act.
The Law of Property (Amendment) Act 1926 c. 11.	Section 5.
The Land Registration Act 1936 c.26.	The whole Act.
The Requisitioned Land and War Works Act 1945 c. 43.	Section 37(3).
The Mental Health Act 1959 c. 72.	In Schedule 7, the entry relating to the Land Registration Act 1925.
The Charities Act 1960 c. 58.	In Schedule 6, the entry relating to the Land Registration Act 1925.
The Civil Evidence Act 1968 c. 64.	In the Schedule, the entry relating to the Land Registration Act 1925.
The Post Office Act 1969 c. 48.	In Schedule 4, paragraph 27.
The Law of Property Act 1969 c. 59.	Section 28(7).
The Land Registration and Land Charges Act 1971 c. 54.	The whole Act.
The Superannuation Act 1972 c. 11.	In Schedule 6, paragraph 16.
The Local Government Act 1972 c. 70.	In Schedule 29, paragraph 26.
The Solicitors Act 1974 c. 47.	Section 75(b).
The Finance Act 1975 c. 7.	In Schedule 12, paragraph 5.
The Local Land Charges Act 1975 c. 76.	Section 19(3). In Schedule 1, the entry relating to the Land Registration Act 1925.
The Endowments and Glebe Measure 1976 No. 4.	In Schedule 5, paragraph 1.
The Administration of Justice Act 1977 c. 38.	Sections 24 and 26.
The Charging Orders Act 1979 c. 53.	Section 3(3). Section 7(4).

Short title and chapter	Extent of repeal
The Limitation Act 1980 c. 58.	In section 17, paragraph (b) and the preceding "and".
The Highways Act 1980 c. 66.	Section 251(5).
The Matrimonial Homes and Property Act 1981 c. 24.	Section 4.
The Administration of Justice Act 1982 c. 53.	Sections 66 and 67 and Schedule 5.
The Mental Health Act 1983 c. 20.	In Schedule 4, paragraph 6.
The Capital Transfer Tax Act 1984 c. 51.	In Schedule 8, paragraph 1.
The Administration of Justice Act 1985 c. 61.	In section 34, in subsection (1), paragraph (b) and the preceding "and" and, in subsection (2), paragraph (b). In Schedule 2, paragraph 37(b).
The Insolvency Act 1985 c. 65.	In Schedule 8, paragraph 5.
The Housing Act 1985 c. 68.	Section 36(3). Section 154(1), (6) and (7). Section 156(3). Section 168(5). In Schedule 9A, paragraphs 2(1), 3 and 5(3).
The Land Registration Act 1986 c. 26.	Sections 1 to 4.
The Insolvency Act 1986 c. 45.	In Schedule 14, the entry relating to the Land Registration Act 1925.
The Building Societies Act 1986 c. 53.	In Schedule 2A, in paragraph 1, sub-paragraph (4) and, in sub-paragraph (5), the definition of "registered land" and the preceding "and". In Schedule 18, paragraph 2. In Schedule 21, paragraph 9(b).
The Patronage (Benefices) Measure 1986 No. 3.	Section 6.
The Landlord and Tenant Act 1987 c. 31.	Section 28(6). In Schedule 4, paragraphs 1 and 2.
The Diplomatic and Consular Premises Act 1987 c. 46.	In Schedule 1, in paragraph 1, the words from "and expressions" to the end.
The Land Registration Act 1988 c. 3.	The whole Act.
The Criminal Justice Act 1988 c. 33.	Section 77(13). In Schedule 15, paragraphs 6 and 7.
The Housing Act 1988 c. 50.	In Schedule 11, paragraph 2(3).
The Finance Act 1989 c. 26.	Sections 178(2)(e) and 179(1)(a)(iv).
The Courts and Legal Services Act 1990 c. 41.	In Schedule 10, paragraph 3. In Schedule 17, paragraph 2.

Short title and chapter	Extent of repeal
The Access to Neighbouring Land Act 1992 c. 23.	Section 5(2) and (3).
The Leasehold Reform, Housing and Urban Development Act 1993 c. 28.	Section 97(3). In Schedule 21, paragraph 1.
The Coal Industry Act 1994 c. 21.	In Schedule 9, paragraph 1.
The Law of Property (Miscellaneous Provisions) Act 1994 c. 36.	In Schedule 1, paragraph 2.
The Drug Trafficking Act 1994 c. 37.	Section 26(13). In Schedule 1, paragraph 1.
The Family Law Act 1996 c. 27.	Section 31(11). In Schedule 8, paragraph 45.
The Trusts of Land and Appointment of Trustees Act 1996 c. 47.	In Schedule 3, paragraph 5.
The Housing Act 1996 c. 52.	Section 11(4).
The Housing Grants, Construction and Regeneration Act 1996 c. 53.	Section 138(3).
The Land Registration Act 1997 c. 2.	Sections 1 to 3 and 5(4) and (5). In Schedule 1, paragraphs 1 to 6.
The Greater London Authority Act 1999 c. 29.	Section 219.
The Terrorism Act 2000 c. 11.	In Schedule 4, paragraph 8(2) and (3).
The Trustee Act 2000 c. 29.	In Schedule 2, paragraph 26.
The International Criminal Court Act 2001 c. 17.	In Schedule 6, paragraph 7(2).

EXPLANATORY NOTES
ON
DRAFT LAND REGISTRATION BILL

PART 1: PRELIMINARY

1.   Part 1 of the Bill is concerned with two preliminary matters, namely the register of title and the scope of title registration.

CLAUSE 1 — REGISTER OF TITLE

2.   This clause provides for the continuation of the register of title. This replicates section 1(1) of the Land Registration Act 1925. There is a power to make rules about how the register is to be kept. This replicates the power in section 144(1)(i) of the Land Registration Act 1925.

CLAUSE 2 — SCOPE OF TITLE REGISTRATION

3.   This provision is descriptive and it explains in relation to which matters the Bill makes provision for registration of title. Clause 2(a) is concerned with the unregistered estates which are capable of being registered. These are dealt with in Part 2, Chapter 1 of the Bill. Clause 2(b) is concerned with those legal interests created by a disposition of land the title to which is registered. These are addressed in Part 3 of the Bill.

PART 2: FIRST REGISTRATION OF TITLE
Chapter 1: First registration

4.   Chapter 1 of Part 2 of the Bill is concerned with the circumstances in which an unregistered estate may or must be registered.

Voluntary registration

CLAUSE 3 — WHEN TITLE MAY BE REGISTERED

5.   Clause 3 makes provision for the voluntary first registration of title and sets out which unregistered legal estates *may* be registered with their own titles.

Subsection (1)

6.   Subsection (1) specifies the unregistered legal estates that may be registered with their own titles under subsection (2).

7.   The first legal estate that may be registered with its own title, is a legal estate in land. As now, it will therefore be possible to register—

(i)   A fee simple absolute in possession.
(ii)   A term of years absolute. However, the right to apply for first registration in respect of a term of years absolute is subject to

463

certain important exceptions: see Clauses 3(3)—(5), 90(1); below, paragraphs 14—19, 394, respectively.

8. The second legal estate that may be registered is a rentcharge. A rentcharge will be legal if it is perpetual or granted for a term of years: Law of Property Act 1925, section 1(2)(b). Subject to certain exceptions, the Rentcharges Act 1977 prevents the creation of new rentcharges after 21 August 1977, and provides for the abolition of most existing rentcharges in 2037. Of the exceptions exempted from the effect of the Act, the most important are "estate rentcharges", created to enable the enforcement of positive covenants and to secure the payment of service charges.

9. The third legal estate that may be registered with its own title is a franchise. A franchise is a royal privilege or branch of the Crown's prerogative, subsisting in the hands of a subject, either by royal grant or prescription. It is an incorporeal hereditament. Examples of franchises still encountered today include those to hold a market or fair, or to take tolls. At present a franchise cannot be registered with its own title. Instead, it has to be protected by means of a notice or caution. However, this is only possible where the encumbered land is itself registered. In view of the potential value of franchises, the Bill enables them to be registered with their own titles.

10. The fourth legal estate that may be registered is a *profit à prendre* in gross. A *profit à prendre* is also an incorporeal hereditament. A profit exists in gross where it has an independent existence and does not exist for the benefit of another piece of land. Examples of profits that can exist in gross include profits of pasture, piscary (fishing) and of hunting and shooting game. At present, a profit in gross cannot be registered with its own title, but can only be protected on the register by an appropriate entry against the title of the land burdened if that land is registered. Profits are often sold and leased and they can be very valuable. The Bill therefore makes provision for them to be registered with their own titles.

Subsection (2)

11. Subsection (2) provides that a person may apply to the registrar to be registered as first registered proprietor of a legal estate in two situations.

12. The first is where the legal estate is vested in him or her. The second is where he or she is entitled to have the legal estate vested in him or her. An example would be where the applicant was absolutely entitled as the sole beneficiary under a trust of land. However, Clause 3(6) provides that a person may not apply to be registered if he or she is a person who has contracted to buy land. This is because the contract will be completed by a conveyance, and that conveyance will be subject to the requirements of compulsory registration under Clause 4. As now, the fees payable on voluntary first registration are likely to be lower than they are on compulsory first registration.

13. First registration involves an application to the registrar. For the general right to object to an application to the registrar and the manner in which such an objection will be disposed of, see Clause 73.

Subsection (3)

14. Subsection (3) forms an important exception to the right to apply for first registration of a lease. Subject to subsection (4), an application in respect of a leasehold estate may only be made if the estate was granted for a term of

464

which more than 7 years remain unexpired. This provision changes significantly the present law. At present only leases with more than 21 years to run may be registered voluntarily: Land Registration Act 1925, section 8(1). The change is in furtherance of the objective that the title to all land in England and Wales should be registered.

15. It should be noted that subsection (3) will apply to *all* leasehold estates. It will therefore apply to the lease of a rentcharge, franchise or profit, as well as to a leasehold estate in land.

16. It sometimes happens that a person holds under one lease but has been granted another lease to take effect on or shortly after the first. Subsection (7) provides that where the reversionary lease is to take effect in possession on, or within one month of, the end of the lease in possession, the terms may be added together. If, taken together, the terms exceed seven years, the lease will be registrable.

17. The Bill confers a power on the Lord Chancellor by order to reduce the length of leases that are capable of being registered: see Clause 116(1) and paragraph 519 below. Before making such an order, the Lord Chancellor must consult such persons as he considers appropriate: see Clause 116(3). It is anticipated that when electronic conveyancing is fully operative, the length of leases that are registrable is likely to be reduced to those granted for a term of which more than three years remain unexpired.

Subsection (4)

18. The effect of subsection (4) is that even where a lease has 7 years or less to run, it may nevertheless be registered if the right to possession is discontinuous. This provision is new. Discontinuous leases are not very common, but they are sometimes used for time-share arrangements under which (for example) the tenant is entitled to occupy premises for a specified number of weeks every year for a certain number of years. Cf *Cottage Holiday Associates Ltd v Customs and Excise Commissioners* [1983] QB 735.

Subsection (5)

19. Subsection (5) provides where there is a subsisting right of redemption, a mortgage term created by demise or sub-demise is never registrable. Subsection (5) replicates the present law except that it applies not only to legal estates in land, but also to rentcharges, franchises, and *profits à prendre* in gross: see Land Registration Act 1925, section 8(1).

Compulsory registration

CLAUSE 4 — WHEN TITLE MUST BE REGISTERED

20. Subsection (1) specifies the events that trigger the requirement of compulsory registration under the Bill. They are as follows.

21. First, compulsory registration is triggered by certain types of transfer of a qualifying estate. The term "qualifying estate" is defined as either a legal freehold estate in land or a legal lease which has more than 7 years to run: see Clause 4(2). The requirement of compulsory registration will apply to the transfer of a qualifying estate made—

(i) For valuable or other consideration. An estate is to be regarded as being transferred for valuable or other consideration even if it has a negative value: see Clause 4(6).

(ii) By way of gift. The Bill provides the following guidance as to what constitutes a gift. First, a transfer by way of gift includes a transfer for the purpose of constituting a trust under which the settlor does not retain the whole of the beneficial interest: Clause 4(7)(a). Thus if S transfers an unregistered estate in land to T1 and T2, to hold on trust of land for S and U in equal shares, that transfer will trigger compulsory registration. However, a transfer by S to T1 and T2 to hold on trust for her as nominee will not trigger compulsory registration. Secondly, a transfer by way of gift includes a transfer for the purpose of uniting the legal title and the beneficial interest in property held under a trust under which the settlor did not, on constitution, retain the whole of the beneficial interest: see Clause 4(7)(b). Thus, if T1 and T2 hold an unregistered estate in land on trust for A for life, thereafter to B absolutely, and A dies, so that the trustees hold the land on trust for B absolutely, a transfer of that land by T1 and T2 to B will trigger compulsory registration. However, where T1 and T2 hold on trust for the settlor absolutely, and the land is transferred either to him or to the person entitled to the interest (as for example, under the settlor's will or intestacy), this will not trigger compulsory registration.

(iii) In pursuance of an order of any court.

(iv) By means of an assent (including a vesting assent). Clause 4(9) makes it clear that "vesting assent" has the same meaning as in the Settled Land Act 1925. For the definition of "vesting assent" in that Act, see section 117(1)(xxxi).

22. A transfer for these purposes does not include a transfer by operation of law: see Clause 4(3). Thus, for example, it would not include the situation where a deceased's property vests in his or her personal representatives. Moreover, the following transfers will not be subject to the requirement of compulsory registration, even if they otherwise would be—

(i) the assignment of a mortgage term (in other words where there is a mortgage by demise or by sub-demise, and the mortgagee assigns the mortgage by transferring the mortgage term): see Clause 4(4)(a); and

(ii) the assignment or surrender of a lease to the owner of the immediate reversion where the term is to merge in that reversion (because the estate transferred disappears): see Clause 4(4)(b).

23. Secondly, the requirement of compulsory registration will apply where there is a transfer of an unregistered legal estate in land in circumstances where section 171A of the Housing Act 1985 applies. Section 171A applies where a person ceases to be a secure tenant because his or her landlord disposes of an interest in a house to a private sector landlord. This replicates the present law: see Housing Act 1985, Schedule 9A, paragraph 2(1).

24. Thirdly, the grant of a legal lease out of a qualifying estate will in some circumstances be subject to compulsory registration. The term "qualifying estate" refers to an unregistered legal estate which is either a legal freehold estate in land or a leasehold estate in land which has more than 7 years to run: see Clause 4(2). The grant out of a qualifying estate of a legal lease for a term of more than seven years from the date of grant will be subject to compulsory registration if it is made—

466

(i)   For valuable or other consideration. If the estate transferred has a negative value it is still to be regarded as transferred for valuable or other consideration: see Clause 4(6).

(ii)   By way of a gift. For these purposes, the same considerations apply as in relation to when a transfer will be regarded as a gift: see above, paragraph 21(ii).

(iii)   In pursuance of an order of any court.

25. There are two exceptions to this provision. A lease will not be subject to compulsory registration if it is the grant of a mortgage term (that is, where there is a mortgage by demise or sub-demise) or if it is a PPP lease: see Clauses 4(5) and 90(2), respectively. For PPP leases, see below, paragraphs 393 and following.

26. Fourthly, compulsory registration will apply where a lease is granted out of a qualifying estate to take effect in possession after a period of more than three months beginning with the date of the grant. Once again, a "qualifying estate" is an unregistered legal estate which is either a legal freehold estate in land or a leasehold estate in land which has more than 7 years to run: see Clause 4(2). This provision is new and is designed to avoid the conveyancing trap that such reversionary leases may create under the present law. At present, a lease granted for a term of 21 years or less, which has not yet taken effect in possession, cannot be registered with its own title nor protected by the entry of a notice on the title of the reversion: see Land Registration Act 1925, sections 19(2), 22(2) and 48(1). Such leases take effect as overriding interests under section 70(1)(k) of the Land Registration Act 1925. A buyer of the land affected may not be able to discover the existence of the lease because the tenant will not be in possession. The Bill remedies this difficulty by requiring such leases to be registered.

27. Fifthly, compulsory registration applies to the grant of a lease out of an unregistered legal estate under the right to buy provisions of Part 5 of the Housing Act 1985. This provision replicates the present law: see Housing Act 1985, section 154(1).

28. Sixthly, compulsory registration will apply to the grant of a lease out of an unregistered legal estate in land in circumstances where section 171A of the Housing Act 1985 applies. Again, this replicates the effect of the present law: Housing Act 1985, Schedule 9A, paragraph 2(1).

29. Seventhly, the creation of a protected first legal mortgage out of a qualifying estate is subject to compulsory registration. The term "qualifying estate" again refers to an unregistered legal estate which is either a legal freehold estate in land or a leasehold estate in land which has more than 7 years to run: see Clause 4(2). A mortgage is protected, if it takes effect on its creation as a mortgage to be protected by the deposit of documents relating to the mortgaged estate: Clause 4(8)(a). A first legal mortgage is one which, on its creation, ranks in priority ahead of other mortgages affecting the mortgaged estate: Clause 4(8)(b).

CLAUSE 5 — POWER TO EXTEND SECTION 4

Subsection (1)

30. Subsection (1) enables the Lord Chancellor, by order, to add new events to those that trigger compulsory registration. He may also make such consequential amendments of any legislation as he thinks appropriate. This

467

power is exercisable by statutory instrument to be laid before Parliament: see Clause 125(2), (3). A similar power may be found in the existing legislation: see Land Registration Act 1925, section 123(4), (5).

Subsection (2)

31. If an event is to be added to the list of those that trigger compulsory registration, it must relate to an unregistered legal estate which is of a kind specified in subsection (2). It may be noted that these correspond to the legal estates that are capable of registration with their own titles under Clause 3(1).

Subsection (3)

32. Subsection (3) expressly provides that the power conferred by subsection (1) may not be exercised to require the compulsory registration of an estate granted to a mortgagee. This is because no benefit would be derived from requiring a charge over land to be registered, if the title to the estate affected remained unregistered.

Subsection (4)

33. Subsection (4) provides that the Lord Chancellor may only exercise the power to add to the list of events that trigger compulsory registration following consultation of such persons as he considers appropriate.

CLAUSE 6 — DUTY TO APPLY FOR REGISTRATION OF TITLE

Subsections (1), (2) and (3)

34. Subsection (1) imposes a duty on the responsible estate owner to apply for registration of a registrable estate within the period of registration if the registration requirement applies.

35. Subsection (2) makes further provision in relation to the situation where compulsory registration is triggered by the creation of a protected legal mortgage under Clause 4(1)(g). Where compulsory registration is triggered by the creation of a protected legal mortgage, the mortgagor must apply for the registration of the estate charged by the mortgage. As now, there is a power by rules to make provision to enable the mortgagee to require the registration of the estate charged by the mortgage to be registered, whether or not the mortgagor consents: see Clause 6(6). Such rules will be land registration rules and will be required to be laid before Parliament only: see Clauses 129(1) and 125(3).

36. Subsection (3) makes further provision where compulsory registration is triggered by any event other than the creation of a protected legal mortgage under Clause 4(1)(g). In such cases, it is the transferee or grantee who must apply for registration of the estate transferred or granted.

Subsections (4) and (5)

37. Subsection (4) provides that where compulsory registration applies, the period for registration is 2 months beginning with the date on which the relevant event occurs. For the effect of non-compliance, see Clause 7.

38. Subsection (5) enables the registrar, on application by an interested person, to specify a longer period for registration if he is satisfied that there is a good

reason for doing so. It should be noted that the registrar may extend the period for registration whether or not the initial period has elapsed. This is apparent from Clause 7(3).

CLAUSE 7 — EFFECT OF NON-COMPLIANCE WITH SECTION 6

Subsections (1) and (2)

39.   Subsection (1) provides that where the requirement of registration is not met, the disposition becomes void as regards the transfer, grant or creation of a legal estate.

40.   Subsection (2) explains the effect of an event becoming void under subsection (1).

    (i)   Where the event is a transfer, the effect of the transfer becoming void is that the transferor holds the legal estate on a bare trust for the transferee.

    (ii)   Where the event is the grant of a lease or the creation of a protected mortgage, the effect of the grant or creation becoming void is that it takes effect instead as a contract made for valuable consideration to grant or create the estate or mortgage concerned.

Subsection (3)

41.   Subsection (3) makes provision for the situation where a transfer, the grant of a lease or the creation of a mortgage has become void and the registrar then makes an order extending the period in which an application for registration can be made under Clause 6(5). In such situations, the disposition is treated as never having become void.

Subsection (4)

42.   Subsection (4) makes it clear that where there is a transfer of a fee simple, the possibility of reverter to which Clause 7(1) gives rise is disregarded for the purposes of determining whether a fee simple is a fee simple absolute. This provision avoids the possibility that Clause 7(1) might have the unintended effect of converting an unregistered fee simple into a determinable fee, which is not a fee simple absolute and so not a legal estate: see Law of Property Act 1925, section 1.

CLAUSE 8 — LIABILITY FOR MAKING GOOD VOID TRANSFERS &C.

43.   Where a disposition has become void because a person has failed to meet the registration requirements, it may be necessary to repeat the disposition. Clause 8 therefore provides that where a disposition has to be repeated—

    (i)   the transferee, grantee or mortgagor is liable to the transferor, grantor or mortgagee for all proper costs of and incidental to the repeated disposition; and

    (ii)   he or she is liable to indemnify the transferor, grantor or mortgagee in respect of any other liability reasonably incurred by him or her because of the failure to comply with the requirement of registration.

Classes of title

CLAUSE 9 — TITLES TO FREEHOLD ESTATES

Subsection (1)

44.   Subsection (1) sets out the classes of freehold title with which an applicant may be registered on first registration. The classes of freehold title which are available under the Bill are the same as those that are available under the Land Registration Act 1925.

45.   For the *effect* of registration with the different classes of freehold title, see Clause 11. For the circumstances in which a title may or must be upgraded, see Clause 62.

Subsections (2) and (3)

46.   Subsection (2) provides that a person may be registered with absolute title if the registrar considers that his or her title is such as a willing buyer could properly be advised by a competent professional legal adviser to accept. Even if the title is defective in some way, subsection (3) provides that the registrar may still register it as absolute if he considers that the defect will not cause the holding under the title to be disturbed. In practice, almost all freehold titles are absolute.

Subsection (4)

47.   Subsection (4) provides that a person may be registered with qualified title, if the registrar considers that the person's title to the estate has been established only for a limited period or subject to certain reservations that are such that the title is not a good holding title. A qualified title might, for example, be appropriate where the transfer to the applicant had been in breach of trust. Qualified title is extremely rare in practice.

Subsection (5)

48.   Subsection (5) provides that a person may be registered with possessory title where he or she is in actual possession of the land, or in receipt of the rents and profits, and there is no other class of title with which he or she may be registered.

49.   In practice the circumstances in which the registrar is most likely to enter a title as possessory are where—

    (i)   the applicant has been in adverse possession of land for 12 years; or
    (ii)   the applicant is unable to prove his or her title because (for example) the documents of title have been lost or destroyed.

CLAUSE 10 — TITLES TO LEASEHOLD ESTATES

Subsection (1)

50.   Subsection (1) sets out the classes of leasehold title with which an applicant may be registered on first registration. The classes of leasehold title which are available under the Bill are the same as those that are available under the Land Registration Act 1925.

51. For the *effect* of registration with the different classes of leasehold title, see Clause 12. For the circumstances in which a title may or must be upgraded, see Clause 62.

Subsection (2)

52. Subsection (2) provides that a person may be registered with absolute title if the registrar considers that his or her title is such as a willing buyer could properly be advised by a competent professional adviser to accept and he approves the lessor's title to grant the lease. A leasehold estate will only be registered with an absolute title therefore where the superior title is either registered with absolute title or, if unregistered, has been deduced to the registrar's satisfaction. Even if the applicant's title is defective, subsection (4) provides that the registrar may register it as absolute if he considers that the defect will not cause the holding under it to be disturbed.

Subsection (3)

53. Subsection (3) provides that a person may be registered with good leasehold title if the registrar considers that his or her title is such as a willing buyer could properly be advised by a competent adviser to accept. Good leasehold title is therefore appropriate where the superior title is neither registered nor deduced. Again, the registrar may register the applicant's title as good leasehold even if it is open to objection, provided that he considers that the defect will not cause the holding under it to be challenged: see Clause 10(4).

Subsection (5)

54. Subsection (5) provides that a person may be registered with qualified title, if the registrar considers that either the applicant's title or the lessor's title to the reversion can only be established for a limited period, or subject to certain reservations that are such that the title is not a good holding title. Cf above, paragraph 47.

Subsection (6)

55. Subsection (6) provides that a person may be registered with possessory title if the registrar considers that he or she is in actual possession, or in receipt of rents and profits of the land and there is no other class of title with which he or she may be registered. Cf above, paragraphs 48 and 49.

Effect of first registration

CLAUSE 11 — FREEHOLD ESTATES

56. Clause 11 makes provision for the effect of first registration of a person as the proprietor of a freehold estate. For the circumstances in which a person will be registered with the different classes of freehold title, see Clause 9; above, paragraphs 44 and following.

Subsections (2), (3), (4) and (5)

57. Subsections (2), (3), (4) and (5) prescribe the effect of registration of a freehold with absolute title.

58. Where a person is first registered as proprietor of a freehold estate, subsection (3) provides that the legal estate is vested in him or her together

with all interests subsisting for the benefit of the estate. The legal estate will therefore vest in the first registered proprietor together with such interests as (for example) the benefit of any easement and *profit à prendre* that is appurtenant to the estate.

59. Subsection (4) provides that on first registration with absolute title, the estate is vested in the proprietor subject only to the following interests affecting the estate *at the time of registration*—

(i) Interests which are the subject of an entry in the register in relation to the estate. As this provision only applies to first registration under the Bill (as opposed to the Land Registration Act 1925), the interests which may be subject to an entry in the register will be registered charges, notices and restrictions.

(ii) Unregistered interests which fall within any of the paragraphs of Schedule 1 (that is, those that override first registration).

(iii) Interests acquired under the Limitation Act 1980 of which the proprietor has notice. This provision is new and is designed to meet the following situation. A takes adverse possession of unregistered land belonging to B. After 12 years' adverse possession, B's title is extinguished and A becomes owner of the land. A then abandons the land and B resumes possession of it. Before B has been back in possession of the land for 12 years he sells it to C. B sells as paper owner in accordance with the title deeds, but A is in fact the true owner. The sale triggers compulsory registration and C applies to be first registered proprietor. Subject to the transitional provisions contained in Schedule 12, paragraph 7, the rights of a squatter will not constitute an overriding interest under the Bill as they presently do. By virtue of Clause 11(4)(c), C will take free of A's rights unless, at the time of registration, he had notice of them. It should be noted that if C is registered as proprietor even though he has notice of A's rights, A will be able to seek alteration of the register. C is bound by her rights and so alteration of the register will not involve rectification. As the register is inaccurate it may be altered to give effect to her rights by registering her as proprietor in place of C: see Schedule 4, paragraphs 2 and 5.

60. Subsection (5) deals with the situation where the first registered proprietor is not entitled to the estate solely for his or her own benefit. The effect of subsection (5) is that where the first registered proprietor holds the land on trust, the estate will be vested in him or her subject to the rights of the beneficiaries under that trust.

Subsection (6)

61. Subsection (6) prescribes the effect of first registration with a qualified freehold title.

Subsection (7)

62. Subsection (7) governs the effect of first registration with a possessory freehold title.

CLAUSE 12 — LEASEHOLD ESTATES

63. Clause 12 makes provision for the effect of first registration of a person as the proprietor of a leasehold estate. For the circumstances in which a

person will be registered with the different classes of leasehold title, see Clause 10, above, paragraphs 50 and following.

Subsections (2), (3), (4) and (5)

64.   Subsections (2), (3), (4) and (5) prescribe the effect of registration of a lease with absolute title.

65.   In most respects, the registration of a leaseholder with absolute title has the same effect as registration of a freeholder with absolute title: see above, paragraphs 57 and following. The only difference is that where a leasehold estate is registered with absolute title, it is vested in the leaseholder subject to implied and express covenants, obligations and liabilities incident to the estate: see Clause 12(4)(a). Thus the first registered proprietor of a lease will take subject to such proprietary interests as restrictive covenants relating to the premises leased.

Subsections (6), (7) and (8)

66.   Subsections (6), (7) and (8) prescribe the effect of the registration of a lease with good leasehold title, qualified title and possessory title respectively.

Dependent estates

CLAUSE 13 — APPURTENANT RIGHTS AND CHARGES

67.   Clause 13 empowers the Lord Chancellor to make rules in relation to the registration of dependent legal estates.

68.   First, rules may make provision for the entry in the register of a registered proprietor as the proprietor of an unregistered legal estate which subsists for the benefit of his or her registered estate. For the definition of a legal estate, see section 1 of the Law of Property Act 1925. Rules made under this provision are meant to cover the situation where, on or subsequent to first registration, a registered proprietor has, or is granted, the benefit of a legal estate, such as an easement or a *profit à prendre*, over unregistered land. Rules will enable the benefit of such an estate to be entered on the register.

69.   Secondly, rules may make provision for the registration of a person as the proprietor of an unregistered legal estate which is a charge on a registered estate. Rules under this provision are intended to cover the situation where—

(i)   on first registration, the land is already subject to a legal mortgage; or

(ii)   subsequent to first registration, a charge is created that does not have to be registered to have effect at law, as in relation to certain local land charges (cf Clause 55 below).

In such circumstances, rules may enable the registration of the mortgagee as the proprietor of a registered charge.

Supplementary

CLAUSE 14 — RULES ABOUT FIRST REGISTRATION

70. Clause 14 confers a power to make rules in relation to various matters concerning first registration. Rules made under this provision will be land registration rules and will be laid before Parliament only: see Clauses 129(1) and 125(3).

CHAPTER 2: CAUTIONS AGAINST FIRST REGISTRATION

71. Chapter 2 of Part 2 of the Bill is concerned with cautions against first registration. Cautions against first registration provide a means by which a person with an interest in *unregistered* land can be informed of an application for first registration of the title to an estate in that land. Under the present law, as it has been interpreted by the registrar, any person having or claiming to have an interest in unregistered land may apply to lodge a caution with the registrar: cf Land Registration Act 1925, section 53(1). Once a caution against first registration has been entered, no registration of the estate affected will be made until notice has been served on the cautioner and he or she has had an opportunity to appear before the registrar and oppose the application for first registration. Under the Bill it will continue to be possible to lodge cautions against first registration, though the circumstances in which this may be done will be both clarified and simplified. The Bill makes certain amendments as to the interests in respect of which a caution may be lodged. It also creates a register of cautions to replace the present system of caution titles that are used to record details about cautions. Cautions against first registration should be distinguished from cautions against dealings, which are a means of protecting interests in registered land under the Land Registration Act 1925. Cautions against dealings are prospectively abolished under the Bill: see below, paragraph 161.

CLAUSE 15 — RIGHT TO LODGE

Subsections (1) and (2)

72. Subsection (1) sets out who may lodge a caution against first registration. The effect of lodging a caution against first registration is explained in Clause 16.

73. Subject to the significant qualification set out in subsection (3), the following persons have a right to lodge a caution against first registration—

    (i)   A person who claims to be the owner of a qualifying estate.
    (ii)   A person entitled to an interest affecting a qualifying estate. For these purposes, an interest is defined as an adverse right affecting the title to the estate or charge: see Clause 129(3)(b).

74. "Qualifying estate" is defined in subsection (2) as a legal estate which relates to land to which the caution relates and which is an interest of any of the following kinds—

474

(i)   An estate in land, which means a fee simple absolute in possession or a term of years absolute: see Law of Property Act 1925, section 1(1).

(ii)   A rentcharge.

(iii)   A franchise.

(iv)   A *profit à prendre* in gross.

75.   It should be noted that the Bill makes special provision in relation to cautions against the first registration of the Crown's demesne land: see Clause 81 and Schedule 12, paragraph 15.

Subsection (3)

76.   Subsection (3) sets out certain exceptions to the right to lodge a caution against first registration.   The effect of subsection (3) is that a caution against first registration may not be lodged by either—

(i)   the owner of a freehold estate in land, in respect of that estate;

(ii)   the owner of a leasehold estate in land where it was granted for a term of which more than seven years remain unexpired, in respect of that estate.

As regards (ii), the owner of such a leasehold estate cannot lodge a caution against its first registration, either as the owner of a qualifying estate under Clause 15(1)(a), or by virtue of his or her interest affecting a qualifying estate under Clause 15(1)(b).

77.   These restrictions are new.   However, the Bill provides that they will not take effect for the period of two years beginning with the day on which Clause 15 is brought into force: see Schedule 12, paragraph 14(1).

78.   The reason behind subsection (3) is that cautions against first registration should not be an alternative to first registration.   Where a legal estate is registrable, the owner of it should apply for first registration rather than for a caution against first registration.   This is part of the ultimate aim to achieve total registration.

Subsection (4)

79.   Subsection (4) provides that the right to lodge a caution against first registration is exercisable by application to the registrar.   For the general power to make rules concerning the form, content and making of applications under the Bill, see Schedule 10, paragraph 6.

80.   There is a general right for anyone to object to an application under the Bill: see Clause 73.   Where such an objection cannot be disposed of by agreement and is not groundless, the registrar must refer the matter to the Adjudicator: Clause 73(6) and (7).   The general right to object is additional to the right contained in Clause 18, which makes specific provision for certain categories of person to apply for cancellation of a caution against first registration.

CLAUSE 16 — EFFECT

81.   Clause 16 sets out the effect of lodging a caution against first registration.

Subsections (1) and (2)

82.   Subsection (1) provides that where a person has lodged a caution against first registration in relation to a legal estate, the registrar must give the cautioner notice of any application for first registration and of his or her right to object. For these purposes, "cautioner" includes not only the person who lodged the caution, but also his or her personal representative: see Clause 22.

83.   Subsection (2) provides that where there has been an application for first registration of an estate, the registrar may not determine that application until the end of such period as rules may provide, unless the cautioner has either—

(i)   exercised his or her right to object to the application; or
(ii)   given the registrar notice that he or she does not intend to object.

84.   Rules under subsection (2) will be land registration rules and will be required to be laid before Parliament only: see Clauses 125 and 129(1).

Subsection (3)

85.   Subsection (3) makes it clear that (as now) the lodging of a caution against first registration has no effect on the validity or priority of any interest that the cautioner may have in the legal estate to which the caution relates. A caution against first registration has the limited effect of giving the cautioner a right to be notified of an application for registration so that he or she can object to it. Such notification will give the cautioner the opportunity to take appropriate steps to protect his or her interest.

Subsection (4)

86.   Subsection (4) makes provision by which an agent acting for the applicant for first registration may give notice to the cautioner and for this notice to be regarded as having been given by the registrar. To take advantage of this provision, notice must be given by a person who is of such a description as rules may provide and the notice must be given in such circumstances as rules may provide. Such rules will be land registration rules and will be required to be laid before Parliament only: see Clauses 125 and 129(1).

87.   Rules made under subsection (4) are likely to enable persons such as solicitors or licensed conveyancers who are acting for the applicant for first registration to give notice to the cautioner at the time at which the application is made. This should expedite the conveyancing process because it will no longer be necessary to wait for the registrar to give notice to the cautioner.

CLAUSE 17 — WITHDRAWAL

88.   This clause enables a cautioner to withdraw a caution against first registration by application to the registrar. By virtue of Clause 22 not only the person who lodged the caution, but also his or her personal representative will be able to apply for it to be withdrawn.

CLAUSE 18 — CANCELLATION

Subsection (1)

89. Subsection (1) gives the owner of a legal estate to which a caution relates and persons of such other description as rules may provide, the right to apply for the cancellation of a caution against first registration. Rules under subsection (1) are likely to enable certain additional categories of persons with an interest in the estate affected, such as mortgagors or receivers, to apply for the cancellation of a caution.

Subsection (2)

90. Subsection (2) provides that, subject to rules, no application may be made to cancel a caution against first registration by the owner of a legal estate who—

    (i)   consented in such manner as rules may provide to the lodging of the caution; or
    (ii)   derived title by operation of law from a person who consented to the lodging of a caution (such as his or her trustee in bankruptcy or personal representative).

91. Even where the caution has been lodged with consent, there may be circumstances where it would be appropriate for the owner to seek its cancellation. The sort of case for which rules might make provision would be where the interest protected by the caution has been terminated. For example, the owner of unregistered land might grant an option to purchase her land, valid for 5 years. If she agreed that the grantee might lodge a caution against first registration in respect of that option, she would still be able to seek the cancellation of that caution after 5 years if the option had not been exercised in that time.

Subsections (3) and (4)

92. Subsection (3) provides that where an application is made to cancel a caution against first registration, the cautioner must be given notice of the application and of the effect of subsection (4).

93. Subsection (4) provides that if the cautioner does not exercise his or her right to object to the application before the end of such period as rules may provide, the registrar must cancel the caution. The right to object to an application for cancellation arises by virtue of Clause 73. Clause 73(2) provides that only the person who lodged the caution to which the application relates, or his or her personal representative, may object to an application for its cancellation.

94. If the cautioner does object to the application, the matter must be referred to the Adjudicator for determination, unless it can be disposed of by agreement or the registrar is satisfied that the objection is groundless: see Clause 73(6) and (7).

CLAUSE 19 — CAUTIONS REGISTER

Subsection (1)

95. Subsection (1) imposes a duty on the registrar to keep a register of cautions against first registration. The formal establishment of a cautions register is

new. However, cautions against first registration will continue to be recorded on the index as they are now: see Clause 68. At present, details of cautions against first registration are kept in paper form on a "caution title". This records certain essential information relating to the caution, such as the name and the address for service of the cautioner, details of the solicitor or licensed conveyancer who lodged the caution, and the estate against which the caution has been registered. It is anticipated that the cautions register will contain similar information. It is intended that it will be kept in dematerialised form, though this may not be the case initially.

Subsection (2)

96. Subsection (2) confers a power to make rules about how the cautions register is to be kept. Such rules will be land registration rules and will be required to be laid before Parliament only: see Clauses 129(1) and 125(3).

CLAUSE 20 — ALTERATION OF REGISTER BY COURT

97. Clauses 20 and 21 contain provisions relating to alteration of the register of cautions against first registration by the court and registrar respectively. These provisions are new and are a necessary concomitant to the formal establishment of a register of cautions against first registration under Clause 9. Cf Schedule 4, which sets out the circumstances in which the court and the registrar can alter the register of title.

98. Subsection (1) enables a court to make an order for alteration of the register of cautions in two situations.

99. First, alteration may be ordered for the purpose of correcting a mistake. An example would be where a caution against first registration is lodged to protect a right of way claimed by prescription over the cautioned land and it can be established that the right of way does not exist.

100. Secondly, alteration may be ordered for the purpose of bringing the register up to date. An example would be where a mortgagee had entered a caution against first registration and the mortgage has since been redeemed.

101. Subsection (3)(a) empowers the Lord Chancellor to make rules specifying the circumstances in which the court will have a duty to exercise the power to make an order for alteration of the register of cautions.

102. Where the court makes an order for alteration, the registrar has a duty to give effect to it when it is served on him: subsection (2). Rules may prescribe the form that such an order should take and how it should be served: subsection (3)(b), (c).

CLAUSE 21 — ALTERATION OF REGISTER BY REGISTRAR

103. The circumstances in which the registrar may alter the register of cautions against first registration are set out in Clause 21(1). These are the same as the grounds upon which the court may order alteration.

104. Where the register of cautions against first registration is altered by the registrar, subsection (3) gives him the power to pay costs. The only restriction on the exercise of this power is that the costs must have been reasonably incurred by a person in connection with the alteration.

105. This clause explains the meaning of "cautioner" in this Chapter. See above, paragraph 82.

PART 3: DISPOSITIONS OF REGISTERED LAND

106. Part 3 of the Bill is concerned with three matters. First, it defines the powers that a proprietor of a registered estate or charge is to be taken to have in the absence of any entry to the contrary in the register and for what purposes. Secondly, it makes provision by which certain dispositions that convey or create a legal estate have to be registered. Thirdly, it sets out the effect that dispositions of registered land have on the priority of interests in such land.

Powers of disposition

CLAUSE 23 — OWNER'S POWERS

107. Clause 23 sets out "owner's powers" of disposition in relation to a registered estate or charge. By Clause 24 these powers are exercisable by the registered proprietor of an estate or charge or, subject to rules, any person who is entitled to be registered as the proprietor.

Subsection (1)

108. In relation to a registered estate, the owner's powers consist of power to—

(i)   make a disposition of any kind permitted by the general law in relation to the interest which the person has, other than a mortgage by demise or sub–demise: Clause 23(1)(a); and

(ii)   charge the estate with the payment of money: Clause 23(1)(b).

There are two points to be noted about these provisions.

109. First, mortgages by demise or sub-demise are in practice obsolete. The effect of Clause 23(1)(a) is that it will no longer be possible to create a legal mortgage over registered land by these means. In future a registered proprietor will only be able to create a legal mortgage by—

(i)   a charge expressed to be by way of legal mortgage; or

(ii)   a charge to secure the payment of money.

110. For the necessary consequential amendments to sections 85 and 86 of the Law of Property Act 1925, see Schedule 11, paragraph 2(6) and (7).

111. Secondly, the power to charge the estate with the payment of money is one that is unique to registered land (cf Land Registration Act 1925, section 25(1)), and it dates back to the Land Transfer Act 1875. There is no equivalent in relation to unregistered land.

Subsection (2)

112. In relation to a registered charge, the owner's powers consist of power to—

(i)   make a disposition of any kind permitted by the general law in relation to the interest which the person has, other than a legal sub-mortgage: Clause 23(2)(a); and

(ii)   charge at law with the payment of money indebtedness secured by the registered charge: Clause 23(2)(b).

113. The exception in relation to legal sub-mortgages, which are defined for these purposes by Clause 23(3), simplifies the present law. In future there will only be one way in which a registered chargee can create a legal sub-charge, namely that specified in Clause 23(2)(b). This method of creating a legal sub-charge is modelled on existing provisions found in the Land Registration Rules 1925: see rule 163(1).

CLAUSE 24 — RIGHT TO EXERCISE OWNER'S POWERS

114. Clause 24 sets out who may exercise owner's powers of disposition under Clause 23, namely either the registered proprietor or a person who is entitled to be registered as proprietor (such as the executor of a deceased registered proprietor, or a disponee who has not yet been registered as proprietor). Cf Land Registration Act 1925, section 37 (powers of persons entitled to be registered).

115. Subsection (2) provides that a person's right to exercise owner's powers by reason of an entitlement to be registered as the proprietor of an estate or charge is subject to rules. Such rules are likely to explain how owner's powers are to be exercised in such a case. Rules under subsection (2) will be land registration rules and will be laid before Parliament only: Clauses 129(1) and 125.

CLAUSE 25 — MODE OF EXERCISE

Subsection (1)

116. Subsection (1) provides that a registrable disposition of a registered estate or charge only has effect if it complies with such requirements as to form and content as rules may provide. For registrable dispositions, see Clause 27. This provision will enable rules to prescribe the form and content that any registrable disposition must take. At present it is not possible to prescribe the form of a registered charge: see Land Registration Act 1925, section 25(2). Nor has any form ever been prescribed for a lease, though it could be: see Land Registration Act 1925, sections 18(1) and 21(1).

117. Rules under this provision will be land registration rules and will be laid before Parliament only: Clauses 129(1) and 125(3).

Subsection (2)

118. Subsection (2) provides that rules may apply Clause 25(1) to any other kind of disposition which depends for its effect on registration. This provision is likely to be particularly important when electronic conveyancing is introduced: see Cl 93.

CLAUSE 26 — PROTECTION OF DISPONEES

Subsections (1) and (2)

119. Subsection (1) sets out the general principle that a person's right to exercise owner's powers in relation to a registered estate or charge is taken to be free

from any limitation affecting the validity of the disposition. This general principle is subject to subsection (2), which provides that it does not apply to a limitation reflected by an entry in the register, or imposed by or under the Bill. It may be noted that in future, the only way to limit owner's powers will be to enter a restriction on the register, because both cautions and inhibitions are prospectively abolished by the Bill. See below, paragraph 161.

Subsection (3)

120. Subsection (3) makes it clear that the principle that a person's right to exercise owner's powers is unlimited unless there is some entry in the register or limitation imposed by, or under, the Bill, has effect for one specific purpose only. That is to prevent the title of a disponee being questioned. However, this will not affect the lawfulness of the disposition.

121. The fact that a disponee's title cannot be called into question, may be illustrated by the following example.

(i)	W and X held on a bare trust as nominee for Y, on terms that they could not make any disposition of the land without Y's written consent;
(ii)	Y, who was in actual occupation of the land held in trust, did not protect her interest by the entry of a restriction;
(iii)	W and X fraudulently charge the land to Z without Y's consent in breach of trust.

Z's charge would be valid and could not be questioned by Y. The fact that Y was in actual occupation at the time of the charge would not change this, because W and X's right to exercise owner's powers is taken to be free of limitation. It follows that Y cannot claim that her beneficial interest under the trust was an overriding interest under Schedule 3, paragraph 2, because her prior consent to the charge was not obtained.

122. Even if a disponee's title cannot be questioned, this does not prevent an action being pursued on the basis that the disposition was unlawful provided that this does not call into question the validity of the disponee's title. This may be illustrated by the following example. Trustees of land, A and B, have limited powers of disposition but no restriction is entered on the register to record this fact. If they transfer land to a buyer, C, in circumstances that are prohibited under the trust, they would commit a breach of trust. Although C's title cannot be called into question, the protection given by Clause 26 does not extend to any independent forms of liability to which she might be subject. Thus if C knew of the trustees' breach of trust when the transfer was made, she might be personally accountable in equity for the knowing receipt of trust property transferred in breach of trust.

Registrable dispositions

CLAUSE 27 — DISPOSITIONS REQUIRED TO BE REGISTERED

Subsection (1)

123. Subsection (1) states the general principle that where a disposition of a registered estate or charge is required to be completed by registration, it

does not operate at law until the relevant registration requirements are met. For the effect of registered dispositions on priority, see Clauses 28—31.

124. With the introduction of electronic conveyancing, the general principle set out in subsection (1) is likely, in time, to be superseded. This is because it is disapplied in relation to dispositions which are required to be communicated electronically to the registrar and which are required to be simultaneously registered under Clause 93: see Clause 93(4). The reason why the general principle is disapplied in this context is that a disposition under Clause 93 has *no* effect, whether at law or in equity, until the relevant registration requirements are met: see Clause 93(2).

Subsection (2)

125. Subsection (2) lists the dispositions of a registered estate which are required to be completed by registration. The registration requirements which apply in relation to each of them are set out in Schedule 2.

126. First, a transfer of a registered estate must be completed by registration. "Registered estate" means a legal estate the title to which is entered in the register, other than a registered charge: see Clause 129(1). For the definition of legal estate, see section 1 of the Law of Property Act 1925. Therefore, where one of the following estates is a registered estate, any transfer of it must be completed by registration—

(i)   a fee simple absolute in possession;
(ii)   a leasehold estate;
(iii) a rentcharge;
(iv)   a franchise;
(v)   a *profit à prendre* in gross; and
(vi)   a manor.

127. The registration requirements in relation to a transfer are as follows. The transferee (or his or her successor in title) must be entered in the register as proprietor: Schedule 2, paragraph 2(1). Where there is a transfer of part of a registered estate, such details as may be provided for by rules, must be entered in the register in relation to the registered estate out of which the transfer is made: Schedule 2, paragraph 2(2). Where the registered proprietor disposes of a part of his or her estate, the Registry currently makes certain entries on the register for example, in relation to rights reserved or granted. It is likely that rules will make provision for this practice to continue.

128. There are three exceptions to the principle that the transfer of a registered estate is a registrable disposition. They all concern dispositions by operation of law.

(i)   The first is a transfer on the death of a sole individual proprietor: see Clause 27(5)(a). A deceased's estate vests by operation of law in his or her executors (if any) or in the Public Trustee until such time as there is a grant of administration. Once the legal title is vested in the personal representatives, they may apply to the registrar to alter the register to bring it up to date, by registering the applicant as proprietor: see Schedule 4, paragraphs 5 and 7.

(ii)   The second is a transfer on bankruptcy of a sole individual proprietor: see Clause 27(5)(a). Where a registered proprietor becomes insolvent, his or her estate will vest by operation of law in his or her trustee in bankruptcy, immediately on his or her appointment (or in the Official Receiver in default of any such appointment): see Insolvency Act 1986, section 306. As in (i), the trustee in bankruptcy may then apply to the registrar to alter the register to bring it up to date, by registering the applicant as proprietor: see Schedule 4, paragraphs 5 and 7.

(iii)   The third is a transfer on the dissolution of a corporate proprietor: see Clause 27(5)(b). When a company is dissolved, its property is deemed to be bona vacantia and therefore vests in the Crown (or one of the Royal Duchies): see Companies Act 1985, section 654. Again, the Crown (or Duchy) will apply to the registrar to alter the register to bring it up to date, by registering the applicant as proprietor: see Schedule 4, paragraphs 5 and 7.

129.   Secondly, the grant of most leases out of a registered estate in land must be completed by registration. The categories of leases which, if granted out of a *registered* estate, must be completed by registration, are the same as those which, if granted out of *unregistered* land may or must be registered and they have been discussed in that context: see above paragraphs 24—28. In respect of two categories of lease granted out of a registered estate, registration is not required—

(i)   a lease granted for seven years or less that does not fall within one of the classes specified in Clause 27(2)(b)(ii)—(v); and

(ii)   a PPP lease granted under the Greater London Authority Act 1999: see Clause 90(3)(a).

Also, in these two cases, the priority of the lease is protected in relation to subsequent registered dispositions without registration: see Clauses 29(2)(a)(ii) and 30(2)(a)(ii); Schedule 3, paragraph 1 and Clause 90(5).

130.   The registration requirements in relation to the grant of a lease which is a registrable disposition are as follows. The grantee of the lease (or his or her successor in title) must be entered in the register as the proprietor of the lease, and a notice in respect of the lease must be entered in the register of the title out of which it is granted: Schedule 2, paragraph 3.

131.   Thirdly, the grant of any lease out of a registered franchise or manor is required to be completed by registration. The grant of such a lease will be registrable regardless of its length. The registration requirements for the lease of a franchise or manor are as follows. If the lease is for a term of more than seven years, the grantee of the lease (or his or her successor in title) must be entered in the register as the proprietor of the lease, and a notice in respect of the lease must be entered: Schedule 2, paragraph 4. If the lease is for seven years or less, a notice in respect of the lease must be entered in the register: Schedule 2, paragraph 5.

132.   Fourthly, the express grant or reservation of an interest of a kind falling within section 1(2)(a) of the Law of Property Act 1925, other than one which is capable of being registered under the Commons Registration Act 1965, is a registrable disposition. In practice the interests that are most likely to be registrable under this provision are easements and *profit à prendre*, whether those are in gross or are appurtenant to an estate. There are two qualifications to this.

(i)   The first is that rights of common which are capable of being registered under the Commons Registration Act 1965 are excluded. This is because section 1(1) of the Commons Registration Act 1965 prohibits the registration under the Land Registration Act

483

1925 of rights of common that are registrable under the 1965 Act. The Bill therefore replicates this prohibition.

(ii) The second is that where an easement, right or privilege is granted as a result of the operation of section 62 of the Law of Property Act 1925, that grant is not regarded as an express grant for these purposes so as to require registration: see Clause 27(7). Section 62 has the effect of implying certain words of grant into a conveyance of land unless its effect is expressly excluded. The current qualification is necessary because for some purposes rights implied by section 62 of the Law of Property Act 1925 are treated as a form of express grant: see, for example, *Quicke v Chapman* [1903] 1 Ch 659.

133. The registration requirements in relation to the fourth category of registrable disposition, depend upon the nature of the grant or reservation.

(i) Where the disposition involves the creation of a legal *profit à prendre* in gross, other than one created by a lease of 7 years or less, the grantee (or his or her successor in title) must be entered in the register as the proprietor of the interest created, and a notice in respect of the interest must be entered: see Schedule 2, paragraph 6.

(ii) Where the disposition involves the creation of any other interest, a notice in respect of the interest must be entered in the register: see Schedule 2, paragraph 7(2)(a). Moreover, where the interest is created for the benefit of a registered estate, the registered proprietor must be entered in the register as the proprietor of the interest: Schedule 2, paragraph 7(2)(b).

134. Fifthly, the express grant or reservation of an interest of a kind falling within section 1(2)(b) or (e) of the Law of Property Act 1925 is required to be completed by registration. This will therefore cover the grant or reservation of the following types of interest—

(i) a rentcharge in possession issuing out of or charge on land being either perpetual or for a term of years absolute; and

(ii) a right of entry exercisable over or in respect of a legal term of years absolute, or annexed, for any purpose to a legal rentcharge.

135. The registration requirements in relation to this category of registrable disposition are as follows—

(i) Where the disposition involves the creation of a legal rentcharge with its own title, and that grant is for an interest equivalent to an estate in fee simple or for a term of more than seven years, the grantee (or his or her successor in title) must be entered in the register as the proprietor of the interest created, and a notice in respect of the interest must be entered: see Schedule 2, paragraph 6.

(ii) In every other case — that is, where a rentcharge is granted or reserved for a term not exceeding seven years, or in the case where a right of re-entry is reserved — a notice in respect of the interest must be entered on the register of the title subject to it: see Schedule 2, paragraph 7(2)(a). Where the interest is for the benefit of a registered estate, the proprietor must also be entered in the register as the proprietor of the interest created: see Schedule 2, paragraph 7(2)(b).

There is, however, a power to modify (ii) in relation to a right of entry over or in respect of a lease: Schedule 2, paragraph 7(3). HM Land Registry does not currently record the benefit of a right of entry on the title of a reversion to a lease. This means that the present practice can continue, but that it would be open to change it at some future date.

136. Finally, the grant of a legal charge is normally a registrable disposition. However, the creation of a legal charge that is also a local land charge is an exception to this principle and does not require registration: see Clause 27(5)(c). For policy reasons, a local land charge is an interest that is binding on a disponee of registered land without registration: see Schedule 3, paragraph 6. It should, however, be noted that a local land charge that secures the payment of money cannot be realised until it is registered as a registered charge: Clause 55.

137. Where the grant of a charge must be completed by registration, the chargee (or his or her successor in title) must be entered in the register as the proprietor of the charge: Schedule 2, paragraph 8.

Subsection (3)

138. Subsection (3) sets out the types of disposition of a registered charge that must be completed by registration.

139. First, a transfer of a charge must be completed by registration. There are certain exceptions in relation to transfers by operation of law: see Clause 27(5). These have already been considered above in relation to the transfer of registered estates: see above, paragraph 128. The registration requirement for the transfer of a charge is that the transferee (or his or her successor in title) must be entered in the register as proprietor: Schedule 2, paragraph 10.

140. Secondly, the creation of a sub-charge must be completed by registration. In this case, the sub-chargee (or his or her successor in title) must be registered as the proprietor of the sub-charge: Schedule 2, paragraph 11.

Subsection (4)

141. Subsection (4) provides that Schedule 2 has effect. Schedule 2 specifies the registration requirements in relation to registrable dispositions.

Subsection (5)

142. This has already been explained: see above, paragraphs 128 and 136.

Subsection (6)

143. Subsection (6) confers power for rules to make provision about applications to the registrar for the purpose of meeting registration requirements under Clause 27. Such rules will be land registration rules, and will be laid before Parliament only: Clauses 129(1) and 125(3).

Subsection (7)

144. This has already been explained: see above, paragraph 132.

145. The Bill states the effect of dispositions of a registered estate or charge on priority. Under the Land Registration Act 1925, the equivalent rules are partly statutory and have in part been supplied by decisions of the courts. Some aspects of the present law are uncertain. Although the provisions of the Bill are similar to the present law, they are not identical. The rules in the Bill are simpler and are intended to avoid some of the difficulties that have arisen under the present law.

CLAUSE 28 — BASIC RULE

Subsection (1)

146. Subsection (1) sets out the general principle that the priority of an interest affecting a registered estate or charge is not affected by a disposition of the estate or charge. The general principle will not apply in two situations—

(i)   where there is a registered disposition for valuable consideration: see Clauses 29 and 30; and

(ii)   in relation to Inland Revenue charges: see Clause 31.

References in the Bill to an interest affecting an estate or charge are to an adverse right affecting the title to the estate or charge: Clause 129(3)(b). For these purposes, an interest does not include a petition in bankruptcy or bankruptcy order: see Clause 86(1).

147. It follows from subsection (1) that where the general principle applies, the priority of *any* interest in registered land will be determined according to the date of its creation. The statutory code laid down by the Bill is absolute: except where the Bill provides otherwise, priority will always fall to be determined in accordance with the general priority principle contained in Clause 28. In particular, it should be noted that the Bill leaves no scope for introduction of the doctrine of notice. Knowledge or notice is *only* relevant to an issue where the Bill expressly so provides. For those situations, see Clauses 11(4)(c), 12(4)(d), 31 and 86(5); Schedule 3, paragraphs 2(1)(c) and 3(1).

Subsection (2)

148. The general principle in Clause 28(1) applies, whether or not the interest or disposition is registered. This is in fact the case under the present law.

CLAUSE 29 — EFFECT OF REGISTERED DISPOSITIONS: ESTATES

Subsection (1)

149. Subsection (1) makes express provision for the effect of a registrable disposition of a registered estate. It forms a significant exception to the general principle of priority under Clause 28.

150. Subsection (1) applies to the registrable disposition of a registered estate for valuable consideration. It provides that completion of the disposition by registration has the effect of postponing to the interest under the disposition any interest affecting the estate immediately before the disposition whose priority is not protected at the time of registration. There are a number of elements of this principle that require explanation.

151. First, it applies only to a *registrable disposition* of a registered estate. A registrable disposition of a registered estate is one which is required to be completed by registration under Clause 27: see Clause 129(1).

152. Secondly it applies only to registrable dispositions made for *valuable consideration*. Where a registrable disposition is made otherwise than for valuable consideration, the general rule of priority under Clause 28 will apply. "Valuable consideration" does not include marriage consideration or a nominal consideration in money: see Clause 129. In relation to marriage consideration, the Bill changes the present law: cf Land Registration Act 1925, section 3(xxxi). Because a transfer of land in consideration of marriage is usually a wedding gift there is no longer any justification for it to be treated differently from other gifts of land.

153. Thirdly, where Clause 29(1) applies it gives the disposition priority over any interest—

  (i)   that affects the estate *immediately prior to the disposition*; and
  (ii)   whose priority is not protected *at the time of registration*.

One effect of this is that, if a disponee creates an interest in favour of a third party before the disposition is registered, he or she will not be able to claim priority over it. The general principle as to priority contained in Clause 28 will apply. In other words, the disponee will not be able to create an interest and then take free of it because it was not protected before he or she happened to be registered as proprietor of the estate. There is one particular interest which requires specific comment in this context because of its unusual character, namely an unpaid vendor's lien. An unpaid vendor's lien arises as soon as a binding contract for the sale of land is made, and not when the transfer is executed. In consequence, the priority of an unpaid vendor's lien in relation to the registered estate will be determined by Clause 28(1). This means that, on registration, the buyer of a registered estate will take free of an unpaid vendor's lien, unless the seller has protected the lien by the entry of a notice against his or her own title before the transfer is made.

Subsection (2)

154. Subsection (2) explains when the priority of an interest will be protected. Such interests are not postponed to the disposition of a registered estate under subsection (1). The interests in question are as follows—

  (i)   Registered charges.
  (ii)   Interests which are the subject of a notice on the register.
  (iii)   Unregistered interests that override registered dispositions by virtue of Schedule 3. Clause 29(3) provides that if an interest has been the subject of a notice in the register at any time since the coming into force of the Bill, it will not be protected under this category. The effect of this provision is that if a notice were entered on the register in respect of an interest that fell within Schedule 3, it could never again be an overriding interest, even if the notice were, by mistake, removed from the register. Where, as a result of such a mistake, a person suffers loss (whether because the register is rectified by restoring the notice or because it is not rectified), they will be entitled to indemnity: see Schedule 8, paragraph 1(1)(b).
  (iv)   Interests that appear from the register to be excepted from the effect of registration. This will be the case where there is a

disposition of an estate which is registered with a title other than an absolute one. For registration with different classes of title, see Clauses 11 and 12.

Subsection (4)

155. The effect of subsection (4) is that the priority principle set out in subsection (1) will apply equally to the grant of a leasehold estate which is not a registrable disposition. This replicates the present law: see Land Registration Act 1925, sections 19(2) and 22(2). For those leases which *are* registrable dispositions, see Clause 27(2)(b) and (c). The priority of other dispositions which are not registrable, will fall to be determined in accordance with the general principle set out in Clause 28.

CLAUSE 30 — EFFECT OF REGISTERED DISPOSITIONS: CHARGES

156. Clause 30 makes express provision for the effect of a registrable disposition of a registered charge. It mirrors subsections (1), (2) and (3) of Clause 29, which govern the registrable disposition of registered estates. The same considerations apply: see above, paragraphs 149—154.

157. For the priority of registered charges *inter se*, see Clause 48.

CLAUSE 31 — INLAND REVENUE CHARGES

158. Clause 31 preserves the existing law as to priorities in relation to Inland Revenue charges under the Inheritance Tax Act 1984.

159. In certain situations an Inland Revenue charge is imposed on specified property in respect of unpaid inheritance tax: see Inheritance Tax Act 1984, section 237. Sections 37(6) and 38 of the Inheritance Tax Act 1984 make express provision for the priority of such charges on the disposal of the property. Those principles of priority are presently applied to registered land by section 73 of the Land Registration Act 1925. Clause 31 similarly provides that, on the disposition of a registered estate or charge, the priority of an Inland Revenue charge in respect of unpaid inheritance tax is to be determined by the provisions of the Inheritance Tax Act 1984, rather than in accordance with Clauses 29 and 30 of the Bill.

PART 4: NOTICES AND RESTRICTIONS

160. Part 4 of the Bill contains provisions on notices and restrictions. It is concerned primarily with the protection of third party rights over or in relation to a registered estate or charge.

161. The Bill introduces a new system of notices and restrictions in relation to third party rights. The main features of the scheme are as follows—

(i) Cautions against dealings are prospectively abolished. Existing cautions will, however, remain in the register by virtue of the transitional provisions contained in Schedule 12, paragraphs 1 and 2(3).

(ii) Notices are retained in an extended form: see Clauses 32—39. Under the Bill there are two types of notice, those that are entered consensually, and those that are entered unilaterally. In relation to the latter, the registered proprietor will be informed of the registration and will be able to apply for its cancellation.

(iii)   Inhibitions are abolished because they are not needed: they are, in reality, just one form of restriction. Under the Bill the only method of restricting the power of the registered proprietor will, therefore, be by the entry of a restriction.

(iv)   Restrictions are retained, but in an altered form: see Clauses 40—47.

Notices

CLAUSE 32 — NATURE AND EFFECT

Subsections (1) and (2)

162.   This clause explains the nature and effect of a notice. The form and content of notices in the register is to be governed by rules: see Clause 39.

Subsection (3)

163.   Subsection (3) provides that the entry of a notice does not necessarily mean that the interest which it is intended to protect is valid. For the equivalent provision in relation to notices under the Land Registration Act 1925, see section 52(1). Where, for example, parties enter into an agreement that is not in fact a valid contract, the entry of a notice in respect of that agreement will not validate it. However, where an interest is valid, the entry of a notice will protect its priority as against a registered disposition of an estate or charge: see Clauses 29(2)(a)(i) and 30(2)(a)(i) respectively.

CLAUSE 33 — EXCLUDED INTERESTS

164.   This clause sets out a number of interests which cannot be protected by the entry of a notice.

165.   First, it is not possible to enter a notice in respect of any interest under a trust of land or a settlement under the Settled Land Act 1925: Clause 33(a). This replicates part of the effect of section 49(2) of the Land Registration Act 1925. Beneficial interests under trusts and settlements should be overreached on a sale or other disposition for valuable consideration. They are not intended to be binding on any buyer of the land. The appropriate form of entry for such interests is therefore a restriction.

166.   Secondly, a notice cannot be entered in respect of leases which are granted for 3 years or less and are not required to be registered: Clause 33(b). At present a notice cannot be entered in respect of a lease granted for 21 years or less, unless it falls within certain statutory exceptions: Land Registration Act 1925, section 48(1). This is because under the 1925 Act such leases take effect as overriding interests: section 70(1)(k). The Bill reduces the length of leases that are required to be registered to those granted for more than 7 years: see Clause 27(2)(b)(i). While it would have been possible to provide that a notice could have been entered in respect of a lease granted for 7 years or less, it has been decided to make the period 3 years or less. First, it is likely that once electronic conveyancing is fully operative, leases granted for more than 3 years will be required to be registered and that only leases of 3 years or less will be overriding. This change will be made by an order under the power conferred by Clause 116. Clause 33(b) anticipates

this likely reduction in the length of registrable leases. Secondly, when leases are granted, it is commonly necessary to grant or reserve easements in respect of them. Under the Bill, all easements that are expressly granted or reserved are registrable dispositions, regardless of the length of the period for which they are granted: see above, paragraph 132. The burden of such easements must be noted in the register. If an easement relating to a lease has to be protected by a notice, the parties to that lease may think it sensible to enter a notice in respect of the lease as well. But there is little point in noting leases granted for three years or less, given that they are readily discoverable.

167. Even if a lease is granted for a term of 3 years or less, a notice may still be entered in the register if the lease is one that is required to be registered. For the registration requirements in relation to leases, see Clauses 4(1)(c)—(f) (compulsory registration) and 27(2)(b) (registrable dispositions).

168. Thirdly, a notice cannot be entered in respect of restrictive covenants made between a lessor and lessee, so far as relating to the property leased: Clause 33(c). Such covenants are normally apparent from the lease, so it is unnecessary for them to be noted in the register. Consequently, the Bill provides that a person to whom a disposition of a registered leasehold estate or of a registered charge in relation to such an estate is made, takes it subject to the burden of any interest that is incident to the estate: see Clauses 29(2)(b) and 30(2)(b) respectively. A restrictive covenant is clearly an interest that is incident to the leasehold estate. There is therefore no reason to enter a notice in respect of one in the register.

169. It should be noted that the third exception is confined to restrictive covenants "so far as relating to the demised premises". This avoids a difficulty that exists under the present law. At present it is not possible to protect any restrictive covenant "made between a lessor and lessee" by the entry of a notice: see Land Registration Act 1925, section 50(1). This means that no notice can be entered in respect of a restrictive covenant made between lessor and lessee that relates to land that is *not* comprised in the lease, such as other adjacent property owned by the landlord: see *Oceanic Village Ltd v United Attractions Ltd* [2000] Ch 234. The Bill reverses this position.

170. Fourthly, it is not possible to enter a notice in respect of an interest which is capable of being registered under the Commons Registration Act 1965: Clause 33(d). This provision is the necessary concomitant of the principle that such rights of common cannot be registered under the Bill: see Clause 27(2)(d).

171. Fifthly, no notice may be entered in respect of an interest in any coal or mine, the rights attached to such interest or the rights of any person under section 38, 49, or 51 of the Coal Industry Act 1994: Clause 33(e). This exception replicates the effect of section 70(4) of the Land Registration Act 1925. Under the Bill these interests override first registration and registered dispositions even though they are not entered in the register: see Schedules 1, paragraph 7; and 3, paragraph 7.

172. The Bill also provides that no notice may be entered in the register in respect of an interest under a PPP lease. For this exception, see Clause 90(4).

CLAUSE 34 — ENTRY ON APPLICATION

Subsection (1)

173. This subsection provides that a person who claims to be entitled to the benefit of an interest in relation to a registered estate or charge that can be registered as a notice may apply to the registrar for its entry.

Subsection (2)

174. Subsection (2) provides that subject to rules, an application may be for either an agreed notice or a unilateral notice. The main distinguishing features of a unilateral notice are that the registered proprietor will be informed of the registration and will be able to apply for its cancellation: see Clauses 35 and 36. Rules may prescribe that in relation to some types of interest, only certain forms of notice are to be available. One example of the sort of situation to which such rules might relate is considered below in paragraph 177.

Subsection (3)

175. Subsection (3) sets out the circumstances in which the registrar may approve an application for an agreed notice. The first two cases are ones where the registered proprietor consents to the entry of the notice.

176. The third situation in which the registrar may approve an application for an agreed notice will arise where the registered proprietor does not consent to the entry of a notice: see subsection (3)(c). The registrar is able to enter an agreed notice where he is satisfied as to the validity of the applicant's claim. An example would be where the applicant could establish to the registrar's satisfaction that the registered proprietor had granted him or her an easement.

177. This third situation is important for other reasons. Where the registrar enters an agreed notice he is not required to notify the registered proprietor of the entry as he is when he enters a unilateral notice. There are currently certain types of interest that can be protected by the entry of a notice without the consent of the registered proprietor: see Land Registration Act 1925, section 64(1)(c), (5)—(7). One example is a spouse's charge in respect of his or her matrimonial home rights under section 31(10) of the Family Law Act 1996. It is likely that rules will prescribe that in such cases, the interests in question should be protected by the entry of an agreed notice rather than by a unilateral notice.

CLAUSE 35 — UNILATERAL NOTICES

Subsection (1)

178. Subsection (1) provides that where a unilateral notice is entered in the register, notice of this will be served on the proprietor of the registered charge or estate to which it relates and such other persons as rules may provide. This provision is necessary because a unilateral notice may be entered without the consent of the registered proprietor.

179. It is anticipated that rules may provide (for example) that notice be served on the liquidator of a company which was the registered proprietor.

180. Subsection (2) provides that a unilateral notice must indicate that it is such a notice and identify who is the beneficiary of it. It is unlikely that anything else will appear in the register. At present, in relation to transactions of a commercially sensitive character, cautions are often entered in preference to notices because the entry of a caution in the register gives no indication as to the matter that lies behind it. The Bill does not replicate the system of cautions. It is, however, anticipated that it will be possible to achieve the same commercial confidentiality by means of a unilateral notice.

Subsection (3)

181. This provision makes it clear that the person who appears in the register as the beneficiary of a unilateral notice may apply for its removal from the register.

CLAUSE 36 — CANCELLATION OF UNILATERAL NOTICES

182. Unilateral notices may be entered without the registered proprietor's consent. In order to protect registered proprietors, Clause 36 makes provision for the cancellation of such notices.

183. Where a registered proprietor applies under subsection (1) for the cancellation of a unilateral notice, the beneficiary of the notice will be entitled to object under the general right conferred by the Bill to object to an application to the registrar: see Clause 73. If the matter cannot be disposed of by agreement, it must be referred to the Adjudicator: see Clauses 73(7) and 106(1).

CLAUSE 37 — UNREGISTERED INTERESTS

184. This clause gives the registrar power to enter a notice in respect of an unregistered interest which falls within Schedule 1, provided that it is not excluded by Clause 33, above. This is part of the strategy of the Bill to ensure that whenever practicable such interests are entered in the register. Clause 37 is similar to, but goes further than, section 70(3) of the Land Registration Act 1925.

CLAUSE 38 — REGISTRABLE DISPOSITIONS

185. In order to register certain registrable dispositions, it is necessary to enter a notice in respect of that interest on the title of a registered estate that is burdened by it: cf Schedule 2, paragraphs 3—7. Clause 38 therefore provides that, where a person is registered as the proprietor of an interest under a disposition falling within Clause 27(2)(b) — (e) the registrar *must* enter a notice in the register in respect of it.

Restrictions

CLAUSE 40 — NATURE

Subsection (1)

186. Subsection (1) defines the nature of a restriction. It is an entry to regulate the circumstances in which a disposition of a registered estate or charge may be the subject of an entry in the register.

187. Because a restriction can only apply to dealings with a registered estate or charge, no restriction can be entered in respect of dealings with interests the title to which is not registered. Thus, for example, it would not be possible to enter a restriction against the assignment of a lease granted for a term of 7 years or less, which takes effect without registration.

188. A restriction, by its nature, operates to restrict the circumstances in which an entry may be made in the register. It follows that the registrar will not make any entry in the register in respect of any disposition except in accordance with the restriction. Since a restriction is only operative in relation to the making of entries in the register, it does not affect the creation of interests whose effect and priority does not depend upon registration. However, if the person having the benefit of such an interest sought to enter a notice in respect of his or her interest, the registrar would have to refuse the application if it were contrary to the terms of a restriction.

Subsections (2) and (3)

189. Subsection (2) gives particular examples of the form that a restriction might take. These examples are non-exhaustive.

190. First, a restriction may prohibit the making of an entry in respect of any disposition or of a disposition of a kind specified in the restriction: Clause 40(2)(a). An example of the kind of case where a restriction might be employed to prohibit any disposition whatsoever would be where a court has granted a freezing injunction over a registered property. An example of the kind of case where a restriction might be employed to prohibit a disposition of a specified kind would be where a registered proprietor (typically a corporation or statutory body) had limited powers of disposition. In this case a restriction would prevent the registration of any disposition that was outside those powers. A further example would be where, under a registered charge, the chargor agrees with the chargee to the exclusion of his or her statutory power of leasing under Law of Property Act 1925, section 99.

191. Secondly, a restriction may prohibit the making of an entry—

(i)   Indefinitely. This would be appropriate where the registered proprietor has limited powers.

(ii)   For a period specified in the restriction. This might be appropriate, for example, where the proprietor had contracted not to make a disposition of the property for that period.

(iii)   Until the occurrence of some specified event. This should be read in conjunction with subsection (3). Subsection (3) provides some examples of the sort of events that might be specified, namely the giving of a notice, the obtaining of consent and the making of an order by the court or registrar.

CLAUSE 41 — EFFECT

Subsection (1)

192. Subsection (1) sets out the general principle that, where a restriction is entered in the register, no entry in respect of a disposition to which the restriction applies may be made in the register, except in accordance with the terms of the restriction. This is subject to the exception set out in subsection (2).

193. The effect of these subsections is that on the application of a person who appears to the registrar to have a sufficient interest in the restriction, the registrar has power by order to disapply or modify a restriction in relation to either—

    (i)   a disposition; or
    (ii)   dispositions of a kind;

    specified in the order.

194. This exception codifies the present practice whereby all restrictions are prefaced by the words "Except under an order of the registrar....".

195. The sort of situation where it might be appropriate for the registrar to exercise his power would be where a disposition of a registered estate could only be made with the consent of a named individual who has disappeared.

CLAUSE 42 — POWER OF THE REGISTRAR TO ENTER

Subsection (1)

196. Subsection (1) provides that the registrar has a power to enter a restriction if it appears to him that it is necessary or desirable to do so for any one of three purposes.

197. The first is to prevent invalidity or unlawfulness in relation to dispositions of a registered estate or charge: Clause 42(1)(a). The following examples illustrate the sort of situations in which such an entry might be made—

    (i)   Where the registered proprietor of an estate or charge is a corporation or statutory body that has limited powers of dealing. If a restriction were not entered to record that limitation, the proprietor's powers of disposition would, in favour of any disponee, be taken to be unfettered, notwithstanding that the disposition is unlawful: see Clauses 26 and 52.
    (ii)   Where the registered proprietor has contracted with some third party that he or she will not make a disposition of land or will only do so with their consent. One example of this would be where the third party has been granted a right of pre-emption. The unlawfulness which the restriction prevents is a breach of contract.
    (iii) Where trustees of land are required to obtain the consent of some person to a disposition. The unlawfulness which the restriction prevents is a breach of trust.

198. The second purpose for which a restriction may be entered is to secure that interests which are capable of being overreached on a disposition of a registered estate or charge are overreached: Clause 42(1)(b). This is directed primarily at trusts of land and settlements under the Settled Land Act 1925. Where the interest of a beneficiary is overreached, it is transferred into the proceeds of sale. On the disposition of a trust of land or settlement, the interests of the beneficiaries will only be overreached if any capital moneys that arise are paid to the trustees or to the trustees of the settlement, of which there must be at least two or a trust corporation. If the beneficial interests are not overreached, normal rules of priority will apply to determine whether the disponee is or is not bound by them: see Clauses 28—30. To ensure that overreaching does take place, the registrar may

enter a restriction to the effect that the proceeds of any registered disposition must be paid to at least two trustees or to a trust corporation.

199. The third purpose is to protect a right or claim in relation to a registered estate or charge: Clause 42(1)(c). A restriction might, for example, be entered to protect the claim by a person that he or she had a beneficial interest in a property under a resulting or constructive trust because he or she had contributed to the cost of its acquisition. Although a restriction under this heading must be for the purpose of protecting a right or claim in relation to the estate or charge, it need not be proprietary. For example, a restriction might be entered in respect of an order appointing a receiver or sequestrator.

Subsection (2)

200. Subsection (2) limits the registrar's power under Clause 42(1)(c) to enter a restriction for the purposes of protecting a right or claim in relation to a registered estate or charge. In exercising it, no restriction may be entered *for the purpose of protecting the priority* of an interest which is, or could be, the subject of a notice. This subsection emphasises the nature and purpose of a restriction. A restriction is simply a means of preventing some entry in the register except to the extent (if any) that is permitted by the terms of the restriction. It is not intended to confer priority.

201. Subsection (2) does not, however, prevent a notice and a restriction being entered in respect of the same interest provided that each serves its proper function. A notice might be entered to protect the priority of an interest against any supervening third party rights while a restriction is entered to ensure the compliance with certain conditions or requirements in relation to any disposition of the property by the registered proprietor. For example the priority of a right of pre-emption might be protected by a notice while a restriction might be entered to ensure that the registered proprietor first offers to sell the land to the grantee of the right before he or she contracts to sell it to anybody else.

Subsection (4)

202. Subsection (4) specifically provides that a person who is entitled to the benefit of a charging order relating to an interest under a trust is, for these purposes, to be treated as a person having a right or claim in relation to the trust property. This means that a restriction can be entered in relation to that order. If it were not for this provision, it would not be possible to make *any* entry in the register to protect such a charging order. This is because to enter a restriction under Clause 42(1)(c) it has to be necessary or desirable to do so for the purpose of protecting a right or claim in relation to a *registered estate*. Formerly such interests were protected by entry of a caution against dealings, but this means of protection is not replicated under the Bill.

CLAUSE 43 — APPLICATIONS

Subsection (1)

203. This subsection sets out who may apply to the registrar for the entry of a restriction.

Subsection (2)

204. Subsection (2)(a) creates a power to make rules that will require that an application be made in such circumstances and by such persons as rules may prescribe. There are currently certain circumstances in which a person has a duty to apply for a restriction. It is likely that in these and perhaps other cases, rules made under the Bill will require an application for a restriction. Examples include the following—

    (i)   Where the powers of trustees of land are limited by virtue of section 8 of the Trusts of Land and Appointment of Trustees Act 1996, the trustees must at present apply for a restriction: see Land Registration Rules 1925, rules 59A and 106A(1).

    (ii)   Where registered land is held by or in trust for a corporation and the corporation becomes a non-exempt charity, the trustees must presently apply for a restriction: Land Registration Rules 1925, rule 124(1).

205. Subsection (2)(c) enables rules to prescribe classes of person who are to be regarded as having a sufficient interest in the making of an entry to apply to the registrar under subsection (1)(c). Such rules will operate without prejudice to the generality of those who may apply under that category. The sort of persons that such rules might cover include—

    (i)   a person having an interest in land that is capable of being protected by the entry of a restriction, such as a beneficiary under a trust of land;

    (ii)   the donee of a special power of appointment in relation to registered land;

    (iii)   the Charity Commission in relation to registered land held upon charitable trusts;

    (iv)   the Church Commissioners in respect of any registered land administered by them under any statute;

    (v)   a receiver (whether or not appointed by the court), administrative receiver, or an administrator or a sequestrator appointed in respect of registered land or a registered charge.

Subsection (3)

206. Subsection (3) provides that if an application for the entry of a restriction is not in one of the forms prescribed by rules under subsection (2)(d), the registrar may only approve it if it meets certain requirements. Subsection (3) replicates an effect of section 58(2) of the Land Registration Act 1925.

CLAUSE 44 — OBLIGATORY RESTRICTIONS

207. If the registrar enters two or more persons in the register as the proprietor of a registered estate, he is required by subsection (1) to enter such restrictions as rules may provide for the purpose of securing that interests which are capable of being overreached on a disposition are overreached. For example, if two registered proprietors were to hold an estate on trust for a number of beneficiaries, a restriction might be entered to ensure that the proceeds of any registered dispositions are paid to at least two trustees or to a trust corporation. If one of the trustees were to die, this would ensure that no disposition could be made until another trustee had been appointed.

208. For another provision of the Bill which imposes a duty on the registrar to enter a restriction, see Clause 86(4) (bankruptcy petitions).

CLAUSE 45 – NOTIFIABLE APPLICATIONS

209. The purpose of this clause is to protect a registered proprietor against the unjustified entry of a restriction against his or her title. The effect of the clause is that where a person applies for a restriction to be entered in the register then, if it is notifiable, the registrar will be under an obligation to serve notice on the registered proprietor and such other persons as rules may prescribe. Clause 45(3) sets out when an application is notifiable, which is, in essence, in any case in which a restriction might be improperly entered. Rules under Clause 45(1)(b) are likely to prescribe that notice be served on registered chargees and other persons who may have a direct interest in any disposition of the property.

210. Where a person receives a notice of an application, he or she may object to it under the general provisions of the Bill that relate to objections: see Clauses 73 and 106. If the objection cannot be resolved by agreement of the parties, it will be referred to the Adjudicator for his decision: Clause 73(7).

CLAUSE 46 — POWER OF COURT TO ORDER ENTRY

Subsection (1)

211. Under this subsection, if it appears to the court that it is necessary or desirable to do so for the purpose of protecting a right or claim in relation to a registered estate or charge, it may make an order requiring the registrar to enter a restriction in the register.

212. The court is most likely to order the entry of a restriction in cases where, under the present law, it would order the entry of an inhibition. However, whereas inhibitions prevent the entry of any dealing in the register, the entry of a restriction under the Bill might be more limited in its effect. For example, if the court determined that a person was entitled to a beneficial interest under a resulting or constructive trust, it might also order the entry of a restriction to ensure that there was no disposition of the registered estate without the prior consent of the beneficiary. An example of the sort of case in which the court might order a restriction on any dealing in the register would be where it grants a "freezing injunction".

Subsection (2)

213. By virtue of subsection (2) the court will not be able to make an order for the purpose of protecting the priority of an interest which is, or could be, the subject of a notice. The reason for this limitation has already been explained in relation to Clause 42(2): see paragraph 200 above.

Subsections (3), (4) and (5)

214. Subsection (3) enables the court to include in an order a direction that a restriction is to have overriding priority.

215. Under the Bill, there are certain situations in which an application for an entry in the register is protected against later entries if it is made within a priority period. This will be the case where there is an official search or a notice is entered in the register in respect of an estate contract: see Clause 72.

216. In the absence of any direction by the court, the priority protection given to an official search or the entry of a notice in respect of an estate contract will prevail over any order of the court that a restriction should be entered in the register. Subsection (3) enables the court to reverse this position by directing that a restriction is to have overriding priority.

217. Subsection (4) provides that where the court directs that a restriction has overriding priority, the registrar will be under a duty to make such entry in the register as rules may provide. This will ensure that it is apparent from the register that the restriction has overriding priority.

218. The effect of subsection (5) is that in exercising its power, the court may impose such terms and conditions as it thinks fit. For example, it might require an undertaking from the applicant that he or she should indemnify any person acting in good faith who had suffered loss as a result of the court's directions. The court might also impose such conditions as requiring the applicant to give security, pay money into court, pay costs, or to withdraw some entry in the register.

CLAUSE 47 – WITHDRAWAL

219. This clause makes provision for the withdrawal of a restriction. The persons who may apply for withdrawal and the circumstances in which such an application may be made will be prescribed by rules.

220. This power is most likely to apply in relation to restrictions that were entered pursuant to a voluntary application rather than those which were entered because there was a duty to do so, or because they were entered on the order of the court or by the registrar. However, even in respect of some restrictions that were entered otherwise than on application, it may be appropriate for an interested person to apply for withdrawal of a restriction, such as where it is spent.

PART 5: CHARGES

Relative priority

221. Part 5 of the Bill contains provisions that relate to charges over registered land. It addresses the following issues—

    (i)   the relative priority of registered charges, including the tacking of further advances;

    (ii)   the powers of chargees;

    (iii)   the realisation of security; and

    (iv)   certain miscellaneous matters.

CLAUSE 48 — REGISTERED CHARGES

Subsection (1)

222. Clause 48 provides that charges on the same registered estate or the same registered charge are to be taken to rank as between themselves in the order shown in the register.

223. For rules concerning the priority of a registered charge relative to prior charges which are registered or the subject of a notice in the register see Clauses 29, 30.

Subsection (2)

224. How such priority should be shown in the register and the manner in which applications for registration of priority of registered charges as between themselves should be made are left for rules.

CLAUSE 49 —TACKING AND FURTHER ADVANCES

225. Clause 49 sets out four circumstances in which the proprietor of a registered charge may make further advances on a security so that they have priority over a subsequent charge. No further means are permitted: Clause 49(6).

Subsections (1) and (2)

226. First, the proprietor of a registered charge may make further advances on the security of its charge that will rank in priority to a subsequent charge if it has not received from the subsequent chargee a notice about the creation of that subsequent charge: Clause 49(1). A notice of this kind is treated as received at the time when, in accordance with rules, it ought to have been received: Clause 49(2). Schedule 10, paragraph 5, confers a general power to make rules concerning the form, content and service of notices to be given under the Bill.

227. These provisions on further advances serve a similar purpose to, but are significantly different from, section 30(1) of the Land Registration Act 1925. Under section 30(1), the registrar serves notice of the second charge on the first lender. This can lead to practical difficulties because the second chargee has no control over the date on which the notice is issued by the registrar. In practice HM Land Registry can only send the notice when it has approved the entry of the second charge in the register. There are cases where, for one reason or another, approval cannot be given for some considerable time. Any further advances made by the first lender in the interim period take priority over the security of the second lender. Lenders do not in fact rely on service of a notice of a further advance by the registrar. The second lender serves the notice itself as it is entitled to do under the common law principles of tacking further advances that still apply to registered land. In accordance with the wishes of the lending industry, the Bill acknowledges and gives effect to the present practice. The registrar will no longer have any responsibility for serving notice of a further advance. It will be a matter for the second lender.

Subsection (3)

228. Secondly, the proprietor of a registered charge may make further advances on the security of its charge that will rank in priority to a subsequent charge if the advance was made in pursuance of an obligation and that obligation was entered in the register in accordance with rules at the time of creation of the subsequent charge. This will be the case where, for example, a lender is contractually obliged to lend further money to a borrower and this is entered in the register.

229. Except that this applies in respect of *any* subsequent charge and not merely a *registered* charge, this provision replicates the effect of section 30(3) of the Land Registration Act 1925.

499

230. Thirdly, the proprietor of a registered charge may make further advances on the security of its charge that will rank in priority to a subsequent charge if the parties to the charge have agreed a maximum amount for which the charge is security and the agreement was entered in the register in accordance with rules at the time of the creation of the subsequent charge: Clause 49(4). This provision is a new one and is intended to offer another means of making further advances.

231. The operation of this third method may be illustrated as follows. X charges land to Y to secure an overdraft to a maximum of £100,000. This is entered in the register. At a time when X is indebted to Y for £50,000, X creates a second charge in favour of Z for the sum of £50,000. X then borrows a further £20,000 from Y. As regards the sum of £20,000 borrowed by X from Y, Y's charge takes priority over Z's because it is within the maximum amount for which it is security. Once, however, advances made by the first lender to the chargor reach the maximum ceiling, any further advances made by it would have to be made under a new charge or the maximum sum for which the charge was security would have to be increased. If a second charge had been created in the interim it would necessarily take priority over the new charge of the first lender or any additional sums secured under its original charge.

232. The maximum sum must necessarily include all principal, interests and costs due under the mortgage, but will not include the costs of enforcing the security, which is additional to the mortgage.

233. The Bill enables rules to be made to provide that in relation to specified types of registered charge this new form of secured charge will not be available at all, or only subject to certain specified conditions: Clause 49(5).

234. Fourthly, the proprietor of a registered charge may make further advances on the security of its charge that will rank in priority to subsequent charges if the subsequent chargees agree. This reflects the general principle that the priority of charges can always be adjusted by agreement between the parties. It involves no change in the law.

CLAUSE 50 — OVERRIDING STATUTORY CHARGES: DUTY OF NOTIFICATION

235. This clause means that on registration of a statutory charge that overrides an existing charge that is registered or is protected by a caution, the registrar is under a duty to give notice of the creation of that charge to such persons as rules prescribe. The persons to be notified are likely to be those who have some form of charge or sub-charge over the registered land. The creation of a statutory charge, other than a local land charge, is a registrable disposition by virtue of Clause 27(5).

236. This provision gives better protection to existing chargees. For example, it would enable a chargee to make an informed decision as to whether or not it should make further advances to a chargor on the security of an existing charge where its security had been eroded because of a statutory charge. In the absence of such a provision the chargee might make further advances ignorant that his security had been diminished.

237. For the registrar's obligation to pay indemnity payable in respect of any loss suffered as a result of any failure by him to perform his duty under this Clause, see Schedule 8, paragraph 1(1)(h).

Powers as chargee

CLAUSE 51 — EFFECT OF COMPLETION BY REGISTRATION

238. Under the Bill, a registered charge may be created either as a charge expressed to be by way of legal mortgage or simply as a charge for the payment of money: see Clause 23(1). By Clause 51, whichever of these two methods is used, the charge takes effect as a charge by deed by way of legal mortgage for the purposes of section 87 of the Law of Property Act 1925, and the chargee has the rights and remedies accordingly.

CLAUSE 52 — PROTECTION OF DISPONEES

239. Subject to any entry in the register to the contrary, Clause 52(1) provides that the registered proprietor of a charge is to be taken to have, in relation to the property subject to the charge, the powers of disposition conferred on a legal mortgagee. For the powers of a legal mortgagee, see Part III of the Law of Property Act 1925.

240. This clause corresponds to Clause 26 (which applies to a disposition of a registered estate). Like Clause 26, its sole purpose is to protect a disponee in a case where the disponor — here the chargee — did not have power to make the disposition, but where there was nothing in the register to indicate this. This could arise, for example, where a chargee purported to exercise a power of sale that had not yet arisen. In the absence of an entry in the register to the contrary, the disponee's title cannot be questioned: Clause 52(2). As the Clause only protects the disponee's title, it will not prevent a chargor from pursuing any other remedies he or she may have, such as bringing an action for damages against the chargee.

241. This clause serves a similar purpose to, but extends the scope of, corresponding provisions found in the Law of Property Act 1925: section 104(2) and (3).

CLAUSE 53 — POWERS AS SUB-CHARGEE

242. Clause 53 is based upon but extends the effect of rule 163(2) of the Land Registration Rules 1925. Whereas rule 163(2) applies only in relation to property subject to the principal charge, Clause 53 also applies to property subject to any intermediate charge.

Realisation of security

CLAUSE 54 — PROCEEDS OF SALE: CHARGEE'S DUTY

243. Clause 54 makes it clear that, for the purposes of a mortgagee's duties in relation to application of proceeds of sale of registered land, "a person shall be taken to have notice of anything in the register".

244. This provision is new. It deals with the following issue. Where a mortgagee exercises its power of sale the proceeds are held in trust. After satisfying certain payments, any surplus is held on trust for "the person entitled to the mortgaged property": Law of Property Act 1925, section 105. The effect is

that a mortgagee will hold the surplus on trust for any subsequent mortgagee of whose mortgage it has notice, actual, constructive or imputed. Where the mortgage relates to unregistered land, the mortgagee should search the Land Charges Register to discover the existence of any subsequent mortgages because registration constitutes actual notice. Under the Land Registration Act 1925 registration does not confer notice. Therefore, under the present law, a chargee should pay any surplus to the chargor unless he has been notified of the existence of a subsequent charge. Clause 54 changes the law. As a result of the provision, the chargee will have to consult the register to determine who is entitled to the surplus. Given the ease with which it is possible to search the register, this is not an onerous requirement.

CLAUSE 55 — LOCAL LAND CHARGES

245. This clause governs the enforceability of any local land charge which is a charge over registered land. Such a charge can only be realised if the title to it is registered. "Charge" is defined by the Bill to mean any mortgage, charge or lien for securing money or money's worth: Clause 129(1). For local land charges generally see the Local Land Charges Act 1975.

246. Although a local land charge to secure the payment of money in respect of registered land cannot be *enforced* until it is registered, prior to registration it will *bind* any disponee of the registered estate as an overriding interest: see Schedule 3, paragraph 6.

247. Clause 55 does not alter the present law: see Land Registration Act 1925, proviso to section 59(2).

Miscellaneous

CLAUSE 56 — RECEIPT IN CASE OF JOINT PROPRIETORS

248. Clause 56 is concerned with the power to give a valid receipt for the money secured by a charge where that charge is registered in the names of two or more proprietors. It replicates in rather simpler terms the effect of section 32 of the Land Registration Act 1925.

CLAUSE 57 — ENTRY OF RIGHT OF CONSOLIDATION

249. Consolidation is the right of a person who holds two or more mortgages granted by the same mortgagor to refuse to permit one mortgage to be redeemed unless the other or others are also redeemed.

250. Clause 57 enables rules to make provision about entry in the register of a right of consolidation in relation to a registered charge. Consolidation is presently regulated by rule 154 of the Land Registration Rules 1925.

PART 6: REGISTRATION: GENERAL

Registration as proprietor

CLAUSE 58 — CONCLUSIVENESS

Subsection (1)

251. Subsection (1) preserves the fundamental principle that the register is conclusive as to the proprietor of a registered legal estate. In other words, a registered legal estate is deemed to be vested in the registered proprietor. This principle is currently found in section 69(1) of the Land Registration Act 1925. "Legal estate" has the same meaning as in the Law of Property Act 1925: Clause 129(1) of the Bill.

252. If, for example, a person is registered as proprietor on the strength of a forged transfer, the legal estate will vest in that transferee even though the transfer is a nullity. Clearly this does not prejudice the right of any person interested to apply for the register to be altered if this is appropriate: see Clause 65 and Schedule 4.

Subsection (2)

253. Subsection (2) creates an exception to the principle set out in subsection (1) where—

   (i)   there is a registrable disposition; and
   (ii)   some further entry is required to meet the registration requirements set out in Schedule 2.

In such circumstances a legal estate is not deemed to be vested in the registered proprietor by virtue of Clause 58(1).

254. Clause 58(2) compliments Schedule 2 by ensuring that the registration requirements set out in that Schedule really are *requirements*.

255. The operation of Clause 58(2) may be illustrated as follows. X applies to be registered as the grantee of a 99-year lease. The lease is registered with its own title. However, the registrar fails to enter a notice of the lease on the superior freehold title. In these circumstances, Clause 58(1) will not operate to vest the legal estate in X, though it will be effective in equity. X can of course apply to the registrar to have the mistake corrected: see Schedule 4, paragraph 5(a).

CLAUSE 59 — DEPENDENT ESTATES

256. This clause sets out where in the register a person should be entered as the proprietor of a dependent estate.

Subsection (1)

257. First, if a legal estate subsists for the benefit of a registered estate, the entry of a person in the register as proprietor must be made in relation to the registered estate. "Legal estate" has the same meaning as in the Law of Property Act 1925: see Clause 129(1). By way of example, where a person is registered as the proprietor of an easement or a *profit à prendre*

appurtenant, he or she must be entered in relation to the registered estate to which the benefit is annexed.

Subsection (2)

258. Secondly, where a person is registered as the proprietor of a charge on a registered estate, that entry must be made in relation to the estate subject to the charge.

Subsection (3)

259. Thirdly, where a person is registered as proprietor of a sub-charge, that entry must be made in relation to the registered charge to which the sub-charge relates.

Boundaries

CLAUSE 60 — BOUNDARIES

Subsections (1) and (2)

260. Subsections (1) and (2) preserve the general boundaries rule presently contained in rule 278 of the Land Registration Rules 1925. Its effect is that the register is not conclusive as to the exact line of boundaries. This is subject to one exception. It is possible to determine the boundaries to a registered estate: see Clause 60(3). Where a boundary is so determined the register *will be* conclusive.

Subsection (3)

261. Subsection (3) contains the power to make provision, by rules, which will enable or require the exact line of the boundary of a registered estate to be determined.

262. At present, the power to fix boundaries is rarely used. This is because the process is expensive and may create boundary disputes because of the need to investigate the titles of all the adjoining landowners.

263. There are two aspects of the rule-making power contained in Clause 60(3) which make it likely that fixed boundaries will become more common in future.

264. First, the rule-making power makes it possible to prescribe a less demanding means of fixing boundaries than is presently employed. The development of modern mapping techniques is likely to make this possible. It is hoped that this will encourage landowners to have boundaries fixed in appropriate cases, such as where a development is laid out.

265. Secondly, Clause 60(3) provides that rules may, in particular, prescribe the circumstances in which a boundary may or must be fixed. The power to *require* boundaries to be fixed is a new one. One example where this might arise is in relation to the new system of adverse possession introduced by the Bill. Under the Bill, a person who has been in adverse possession of a registered estate for a period of 10 years may usually apply to be registered as proprietor of it: Schedule 6, paragraph 1. If the proprietor (or certain other interested persons) serves a counter-notice, the application will be rejected: Schedule 6, paragraphs 2 and 3. There are certain exceptions to

this: Schedule 6, paragraph 5. In particular, a person will be entitled to be registered where—

(i)   he or she has been in adverse possession of land adjacent to his or her own; and

(ii)   for at least 10 years of that period of adverse possession, the squatter or his or her predecessor in title reasonably believed that the land to which the application relates belonged to him or her: Schedule 6, paragraph 5(4).

The reason for this exception is that legal and physical boundaries do not always coincide, as where physical features marked on the plan, such as fences, are no longer there. Where this is the case, and a neighbour reasonably believed that he or she owned the land, his or her claim should succeed. The exception in Schedule 6, paragraph 5(4), does not, however, apply where the boundary has been determined in accordance with rules under Clause 60(3): Schedule 6, paragraph 5(4)(b). Rules under Clause 60(3) are likely to require that where an applicant comes within the exception and acquires title to the land, the boundaries be fixed. This will ensure that he or she (or any successor in title) can never invoke this exception in relation to that registered estate again.

CLAUSE 61 — ACCRETION AND DILUVION

Subsection (1)

266. Subsection (1) makes it clear that the fact that a registered estate is shown in the register as having a particular boundary does not affect the operation of accretion or diluvion.

267. The principles of accretion and diluvion may be explained as follows. Where land is adjacent to water, erosion and other natural processes are likely to cause changes to the boundary between the land and the water. If land is added or lost by a gradual and imperceptible process of change, the legal boundary will shift in accordance with the physical boundary between the land and the water: see *Southern Centre of Theosophy Inc v State of South Australia* [1982] AC 706. Where an owner gains land in this manner it is called accretion. Where an owner loses land this is called diluvion.

268. It follows from Clause 61 that the doctrines of accretion and diluvion will apply whether the general boundaries rule applies or whether the exact line of the boundary has been determined in accordance with Clause 60.

Subsection (2)

269. Subsection (2) provides that an agreement about the operation of the doctrine of accretion and diluvion in relation to a registered estate has effect only if registered in accordance with rules. This subsection recognises the possibility that parties may, by agreement, exclude the operation of the doctrines of accretion and diluvion. For example, if the boundary between two registered estates is a stream, and the respective owners agree that the boundary should be in a particular place notwithstanding changes that might otherwise be made by movement of the stream, that arrangement will only be effective if it is recorded on the register in accordance with rules.

Quality of title

CLAUSE 62 — POWER TO UPGRADE TITLE

270. Clause 62 confers on the registrar power to upgrade the quality of any title that is not absolute. This is currently governed by section 77 of the Land Registration Act 1925 (substituted by the Land Registration Act 1986, section 1(1)). The Bill replicates the effect of the current provisions with some amendments.

Subsection (1)

271. Where a freehold estate is registered with a possessory or qualified title, subsection (1) enables the registrar to enter it as absolute if he is satisfied as to the title to the estate. For the different classes of freehold title that may be entered on first registration, see Clause 9. In determining whether he is satisfied as to the title, the registrar must apply the same standards as those which apply under Clause 9: see Clause 62(8).

272. The following example illustrates the type of situation in which a possessory title might be upgraded under Clause 62(1). On first registration X is registered with a possessory title because he is unable to prove title for the statutory period of at least 15 years: see Law of Property Act 1925, section 44(1). This may happen because X has lost the documents of title or believes them to have been destroyed. If they subsequently come to light, the registrar may enter X's title as absolute if he is satisfied as to the title to the estate.

273. Registration with a qualified title is rare and will only occur when the registrar considers that title can only be established for a limited period or subject to certain reservations that may disturb the holder under that title: see Clause 9(4). Before he could upgrade a qualified title to an absolute one under Clause 62(1), the registrar would therefore have to be satisfied that the cause of the original objections no longer threatened the holding under that title.

Subsection (2)

274. Subsection (2) gives the registrar the power to upgrade a leasehold title which has been registered as good leasehold. A leasehold title will be registered as such if the registrar is unable to satisfy himself as to the superior title. Subsection (2) therefore enables the registrar to upgrade a good leasehold title if he subsequently becomes satisfied as to the superior title. This might, for example, happen where the reversion expectant on a lease is registered for the first time. In determining whether he is satisfied as to the title, the registrar will have to apply the same standards as those which apply under Clauses 9 and 10: see Clause 62(8).

Subsection (3)

275. Subsection (3) provides that where the title to a leasehold estate is possessory or qualified, the registrar may upgrade it to—

    (i)   good leasehold, if he is satisfied as to the title to the estate; or
    (ii)   absolute, if he is satisfied both as to the title to the estate and as to the superior title.

506

276. When determining whether he is satisfied as to the title, the registrar will again have to apply the same standards as those which apply under Clauses 9 and 10: see Clause 62(8).

Subsection (4)

277. Where a freehold estate is registered with possessory title, subsection (4) confers a power on the registrar to enter it as absolute if—

(i)   it has been registered as possessory for at least 12 years; and
(ii)   he is satisfied that the proprietor is in possession of the land

278. A proprietor is in possession for these purposes in the circumstances set out in Clause 128. See below, paragraphs 559.

279. The reason for this provision is as follows. If a proprietor has been in possession for 12 years after first registration, the likelihood that any adverse rights could be successfully asserted is significantly reduced. Even if they were not barred by adverse possession at the time of first registration, it is probable that they will be 12 years later. This is because most (though not all) estates in unregistered land are extinguished by 12 years' adverse possession: see Limitation Act 1980, sections 15, 17. (Any rights adverse to the proprietor of the possessory title will necessarily be unregistered because possessory title is only given on first registration. The Bill creates a new system for dealing with adverse possession of registered land: see Clauses 95—97; and Schedule 6). The Lord Chancellor is given the power by order to change the period of 12 years to some other period: see Clause 62(9). This rule-making power will enable the period of 12 years to be kept in line with any changes that may be made to the 12 year period of limitation that currently applies in relation to unregistered land.

Subsection (5)

280. Where a leasehold estate is possessory, subsection (5) confers a power on the registrar to enter it as good leasehold if—

(i)   it has been registered as possessory for at least 12 years; and
(ii)   he is satisfied that the proprietor is in possession of the land.

281. Once again, the circumstances in which a proprietor is in possession for these purposes as explained in Clause 128. See below, paragraphs 559 and following.

282. The Lord Chancellor is again given the power by order to change the period of 12 years to some other period: see Clause 62(9). This is explained above: see paragraph 279.

Subsection (6)

283. Subsection (6) replicates the effect of section 77(4) of the Land Registration Act 1925. It operates to ensure that any such adverse claims which are outstanding are resolved before any application to upgrade the title is made.

Subsection (7)

284. Subsection (7) sets out the categories of persons who may apply to the registrar to have a title upgraded. It includes a wider class of persons than

fall within section 77 of the Land Registration Act 1925. The following persons may apply—

(i) The proprietor of the estate to which the application relates.

(ii) A person entitled to be registered as the proprietor of that estate. The executor of a deceased registered proprietor would, for example, be able apply for the deceased's title to be upgraded.

(iii) The proprietor of a registered charge affecting that estate. For example, a mortgagee in possession could apply to have the title upgraded before exercising its power of sale.

(iv) A person interested in a registered estate which derives from that estate. For example, a tenant would be able to apply for the landlord's freehold title to be upgraded. This might be desirable where, say, the tenant wishes to have his or her own title upgraded from good leasehold to absolute: see Clause 62(2).

As now, a person who is interested in some other way in a registered estate will be able to *request* the registrar to exercise his power to upgrade title. This is so, even though that person may have no right to apply to him to do so and he would, therefore, be under no obligation to consider his or her request.

CLAUSE 63 — EFFECT OF UPGRADING TITLE

285. Clause 63 explains the effect of upgrading title (it is left to be inferred under the Land Registration Act 1925). If a person suffers loss when a title is upgraded, he or she will be regarded as having suffered loss by reason of the rectification of the register and will therefore be entitled to indemnity: see Schedule 8, paragraph 1(1)(a) and 1(2)(a). See below, paragraphs 731 and 732.

Subsection (1)

286. Subsection (1) sets out the effect of upgrading a registered freehold or leasehold title to absolute title. On such an upgrading, the proprietor will cease to hold the estate subject to any estate, right or interest whose enforceability was preserved by virtue of the previous entry about the class of title. For the estates, rights and interests, the enforceability of which is preserved under the different classes of title, see Clauses 11 and 12.

Subsection (2)

287. Subsection (2) sets out the effect of upgrading a leasehold title from possessory or qualified to a good leasehold title. Once again, the proprietor ceases to hold the estate subject to any estate, right or interest whose enforceability was preserved by virtue of the previous entry about class of title. For the estates, rights and interests whose enforceability is preserved under the various classes of leasehold title, see Clause 12. However, the upgrading of a title to good leasehold does not affect or prejudice the enforcement of any estate, right or interest affecting, or in derogation of, the title of the lessor to grant the lease.

CLAUSE 64 — USE OF REGISTER TO RECORD DEFECTS IN TITLE

Subsection (1)

288. Subsection (1) provides that, if it appears to the registrar that the right to determine a registered estate in land has become exercisable, he may enter

the fact on the register. This power is new and is one of the provisions of the Bill that is intended to make the register as complete a source of information about title as possible.

Subsection (2)

289. Subsection (2) contains a rule-making power in relation to entries made under subsection (1). It specifies certain particular matters for which rules may make provision. The first of these — the circumstances in which there is a duty to exercise the power conferred by that subsection — requires further explanation. In most of the limited number of cases in which an estate may determine on the occurrence of an event, there are already simple and well-developed practices for protecting buyers of the land affected. In such cases there is no need to record the defect in title in the register, as there are already satisfactory solutions. One example is on an assignment of a lease. There is a risk that the assignor is in breach of covenant and that the landlord will, therefore, be able to exercise his or her right to re-enter and determine the lease. However, where a landlord accepts rent from a tenant whom he or she knows to be in breach of covenant, he or she will be taken to have waived the breach of covenant. Conveyancers take advantage of this principle and require the assignor of a lease to produce the last receipt for rent prior to the assignment. This creates a rebuttable presumption that all the covenants and provisions of the lease have been fully performed: Law of Property Act 1925, section 45(2) and (3). Because there is already a procedure for dealing with this situation, there is little point in empowering the registrar to enter on the register the fact that the lease might be determined.

290. Rules are likely to confine the exercise of the power under subsection (1) to those cases where there is presently no established procedure for dealing with the problem, and in particular to cases concerning rentcharges. An example might be where X purchases a registered freehold estate from Y which is subject to a rentcharge in favour of Z. Z has a right of re-entry in the event of the non-payment of the rentcharge. In the course of undertaking the conveyancing work, X's solicitor discovers that the rentcharge has not been paid by Y for some years. X is prepared to take the risk of acquiring the land nonetheless. X's title is, in law, a bad one. If X decides to sell the land, an intending buyer may not enquire as to whether the rentcharge has been paid until after he or she has expended money in relation to the purchase, as by making local searches or engaging a surveyor. Under the present law, there will be nothing on the register to indicate the defect in title. Clause 64 of the Bill is intended to meet this shortcoming.

291. Rules made under subsection (2) will be land registration rules such that they will be laid before Parliament only: see Clauses 129(1) and 125(3).

Alteration of register

CLAUSE 65 — ALTERATION OF REGISTER

292. Under this provision, Schedule 4 to the Bill, which contains the provisions on the alteration of the register, has effect. The provisions of the Bill on alteration and rectification are discussed in the notes to Schedule 4.

Information etc.

CLAUSE 66 — INSPECTION OF THE REGISTERS ETC

293. Clause 66 is one of the most important provisions in the Bill. It replaces, and extends the scope of, section 112 of the Land Registration Act 1925 (as substituted by the Land Registration Act 1988), which first made provision for an open register. The open register is an essential element in the move to a system of electronic conveyancing under which virtually all enquiries can be made on-line.

Subsection (1)

294. Subsection (1) provides that a person may inspect and make copies of, or of any part of, the following—

(i)   The register of title. This replicates the effect of section 112(1)(a) of the Land Registration Act 1925.

(ii)   Any document kept by the registrar which is referred to in the register of title. The Bill does not replicate the present exception in relation to leases or charges (or copies of leases or charges): cf Land Registration Act 1925, section 112(1)(b). However, it is anticipated that rules made under Clause 66(2) will restrict this right of access to protect private information in a manner that is similar to the Freedom of Information Act 2000.

(iii)   Any document kept by the registrar which relates to an application to him. At present, such documents can usually only be inspected at the discretion of the registrar: Land Registration Act 1925, section 112(2)(b). Once again, rules under Clause 66(2) are likely to qualify this right.

(iv)   The register of cautions against first registration. The formal establishment of a register of cautions against first registration is new: see Clause 19. The register is to be open. Although new in form, this is not in fact a novelty. Currently, cautions against first registration are recorded in the Index Map and there is a right to search the Index Map and also to obtain copies of a caution title: see Land Registration (Open Register) Rules 1991, rules 8 and 9.

Subsection (2)

295. Subsection (2) provides that the right to inspect and copy in Clause 66(1) is subject to rules. These rules may, in particular, provide for exceptions to the right and impose conditions including conditions requiring the payment of fees. It is likely that rules made under Clause 66(2) will restrict access to documents which are of a private nature or which contain commercially sensitive information to those who have a good reason to see them.

296. Rules made under subsection (2) will be land registration rules such that they will be laid before Parliament only: see Clauses 129(1) and 125(3).

CLAUSE 67 — OFFICIAL COPIES OF THE REGISTERS ETC

Subsection (1)

297. Subsection (1) provides that an official copy is admissible in evidence to the same extent as the original. It replicates part of the effect of section 113 of the Land Registration Act 1925, which provides that "office copies" are

admissible in evidence to the same extent as the original. In practice, "office copies" are copies made by the land registry which take a particular form and which are certified, by statute, to be accurate. The Bill replaces the old terminology of "office copy" with the more descriptive term "official copy".

298. The matters in respect of which an official copy may be obtained under Clause 67(1) mirror those listed in Clause 66. The things of which copies are admissible under Clause 67 are the things of which copies may be taken under Clause 66.

Subsection (2)

299. Subsection (2) makes it clear that a person who relies on an official copy in which there is a mistake is not liable for loss suffered by another by reason of that mistake. However, where a person suffers loss by reason of a mistake in an official copy he or she will be entitled to indemnity under Schedule 8, paragraph 1(1)(d).

Subsection (3)

300. Subsection (3) contains the power to make rules concerning the issue of official copies. Rules may, in particular, make provision about who may issue them: Clause 67(3)(b). In this respect, it may be noted that, following the introduction of electronic conveyancing, there will be a power to authorise persons such as solicitors and licensed conveyancers to issue official copies pursuant to a network access agreement: Schedule 5, paragraph 1(2)(d).

301. Rules made pursuant to subsection (3) will be land registration rules: Clause 129(1). As such, they will be laid before Parliament only: see Clause 125(3).

CLAUSE 68 — INDEX

Subsection (1)

302. This subsection imposes a duty on the registrar to keep an index for the purpose of enabling the matters mentioned in the subsection to be ascertained in relation to any parcel of land. Under the present law, this duty is found in rule 8 of the Land Registration Rules 1925. It more properly belongs in primary legislation which is why it is included in the Bill. Clause 68 does not require the index to be specifically tied to a map as such. It suffices that the information is ascertainable from the index. This will mean that the index can be kept in dematerialised form.

Subsection (2)

303. Subsection (2) enables rules to be made about various matters in relation to the index. In particular, rules may make provision as to how the index is to be kept, including the following matters—

(i)   The information to be included in it. This might be wider than it is at present and might, for example, include land use.
(ii)   The form in which such information is to be kept. This power would enable the index to be kept in electronic form.
(iii)   The arrangement of information.

304. Secondly, rules may make provision about official searches of the index. Official searches of the Index Map can already be made electronically through Direct Access: see Direction of the Chief Land Registrar, 12 May 1997.

305. Rules made under subsection (2) will be land registration rules and will be laid before Parliament only: Clauses 125(3) and 129(1).

CLAUSE 69 — HISTORICAL INFORMATION

Subsection (1)

306. Subsection (1) provides that the registrar may on application provide information about the history of a registered title.

307. The power contained in Clause 69(1) is a new one. The reason for this provision may be explained as follows. The register of title only provides details of the title as it stands at any given time. It is a snapshot, not a chronology of the title. It does not provide any details as to the historical devolution of that title. There may, however, be occasions when a person has a reason for wishing to know the historical devolution of a registered title, as for example where—

   (i)   an issue has arisen as to whether a former proprietor is liable on the covenants for title which were implied on an earlier transfer (the benefit of such covenants is annexed to the land benefited and runs with it);
   (ii)   it is necessary to discover more about the ownership of land at the time when a restrictive covenant was entered into in order to determine the extent of the land that it was intended to benefit; or
   (iii) there is an issue as to whether certain freeholds had at some stage been in common ownership so as to extinguish certain easements or covenants.

308. HM Land Registry does in fact keep a computerised record of the history of registered titles for its own purposes, although it is not necessarily complete. Although there is at present no right to inspect that record, the registrar does sometimes provide information as to the devolution of a registered title if the applicant can show a good reason for wishing to see it. Clause 69 places this practice on a statutory footing.

309. It should be noted that Clause 69(1) does *not* impose any obligation on the registrar to compile or keep an historical record of titles. The record that the registrar may disclose is such as the Registry may happen to have.

Subsection (2)

310. Subsection (2) provides that rules may make provision about applications for the exercise of the registrar's power to provide historical information.

311. It is likely that rules will restrict the categories of persons who may apply for the registrar to exercise his power. An investigation of the history of a title will necessarily add time and expense to the conveyancing process and it should only be carried out where there is a sound reason for doing so. Moreover, it should *never* become a routine inquiry that a buyer's solicitor or licensed conveyancer feels that he or she is bound to make.

312. Rules under subsection (2) will be land registration rules and will be laid before Parliament only: Clauses 125(3) and 129(1).

CLAUSE 70 —OFFICIAL SEARCHES

313. This clause confers a rule-making power to make provision for official searches of the register, including searches of pending applications for first registration. Where an applicant makes an official search he or she will obtain an official copy of the register of title and of any documents abstracted in it. There are certain specific matters for which rules may, in particular, be made. These are—

(i)   The form of applications for searches.

(ii)   The manner in which such applications may be made. Under the present law, an application for an official search can already be made electronically by means of the Direct Access system: see Notice of the Chief Land Registrar, 12 May 1997.

(iii)   The form of official search certificates.

(iv)   The manner in which such certificates may be issued. With the introduction of electronic conveyancing, persons such as solicitors and licensed conveyancers may be authorised to issue official search certificates pursuant to a network access agreement: see Schedule 5, paragraph 1(2)(c).

314. For the provisions of the Bill relating to official searches with priority protection, see Clause 72, below paragraphs 317 and following.

Applications

CLAUSE 71 — DUTY TO DISCLOSE UNREGISTERED INTERESTS

315. The purpose of this provision is to ensure that an applicant for registration — whether for first registration or in respect of a registrable disposition — discloses to the registrar any unregistered interests which fall within Schedule 1 or 3 affecting the property, so that they can be entered on the register. As such, it forms part of the machinery to ensure that the register becomes as complete a record of title as is reasonably practicable. The registrar will only wish to enter in the register such rights as are clear and undisputed. Rules will therefore provide guidance as to when an applicant for registration is obliged to provide information and in respect of which unregistered interests. The rules will be land registration rules and will be laid before Parliament only: Clauses 125(3) and 129(1). For unregistered interests that override first registration and registered dispositions respectively, see below Schedules 1 and 3.

316. There will be no direct sanction for breach of an obligation to disclose information under rules made pursuant to Clause 71. However, when electronic conveyancing becomes operative, compliance with such rules is likely to be a condition of any network access agreement. For network access agreements and the sanctions for breaching their terms, see Schedule 5, below, paragraphs 645 and following.

CLAUSE 72 — PRIORITY PROTECTION

317. This clause makes provision for priority protection in relation to official searches and the noting in the register of certain types of contract.

318. At present, priority protection can only be obtained in relation to official searches. Priority protection is a matter of considerable importance in relation to registered conveyancing. Where a purchaser obtains an official copy of the register, this will be a statement of the title on the date on which the search is made. Between the date on which that copy is made and completion, third party rights might supervene. But for priority protection, the buyer might—

    (i)   complete and find him or herself bound by such rights; or

    (ii)   conduct a search just before completion, discover the existence of such rights and refuse to complete at all or until the defect in title has been removed.

However, where an official search is made with priority protection, this enables a purchaser to obtain an official copy of the register and to ensure that his or her interest takes priority over any other entry made during the priority period. Official searches with priority protection are currently governed by the Land Registration (Official Searches) Rules 1993. Given its importance, the main principles governing priority protection are included in the Bill leaving matters of technical detail only to rules.

Subsection (1)

319. Subsection (1) makes provision as to when an application for an entry in the register will be protected. It should be read with subsection (6)(a), which, by means of a rule-making power indicates the two situations under the Bill in which priority protection will be available, namely on an official search (as now) and when an estate contract is noted in the register. The latter is new and is linked to the introduction of electronic conveyancing. With the introduction of electronic conveyancing, it is likely that—

    (i)   any disposition of a registered estate or charge or a contract to make such a disposition will take effect only when it is registered; but

    (ii)   the making and registration of a contract or disposition will occur simultaneously.

It follows that it will become necessary to enter a notice in the register in respect of any estate contract. At present it is unusual to enter a notice in respect of estate contracts. Because it will become necessary to enter a notice for any contract to be valid, it is reasonable that this should confer the additional advantage of priority protection.

Subsection (2)

320. This subsection sets out the effect of priority protection. Where an application for an entry in the register is protected, any entry made in the register during the period relating to the application, is postponed to any entry that is made in pursuance of the application. There are two exceptions to this protection. These are set out in subsections (3) and (4), explained below.

321. The following example may be taken to illustrate the manner in which priority protection operates—

    (i)   X is the registered proprietor of a parcel of land.

    (ii)   On 1 March Z obtains a charging order over X's land.

(iii)	On 1 April, X contracts to sell his land to Y. Y's estate contract is protected by a notice and the entry of that notice also confers priority for the priority period which is, say, 30 days.
(iv)	On 7 April, Z applied for the entry of a notice in the register in respect of her charging order: see Clause 87(1)(b).
(v)	On 21 April, X executes a transfer on sale of the land to Y. Within the 30-day priority period, Y applies to register that transfer and is then registered.

In these circumstances, Y takes free of Z's charging order. Even though Z's charging order had priority over Y's estate contract (because it predated it), Y will take free of it because it was not protected on the register at the time of transfer. If it were not for the priority protection that was conferred when Y entered a notice of the estate contract, Z's application for a notice would have been effective and her charging order would have bound Y on registration. In other words, the protection given to Y's estate contract will prevent an entry on the register of Z's prior interest which, if it were entered on the register prior to the registration of the disposition to Y, would otherwise have priority.

Subsection (3)

322. Subsection (3) forms an exception to the principle that where an entry in the register is made in pursuance of an application to which a priority period relates, any entry made in the register during the priority period relating to the application is postponed to any entry that is made in pursuance of the application. If A had made an official search with priority on 1 April, and B then made an official search with priority on 10 April, A's application to register a transfer in her favour would not be postponed to, but would take priority over, B's application.

Subsection (4)

323. Subsection (4) forms a further exception to the principle of priority protection. This exception applies where the court makes a direction pursuant to Clause 46(3) that a restriction be entered with overriding priority: see above, paragraph 214. This overrides the priority that the application would otherwise have.

Subsection (5)

324. This subsection enables the registrar to wait until the end of the priority period to determine whether in fact it is necessary for him to make any entry at all, or, if it is, in what form. Where subsection (2) applies, it may have the effect that the interest in respect of which registration is sought may have been defeated by the disposition that has priority protection whether in whole or in part. Thus, for example, if the priority period related to a leasehold estate, and an application was made to enter a notice of a restrictive covenant during that period, the notice of the covenant would affect the title of the reversion, but not of the lease.

Subsection (6)

325. Subsection (6)(a) was considered above in relation to the explanatory notes on subsection (1): see above, paragraph 319. Subsection (6)(b) enables rules to be made that make provision for the keeping of records in relation to priority periods and the inspection of such records. This will make it

possible for a person to discover whether there is any priority period in place in respect of another application.

Subsection (7)

326. It was explained above that subsection 6(a) confers the power to make rules concerning the two cases in which priority protection may be given: see above, paragraph 319. Subsection (7) specifies four particular matters in relation to which rules may be made under that power. Two of these require some explanation. First, as regards subsection (7)(b) (the applications for registration to which such a period relates), a purchaser will commonly be buying land with the aid of a mortgage so that both the transfer and the charge will require protection. Secondly, subsection (7)(d) (the application of subsections (2) and (3) in cases where more than one priority period relates to the same application), is intended to meet the following situation. In some cases a person might, for example, make an official search with priority before contracting to buy certain land. When a second search is made with priority or the estate contract is noted on the register, this will result in a further period of priority. Subsections (6)(a) and (7) will enable rules to be made about how the two periods interrelate and what happens where a third party makes a priority search in between the two events.

CLAUSE 73 — OBJECTIONS

Subsection (1)

327. Subsection (1) lays down the principle that, subject to subsections (2) and (3), anyone may object to an application to the registrar under the Bill.

328. The Bill makes provision for the making of applications in many circumstances. Clause 73 sets out the means by which an application may be challenged. The right to challenge applications under Clause 73 is referred to in the Bill as the "right to object": Clause 129(3)(c).

329. It should be noted that where a person exercises his or her right to object to an application to the registrar without reasonable cause, he or she will be in breach of statutory duty under Clause 77.

Subsections (2), (3) and (4)

330. The principle that *anyone* may object to an application to the registrar, is subject to two exceptions which are set out in subsections (2) and (3).

    (i)   In relation to an application for the cancellation of a caution against first registration under Clause 18, only the person who lodged the caution or his or her personal representative may object: Clause 73(2).

    (ii)   Where an application is made for the cancellation of a unilateral notice under Clause 36, only the person shown on the register as the beneficiary of it may object: Clause 73(3).

Furthermore, the right to object is subject to any rules that may be made under subsection (4). Such rules will be land registration rules and are required to be laid before Parliament only: Clauses 125 and 129(1).

331. As a result of subsection (5), where an objection is made, the registrar must give notice of it to the applicant and may not determine the application until the objection is disposed of. Paragraph 5 of Schedule 10 contains a general rule-making power concerning the form, content and procedure to be adopted in relation to notices under the Bill. Such rules will be land registration rules and are required to be laid before Parliament only: Clauses 125 and 129(1).

332. Subsection (5) will not apply where the registrar is satisfied that the objection is groundless: see Clause 73(6). If a person wishes to challenge the registrar's decision, he or she must seek judicial review of it.

Subsections (7) and (8)

333. Where an objection is made to an application and this cannot be disposed of by agreement, subsection (7) requires the registrar to refer the matter to the Adjudicator to HM Land Registry. For the main provisions of the Bill that govern adjudication and the Adjudicator, see Part 11 and Schedule 9.

334. Subsection (8) enables rules to make provision about references to the Adjudicator under subsection (7). Such rules are land registration rules and are therefore required to be laid before Parliament: see Clauses 125(3) and 129(1).

CLAUSE 74 — EFFECTIVE DATE OF REGISTRATION

335. This clause makes provision for the effective date of registration. At present, registration is deemed to occur when an application is delivered to the Registry: see Land Registration Rules 1925, rules 24, 42 and 83.

336. Clause 74 provides that an entry made in the register pursuant to an application for first registration or an application to register a registrable disposition has effect from the time of the making of the application. Rules may make provision about when an application under the Act is to be taken as made: see Schedule 10, paragraph 6(c).

337. With the development of electronic conveyancing, Clause 74 may become obsolete in the fairly near future. This is because, under the system of electronic conveyancing, it is likely that a disposition and its registration will occur simultaneously: see Clause 93 and paragraphs 421 and following, below.

Proceedings before the registrar

CLAUSE 75 — PRODUCTION OF DOCUMENTS

Subsections (1) and (2)

338. Subsection (1) gives the registrar the power to require a person to produce a document for the purposes of proceedings before him. He might (for example) exercise it in the following circumstances. X, the registered proprietor of a property applies for the cancellation of a consensual notice in respect of an option which he claims is spent. The option was entered into by X's predecessor in title. Neither X nor the registrar has a copy of the option agreement. Y, having the benefit of the option, has a copy but is

unwilling to produce it. In this situation the registrar might require Y to produce the document.

339. Subsection (2) provides that the power to require the production of documents is subject to rules. Rules made under subsection (2) will be land registration rules and are required to be laid before Parliament only: see Clauses 125(3) and 129(1).

Subsection (3)

340. Subsection (3) provides that where the registrar requires a person to produce a document, this will be enforceable as an order of the court. It follows that non-compliance will be enforceable as contempt. Under the Bill references to the court are to the High Court or a county court: see Clause 129(3)(a).

Subsection (4)

341. Subsection (4) enables a person who is aggrieved by a requirement to produce a document to appeal to a county court, which may make any order which appears appropriate.

CLAUSE 76 — COSTS

Subsections (1) and (2)

342. Subsection (1) gives the registrar the power to make orders about costs in relation to proceedings before him, as for example in connection with such matters as applications and procedures before the registrar.

343. Subsection (2) provides that the power to make orders about costs is subject to rules. Such rules will be land registration rules and are required to be laid before Parliament only: see Clauses 125(3) and 129(1).

Subsection (3)

344. Subsection (3) makes it clear that rules made under subsection (2) may include provision about costs incurred by the registrar and liability for costs thrown away as the result of neglect or delay by a legal representative of a party to proceedings. This will serve the same purpose as a "wasted costs order" does in court proceedings.

Subsection (4)

345. Subsection (4) provides that where the registrar makes an order about costs, the order will be enforceable as an order of the court. It follows that non-compliance will be enforceable as contempt. Under the Bill references to the court are to the High Court or a county court: see Clause 129(3)(a).

Subsection (5)

346. Subsection (5) enables a person who is aggrieved by a costs order to appeal to a county court, which may make any order which appears appropriate.

CLAUSE 77 — DUTY TO ACT REASONABLY

347. Under section 56(3) of the Land Registration Act 1925, a person who, without reasonable cause, lodges a caution, whether against first registration or dealings, is liable to compensate any person who suffers damage in consequence. Cautions against dealings are prospectively abolished under the Bill: see above, paragraph 161. However, it is possible to enter both notices and restrictions unilaterally. It is therefore necessary to have some equivalent to section 56(3) to discourage improper entries, particularly given their potential to disrupt conveyancing transactions. This is found in Clause 77.

348. Subsection (1) creates a statutory duty not to exercise any of the following rights without reasonable cause—

    (i)   The right to lodge a caution against first registration under Clause 15.
    (ii)   The right to apply for the entry of a notice or a restriction. For the provisions of the Bill that govern notices and restrictions, see Part 4.
    (iii)   The right to object to an application to the registrar. For this right, see Clause 73.

It will be apparent from this that Clause 77 extends the present law. Not only does it apply to applications to enter notices and restrictions without reasonable cause (for the reasons mentioned in paragraph 347), but it also applies to those who abuse the right to object in Clause 73.

349. Subsection (2) means that where a person is in breach of this statutory duty he or she will be liable in damages to any person who suffers loss in consequence.

CLAUSE 78 — NOTICE OF TRUST NOT TO AFFECT REGISTRAR

350. Clause 78 replicates the principle, presently found in Land Registration Act 1925, section 74, that the registrar shall not be affected with notice of any trust.

PART 7: SPECIAL CASES

The Crown

CLAUSE 79 — VOLUNTARY REGISTRATION OF DEMESNE LAND

Subsection (1)

351. This clause addresses an anomaly that arises from the survival of certain ancient feudal principles. Most land in England and Wales is held by a landowner for a legal estate in fee simple. The only exception is the land held by the Crown in demesne. Demesne lands are those held by the Crown as sovereign or lord paramount in which it has no estate. The Crown has substantial holdings of demesne land which include—

(i)   the foreshore around England and Wales except where it has been granted away or is in some other way vested in a private owner;

(ii)   land which has escheated to the Crown (for an explanation of escheat, see below paragraph 366); and

(iii)   the ancient lands of the Crown which it has never granted away.

352. At present it is not possible for the Crown to register its title to land held in demesne. This is because section 2(1) of the Land Registration Act 1925 provides that "estates capable of subsisting as legal estates shall be the only interests in land in respect of which a proprietor can be registered". As the Crown has no estate in its demesne land, it cannot register the title: see *Scmlla Properties Ltd v Gesso Properties (BVI) Ltd* [1995] BCC 793, 798. Moreover, it is doubtful whether the Crown could ever make an infeudatory grant of an estate to itself out of its paramount lordship. The Crown is one and indivisible and it cannot, therefore, hold land directly of itself as feudal lord. The Bill makes provision to overcome this difficulty.

353. Subsection (1) provides that Her Majesty may grant an estate in fee simple absolute in possession out of demesne land to Herself. For the purposes of the Bill, demesne land means land belonging to Her Majesty in right of the Crown which is not held for an estate in fee simple absolute in possession: see Clause 129(1). It does not include land which has escheated unless there has been an act of entry or management by the Crown: see Clause 129(2). It should be noted that the *only* purpose for which Her Majesty may grant Herself a fee simple is so that the estate can be registered: see below, paragraph 354. In this way the Crown will be able to obtain the substantial benefits that registration under the Bill offers. In particular, it will give the Crown better protection from encroachment by squatters because of the provisions of the Bill on adverse possession: see below, Part 9 and Schedule 6. It also accords with one of the aims of the Bill which is to seek to encourage total registration.

Subsections (2), (3), (4) and (5)

354. Subsection (2) provides that where Her Majesty grants Herself a fee simple under subsection (1), that grant will not be treated as having been made unless an application for voluntary first registration under Clause 3 is made before the end of the period for registration. The basic period for registration is 2 months from the date of grant: see Clause 79(3). The registrar may on application by Her Majesty extend that period by order if he is satisfied that there is a good reason for doing so: see Clause 79(4).

355. If the registrar makes an order extending the period for registration after the initial period has elapsed, the grant will not be treated as having been invalidated by the failure to register within the initial period: Clause 79(5).

356. Although Clause 79 is concerned with *voluntary* registration of land held in demesne, the effect of a failure to register the grant of a fee simple is to invalidate it. The position is analogous to the situation where a disposition of unregistered land that is subject to compulsory registration is not registered within the period of registration: cf Clauses 6 and 7, above. As indicated in paragraph 353 above, these provisions are intended to ensure that the power to grant a fee simple can *only* be employed to secure the registration of title to the land.

357. This clause makes special provision for compulsory first registration where the Crown grants an estate out of demesne land (other than to itself under the power under Clause 79). At present, such grants are subject to compulsory registration under section 123 of the Land Registration Act 1925. However, they do not fall within the wording of Clause 4, which only applies to—

(i)   the *transfer* of; or
(ii)   the *grant* of certain leases out of;

an estate in fee simple or of a leasehold estate which has more than seven years to run: see Clause 4(1) and (2).

Subsections (1) and (2)

358. In addition to the list of events that trigger compulsory first registration under Clause 4, subsection (1) adds the following grants by Her Majesty out of demesne land—

(i)   The grant of an estate in fee simple absolute in possession, other than a voluntary grant to Herself under Clause 79.
(ii)   The grant of a term of years absolute of more than seven years from the date of grant that is made for valuable or other consideration, by way of gift or in pursuance of an order of the court. A grant by way of gift includes a grant for the purpose of constituting a trust under which Her Majesty does not retain the whole of the beneficial interest: see Clause 80(2).

For the meaning of demesne land, see Clause 129(1) and (2).

Subsection (3)

359. Subsection (3) excepts from the requirement of compulsory registration the grant by the Crown of mines and minerals held apart from the surface. It corresponds to Clause 4(9), and is associated with the difficulties that, for historical reasons, apply to the registration of mineral rights.

Subsection (4)

360. Subsection (4) confers a power on the Lord Chancellor, by order, to add to the events relating to demesne land that trigger compulsory registration and to make such consequential amendments as he thinks fit. This power is exercisable by statutory instrument that is subject to annulment in pursuance of a resolution of either House of Parliament: see Clause 125(2) and (4). Cf Clause 5.

Subsection (5)

361. The effect of subsection (5) is that if a grant is required to be registered within the period for registration stipulated by Clause 6, but is not, it takes effect as a contract made for valuable consideration to grant the legal estate concerned.

CLAUSE 81 — DEMESNE LAND: CAUTIONS AGAINST FIRST REGISTRATION

362. Under Clause 15, a caution against first registration can only be lodged against the registration of a title to an unregistered estate. As the Crown holds no estate in its demesne land, it would not be possible to lodge a caution against the first registration of demesne land in the absence of some express provision. To meet this difficulty, subsection (1) provides that Clause 15, which concerns the right to lodge a caution against first registration, shall apply as if demesne land were held by Her Majesty for an unregistered estate in fee simple absolute in possession. For the definition of demesne land, see Clause 129(1) and (2).

363. It has been explained in relation to Clause 15 that two years after that clause is brought into force, it will cease to be possible for a person who holds either a freehold or leasehold estate that is capable of being registered with its own title, to lodge a caution against first registration of that title: see above, paragraphs 72 and following. This is because cautions against first registration are not intended to be a substitute for first registration. In relation to the Crown, the Bill makes special provision. The Crown has not hitherto been able to register the title of land that it holds in demesne. Given the extent of the Crown's demesne land, it will take some time to register it using the procedure set out in Clause 79. In the interim the Crown may wish to protect such land by lodging a caution against first registration. Paragraph 15 of Schedule 12 therefore permits it to lodge cautions against the first registration of any demesne land for 10 years after Clause 15 comes into force, or such longer period as may be provided for by rules. Such rules will be land registration rules and will be required to be laid before Parliament only: see Clauses 129(1) and 125. It is anticipated that an extension of the 10-year period is likely to be necessary. The reason for specifying a 10-year period is to ensure that the process of registration is kept under review. After 10 years it will be possible to make a better estimate as to how long it will take to register the Crown's demesne land and to extend the period accordingly.

364. It should be noted that, under Clause 81, it will be possible for cautions against first registration in respect of demesne land to be lodged not only by the Crown, but also by other persons having an interest in demesne land.

Subsection (2)

365. Subsection (2) enables modifications to be made to the provisions on cautions against first registration should this be necessary to adapt them to demesne land. Rules made under this subsection will be land registration rules and will be required to be laid before Parliament only: see Clauses 129(1) and 125.

CLAUSE 82 — ESCHEAT ETC

366. Clause 82 is intended to solve a specific problem that currently arises in relation to escheat. Escheat occurs on the determination of a freehold estate. The owner's estate having determined, the feudal lord of whom he or she held the land — which will in practice be the Crown or one of the Royal Duchies (Cornwall and Lancaster) — becomes entitled to the land, but freed from the estate that previously encumbered it. However, the lord takes the land subject to subsisting charges or other incumbrances created by any former owner of the defunct fee simple. Although escheat occurs automatically on the determination of a freehold estate, it is only completed when the lord to whom the land reverts takes possession or control of it, or

takes proceedings for its recovery. Until that time, the lord will not be subject to liabilities that affect the land, such as the burden of a landlord's covenants where the land is subject to a subsisting tenancy.

367. Escheat can occur whenever, and for whatever reason, a legal estate in fee simple determines. The most common circumstances involve the disclaimer of such an estate. In particular, when a company is dissolved, its property vests in the Crown as bona vacantia. By section 656 of the Companies Act 1985, the Crown is permitted to disclaim such property. In practice, where the property is onerous (as it often is), the Treasury Solicitor will disclaim it. The effect of disclaimer is that the freehold determines and the land escheats to the Crown or one of the Royal Duchies. For other situations in which escheat occurs on disclaimer, see sections 178 and 315 of the Insolvency Act 1986. Although the land will automatically vest in the Crown Estate or one of the Royal Duchies, they will not be subject to liabilities attaching to the property unless and until there is some act of entry or management.

368. At present, where a registered estate escheats, its title will be removed from the register. This is because the estate no longer exists. Where the land escheats to the Crown, it will be held in demesne and (as the law now stands) cannot be registered. If it passes to one of the Royal Duchies, that Duchy will hold the land by virtue of its own unregistered fee simple estate. Under the Bill it would in theory be possible for land that has escheated to be registered voluntarily under Clause 3 (where the lord by escheat holds a freehold estate) or Clause 79 (where the land escheats to the Crown and forms part of its demesne). However, in practice it is unlikely that the land would be registered voluntarily, because to do so would constitute an act of management. The Crown or Royal Duchy would then become subject to the liabilities attaching to the property.

369. Consistently with the ultimate goal of total registration, the Bill therefore provides a mechanism for keeping on the register a registered freehold estate that has escheated. The rule-making power contained in Clause 82 is intended to ensure that such an estate may remain on the register until such time as there is a disposition of the land by the Crown or Duchy, or by order of the court.

370. It is envisaged that rules under this provision might operate in the following way. Where a registered freehold escheats, its title will not be closed. Instead, either the Treasury Solicitor (if he or she disclaims) or the Crown Estate or Royal Duchy (in other cases) will apply for the entry of a restriction in the register. Such a restriction is likely to prohibit the entry of a disposition in the register unless it is made by order of the court or by or on the direction of the Crown Estate. When such a disposition is made, it will necessarily create a new fee simple and it will be registered with a new title number. The old title will then be closed. Any encumbrances to which the former title was subject and which still subsist in relation to the new estate will be entered in the register of the new title.

371. Rules under Clause 82 will be land registration rules and will be required to be laid before Parliament only: Clauses 129(1) and 125.

372. Subsection (2) provides that rules may, in particular, make provision about various matters. An example of what is likely to be required under (a) is that the appropriate restrictions are entered in the register when a disclaimer occurs. As regards (b), the rules will ensure that encumbrances on the former title will subsist in relation to the new estate when it is entered in the register. The rules made under (c) are likely to provide that the fact of

escheat is recorded on the register. This will ensure that as and when a new freehold estate is granted, the subsisting encumbrances are transferred and that the old title is closed. The sort of requirements that may be required under (d), are that it should be necessary to refer to the number of the former title in the application to register the new estate.

CLAUSE 83 — CROWN AND DUCHY LAND: REPRESENTATION

373. Clause 83 sets out which bodies or persons may represent the owner of Crown or Duchy interests for the purposes of the Bill. It also sets which bodies or persons are entitled to receive notices and make applications under the Bill in respect of such interests. Clause 83 performs the same function as section 96 of the Land Registration Act 1925 does under the present law.

CLAUSE 84 — DISAPPLICATION OF REQUIREMENTS RELATING TO DUCHY LAND

374. The law governing sale and acquisition of land by the Royal Duchies of Cornwall and Lancaster is based upon a series of complex mid-19th century Acts of Parliament that reflect the uncertainties of conveyancing at that time. Dispositions to and by the Duchies have to comply with certain requirements that are incompatible with registered conveyancing. In particular, deeds or instruments relating to a disposition either to a Duchy, or of Duchy land, are required to be enrolled in the relevant Duchy office within six months if they are to be valid. The certainty that this was originally designed to achieve is now much more effectively attained by registration of title under the Land Registration Act 1925. Clause 84 is intended to provide some alleviation of the position. Its effect is that a disposition of a registered estate or charge by or to either the Duchy of Cornwall or the Duchy of Lancaster can be made in the usual way, regardless of the requirements that would otherwise apply under the legislation governing the Duchies.

CLAUSE 85 — BONA VACANTIA

375. The Bill does not affect the operation of bona vacantia. The rule-making power contained in Clause 85 is included so that specific provision may be made, should it be necessary, as to how the passing of a registered estate or charge is to be dealt with for the purposes of the Bill. Rules under Clause 85 will be land registration rules and will be required to be laid before Parliament only: Clauses 129(1) and 125.

Pending actions etc.

CLAUSE 86 — BANKRUPTCY

376. Clause 86 makes special provision for the effect of bankruptcy. This is necessary to reflect the provisions of the Insolvency Act 1986.

Subsection (1)

377. Because of the special rules of priority that apply in relation to dispositions of a bankrupt's property (explained below, at paragraph 381), subsection (1) has the effect of isolating the general rules of priority found in Clauses 28—30 of the Bill.

378. Subsection (2) sets out the procedure to be followed in relation to bankruptcy petitions. When a petition in bankruptcy is filed against a debtor, the relevant court official must apply to register the petition as a land charge in the register of pending actions: see Insolvency Rules 1986. If the debtor is proprietor of any registered land, this can have no direct effect, for a person to whom a registrable disposition is made is not required to make a search under the Land Charges Act 1972: see Clause 86(7). However, the registration of such a land charge will trigger a procedure for ensuring that an appropriate entry is made in the register of title. The registrar, who maintains both the register of land charges and the register of title, will search the index of proprietors' names in an attempt to ascertain whether the debtor is the registered proprietor of any land or charge in the register of title. If it *appears* to him that any registered estate or charge is affected he must register notice against that title. This procedure is similar, but not identical, to that which presently applies under section 61(1) of the Land Registration Act 1925.

379. Subsection (3) provides that, unless cancelled in accordance with rules, a notice which is entered in respect of a bankruptcy petition must remain in the register until either a restriction is entered under Clause 86(4) or the trustee in bankruptcy is registered as proprietor. The rules in question will be land registration rules and will be required to be laid before Parliament only: Clauses 129(1) and 125.

Subsection (4)

380. Subsection (4) sets out the procedure to be followed in relation to bankruptcy orders: cf Land Registration Act 1925, section 61(3). It is intended to ensure the entry in the register of a restriction that reflects the limitation under section 284 of the Insolvency Act 1986, by which a disposition by a bankrupt is void unless made with the consent of the court, or is subsequently ratified by the court. The way in which this procedure will operate is analogous to the procedure that was explained above in relation to bankruptcy petitions: see above, paragraph 378.

Subsection (5)

381. Subsection (5) explains the circumstances in which the title of a trustee in bankruptcy will be defeated by a registrable disposition of the bankrupt's registered estate or charge. As explained above, the normal rules of priority contained in the Bill do not apply: see above, paragraph 377. Subsection (5) follows the rule laid down in section 284(4) of the Insolvency Act 1986.

Subsection (6)

382. Subsection (6) provides that subsection (5) will only apply if the relevant registration requirements are met in relation to the disposition, but, when they are met, has effect as from the date of the disposition. For those registration requirements, see Clause 27 and Schedule 2.

CLAUSE 87 — PENDING LAND ACTIONS, WRITS, ORDERS AND DEEDS OF ARRANGEMENT

383. Amongst other matters, section 59 of the Land Registration Act 1925 presently makes provision for the protection of certain writs, orders, deeds of arrangement and pending actions by means of lodging a caution against

dealings. Cautions against dealings are prospectively abolished under the Bill: see above, paragraph 161. It is therefore necessary for the Bill to make other provisions for the protection of these matters.

Subsection (1)

384. Subsection (1) makes it clear that the matters that it lists are all to be regarded as interests for the purposes of the Bill. This is relevant to the effect of registered dispositions on their priority and to the application of the provisions about notices and restrictions. Pending land actions and the relevant writs and orders are defined by reference to the meaning given to them in the Land Charges Act 1972: see respectively sections 5(1)(a), 17(1) (pending land actions) and 6(1)(a) (writs and orders). The words "an order appointing a receiver or sequestrator" in Clause 87(1)(c) echo those in section 6(1)(b) of the 1972 Act. A deed of arrangement is defined by reference to the Deeds of Arrangement Act 1914, section 1: see Clause 87(5).

Subsection (2)

385. The effect of this subsection is that an order appointing a receiver or sequestrator and a deed of arrangement can only be protected by the entry of a restriction. Some orders appointing a receiver or sequestrator will be regarded as a proprietary right and some will not: see *Clayhope Properties Ltd v Evans* [1986] 1 WLR 1223, 1228. It was felt better to avoid difficult questions as to which side of the line a particular order fell, and whether or not it could, therefore, be protected by the entry of a notice. The Bill therefore treats all such orders as interests for the purposes of the Bill, but they can only be protected by the entry of a restriction. A deed of arrangement protects creditors in the period before the debtor's assignment of his or her property to a trustee for his or her creditors. It is therefore analogous to a bankruptcy order, and like such orders, is to be protected by the entry of a restriction.

386. A pending land action (under Clause 87(1)(a)) and a writ or order (under Clause 87(1)(b)) may be protected by the entry (as appropriate) of a notice, a restriction or both.

Subsection (3)

387. The effect of this subsection is that the four matters listed in subsection (1) can only be protected by the appropriate entry in the register and cannot override first registration or a registered disposition under Schedule 1 or 3. In practical effect, this means that they could not be protected merely because the person having the benefit of any of them was in actual occupation of the land affected for the purposes of paragraph 2 of either Schedule 1 or 3.

Subsection (4)

388. The power by rules to modify its application to any of the matters listed in Clause 87(1) is included because there may be cases where such matters may not readily fall within the wording of the provisions of the Bill without some modification to accommodate them. The rules in question will be land registration rules and will be required to be laid before Parliament only: Clauses 129(1) and 125.

CLAUSE 88 — INCORPOREAL HEREDITAMENTS

389. Each of the interests listed in this clause may be registered with its own title. At present, only rentcharges and manors can be so registered. Under the Bill, franchises and *profits à prendre* in gross will be registrable with their own titles. However, as regards manors, it will not be possible to register with their own titles any that have not hitherto been registered. Cf Clauses 3, 4. The reason for the power in Clause 88 is that, in applying the provisions about interests that may be registered with their own titles, it may be necessary to make modifications to take account of the incorporeal nature of the interests listed in the clause.

390. Any such rules will be land registration rules and will be required to be laid before Parliament only: Clauses 129(1) and 125.

CLAUSE 89 — SETTLEMENTS

391. Clause 89 contains a rule-making power to make provision for the purposes of the Bill in relation to the application to registered land of the various enactments relating to settlements under the Settled Land Act 1925 (such as the Trustee Act 1925 and the Administration of Estates Act 1925). The Land Registration Act 1925 contains detailed provisions relating to its application to settlements under the Settled Land Act 1925. It ceased to be possible to create new settlements under the Settled Land Act 1925 after 1996: see Trusts of Land and Appointment of Trustees Act 1996, section 2. Even before 1997 settlements had become uncommon and they will eventually disappear. It is for this reason that the Bill enables settlements to be dealt with by rules rather than making detailed statutory provision.

392. Rules under Clause 89 will be land registration rules and will be required to be laid before Parliament only: see Clauses 129(1) and 125.

CLAUSE 90 — PPP LEASES RELATING TO TRANSPORT IN LONDON

393. Clause 90 makes special provision in relation to various matters concerning PPP leases. For these purposes, a "PPP lease" has the meaning given by section 218 of the Greater London Authority Act 1999: Clause 90(6). In future, it is intended that arrangements for the operation and development of the London underground railway network will be made by means of public-private partnership agreements. PPP leases will be employed as part of that strategy. They will be leases of underground railways and other ancillary properties. The 1999 Act makes special provisions in relation to land registration and PPP leases: see Greater London Authority Act 1999, section 219 (amending the Land Registration Act 1925). Clause 90 replicates the effect of those provisions.

394. The effect of these provisions is that PPP leases—

    (i)   may not be registered with their own titles voluntarily: Clause 90(1);

    (ii)   do not trigger the requirement of registration when granted or transferred: Clause 90(2);

    (iii)   are not registrable dispositions: Clause 90(3); but take effect as if they were: Clause 29(4);

(iv) cannot be protected by means of the entry of a notice: Clause 90(4); and

(v) override both first registration and registered dispositions: Clause 90(5).

Furthermore, the grant of a sublease under a PPP lease is not registrable, nor is the grant for the benefit of a PPP lease of any right falling within section 1(2) of the Law of Property Act 1925 (such as a legal easement): Clause 90(3).

395. The reason for taking PPP leases outside the registered system in this way is as follows. Such leases are likely to be granted for a comparatively short period, namely 30 years. They will be virtually inalienable. Although it would no doubt be possible to produce accurate plans for such leases, it is thought that the costs would be enormous and disproportionate to the benefits that would accrue from so doing. There are similarities with the treatment of rights of coal in the Bill: cf paragraph 7 of Schedules 1 and 3.

PART 8: ELECTRONIC CONVEYANCING

396. Part 8 and Schedule 5 of the Bill contain the provisions that govern electronic conveyancing. These are of the greatest importance in the scheme of the Bill. Electronic conveyancing is the process whereby the transfer of land and the creation of interests in or over land will be effected electronically rather than, as at present, in paper form. Electronic conveyancing will necessarily be confined to dealings with registered land or with unregistered land that trigger the requirement of compulsory registration under Clauses 4 and 80 of the Bill. In the system of registered land that exists in England and Wales, there are two stages in the making of a transfer, grant or reservation. The first is the instrument which effects the transfer, grant or reservation. The second is the registration by the registrar of that transfer, grant or reservation after it has been submitted to him for registration. It is the process of registration that confers legal title in the case of registrable dispositions.

397. The aim of the Bill is to ensure not only that dispositions can be effected electronically where presently a written instrument of some kind is required, but also to bring about the situation in which the making of the disposition and its registration occur simultaneously. It is intended that it will, in time, be impossible to create or transfer many interests in or over registered land, whether legal or equitable, except by the simultaneous registration of the electronic instrument that effects the transfer, grant or reservation. This reflects an essential part of the strategy of the Bill, which is to make the register as conclusive as to title as it can be. (It can never be wholly conclusive because interests in registered land can be created informally, as by proprietary estoppel or prescription.)

CLAUSE 91 — ELECTRONIC DISPOSITIONS: FORMALITIES

398. This clause sets out the formal requirements which, if met, will enable certain dispositions of registered land to be effected electronically when they would otherwise have to be made in writing or by deed. It is derived (with modifications) from section 144A of the Land Registration Act 1925 proposed to be inserted by the draft Law of Property (Electronic Communications) Order.

399. Clause 91 sets out a uniform requirement for making any electronic document, whether that document does the work of a deed or of signed writing. In this respect it greatly simplifies the present law. At the same time, the requirements are such that they will continue to fulfil the cautionary and evidential functions that the existing requirements of signed writing or of a deed are intended to achieve.

Subsections (1), (2) and (3)

400. The effect of subsection (1) is that Clause 91 will only apply where the following requirements are met.

401. First, there must be a document made in electronic form that purports to effect a disposition: Clause 91(1)(a).

402. Secondly, that disposition must fall within subsection (2), that is to say it must be—

(i)   a disposition of a registered estate or charge;
(ii)   a disposition of an interest which is the subject of a notice in the register such as an equitable charge or an option; or
(iii)   a disposition which triggers the requirement of compulsory registration under Clause 4 of the Bill;

which is of a kind specified by rules: Clause 91(2). It is likely that, in due course, there will be a prescribed form of electronic disposition for *all* dispositions that could be made in electronic form under the clause. These forms are likely to be similar to those that have been successfully employed in paper form since 1997 in relation to applications for registration: see Land Registration Rules 1925, Schedule 1.

403. Thirdly, the document in electronic form must meet the four conditions that are set out in Clause 91(3), namely—

(i)   The document must make provision for the time and date when it takes effect: Clause 91(3)(a). At present it is usual practice for conveyancing documents to be signed and otherwise executed by the parties to them, but not actually dated. Documents are usually dated by the conveyancers shortly before they are intended to take effect. With a deed, this will be signified by delivery. An electronic document is not a deed, but merely regarded as one for the purposes of any enactment: see Clause 91(5). The concept of delivery is therefore inapplicable to electronic documents. The requirement that an electronic document must make provision for the time and date when it takes effect provides the necessary means of determining the date on which an instrument is to take effect. It will also enable the continuation of the present practice of completing when all parties are ready to do so.

(ii)   The document must have the electronic signature of each person by whom it purports to be authenticated: Clause 91(3)(b). References to an electronic signature are to be read in accordance with section 7(2) of the Electronic Communications Act 2000: see Clause 91(10). An electronic signature is a means by which an electronic document can be authenticated as that of the party making it. Normally it will only be the disponor whose electronic signature will be required. However, Clause 91(3)(b) specifies that the electronic signature is needed "of each person by whom it purports to be authenticated". This is because a disponee may sometimes need to be a party to the document, as where there is a disposition of registered land and the disponees are to be joint proprietors. In this case, both the disponor and the disponees will execute the transfer or application, because it will set out the trusts on which the land is to be held. A declaration of trust must be manifested and proved in writing and signed "by some person who is able to declare such trust": section 53(1)(b) of the Law of Property Act 1925.

(iii)   Each electronic signature must be certified: Clause 91(3)(c). Certification is the means by which an electronic signature can be linked to a particular individual. For these purposes certification has the meaning given to it in section 7(3) of the Electronic Communications Act 2000: Clause 91(10).

(iv)   There must be compliance with such other conditions as rules may provide: Clause 91(3)(d). This requirement provides some flexibility in relation to the creation of dispositions in electronic form. In light of experience with electronic documents, it might be thought advisable to impose further requirements. For example, there are various levels of assurance that can be achieved in relation to the security of electronic signatures, and it might be appropriate to require compliance with a specified standard. Any such rules will be land registration rules and will be required to be laid before Parliament only: see Clauses 129(1) and 125.

Subsection (4)

404.   Subsection (4) is the operative part of Clause 91. It provides that an electronic document which satisfies the requirements in subsections (1), (2) and (3) is to be regarded as—

(i)   in writing; and
(ii)   signed by each individual, and sealed by each corporation, whose electronic signature it has.

405.   This provision is not subject to the constraints imposed by the Electronic Communications Act 2000 (which only permits alterations to statutory requirements and not to rules of common law). It is therefore able to go further than its equivalent in the draft Law of Property (Electronic Communications) Order: see the proposed Land Registration Act 1925, section 144A(4). Clause 91(4) not only deems the document to comply with any *statutory* requirements of formality, but also with those that apply *at common law*. This is important in the context of those corporations that have no statutory powers of execution: see below paragraph 407.

406.   Subsection (4) will enable corporations (whether corporate or sole) to execute documents in electronic form.

407.   Where a corporation is able to execute a document by affixing its common seal, an electronic document which complies with Clause 91 will take effect as though it were sealed. This will apply in respect of the following types of corporation—

(i)   A corporation that is governed by the Companies Act 1985: see Companies Act 1985, section 36A(2). For corporations to which the Companies Act 1985 applies, see sections 735(1), 718 and Schedule 22 and the Foreign Companies (Execution of Documents) Regulations 1994: SI 1994 No 950 (as amended).

(ii)   A corporation that has an express statutory power to execute documents by affixing its common seal: see, for example, Charities Act 1993, section 62(2) and Friendly Societies Act 1992, Schedule 6, paragraph 2(2).

(iii)   A corporation that has no express statutory powers of execution, but to which the common law rules apply. At common law any instrument that effects a disposition of property by a corporation must be executed under that corporation's seal. In this respect the Bill goes further than the draft Law of Property (Electronic Communications) Order which does not alter the common law: see above, paragraph 405.

408. Where a corporation does not have a common seal, it must execute instruments in some other way. Some corporations have express statutory powers that enable them to execute a document where it is signed by certain specified persons. For example, in respect of corporations governed by the Companies Act 1985, section 36A(4) of that Act provides that "a document signed by a director and the secretary of a company, or by two directors of a company, and expressed (in whatever form) to be executed by the company has the same effect as if it were executed under the common seal of the company". Equivalent provisions are found (for example) in the Charities Act 1993, section 62(3) and Friendly Societies Act 1992, Schedule 6, paragraph 2(4). Where a document is in electronic form and is signed electronically by the specified persons, Clause 91 has the effect that it will be regarded as being signed by each of those individuals.

409. In any event, any corporation can appoint an individual to sign a document in electronic form as its agent.

Subsection (5)

410. This subsection provides that any document to which Clause 91 applies is to be regarded as a deed for the purposes of any enactment. It should be stressed that the effect of subsection (5) is that the document is *regarded as* a deed, not that it *is* a deed. Thus the rule at common law, that an agent can execute a deed on behalf of his or her principal only if authorised to do so by deed, has no application.

411. It should be noted that where a document is signed electronically by joint disponees or by their agent, it will necessarily satisfy the requirements for a valid declaration of trust under section 53(1)(b) of the Law of Property Act 1925.

Subsection (6)

412. Certain statutory provisions require a disposition by an agent acting by or on behalf of his or her principal to be authorised in writing: see, for example, Law of Property Act 1925, section 53(1)(a) in relation to the creation or disposition of interests in land. The effect of subsection (6) is that where an agent makes an electronic disposition, it will not be possible to question whether the agent did in fact have *written* authority to make it. Cf Schedule 5, paragraph 8.

Subsection (7)

413. Under the Bill it will be possible to assign electronically certain legal and equitable interests in registered land that are not registered estates but are merely protected by the entry of a notice: see Clause 91(2)(b). Such

assignment will be completed by a change in the terms of the notice. This is new. At present only the transfer of registered estates and charges is required to be completed by registration. In relation to an interest which is a debt or legal chose in action — such as the benefit of an option or other estate contract — it is necessary to give "express notice *in writing*" of the assignment to the debtor or other contracting party: Law of Property Act 1925, section 136. Clause 91(7) therefore enables such notices to be served in an electronic form in accordance with rules.

Subsection (8)

414. Subsection (8) disapplies section 75(1) of the Law of Property Act 1925 in relation to electronic dispositions under Clause 91. Section 75(1) of the Law of Property Act 1925 provides that a purchaser is "entitled to have, at his own cost, the execution of a conveyance [to him] attested by some person appointed by him, who may, if he thinks fit, be his solicitor". This provision is not thought to be widely (if ever) employed nowadays. In any event, attestation is not appropriate to forms of electronic disposition.

Subsection (9)

415. Where an electronic document has apparently been executed in accordance with section 36A(4) of the Companies Act 1985 (see above, paragraph 408), section 36A(6) of the Companies Act may be relevant. Section 36A(6) provides that "in favour of a purchaser a document shall be deemed to have been duly executed by a company if it purports to be signed by a director and the secretary of the company, or by two directors of the company...". Clause 91(9) makes it clear that if section 36A(4) of the Companies Act 1985 applies to a document because of Clause 91(4), section 36A(6) shall have effect in relation to the document with the substitution of "authenticated" for "signed". This reflects the requirement contained in Clause 91(3)(b) that an electronic document must have the electronic signature of each person by whom it purports to be authenticated.

Subsection (10)

416. Subsection (10) defines the terms "electronic signature" and "certification of an electronic signature" by reference to section 7(2) and (3) of the Electronic Communications Act 2000. Section 7(2) provides that for the purposes of that section, an electronic signature "is so much of anything in electronic form as—

    (i)   is incorporated into or logically associated with any electronic communication or electronic data; and

    (ii)   purports to be incorporated or associated for the purpose of being used in establishing the authenticity of the communication or data, the integrity of the communication or data, or both".

417. Section 7(3) of the Electronic Communications Act 2000 provides that "an electronic signature incorporated into or associated with a particular electronic communication or particular electronic data is certified by any person if that person (whether before or after the making of the communication) has made a statement confirming that—

    (i)   the signature,

    (ii)   a means of producing, communicating or verifying the signature, or

    (iii)   a procedure applied to the signature,

is (either alone or in combination with other factors) a valid means of establishing the authenticity of the communication or data, the integrity of the communication or data, or both".

CLAUSE 92 — LAND REGISTRY NETWORK

Subsection (1)

418. Subsection (1) enables the registrar to provide an electronic communications network or to arrange for its provision (the provision of the network may, therefore, be contracted out). The land registry network will facilitate the transfer and creation of rights and interests in registered land by electronic conveyancing. The land registry network is to be used for such purposes as the registrar thinks fit relating to registration or the carrying on of transactions which involve registration and are capable of being effected electronically.

419. As such, the purposes will include—

   (i)   the provision of information to the registrar or to any party to a transaction or proposed transaction that will involve—

       (a)   a disposition of registered land or of an interest in registered land; or

       (b)   a disposition of unregistered land that will trigger compulsory first registration;

   (ii)   the preparation of conveyancing documents in electronic form in relation to (i)(a) or (b); and

   (iii)   the registration of any disposition.

Subsection (2)

420. Subsection 2 provides that Schedule 5 has effect. Schedule 5 makes detailed provision for the working of the land registry network, and is explained below, at paragraphs 645 and following. That Schedule is central to the provision of electronic conveyancing.

CLAUSE 93 — POWER TO REQUIRE SIMULTANEOUS REGISTRATION

421. Clause 93 contains the power — that will not be exercised lightly — to make electronic conveyancing compulsory and to require that electronic dispositions should be simultaneously registered. It will be noted that there are two elements that can be made compulsory — the use of electronic conveyancing and the requirement that dispositions should be made and registered simultaneously. The reasons why such a power is necessary are as follows.

422. *Requiring dispositions to be effected electronically.* It is inevitable that the move from a paper-based to an all-electronic system of conveyancing will take some years and that the two systems will have to exist side by side during that time. However, that period of transition needs to be kept to a minimum. Not only will it be very difficult for practitioners and the land registry to operate the two systems in tandem, but also, if electronic conveyancing is to achieve its true potential and deliver the savings and benefits that it promises, it must be the only system. For example, it will be possible under a system of electronic conveyancing to manage the typical chain of domestic sales. However, if just one link in that chain is conducted in the conventional paper-based manner, the advantages of electronic chain

management are likely to be lost. A chain moves at the speed of the slowest link. A paper-based link is in its nature likely to be slower than an electronic one and will not be subject to the scrutiny and controls of those links in the chain that are electronic and therefore managed. It is anticipated that the exercise of this power to require transactions to be conducted in electronic form will be merely a formality. Solicitors and licensed conveyancers are likely to choose to conduct conveyancing electronically in view of the advantages that it has to offer.

423. *Simultaneous registration of dispositions.* When solicitors and licensed conveyancers enter into network access agreements with the Registry, they will be required to conduct electronic conveyancing in accordance with network transaction rules: see Schedule 5, paragraphs 2 and 5. Those transaction rules are likely to ensure that electronic dispositions are simultaneously registered, which is the single most important technical objective of the Bill. However, it is necessary to go beyond that and make an inextricable link as a matter of law between the making of a transaction and its registration. Network transaction rules made under Schedule 5, paragraph 5 can be used to ensure that a transaction and its registration coincide. But it is conceivable that, due to some mischance in a particular case, this might not happen. The transaction might then still have some effect between the parties (as it would now) though not registered. There is a risk that the mere fact that this could happen might undermine one of the goals of ensuring simultaneity of transaction and registration, namely that a person could rely on the register as being conclusive as to priority. It is therefore necessary to have statutory provision that will ensure a transaction can have no effect unless simultaneously registered.

Subsection (1)

424. By virtue of subsection (1), compulsory electronic conveyancing and simultaneous registration will only apply in respect of a disposition of—

(i)   a registered estate or charge; or
(ii)   an interest which is the subject of a notice in the register;

where the disposition is of a description specified by rules. This means that compulsory electronic conveyancing can be brought in gradually. As the use of electronic conveyancing becomes the norm in relation to particular transactions, the power to require them to be made electronically and simultaneously registered could then be exercised.

425. Rules under this subsection must be made by the Lord Chancellor by statutory instrument and will be subject to annulment in pursuance of a resolution of either House of Parliament: see Clause 125(2) and (4). Given the considerable importance of this power, the Lord Chancellor is required to consult such persons as he thinks appropriate before he exercises it: Clause 93(5). There will, therefore, be wide consultation before this step is taken.

426. For the purposes of Clause 93, "disposition", in relation to a registered charge, includes postponement: Clause 93(6). Under the Bill, registered charges are to be taken to rank, as between themselves, in the order shown in the register: Clause 48. However, chargees may by agreement alter the priority of their relative charges. For example, they may agree that charge A is to be postponed to charge B, over which it would otherwise have priority. The effect of Clause 93(1) and (6) is that rules may require the postponement of a charge to be made and registered electronically.

427. Clause 93(1) also makes it possible to require a disposition of an interest protected by a notice to be made and registered electronically. This is something new under the Bill: see above, paragraph 413. It is not at present possible to register transfers of such interests. The types of interest to which this power is likely to be applied include—

    (i)   a *profit à prendre* in gross that has not been registered with its own title;

    (ii)   a franchise that has not been registered with its own title;

    (iii)   an equitable charge;

    (iv)   the benefit of an option or a right of pre-emption.

Subsections (2) and (3)

428. The effect of subsections (2) is that not only will a disposition (or contract to make a disposition) be required to be made electronically, but it will also only have effect when it is entered in the register in the appropriate way (ie the relevant registration requirements are met). These events will occur simultaneously with the result that—

    (i)   There will no longer be the possibility of any period of time between a transaction and its registration (the so-called "registration gap"). It will no longer be possible to create or dispose of rights and interests off the register (as it is at present). The absence of the registration gap eliminates any risk of the creation of third party interests in the interim. It also means that there is no risk that the transferor may destroy the interest after its transfer but before its registration, as where X Plc assigns its lease to Y Ltd and X Plc then surrenders the lease to its landlord after assigning it but before the assignment is registered. Cf *Brown & Root Technology Ltd v Sun Alliance and London Assurance Co* [2000] 2 WLR 566.

    (ii)   The register will become conclusive as to the priority of many interests in registered land. The Bill provides that the priority of an interest in registered land, other than a registrable disposition that has been registered, depends upon the date of its creation, not the date that it is entered on the register: see Clause 28. However, if the power under Clause 93 is exercised, any transaction will be made and registered simultaneously. As the register will reflect the date of the transaction, for all practical purposes it will be conclusive as to the priority of competing interests that are expressly created.

Subsection (4)

429. In relation to any disposition to which Clause 93 applies, subsection (4) disapplies Clause 27(1) (which provides that a registrable disposition does not operate at law until the registration requirements are met). Clause 27(1) does not apply because under Clause 93 a disposition has *no* effect, whether at law or in equity, until the registration requirements are met.

CLAUSE 94 — SUPPLEMENTARY

430. The rule-making power contained in Clause 94 relating to both the communication and storage of electronic documents ensures the necessary flexibility in relation to both these matters. Not only are such rules likely to be technical in character, but also it can reasonably be anticipated that they

will change from time to time to reflect developments in information technology.

431. The rules made under Clause 94 will be land registration rules and will be required to be laid before Parliament only: see Clauses 129(1) and 125.

PART 9: ADVERSE POSSESSION

432. The Bill establishes a new scheme of adverse possession in relation to registered land. Under this new scheme, adverse possession of an estate in land will never of itself bar the registered proprietor's title. Instead, adverse possession for a period of 10 years will entitle a squatter to apply to be registered as proprietor. The Bill sets out the circumstances in which such an application will succeed.

433. The effect of the new scheme is that it will be considerably more difficult for a squatter to obtain title by adverse possession to land with registered title. The doctrine of adverse possession in English law rests on the principle that title to land is relative and ultimately rests on possession. That is true in relation to land with unregistered title. The fact that a squatter can usually extinguish a landowner's title by 12 years' adverse possession undoubtedly assists in the deduction of title to unregistered land and shortens the period for which such title has to be investigated (presently at least 15 years). However, the basis of title to registered land is not possession but the fact of registration. The register alone proves ownership. In many Commonwealth countries where there is a system of title registration, doctrines of adverse possession have therefore either been completely abandoned or modified. However, there is a danger of jettisoning the doctrine completely. Sometimes a registered proprietor dies and nobody administers his or her estate. In other cases, he or she simply disappears and cannot be traced. It is important that land should be kept in commerce. In such circumstances, if a squatter takes over the property and is able to acquire title to it by his or her adverse possession, that aim may be secured. The Bill recognises these competing policies. It creates what is, in essence, a system by which the registered proprietor will normally be given the opportunity to object to the squatter's claim to be registered and will have two years in which to put an end to his or her adverse possession. If the registered proprietor does not object or fails to take steps to put an end to the squatter's adverse possession, the squatter will be entitled to be registered as proprietor of the land affected instead.

434. The following is a summary of the main provisions of the Bill that deal with adverse possession—

(i)   Clause 95 disapplies various provisions contained in the Limitation Act 1980 in so far as they relate to registered land.
(ii)   Schedule 6 explains the circumstances in which a squatter may apply to be registered as proprietor and the circumstances in which such an application will succeed.
(iii)   Clause 97 deals with defences based on adverse possession in relation to possession proceedings.
(iv)   Schedule 12, paragraph 18 contains transitional provisions.

CLAUSE 95 — DISAPPLICATION OF PERIODS OF LIMITATION

Subsection (1)

435. The effect of this subsection is that where the title to an estate in land or rentcharge is registered, no period of limitation shall run in relation to an action for the recovery of land other than against a chargee. For the meaning of "estate in land", see Law of Property Act 1925, section 1(1).

436. The disapplication of limitation periods for actions to recover land is confined to estates in land or rentcharges the title to which is registered. The Limitation Act 1980 will therefore continue to apply to the following situations concerning registered land.

(i)   Where a squatter has been in adverse possession against a tenant and the lease was granted for a term of 21 years or less prior to the Bill coming into force. Subsection (1) will not apply to such leases because they will not be registered estates, unless voluntarily registered after the Bill comes into force. This is because under the Bill only leases granted for a term seven years or less will be overriding interests: Schedules 1, paragraph 1 and 3, paragraph 1. The title to such leases clearly cannot be barred by adverse possession (since the period of adverse possession required under the Limitation Act 1980 is 12 years). The title to a lease granted for a term of more than seven years will have to be registered: Clauses 3(3) and 4(1). As such, it will fall within Clause 95(1).

(ii)   Where a licensee or tenant at will brings a claim to recover the possession of land. As such persons are not registered proprietors, the Limitation Act 1980 will continue to apply to them.

(iii)   Where a lease becomes liable to forfeiture for breach of some covenant or condition in the lease, or a right of re-entry becomes exercisable in respect of a fee simple for breach of condition or on the occurrence of some event. An example of the latter would be where the owner of a rentcharge is entitled to exercise a right of re-entry because the registered proprietor of a fee simple has failed to pay rent which is due. The Limitation Act 1980 will continue to apply to rights of re-entry. The Bill achieves this effect by providing that no period of limitation under section 15 of the Limitation Act 1980 shall run against any person "in relation to an estate in land". A right of re-entry is not an estate *in land*: see section 1(1) of the Law of Property Act 1925. Consequently, section 15 of the Limitation Act 1980 will continue to apply to such rights.

(iv)   Where a squatter is dispossessed by a second squatter. In this situation, time will run against Squatter 1 for the purposes of section 15 of the Limitation Act 1980. After 12 years have elapsed, Squatter 1 will not be able to bring an action to recover the land from Squatter 2. The Limitation Act 1980 applies in this situation because Squatter 1 relies on his or her own freehold estate, which arose by adverse possession: this is clearly not registered.

437. Subsection (1) makes it clear that where a chargor is in possession, the rights of the chargee to recover possession or to foreclose remain subject to the provisions of the Limitation Act 1980. As such, a 12-year limitation period will continue to apply to the chargee's right to recover moneys due under the charge, to possession and to foreclosure. For the relevant provisions of the Limitation Act 1980, see sections 15, 20 and 29, and Schedule 1.

Subsection (2)

438. Subsection (2) has the effect that, in relation to a registered estate in land or registered rentcharge, no period of limitation will run in relation to an action for redemption.

439. This subsection makes a significant change to the law. Under section 16 of the Limitation Act 1980, where a mortgagee has been in possession of land for 12 years or more, the mortgagor loses his or her right to redeem the mortgage. This is anomalous and, given the remedies available to the mortgagee, unnecessary. The Bill disapplies section 16 in relation to a registered estate in land or registered rentcharge.

440. A mortgagee in possession will not be able to rely on his possession as mortgagee to found an application under the Bill to be registered as the proprietor of an estate. This is because to make such an application a claimant must be in adverse possession: see Schedule 6, paragraph 1. A mortgagee will never be in adverse possession because he will either—

(i)   be the tenant under a lease, if the mortgage was made by demise or sub-demise prior to the Bill coming into force: Law of Property Act 1925, sections 85 and 86; or

(ii)   have the same rights as if he were such a person, if the mortgage was a charge by way of legal mortgage: Law of Property Act 1925, section 87.

Possession by a mortgagee is clearly not adverse, for it is attributable to the legal relationship between mortgagor and mortgagee.

Subsection (3)

441. This subsection is a necessary concomitant to subsections (1) and (2). Its effect is that section 17 of the Limitation Act 1980 will not operate to extinguish the title of a person against whom, under Clause 95, a period of limitation does not run.

CLAUSE 96 — REGISTRATION OF ADVERSE POSSESSOR

442. Clause 96 provides that Schedule 6 has effect. Schedule 6 sets out in detail the working of the new system of adverse possession applicable to registered estates in a case where the squatter applies to be registered.

CLAUSE 97 — DEFENCES

443. This clause ensures that, in relation to proceedings for the possession of land, the position of a squatter mirrors that which applies in relation to an application for registration under Schedule 6. The clause sets out a number of defences in relation to proceedings for the possession of registered land. Like the provisions of Schedule 6, Clause 97 is designed to ensure that the issue of entitlement to the registered estate will be resolved one way or the other, and within a comparatively short period. Once a registered proprietor commences proceedings against a person who has been in adverse possession for 10 years or more, that step will necessarily lead to a result.

Subsection (1)

444. Under this subsection, it is a defence to an action for the possession of land if the squatter has been in adverse possession of land adjacent to his or her

own for 10 years under the mistaken but reasonable belief that he or she was the proprietor of it and could have satisfied the condition set out in Schedule 6, paragraph 5(4).

Subsection (2)

445. This subsection has the effect that where a judgment for the possession of land is obtained against a squatter who has been in adverse possession of land for 10 years (and could, therefore, have applied to be registered as proprietor under Schedule 6, paragraph 1), it will cease to be enforceable at the end of a further two-year period. But for this provision, the registered proprietor or chargee who had obtained the judgment would have six years within which either to bring an action on the judgment for possession (Limitation Act 1980, section 24(1)) or to execute the judgment without the leave of the court (CPR, Schedule 1, R46.2(a); Schedule 2, C26.5(1)(a)).

Subsection (3)

446. Under this subsection, a squatter also has a defence to an action for the possession of land if he or she—

    (i)   has been in adverse possession of land for at least 10 years;

    (ii)   has made an application for registration which was rejected; and

    (iii)   would have been entitled to re-apply to be registered under paragraph 6 of Schedule 6.

447. The requirement in paragraph 446(iii) will be satisfied where—

    (i)   no steps were taken to terminate the squatter's adverse possession within two years of that rejection and during that period he or she remained in adverse possession;

    (ii)   a judgment was obtained against the squatter but it was not enforced within two years; or

    (iii)   although possession proceedings were brought against the squatter they were discharged or struck out within two years of the rejection of the squatter's application.

Subsection (4)

448. Under this subsection a judgment for possession will cease to be enforceable against a squatter where—

    (i)   he or she has been in adverse possession of land for at least 10 years;

    (ii)   he or she has made an application for registration which was rejected;

    (iii)   the judgment was obtained in possession proceedings against the squatter within two years of that rejection; and

    (iv)   two years have elapsed since that judgment was obtained but no steps have been taken to enforce it.

Subsection (5)

449. The effect of this subsection is that, where the court determines either—

    (i)   that a squatter has a defence under Clause 97; or

(ii)   that a judgment for possession has ceased to be enforceable against him or her under Clause 97(4);

it must order the registrar to register the squatter as proprietor. This ensures that the circumstances in which a squatter can be registered as proprietor are the same whether that squatter applies for registration under the provisions of Schedule 6 or the registered proprietor takes proceedings against him or her to recover possession.

Subsection (6)

450. Subsection (6) provides that the defences under Clause 97 are additional to any other defences a person may have. In other words, if the squatter has some independent right to possession of the land, he or she is entitled to raise it by way of defence. If, for example, X enters into possession under a contract to purchase the land from Y and he has paid the consideration, that would, as now, be a defence to possession proceedings brought by Y. Similarly, if A has an equity in her favour by proprietary estoppel, she can raise that equity as a defence in possession proceedings brought by B, the registered proprietor.

Subsection (7)

451. The application of the provisions of the Bill on adverse possession to rentcharges is likely to be rather technical and complex. It is considered that it would be more appropriate to make such provision in rules (see too Schedule 6, paragraph 14) for the following reasons. First, the necessary provisions are likely to be technical and of a length that is disproportionate to their importance. Secondly, the incidence of rentcharges tends to be rather localised (they are most common in Greater Manchester, Lancashire, Sunderland and Bristol). Thirdly, most rentcharges will terminate in 2037 (Rentcharges Act 1977, sections 2 and 3), which may occur within the lifetime of the present Bill. The rules under this subsection will be land registration rules and will be required to be laid before Parliament only: see Clauses 129(1) and 125.

PART 10: LAND REGISTRY

452. Part 10 of the Bill, together with Schedules 7 and 8, make provision for the administration of HM Land Registry, for the charging of fees and the payment of indemnities, and for other miscellaneous matters.

Administration

CLAUSE 98 — THE LAND REGISTRY

Subsection (1)

453. Subsection (1) makes provision for the continuance of HM Land Registry which is to deal with the business of registration under the Bill. Cf Land Registration Act 1925, section 1.

454. Paragraph 5 of Schedule 7 provides that the registry is also to continue to have a seal and any document purporting to be sealed with it is to be

admissible in evidence without any further proof. This replicates the effect of the Land Registration Act 1925, section 126(7).

Subsection (2)

455. Subsection (2) provides that the land registry is to consist of the Chief Land Registrar and the staff of the registry who are to be appointed by him. Subsection (2) should be read in conjunction with paragraph 3 of Schedule 7 which provides that the registrar may appoint such staff as he thinks fit. The terms and conditions of such appointments require the approval of the Minister for the Civil Service.

456. By paragraph 4 of Schedule 7, any member of the land registry is protected from a claim in damages for any act or omission in the discharge or purported discharge of any function relating to land registration, unless it is shown that the act or omission was in bad faith. This provision substantially replicates the effect of the Land Registration Act 1925, section 131.

Subsection (3)

457. Under this subsection, the Chief Land Registrar is to be appointed by the Lord Chancellor. Paragraphs 1 and 2 of Schedule 7 make provision for the Chief Land Registrar's resignation, removal, re-appointment and remuneration.

458. Under the Bill, the office of Chief Land Registrar will be a disqualifying office for the purpose of membership of the House of Commons and the Northern Ireland Assembly: see Schedule 7, paragraph 7, amending the House of Commons Disqualification Act 1975 and the Northern Ireland Assembly Disqualification Act 1975. At present the office of Chief Land Registrar is not a disqualifying office. The change reflects the view that it should be.

Subsection (4)

459. Subsection (4) provides that Schedule 7 has effect. That Schedule sets out in further detail matters relating to the Chief Land Registrar, the staff of HM Land Registry, and other matters.

CLAUSE 99 — CONDUCT OF BUSINESS

Subsections (1) and (2)

460. Subsection (1) permits the Chief Land Registrar to delegate any of his functions to any member of the land registry.

461. Subsection (2) replicates the effect of section 126(6) of the Land Registration Act 1925.

Subsection (3)

462. The land registry operates through a series of district registries. The effect of subsection (3) is that a particular district land registry can be designated by the Lord Chancellor to receive applications from particular areas of England and Wales (as happens now), or indeed a specific type of application. For example, as applications for first registration become increasingly rare, it might be desirable to designate one or more particular land registries to deal with all such applications.

463. An order under this subsection is required to be made by statutory instrument and is to be laid before Parliament only: see Clause 125(2) and (3).

Subsection (4)

464. Subsection (4) replicates the effect of section 127 of the Land Registration Act 1925. That provision has been used for a variety of matters, such as for the giving of guidance as to how to conduct official searches of the register by fax and telephone and prescribing conditions of use of the registry's direct access service.

465. The Bill provides that forms and directions issued by the registrar, or any person authorised to act on his behalf, are admissible in evidence under the Documentary Evidence Act 1868: see Schedule 7, paragraph 6.

CLAUSE 100 — ANNUAL REPORT

466. Subsection (1) imposes a duty on the registrar to make an annual report on the business of the land registry to the Lord Chancellor. This places the current practice on a statutory footing. He must also publish that report: Clause 100(2). The Bill also requires the Lord Chancellor to lay copies of every such report before Parliament: Clause 100(3).

Fees and indemnities

CLAUSE 101 — FEE ORDERS

467. Clause 101 makes provision for the power to charge fees. It simplifies the equivalent provisions found in section 145 of the Land Registration Act 1925 and section 7 of the Land Registration Act 1936.

468. Under the general provisions of the Bill, the power to make a fee order under Clause 101 includes the power to make different provision for different cases: see Clause 125(1).

469. The Bill does not prescribe the method for assessing fees as section 145 of the Land Registration Act 1925 presently does. It is in fact likely that the method of assessment will change from its present *ad valorem* basis to one based on the work involved in the particular transaction.

CLAUSE 102 — INDEMNITIES

470. Schedule 8 makes provision for the payment of indemnities by the registrar and other related matters.

Miscellaneous

CLAUSE 103 — GENERAL INFORMATION ABOUT LAND

471. Clause 103 gives the registrar the power to publish information about land in England and Wales if it appears to him to be information in which there is a legitimate public interest. The registrar does in fact already publish information about changes in residential property prices on a quarterly basis. These are widely used, owing to their accuracy. In future, it is likely to

become possible to publish further information that can be ascertained either from the register itself or from applications for registration.

CLAUSE 104 — CONSULTANCY AND ADVISORY SERVICES

Subsection (1)

472. Subsection (1) empowers the registrar to provide consultancy and advisory services about the registration of land in England and Wales or elsewhere. It is likely that his expertise may be in demand in relation to the development of electronic registration systems in other countries.

Subsection (2)

473. Where the registrar provides such services they are to be provided on such terms, including terms as to payment, as he thinks fit. This means that the registrar will be free to negotiate the amount of such fees. They will not be constrained by the terms of any fee order made pursuant to Clause 101(a).

PART 11: ADJUDICATION

474. Part 11 contains provisions relating to adjudication and establishes a new office, that of Adjudicator to HM Land Registry. This office is independent of the Registry. It will be the Adjudicator's principal function to determine any contested applications to the registrar that cannot be determined by agreement between the parties to the dispute. At present this function is performed by the Solicitor to HM Land Registry, who is the land registry's senior lawyer. The Solicitor only deals with disputes between applicants and objectors, not with disputes between applicants and the registrar. However, issues can arise in such cases which concern the conduct of land registry officials. It is therefore appropriate that an independent office should be created for the purposes of adjudication.

CLAUSE 105 — THE ADJUDICATOR

Subsection (1)

475. Subsection (1) requires the Lord Chancellor to appoint a person to be the Adjudicator to HM Land Registry.

Subsection (2)

476. Subsection (2) stipulates the qualifications that a person must have to be appointed as Adjudicator. A person must have a 10 year general qualification within the meaning of section 71 of the Courts and Legal Services Act 1990. By section 71(3)(c) of that Act, a person has a "general qualification" if "he has a right of audience in relation to any class of proceedings in any part of the Supreme Court, or all proceedings in county courts or magistrates' courts."

Subsection (3)

477. Subsection (3) gives effect to Schedule 9 to the Bill, which makes further provision about the new office of Adjudicator.

478. Paragraphs 1 and 2 of Schedule 9 make provision for the resignation, removal, reappointment and remuneration of the Adjudicator. Paragraph 1(3) reflects the provision made by paragraph 28 of Schedule 11 which has the effect of attracting the retirement date provisions in section 26 of the Judicial Pensions and Retirement Act 1993.

479. Paragraph 3 of Schedule 9 gives the Adjudicator a power to appoint such staff and, subject to the approval of the Minister for the Civil Service, on such terms as he thinks fit.

480. In general, any function of the Adjudicator may be carried out by any member of his staff who is authorised by him for the purpose: see Schedule 9, paragraph 4(1). However, the Adjudicator may only delegate functions which are not of an administrative character to a member of staff who has a 10 year general qualification within the meaning of section 71 of the Courts and Legal Services Act 1990: see Schedule 9, paragraph 4(2). For the definition of a 10 year general qualification, see above, paragraph 476.

481. The Lord Chancellor has the power by regulations to make provision about the carrying out of functions during any vacancy in the office of Adjudicator: Schedule 9, paragraph 5. Such regulations are required to be made by statutory instrument and laid before Parliament only: see Clause 125(2) and (3)(c).

482. The Lord Chancellor is to meet costs incurred by the Adjudicator, but may require the registrar to contribute towards these expenses: Schedule 9, paragraphs 6 and 7.

483. Paragraph 8 of Schedule 9 places the Adjudicator under the supervision of the Council on Tribunals. The effect is to apply to the Adjudicator the various requirements which under the Tribunals and Inquiries Act 1992 apply to tribunals subject to the Council's supervision. For example, the Adjudicator will be subject to the duty under section 10 of that Act to give reasons for his decisions.

484. Paragraph 9 of Schedule 9 ensures that the office of Adjudicator is a disqualifying office for the purpose of membership of the House of Commons or the Northern Ireland Assembly.

CLAUSE 106 — JURISDICTION

Subsection (1)

485. Subsection (1) sets out the Adjudicator's two principal functions—

(i) The first is to determine matters referred to him under Clause 73(7). A matter will be referred to the Adjudicator under Clause 73(7) where an objection is made to an application to the registrar and this cannot be disposed of by agreement between the parties: see above, paragraph 333. This function is confined to disputes between a person who has made an application to the registrar and some other person.

(ii) The second is to determine appeals under paragraph 4 of Schedule 5. Paragraph 4 of Schedule 5 concerns the right to appeal from a decision of the registrar with respect to entry into, or termination of, a network access agreement: see below, paragraphs 665 and following.

486. Subsection (2) makes provision for the Adjudicator to rectify or set aside certain documents. On an application to him, the Adjudicator may exercise this power in relation to any document which—

(i) Effects a qualifying disposition of a registered estate or charge. "Qualifying disposition" is defined in subsection (3) as a registrable disposition or a disposition which creates an interest that may be the subject of a notice on the register. This will, therefore, include documents such as a transfer or grant of a legal estate or an instrument creating a restrictive covenant.

(ii) Is a contract to make a qualifying disposition of a registered estate or charge.

(iii) Effects a transfer of an interest which is the subject of a notice on the register. An example might be where there is an assignment of a *profit à prendre* that was noted on the register but not registered with its own title, and there was an error in that assignment. With the introduction of electronic conveyancing, the registrar will also be able to rectify or set aside documents in electronic form under this power. This will be of particular importance if, as anticipated, it becomes possible to transfer electronically certain interests that do not have their own titles, such as options and equitable charges, and to complete those transfers by an entry in the register: see Clause 93(1)(b).

487. At present, the registrar has no power to rectify or set aside documents. This has sometimes meant that he has had to refer a matter to the High Court that he could otherwise have dealt with himself. Clause 106 is intended to obviate the cost and delay that such a reference might entail. Thus the Adjudicator has a limited power to set aside the conveyancing documents listed above.

Subsection (4)

488. Subsection (4) makes it clear that the general law about the effect of an order of the High Court for the rectification or setting aside of a document applies to an order made by the Adjudicator. This means, for example, that—

(i) Rectification relates back to the time when the instrument was executed: see *Earl of Malmsbury v Countess of Malmsbury* (1862) 31 Beav 407; 54 ER 1196.

(ii) After rectification the instrument is to be read as if it had been drawn up in its rectified form: see *Craddock Bros v Hunt* [1923] 2 Ch 136.

CLAUSE 107 — PROCEDURE

Subsection (1)

489. Subsection (1) provides that hearings before the Adjudicator are to be held in public, except where he is satisfied that it is just and reasonable to exclude the public.

490. It should be noted that, although the Bill makes provision for hearings to be held in public, it is not intended that there should be any requirement for the Adjudicator to hold a hearing unless one or both of the parties wish to

have one. When hearings are to be held will be the subject of rules under subsection (3). It is envisaged that he may, instead, determine a matter on the papers submitted to him by the parties. This is the case now when a matter is determined by the registrar.

Subsections (2) and (3)

491. Subsection (2) confers a power to make rules to regulate—

(i)   the practice and procedure to be followed with respect to proceedings before the Adjudicator; and

(ii)   matters that are incidental to or consequential on such proceedings.

492. Subsection (3) lists the matters in relation to which rules may, in particular, make provision.

493. The power to make rules under Clause 107 is exercisable by the Lord Chancellor: see Clause 112. Such rules are to be made by statutory instrument and will be laid before Parliament only: Clause 125(3). They will *not* be made with the advice and assistance of the Rule Committee under Clause 124. This is because they are not land registration rules: see Clause 129(1). But the Lord Chancellor must consult the Council on Tribunals before making such rules: see above, paragraph 483.

CLAUSE 108 — FUNCTIONS IN RELATION TO DISPUTES

Subsection (1)

494. Subsection (1) provides that in proceedings on a reference to the Adjudicator under Clause 73(7), he may, instead of deciding a matter himself, direct a party to the proceedings to commence proceedings within a specified time in the court to obtain the court's decision on the matter. A reference is made to the Adjudicator under Clause 73(7) where a person objects to an application to the registrar and that dispute cannot be disposed of by agreement between the parties. Under the Bill, references to "the court" are to the High Court or a county court: Clause 129(3)(a).

495. It may be appropriate for the Adjudicator to direct a reference to the court under this provision where, for example—

(i)   the application raises an important or difficult point of law;

(ii)   there are substantial or complex disputes of fact that are more appropriate for a court hearing;

(iii)   there are other issues between the parties already before the court (such as matrimonial proceedings); or

(iv)   the court has powers not available to the Adjudicator, as for example, the power to award damages for objecting to an application without reasonable cause: see Clause 77.

496. At present, the registrar has an equivalent power to refer matters to the court under rule 299(3) of the Land Registration Rules 1925.

Subsection (2)

497. Subsection (2) confers a rule-making power to make provision about references to the court. In particular, rules may make provision about—

<dl>
<dt>(i)</dt>
<dd>Adjournment of proceedings before the Adjudicator pending the outcome of proceedings before the court. For example, proceedings before the Adjudicator could be adjourned, pending the determination of a preliminary point of law which had been referred to the court.</dd>
<dt>(ii)</dt>
<dd>The powers of the Adjudicator in the event that a party fails to comply with a direction to commence proceedings in the court. Rules might, for example, empower the Adjudicator to dismiss an application in whole or in part if the applicant has failed to comply with a direction to commence proceedings. Conversely, they might authorise the Adjudicator to give effect to an application in whole or in part if the person who objected to the application has failed to comply with a direction to commence proceedings.</dd>
</dl>

498. The power to make rules under Clause 108(2) is exercisable by the Lord Chancellor: see Clause 112. Such rules are to be made by statutory instrument and will be laid before Parliament only: Clause 125(3). However, they will *not* be made with the advice and assistance of the Rule Committee under Clause 124. This is because they are not land registration rules: see Clause 129(1).

Subsection (3)

499. Subsection (3) confers the power to make rules about the functions of the Adjudicator in consequence of a decision on a reference under Clause 73(7). In particular, rules may make provision enabling the Adjudicator to determine or to make directions about the determination of—

<dl>
<dt>(i)</dt>
<dd>The application to which the reference relates.</dd>
<dt>(ii)</dt>
<dd>Such other present or future applications as rules may provide. Rules may therefore enable the Adjudicator to give general directions in relation both to pending and future applications. This will, of course, obviate the need for further references to him on the same point and will provide guidance to the registrar.</dd>
</dl>

500. Again, such rules must be made by the Lord Chancellor: see Clause 112. The procedure that must be followed is the same as that in respect of rules under subsection (2): see above, paragraph 498.

Subsection (4)

501. Subsection (4) deals with the case where an application by a squatter for registration under paragraph 1 of Schedule 6 falls to be dealt with under paragraph 5 of that Schedule and there is an unresolved dispute between the applicant and an objector to the application. It applies if the Adjudicator takes the view that it would be unconscionable for the registered proprietor to seek to dispossess the applicant, but that the circumstances are not such as to make it appropriate to register the applicant as proprietor. In those circumstances, the Adjudicator must decide what should be done to satisfy the equity in the applicant's favour and make the appropriate order.

CLAUSE 109 — APPEALS

Subsection (1)

502. Subsection (1) gives a person aggrieved by a decision of the Adjudicator the right to appeal to the High Court. Subject to subsection (2), the right to appeal is unqualified and is, therefore, a right to appeal on a point either of

law or of fact. However, it is subject to the power contained in section 54 of the Access to Justice Act 1999, to provide by rules of court that any right of appeal may be exercised only with permission.

Subsection (2)

503. Subsection (2) qualifies the right to appeal from a decision of the Adjudicator on an appeal by a person who is aggrieved by a decision of the registrar with respect to entry into, or termination of, a network access agreement. In such cases there is a right to appeal on a point of law only. This is because it is a second appeal, and it is not considered to be appropriate to permit unlimited rights to make a second appeal.

Subsection (3)

504. Subsection (3) mirrors clause 108(4) and imposes on the court a duty corresponding to that imposed on the Adjudicator in relation to a disputed application by a squatter for registration under paragraph 1 of Schedule 6.

CLAUSE 110 — ENFORCEMENT OF ORDERS ETC

505. This clause provides that a requirement of the Adjudicator shall be enforceable as an order of the court. It follows that where a person fails to comply with a requirement of the Adjudicator he or she will be in contempt.

CLAUSE 111 — FEES

506. This clause gives the Lord Chancellor the power by order both to prescribe the amount of fees to be paid in respect of proceedings before the Adjudicator, and to make provision about their payment.

PART 12: MISCELLANEOUS AND GENERAL

Miscellaneous

CLAUSE 113 — RIGHTS OF PRE-EMPTION

Subsection (1)

507. Subsection (1) provides that a right of pre-emption in relation to registered land has effect from the time of creation as an interest capable of binding successors in title (subject to the rules about the effect of dispositions on priority). In other words, it will take its priority from the date of creation. For the provisions of the Bill that govern priority, see Clauses 28—31.

508. A right of pre-emption is a right of first refusal. It imposes an obligation on the grantor not to sell the land without first offering it to the grantee. The precise status of a right of pre-emption is at present uncertain. In *Pritchard v Briggs* [1980] Ch 338 a majority of the Court of Appeal held (obiter) that a right of pre-emption did not of itself confer on the grantee any interest in land. However, when the grantor chose to sell the property the right of pre-emption became an option and, as such, an equitable interest in land. If correct this might lead to unfortunate results. For example, although the grantee of a right of pre-emption would be able to register it at the time of its

creation, the right would not be effective for the purposes of priority until the grantor evinced a desire to sell the land. Similarly, if the grantee of the right of pre-emption is in actual occupation of the land to which it relates, the right of pre-emption presently takes effect as an overriding interest only when the grantor does something to indicate an intention to sell. The precise time when that occurs is uncertain. Clause 113 clarifies and simplifies the law by providing in relation to registered land that a right of pre-emption takes effect from the time of creation as an interest in land. On the basis that the dicta in *Pritchard v Briggs* represent the present law, the Bill changes it in relation to registered land.

Subsection (2)

509. Subsection (2) ensures that the principle in subsection (1) is prospective only. Therefore, it will not apply to rights of pre-emption created before Clause 113 is brought into force.

CLAUSE 114 — PROPRIETARY ESTOPPEL AND MERE EQUITIES

510. Clause 114 declares for the avoidance of doubt that, in relation to registered land, an equity by estoppel and a mere equity have effect from the time when the equity arises as an interest capable of binding successors in title (subject to rules about the effect of dispositions on priority). For the provisions of the Bill that govern priority, see Clauses 28—31.

511. In relation to equities arising by estoppel, Clause 114 removes present uncertainty as to the status of such rights. An equity by estoppel will arise in the following circumstances. A, the owner of land, encourages or allows the claimant, B, to believe that he or she has some right or interest over A's land. To A's knowledge, B acts to his or her detriment relying upon that belief. A then seeks to deny B the anticipated right or interest in circumstances that make this refusal unconscionable. In these circumstances B has an "equity" which gives him or her the right to go to court to seek relief. The court has a wide discretion in determining the minimum relief necessary to satisfy this equity. At present, there is uncertainty as to the precise status of B's "inchoate equity" after he or she has relied to his or her detriment but before the court has given effect to it. The weight of authority is probably in favour of the view that such an equity is proprietary and not merely personal. HM Land Registry already treats it as such, permitting the entry of a caution or notice in relation to such equities. Clause 114 removes the present uncertainty by confirming the proprietary status of an equity arising by estoppel in relation to registered land.

512. In relation to "mere equities" the Bill clarifies the present law. A "mere equity" is difficult to define with any clarity. The term is used to denote a claim to discretionary equitable relief in relation to property, such as a right to set aside a transfer for fraud or undue influence, a right to rectify an instrument for mistake, or a right to seek relief against the forfeiture of a lease after a landlord has peaceably re-entered.

513. For the avoidance of doubt, Clause 114 makes it clear that a mere equity has effect from the time when it arises as an interest capable of binding purchasers. Because a mere equity is an interest for the purposes of the Bill, it is brought within the general principles of priority applicable to registered land that are contained in Clauses 28—31. This means that a mere equity will not be defeated by the buyer of a later equitable interest in registered land without notice of that equity.

CLAUSE 115 — REDUCTION IN UNREGISTERED INTERESTS WITH AUTOMATIC PROTECTION

Subsection (1)

514. Under the Bill, as now, there are certain categories of unregistered interests which will nevertheless override first registration and registered dispositions. These are set out in Schedules 1 and 3, respectively: see below, paragraphs 570 and following and 599 and following. In accordance with the aim of total registration, the Bill seeks to restrict such interests so far as possible.

515. Subsection (1) makes provision for the phasing out of certain categories of unregistered interest which override first registration and registered dispositions. The following interests will cease to be overriding 10 years after Schedules 1 and 3 are brought into force—

    (i)   franchises;
    (ii)   manorial rights;
    (iii)   crown rents;
    (iv)   certain rights in relation to embankments and sea walls; and
    (v)   what are commonly called corn rents.

516. The rights that are covered by these categories of interest are all linked in that—

    (i)   they are of ancient origin;
    (ii)   they are of an unusual character that a buyer would not normally expect to encounter;
    (iii)   they can be very difficult to discover; and
    (iv)   they may be exceptionally onerous.

Subsection (2)

517. Subsection (2)(a) means that where a person has the benefit of a right over *unregistered* land which is to be deprived of its status as an interest which overrides first registration 10 years after Schedule 1 comes into force, he or she will be able to lodge a caution against first registration by virtue of that interest during that 10 year-period without the payment of any fee.

518. Subsection (2)(b) means that where a person has the benefit of a right over *registered* land which is to be deprived of its status as an interest which overrides registered dispositions 10 years after Schedule 3 comes into force, he or she will be able to register a notice in respect of that right during that 10-year period without the payment of any fee.

CLAUSE 116 — POWER TO REDUCE QUALIFYING TERM

519. Subsection (1) confers a power on the Lord Chancellor by order to reduce the length of the term specified in any of the following provisions—

    (i)   Clause 3(3) (length of leases which may be registered): cf paragraphs 14 and following, above;
    (ii)   Clause 4(1)(c)(i) (length of leases the grant of which triggers compulsory first registration) and 2(b) (length of leases the transfer of which triggers compulsory first registration): cf paragraphs 24 and 21, above;

(iii)   Clause 15(3)(a)(ii) (length of leases in respect of which the owner cannot lodge a caution against first registration): cf paragraphs 76 and following, above;

(iv)   Clause 27(2)(b)(i) (length of leases granted out of registered estates in land which are required to be registered): cf paragraphs 125 and 129, above;

(v)   Clause 80(1)(b)(i) (length of leases granted out of the Crown's demesne land which are required to be registered): cf paragraph 358, above;

(vi)   Paragraph 1 of Schedule 1 (length of unregistered leases which override first registration): cf paragraphs 574 and following, below;

(vii)   Paragraphs 4(1), 5(1) and 6(1) of Schedule 2 (registration requirements in respect of certain leases): cf paragraphs 131 and following, above;

(viii)   Paragraph 1 of Schedule 3 (length of unregistered leases which override registered dispositions): cf paragraphs 603 and following, below.

520.   Before making such an order, the Lord Chancellor must consult such persons as he considers appropriate: see Clause 116(3). The power to make an order under this clause is exercisable by statutory instrument which is subject to annulment in pursuance of a resolution either House of Parliament: Clause 125(2) and (4).

CLAUSE 117 — POWER TO DEREGISTER MANORS

521.   Clause 117 confers a power on the registrar to remove the title to a manor from the register on the application of the registered proprietor of that manor.

522.   At present a manor — that is, the lordship of a manor — is registrable with its own title: Land Registration Rules 1925, rules 50 and 51. The manorial rights of a lord are wholly incorporeal and are commonly owned separately from the land that was originally comprised in the manor. The registration of manors gives rise to many practical difficulties at HM Land Registry and offers few, if any, benefits in return. Therefore, the Bill does not replicate the present power to register a manor and Clause 117 makes it possible to deregister manors which are currently registered.

CLAUSE 118 — CONCLUSIVENESS OF FILED COPIES ETC

523.   This clause creates a presumption as to the conclusiveness of certain documents kept by the registrar which are not originals. It is designed to prevent persons from going behind the register. Clause 118 replaces section 110(4) of the Land Registration Act 1925 and makes certain adjustments to take account of the open register.

Subsection (1)

524.   Clause 118 will apply where—

(i)   a disposition relates to land to which a registered estate relates; and
(ii)   an entry in the register relating to the registered estate refers to a document kept by the registrar which is not an original.

525.   A disposition may relate to land to which a registered estate relates not only where the disposition requires registration, but also in some cases where it

551

does not. Because the register is open, it may be relied upon not only by those who are parties to a disposition of a registered estate that is capable of being protected on the register, but also by—

(i)   those who are granted an interest out of a registered estate which is not registrable; and

(ii)   those who are parties to any subsequent dealings with such an interest.

For example, where a freeholder grants a lease for seven years or less, the lease will not ordinarily be required to be registered, nor will its priority need to be protected by means of a notice in the register: see Schedule 3, paragraph 1. However, the grantee of the lease may search and rely upon copies of documents referred to in the register of the freehold title to ascertain what incumbrances (if any) affect it. Similarly, on an assignment of that lease, the intending assignee may search the register of the freehold title out of which the lease has been granted. The presumption of conclusiveness in Clause 118 will therefore apply to such dealings.

526.   Where the register refers to an *original* document that is kept by the registrar, Clause 118 will not apply. Where the register refers to any document the original of which is kept by the registrar, any person may inspect and copy it, except to the extent that rules may provide otherwise: see Clause 66. As such, there is no need for any provision as to the conclusiveness of the document. Clause 118 is intended to meet the sort of cases where the registrar has retained a copy of (or parts of) a document, but has not retained the original.

Subsections (2), (3) and (4)

527.   Where Clause 118 applies, the effect of subsection (2) is that the document concerned has to be taken to be accurate and complete. Subsection (3) accordingly prevents a party to the disposition requiring production of the original, while subsection (4) shields the parties to the disposition from any discrepancy between the original and the copy kept by the registrar.

528.   It may be noted that a person who suffers loss by reason of a mistake in a document kept by the registrar which is not an original and which is referred to in the register will be entitled to indemnity: see Schedule 8, paragraph 1(1)(e). See below, paragraph 736.

CLAUSE 119 — FORWARDING OF APPLICATIONS TO REGISTRAR OF COMPANIES

529.   This clause confers a power on the Lord Chancellor to make provision by rules about the transmission by the registrar to the registrar of companies of applications under—

(i)   Part 12 of the Companies Act 1985 (registration of charges); or

(ii)   Chapter 3 of Part 23 of that Act (corresponding provision for oversea companies).

530.   This provision may be explained as follows. Where a company creates a registered charge over its property, that charge will not only be registrable under the Bill, but it will also be required to be registered under the Companies Act 1985. Registration under the Companies Act 1985 fulfils an entirely different function from registration of title. It does not affect the priority of competing charges. Instead, it is intended to protect actual or

intended creditors by making it apparent on the face of the Companies Register what the liabilities of a company are. Notwithstanding the different functions of registration of title and registration in the Companies Register, it is highly desirable that it should be possible to make a combined application to the land registry to register the charge and for that application then to be forwarded to Companies House for registration in the Companies Register. Rules under paragraph 6(a) of Schedule 10 should make it possible to have a combined form of application for this purpose. Clause 119 will enable rules to make provision for the transmission of such applications from the registrar to the Companies Registrar.

531. Rules made under Clause 119 will be laid before Parliament only, but they will not be land registration rules: Clauses 125(3)and 129(1). This means that they will not be considered by the Rule Committee: cf Clause 124. There is no reason why rules concerning the transmission of information from one Government department to another should have to be considered by the Rule Committee.

Offences etc

CLAUSE 120 — SUPPRESSION OF INFORMATION

Subsection (1)

532. Clause 120 creates a new offence. A person commits an offence where, in the course of proceedings relating to registration under the Bill, he or she suppresses information with the intention of—

(i) concealing a person's right or claim; or
(ii) substantiating a false claim.

533. This offence applies in relation to any proceedings under the Bill. Thus it will include not only contentious proceedings before the court or the Adjudicator to HM Land Registry, but also any procedure under the Bill which may involve the making of some change in the register.

534. The offence under this subsection is similar, but not identical, to the offence presently found in section 115 of the Land Registration Act 1925.

Subsection (2)

535. Subsection (2) sets out the penalties for an offence committed under subsection (1).

CLAUSE 121 — IMPROPER ALTERATION OF THE REGISTERS

Subsection (1)

536. Subsection (1) creates a new offence in relation to improper alterations of the registers. A person will commit an offence if he or she dishonestly induces another—

(i) to change the register of title or the cautions register; or
(ii) to authorise the making of such a change.

537. Subsection (4) makes it clear that for these purposes a change to the register includes a change to a document referred to in it.

538. This offence is similar, but not identical, to the offence presently found in section 116 of the Land Registration Act 1925.

539. The sort of situation in which a person might (for example) commit an offence under this subsection would be where he or she deliberately makes a false statement in an application for registration.

540. With the introduction of electronic conveyancing, a person who enters into a network access agreement may be authorised to change the register: see Schedule 5, paragraph 1. However, it is likely that any changes to the register will have to be approved in advance by the registrar. The offence in subsection (1)(b) will therefore cover the case of a party to a network access agreement who dishonestly induces the land registry to agree to a particular change in the register that he or she then makes.

Subsection (2)

541. Subsection (2) creates a further offence in relation to improper alterations of the register. A person will commit an offence if he or she intentionally or recklessly makes an unauthorised change in the register of title or cautions register.

542. Again, for these purposes a change to the register includes a change to a document referred to in it: Clause 121(4).

543. The offence created by subsection (2) will in fact cover two distinct situations.

   (i)   First, where a person who is not authorised to change the register does so, knowing that he or she is not authorised to do so, or being reckless as to that fact.
   (ii)   Secondly, where a person who has authority to make a particular change to the register intentionally or recklessly makes some other change that he or she is not authorised to make.

Subsection (3)

544. Subsection (3) sets out the penalties for offences committed under Clause 121(1) or (2).

CLAUSE 122 — PRIVILEGE AGAINST SELF-INCRIMINATION

545. Clause 122 replicates the effect of section 119(2) of the Land Registration Act 1925. It provides that the privilege against self-incrimination, so far as relating to offences under the Bill, does not entitle a person to refuse to answer any question or produce any document or thing in any legal proceedings other than criminal proceedings.

546. However, subsection (2) provides that no evidence so obtained shall be admissible in any criminal proceedings under the Bill against either the person from whom it was obtained or his or her spouse.

Land registration rules

CLAUSE 123 — MISCELLANEOUS AND GENERAL POWERS

547. Clause 123 provides that Schedule 10 has effect. Schedule 10 contains a series of miscellaneous and general land registration rule-making powers. See below, paragraphs 759 and following.

CLAUSE 124 — EXERCISE OF POWERS

Subsection (1)

548. Subsection (1) provides that the power to make land registration rules is, as now, exercisable by the Lord Chancellor with the advice and assistance of a body called the Rule Committee. For the equivalent provision in the Land Registration Act 1925, see section 144. For the definition of land registration rules under the Bill, see Clause 129(1).

Subsections (2) and (3)

549. Subsections (2) and (3) deal with the composition of the Rule Committee. In this respect the Bill makes two changes.

    (i)   First, the Ministry of Agriculture Fisheries and Food will cease to be represented on the Rule Committee. In its place, the Council of Mortgage Lenders will nominate a member. This change takes account of the importance of secured lending on land which has developed since 1925.

    (ii)   Secondly, the Lord Chancellor may nominate to be a member of the Rule Committee any person who appears to him to have qualifications or experience which would be of value to the committee in considering any matter with which it is concerned.

Supplementary

CLAUSE 125 — RULES, REGULATIONS AND ORDERS

Subsection (1)

550. Subsection (1) provides that any power of the Lord Chancellor to make rules, regulations or orders under the Bill, includes power to make different provision for different cases. This power may be used, for example, in relation to fee orders: see above, paragraph 468.

Subsection (2)

551. Subsection (2) requires *all* rules, regulations or orders made under the Bill by the Lord Chancellor to be made by statutory instrument.

Subsection (3)

552. Subsection (3) provides that where a statutory instrument contains the following, it will be required to be laid before Parliament after being made—

    (i)   Land registration rules. For the definition of land registration rules, see Clause 129(1).

(ii)   Rules relating to adjudication or to the forwarding of applications to the Registrar of Companies.

(iii)   Regulations under the Bill.

(iv)   An order designating a particular office of the land registry as the proper office for the receipt of applications or a specified kind of application.

Subsection (4)

553.   Subsection (4) provides that where a statutory instrument contains the following, it will be subject to annulment in pursuance of a resolution of either House of Parliament—

(i)   Rules requiring transactions to be made in electronic form and simultaneously registered and rules concerning network access agreements.

(ii)   Any order made under the Bill other than—

(a)   an order designating a particular office of the land registry as the proper office for the receipt of applications or a specified kind of application;

(b)   a fee order prescribing fees to be paid in respect of dealings with the land registry;

(c)   a fee order prescribing fees to be paid in respect of proceedings before the Adjudicator;

(d)   an order making transitional provision in relation to the operation of the Bill;

(e)   an order bringing any provisions of the Bill into force.

CLAUSE 126 — CROWN APPLICATION

554.   Clause 126 provides that the Bill binds the Crown.

CLAUSE 127 — APPLICATION TO INTERNAL WATERS

555.   This clause defines the application of the Bill to land covered by internal waters.

556.   First, the Bill applies to land covered by internal waters which are within England or Wales: Clause 127(a). For the definition of "England" or "Wales" respectively, see Schedule 1 to the Interpretation Act 1978. As now, land registration will therefore apply to land covered by internal waters within local government administrative areas, ie the counties of England or Wales (as defined by Local Government Act 1972), Greater London and the Isles of Scilly. It may be noted that the seaward limit of a county (or other administrative area) is usually the low water mark. However, in some cases, other tidal waters are included within a county as (for example) where there is an estuary. In the case of an estuary, the county boundary is at the seaward limit of that estuary as determined by the Ordnance Survey.

557.   Secondly, the Bill applies to land covered by internal waters of the United Kingdom that are adjacent to England or Wales and which are specified by order made by the Lord Chancellor for these purposes: Clause 127(b). An order made pursuant to this provision must be made by statutory instrument which will be subject to annulment by a resolution of either House of Parliament: Clause 125(2) and (4).

558. If exercised, the power contained in Clause 127(b) will enable the Crown Estate to register its submarine land out to the baselines which define the territorial limits of the United Kingdom: see Convention on the Territorial Sea of 1958, Article 4. This, in turn, will enable it to protect such land against encroachments by adverse possessors who might (for example) lay cables or pipelines within internal waters but outside the body of a county. For the provisions of the Bill on adverse possession see Part 9 and Schedule 6. At present, the land which can be registered under the Land Registration Act 1925 is, in practice, determined by reference to local government administrative areas. Although HM Land Registry could in theory resource the registration of submarine land within a county, it would be in difficulties if land became registrable as far out as the baselines. The fact that the extension of land registration beyond county boundaries is dependent on the exercise by the Lord Chancellor of an order-making power means that extension can be phased in. It will be necessary for extension to be phased in because of the effect of extension on land registry resources.

CLAUSE 128 — "PROPRIETOR IN POSSESSION"

559. Clause 128 sets out the circumstances in which a proprietor will be regarded as being a proprietor in possession for the purposes of the Bill. The Bill employs this term in Clause 62 (Power to upgrade title) and Schedule 4 (Alteration of the register).

Subsection (1)

560. The first situation where land is in the possession of the proprietor is where the land is physically in his or her possession.

561. The second situation where land is in the possession of the proprietor is where the land is physically in the possession of a person who is entitled to be registered as proprietor. An example would be where a beneficiary under a bare trust is in physical possession of land and the registered proprietor was his or her nominee. For these purposes, Clause 128(3) makes it clear that a squatter who is entitled to apply to be registered under Schedule 6 is not regarded as a person who is entitled to be registered as proprietor.

Subsection (2)

562. The third situation in which land is in the possession of the proprietor is where the possession of a person other than the proprietor is attributed to the proprietor by virtue of one of the relationships specified in subsection (2). The effect of this provision is to attribute the possession of the second-named person to the first-named person not only where the second-named person is in physical possession, but also where he or she is *treated* as being in possession. This would, for example, cover the case where a tenant has sublet.

CLAUSE 129 — GENERAL INTERPRETATION

563. This clause sets out the definitions of those expressions which are defined generally for the purposes of the Bill.

Final provisions

CLAUSE 130 — MINOR AND CONSEQUENTIAL AMENDMENTS

564. Clause 130 provides that Schedule 11 has effect. Schedule 11 makes minor and consequential amendments. See below, paragraphs 779 and following.

CLAUSE 131 — TRANSITION

Subsection (1)

565. Subsection (1) empowers the Lord Chancellor by order to make such transitional provisions and savings as he thinks fit in connection with the coming into force of the Bill. Such an order will be made by statutory instrument and is not subject to any Parliamentary procedure: see Clause 125(2) and (4)(b).

Subsections (2) and (3)

566. Subsection (2) provides that Schedule 12 has effect. Schedule 12 contains transitional provisions and savings. See below, paragraphs 790 and following. However, subsection (3) makes it clear that nothing in Schedule 12 affects the Lord Chancellor's power by order to make transitional provisions and savings under subsection (1). Moreover, he may use that power to modify any provision of Schedule 12.

CLAUSE 132 — REPEALS

567. Clause 132 provides that Schedule 13 has effect. Schedule 13 lists repeals made to other Acts.

CLAUSE 133 — SHORT TITLE, COMMENCEMENT AND EXTENT

Subsection (2)

568. Subsection (2) provides that the Bill will come into force on such day as the Lord Chancellor may by order appoint, and different days may be appointed for different purposes. For an example of a provision which might be brought into force at a later stage, see below paragraph 702. An order made under this subsection must be made by statutory instrument, but is not subject to any Parliamentary procedure: Clause 125(2) and (4)(b).

Subsections (3) and (4)

569. Subsection (3) provides that, subject to subsection (4), the Bill applies to England and Wales only. Subsection (4) deals with the point that some of the amendments and repeals made by the Bill need to extend to other parts of the United Kingdom because the enactments amended or repealed do so (e.g. the amendments of the House of Commons Disqualification Act 1975).

SCHEDULE 1
UNREGISTERED INTERESTS WHICH OVERRIDE FIRST REGISTRATION

570. Schedule 1 lists the interests which bind the first registered proprietor even though they are not entered on the register.

571. Where a person is registered as first registered proprietor, he or she takes the estate subject to certain interests, including "interests which are the subject of an entry in the register" and "unregistered interests which fall within any of the paragraphs of Schedule 1": see Clauses 11(4)(a) and (b); 12(4)(a) and (b). Schedule 1 lists fourteen such interests. A fifteenth (a PPP lease) is listed in Clause 90, which takes effect as if it were included in Schedule 1.

572. Under the present law, section 70 of the Land Registration Act 1925 lists, without differentiating between them, those interests that override—

    (i)   first registration; and
    (ii)   registered dispositions.

The Bill distinguishes between these two categories of interest. Interests that override registered dispositions are set out separately in Schedule 3.

573. The rights set out in paragraphs 10—14 will lose their overriding status 10 years after the date on which Schedule 1 is brought into force: see Clause 115. This is in accordance with one of the aims of the Bill, which is to eliminate overriding interests so far as possible. Clause 115 is one element of that strategy.

Paragraph 1

574. Under paragraph 1 a leasehold estate granted for a term not exceeding seven years from the date of grant overrides first registration.

575. The principle that short leases (which under the present legislation means leases granted for 21 years or less) should take effect as overriding interests is currently embodied in section 70(1)(k) of the Land Registration Act 1925.

576. Paragraph 1 lists three situations in which a lease cannot override first registration even if it is granted for a term of seven years or less. In each of these situations, the grant of a lease is required to be completed by registration: Clause 4(1)(d), (e) and (f), namely—

    (i)   A reversionary lease granted to take effect in possession more than three months after the date on which it was granted. The reason for this exception is that a reversionary lease can be very difficult to discover. Under the Bill, therefore, such a lease will be required to be registered substantively. There is no equivalent to this provision under the present law.

    (ii)   A lease granted out of an unregistered legal estate under the right to buy provisions of Part 5 of the Housing Act 1985. This exception replicates part of the effect of section 154(7) of the Housing Act 1985.

    (iii)   A lease granted by a private sector landlord out of an unregistered legal estate to a person who was formerly a secure tenant and has preserved a right to buy. This exception replicates part of the effect of section 171G of, and Schedule 9A, paragraph 3 to, the Housing Act 1985.

577. Under the transitional provisions of the Bill, all leases that had overriding status under section 70(1)(k) of the Land Registration Act 1925 before the coming into force of the Bill retain their overriding status: see Schedule 12, para 12.

Paragraph 2

578. This category of unregistered interest substantially replicates the effect of section 70(1)(g) of the Land Registration Act 1925 in relation to first registration but with some significant changes.

579. The effect of sub-paragraph (1) is that, subject to one exception, an interest belonging to a person in actual occupation, so far as relating to land of which he or she is in actual occupation, overrides first registration.

580. The exception is an interest under a settlement under the Settled Land Act 1925. This exception replicates the effect of section 86(2) of the Land Registration Act 1925 which provides that such interests take effect "as minor interests and not otherwise".

581. It should be noted that where a person is in actual occupation of part of the land, his or her rights will be protected only insofar as they relate to the land of which he or she is in actual occupation. This was thought to be the law until recently: see *Ashburn Anstalt v Arnold* [1989] Ch 1, 28. However, that decision was not followed by the Court of Appeal in *Ferrishurst Ltd v Wallcite Ltd* [1999] Ch 355. The Bill reverses that latter decision: see further below, paragraph 612.

582. Sub-paragraph (2) provides some guidance as to what is meant by "actual occupation"—

 (i) First, actual occupation requires physical presence. This reflects the way in which the concept of "actual occupation" under section 70(1)(g) of the Land Registration Act 1925 has been judicially interpreted. The requirement of physical presence means that a mere legal entitlement to occupy will not suffice. For example, a person who has merely contracted to take a lease or licence of the property, but has not yet entered into possession, will not be in actual occupation. Obviously, as under the present law, what constitutes physical presence will depend upon the nature and state of the property and does not require residence.

 (ii) Secondly, the Bill confirms the view that a person will be regarded as being in actual occupation if his or her agent or employee is physically present there: cf *Lloyds Bank Plc v Rosset* [1989] Ch 350, 377, 405.

583. There are two aspects of section 70(1)(g) of the Land Registration Act 1925 which are not found in paragraph 2 of Schedule 1—

 (i) First, it does not replicate the words "save where enquiry is made of such persons and the rights are not disclosed". Subject to one exception (in relation to interests acquired under the Limitation Act 1980 of which the first registered proprietor does not have notice: see Clauses 11(4)(c), 12(4)(d)), the process of first registration does not change existing priorities. Its function is to record the state of the title at the date of registration. There is, therefore, no occasion on which any inquiry of the occupier could be made and no issue of priority to which such an inquiry would be relevant.

(ii)   Secondly, overriding status has been removed from the rights of persons who are not in actual occupation but who are in receipt of the rents and profits of the land.

Paragraph 3

584.   The effect of paragraph 3 is that a legal easement or *profit à prendre* ranks as an overriding interest on first registration.

585.   The overriding status of easements and *profits à prendre* is currently governed by section 70(1)(a) of the Land Registration Act 1925 and rule 258 of the Land Registration Rules 1925.

586.   The effect of the Bill is that an *equitable* easement will no longer rank as an overriding interest. At present, an equitable easement which is openly exercised and enjoyed by the dominant owner as appurtenant to the land will take effect as an overriding interest: *Celsteel Ltd v Alton House Holdings Ltd* [1985] 1 WLR 204. That creates an anomaly, as the following examples illustrate. In each case unregistered land is subject to an equitable easement which is openly exercised and enjoyed by the dominant owner but which has not been registered as a Class D(iii) land charge under Land Charges Act 1972, section 2(5)(iii).

(i)   In the first case, the owner voluntarily registers the land, and then makes a disposition of it to a buyer who is duly registered as proprietor. The buyer is, at present, bound by the equitable easement as an overriding interest.

(ii)   In the second case, the unregistered land is sold to a buyer who takes it free of the easement because it was not registered as a land charge: see the Land Charges Act 1972, section 4(6).

The Bill removes this anomaly. Although, in (i), the first registered proprietor remains subject to the unprotected equitable easement, any buyer from him or her will take free of it.

Paragraphs 4 and 5

587.   These paragraphs preserve the overriding status of customary and public rights. They replicate the effect of part of section 70(1)(a) of the Land Registration Act 1925.

588.   The term "customary rights" refers to ancient rights enjoyed by members of a local community or a particular defined class of such persons.

589.   The term "public rights" refers to present (not future) rights which can be exercised by any member of the public: see *Overseas Investment Services Ltd v Simcobuild Construction Ltd* (1995) 70 P & CR 322. "Public rights" include such rights as the right of passage along a highway or navigable waterway or the right to discharge into a public sewer.

Paragraph 6

590.   The effect of paragraph 6 is that a local land charge will have the status of an interest which overrides first registration. This replicates the effect of

section 70(1)(i) of the Land Registration Act 1925. It should, however, be noted that a local land charge that secures the payment of money cannot be realised until it is registered as a registered charge: see Clause 55. An interest which immediately before the coming into force of this Schedule is an overriding interest under section 70(1)(i) of the Land Registration Act 1925, and whose status was preserved by section 19(3) of the Local Land Charges Act 1975 (which is a transitional provision in relation to the change in the definition of "local land charge"), will override first registration under this Schedule: see Schedule 12, paragraph 13.

Paragraph 7

591. This paragraph replicates the effect of section 70(1)(m) of the Land Registration Act 1925 as inserted by the Coal Industry Act 1994.

Paragraphs 8 and 9

592. These paragraphs achieve the same effect as part of section 70(1)(l) of the Land Registration Act 1925.

Paragraphs 10 and 11

593. These paragraphs preserve the overriding status of franchises and manorial rights and replicate the effect of part of section 70(1)(j) of the Land Registration Act 1925.

594. The meaning of "manorial rights" is a precise one. The rights in question were listed in some detail in paragraphs 5 and 6 of Schedule 12 to the Law of Property Act 1922. Those provisions have since been repealed, but it may be taken that the list found in Schedule 12 to the 1922 Act was a comprehensive statement of these rights. The rights include—

(i)   the lord's sporting rights;
(ii)   the lord's or tenant's rights to mines and minerals;
(iii)   the lord's right to fairs and markets;
(iv)   the tenant's rights of common; and
(v)   the lord's or tenant's liability for the construction, maintenance, and repair of dykes, ditches, canals and other works.

Paragraph 12

595. This paragraph replicates the effect of part of section 70(1)(b) of the Land Registration Act 1925.

Paragraph 13

596. This paragraph replicates the effect of section 70(1)(d) of the Land Registration Act 1925 in preserving the overriding status of non-statutory rights in respect of embankments and sea and river walls. This form of liability is one which falls on a person whose property fronts the sea or a river and which has arisen by prescription, grant, a covenant supported by a rentcharge, custom or tenure.

Paragraph 14

597. This paragraph replicates the effect of part of section 70(1)(e) of the Land Registration Act 1925. The other interests set out in section 70(1)(e) are not included in paragraph 14 because they are now obsolete.

Schedule 2
Registrable Dispositions:
Registration Requirements

598. Schedule 2 sets out the registration requirements for those cases where a disposition of a registered estate or charge has to be completed by registration. Schedule 2 has already been considered in the context of Clause 27 which sets out those dispositions which are required to be completed by registration: see above, paragraphs 125 and following.

Schedule 3
Unregistered Interests Which
Override Registered Dispositions

599. Schedule 3 lists those interests which will bind the disponee of a registered estate or charge for valuable consideration, even though they are not protected by an entry on the register.

600. By virtue of Clauses 29(2)(a)(ii) and 30(2)(a)(ii), a registered disposition for valuable consideration of a registered estate or a registered charge takes subject to those interests affecting the estate or charge that are listed in Schedule 3. Schedule 3 lists fourteen such interests. A fifteenth (a PPP lease) is found in Clause 90, which takes effect as if it were included in Schedule 3.

601. As has been explained in paragraph 572, above—

   (i)   section 70 of the Land Registration Act 1925, which contains a list of those interests that are overriding under the present law, does not differentiate between interests that override first registration and those that override a registered disposition; but

   (ii)   the Bill distinguishes between these two categories of interest.

   Interests that override first registration are set out separately in Schedule 1 and have already been explained.

602. The rights set out in paragraphs 10—14 will lose their overriding status 10 years after the date on which the Schedule is brought into force: see Clause 115.

Paragraph 1

603. Under this paragraph, a leasehold estate granted for a term not exceeding seven years from the date of grant, overrides a registered disposition.

604. The principle that short leases (which under the present legislation means leases granted for 21 years or less) should take effect as overriding interests is currently embodied in section 70(1)(k) of the Land Registration Act 1925.

605. There are two exceptions to the general principle that a short lease will override a registered disposition.

606. The first exception (paragraph 1(a)) covers three situations where a lease granted out of an *unregistered* legal estate is required to be completed by registration: see Clause 4(1)(d), (e) and(f), namely—

(i)   A reversionary lease granted out of an unregistered legal estate to take effect in possession more than three months after the date on which it was granted. The reason for this exception is that a reversionary lease can be very difficult to discover. There is no equivalent to this provision under the current law.

(ii)   A lease granted out of an unregistered legal estate under the right to buy provisions of Part 5 of the Housing Act 1985. This exception replicates part of the effect of section 154(7) of the Housing Act 1985.

(iii) A lease granted by a private sector landlord out of an unregistered legal estate to a person who was formerly a secure tenant and has preserved a right to buy. This exception replicates part of the effect of section 171G of, and Schedule 9A, paragraph 3 to, the Housing Act 1985.

607. The second exception covers five cases where a lease granted out of a *registered* legal estate or charge constitutes a registrable disposition that must be completed by registration: see Clause 27(1), (2)(b) and(c). They are as follows—

(i)   A reversionary lease granted to take effect in possession more than three months after the date of the grant of the lease. There is no equivalent to this exception under the current law.

(ii)   A lease under which the right to possession is discontinuous, such as a timeshare lease. There is no equivalent to this exception under the present law because there is no requirement to register such leases under the Land Registration Act 1925.

(iii) A lease granted in pursuance of the right to buy provisions of Part 5 of the Housing Act 1985. This exception replicates part of the effect of section 154(7) of the Housing Act 1985.

(iv)   A lease granted by a private sector landlord to a person who was formerly a secure tenant and has preserved a right to buy. This exception replicates part of the effect of section 171G of, and Schedule 9A, paragraph 3 to, the Housing Act 1985.

(v)   A lease of a franchise or manor. Again, there is no equivalent to this exception under the present law because there is no requirement to register such leases under the Land Registration Act 1925.

608. Under the transitional provisions of the Bill, all leases that had overriding status under section 70(1)(k) of the Land Registration Act 1925 before the coming into force of the Bill retain their overriding status: see Schedule 12, paragraph 12.

Paragraph 3

609. This category of interest substantially replicates the effect of section 70(1)(g) of the Land Registration Act 1925 in relation to registered dispositions but with some significant changes.

610. The effect of sub-paragraph (1) is that, subject to four exceptions, an interest belonging to a person in actual occupation, so far as relating to land of which he or she is in actual occupation, overrides a registered disposition.

611. Sub-paragraph (2) makes it clear that a person is to be regarded as in actual occupation if he or she, or his or her agent or employee is physically present there. It has already been explained in relation to Schedule 1 that this restates the present law: see above, paragraph 582.

612. Under paragraph 2, where a person is in actual occupation of part of the land, his or her rights will be protected only insofar as they relate to the land of which he or she is in actual occupation. The effect of this provision is to reverse the effect of *Ferrishurst Ltd v Wallcite Ltd* [1999] Ch 355. The provision will restrict the inquiries that a buyer of registered land will have to make. As a result of the *Ferrishurst* case they are, paradoxically, greater in relation to registered land than where the title is unregistered. This limitation of the scope of inquiries is in line with the general policy of the Bill, which is to bring about faster and simpler conveyancing. It will encourage those who have rights in land to register them.

613. There are four situations in which a person's rights will not override a registered disposition even if he or she is in actual occupation of the land to which the rights relate. They are as follows.

614. The first (paragraph 2(1)(a)) is an interest under a settlement under the Settled Land Act 1925. As explained above, this replicates the present law: see paragraph 580.

615. The second exception (paragraph 2(1)(b)) is a reformulation of one that presently applies under section 70(1)(g) of the Land Registration Act 1925. An interest of a person of whom inquiry was made before the disposition and who failed to disclose the right when he or she could reasonably have been expected to do so will not be protected as an overriding interest by virtue of his or her actual occupation.

616. The third exception (paragraph 2(1)(c)) is new. It is designed to protect buyers and other registered disponees for valuable consideration in cases where the fact of occupation is neither subjectively known to them nor readily ascertainable. Under this exception, the priority of an interest will not be protected by virtue of a person's actual occupation where—

(i)   it belongs to a person whose occupation would not have been obvious on a reasonably careful inspection of the land at the time of the disposition; and

(ii)   the person to whom the disposition is made does not have actual knowledge of it at that time.

617. The following points should be noted about the third exception—

(i)   For the purposes of the exception, it is not the *interest* that has to be apparent (as in relation to contracts for the sale of land), but the *occupation* of the person having the interest.

(ii)   The test is not one of constructive notice of the occupation. It is the less demanding one (derived from the test as to which encumbrances a seller has to disclose to an intending buyer of land) that it should be obvious on a reasonably careful inspection of the land.

(iii)   Even if a person's occupation is not apparent, the exception will not apply where a buyer has actual knowledge of that occupation.

618. The fourth exception (paragraph 2(1)(d)) is where a leasehold estate is granted to take effect in possession more than three months from the date of

the grant and has not taken effect in possession at the time of the disposition. This exception is a corollary to the provision of the Bill that requires such leases to be registered: see Clause 4(1)(d). This exception is not likely to occur very often. It would only be relevant where—

(i)   a reversionary lease had been granted to take effect in possession more than three months after the date of the grant but had not been registered; and

(ii)   the grantee was in actual occupation of the land to which the lease related, but at a time when the lease has necessarily not taken effect in possession.

619. Paragraph 2 removes the overriding status of the rights of persons who are not in actual occupation but who are in receipt of the rents and profits of the land. The transitional provisions in relation to this change are as follows. Where a person is not in actual occupation, but in receipt of rents and profits, he or she will have the benefit of the transitional provision contained in Schedule 3, paragraph 2A(1) inserted by Schedule 12, paragraph 8. However, that interest will cease to be overriding for these purposes, if at any time thereafter the person having the interest ceases to be in receipt of the rents and profits: see Schedule 3, paragraph 2A(2).

Paragraph 3

620. The effect of paragraph 3 is that, subject to one exception, a legal easement or *profit à prendre* will override a registered disposition.

621. The overriding status of easements and *profits à prendre* is currently governed by section 70(1)(a) of the Land Registration Act 1925 and rule 258 of the Land Registration Rules 1925.

622. Under the Bill, only a *legal* easement or *profit à prendre* will override a registered disposition. It follows that where an easement or profit is expressly granted or reserved out of registered land it will never be an overriding interest. This is because the grant or reservation of such a right is a registrable disposition and will not take effect at law until so registered: Clause 27(1), (2)(d). Once a notice has been entered in the register in respect of an easement it cannot fall within Schedule 3: see Clauses 29(3), 30(3).

623. The exception operates to exclude certain categories of legal easements and profits from those that can be overriding. Its effect may be summarised as follows. Any person who acquires an interest for valuable consideration under a registered disposition will only be bound by a legal easement or profit if—

(i)   it is registered under the Commons Registration Act 1965;
(ii)   he or she actually knows of it;
(iii)   it is patent: in other words, it is obvious on a reasonably careful inspection of the land over which the easement or profit is exercisable, so that no seller of land would be obliged to disclose it; or
(iv)   it has been exercised in the period of one year ending on the day of the disposition.

624. The fourth case is important and will cover, in particular, "invisible" easements such as rights of drainage or the right to run a water supply over a neighbour's land. These rights have often existed for many years, but

because they were commonly not the subject of any express arrangement between the parties are not recorded on the register.

625. The exception is likely to encourage a straightforward system of standard inquiries in relation to easements and profits that will prompt sellers to disclose what they can reasonably be expected to know. This in turn will help to ensure that such rights are disclosed to the registrar by virtue of rules made pursuant to Clause 71. The rights will then be entered in the register.

626. For the transitional provisions in relation to this category of overriding interests, see Schedule 12, paragraphs 9 and 10. The effect of those two paragraphs is as follows—

(i)   an easement or *profit à prendre* that was an overriding interest in relation to a registered estate immediately before the coming into force of Schedule 3 remains an overriding interest, even though it would not fall within paragraph 3 of Schedule 3; and

(ii)   the exception in Schedule 3, paragraph 3(1) will not apply for three years after the coming into force of that Schedule.

Paragraphs 4—14

627. The interests set out in paragraphs 4—14 are identical to those that were considered in relation to paragraphs 4—14 of Schedule 1 and the same considerations apply: see above, paragraphs 587—597.

SCHEDULE 4
ALTERATION OF THE REGISTER

628. Schedule 4 makes provision for alteration of the register of title. It differs significantly in form from the present provisions found in section 82 of the Land Registration Act 1925. It is intended to achieve two objectives. The first is to make a number of changes to the present law in order to improve its working. The second is to recast the legislation so that it reflects the practice of rectification as it has developed under section 82.

Paragraph 1

629. The basic concept which the Bill employs is that of *alteration* of the register. Paragraph 1 defines "rectification" and makes it clear that it is just one form of alteration, namely one which involves the correction of a mistake and prejudicially affects the title of a registered proprietor. Where an alteration amounts to rectification special considerations apply under the Bill.

Paragraph 2

630. Paragraph 2(1) sets out the three circumstances in which a court may make an order for alteration of the register.

   (i) The first is for the purposes of correcting a mistake. For example, if X has forged Y's signature on a certificate of transfer and has been registered as the proprietor of Whiteacre, the court could make an order for Y to be reinstated as registered proprietor.

   (ii) The second is for the purpose of bringing the register up to date. For example, if a court ordered the forfeiture of a registered leasehold title for breach of covenant, it should also order that the title to the lease be deleted from the register.

   (iii) The third is to give effect to any estate or interest excepted from the effect of registration: compare Clauses 11(6), (7), 12(6)—(8), 29(2)(a)(iii) and 30(2)(a)(iii). An example would be where Blackacre is registered with a possessory freehold title on the basis of the first registered proprietor's adverse possession. It subsequently transpires that the estate against which she adversely possessed was not in fact freehold but leasehold. The court may order that the registered title be altered from freehold to leasehold.

631. The Lord Chancellor has a power under paragraph 4 to make rules to specify circumstances in which the court will be required to exercise its power to make an order for the register to be altered in cases that do not involve rectification. Such rules are likely to impose a *duty* on the court to make an order for alteration where it has made a determination in proceedings. They are unlikely to *require* the court to make an order where it incidentally discovers in the course of proceedings that some entry on the register is incorrect.

632. The effect of paragraph 2(2) is that where a court makes an order for the register to be altered, the registrar will be under a duty to give effect to that order once it has been served on him. The Lord Chancellor has a power under paragraph 4 to make rules as to the form of the court's order and as to its service on the registrar.

Paragraph 3

633. Paragraph 3(2) restricts the circumstances in which it is possible for a court to make an order for alteration of the register that affects the title of a proprietor of a registered estate in land who is in possession. Paragraph 3(1) makes it clear that this restriction applies only where alteration of the register amounts to rectification. In the absence of the proprietor's consent, such alteration will only be possible in two cases. Those are—

(i)   where the proprietor has by fraud or lack of proper care caused or substantially contributed to the mistake; or

(ii)   where it would for any other reason be unjust for the alteration not to be made.

These two exceptions achieve the same effect as section 82(3)(a) and (c) of the Land Registration Act 1925 respectively. Paragraph 3(2) must be read in conjunction with Clause 128 which sets out the circumstances in which a proprietor will be regarded as being a "proprietor who is in possession" for the purposes of the Bill (compare Clause 62(4), (5)). The title to a registered estate in land includes the benefit of any registered estate, such as an easement, that subsists for the benefit of that title: paragraph 3(4).

634. Paragraph 3(3) requires the court to make an order for rectification of the register in all cases where it is able to so, "unless it considers that there are exceptional circumstances which justify its not doing so".

Paragraph 5

635. Paragraph 5(1) sets out circumstances in which the registrar may alter the register. The first three circumstances are identical to those in which the court may order alteration of the register under paragraph 2(1). The registrar will also be able to alter the register for the purpose of removing a superfluous entry. This would, for example, enable him to remove an entry on the register that protected an interest that was adequately protected by another entry. Where there is an application for an alteration to the register that would, if made, amount to rectification within paragraph 1 of Schedule 4, the registrar must refer that application to the Adjudicator to HM Land Registry if the proprietor objects to it. This reference is under the general provisions of the Bill about objections to applications: see Clauses 73 and 106. Rectification by the registrar other than with the consent of the proprietor will, therefore, always be a matter for the Adjudicator.

Paragraph 6

636. Paragraph 6(2) restricts the circumstances in which the register may be rectified against the proprietor of a registered estate who is in possession of land. The same considerations apply under this paragraph as apply under paragraph 3(2) in proceedings before the court: see above, paragraphs 633 and 634.

Paragraph 7

637. Paragraph 7 contains a power for the Lord Chancellor to make rules regulating alteration of the register.

638. Paragraph 7(a) gives the power to specify when the registrar is under *a duty* to alter the register other than in cases of rectification. It is likely that the registrar will be under a duty to alter the register in all cases where he

569

discovers grounds for doing so regardless of the circumstances in which those grounds came to light.

639. Paragraph 7(b)—(d) enables rules to be made dealing with the manner in which the registrar should exercise the power of alteration, applications for alteration of the register and the procedure for exercising the power of alteration whether on application or otherwise.

Paragraph 8

640. Paragraph 8 makes it clear that rectification of the register can affect derivative interests but that any such changes are prospective only. This reflects the position under the current law: see Land Registration Act 1925, section 82(2).

Paragraph 9

641. Paragraph 9 contains provisions for the payment of costs where the register is altered and the case is not one of rectification.

642. Paragraph 9(1) enables the registrar to pay such amount as he thinks fit in respect of any costs or expenses reasonably incurred in connection with alteration. Where the costs or expenses were incurred with his consent the registrar may always exercise this power.

643. Even if the registrar did not give his prior consent, by virtue of paragraph 9(2), he may nevertheless pay costs and expenses where—

(i)   it appears to him that they had to be incurred urgently or that it was not reasonably practicable to apply for his consent in advance; and

(ii)   he has subsequently approved the incurring of them.

644. The power contained in paragraph 9 is new and remedies a deficiency in the present law. There is currently no power to pay a party's costs in relation to an alteration that does not amount to rectification of the register. The sort of case in which the power may be exercised is where it appears that there may be a reason to alter the register and an interested party incurs expenses in making investigations into the matter.

SCHEDULE 5
LAND REGISTRY NETWORK

645. Schedule 5 makes detailed provision in relation to the land registry network that may be provided under Clause 92. In particular, it makes provision for access to the land registry network by persons other than the registrar and land registry staff. This marks a fundamental change in the current practice of registered conveyancing. Instead of the registrar registering dispositions on application, with the introduction of electronic conveyancing, solicitors and licensed conveyancers will register dispositions at the same time as they are made. In this way it will be possible to ensure that when a transaction is made it is simultaneously registered: cf Clause 93

Paragraph 1

646. Paragraph 1(1) provides that a person who is not a member of the land registry will only have access to a land registry network if he or she is authorised by means of an agreement with the registrar. A network access agreement of this kind will normally be a contract and enforceable as one. The only such agreements that will not be contracts will be those where the other party to be given access is some other manifestation of the Crown, such as the Treasury Solicitor or the Crown Estate. This is because the Crown is one and indivisible and cannot, therefore, contract with itself.

647. Paragraph 1(2) sets out the purposes for which the agreement may authorise access. It permits the level of access to be varied according to the purposes for which it is required. For example, a solicitor or licensed conveyancer who is authorised to conduct electronic conveyancing might be granted access for all or most of the purposes listed in paragraph 1(2). In contrast an estate agent might only be authorised to have access for the first of them and a mortgage lender might have access for, say, the first three, and then only in relation to a charge in its favour.

648. Paragraph 1(3) provides that rules may regulate the use of network access agreements to confer authority to carry out functions of the registrar. Many of the purposes for which access is authorised under paragraph 1(2) will be functions of the registrar. Paragraph 1(3) makes it clear that a solicitor or licensed conveyancer who is appropriately authorised for one of the purposes listed in paragraph 1(2) will, within the limits of that authority, be able to carry out the functions that are conferred by the Bill on the registrar. For example, a solicitor or licensed conveyancer who has authority to do so will be able to perform the registrar's function of registering dispositions and making other entries in the register. Likewise, he or she will be able to carry out the registrar's function of issuing official search certificates or official copies.

649. Paragraph 1(4) provides that the registrar *must*, on application, enter into a network access agreement with an applicant if the applicant meets such criteria as rules may provide. For appeals by a person aggrieved by the registrar's decision with respect to entry into a network access agreement, see paragraph 4: below, paragraphs 665 and following.

650. The power to make rules under paragraph 1 will be exercisable by the Lord Chancellor: see paragraph 11(1). Before making such rules, he must consult such persons as he considers appropriate: see paragraph 11(2). Paragraph 11(3) specifies certain matters to which the Lord Chancellor must have regard in making such rules. Such rules will be made by statutory

instrument which is subject to annulment in pursuance of a resolution of either House of Parliament: see Clause 125(4).

Paragraph 2

651. Paragraph 2(1) sets out the general principle that the terms on which access to the land registry network is authorised will be such as the registrar thinks fit, and may, in particular, include charges for access. That principle is, however, qualified by paragraph 2(3) and (4): see below, paragraphs 656 and 657.

652. By virtue of paragraph 2(2), the power to authorise access to the land registry network on terms may be used not only for regulating the use of that network, but also for three other purposes.

653. First, the terms may require that the person granted access should *have* to use the network to carry on such qualifying transactions as may be specified in the agreement: paragraph 2(2)(a). The term "qualifying transaction" is defined in paragraph 12 as meaning a transaction which involves registration and is capable of being effected electronically. By this means, the registrar can ensure that those who use the network carry out all (or all specified) registrable transactions electronically. This may be used to ensure the speedy transition from a paper-based system of conveyancing to an electronic one. As such, it complements Clause 93, which contains the power to require dispositions to be made electronically, but which is unlikely to be used until electronic conveyancing has become the norm.

654. Secondly, the terms on which a person is granted access may include such other purpose relating to the carrying on of qualifying transactions as rules may provide: paragraph 2(2)(b). For the meaning of a "qualifying transaction", see paragraph 12: above, paragraph 653. This power might be used for a variety of purposes, such as to require the person authorised to issue land certificates or official copies to do so when requested.

655. Thirdly, the terms may be used to enable network transactions to be monitored: paragraph 2(2)(c). This provision should be read in conjunction with paragraph 9 of the Schedule, which makes provision for the monitoring of network transactions: see below, paragraphs 678 and following. In relation to a transaction that was part of a chain, the terms of the network access agreement might, for example, require the solicitor or licensed conveyancer to provide the registrar with information, such as the following, as soon as it became available—

(i)   that his or her client was proposing to enter into a transaction that appeared to be part of a chain;
(ii)   that he or she had performed a specified conveyancing step, such as having completed local searches or that his or her client had received a mortgage offer.

656. Paragraph 2(3) provides that where a person is authorised by a network access agreement to carry on qualifying transactions it will be a condition of that agreement that he or she will comply with rules for the time being in force under paragraph 5. The term "qualifying transaction" is defined in paragraph 12: above, paragraph 653.

657. Paragraph 2(4) enables rules to regulate the terms on which access to a land registry network is authorised. It is likely that rules will specify terms that

should be included in any network access agreement and that these will vary according to the level of access granted.

658. Rules made under paragraph 2 are required to be made by statutory instrument, which is subject to annulment in pursuance of a resolution of either House of Parliament: Clause 125(4). Before the Lord Chancellor makes such rules, he must consult such persons as he considers appropriate: see paragraph 11(2).

Paragraph 3

659. Paragraph 3 makes provision for the termination of network access agreements.

660. Paragraph 3(1) makes provision for the termination of a network access agreement on notice to the registrar by a person who has been granted access under such an agreement.

661. Paragraph 3(2) enables rules to be made governing the circumstances in which the registrar may terminate a network access agreement. These rules may, in particular make provision about three matters. As regards the first of these, the grounds of termination, the Lord Chancellor is required to have regard to the three matters listed in paragraph 11(3) in making any such rules. Furthermore, paragraph 3(3) provides that rules made under paragraph 3(2)(a) may, in particular, authorise the registrar to terminate a network access agreement in the circumstances there listed. One effect of paragraph 3(3) is that a person who has been granted access must comply with the conditions of access as they stand *at any given time* and not merely at the time when the network access agreement was first made. If he or she fails to do so, he or she is liable to have his or her access withdrawn.

662. To ensure both transparency and fairness, paragraph 3(2)(b) authorises rules to be made about the procedure to be followed in relation to termination by the registrar. By virtue of paragraph 3(2)(c), rules may also provide for the suspension of termination pending an appeal to the Adjudicator from the registrar's decision.

663. Rules made under paragraph 3 are required to be made by statutory instrument, which is subject to annulment in pursuance of a resolution of either House of Parliament: Clause 125(4). Before the Lord Chancellor makes such rules, he must consult such persons as he considers appropriate: see paragraph 11(2).

664. Termination of a network access agreement is likely to be a remedy of last resort. Because network access agreements will usually be contractual (see above, paragraph 646), the registrar may have contractual remedies short of termination available to him.

Paragraph 4

665. The termination of a network access agreement by the registrar or a refusal by him to enter into such an agreement has potentially very serious consequences. The Bill therefore provides for a right of appeal to the Adjudicator by any person aggrieved by a decision of the registrar either with respect to entry into, or termination of, a network access agreement: see paragraph 4(1).

666. This right of appeal is unique in the Bill, because it is the only matter on which there is a right of appeal to the Adjudicator from a decision of the registrar: see Clause 106(1). But for this right of appeal, the only way of challenging the registrar would have been by judicial review. An appeal to the Adjudicator will not only be much cheaper and less formal than proceedings for judicial review, but it will also be a full appeal from, and not merely a review of, the decision of the registrar. However, contrary to the general rule, an appeal will lie from the Adjudicator's decision to the High Court only on a point of law and not on a point of fact: see Clause 109(2).

667. There is a power under paragraph 4(2) for the Adjudicator to give directions as to how any determination which he makes is to be carried out.

668. Paragraph 4(3) enables rules to make provision about appeals. The rules that may be made under paragraph 4(3) will be land registration rules: see Clause 129(1). As such they will be required to be made by statutory instrument to be laid before Parliament only: Clause 125(2), (3).

Paragraph 5

669. Network transaction rules under paragraph 5 will be the technical rules which specify how electronic conveyancing is to be conducted. Paragraph 5(1) enables the Lord Chancellor to make provision by such rules "about how to go about network transactions". Paragraph 5(2) stipulates that these rules may, in particular, make provision about dealings with the registry, including provision about the procedure to be followed and the supply of information. The rules are likely to require an authorised solicitor or licensed conveyancer to provide specified information about any dealing and, in particular, about unregistered interests. Rules may also be used to ensure the disclosure of information that the registered proprietor would be reluctant to reveal, such as that a right to determine a registered estate in land has become exercisable: see Clause 64.

670. Rules under paragraph 5(1) may further require that, when a disposition or contract is made, it is simultaneously registered. Although Clause 93 contains the power to make simultaneous registration compulsory, the network transaction rules will be another means of achieving this aim in advance of the exercise of that power. It should be noted, however, that the effect of failure to observe a requirement about simultaneous disposition and registration imposed by rules under paragraph 5 is not the same as the effect of failure to observe such a requirement under Clause 93. Clause 93 prevents the disposition having any effect. If a solicitor or licensed conveyancer failed to observe rules under paragraph 5, he or she would be in breach of the terms of his or her network access agreement. However, that breach would not effect the validity of the disposition.

671. Rules made under paragraph 5 will be land registration rules: see Clause 129(1). As such they will be required to be made by statutory instrument and laid before Parliament only: Clause 125(2) and (3).

Paragraph 6

672. To the extent that an obligation owed by an authorised person conflicts with his or her obligations not owed under a network access agreement, paragraph 6 provides that the obligation not owed under the network agreement is discharged. This provision covers the kind of situation where, say, a solicitor or licensed conveyancer has entered into a network access

agreement, and finds herself in a position where she is required to act contrary to the wishes of her client. For example—

   (i)   she might have to register an unregistered interest affecting the property that her client is purchasing which he would prefer to keep off the title; or

   (ii)   she might have to disclose under paragraph 2(2) of Schedule 5 that she is acting in a transaction which involves registration and is capable of being effected electronically notwithstanding the duty of confidentiality which she might otherwise owe to her client.

673. In such situations a solicitor or licensed conveyancer will have an overriding duty to fulfil his or her obligation under the network access agreement and will incur no liability to his or her client by so doing.

Paragraph 7

674. If there is a land registry network, paragraph 7(1) imposes a duty on the registrar to provide such assistance as he thinks appropriate for the purpose of enabling persons engaged in qualifying transactions who wish to do their own conveyancing to do so by means of the network. For the meaning of "qualifying transaction", see paragraph 12: above paragraph 653. This will enable persons who conduct their own conveyancing to take advantage of the new scheme. It is envisaged that the registrar will carry out the necessary transactions in electronic form on the instructions of the person who is undertaking his or her own conveyancing. That person will be required to pay an appropriate fee for this service.

675. Paragraph 7(2) makes it clear that the registrar's duty to provide assistance for "do-it-yourself" conveyancers does not extend to the provision of legal advice.

Paragraph 8

676. It is probable that, at least when electronic conveyancing is first introduced, solicitors and licensed conveyancers will authenticate documents electronically on behalf of their clients. If the requirements of paragraph 8(a) and (b) are met, an agent authorised under a network access agreement will, in favour of the other party, be deemed to be acting under the authority of his or her principal.

677. If it were not for paragraph 8, a solicitor or authorised conveyancer acting for one party would be entitled to see written authority from the other party to his or her solicitor or licensed conveyancer and *vice versa*. This is because a solicitor (and therefore, presumably, a licensed conveyancer) has no *implied* authority to sign a contract for the sale or purchase of an interest in land on behalf of his or her client: *Smith v Webster* (1876) 3 ChD 49; *H Clark Doncaster Ltd v Wilkinson* [1965] Ch 694, 702. He or she can only conclude such a contract if he or she has *actual* authority. By applying a presumption of authority, paragraph 8 ensures that paper-based written authorities do not have to be exchanged before contracts can be concluded electronically. However, it is intended that, under the network transaction rules made under paragraph 5, there will be a standard form of authority which a practitioner will be required to use to obtain his or her client's agreement where that practitioner is to execute an electronic instrument as agent for that client.

Paragraph 9

678. Paragraph 9 makes provision for the management of network transactions. It forms part of the machinery of the Bill that is particularly designed to expedite chains of domestic sales and to reduce the risk of any break in them.

679. Paragraph 9(1) provides that the registrar may use monitoring information for the purpose of managing network transactions. In particular, he may disclose such information to persons authorised to use the network, and authorise the further disclosure of that information if he considers it necessary or desirable to do so. By paragraph 9(2), the registrar may delegate these functions subject to such conditions as he thinks fit. The monitoring information referred to in this paragraph is the information provided in pursuance of provision in a network access agreement included under paragraph 2(2)(c) of Schedule 5 (above, paragraph 655): paragraph 9(3).

680. It is envisaged that the sort of information that paragraph 9 will enable the registrar (or his delegate as "chain manager") to disclose will be the state of progress of transactions in a chain to other parties in that chain. Although the "chain manager" will not have any direct coercive powers, he or she will be able to identify the link in the chain that is causing the delay. He or she will then be able to encourage that party to proceed with due despatch.

Paragraph 10

681. As a means of assisting those who have entered into network access agreements to continue to meet the requirements of such agreements, paragraph 10 empowers the registrar to provide education and training in relation to the use of a land registry network. It is likely that this will include on-line training and education programmes. Indeed, continued participation in such programmes is likely to be a condition of a network access agreement: cf paragraph 2(4).

Paragraph 11

682. Paragraph 11 relates to rules made under paragraphs 1—3. These rules are not land registration rules and they are subject to a higher level of scrutiny in that—

(i) before making the relevant rules, the Lord Chancellor must consult such persons as he considers appropriate: see paragraph 11(2); and

(ii) they are subject to annulment in pursuance of a resolution of either House of Parliament: Clause 125(4). In contrast, land registration rules merely have to be laid before Parliament: Clause 125(3).

SCHEDULE 6
REGISTRATION OF ADVERSE POSSESSOR

683. Schedule 6 contains provisions concerning the registration of adverse possessors. These provisions represent a major departure from the present law and the thinking behind them has already been explained: see above, paragraph 432.

Paragraph 1

684. Paragraph 1(1) sets out the basic principle that a person may apply to be registered as the proprietor of a registered estate in land if he or she has been in adverse possession of that estate for the period of ten years ending on the date of the application. There is a specific power to make rules about the procedure to be followed pursuant to an application under Schedule 6: see paragraph 15. Any such rules will be land registration rules: Clause 129(1). They will be made by statutory instrument to be laid before Parliament only: Clause 125(2) and (3).

685. Adverse possession is defined in paragraph 11 (see below, paragraph 717). In general, adverse possession has the same meaning as it does for the purposes of section 15 of the Limitation Act 1980: see paragraph 11(1). This means that, for example, neither a trustee nor a beneficiary will ever be able to apply to be registered as proprietor of trust land by reason of his possession of that land. A trustee of a trust of land cannot be in adverse possession against a beneficiary, nor can a beneficiary be in adverse possession against the trustee(s) or any other beneficiary.

686. Paragraph 1(2) deals with the situation where a person who has a right to apply to be registered as proprietor under paragraph 1(1) is then evicted, other than pursuant to a judgment for possession, by the registered proprietor or a person claiming under that proprietor (such as a registered chargee). In those circumstances, the ejected squatter may, notwithstanding his or her ejection, apply to be registered within six months. Were it not for this provision, it would be more advantageous for a registered proprietor (or registered chargee) to terminate a squatter's adverse possession by re-entering rather than by seeking a court order for possession. The Bill seeks to ensure that, whether a squatter applies to be registered, is ejected at a time when he or she could have applied to be registered, or is a defendant to possession proceedings, the outcome is the same. See too paragraph 703 below.

687. Paragraph 1(3) precludes an application to register by a squatter who is a defendant in possession proceedings or against whom a judgment for possession has been given within the last two years. Cf Clause 97(2) and above paragraph 445.

688. Paragraph 1(4) provides that a person may apply to be registered as the proprietor of a registered estate even though the estate was not registered throughout the period of adverse possession. For example, if a squatter goes into adverse possession when the title to an estate is unregistered, but four years later the owner voluntarily registers it, the squatter may apply to be registered after a further six years of adverse possession. In one specific set of circumstances, however, an application will not be successful unless the estate to which it relates was registered for more than one year prior to the date of the application: see paragraph 5(4)(d). See below, paragraph 700.

689. Paragraph 2(1) provides that where a person makes an application to be registered under paragraph 1, the registrar must give notice of that application to the persons listed. As regards paragraph 2(1)(b), for the effect of the registration of an adverse possessor on chargees, see paragraph 9 (below, paragraph 710). Paragraph 2(1)(d) is likely to encompass those persons who can satisfy the registrar that they have some right or interest in land that would be prejudicially affected if the squatter's application were successful. Examples might include an equitable chargee or someone entitled to the benefit of a rentcharge. As regards paragraph 2(1)(e), there may be certain categories of body or other person who should be notified of the squatter's application to be registered as proprietor even though they have not registered any interest under the previous paragraph. This category might, for example, include the Charity Commission in relation to land held upon charitable trusts, or a trustee in bankruptcy in relation to a bankrupt.

690. Rules made under paragraph 2(1)(d) and (e) will be land registration rules: Clause 129(1). They will be made by statutory instrument to be laid before Parliament only: Clause 125(2) and (3).

691. The effect of paragraph 2(2) is that the notice served under sub-paragraph (1) must inform the recipient that if an application for registration is not required by him or her to be dealt with under paragraph 5, the applicant is entitled to be registered as proprietor.

Paragraph 3

692. Where a notice has been served on a person under paragraph 2, he or she may serve a counter-notice on the registrar requiring him to deal with the application under paragraph 5. The notice must be served within the time prescribed by rules. The period is likely to be three months initially. However, that period may be reviewed once there has been some experience of how the procedure works in practice. Rules made under paragraph 3(2) will be land registration rules: Clause 129(1). They will be made by statutory instrument to be laid before Parliament only: Clause 125(2) and (3).

Paragraph 4

693. Where notice is served by the registrar and no counter-notice is served on him within the time prescribed, paragraph 4 requires the registrar to approve the squatter's application and to register him or her in place of the existing proprietor.

Paragraph 5

694. If, but only if, a squatter can establish any one of the three conditions set out in paragraph 5, the registrar must approve his or her application and register the applicant as proprietor notwithstanding that he has received a counter-notice from a person who was notified of the squatter's application: paragraph 5(1). If there is a dispute as to whether the squatter is entitled to be registered then, unless it can be disposed of by agreement, the matter will be referred by the registrar to the Adjudicator for resolution: see Clauses 73(1) and (7); 106(1)(a). It is anticipated that, in practice, most such cases will be referred to the Adjudicator.

695. The first condition is set out in paragraph 5(2). Its effect is to state in statutory form the equitable principle of proprietary estoppel. To succeed, the applicant will have to show that an equity has arisen in his or her favour, because—

    (i)   the registered proprietor encouraged or allowed him or her to believe that he or she owned the parcel of land in question;

    (ii)   in this belief, the applicant acted to his or her detriment to the knowledge of the registered proprietor; and

    (iii)   it would be unconscionable for the proprietor to deny him or her the rights which he or she believed that he or she had.

696. When granting relief on the basis of proprietary estoppel, a court will ascertain the minimum equity necessary to do justice to the claimant, and it has a wide discretion as to what order it should make. This principle is applied by the Bill. By Clause 108(4), where the Adjudicator determines that an equity has arisen but that the circumstances are not such that the applicant ought to be registered as proprietor, he must determine how effect should be given to it. For that purpose, he is empowered to make any order that could be made by the High Court in exercise of its equitable jurisdiction. He might, for example, order the registered proprietor to grant the applicant an easement over the land or to pay him monetary compensation. For analogous provision governing the situation where an appeal is made to the High Court from the Adjudicator's decision in such cases of proprietary estoppel, see Clause 109(3).

697. The following examples illustrate the type of case where the first condition may be in issue.

    (i)   X has built on a plot of land in the mistaken belief that she is the proprietor of it. Y, the registered proprietor, knowingly acquiesced in X's mistake. X finally discovers the true facts and after 10 years applies to be registered as proprietor.

    (ii)   A entered into an unenforceable oral agreement to sell a parcel of land to B for valuable consideration. A paid the price for the land and went into possession. A finally discovers that he has no title to the estate. If he has been in possession for 10 years he may apply to be registered as proprietor.

698. The second condition is set out in paragraph 5(3). This makes provision for the case where a squatter can establish some other right that would entitle him or her to be registered as proprietor irrespective of any adverse possession. This might be the case where, for example—

    (i)   The applicant is entitled to the land under the will or intestacy of the deceased registered proprietor but no assent was executed in his or her favour.

    (ii)   The applicant contracted to buy the land and paid the purchase price, but the legal estate was never transferred to him or her.

699. The third condition, which concerns disputed boundaries, is set out in paragraph 5(4). In practice, it is the most significant of the three cases, because it is the one situation in which a squatter may acquire title solely by virtue of his or her adverse possession and notwithstanding objection by the registered proprietor (or others on whom a notice is served under paragraph 2).

700. It will apply where all of the following requirements are met—

(i) The land to which the application relates is adjacent to land belonging to the applicant.

(ii) The exact line of the boundary has not been determined under rules made under Clause 60(3). Where a boundary has been determined under such rules, that fact will be apparent from the register, which will then be conclusive as to the boundary.

(iii) For a period of 10 years the squatter or his or her predecessor in title reasonably believed that the land to which the application relates belonged to him or her. In practice, where X has been in possession of a parcel of land for 10 years in circumstances where the physical boundaries of the land suggest that it belongs to X, this is likely to raise a rebuttable presumption that X had the reasonable belief. It will then be incumbent on the registered proprietor to show that X knew or ought to have known that the parcel of land did not belong to him or her.

(iv) The estate to which the application relates was registered more than one year prior to the date of the application. The reason for this requirement is as follows. Title to *unregistered* land is normally extinguished by 12 years' adverse possession. Under this third condition, title to *registered* land may be acquired after 10 years' adverse possession. A case might arise where—

(a) a squatter had been in adverse possession of a parcel of unregistered land for more than 10, but less than 12 years;
(b) the title to the land was then registered;
(c) the requirements of paragraph 5(4) were otherwise met.

But for this fourth requirement, the squatter would be able to apply to be registered as soon as the land was registered and the owner would have no opportunity to evict him or her.

701. This condition is likely to cover the following types of case.

(i) The first is where the boundaries as they appear on the ground and as they are according to the register do not coincide. This may happen because (for example)—

(a) the physical features (such as the position of trees and other landmarks) suggest that the boundary is in one place but where, according to the plan on the register, it is in another; or
(b) when an estate was laid down, the dividing fences or walls were erected in the wrong place and not in accordance with the plan lodged at the land registry.

(ii) The second is where the registered proprietor leads the squatter to believe that he or she is the owner of certain land on the boundary when in fact it belongs to the registered proprietor. In some cases there will be detrimental reliance in which case the squatter will be able to rely on the condition in paragraph 5(2), but where there is not, the applicant will have to rely on the condition in paragraph 5(4).

702. It is envisaged that paragraph 5(4) will be brought into force one year after the rest of Schedule 6. If this were not so, a squatter might find that he or she is entitled to be registered as proprietor of the estate under paragraph 5(4) on the day that the legislation is brought into force, even though he or

she had only been in adverse possession for 10 years and, the day before, the registered proprietor could successfully have initiated possession proceedings. This would clearly be undesirable. The proposed course of action will give a registered proprietor one year to take proceedings against any squatter or to regularise his or her position. For the Lord Chancellor's power to appoint the dates on which the Bill is to come into force, see Clause 133(2).

703. Paragraph 5(5) applies in the case of a squatter who could have applied to be registered under paragraph 1 but is evicted before so doing. Cf paragraph 1(2) and above, paragraph 686. It ensures that the ten year period of adverse possession mentioned in paragraph 5(4)(c) is measured by reference to the day before the applicant was evicted rather than from the date of his or her application.

Paragraphs 6 and 7

704. Subject to the qualifications contained in paragraph 6(2), paragraph 6(1) permits a squatter, whose application under paragraph 1 has been rejected, to make a further application to be registered, provided that he or she has remained in adverse possession for two years following the date of the rejection of that application. For the meaning of "adverse possession", see paragraph 11, (below paragraph 717). If the squatter does make such an application, he or she is entitled to be registered as the new proprietor of the land: see paragraph 7.

705. The general principle is subject to certain important qualifications contained in paragraph 6(2). An application cannot be made under paragraph 6(1) in any of the three situations mentioned in that sub-paragraph. The reason for each of them is obvious. It would plainly be wrong to allow an application for registration to be made when proceedings to evict the squatter were pending, or where judgment had been given, but had not yet been enforced within the two year period that the Bill allows (see Clause 97(2)), or where the squatter has been evicted pursuant to a judgment for possession.

Paragraph 8

706. Paragraph 8 sets out two situations in which a squatter cannot make a valid application to be registered under paragraph 1 even though he or she may have been in adverse possession for 10 years. Where it appears that one of these two situations applies, the registrar may include a note on the register to that effect: paragraph 8(4).

707. First, no application can be made during, or before the end of twelve months after the end of, any period during which the existing registered proprietor is for the purposes of the Limitation (Enemies and War Prisoners) Act 1945 either an enemy or detained in enemy territory: paragraph 8(1). This provision ensures that the protection conferred by the 1945 Act is carried forward to the present Bill.

708. The second situation provides protection in some cases where a registered proprietor is suffering from mental disability or physical impairment: see paragraph 8(2) and (3). The purpose of these provisions is to guard against the danger that, where the registered proprietor is disabled, an application to be registered might be successful because no one responds when the registrar serves a notice under paragraph 2. The protection afforded by this provision goes beyond that which applies to a person under a disability under the Limitation Act 1980 in the following respects—

(i)   Under the Limitation Act 1980, the time at which the person has to be subject to a disability is when the cause of action accrues, that is when adverse possession commences: Limitation Act 1980, section 28(1). Under the Bill, the time at which the registered proprietor has to be subject to a disability is when the squatter applies to be registered, which is when the registered proprietor therefore needs to be able to act to protect his or her position.

(ii)   The Limitation Act 1980 offers protection only to those subject to a mental disability: Limitation Act 1980, section 38(2)—(4). The Bill goes further and protects also those who are so physically impaired that they cannot communicate their decisions.

709. If the registrar mistakenly registers a squatter in either of these two situations (if, for example, he is unaware of the registered proprietor's disability), the registered proprietor may be able to seek rectification of the register under the provisions of Schedule 4.

Paragraph 9

710. Where a squatter's application for registration is successful, the registrar will register him or her as the new proprietor of the estate which he or she had adversely possessed: see paragraphs 1(1), 4 and 7. Paragraph 9(1) is the concomitant of this. The fee simple absolute in possession which the squatter has hitherto had by virtue of his or her adverse possession is expressly extinguished.

711. The effect of paragraph 9(2) is that, as now, when a squatter is registered as proprietor, he or she takes the land subject to the same estates, rights and interests that bound the previous proprietor.

712. The basic principle that registration of a squatter as proprietor will not affect the priority of interests affecting the estate is subject to one significant exception. A squatter will take free of any charge which affected the registered estate immediately before his or her registration (see paragraph 9(3)) *unless* his or her application was determined by reference to one of the conditions set out in paragraph 5 (see paragraph 9(4)). The reason for this exception is that in those cases where a chargee has had the opportunity to prevent the registration of the squatter (by serving a counter-notice under paragraph 3 and, if necessary, evicting the squatter) but has failed to do so, the squatter should not be bound by the charge. If the proprietor of the registered estate loses his or her title, so too should the chargee. This will facilitate subsequent dealings with the land by the squatter and so promote one of the aims of the provisions of the Bill on adverse possession, which is to ensure that land remains in commerce. By contrast, in those cases where a chargee *has* objected to the squatter's application to be registered, but the squatter has, nonetheless, been registered because his or her case fell within paragraph 5, the squatter will *not* take free of the charge unless his or her case fell within paragraph 5(2) or (3) and his or her interest in the land had priority over the charge in accordance with the rules about the effect of dispositions on priority.

Paragraph 10

713. As explained above, a squatter whose application to be registered is successful will commonly take free of any registered charge. However, there will be cases where a squatter is bound by a registered charge or some other form of charge (such as a charging order). That charge may also affect

property other than the estate of which the squatter has been registered as proprietor. Paragraph 10 reverses the current position whereby a squatter can only redeem the mortgage if he or she pays the full amount of the debt secured by it: see *Caroll v Manek* (1999) 79 P & CR 173. Once again, the object is to facilitate subsequent dealings with the land and to ensure that land is kept in commerce.

714. Paragraph 10(1) enables a squatter who is registered as proprietor of an estate which is subject to a charge that continues to be binding on him or her to require the chargee to apportion the charge. A charge means any mortgage, charge or lien for securing money or money's worth: see Clause 129(1). Apportionment is to be on the basis of—

(i)   the respective values of the parcels of land subject to the charge; and

(ii)   the amount secured by the charge at the time when the squatter requires the chargee to make the apportionment.

715. By paragraph 10(2), the person who requires the apportionment to be made is entitled to have his or her estate discharged from the charge if he or she pays the chargee the amount apportioned to that estate together with its costs in making the apportionment. The corollary of this is that the liability of the chargor to the chargee will be reduced accordingly: paragraph 10(3).

716. Paragraph 10(4) confers a power to make rules concerning apportionment. In particular, it should be noted that sub-paragraph (4)(d) envisages that rules may be made which will enable the chargor to recover from the squatter any costs that he or she incurs in the course of the making of the apportionment. Any such rules will be land registration rules: Clause 129(1). They will be made by statutory instrument to be laid before Parliament only: Clause 125(2) and (3).

Paragraph 11

717. Paragraph 11(1) lays down the general principle that for the purposes of Schedule 6 a person is in adverse possession if, but for Clause 95, a period of limitation would run in his or her favour under the Limitation Act 1980. However, this is qualified in three ways.

718. First, in certain circumstances a person can satisfy the requirement of adverse possession even though he or she has not personally been in adverse possession for the whole 10-year period. This will be the case where the applicant—

(i)   Is the successor in title to an earlier squatter (as, for example, where the applicant purchased the land from him or her) and, taken together, the total period of adverse possession amounts to 10 years: see paragraph 11(2)(a).

(ii)   Has been in adverse possession, has been dispossessed by a second squatter, and has then recovered the land from the second squatter. In this case the applicant can add the second squatter's period of adverse possession to his or her own to make up the necessary 10-year period: see paragraph 11(2)(b).

719. It should be noted that where a squatter is dispossessed, the second squatter will not be able to add the prior period of adverse possession to his or her own to make up the necessary 10-year period. Thus, for example, if X has been in adverse possession for 6 years and Y dispossesses her, Y will not be

able to apply to be registered as proprietor until he has been in adverse possession for a further period of 10 years. He cannot add X's period of adverse possession to his own. This is because in this situation Y is not X's successor in title, but has a freehold estate of his own by virtue of his adverse possession. Nor did X's period of adverse possession come between two periods of adverse possession by Y.

720. The second qualification to the principle stated in paragraph 11(1) is that, in determining whether a period of limitation would run under section 15 of the Limitation Act 1980, the commencement of any legal proceedings is to be disregarded: paragraph 11(3)(a). The principle that would otherwise apply is that the commencement of proceedings against a squatter prevents time running against the squatter for the purposes of that action: see *Markfield Investments Ltd v Evans* [2001] 2 All ER 238.

721. The third qualification is the disapplication of a technical rule about the adverse possession of a reversion, that is not needed in the scheme created by Schedule 6: see paragraph 11(3)(b).

Paragraph 12

722. Paragraph 12 provides that where an estate is held in trust, a squatter will not be regarded as being in adverse possession unless the interest of each of the beneficiaries in the estate is an interest in possession. In other words, a squatter will not be regarded as being in adverse possession at any time when a registered estate is held in trust as long as there are successive interests in the land. This provision achieves the objective that where there are successive interests, adverse possession by a squatter should not prejudice the rights of beneficiaries who are not yet entitled in possession.

723. The effect of paragraph 12 may be illustrated as follows. Land is held on trust of land for A for life, thereafter for B for life, thereafter for C absolutely. S, a squatter, goes into possession of the land during A's lifetime and remains there. For as long as either A or B is alive, S is not regarded as being in adverse possession. It is only once C's interest has fallen into possession that S may be treated as being in adverse possession. Thereafter, S will have to remain in possession for a further 10 years before he or she can make an application to be registered as proprietor under paragraph 1.

Paragraph 13

724. Paragraph 13 contains special provisions dealing with adverse possession against foreshore belonging to the Crown. By virtue of paragraph 1 of Schedule 6, this provision will only apply where Crown foreshore is registered. For registration by the Crown of its demesne lands, see Part 7 of the Bill.

725. Under paragraph 13(1) a squatter must be in adverse possession for 60 years instead of 10 before he or she can apply to be registered in place of the Crown as the proprietor of any foreshore. The longer period has been chosen because of the difficulties that the Crown faces in monitoring the very substantial areas of foreshore which it holds to ensure that there are no persons in adverse possession of it. Foreshore is defined by paragraph 13(3).

726. The effect of paragraph 13(2) is that where land ceases to be foreshore, the squatter may apply to be registered after he or she has been in adverse possession for the shorter of—

(i)   60 years; or

(ii)   10 years from the time when the land ceased to be foreshore.

Paragraph 14

727. Paragraph 14 enables rules to be made which will apply to registered rentcharges the new scheme for adverse possession contained in the Bill, with such modifications and exceptions as may be prescribed in those rules. It should be noted that without such rules the scheme would not apply to rentcharges. This is because paragraph 1 only enables a squatter to apply to be registered as proprietor of an estate *in land*. A rentcharge is not an estate *in land*: see Law of Property Act 1925, section 1(1).

SCHEDULE 7
THE LAND REGISTRY

728. Schedule 7 makes further provision in relation to the land registry, the office of Chief Land Registrar and land registry staff. Schedule 7 has already been considered in the context of Clauses 98 and 99: see above, paragraphs 453 and following.

SCHEDULE 8
INDEMNITIES

729. Schedule 8 contains provisions relating to the payment of indemnity. Although recast, this Schedule achieves substantially the same effect as section 83 of the Land Registration Act 1925 (as substituted by section 2 of the Land Registration Act 1997).

Paragraph 1

730. This paragraph sets out eight circumstances in which a person who suffers loss is entitled to be indemnified by the registrar.

731. The first is where a person suffers loss by reason of rectification of the register of title: paragraph 1(1)(a). For the meaning of "rectification" see paragraph 11(2).

732. Paragraph 1(2) extends the scope of paragraph 1(1)(a) to cover two situations in which a person will be treated as if he or she has suffered loss by reason of rectification, even though this might not otherwise be so. This is the case where—

   (i)   he or she suffers loss by reason of the registrar exercising his power to upgrade title under Clause 62 of the Bill; or

   (ii)   the register is rectified in relation to the proprietor of a registered estate or charge claiming in good faith under a forged disposition.

733. The second circumstance in which a person is entitled to indemnity is where he or she suffers loss by reason of a mistake, whose correction would involve rectification of the register: paragraph 1(1)(b). This will cover two situations—

   (i)   Where there is a mistake but the register is not rectified because, for example, there is a proprietor in possession. This deals with the situation presently covered by section 83(2) of the Land Registration Act 1925.

   (ii)   Where the register is rectified, but the person in whose favour it is rectified still suffers loss as a result of the mistake. This achieves the same effect as section 83(1)(b) of the Land Registration Act 1925.

Under paragraph 1(1)(b) no indemnity is payable until a decision has been made whether or not to alter the register and the loss suffered by reason of the mistake will be determined in light of that decision: paragraph 1(3). For the definition of mistake, see paragraph 11(1).

734. The third situation is where a person suffers loss by reason of a mistake in an official search: paragraph 1(1)(c). This replicates the effect of part of section 83(3) of the Land Registration Act 1925 and is a necessary corollary to Clause 70 of the Bill which governs official searches.

735. The fourth situation is where loss is suffered by reason of a mistake in an official copy: paragraph 1(1)(d). This replicates the effect of part of section 133 of the Land Registration Act 1925. For the provisions of the Bill relating to the issue of official copies and their legal consequences, see Clause 67.

736. The fifth situation is where a person suffers loss by reason of a mistake in a document kept by the registrar which is not an original and is referred to in the register of title: paragraph 1(1)(e). The right to indemnity in this situation is a natural corollary to the presumption created by Clause 118 that such a copy is to be taken as correct and to contain all material parts of the original document. Paragraph 1(1)(e) is based upon, but substantially extends the scope of, section 110(4) of the Land Registration Act 1925.

737. The sixth situation is where a person suffers loss by reason of the loss or destruction of a document lodged at the registry for inspection or safe custody: paragraph 1(1)(f). This reproduces part of the effect of section 83(3) of the Land Registration Act 1925.

738. The seventh situation is where a person suffers loss by reason of a mistake in the register of cautions against first registration: paragraph 1(1)(g). This provision is novel. It is a natural concomitant of the formal establishment of a register of cautions against first registration under the Bill and the provisions which govern alteration of that register: see Clause 19 and Clauses 20 and 21, respectively.

739. The eighth situation is where there is a failure by the registrar to perform his duty under Clause 50 to give notice of the creation of an overriding statutory charge: paragraph 1(1)(h). For example, where a prior chargee makes a further advance to the registered proprietor because the registrar has failed to notify him of the creation of an overriding statutory charge, he or she may be entitled to indemnity if the security proves to be insufficient to meet the advance.

Paragraph 2

740. This paragraph replicates the effect of section 83(5)(b) of the Land Registration Act 1925.

Paragraph 3

741. Paragraph 3 makes provision for the payment of costs or expenses incurred where an indemnity is paid. It reproduces the effect of section 83(5)(c) and (9) of the Land Registration Act 1925.

742. The general rule is that costs or expenses may only be recovered if they are reasonably incurred by the claimant with the registrar's consent: paragraph 3(1). This is subject to exceptions. Where the registrar's prior consent is not obtained, costs or expenses may still be recovered if—

(i)   they were incurred by the claimant urgently and it was not reasonably practicable to apply for the registrar's consent in advance: paragraph 3(2); or

(ii)   the registrar subsequently approved the incurring of them: paragraph 3(3).

743. Legal costs or expenses may also be recovered without the registrar's prior consent where the claimant made an application to the court to determine whether he or she was entitled to an indemnity or to determine the amount of any indemnity: paragraph 7(2). This latter provision replicates part of the effect of section 2(2) of the Land Registration and Land Charges Act 1971.

Paragraph 4

744. The effect of paragraph 4 is new and remedies a deficiency in the present law. It gives the registrar a discretion to pay the costs or expenses of a claimant who fails to obtain indemnity. Generally, such costs or expenses must be incurred reasonably in connection with the claim and with the consent of the registrar: paragraph 4(1). Where prior consent was not obtained, the registrar may still exercise his power to pay costs or expenses if—

  (i)   it appears to him that they were incurred by the claimant urgently and it was not reasonably practicable to apply for his consent in advance: paragraph 4(2)(a); or
  (ii)   the registrar subsequently approved the incurring of them: paragraph 4(2)(b).

Paragraph 5

745. Paragraph 5 sets out factors that will bar a claim for indemnity or reduce the amount that can be recovered. This paragraph is intended to replicate the effect of section 83(5)(a), (6) and (7) of the Land Registration Act 1925.

Paragraph 6

746. Where a party is seeking indemnity for the loss of an estate, interest or charge, paragraph 6 has the effect of limiting the maximum value of indemnity payable in respect of that estate, interest or charge. It does not, however, limit the entire claim for indemnity to that sum. For example, the claimant may be able to recover his or her additional costs.

747. Where the claimant is entitled to indemnity by reason of loss suffered by rectification, the maximum value of the estate, interest or charge for the purposes of indemnity is taken to be its value before rectification of the register of title, but as if there were to be no rectification: paragraph 6(a).

748. Where the claimant is entitled to indemnity by reason of loss suffered because of a mistake whose correction would involve rectification of the register, the maximum value of the estate, interest or charge for the purposes of indemnity is taken to be its value at the time when the mistake which caused the loss was made: paragraph 6(b).

Paragraph 7

749. Paragraph 7(1) replicates the effect of section 2(1) of the Land Registration and Charges Act 1971.

Paragraph 8

750. Paragraph 8 reproduces the effect of section 83(12) of the Land Registration Act 1925.

751. Paragraph 8 makes the liability to pay indemnity a simple contract debt for the purposes of the Limitation Act 1980. It will therefore be barred six years after the date on which the cause of action arose: Limitation Act 1980, section 5.

752. This paragraph confers a new power on the Lord Chancellor to make rules about the payment of interest on an indemnity. Such rules will be land registration rules and will be required to be laid before Parliament only: see Clauses 129(1) and 125(3).

753. Amongst other things, paragraph 9 will help to place current land registry practice on a more formal and transparent basis. At present, where the register is not rectified the land registry tends to pay interest on indemnity from the date of the mistake. This practice is based upon section 2(5) of the Land Registration and Land Charges Act 1971, which gives the registrar the power to settle claims for indemnity by agreement.

Paragraph 10

754. Paragraph 10 replicates the effect of section 83(10) and (11) of the Land Registration Act 1925. It sets out the circumstances in which the registrar may recover from a third party the amount of any indemnity that he has paid to a claimant. These are set out below.

755. First, the registrar may recover the amount paid from any person who caused or substantially contributed to that loss by fraud: paragraph 10(1)(a). An example would be where a mistake in the register was caused by impersonation of the registered proprietor.

756. Secondly, he is entitled to enforce the rights of action (of whatever nature and however arising) which the claimant would have been entitled to enforce had the indemnity not been paid: paragraph 10(1)(b) and (2)(a). An example would be where a mistake in the register is caused by the negligence of the claimant's solicitor.

757. Thirdly where the register has been rectified, the registrar is entitled to enforce any right of action (of whatever nature and however arising) which the person in whose favour the register has been rectified would have been entitled to enforce had it not been rectified: paragraph 10(1)(b) and (2)(b). This situation may be illustrated by the following example. Rectification is ordered in favour of X because his solicitor negligently lodged inaccurate documents. Y obtains indemnity from the registrar because she has suffered loss as a result of the rectification. The registrar can recover from X's solicitor the amount of the indemnity paid to Y. This is the case even if Y would have had no cause of action against X's solicitor, so long as X would have had a cause of action against the solicitor in the absence of rectification.

SCHEDULE 9
THE ADJUDICATOR

758. Schedule 9 makes provision about the new office of Adjudicator to HM Land Registry. Schedule 9 has already been considered in the context of Clause 105: see above, paragraphs 475 and following.

SCHEDULE 10
MISCELLANEOUS AND GENERAL POWERS

Part 1: Miscellaneous

Paragraph 1

759. Paragraph 1 provides that rules may make provision applying the Bill to a pre-registration dealing with an estate which triggers compulsory first registration under Clause 6 as if the dealing had taken place after the date of the first registration of the estate, and about the date on which registration of the dealing is effective. This power replicates a power under section 123A(1)(a) of the Land Registration Act 1925. Rules under that power have provided that the provisions of the Land Registration Act 1925 apply to such pre-registration dealings as if they had taken place after the date of first registration: see Land Registration Rules 1925, rule 73. Rules under paragraph 1 of Schedule 10 will be land registration rules and will be required to be laid before Parliament only: see Clauses 129(1) and 125(3).

Paragraph 2

760. Paragraph 2(1) concerns the obligation that a seller of land owes to prove his or her title. It confers a power on the Lord Chancellor to make provision about the obligations with respect to—

(i)   proof of title; or
(ii)   perfection of title;

of a seller under a contract for the transfer, or other disposition, for valuable consideration of a registered estate or charge. The reference to provision about the perfection of title is intended to cover the case of a seller who is not the registered proprietor, as where he or she is executor of a deceased registered proprietor or the registered proprietor holds the registered estate or charge on trust for the seller. In such cases rules may provide for the steps that a seller is required to take to perfect his or her title.

761. Proof of title to registered land is presently governed by section 110 of the Land Registration Act 1925, which sets out in detail the documents that a purchaser can require a vendor to produce. It also deals with the situation where a seller of land is not in fact registered as proprietor of the land.

762. Section 110 of the Land Registration Act 1925 reflects the state of the law when it was first enacted. At that stage, searching the register and obtaining office copies could be both costly and time consuming. In contrast, the register is now open so that it is no longer necessary to obtain a seller's consent to search the register or to obtain copies of documents referred to in the register. Moreover, the system of searching the register has become much simpler and cheaper than was formerly the case, in particular with the availability of direct access official searches by computer. In light of these developments, the prescriptive nature of section 110 and its inflexibility can produce unnecessary difficulties for the parties.

763. Paragraph 2 of Schedule 10 achieves a high degree of flexibility in relation to the law governing proof of title to registered land.

764. Paragraph 2(2) provides that any rules made under the power contained in paragraph 2(1) may be expressed to have effect notwithstanding any stipulation to the contrary. This leaves open the possibility that, if appropriate, rules as to proof of title might prevent the parties from excluding them. Rules under paragraph 2 will be land registration rules and will be required to be laid before Parliament only: see Clauses 129(1) and 125(3).

Paragraph 3

765. Paragraph 3 makes provision for rules to be made in relation to implied covenants for title. Covenants as to title are a kind of warranty given by the seller as to his or her title. Often, they are the only remedy that a grantee or transferee of land has for any defects in title that emerge after completion.

766. In relation to registered land, section 38(2) of the Land Registration Act 1925 currently contains a rule-making power for "prescribing the effect" of covenants for title implied under the Law of Property (Miscellaneous Provisions) Act 1994. The rule-making powers contained in paragraph 3 of Schedule 10 are more precisely defined.

767. Paragraph 3(a) enables rules to make provision about the form of provisions that extend or limit any covenant that is implied by virtue of Part 1 of the Law of Property (Miscellaneous Provisions) Act 1994. There are certain rules in the Land Registration Rules 1925 that have this effect: see Land Registration Rules 1925, rules 76A(5) and 77A(3). The power contained in paragraph 3(a) will enable similar provisions to be made.

768. Paragraph 3(b) allows rules to make provision about the application of section 77 of the Law of Property Act 1925 to transfers of registered estates. Section 77 is concerned with covenants that are to be implied on a conveyance of land which is subject to a rentcharge. Rules might, for example, enable the implication of the covenants to be modified or negatived: cf Land Registration Rules 1925, rule 109(6).

769. Paragraph 3(c) confers the power for rules to make provision about reference in the register to implied covenants, including provision for the state of the register to be conclusive in relation to whether covenants have been implied. This rule-making power may be used to effect a change to the present law. Subject to one exception, rule 76A(4) of the Land Registration Rules 1925 currently provides that no reference shall be made in the register to any covenant implied under Part 1 of the Law of Property (Miscellaneous Provisions) Act 1994.

Paragraph 4

770. Paragraph 4 confers the power to make various rules about land certificates.

771. At present, section 63(1) of the Land Registration Act 1925 makes provision for the issue of land and charge certificates. Charge certificates are not retained under the Bill and the role of land certificates is to be greatly reduced. In particular, it will no longer be necessary to produce a land certificate in order to secure the entry of a notice or a restriction in the register: see above, paragraphs 173 and following.

772. In future land certificates are unlikely to play any part in the conveyancing process. A land certificate will simply be a document certifying that the registration of a registered estate has taken place and that a named person is

the registered proprietor. Nevertheless, land certificates will continue to perform a useful function. A land certificate might, for example, alert a personal representative that the deceased was the registered proprietor of a property, when this would not otherwise have been apparent to him or her.

773. Rules made pursuant to paragraph 4 will be land registration rules and will be laid before Parliament only: Clauses 125(3) and 129(1).

Part 2: General

Paragraph 5

774. Paragraph 5 confers the power for rules to make provision about the form, content and service of any notice under the Bill. This replicates the effect of provisions contained in the Land Registration Act 1925, section 79.

Paragraph 6

775. Paragraph 6 confers a general power to make certain rules in relation to applications under the Bill. There are numerous applications that can be made to the registrar under the Bill: see, for example, Clauses 3 and 4 (first registration); Clause 67 (application for official copies); Schedule 6, paragraphs 1 and 6 (applications by a squatter to be registered as proprietor).

776. Rules under paragraph 6 may—

(i) Make provision about the form and content of applications under the Bill. It is likely that all applications in electronic form will be in a prescribed form to ensure the effective working of the system: see above, paragraph 402.

(ii) Make provision requiring applications under the Bill to be supported by such evidence as rules may prescribe.

(iii) Make provision about when an application under the Bill is to be taken as made. This will ensure that there is a power to allocate priority to competing applications that come into the land registry.

(iv) Make provision about the order in which competing applications are to be taken to rank. Again, this will ensure that there is a power to allocate priority to competing applications that come into the land registry.

(v) Make provision for alteration by the registrar to correct a mistake in any application or accompanying document. The purpose of this power is to ensure that the registrar is able to correct clerical errors without the need to obtain the consent of the applicant. Rules are likely, for example, to enable the registrar to correct a property description or a detail in an address where it is established elsewhere in the application and the parties do not object. It is considered that there should be a statutory foundation for the registrar's power to make such alterations. At present, the power is found in rules: see Land Registration Rules 1925, rule 13.

Paragraph 7

777. Paragraph 7 provides that rules may make provision about the form of any statement required under an enactment to be included in an instrument effecting a registrable disposition or a disposition which triggers compulsory first registration of title. A number of statutes require that an instrument which makes a disposition contains certain particulars. This is so (for

example) in relation to certain dispositions by charities, and in relation to vesting deeds which convey the legal estate to the tenant for life of a settlement under the Settled Land Act 1925: see Charities Act 1993, sections 37 and 39 and Settled Land Act 1925, section 5, respectively.

Paragraph 8

778. This paragraph contains a residual rule-making power. It replicates the power presently found in the Land Registration Act 1925, section 144(1)(xxxi). However, because the rule-making powers conferred by the Bill are more sharply focussed than those found in the 1925 Act, it is anticipated that it will not be necessary to employ this residual power as often as has been the case under the present legislation.

SCHEDULE 11
MINOR AND CONSEQUENTIAL AMENDMENTS

779. Schedule 11 makes minor and consequential amendments to other enactments. These notes refer to a few of the more significant.

Paragraph 2

780. Paragraph 2(2) inserts a new subsection (4A) in section 44 of the Law of Property Act 1925. This provides that subsections (2) and (4) of that section do not apply to contracts to grant leases that trigger compulsory first registration under Clause 4 of the Bill.

781. Section 44(2) and (4) of the Law of Property Act 1925 provide that subject to express provision to the contrary—

   (i)   under a contract to grant or assign a lease, there is no right to inspect title to the freehold;

   (ii)   under a contract to grant a sublease, there is no right to inspect title to the leasehold reversion.

As a result of paragraph 2(2), where the owner of an *unregistered estate* contracts to grant a lease or sublease that will be subject to the requirement of compulsory first registration, he or she will have to deduce his or her title for the statutory period, unless the parties agree to the contrary. This will help to secure one of the aims of the Bill which is to ensure that, where appropriate, leases are registered with absolute title.

782. Paragraph 2(4) inserts a new subsection (12) at the end of section 44 of the Law of Property Act 1925. This provides that the section does not apply to the transfer of a *registered estate* or to a lease derived out of a *registered estate*. Section 44(1) of the 1925 Act provides that the statutory period for commencement of title is fifteen years. Section 44(2) and (4) have already been considered above: see above, paragraph 781. Although section 44 does currently apply to registered land, it has little significance in relation to the transfer of a registered estate or the grant of a lease out of such a registered estate. This is because the register of itself is proof of the title to a registered estate so that any transferee or grantee can inspect the title of the estate that is to be transferred or out of which the grant is to be made: see Land Registration Act 1925, section 112; see also, Clause 66 of the Bill. Therefore, the restrictions imposed by section 44 of the Law of Property Act 1925 no longer have any real practical effect on the right to inspect title to registered land. This is why they are disapplied by the amendment made under paragraph 2(4).

Paragraph 28

783. Paragraph 28 adds the Adjudicator to HM Land Registry to Schedule 5 of the Judicial Pensions and Retirement Act 1993. This has the effect of attracting to the Adjudicator the retirement date provisions in section 26 of that Act. Accordingly, the Adjudicator must retire at the age of 70, but may be authorised to continue in office on a yearly basis until the age of 75: Judicial Pensions and Retirement Act 1993, section 26(1), (4), (5) and (6).

784. Paragraph 31(2) inserts a new subsection (4) in section 6 of the Law of Property (Miscellaneous Provisions) Act 1994.

785. The Law of Property (Miscellaneous Provisions) Act 1994 makes provision for covenants of title which are to be implied into dispositions of property. These are a kind of implied warranty given by the seller as to his or her title. Often, they are the only remedy that a grantee or transferee of land has for any defects in title that emerge after completion.

786. Section 6 of the Law of Property (Miscellaneous Provisions) Act 1994 provides that there is no liability in relation to *some* of the covenants implied by Part 1 of that Act in certain circumstances. In particular, under section 6(2), the person making the disposition is not liable under any of the relevant covenants for anything that is either within the actual knowledge, or is a necessary consequence of facts that are within the actual knowledge, of the person to whom the disposition is made.

787. Rule 77A(2) of the Land Registration Rules 1925 makes additional provision as to implied covenants in relation to registered land. The effect of rule 77A(2) is that *any* covenant implied by virtue of Part 1 of the 1994 Act takes effect as if the disposition had been expressly made subject to—

    (i)   anything that was entered in the register at the time when the disposition was executed; and
    (ii)   any overriding interest of which the person to whom the disposition was made had notice at the time the disposition was registered.

As such, there will be no breach of an implied covenant in relation to these matters.

788. Paragraph 31(2) inserts section 6(4) into the Law of Property (Miscellaneous Provisions) Act 1994 to deal with matters currently covered by rule 77A(2) of the Land Registration Rules 1925. It provides that where the disposition is of an interest the title to which is registered under the Bill, the covenantor is not liable for anything which was at the time of the disposition entered in relation to that interest in the register of title.

789. The effect of paragraph 31(2) is similar, but not identical, to rule 77A(2) of the Land Registration Rules 1925. The key changes are as follows—

    (i)   There is nothing in the new subsection that corresponds to rule 77A(2)(b) in relation to overriding interests. Section 6(2) of the Law of Property (Miscellaneous Provisions) Act 1994 makes that provision unnecessary.
    (ii)   Paragraph 31(2) will only apply to those covenants listed in section 6 of the 1994 Act, whereas rule 77A(2) currently applies in relation to all of the covenants implied under Part 1 of that Act. This change is unlikely to be material and greatly simplifies the present law.

SCHEDULE 12
TRANSITION

790. Schedule 12 contains the transitional provisions applicable to the Bill. It addresses the following matters—

(i)   existing entries in the register;
(ii)   existing cautions against first registration;
(iii)   pending applications;
(iv)   former overriding interests;
(v)   cautions against first registration;
(vi)   certain applications by cautioners;
(vii)   adverse possession;
(viii) indemnities;
(ix)   implied covenants on transfers of pre-1996 leases.

Some of these matters have already been explained and, where this so, a cross reference is made to the earlier discussion.

Paragraph 1

791. Under paragraph 1, the validity of existing entries on the register is unaffected by any repeal made by the Bill.

Paragraph 2

792. Under paragraph 2(1), notices entered under the Land Registration Act 1925 are treated in the same way as a notice entered on application under Clause 34(2)(a) of the Bill. For the provisions of the Bill relating to notices, see Clauses 32—39.

793. Under paragraph 2(2), existing restrictions and inhibitions are treated in the same way as restrictions entered under the Bill. For the provisions of the Bill relating to restrictions, see Clauses 40—47. It was explained above that under the Bill inhibitions are to be abolished because they are, in reality, just one form of restriction: see above, paragraph 161.

794. Paragraphs 2(3) and (4) contain provisions relating to cautions against dealings. Under the Bill there is no power to lodge further cautions against dealings: see paragraph 161. Paragraph 2(3) provides that sections 55 and 56 of the Land Registration Act 1925 shall continue to have effect in relation to existing cautions against dealings. Paragraph 2(4) confers power to make rules in relation to existing cautions. It is likely that such rules will replicate the effect of existing rules relating to the operation of cautions: cf Land Registration Rules 1925, rules 217—219, 221 and 222.

Paragraph 3

795. Prior to April 3, 1995, it was possible to create a lien by depositing a land or charge certificate with the lender. Such a lien could be protected on the register by a notice of deposit or a notice of intended deposit: Land Registration Rules 1925, rules 239—243. Since April 2, 1995, it has not been possible to protect a lien by these means. At present, rule 239 of the Land Registration Rules 1925 provides that where a lien protected by a notice of deposit or a notice of intended deposit of a land or charge certificate was entered on the register prior to April 3, 1995, it shall take effect as a caution against dealings under section 54 of the Land Registration

Act 1925. Paragraph 3 therefore preserves the effect of rule 239 of the Land Registration Rules 1925.

Paragraph 4

796. Paragraph 4 preserves the effect of section 56(3) of the Land Registration Act 1925 in relation to cautions against first registration lodged under that, or any earlier, Act. Section 56(3) provides that where a person causes damage to another by entering a caution without reasonable cause he or she will be liable in damages. For the equivalent provision in relation to cautions entered under the Bill, see Clause 77.

Paragraphs 5 and 6

797. Paragraph 5 preserves the effect of the Land Registration Act 1925 in relation to applications for the entry of a notice, restriction, inhibition or caution pending at the time of the repeal of the provision under which the application is made.

798. Paragraph 6 provides that where an application for a caution against first registration is pending at the time of the repeal of section 56(1) and (2) of the Land Registration Act 1925, those provisions shall continue to apply to that application. Section 56(1) enables a person aggrieved by an act of the registrar in relation to a caution to appeal to the court. Section 56(2) expressly provides that a caution shall not prejudice the claim or title of any person and shall not have any effect except as provided by the Land Registration Act 1925.

Paragraph 7

799. Paragraph 7 creates an additional category of unregistered interests which override first registration by inserting paragraph 15 in Schedule 1 for a period of three years.

800. Under section 70(1)(f) of the Land Registration Act 1925 the rights of a squatter are protected as overriding interests. On first registration such rights are protected as overriding interests even if the squatter is not in actual occupation of the land at that time. The Bill does not replicate the effect of section 70(1)(f). Under the Bill, a squatter's rights will only be protected as an interest which overrides first registration if he or she is in actual occupation so that they come within paragraph 2 of Schedule 1. However, paragraph 7 continues for the first three years of the new regime the automatic protection which the existing regime affords to a person who has acquired title by adverse possession, but who is no longer in actual occupation.

801. Paragraph 7 means that for three years after Schedule 1 is brought into force, a squatter will have an interest which overrides first registration where he or she had, before the coming into force of the Schedule, extinguished the title of the person who is registered as first registered proprietor. This will provide a reasonable opportunity for any squatter who is no longer in actual occupation of the land which he or she claims, to register his or her rights.

Paragraph 8

802. Paragraph 8 creates a further category of unregistered interests which override registered dispositions by inserting paragraph 2A in Schedule 3. This provision is necessary because under the Bill overriding status will be removed for the rights of persons who are in receipt of rents and profits in respect of land. The rights of such persons are currently protected as overriding interests under section 70(1)(g) of the Land Registration Act 1925.

803. Paragraph 2A(1) provides that an interest which, immediately before the coming into force of Schedule 3, was an overriding interest under section 70(1)(g) of the Land Registration Act 1925 by virtue of a person's receipt of rents and profits, continues to be so for the purpose of Schedule 3. However, by virtue of paragraph 2A(2), that interest will cease to be overriding for these purposes if, at any time thereafter, the person having the interest ceases to be in receipt of the rents and profits. If, for example, X holds the residue of an unregistered 99-year lease and, before the Bill came into force, granted an underlease to Y, X would continue to have an interest capable of overriding a registered disposition for the purposes of the Bill. If, however, Y's underlease determined and X then granted a new underlease to Z, X would at that point cease to have an overriding interest. However, an interest of the kind described above will not override a registered disposition if inquiry is made of the person with the benefit of the interest before the disposition, and he or she unreasonably fails to disclose it.

Paragraphs 9 and 10

804. Paragraphs 9 and 10 are transitional provisions relating to easements and *profits à prendre* which override registered dispositions.

805. Under the Bill the class of easements and profits that override a registered disposition will be narrower than at present. In particular the following easements and profits will cease to be such interests—

    (i)   equitable easements or profits;

    (ii)   easements and profits expressly granted or reserved out of registered land; and

    (iii)   legal easements and profits that fall within one of the exceptions set out in Schedule 3, paragraph 3.

806. By virtue of paragraph 9 any easement or profit that is an overriding interest at the time when Schedule 3 comes into force, but would not have been overriding by virtue of paragraph 3 of that Schedule if it had been created thereafter, will retain its overriding status. Those who have the benefit of such rights are not at risk of losing them.

807. The effect of paragraph 10 is that for a period of three years after Schedule 3 is brought into force *any* legal easement or profit that is not registered will be capable of overriding a registered disposition. This will, therefore, cover all legal easements and profits that arise before or after the Schedule is brought into force. However, that overriding status will cease three years after the date on which the Schedule is brought into force. Thereafter the priority of an unregistered legal easement will only be protected as an overriding interest if either—

(i)   it falls within paragraph 3 of Schedule 3; or
(ii)   it is an overriding interest at the time when the Schedule comes into force and continues to be so by virtue of paragraph 9 of Schedule 12.

Except in relation to equitable easements or profits, paragraph 10 ensures that there is a period of three years' grace before the new provisions take effect. It should be noted that under the Bill easements and profits that are expressly granted or reserved after the Bill comes into force will only be *equitable* unless and until they are registered: Clause 27(1) and 2(d). As such they will never gain protection under the transitional provision in paragraph 10.

Paragraph 11

808. Paragraph 11 creates an additional category of interests which override registered dispositions by inserting paragraph 15 into Schedule 3 for the period of 3 years from the commencement of that Schedule. This provision is similar to paragraph 7 of Schedule 12, except that it deals with the position where a squatter is entitled to be registered as proprietor of a *registered* estate by virtue of his or her adverse possession immediately before Clause 96 is brought into force: cf above, paragraphs 571 and following.

Paragraph 12

809. Paragraph 12 provides that paragraph 1 of Schedules 1 and 3 shall be taken to include an interest which immediately before the coming into force of the Schedule, was an overriding interest under section 70(1)(k) of the Land Registration Act 1925. At present, leases granted for a term of 21 years or less are protected as overriding interests: see Land Registration Act 1925, section 70(1)(k). Under the Bill, a lease will not override first registration or a registered disposition unless it was granted for a term of 7 years or less: see paragraph 1 of Schedules 1 and 3. Paragraph 12 therefore preserves the overriding status of legal leases which are granted before Schedules 1 and 3 come into force and which fall within section 70(1)(k).

Paragraphs 14, 15 and 16

810. Paragraph 14 makes transitional provision in relation to cautions against first registration. It has already been considered in relation to Clause 15: see above, paragraphs 76 and 77.

811. Paragraph 15 makes provision in relation to cautions against first registration in respect of the Crown's demesne land. It has already been considered in relation to Clause 81: see above, paragraph 363.

812. Paragraph 16 ensures that existing cautions against first registration entered under section 53 of the Land Registration Act 1925 are treated in the same way as cautions entered under Clause 15 of the Bill. For the main

provisions of the Bill that deal with cautions against first registration see Clauses 15—22.

Paragraph 17

813. Paragraph 17 means that where a person has lodged a caution against dealings under section 54 of the Land Registration Act 1925 in respect of an estate, he or she may only apply for the entry of a notice or restriction in respect of that estate under the Bill if he or she also applies to withdraw the caution. This provision is a natural concomitant to the prospective abolition of cautions against dealings: see above, paragraph 161.

Paragraph 18

814. Paragraph 18 makes transitional provision for the situation where, prior to Clause 96 coming into force, a squatter had become entitled to be registered as proprietor of an estate by virtue of section 75 of the Land Registration Act 1925.

815. Paragraph 18(1) confers an entitlement to be registered on any squatter who is a beneficiary under a trust under section 75 of the Land Registration Act 1925 immediately before Clause 96 comes into force. That entitlement is a proprietary right and will be protected without the need for registration if the squatter remains in actual occupation: see Schedule 3, paragraph 2.

816. Paragraph 18(2) provides that the entitlement to be registered under paragraph 18(1) will constitute a defence to any proceedings for possession. If a person successfully claims the benefit of this defence, the court must order the registrar to register the squatter as proprietor of the estate to which he or she is entitled: see paragraph 18(3).

817. Paragraph 18(5) enables rules to make transitional provision for rentcharges held in trust under section 75 of the Land Registration Act 1925. This situation is not covered by paragraph 18(1) because that provision applies only to estates *in land*. A rentcharge is not an estate *in land*: see Law of Property Act 1925, section 1(1).

Paragraph 19

818. Paragraph 19(1) applies Schedule 8 to claims made before the commencement of the Schedule which have not been settled by agreement or finally determined by that time. Schedule 8 makes provision for the payment of indemnities and, although recast, substantially replicates the effect of section 83 of the Land Registration Act 1925 (as substituted by section 2 of the Land Registration Act 1997).

Paragraph 20

819. Paragraph 20 replicates the effect of section 24(1)(b) and (2) of the Land Registration Act 1925 in relation to the assignment of leases which are not "new tenancies" for the purposes of section 1 of the Landlord and Tenant (Covenants) Act 1995.

820. In relation to a lease granted prior to 1996, the tenant remains liable for the tenant covenants contained in the lease for its whole duration, regardless of any assignments that might take place. As regards leases granted prior to 1996, section 24(1)(b) and (2) of the Land Registration Act 1925 makes provision for implied indemnity covenants on the part of the transferee in

favour of the transferor, and, in relation to a transfer of part, implied indemnity covenants on the part of the *transferor* in favour of the *transferee*. The continuing liability of the first tenant for the duration of the lease regardless of assignments was prospectively abolished by the Landlord and Tenant (Covenants) Act 1995. However, section 24(1)(b) and (2) was preserved by the Landlord and Tenant (Covenants) Act 1995, in relation to leases granted before 1996: see Landlord and Tenant (Covenants) Act 1995, sections 14(b) and 30(3). Paragraph 20 of Schedule 12 replicates the effect of the present law in this respect.

SCHEDULE 13
REPEALS

821. Schedule 13 lists repeals of provisions in other enactments.

APPENDIX B

LIST OF PERSONS AND ORGANISATIONS WHO RESPONDED TO CONSULTATIVE DOCUMENT LAW COM NO 254

Organisations who responded to our Consultative Document

Abbey National Plc

Advisory Service for Squatters

Birmingham Law Society

Bond Pearce

Bradford and Bingley

Bristol Law Society

British Property Federation

Butler and Evans

Chancery Bar Association

Charities Property Association

City of London Law Society

Clifford Chance

Cobbetts

Council of Mortgage Lenders

Country Landowners' Association

Crown Estate

The Crown Estate Commissioners

Davies and Partners

Decherts

Departmental Trade Union Side, HM Land Registry

Falcon Chambers

Farming and Rural Conservation Agency

Farrer and Co

Funnell and Perring

General Council of the Bar

Holborn Law Society

Institute of Legal Executives

The Law Society

Lloyds TSB

Lovell White Durant

Ministry of Agriculture Fisheries and Food

Ministry of Defence

Moss Solicitors

National Association of Estate Agents

National Farmers Union

National Trust

Palser Grossman

Property Litigation Association

Robert Hitchins Ltd

Royal Institution of Chartered Surveyors

Simmons and Simmons

Society of Public Teachers of Law

Warwickshire Law Society
Woolwich Plc
Wragge and Co

Individuals who responded to our Consultative Document
Professor D G Barnsley
Mrs E E Bennett
Ms Susan Bright
Professor E H Burn
Cliff Campbell Esq
Ian Clyde Esq
Dr Elizabeth Cooke
Dr Patricia Critchley
Martin Dixon Esq
Dr John Greed
Nick Hopkins Esq
Dr Jean Howell
David Hunt Esq
Stephen Jourdan Esq
Ian Leeming Esq QC
G L Leigh Esq
Dr Paul McHugh
John Manthorpe Esq CB
The Lord Marcher of Trelleck
Olle Millgård Esq
Robert Moseley Esq
Glenn Pearce Esq
Robert Roper Esq
J S Shaw Esq
Roger Smith Esq
Peter Sparkes Esq
Colin Sydenham Esq
Ms Louise Tee
John Thirwell Esq
Andrew Turek Esq
David Watkinson Esq
Derek Wood Esq CBE QC

Printed in the UK for The Stationery Office Limited
On behalf of the Controller of Her Majesty's Stationery Office
Dd5070151 7/01 019585 Ord TJ00 5026